Scotland's Lost Gardens

From the Garden of Eden to the Stewart Palaces

Scotland's Lost Gardens

From the Garden of Eden to the Stewart Palaces

Marilyn Brown

Royal
Commission on the
Ancient and
Historical
Monuments of
Scotland

First published in 2012
Re-printed in paperback in 2015 by the
Royal Commission on the Ancient and
Historical Monuments of Scotland

RCAHMS

**Royal Commission on the Ancient
and Historical Monuments of Scotland**

John Sinclair House
16 Bernard Terrace
Edinburgh EH8 9NX
0131 662 1456

info@rcahms.gov.uk
www.rcahms.gov.uk

Registered Charity SC026749

British Library Cataloguing-in-Publication Data.
A catalogue record for this book is available from
the British Library.

ISBN 978 1 902419 94 7

Printed by Skleniarz, Poland

Layout by Mitch Cosgrove

Frontispiece: 'A Young Daughter of the Picts'
attributed to Jacques Le Moyne de Morgues and
painted about 1585. This imaginary Pictish amazon
celebrates the cultivation of flowers which was
stimulated by the knowledge in Europe of new plants
from east and west. Le Moyne de Morgues was a
Huguenot refugee in London, who had taken part in
a French expedition to establish a colony in Florida,
which was overrun by the Spanish in 1565. It shows
a girl carrying a spear and wearing a sword, and
tattooed all over her body with symmetrically arranged
flowers: peonies, hollyhocks, lilies, cornflowers, irises,
horned poppies, columbines, rose campion, narcissus
and tulips. Watercolor and gouache, touched with
gold, on parchment. © Yale Center for British Art,
Paul Mellon Collection B1981.25.2646

Contents

Editorial Notes · vi

Acknowledgements · vii

Introduction · 1

Chapter 1:   The Monastic Garden 500 to 1560 · 17

Chapter 2:   The Royal and Noble Garden 1100 to 1560 · 53

Chapter 3:   The Renaissance Garden 1560 to 1603 · 97

Chapter 4:   The Union Garden 1603 to 1660 · 143

Chapter 5:   The Restoration Garden 1660 to 1714 · 213

Chapter 6:   Evolution and Innovation 1714 to 1750 · 313

Afterword · 337

Distribution Maps · 338

Gazetteer · 340

Bibliography · 343

Index · 357

Editorial Notes

All names highlighted in bold within the body of the text refer to gardens which are discussed in detail in the course of the volume. They appear on the distribution maps at the end of the volume on pages 338–9 and are listed in alphabetical order in the Gazetteer on pages 340–3 where the name of the historic county and the present council area are given along with the National Grid Reference. Monetary values are in Scots currency unless otherwise specified.

Bibliographical References
Harvard-style short titles are used throughout the text and are expanded in the full bibliography at the end of the volume. The main body of the text contains only those references which are relevant to the point under discussion; the bibliography also contains reference to other works of interest.

Illustrations
All illustrations are treated as Figures. The distribution maps are aligned to Grid North and the National Grid is marked along the margin. All maps are based on information derived from the OS and are reproduced by permission of Ordnance Survey on behalf of HMSO: © Crown Copyright 2012. All rights reserved. Ordnance Survey Licence Number 100020548.

Copyright
Unless otherwise specified, the contents of this volume are Crown Copyright: Royal Commission on the Ancient and Historical Monuments of Scotland. Copies of RCAHMS photographs have a unique catalogue number appended at the end of the caption (eg SC672596) which serves to identify the item in the National Collection. These may be purchased online, although it should be noted that many, particularly aerial views, appear in the volume in a cropped form.

Plan Conventions

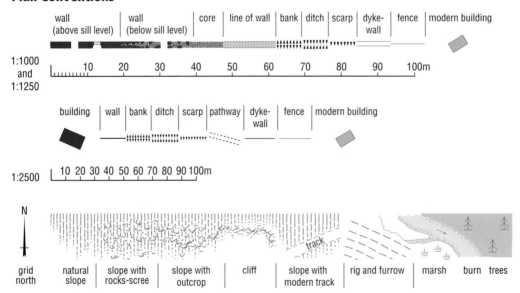

Acknowledgements

The Royal Commission and the author wish to acknowledge the assistance of all the individuals who contributed to the preparation of this volume.

The photographs were taken and processed by Robert Adam, Georgina Brown, Marilyn Brown, Tahra Duncan-Clark, Dennis Gallagher, Zoe Gibson, John Keggie, Angus Lamb, Anne Martin, Derek Smart and Stephen Wallace, as well as by earlier photographers and surveyors whose work forms part of the collections of RCAHMS. The drawn surveys were carried out by John Borland, Georgina Brown, Alan Leith and Ian Parker in addition to those surveyed and published in RCAHMS *Inventories* before 1967. Design and production work was carried out by Oliver Brookes and Mitch Cosgrove. Many other members of the staff of RCAHMS, in particular Peter McKeague and Kristina Watson, made important contributions to assembling the illustrations. James Crawford provided editorial support and looked after marketing and sales for the book.

Editorial work has been carried out by David Gallagher, Dennis Gallagher, Stratford Halliday, Mira Knoche, Philippa Lewis, Jack Stevenson and Robin Turner.

Particular thanks are due to Christopher Dingwall, Dennis Gallagher and John Harrison for their helpful criticisms and contributions to the volume.

The staff of the National Trust for Scotland, Historic Scotland, the National Library of Scotland, the National Records of Scotland and the librarians of the Special Collections of the universities of Edinburgh and Glasgow have all kindly contributed information and illustrations.

Finally we would like to thank the many owners and occupiers who allowed access to the gardens and sites celebrated here and gave of their time and knowledge.

Introduction

The garden and its companion, the designed landscape, are important elements in the cultural history of Scotland. They also form one of its more ephemeral elements; subject to constant variation on a small scale, they are, on a larger scale, relatively easily changed or abandoned, leaving little or no trace. The creation of gardens, and the form of garden adopted, provides insights into the culture and philosophy of the society that designed and produced them. Like any other art form the style of a garden mirrors the aesthetic, social, technological, economic and political attitudes of the time (Fig 1). More than this, they intimately reflect the personality and ideals of the individuals who created them, and chart the changing fortunes and ambitions of successive generations. Through its gardens Scotland may be seen as part of a wider European movement, drawing on the same literary and visual influences and sharing a common medieval, renaissance and early modern heritage. This approach to the understanding of Scotland's culture reflects the wider approach to the writing of the history of Scotland which has emerged during the later twentieth and early twenty-first centuries, encouraging a reconsideration of its institutions and cultural achievements (MacIntosh 2007, 223; Stevenson and Davidson 2009).

Fig 1 The oil painting of the estate of Yester by an unknown Dutch or Flemish artist and probably dating from the 1690s focuses on the long drive leading from Gifford Village to Yester House. The planned village with its extensive green and its cross occupy the foreground with a mill situated on the Gifford Water. On the right is a walled garden overlooked by an upper terrace. Below the terrace a stretch of the Gifford Water has been converted into a canal. The planting of the lower garden would appear to be incomplete but it may be an orchard or a decorative kitchen garden or perhaps a nursery for trees. DP109179

Scope and Range of the Study

The *Shorter Oxford English Dictionary* describes a garden as 'an enclosed piece of ground devoted to the cultivation of flowers, fruit or vegetables'. This seems a very limited and rather unsatisfactory definition, and another more useful one, 'any purposeful arrangement of natural objects ... with exposure to the open air, in which the form is not fully accounted for by purely practical considerations such as convenience', was put forward by David Cooper in his discussion of the term in his *A Philosophy of Gardens* (2006). For the purposes of this book I have adopted a wide and tolerant use of the term 'garden'. It encompasses at various times all of the above plus the immediate surroundings of the dwelling house, the policies, the kitchen garden, the orchard and, on occasion, the park, and includes the wider setting of the house, where the concept of the garden included and gave meaning to features at a distance from it.

The chronological span of this book covers the period from Early Christian times to the end of the reign of the last member of the Stewart dynasty, Queen Anne, in 1714, with a consideration of later developments in the designed landscape, before the widespread adoption of the principles of the informal garden in the later eighteenth century. It examines the evidence for the existence and nature of gardens in Scotland with a concentration on their form, appearance and location. This way of looking at gardens in Scotland draws on the approaches and attitudes to the study of sites and monuments in the landscape maintained by the Royal Commission on the Ancient and Historical Monuments of Scotland. For more than a century the Royal Commission has been recording all aspects of the heritage of Scotland, both through its own programme of surveying and through

Fig 2 A detail from the plan of a ninth century monastery drawn at Reichenau, a monastery on an island in Lake Constance, which has been preserved at the monastery of St Gall in Switzerland, showing the unroofed area beyond the abbey church designated 'Paradise'. Codex Sangallensis 1092 recto. © Abbey Library of St. Gallen, Switzerland / Codices Electronici Sangallenses

Fig 3 Aerial view of Sgor nam Ban-Naomha, the site of a possible Early Christian eremitic settlement on Canna. The garden would help to provide a basic diet. SC663865

the creation of the collections of drawings, photographs and descriptions of the heritage to create an inventory of Scotland (Fig 3 etc). The gardens were considered along with the buildings for which or perhaps with which they were designed, and this approach allows the gardens to be viewed in their wider context. Some of this evidence for the presence of gardens is derived from the plans and written accounts of earthwork remains recorded in the series of county inventories published between 1908 and 1992.

Little is said here of the plants within the garden, a subject which has recently been examined by Forbes Robertson (Robertson 2000, 2007), and the present twenty-first century state of these gardens is only briefly touched on. *Early Scottish Gardens* by Sheila Mackay (2001) and *The Scottish Gardener* by Suki Urquhart (2005) both take, for the most part, a selection of present day gardens, often with early antecedents, and consider them in the light of their development over the centuries. The division of this account of gardens in Scotland into chapters based on the reigns of monarchs is a matter of convenience rather than a desire to attribute developments in design to the individual rulers or even specifically to their reigns.

Sources of Information

By their very nature the remains of gardens tend to be ephemeral and subject to constant change, ranging from minor alteration and modification to wholesale reconstruction or even obliteration. They did not form an important element in the earlier volumes of the RCAHMS county inventory series, although a garden is recorded at Plunton in Kirkcudbrightshire in 1911 and a garden mount at Lochwood Castle in Dumfriesshire in 1912 (RCAHMS 1914, lii, 38–40; RCAHMS 1920, 117); the garden at Pinkie House in Musselburgh was the first to be described, along with the architecture of the house, in the Midlothian and West Lothian inventory of 1929, and it was only with the publication of *Roxburgh* in 1956 that the remains of gardens in the form of earthwork banks and hollows became an occasional element in the record; the skills of generations of fieldworkers have allowed the identification of a series of low mounds with the site of a garden, which previously may have been considered as defensive works or settlement remains or were just ignored. Ground surveys of some gardens surviving in this form have been prepared specifically for this volume (Figs 167, 170, 175 etc).

Much of the impetus for this work is drawn from the programme of aerial survey which the Royal Commission has carried out since 1976, discovering and recording a range of sites and landscapes, from the earliest times to the present day. Garden features were identified from the air and these discoveries stimulated research into their form and development. From the air the remains of the gardens may appear as

Fig 4 The treble singer from the Wode Partbooks, dressed in green and holding a book, stands between depictions of large flowers. These psalm settings were compiled by Thomas Wode, a former monk of Lindores Abbey which was well known for its horticultural skills. University of Edinburgh Library Special Collections, La.III.1.iv. © Edinburgh University Library.

slight earthworks, whose visibility is enhanced by the shadows cast by slanting sunlight, allowing the pattern of the garden to be identified; the gardens at Muness were recognised in this way (Fig 161). They may also emerge in the form of a pattern of cropmarks in areas of grass or arable farmland (Fig 7). Although cropmarks of the type known as negative cropmarks, reflecting the position of features such as ditches and post holes,

Fig 5 An initial L at the beginning of Psalm 35 incorporating a gillyflower or pink, a flower associated with the Virgin Mary, from the later sixteenth century Wode Partbooks. University of Edinburgh Library Special Collections, EUL Dk.5.15.125 © Edinburgh University Library

Fig 6 The early seventeenth century terraced gardens at Elibank Castle in Selkirkshire with shadows emphasising the stone and earthwork remains. DP060997

Fig 7 Cropmark evidence for the late sixteenth century walled gardens to the east of Castle Menzies in Perthshire, now an arable field, was recorded from the air during dry summers. SC672596

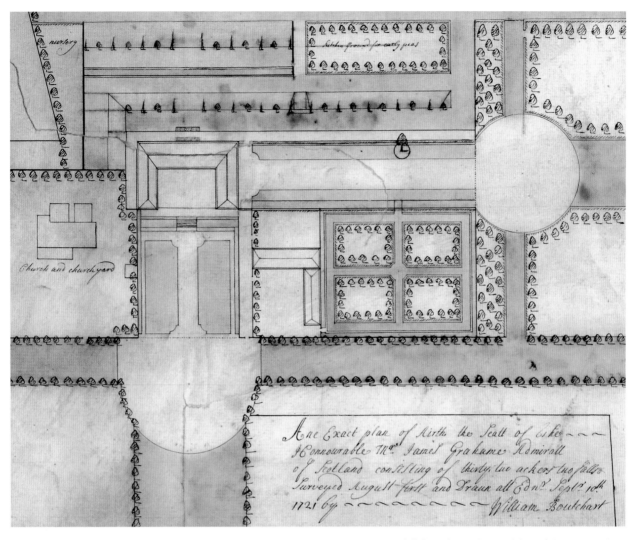

Fig 8 A detail from a survey of Airth in Stirlingshire with its parterres and terraces drawn by William Boutcher in 1721. DP090704

which were excavated during their original construction, do emerge with clarity, markings in grass indicating the site of an earlier garden often emerge in the form referred to as positive cropmarks, appearing as lighter marks. These are caused by the presence of a surface below the ground, such as a wall, a path or a bank formed of a relatively impermeable material such as a mixture of earth and stone or clay. The identification of the terraces at Monzie Castle was first made from the air. Close cropping of the turf, in particular by sheep, or close cutting by gardeners usually provides the most likely conditions in which features below the turf may be visible (Fig 47). The areas of carefully tended grass around properties in the care of Historic Scotland, for example, provide some of the most regular locations for revealing underlying walls. The evidence of cropmarking does not directly allow the identification of one feature as either earlier or later than another, but rather reveals a palimpsest. The analysis of different forms may allow features to be associated and dated on stylistic grounds, although excavation may be the only means to establish a chronology with certainty (Hynd and Ewart 1983; Taylor 1983, 50).

The most usual stimulus for the formation of cropmarks in Scotland is the creation of a soil moisture deficit, brought about by the relative absence of rainfall, possibly accompanied by wind and sunshine, increasing the rate of evapo-transpiration from the crop growing on freely draining soil. When this occurs at a critical period in the growth of the crop, the crop reflects below-ground disturbance. The reason for this may be agricultural, often from recent activity, or geological; both of these factors are far more common than the disturbance caused by buried archaeological features, which are the type of cropmark feature selected for recording during summer reconnaissance (Wilson 2000, 53–6). While grass can be very responsive to growth stress, the proportion of sites discovered in pasture is low in comparison with those in wheat and barley and often requires the features to lie only at a shallow depth below the turf or to contrast sharply with the soil in which it lies.

The Royal Commission holds large collections concerned with all aspects of the built heritage of Scotland from the earliest times to the twenty-first

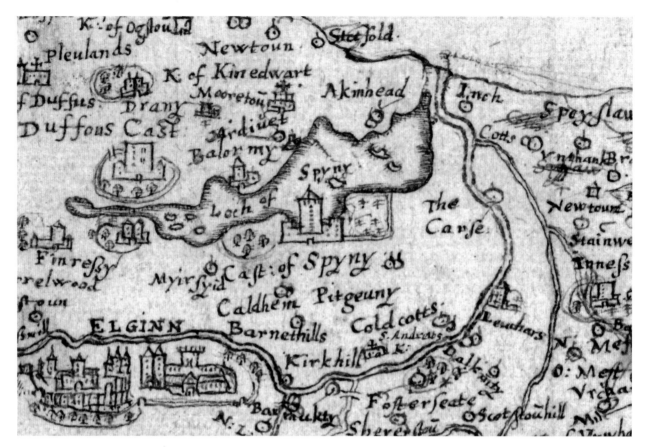

Fig 9 Part of the manuscript map of Moray made by Timothy Pont in the late sixteenth century. The depiction of the surroundings of castles such as Spynie can reveal evidence for their gardens, orchards and parks (Gordon 23). © NLS

century. They include a huge range of books, prints and drawings, which have provided much of the illustrative material in this book, and one of the aims of this work is to make these collections more widely known (Fig 8). The material associated with buildings may include much information about their gardens as well as their architects and owners.

Other important source material is held by the Map Library, part of the National Library of Scotland, whose staff have organised the digitisation of many of the early manuscript maps of Scotland (Webster 2004, 93–108). While previously these maps could be consulted at the Map Library, and copies of some of them were available in the Royal Commission's collections, the ability to examine these sources as a whole and in great detail has opened up the study of the topography of Scotland in the sixteenth, seventeenth and eighteenth centuries and has played an important part in the development of this book. The realisation that the cropmark features which had been recorded from the air at Castle Menzies, and which had been thought to be those of a garden, could be identified with a depiction of a garden on a manuscript map by Timothy Pont (NLS Pont 23), dating from the late sixteenth century was an important encouragement in this attempt to take forward the study of gardens in Scotland (Stone 1989) (Fig 7).

The presentation of other maps and plans has followed. Of particular value have been those by Adair (NLS Adv. MS.70.2.11), Gordon of Rothiemay (NLS EMS.s.52; EMS.s.249) and the Military Survey of 1747 to 1755 carried out under the auspices of William Roy and now housed in the British Library (Maps K.Top.48.25–1.a–f); all these maps are available through the National Library of Scotland website (Figs 10–12).

The presentation of the evidence for the presence of gardens in Scotland, whether it is derived from the physical remains on the ground or from documentary sources, underlies this approach to their history (Fig 13). This is especially relevant to the earlier chapters on gardens in Scotland covering the period before 1560, when pictorial evidence is for the most part lacking. Analogies have been made with illustrations derived from elsewhere in Europe, particularly in relation to the early medieval period. Archaeological excavations may provide a source of additional evidence for types of plants grown (Dickson and Dickson, 2000).

The work of earlier generations in producing printed editions of the ecclesiastical and secular records of Scotland has been invaluable in the study of gardens from medieval times. While further publication of surviving monastic and lay documents might well allow a more positive view of this period, enough material is available to allow the presumption that the presence of gardens and orchards was a normal feature of monastic houses, friaries, bishop's residences and universities in Scotland. The role of the garden extended beyond the

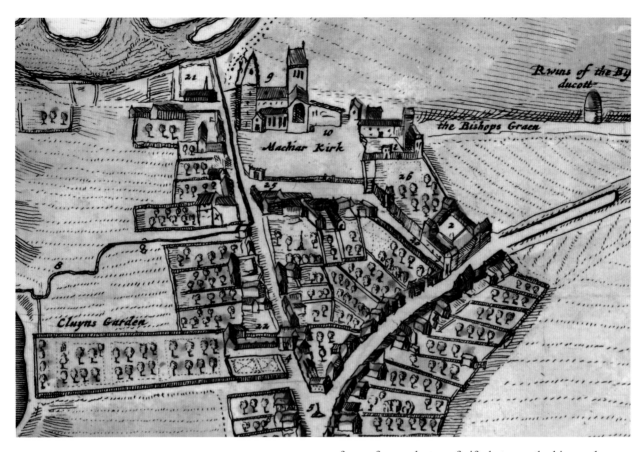

Fig 10 Gardens in Old Aberdeen from the map of Aberdeen by Gordon of Rothiemay of 1661. The garden near the centre with what appears to be a sundial in it belonged to the Marquess of Huntly (EMS.s.249). © NLS

essential function of providing food for the inhabitants of the monasteries; the opportunity for manual work and a place for pleasant refreshment had emblematic, theological and spiritual dimensions. The identification of the garden with Paradise evoked ideas of innocence, but it was also seen as the seat of more earthly pleasures (Figs 4 and 5).

There is far more evidence for the gardens belonging to the kings of Scotland than for those belonging to any of their subjects (Fig 14). Early Scottish documentary sources can scarcely be reckoned plentiful, but they are present, particularly in the later medieval period. The role of chance in the survival of documents is remarkable and the loss of the *Accounts of the Lord High Treasurer of Scotland* for the period between May 1498 and February 1500 is a source of great regret, for the payments in the *Exchequer Rolls* reveal that these years saw the beginnings of the gardens below the castle at Stirling near the area where the King's Knot now stands. Such information is often concerned with regular entries for wages and supplies for the gardens, but developments can be traced through payments for exceptional services; much of the evidence for the inception of the royal gardens at Holyrood emerges from such sources. They also reveal an active trade in trees, plants and seeds; in many cases this may have had the

form of an exchange of gifts between the king and one of his subjects, usually an abbot or a nobleman, who would receive or expect in the future an appropriate gift or favour in return for a donation of plants, but there are some indications of more conventional commercial acquisitions. The planting of *wyne treis* at Stirling suggests some more exotic species in the king's orchard. Information about the gardens belonging to the great lords is more random in its survival, but further work on estate papers might allow a wider perspective to be achieved. When there are documentary sources available, as in the case of the gardens of the Seton family, the information given may be startling; the gardens at Winton created by George Seton, who died in 1508, included one set with a hundred painted timber posts some twenty-five years before Henry VIII established the Privy Orchard at Hampton Court or the garden of Whitehall Palace (Fig 15). Gardens belonging to the Seton family were targeted for destruction during the English invasions of the 1540s.

The personal rules of Mary Queen of Scots and James VI and his governors during his minority see the evidence for gardens of the nobles and gentry becoming more prominent, although there is little evidence that James VI was interested in elaborating his palaces with such features. If more of the Masters of Works' account books (*MW*) had survived for the latter part of James VI's rule in Scotland the picture presented might have looked different, but his most remarkable creation was the Chapel Royal at Stirling Castle, designed for the

Fig 11 Biel, Belton, Tyningeham, Lochend and Broxmouth near Dunbar in East Lothian with their gardens as they were depicted on the manuscript map of East Lothian by John Adair in 1682 showing the enclosure walls, the tree planting and the gardens around the houses. Adv.MS.70.2.11 (Adair 10) © NLS

Fig 12 The formal gardens around Drum in Midlothian from Roy's Military Survey 1747–55 with its array of decorative plantations. © British Library Licensor Scran

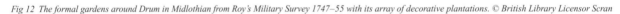

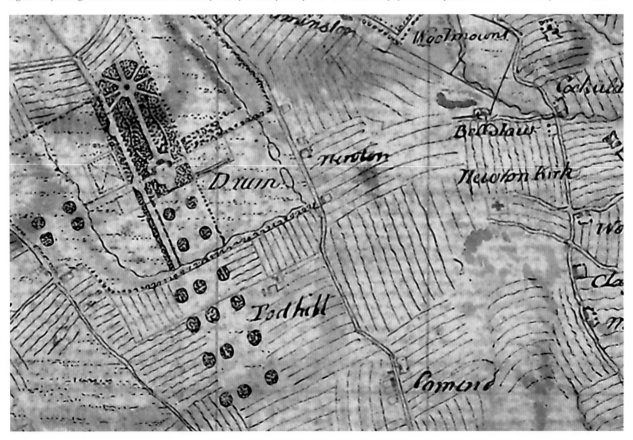

Fig 13 Aerial view of Dundrennan Abbey in Kirkcudbrightshire showing the enclosures around the monastery, the site of the former gardens or yards of the abbey. SC1291613

occasion of the christening of his heir, Prince Henry. He visited and spent time at the houses of his wealthy subjects, as he did later in England, and there are clear indications for the development of their gardens during this period.

Evidence for Dating

The surviving manuscript maps of Timothy Pont, for example, do provide evidence for gardens, or at least walled enclosures with trees growing in them, around many of the castles and mansions across much of the country apart from those in north-west Scotland. In the absence of a depiction on the Pont maps, the dating tends to be aligned with the date of the building with which the garden is associated, when its design is congruent, although there are several examples where the creation of the garden preceded the building of the house, sometimes, as in the case of Castle Kennedy, by over a century. An example of a simple use of axiality in which the house and garden are aligned appears at Castle Menzies in the 1580s and such a design

had strong practical advantages, with the mansion providing a fourth wall for the walled garden. A date for a particular garden may be put forward because of an association with a particular patron and owner, whose education, interests and wealth would suggest the probability he had played a part in its creation. The increasing number of printed books available in Scotland from the later fifteenth century favoured the prestige of the classics and the enjoyment of gardens believed to be designed on classical models. Important changes in land holding and security of tenure at this time probably played their part in encouraging gardening: the passing of land from monastic ownership into lay ownership or management, although only completed in the seventeenth century, also had an impact on secular gardens and gardening.

James VI's 'government by pen' after he had established himself in England was managed by a group of Scottish councillors and office holders of various ranks, many of whom have left evidence of their interest in gardening and in some cases the remains of their gardens. A number of men belonging to noble and gentry families accompanied James to England and prospered there, managing the developments of their estates in Scotland at a distance or during visits home.

Fig 14 Linlithgow Palace, formerly surrounded by gardens with its park on the north side of Linlithgow Loch, one of the principal residences of the kings and queens of Scotland. DP013242

There was no sudden change in design or purpose. It is difficult to imagine that the garden at Edzell, for example, dated to 1604, was not designed and planned over a period which covered the years on both sides of James' accession to the English throne (Fig 181). The gardens that have survived to be recognised as belonging to the late sixteenth and seventeenth centuries are for the most part those with strong earthwork or masonry elements, enclosing stone walls, terracing and decorative ponds. The survival of these gardens in such cases as Brunston or Elibank is often owing to their neglect or abandonment by their owners or the confiscation of the estate following opposition to the government particularly in the 1715 and 1745 rebellions. Many of the houses had been first built as defensible structures. Brunston (Fig 196) declined to a farmhouse when its owners favoured another property as their principal dwelling house. Elibank (Fig 204) stands at a height of 200m and its later owners would appear to have preferred to live at their house in East Lothian rather than at the property from which they derived their title. Edzell was preserved from a redesign as a landscape garden after its loss to the Lindsay family in 1715 and the sale to the York Buildings Company. The owners of Whytbank, which is situated at 260m above sea level, where fruit growing would be difficult, moved down to Yair on the banks of the Tweed in the

eighteenth century (Fig 215). Climate changes may have had a role in desertion (Morrison 1995, 8–12). The intellectual delight taken in gardens with their inscriptions, sculpture, fountains, garden houses and sundials is paralleled in the houses of earlier seventeenth

Fig 15 'Whitehall Stairs' by the Flemish artist Antonis van Wyngaerde, drawn between 1558 and 1562, showing the garden of Whitehall Palace in London with a fountain surrounded by painted posts. The design recalls the painted posts in the earlier garden at Seton Castle. WA.C.IV*.99a. © Ashmolean Museum, University of Oxford

century date, of which Pinkie is an outstanding example (Fig 193). An engagement with the arts and sciences was part of the pleasure which the enlightened owner would take in his garden, and the house and the garden should be considered together, each playing an essential part in their owner's view of himself and his world. Many earlier houses were remodelled and extended in the seventeenth century, and gardens were constructed to match the changing demands of style and status.

There are many more gardens surviving in Scotland whose design originated in the period following the Restoration of Charles II in 1660. Information on garden layout and planting, both theoretical and practical, became far more widely available and books on garden and estate design proliferated. The overall scale of gardening and planting increases dramatically, and the surviving traces in the landscape can be read with greater certainty. For the first time gardeners could see themselves as outdoing their Roman predecessors. The importance of French culture and its expression in the design of gardens shape the predominating style adopted by major landowners, but the retention of walled enclosures close to the house, albeit on a larger scale, which had been an important feature of gardens earlier, remained an important element in the overall design. The integration of the garden and the wider estate was an aim which was satisfying to the landowner philosophically as well as practically. The park at Yester in East Lothian, discussed in Chapter 6, was the subject of a series of five paintings covering different aspects of the Earl of Tweeddale's estate and encapsulate this development (Figs 1, 19 etc). Many more individual gardens survive, but the estate plans which begin to appear about 1700 and the Roy Military Survey show how many were swept away as the principles governing garden design underwent major changes later in the eighteenth century. The focusing of a garden, and indeed a house, on a distant monument of historic significance or remarkable natural features was a particular aspect of the work of Sir William Bruce, the most influential architect in later seventeenth century Scotland, and was taken up by his successors. Evidence for the planning of the garden as part of the total conception of the house and its policies becomes more frequent in this period.

Fig 16 The sundial now in the garden of Broughton House, Kirkcudbright, probably came from MacLellans Castle in Kirkcudbright and dates from 1636. As well as indicating the time it is concerned with astronomical observation. SC801548

Contemporary Descriptions

One source which has been quarried for information about the state of gardens in Scotland is the accounts of travellers to the country. In 1891 Peter Hume Brown drew together a very useful collection dating from before 1700 which has subsequently been reprinted (1978). His selection begins with Edward I in 1295 and concludes with an extract from Thomas Morer's *A short history of Scotland* of 1689. John Macky and Daniel Defoe published their descriptions of Scotland in 1723 and 1724 respectively, although some of the material was gathered several years earlier. Their descriptions of gardens are frequently cited in the later chapters of this book. A problem with the use of these accounts is achieving an understanding of the motives and underlying prejudices of their authors, a matter which must be considered in all documentary sources, but which may be less obvious in these sometimes artless narratives. Various writers including Andrew Boorde, Defoe and Macky formed their impressions while they were acting as spies or agents of a foreign government, in all these cases that of England (Fig 17) (Scott 1995, 3–17; 40–8). Fortunately a summary and review of sixteenth century and earlier accounts by travellers to

Fig 17 Andrew Boorde was a well known doctor and writer on medical and other subjects during the reign of Henry VIII; he named Orleans, Poitiers, Toulouse, Montpellier and Wittenberg as his places of study. He spent about a year in Glasgow and wrote in a letter to Thomas Cromwell on 1 April 1536 from Leith, 'I am now in skotland, in a lytle vnyuersyte or study namyd Glasco, wher I study & practyce physyk as I haue done in dyuerce regyons & prouynces, for the sustentacyon off my lyuyng.' He was also acting as an agent for Cromwell, reporting on foreign views of the actions of Henry VIII. © Edinburgh University Library: Licensor Scran

Scotland provide a useful context for these writings (Rackwitz 2007, 73–114). Some writers provide detailed descriptions which are of considerable value when used with caution, but the desire to denigrate Scottish customs in this form of literature should be considered in its context.

One of the earlier descriptions was that by Fynes Moryson, who visited Edinburgh, Leith and Falkland on a brief visit in 1598 (perhaps four or five days in all including the journey from Berwick and back again) and published his description of Scotland, *An Itinerary written by Fynes Moryson, gent. First in the Latin tongue and then translated by him into English: containing his ten yeeres travell through the twelve Dominions of Germany, Boermerland, Sweitzerland, Netherland, Denmarke, Poland, Jtaly, France, England, Scotland and Ireland* in 1617. His limited acquaintance with the country is, however, informed by his wide experience of other countries, including a journey through the Levant. On his one day journey from Berwick to Edinburgh he passed by 'the ancient and (according to the building of that Kingdome) stately Pallace of L. Seton, beautified with faire Orchards and Gardens and for that clime pleasant'. Of Fife he writes that it was 'full of Noblemen's and gentlemens dwellings commonly compassed with little groves, though trees are so rare in those parts, as I remember not to have seen one wood' (Moryson 1617, Pt1 Bk 3, Ch 5, 272–4). Moryson was, like William Lithgow (1640) and Thomas Coryate (1611), an almost obsessive traveller and writer. Among other writers of seventeenth and eighteenth century accounts there is a tendency to repeat what earlier visitors had previously published; the wondrous tale of the barnacle geese that grow on trees recurs frequently in these narratives.

The intention to publish would seem to have had a bearing on the description of the country. One of the more curious examples of this tendency is Thomas Kirke, who produced two accounts of his three month travels in Scotland in 1677. The first of these was his diary; the second a diatribe against Scotland entitled *A modern account of Scotland; : being, an exact description of the country, and a true character of the people and their manners. Written from thence by an English gentleman* and printed in London anonymously in 1679. It was an imitation of Antony Weldon's *A perfect description of the people and country of Scotland* printed in 1644 in London, supposedly an account of Scotland by someone who accompanied James on his visit to Scotland in 1617. Kirke's diary, never intended to be printed, was moderate in tone and reflected his appreciation of the kind and helpful way in which he was treated in Scotland, as well as providing some useful information about gardens. In contrast in his published account he presented a distorted picture that in no way reflected his own experiences. It was a popular image and Martin Rackwitz has pointed out that the four reprints of the pamphlet between 1699 and 1746 were published at times of extreme tension between England and Scotland, namely the Darien disaster, the Jacobite rebellion of 1708, the Hanoverian succession and the 1745 rebellion (Rackwitz 2007, 118–21).

The earliest book on gardening by a Scot and specifically concerned with the weather conditions and the topography of Scotland was *The Scots Gard'ner Published for the Climate of Scotland* written by John

Reid and printed by David Lindsay in Edinburgh in 1683 (Fig 18). His aim as a writer was 'the good of my country'. Like many of his successors, Reid was concerned about the weather in Scotland. His reference to earlier writers, that 'the many books on Gard'nery were for other countries and climates' (Reid 1988, A2), reflects the perception in Scotland in the seventeenth century that books on gardening in English were designed for England and that English gardening practice was the norm against which Scottish gardens were judged, a position which has been maintained until relatively recent years.

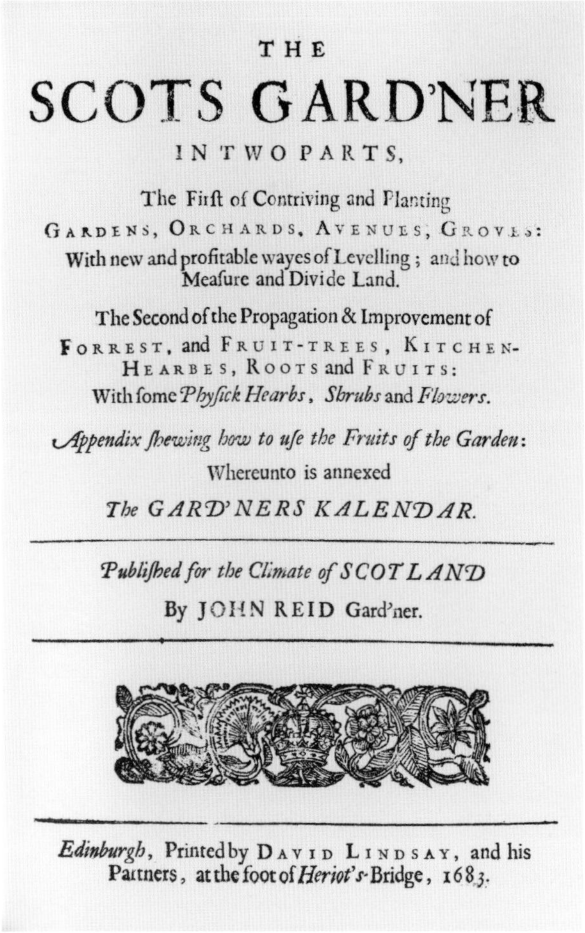
THE

SCOTS GARD'NER

IN TWO PARTS,

The Firſt of Contriving and Planting GARDENS, ORCHARDS, AVENUES, GROVES: With new and profitable wayes of Levelling; and how to Meaſure and Divide Land.

The Second of the Propagation & Improvement of FORREST, and FRUIT-TREES, KITCHEN-HEARBES, ROOTS and FRUITS: With ſome *Phyſick Hearbs*, *Shrubs* and *Flowers*.

Appendix ſhewing how to uſe the Fruits of the Garden: Whereunto is annexed *The GARD'NERS KALENDAR.*

Publiſhed for the Climate of SCOTLAND By JOHN REID Gard'ner.

Edinburgh, Printed by DAVID LINDSAY, and his Partners, at the foot of *Heriot's*-Bridge, 1683.

Fig 18 The title page of the The Scots Gard'ner Publish'd for the Climate of Scotland *by John Reid Gard'ner in 1683, the first book on gardening published in Scotland.*

Modern Works

Writers of the twentieth century, particularly those with a historical perspective, such as Sir Herbert Maxwell in *Scottish Gardens being a representative selection of different types, old and new* (1908) and Euan Cox in *A History of Gardening in Scotland* (1935) view Scottish gardening practice in relation to an English background, although with a stated desire to present gardens in Scotland in their own right. In contrast to this is Elizabeth Haldane's *Scots Gardens in Old Times (1200–1800)* published in 1934, which makes a point of recognising Scotland's European links and puts forward a more sanguine and, despite its rather cosy tone, a more accurate impression of the progress of gardens in Scotland. Unfortunately none of these authors have provided specific references for most of their statements and suggestions, and the reader is unable to gain an informed opinion on the subject.

Sir Herbert Maxwell of Monreith was born in 1845. In 1908 on the establishment of the Royal Commission on the Ancient and Historical Monuments of Scotland he became its first chairman and held this post for twenty-six years (Murray 2008, 115–35). His family estates lay in Wigtownshire and he was deeply concerned in their management. He was MP for the county from 1880 to 1906 and had a career as a politician, becoming a Junior Lord of Treasury with responsibility for pensions. He wrote popular books on a wide variety of scholarly subjects which included topography, Scottish and local history, archaeology, natural history and horticulture. He was responsible for two series of Rhynd Lectures for the Society of Antiquaries of Scotland of which he was president between 1900 and 1913. He was closely involved in the passing of the original Ancient Monuments Act in 1882 and was the first person in Scotland to put forward various sites on his own land for guardianship under the Act. His book *Scottish Gardens* appeared in 1908, the same year he became chairman of the Royal Commission, and included coloured illustrations prepared by Mary Wilson of selected contemporary gardens, which had, for the most part, predecessors in the sixteenth and seventeenth centuries. It took a positive if romantic view of what had been achieved in these gardens and a nuanced perception of the differences in climatic conditions between England and Scotland as well as displaying a keen sense of place. It is possible that the reference to the garden at Plunton Castle in Kirkcudbrightshire, the first to occur in any inventory, may be owing to his interests (RCAHMS 1914, 39–40).

Elizabeth Haldane was born in Edinburgh in 1862, an only daughter with five brothers, who was destined from the age of fifteen to be the unmarried companion of her widowed mother, a role which she performed for forty-eight years. The family had a country house at Auchterarder in Perthshire. She was well educated and her achievements in public life were remarkable, aided by her brothers' careers and connections, and perhaps helped by her unmarried state. She was involved with Octavia Hill in the improvement of housing conditions for the poor, met Sidney and Beatrice Webb and George Bernard Shaw and studied the writings of Arnold Toynbee and John Ruskin. In 1890 she helped to found the Scottish Women's Benefit Society, pioneers of old-age pensions for women in Scotland. She also produced with Frances Stimson *The History*

Fig 19 Detail from a painting of the garden of Yester House probably dating from the 1690s. A lady and her dog walk towards the gate leading into the wider park. The beds have been cut out in a simple pattern and planted with colourful flowers. The gate posts are topped with urns. DP109178

of Philosophy and several works on Hegel. Her *Life of Descartes* published in 1905 led to her being awarded an honorary LLD by the University of St Andrews in 1906. She served on many committees on social welfare, particularly those concerned with schools and hospitals, and was appointed a Companion of Honour in 1918. A supporter of women's suffrage, in 1912 she was appointed a member of a royal commission on the civil service, and wrote a memorandum of dissent from the recommendations of the majority on the question of women's conditions of employment; she was concerned that women should receive equal pay. Her book on Scottish gardens, also with illustrations by Mary Wilson, was published when she was in her seventies. She did use published sources, including the *Exchequer Rolls* and Brown's *Early Travellers in Scotland*, and considered a range of writers on Scotland and their descriptions of agriculture and horticulture. She fully acknowledged the difficulties of putting forward a complete account because of lack of information, but was not tempted to take the opportunity to argue from absence of knowledge (*DNB* 2004, 24, 503–5).

Euan Cox was a gardener and plant collector, born in 1893 to a family of jute manufacturers who owned the Camperdown Works in Dundee. He read history at Cambridge, and after being wounded in World War I, became secretary to John Buchan at the Foreign Office. In 1919 he took part in a plant collecting expedition to Burma, which led to the introduction of new plant species into Britain. His choice of authorship as a career was influenced by a declining financial situation – jute manufacturing was moving to India – and in addition to *The History of Gardening in Scotland* in 1935, he published works on plant hunting in the Far East and wild gardening. He became garden editor of *Country Life* and edited another magazine, *New Flora and Silva*, which was concerned with the introduction of new plants into Britain. He returned to Scotland in 1931 and in 1943 moved into the family house at Glendoick in Perthshire, where he had already planted many rhododendrons, and the collection was extended through the following decades. The nursery, which still continues as a major supplier of plants, was established in the early 1950s (Urquhart 2005, 153). *The History of Gardening in Scotland* is still the only work which attempts to cover gardens and gardening in Scotland before the latter part of the reign of Queen Victoria but is, on the whole, a gloomy and disparaging work. For example Cox's comment on the garden at Edzell, one of the most remarkable survivals of a seventeenth century garden in any country, is 'It is unfortunate that only the walls and the garden house are standing. Flower-beds there must have been, but no trace of them survives' (Cox 1935, 32). The area where Cox expresses most enthusiasm is the section on 'Seedsmen, Nurserymen and Market Gardeners' and that only in the period after 1660. A tendency to argue from lack of information is an unfortunate element in the work, particularly in relation to the period before the eighteenth century.

Many of the twentieth century authors drew on the very useful report prepared by Patrick Neill for the Board of Agriculture, published in 1813. Neill was the Secretary of the Caledonian Horticultural Society for forty years; he was deeply affected by the contemporary view of garden design (Neill 1813, 3) and highly critical of formal gardens, somewhat inaccurately attributing them to the early eighteenth century rather than the previous century:

> ...ornamental gardening [was] more generally introduced into Scotland in the beginning of the eighteenth century. The garden was laid out into squares, planes and slopes, circles, ovals and various fanciful figures; with trees pruned into particular and grotesque shapes.

He continues expressing his relief 'that the ground is no longer planned into regular mathematical figures and topiary work is altogether exploded'. Instead there is 'the substitution of imitations of natural scenery in place of exact squares and faultless circles' (Fig 19) (Neill 1813, 5, 6).

An apologetic vein and a tendency to an automatic comparison with England run through many of the books and articles on gardens in Scotland. Even Kitty Cruft of Royal Commission, writing in 1988, says, 'In England the examination of vanished manorial houses has resulted in an interesting series of abandoned formal gardens with designed parterres, long canals, ponds and wildernesses. These important manor houses are absent in Scotland,' before going on to provide remarkable examples of survival in Scotland, comparable with those in England (Cruft 1991, 175). The work of Alan Tait, particularly his deeply scholarly volume *The Landscape Garden in Scotland 1735–1835* (1980), which covers the period following that which forms the main part of this book, provides a detailed and brilliantly researched account of later developments in the culture of gardening. He addresses the habitual deference to English superiority in this field and begins with the sentence, 'The landscape garden in Scotland has been inevitably accepted as the poor relation of that in England.' He goes on to record how 'as a child of the Edinburgh Enlightenment, the landscape garden was indeed very much part of the wider culture of North Britain' and demonstrates how it has evolved. Behind such attitudes are the words of Fynes Moryson, who visited Scotland in April 1598: 'As in the Northerne parts of England, they have small pleasantness, goodness, or abundance of Fruites and Flowers, so in Scotland, they must have lesse or none at all,' an opinion, based in his case, on very restricted observation.

Reassessment and Review

The two writers who have done most to alter the perception of early gardens in Scotland are Neil Hynd of Historic Scotland and Forbes W Robertson, Emeritus Professor of Genetics at the University of Aberdeen. Neil Hynd wrote a short paper 'Towards a study of gardening in Scotland' (Hynd 1984, 269–84), arising from his own involvement in the excavations at Aberdour Castle. He brought together information about various sites in the care of what is now Historic Scotland and the accounts and references in the RCAHMS county inventories to rectify the prevailing picture of gardening in Scotland in the sixteenth and seventeenth centuries and produce a more measured view. Forbes W Robertson's *Early Scottish Gardeners and their Plants*, published in 2000, had its origins in his studies of the plants, shrubs, vegetables and fruit trees grown in the seventeenth and eighteenth centuries and the men who were responsible for them.

In addition to these broader works, there is a series of excellent recent papers on the history and development of individual gardens, among which might be singled out that on the gardens at Holyrood before 1700 by Fiona Jamieson (1994) and the discussion by David Allan (1997) of the role of philosophy in the garden in the seventeenth century as exemplified by Edzell. For the later seventeenth century the work of the architect Sir William Bruce has been the subject of studies by John Dunbar (1970 and 1975) and Hugh Fenwick (1970). Margaret Stewart has written illuminatingly on the Earl of Mar's garden at Alloa (1989) and John Lowrey has elucidated later garden achievements at Hamilton Palace prior to William Adam's work there (1989). Lowrey has also charted the career of Alexander Edward, a dispossessed Episcopalian minister, architect and designer who has been associated with the gardens at Kinross, Hamilton, Hopetoun and Brechin (Lowrey 1989) and who frequently worked with Bruce. This partnership provides the first proof of a professional approach to the whole building and its landscape setting.

Writers of the twenty-first century, such as Suki Urquhart (2005), whose particular concern is gardeners and their gardens, do not seem to have the need, unlike their predecessors, to look to the south, concentrating on individual gardens of the present day and taking an unapologetic stance. This positive attitude to Scottish culture and institutions is not confined to subjects such as gardening; the history, constitution, philosophy, architecture, music and drama of the medieval, renaissance and early modern period have all undergone recent reassessment in the light of new research. While continuity is an important element, the period before 1750 saw important changes in the physical relationship between the house and garden and major changes in the intellectual approaches to the enjoyment of gardens.

Chapter 1: The Monastic Garden 500 to 1560

'In recording the story of gardening the historian can look with envy on the history of gardening south of the Border... The truth is that gardening, as we know it, was little practiced before the reign of James VI.' With this rather depressing prologue EHM Cox began, in 1935, his work *A History of Gardening in Scotland*. The materials for studying early gardening are neither so plentiful in England nor so lacking in Scotland in the medieval period as the author seemed to believe. Scotland was exposed to the same writings on classical gardening as the rest of Western Europe. The Roman villa was a place for agricultural production and recreation in the country; as an institution it ceased to be viable during the unsettled period after the fall of Rome, but the traditions which underlay it survived, to some degree, in the Christian monasteries which followed the Rule of St Benedict, some of which were founded on the sites of earlier villas, and so came to form part of the common monastic practice in Europe. As in most of Western Europe, there was no settlement by Moslem conquerors from North Africa and the Near and Middle East, although some acquaintance with the gardens created for them in Spain and Sicily – where there were surviving remains at Cordoba, at Seville, at Granada and in the environs of Palermo – is possible (Harvey 1990, 44–51; Harvey 1992, 76). Scotland, like the rest of Western Europe, had its spiritual ties to Rome, and Latin was the common language of the educated classes, with French as the medium for cultured and courtly conversation. This common cultural background is more important than the differences between the various countries in climate and the differences in their relative wealth. By comparison with buildings, gardens are, for the most part, relatively inexpensive creations and means of expressing a cultural identity. Because of the nature of the ownership of the early gardens that can be traced in Scotland and of their subsequent history, it is convenient to treat gardens belonging to religious foundations and those belonging to the Crown and the greater landowners in Scotland in separate chapters, although as becomes evident in the later fifteenth and early sixteenth centuries, when the survival of records is greater, there was a certain fluidity between the two, both in terms of the gardens themselves and those who designed and worked in them.

Fig 20 Aerial view of Iona Abbey from the south-east showing the remains of the monastic vallum or boundary bank which enclosed the monastery, and the level fertile land around it. SC738555

Gardens Before the Twelfth Century

Facing the south for warmth, a little stream across its enclosure, a choice ground with abundant bounties which would be good for every plant...

The wish of Manchan of Liath (Jackson 1971, 280).

There is no archaeological record of the existence of gardens in the prehistoric or Roman periods in Scotland, although there is evidence for cultivation, normally associated with the growing of plants for food and drink, as well as, perhaps, for medicinal reasons (Zeepvat 1991, 53–9; Dickson and Dickson 2000, 204–210). Camilla and James Dickson in *Plants and People in Ancient Scotland* describe the evidence for plant species recovered from excavation and analysis in the first millennium AD (Dickson and Dickson 2000, 128–176). Widely separated sites, monastic and domestic, have yielded finds suggesting the cultivation of plants which would require careful attention and skills of a kind which might be equated with that provided by a gardener. The excavation of the monastery at Whithorn in south-west Scotland produced evidence for a possible herb garden of a date prior to the middle of the ninth century (Hill 1997, 593), with dill, coriander and mustard present, although it is possible that the seeds found there may have been imported (Dickson and Dickson, 2000, 137–8). If the plants were grown at the monastery, this would be the earliest evidence for a herb garden in Britain. Coriander and dill are also known from the excavation of the crannog at Buiston in Ayrshire (Holden 1996, 957–8). Far to the north, henbane, juniper and lesser celandine, plants with medicinal uses, with antiseptic, anti-inflammatory, diuretic and emmenagogic (promoting menstruation) qualities, are known from excavations at the broch site of Howe in Orkney in contexts belonging to the first millennium AD.

The first gardens usually discussed in Scotland are those of the monastic communities, which colonised the west of Scotland, and the islands of the Hebrides in particular, from abbeys in Ireland. **Iona**, the most prominent of these, was founded by St Columba about 563. The site of the early monastery, which was presumably approved by Columba himself, lies on the gently sloping eastern plain (Figs 20, 21). The central area is sheltered from the west by the rocky outcrop known as Cnoc nan Carnan. Discussion of the layout of the Early Christian monastery in Volume 4 of *Argyll: An Inventory of the Monuments* (RCAHMS 1982, 31–43) indicates an organised series of enclosures within the monastic *vallum* or surrounding bank, serving different functions necessary to the running of the community. Chapter 66 of the Rule of St Benedict declares that the monastery should, if possible, be so arranged that 'all necessary things such as water, mill, garden and various crafts may be within the enclosure, so that the monks may not be compelled to wander outside it, for that is not at all expedient for their souls' (Benedict 1995, 74). The *Life of St Columba* compiled by Adomnan, who became one of Columba's successors as abbot of Iona in 679, survives in a copy made there during the author's lifetime. It records that Columba sent one of his monks, a man called Trenan, as a messenger to Ireland (Adomnan 1995,125, 279). Finding himself to be one man short of a full boat crew, he complained to the saint, who replied that he would have a fair following wind to Ireland and that the first man he met on landing would return with him to Iona. This was Lasren, described as a gardener and holy man, who spent the rest of his life in the monastery, presumably in charge of the herb garden and other crops required for the monks. Excavations on the island have not, to date, revealed surviving pollen of plants appropriate to such a garden. They do suggest the presence of wooden buildings, enclosed within a bank topped with bushes and small trees, which would provide some shelter from the persistent winds. The conditions for much of the year on Iona would contrast with the ideal setting for a monastery or hermitage epitomised in verses attributed to a monk of the tenth century in *The wish of Manchan of Liath* (Jackson 1971, 280).

> I wish, O son of the Living God, ancient eternal King, for a secret hut in the wilderness that it may be my dwelling.
> A very blue shallow well to be beside it, a clear pool for washing away sins through the grace of the Holy Ghost.
> A beautiful wood close by around it on every side, for the nurture of many-voiced birds, to shelter and hide it.
> Facing the south for warmth, a little stream across its enclosure, a choice ground with abundant bounties which would be good for every plant...
> This is the housekeeping I would undertake, I would choose it without concealing; fragrant fresh leeks, hens, speckled salmon, bees.

The verses in Gaelic and Latin, believed to have been written on Iona itself in the seventh and eighth centuries, are concerned more directly with devotion to God, Columba and the saints (Clancy and Markus 1995).

From the sixth and seventh centuries onwards monasteries and hermitages were founded across Scotland. The ideal was a remote place, cut off from the world, where the monks and nuns would be undisturbed by secular affairs. Some of these

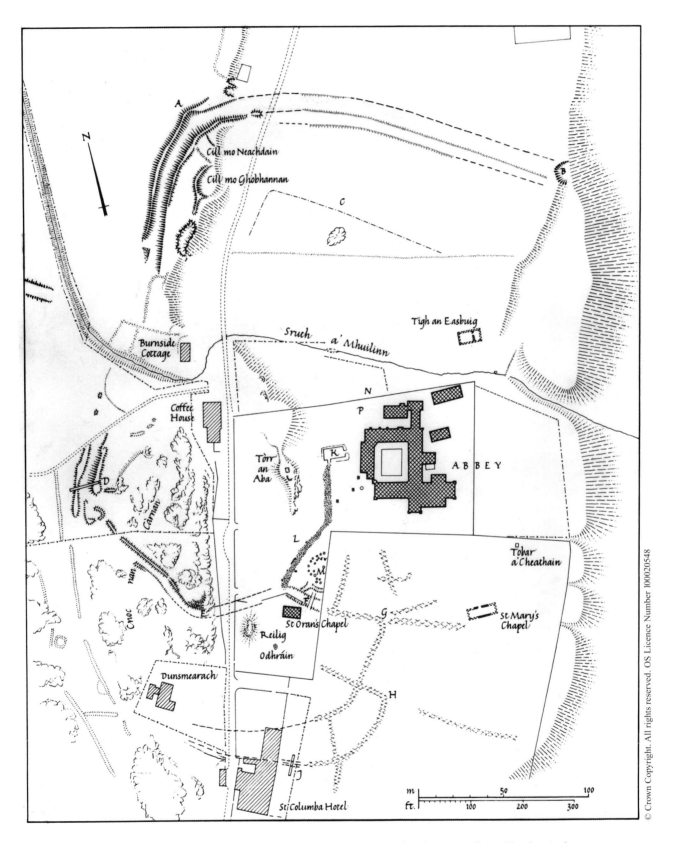

Fig 21 Plan of Iona Abbey showing the monastic vallum and other enclosures of the Early Christian period revealed by geophysical survey. SC366785

monasteries probably lie beneath later buildings and others cannot be traced, but some, particularly those in remote areas, not subject to stone robbing, survive as low turf and stone walls and banks. A site on Canna, in the Inner Hebrides, known as Sgor nam Ban-Naomha or Skerry of the Holy Women, provides a picture of what an early eremitic site in Scotland might look like (Fig 22). The site lies at the foot of a cliff, with a landing from the sea possible only in

Fig 22 Aerial view of Sgor nam Ban-Naomha, the site of a possible Early Christian eremitic settlement on Canna. SC378367

Fig 23 The site of the Anglian monastery of Coldingham situated on the cliffs of St Abbs Head in Berwickshire, high above the North Sea. SC1237351

good weather, and a difficult path down the scree slopes from above. It measures about 37m across within a massive drystone wall, with a chapel in the interior. Some early monasteries in Scotland, such as the monastery of Coldingham on the sea cliffs of St Abbs Head, were founded in remote places, in that case within an earlier fort (Fig 23). Others were located on sites, such as promontories, which could with relatively little labour be enclosed by a bank and ditch. Old Melrose was founded in a meander of the River Tweed (Fig 24), while the monastery at Hoddom in Annandale, which is associated with St Mungo or Kentigern, is enclosed by a ditch; it appears in the form of a cropmark, with faint traces of other smaller enclosures within it, near the site of the later medieval church (Fig 25). All would have had a garden as a normal element of a monastery.

The plan of an ideal monastery (MS Codex Sangallensis 1092) (Figs 26, 27, 28, 29), preserved at the monastery of St Gall, an abbey founded by an Irishman in the seventh century in what is now Switzerland, was addressed to Gozbert who was abbot between 816 and 836, and it may have been drawn up by Haito, abbot of the nearby house of Reichenau. The plan is in some sense that of an ideal

Fig 24 The site of the Anglian monastery at Old Melrose, lying in a meander of the River Tweed. SC449851

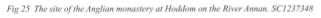

Fig 25 The site of the Anglian monastery at Hoddom on the River Annan. SC1237348

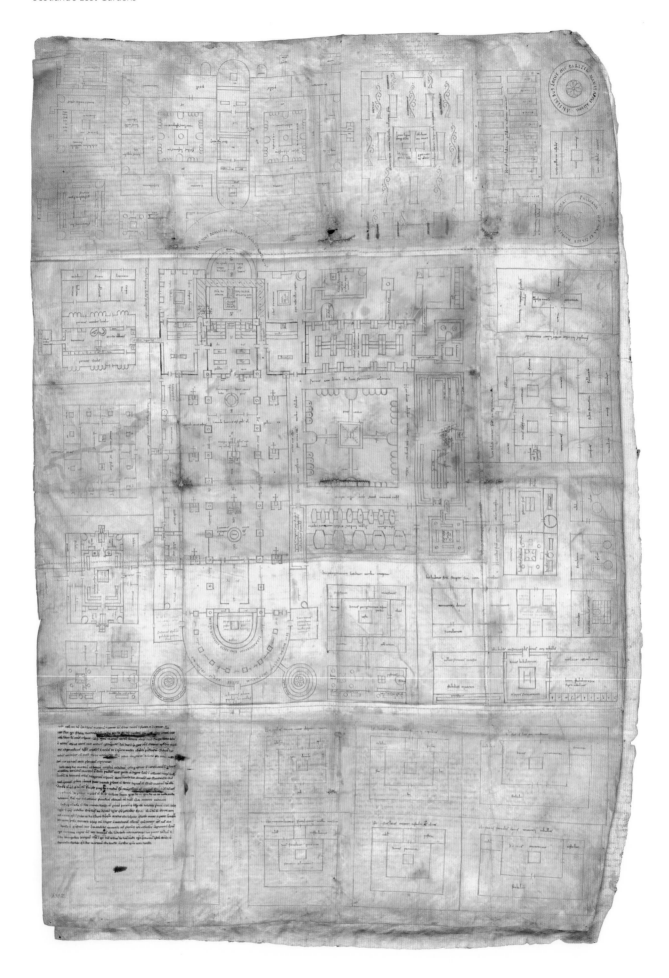

monastery: the monastery complex could not, for instance, be constructed on the site of St Gall itself, and it may be that it was an exemplar devised by these senior churchmen of the Carolingian period, for an ideal or typical monastery, reflecting the complex roles of monastic houses of the ninth century. This extremely geometrical plan shows two gardens; one, the infirmary garden, *herbularius*, next to the physician's house, contains sixteen beds, each with a named herb, while the other, next to the poultry yard, was a larger kitchen garden, the *hortus*, with eighteen beds, growing dill, coriander, onions, garlic, leeks, shallots, celery, parsley, chervil, poppy, savory, radishes, possibly carrots, parsnips, coleworts, beets and black cumin (Fig 29). The orchard was laid out in the monks' cemetery (Harvey 1990, 32–3) with trees and graves alternating (Fig 27). The movement of scholars and pilgrims across Europe would have allowed knowledge of such a scheme to reach monastic houses throughout Britain and the rest of Europe. At the Benedictine monastery of Fleury on the River Loire, a house which had considerable contact with Anglo-Saxon monasteries in the tenth century, after the Viking incursions, the gardener is described as follows:

The one appointed to be gardener (called hortulanus and viridarius) should be a spiritual man, of mature years, physically strong, and an enemy of idleness, who during the whole spring and summer will attentively busy himself with the garden, digging, manuring and planting useful vegetables from which dishes can be prepared for the brethren, namely cabbages, leeks, turnips, squash, pumpkins and melons. The other kinds of herbs used to season dishes or sweeten food are too many to enumerate. Let him take diligent care of the orchard and each year, at the full moon that precedes Easter, skilfully graft or plant new tree shoots. He is also to cultivate under the largest trees the radishes that produce such pungent belches. He should obtain sufficient bread from the baker and other food from the cellarer for his workers. He must also provide the cellarer with a certain number and variety of fruits and with vegetables for the daily meals. (Meyvaert 1986, 30, n. 25)

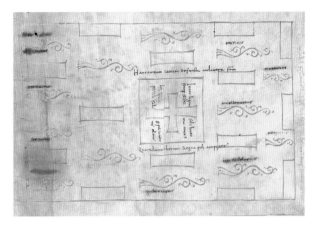

Fig 27 Detail of the St Gall plan showing the design of the orchard where the fruit trees are interspersed with the graves of the monks. Codex Sangallensis 1092 recto. © Abbey Library of St. Gallen, Switzerland / Codices Electronici Sangallenses

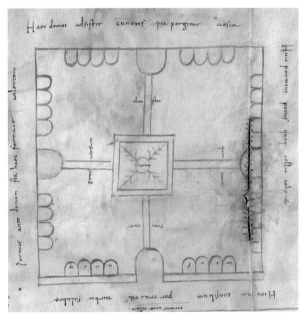

Fig 28 Detail of the St Gall plan showing the design of the cloister. Codex Sangallensis 1092 recto. © Abbey Library of St. Gallen, Switzerland / Codices Electronici Sangallenses

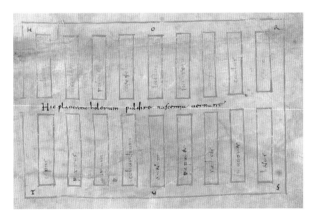

Fig 29 Detail of the St Gall plan showing the design of the plots in the vegetable garden. Codex Sangallensis 1092 recto. © Abbey Library of St. Gallen, Switzerland / Codices Electronici Sangallenses

Fig 26 Plan of an ideal layout for an early ninth century monastery drawn at Reichenau, a monastery on an island in Lake Constance, which has been preserved at the monastery of St Gall in Switzerland. The infirmary garden appears at the top right of the plan and vegetable garden at the top left. Codex Sangallensis 1092 recto. © Abbey Library of St. Gallen, Switzerland / Codices Electronici Sangallenses

Monastic Gardening From the Twelfth to the Sixteenth Century

Allone as I went up and doun
In an abbay was fair to see

The Abbay Walk (Henryson 1968, 195)

During the twelfth century many of the religious houses, which survive as notable ruins in the landscape and townscapes of Scotland, were founded or refounded, often with the direct support of the Crown. There was strong influence from both England and France, with daughter houses established by monks from both countries. While some, such as Dunfermline and Iona, followed the Benedictine Rule, others such as Holyrood, which was established by canons from Merton, belonged to the Augustinian order. Jedburgh, also an Augustinian house, was probably founded from the abbey of St Quentin, near Beauvais in northern France. Kelso belonged to the Tironensian Order, founded from Tiron near Chartres in western France,

with Kilwinning and Arbroath founded from Kelso; Paisley belonged to the Cluniac Order colonised by monks from Much Wenlock in Shropshire, Dryburgh (Fig 30) to the Premonstratensian with canons coming from Alnwick in Northumberland, and Melrose to the Cistercian Order founded with an abbot and monks coming from Rievaulx in North Yorkshire. Pluscarden, Ardchattan in Argyll and Beauly belonged to the Valliscaulian order from Val-des-Choux in Burgundy and followed in the thirteenth century (Cowan and Easson 1976, 7–15).

Monastic government ensured contact between the houses belonging to the same order. In the case of the Cistercians, abbots of all the daughter houses were supposed to meet at Cîteaux for the general chapter each year, although from about 1180, abbots from Scotland were allowed to attend every four years because of the arduous nature of the journey (Kerr 2008, 50). One aim of the annual chapters was to preserve a degree of uniformity among Cistercian houses. The opportunities for discussion of matters pertaining to the monastic life across the whole of Europe were allied to visits to monasteries en route, so that knowledge of the organisation, including the cultivation and maintenance

Fig 30 Dryburgh Abbey beside the River Tweed in Berwickshire. Yards and orchards formerly surrounded the abbey. DP073387

of gardens, would be extended across all the houses of the order. Most of the other orders did not hold such regular meetings, but the conduct of the individual houses required travel, at least for the abbots and major office holders, to conduct business, legal, economic and spiritual, in the world beyond the boundaries of the house.

Elizabeth Haldane, whose *Scots Gardens in Olden Times* was published in 1934, takes a relatively sanguine view of gardening in Scotland in the 'days of the monks and the castles', but gives little in the way of specific references before the sixteenth century, and cites late eighteenth and nineteenth century works recording the presence of ancient trees and particularly fruit trees on monastic sites as evidence for gardens (Haldane 1934, 1–37). Cox sees Scotland as a backwater, out of touch with the rest of the world, as well as riven by internal strife, preventing gardening from developing there. He remarks that the siting of castles usually made the formation of a garden a physical impossibility and comments on the small scale of castles in Scotland compared with those in England. This does not seem to indicate a detailed understanding of the history or of the architecture of either country. He does, however, see the monastic houses, with the exception of the abbeys in the Borders, as exempt from this constant warfare. The argument from an absence of evidence is unsound and partakes of the general view of all good things, including knowledge of agriculture and fruit growing, coming from the 'large monasteries of the south' (Cox 1935, 2–4).

The lack of specific references makes it difficult to consider this claim, but something of the same lack of confidence here transferred to another country, can be seen in the first chapter of Miles Hadfield's *A History of British Gardening* published in 1960. Here, from an English point of view, the practice of gardening was more successfully undertaken outside England, in this case on the other side of the Channel. There is little about gardens or gardening in the medieval period in Scotland in this volume, which drew mainly upon Cox's and Haldane's works. After a consideration of the documentary evidence for monastic gardens in England before the end of the fifteenth century (Hadfield 1979, 28), Hadfield states that little is known about monastic gardening, which is undoubtedly true, but concludes that it may have been generally a second-rate version of contemporary continental gardening and 'that is about all', giving no reference to sources, which he might have employed to support this view. John Harvey, an architectural and garden historian, mentioned only one gardener in his *English Mediaeval Architects* of 1954. This was used by Hadfield as supporting evidence of the lack of gardening skills and notable gardens in England (Hadfield 1979, 36), but Harvey went on to publish his *Mediaeval Gardens* in 1981, where his Appendix One directly contradicts this perception (Harvey 1990, 155).

Fig 31 The Temptation in the Garden of Eden from the late twelfth century Hunterian Psalter, possibly commissioned by Roger de Mowbray, a Yorkshire magnate who fought against the Scots at the Battle of the Standard in 1138. MS Hunterian 229 7v. © University of Glasgow Library, Department of Special Collections.

This book, with its wide-ranging title, does consider the whole of Europe, but with a greater concentration on England in its later chapters. There are few references to Scotland. His map marking the principal gardens discussed in the text (Harvey 1990, 55) includes lowland Scotland and marks gardens there at a density that equals or surpasses any area of England or Wales north of a line from the Wash to the Severn. Unfortunately despite its inclusion of eleven sites in Scotland, only two, Stirling and Dunblane, receive a brief mention and the latter reference is only a dismissive comment on an old sycamore tree (Harvey 1990, 124). This is perhaps a fair proportion in the context of the whole of Europe. Harvey stresses the close ties of England with the Continent after the Norman Conquest of 1066 and the importance of links between mother and daughter houses in the transmission of fruit and plants, with documentary evidence coming from Germany and Denmark (Harvey 1990, 55–8).

The Garden of Eden, the creation by God for Adam and Eve before the Fall, serves as parallel for gardens throughout their history (Fig 31). *Genesis* 2, verses 8–9, describes a garden, shaded by trees and cooled by four rivers (Harrison 2008, 135–48). Spiritual and mystical uses of the garden as a metaphor are common in the writings of the Fathers of the early church (McLean 1989, 20–2). The monastery could be likened to Paradise, as could the monastic cloister with a tree at its centre (Figs 28, 38). The sacrist was the ecclesiastical and monastic official, who was responsible for the keeping of the sacred vessels and vestments of the church and their preparation for the church services. By extension he cared for the church and its furnishings, including the provision of flowers to decorate the altar and for festivals such as Pentecost, when rose petals might be scattered during the procession. The cloister garden would probably contain red roses, white lilies, violets, and perhaps columbines. These possessed both beauty and symbolic values (Figs 32, 33). There is evidence for a garden at the Abbey of Holyrood pertaining to the sacrist. On 6

Fig 32 The Crowned Lily, a symbol of the Virgin Mary, an initial in the later sixteenth century Wode Partbooks. University of Edinburgh Library Special Collections, EUL Dk.5.14.52 © Edinburgh University Library

Fig 33 An initial incorporating a rose, also a symbol of the Virgin Mary, from the later sixteenth century Wode Partbooks. University of Edinburgh Library Special Collections, EUL Dk.5.14.113 © Edinburgh University Library

July 1507 George Kincaid, Baillie of Canongate, gave sasine (possession) to David Rouch of 'a waste land lying near the monastery of Holyrood, on the north side of the High Street, between the common north port of the burgh and the highway, on the west, the land or garden of the abbot and convent, pertaining to the chaplain of the chapel of St Leonard, on the east, the garden of the sacrist of the said monastery on the north, and the common way on the south' (Donaldson 1952, 387 no 1755).

Gardens provided an allegory both for seductive pleasures, which would bring about the destruction of the soul, and for spiritual fulfilment (Pearsall 1986, 237). The *Song of Songs* was interpreted with reference to the relationship of Christ with his Church. The Virgin Mary was identified with a *hortus conclusus* or enclosed garden, a *fons signatus* or sealed fountain, a well of living waters, a rose bush and a lily among thorns; and these epithets became over time a part of the liturgy (Daley 1986, 261–5).

References to gardens known as Paradise are widespread throughout Europe. According to the St Gall plan there was a Paradise at both the east and west ends of the church, which appears to be part of the church building, but, as the space is not roofed, its identification as a garden or not is uncertain (Fig 2). The term is believed to have been derived from the name given to the atrium of the Old St Peter's Basilica in Rome because of the mosaic over the entrance door, which depicted the Lamb of the Apocalypse with the Elders in adoration, a vision of heaven (Meyvaert 1986, 50). A Paradise survives at the Benedictine house of Maria Laach near Koblenz; one awaits restoration at the Minorite house at Cesky Krumlov in the Czech Republic; another is known to have existed at Winchester Cathedral, where the name is still preserved, and one is recorded at Cambuskenneth Abbey in Scotland (Fraser 1872, 310, no 214). The Dominican monastery in Glasgow, next to the university, had gardens named Paradise and 'Ower Paradise' (NRS RH1/2/392).

Medieval monastic houses in Scotland were, for the most part, provided with adequate land to support their relatively small number of monks through the provision of goods and labour. Lees in his account of Paisley Abbey (Lees 1878, 159–60) paints an idyllic picture of the life of the monastic tenants. Within the monastery the cellarer had the responsibility for the material needs of the monks, but the gardener or *hortulanus* would be responsible for the gardens. Once a year, the gardener had a specific role in the celebration of Vespers. During Advent from 17 December to 23 December a series of antiphons was sung in preparation for the celebration of the birth of Christ. These were known as the Great O-Antiphons because the series of seven were in turn: O Wisdom, O Adonai, O Root of Jesse, O Key of David, O Orient, O King of Nations and O Emanuel, a

Fig 34 The Abbey of Cambuskenneth from the air. The boundaries may reflect those of earlier monastic gardens. SC1237350

sequence recalled in the popular advent carol, *O come, O come, Emanuel*. The intoning of the antiphon was assigned to an official of the monastery. The abbot began with O Wisdom, the cellarer had O Key of David and the gardener O Root of Jesse (Meyvaert 1986, 30). The gardens immediately around the monastic houses appear to have been devoted to the growing of vegetables, fruit and flowers (Meyvaert 1986, 35, 38, 41, 46) (Fig 13).

The monastic house of **Cambuskenneth**, also known as St Mary of Stirling, was founded around 1140 by David I for monks of the Arrouaisian order, later becoming a house of Augustinian canons regular (Fig 34). The monastery was used by the Crown as an occasional lodging, and, in the later fifteenth century, was chosen as the burial place of James III and Margaret of Denmark. In 1314, after Bannockburn, the Scottish parliament met there (RPS, 1314, 1). In 1451 the prior, Alexander Cliddesdale, was in the position to provide herbs from his garden for the king's horses, for which he was £3 7s (*ER* 5, 477). Whether these were for veterinary purposes, or just for fodder, is not known. The site, visible from the castle of Stirling, lies within one of the meanders of the River Forth, with the river providing most of the monastic enclosure. The garden called Paradise is referred to in a charter of 1445 (Fraser 1872, 310, no 214), and the sale of its produce

supported an altar in the abbey church. Close to the north-east corner of the south transept, foundations survive, which may represent the enclosing wall of a garden or orchard. The name of St James' Orchard, which lies to the north of the tower, suggests that this ground was part of the monastery (RCAHMS 1963, 129). When lands belonging to Cambuskenneth Abbey were feued to John Abercrombie in 1558, part of the feu duty included a payment of a thousand apples and pears (*RMS* 5, 1292). According to Sir James Alexander, who wrote the account of excavations at Cambuskenneth in 1864 (Alexander 1864, 16), there were still orchards on two sides of the abbey, long celebrated for their delicious pears, apples and geans or wild cherries. Other gardens at Cambuskenneth were used by members of the convent (Fraser 1872, 310, no 214). The Pont manuscript map (NLS Pont 32) (Fig 37) shows the enclosure wall or bank, which is not visible on the aerial photographs, still cutting off the monastery from the north, with the meander of the Forth providing the boundary on the other sides. What does appear is a tree symbol beside the representation of the bell tower and down by the bank of the river to the south. A curious feature of the site, which may relate to the layout of the monastery and its gardens, is a series of earthwork divisions running from the west of the church towards the site of the Watergate. These are depicted in the foreground of an engraving by John Slezer of 'The prospect of the Town of Sterling from the East' (Slezer 1718) (Fig 36), which was taken from

Fig 36 *The Abbey of Cambuskenneth from the late seventeenth century engraving in* Theatrum Scotiae *by Slezer shows the areas around the monastery used for cultivation. DP101336*

the ruins of Cambuskenneth. An enclosure, surrounded by a wall of stone, or possibly brick, is depicted on the north side of the monastic church. Francis Grose recorded that, on his visit to Cambuskenneth prior to the publication of *The Antiquities of Scotland* in 1791 (Grose 1791, 2, 308), there were still some remains of the gardens visible.

For the most part monastic life in Scotland came to an end in 1560, when the Confession of Faith was ratified by Parliament. This abrogated papal authority and forbade the celebration of mass, sounding a death knell for monasteries and other religious communities, where the saying of the office was their central function. This might happen suddenly, in the case of many friaries, or more gradually, in the case of some monasteries, such as Crossraguel, and even St Andrews (Fergusson 1963, 55–66). Because of the complicated legal situation much of the information about the physical layout of monasteries comes from the later sixteenth century. Monastic houses in England had been dissolved in 1536 and 1539, and Henry VIII of England had encouraged his nephew, James V, to follow his example and abolish the monasteries in Scotland,

and this possibility may have influenced monastic management of their property, leading to the feuing of land, a change from tenancy to a form of proprietorship.

The canons of St Andrews Priory, which was founded from Scone Abbey, formed the chapter of **St Andrews Cathedral**, and lived within the large precinct, much of the wall of which still survives. The map of St Andrews drawn in about 1580 by John

Fig 37 *The Abbey of Cambuskenneth as it appears on the manuscript map of Timothy Pont about 1590 some thirty years after its dissolution, with the monastic boundary cutting across the meander of the River Forth (Pont 32). © NLS*

Fig 35 *Aerial view of St Andrews Cathedral and Priory from the west. SC1037619*

Fig 38 *St Andrews Cathedral and the priory buildings before their destruction during the Reformation. The cloister has a symbolic Tree of Life at its centre. The enclosed gardens which would be cultivated by the canons can be seen within the precinct wall. The manuscript map dates from about 1580 and is probably by John Geddy. S. Andre sive Andreapolis Scotiae Universitas Metropolitana MS.20996. © NLS*

Geddy (NLS MS. 20996) (Figs 35, 38) shows the layout of the priory in detail, with the cathedral and the cloister depicted as roofed and complete, and so may reflect the arrangement before the attack by reformers on the fabric of the cathedral and priory in 1560. It has been suggested that it was based on sketches made in the 1550s by a scholar in St Andrews in response to an invitation from Georg Braun of Cologne to send images of the city to form part of his collection of views of great cities of the world which was published in 1572 as *Civitates orbis terrarium*. The picture of the city is very recognisable, and there was obviously sufficient interest in cartography in St Andrews at this period to produce a useful plan. St Andrews was the university where Timothy Pont studied some thirty years later, and the interest in cartography may have been maintained there (McRoberts 1976b, 151–2), encouraging his decision to undertake his survey of Scotland. In the centre of the cloister garth is a tree, possibly a symbolic Tree of Life. There are many enclosed plots within the precinct which represent the gardens of the canons. Although they appear on the map only as grass plots, they continued to be cultivated by the canons who remained after the dissolution of the monastery in 1560, such as David Peebles, the composer, who lived with his wife and sons in a house with a garden there, possibly the one that had been assigned to him as a canon, while the priory still functioned as a monastery (Fleming 1910, 614).

While the layout of monastic houses followed the same general pattern, the individual nature of each site led to modifications. The plan of the precinct of **Melrose Abbey** (RCAHMS 1956, 269) (Figs 39, 40) shows the extent of the area included within the boundary wall. It was irregular in form and covered about 16ha (Fawcett and Oram 2004, 69). As a Cistercian house, Melrose was required to be as self-sufficient as possible, avoiding contact with the world outside the precinct. It is likely that considerable areas were used by the monks as gardens and much of the area was, in the centuries after its dissolution, colonised by houses with large gardens, perhaps centring on the remains of a particular monastic structure or enclosure (Curle 1935, 46–9).

The maintenance of the domestic life of an abbey such as Melrose required a standard set of buildings and other features, and the majority of charters tend to refer to these in general phrases, confirming grants of property with all their appurtenances in a conventional format. All property at monastic houses was intended to be held in common, and details of gardens usually emerge when there was some need for reform or for the settling of disputes. If gardens were held by individual monks they could yield fruit, flowers and vegetables which could be sold for the financial benefit of the cleric to whom the garden had been assigned; this practice was against the spirit and letter of the monastic rule, and it was the subject of regular criticism during visitations. King James V had called for church

Fig 39 Aerial view of Melrose Abbey showing the enclosed areas, formerly the sites of the monks' yards within the monastic precinct. SC1002164

reform and for measures to reverse the decline of the spiritual life in monasteries (Cowan and Easson 1976, 21–3). As a response to this, the Cistercian chapter-general gave Walter Malin, the abbot of Glenluce, a commission as visitor or inspector for Scotland (Dilworth 1995, 37–8). His attempts at reform proved too extreme, and the houses where he had carried out his visitations complained. In 1531 the king wrote to the abbot of Citeaux to request a special visitor from outside Scotland, Simon Postel, the French abbot of the monastery of Chaalis, which lies to the north of Paris. Postel's reaction was even more severe, ordering disciplinary action against various monks, including the abbot of Melrose, Andrew Durie, who was summoned to Citeaux to answer charges of negligence in the performance of his duties. Although the king acted to prevent this, the chapter-general decided to institute an internal reform, granting the rights of visitation to the abbots of Glenluce and Coupar Angus. These official visitors required similar action, with a demand for the return to the holding of all things in common. An end was decreed to private habitations and gardens; all the monks' food and clothing was to be dispensed centrally to the same standard. In 1534 at Melrose it was ordered, under threat of excommunication, that the monks should no longer have private gardens (Fawcett and Oram 2004, 57–8). This decision led to protests from several

Scottish houses, led by Melrose. In 1535 a compromise was reached: the monks were allowed to keep their gardens, but only if the produce was used in common, and it could not be sold for the profit of the individual monk-gardener. Apparently this agreement was ignored, and fines were imposed. Abbot Andrew Durie was

Fig 40 Plan of the precinct of the Cistercian monastery at Melrose showing possible boundaries between the gardens. DP103104

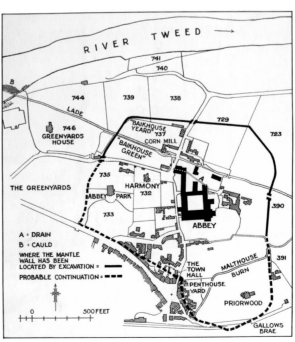

Fig 41 Aerial view of Coupar Angus Abbey. Little survives on the ground of the buildings and plan of this relatively well documented Cistercian monastery. SC397521

in favour with the king, and James' own attitude to the question is illustrated by his award in 1535 of the commendatorship of Melrose to his own five-year old bastard son, another James, Mary Queen of Scots' half brother and later regent of Scotland, who was also commendator of Kelso. Holyrood and the priories of St Andrews and Coldingham were held on behalf of other illegitimate sons (Thomas 2005, 11). This arrangement secured a proportion of the revenues of the abbey to the Crown. This system of the Crown providing a protector for abbeys in the years before the Reformation resulted in the loss of effective ownership by the monks, and the decline in their numbers and in the maintenance of the monastic life (Murray 1983, 58–9). It was sometimes the family of the last commendators in post before 1560, which succeeded in gaining much of the holdings of the monastery, either because the lands of the abbey or priory were erected into a temporal lordship in their favour or because the commendator feued out abbey lands to his kin (Cowan and Easson 1976, 24; Dilworth 1995, 83–6).

The monks of Balmerino Abbey in Fife, another Cistercian house, faced similar criticism during the visitation, and in response to their petition to retain their gardens were permitted to do so as long as no garden was larger than another, that there was a common way through the gardens, and that the produce of the gardens was employed for the common benefit of the monks. Newbattle Abbey faced a comparable problem (Dilworth 1994, 219). That the produce of gardens was a common occasion for minor personal profit is illustrated by a throw-away line about the selling of cabbages without leave of the abbot at Kinloss (Stuart, 1872 xvii).

The Cistercian house of **Coupar Angus Abbey** (Figs 41, 42), whose abbot was one of the official visitors of the order, rented out the monks' yards or gardens to be worked by laymen, listing a specific layout to be followed. In 1542 the instructions given to the gardener say:

> ... for Dene James Michelsonis zard, the sowm of five pund, sex schillingis aucht penneys; for Dene Robert Dunbrekis zarde, the sowm of four pund; and for Dene Johne Hwgonis zard, four pund xiijs iiijd; and sall have reddy to all common labour ane seruand for ilk zard; and for the said Dene James zard, sal furnish to the abbot and conuent caill and herbis his xv days about; and sall haif twa beddis of herbis, sic as percell, betis and latows; and sall furnish to the warden in the zeir, four beddis of vnzeonis, bowcaill, and half of fructis at growis on the treis in zeir; and sall haue twa beddis of eschis, of xxiiii fuit lang, weille wede and nurist quhill thai [be] four or five zeire auld; and sall wphald the heggis, dykis and alais, and sall draw and clenge the stankis

Fig 42 The site of the former yards of Coupar Angus Abbey. SC335752

within his bounds of the said zard sufficientlie ... for the quhilk and his seruice, he sall have dailie, to him and his bois, ane point aile, ane ait laif, and efferand of fysche and flesche to ane zeman man in the abbotis hall, of the conuentis leiffingis. (Rogers 1879–80, 2, 208)

The yard of Dean Johne Hugonis was to have:

five beddis of unzeonis and caill in the zeire... two beddis of percell betis and lattows with two beddis of zong eschis of xxiiii fuit lang, well weid and nurist, quhill thai be four or five year auld ... and that he will grub the trees and clenge the stank weil and sufficiently with the avis of the maister of werke. (Rogers 1879–80, 2, 209)

Another of the yards was to have eight beds of onions and bowcaill and four beds of ashes. On the same day the convent for a sum of £6 4s 3d:

componit with Georde Tailzeour, *alias* Act, in manneris efter follows, that is to say, that the said Georde sall laubour and graitht in all sortis our garding, herbe garding, orcheat treis and alleris thairin haldin the stankis clene begynnand at the new dyke quhill it cum to the est syd of

the mustard zard ... and in fruit tyme sall walk and keipe the sammyne, quhilk we reserue alhaille to our self, and sall furnish the abbot caille and herbis, with helpe vsit of the laif of the gardenaris, dischargeand hym of all commoun labour except quhen he is chargit in speceale be my lord. (Rogers 1879–80, 2, 210–11)

In 1553 the community resolved 'to lead a regular life and to order our manners according to the reformers of the Cistercian order', and that the abbot and convent should possess and use in common the fruits, income and provision of the monastery (Cowan and Easson 1976, 26). Only a few years later in 1558 a charter was issued to Robert Alexander of the third part of the lands of Gallowraw (later Gallery) to the north of Coupar Angus, which can perhaps be seen as an attempt to guarantee their assets into the uncertain future faced by the abbey in the years immediately before 1560. It shows that the amenities regarded as appropriate for the abbot and monks included not only the practical, if pleasant, orchards and herb garden, but also the flower garden:

Moreover the said Robert and Margaret and Alexander shall build and have always in readiness ample buildings on their eastern plot of ground, viz a large hall, chambers with well-appointed tables, stable with straw, hay and oats, a cellar stored with victuals, drinks and wines, when they can be had, always ready to be sold

Fig 43 Aerial view of Jedburgh Abbey and Jedburgh Friary. SC973204

to the convent and successors, and their servants and guests arriving on the sea-coast of Angus; also they shall plant orchards, herb-gardens, flower-gardens and other things suitable to the soil ... (Rogers 1879–80, 2, 168–9)

A large part of the abbey precinct at **Jedburgh** to the east of the church was devoted to gardens and orchards (Fig 43). This area was referred to in a charter of 1588, when the commendator of Jedburgh was asked to surrender into the king's hands the lands known as the Orchard, the Convent Yard and the lands called Selraw yardis and Vergene (CH6/6 1.f 86v). In a further reference in 1596 'the orchards and convent yards' were identified as lying to the south side of the burgh, between the houses and lands commonly called the Canongate and the river (*ER* 23, 456). In 1813 a report was drawn up by Patrick Neill 'by desire of the Board of Agriculture' on Scottish gardens and orchards (Neill 1813, 127, 131, 135). His particular concern was the identification of commercial orchards and fruit varieties, and his visits to the orchards of long dissolved monasteries arose from this consideration. He recorded that there were a number of very old trees at Jedburgh, chiefly pears of French extraction. Several of these trees were of a large size '30 to 40 feet high [9.14m to 12.19m] with huge trunks and spreading branches. ... One tree, a Red Honey pear is of preeminent bulk

rising between 50 and 60 feet [15.24m and 18.29m] and having a trunk, which measures nine foot in circumference [2.74m]. Many of the oldest trees are now much decayed and supported with props' (Neill 1813, 127). He also mentioned the apple varieties of 'white and Carlisle codlings' (Neill 1813, 126).

There are many references to gardens and orchards in monasteries across Scotland. Three gardens are referred to at **Monymusk** Priory in 1534 (Simpson 1925, 43), one of which, just to the north of the parish church, was later associated with the provision for the schoolmaster (Fig 44). At **Scone Abbey** the abbot was able to supply the king's master cook with cherries and strawberries in 1496 (*TA*, I, 288) (Fig 45). In 1567 *The Register of the Great Seal of Scotland* (*RMS*) records the manor or mansion of Clien in 1567 as reserved to the monastery of Scone; Clien with its chapel, gardens, orchards and the three acres called *the gardnaris-land* is situated near Kinfauns in Perthshire not far from Scone (*RMS*, 4, 444, No 1778), a site which may now be occupied by Glendoick House (RCAHMS 1994, 112).

In 1501 the gardener at Scone carried herbs to the king to be planted in the garden at Stirling and received two shillings (*TA*, 2, 97). Scone was one of the monastic houses which suffered considerably from the riots of June 1559, when it was attacked by the townsmen of Dundee, to whom James Hepburn, the abbot *in commendam*, was particularly odious because of his part in the execution for heresy of Walter Myln,

Fig 44 Aerial view of the parish church of Monymusk, which was formerly the church of the Augustinian Priory. A garden belonging to the priory lay to the north of the church. SC961129

the priest of Lunan, in 1558 (Fawcett 2003, 172–3). The house of the prior of the abbey, Henry Abercromby, had a garden where the remaining monks held a formal meeting in January 1568 (NRS GD90/2/9) to register their protest against the disposal of their income by the Regent, James, Earl of Moray (Fig 45).

The witnessing of documents out of doors has led to evidence for the existence of gardens not otherwise recorded. The transfer of the superintendence of the building of the hospital of St Martha at Aberdour to four sisters of the Third Order of St Francis took place in the east garden of **Inchcolm Abbey** in 1486 (NRS GD 150/206), suggesting that there were at least two distinct gardens there. The probable outline of this east garden is still visible on the ground and from the air (Fig 46) and this is possibly the most promising candidate for discovering something of the form of a monastic garden surviving. Over a hundred years after the monastery was dissolved, Sir Robert Sibbald, who was concerned with collecting plants for the Physic Garden in Edinburgh noted 'In the Garden adjacent to the Monastery, I found the female Paeonie, bearing seed, common Borage and Pellitorie, the dwarf Elder and Echium flore albo, Solanum dictum Bella Donna and the Malva Pomilaflore albo'; some of these plants would certainly be used for medicinal purposes (Sibbald 1710, 40).

James IV visited **Glenluce Abbey** in the course of his pilgrimages to Whithorn Priory and, in 1507, he is recorded as making a gift of four shillings to the gardener there (*TA*, 3, 404) (Fig 47). The precise location of the monastic gardens there is uncertain, but aerial survey in the dry summer of 1992 revealed the

Fig 45 Scone Abbey as it was depicted on the manuscript map of Timothy Pont about 1590, some thirty years after its dissolution (Pont 26). © NLS

Fig 47 Aerial view of Glenluce Abbey in drought conditions. In addition to the outlines of now demolished monastic buildings, the former manse garden, which lies towards the bottom of the photograph, reveals the line of former paths dividing it into four. After the Reformation the minister's glebe lands included the garden of the monastery. SC1237345

layout of the garden of the former manse to the west of the abbey. The *Statistical Account* provided by the parish minister, William Learmont, in the late eighteenth century (*Stat Acct*, 14, 497), states that his glebe included the garden of the abbey. The abbey was still in a condition to receive Mary Queen of Scots and her train when she made her progress through the south-west of Scotland in 1563 (Breeze 1987, 49). At Crossraguel Abbey the yards or gardens of the monks were given by James VI in 1602 to the son of his former nurse, John Gray, who took possession of them in the presence of one of the surviving monks, who was still living in the abbey (Fergusson 1963, 65) (Fig 48).

Some Scottish medieval gardeners are known by name, usually through payments made to them by the royal household; the account of **Kinloss Abbey** by Giovanni Ferrerio introduces a gardener from Dieppe in Normandy called William Lubias. Ferrerio or Ferrerius, an Italian from Piedmont, was studying at the University of Paris when he was introduced to Robert Reid, abbot of Kinloss, who was travelling back from Rome, where he had collected the bulls of provision

Fig 46 Aerial view of the Augustinian priory of Inchcolm. A charter was signed in the east garden of the monastery, which probably occupied the level area near the centre of the photograph. SC1237349

to the abbacy; Robert Reid later became Bishop of Orkney. Ferrerius accompanied Reid back to Scotland in 1528 (Stuart 1872, xiv–v). He wrote a *History of the Abbots of Kinloss*, which provides some information pertaining to gardens and gardeners. One abbot, William of Culross, who died in 1504, is recorded as labouring, even to fatigue in the gardens, in planting and grafting trees (Stuart 1872, xlii–xliii) (Fig 49). Lubias seems to have had an eventful life, losing a foot in a sea fight against the Spaniards near Marseilles. No mention is made of his qualifications for the post of gardener, but he is described as also skilled in the dressing of wounds and was consulted by people from all parts of Moray (Wilson 1839, 48). It has been suggested (Wilson 1839, xv–xvi), that some ancient pear trees blown down during a violent storm early in the eighteenth century had been planted with a carefully laid pavement under their roots, a horticultural practice designed to prevent the fruit trees rooting too deeply, and that the owners of the nearby **Kilravock Castle** used the trees at Kinloss as a resource for their own orchard. The owner of Kilravock in 1536, Hugh Rose, was confined in Dumbarton Castle for seizing and imprisoning William Galbraith, abbot of Kinloss. While he was in prison a contract was drawn up by which Thom Daueson, a burgess of Paisley, and a serving man were to travel to Kilravock to 'werk and lawbour to the said huchoun his yardis, gardingis, orchardis, ayles, heggingis, and stankis, and werkis pertening to ane gardner to do to siclyk thingis of the best fassoun may be deuisit' (Wilson 1839, xvi).

Fig 48 Aerial view of Crossraguel Abbey. Most of the gardens are now taken into arable cultivation. SC798447

Fig 49 Kinloss Abbey as it appears on the manuscript map by Timothy Pont in the late sixteenth century with what may be a representation of the site of its orchard to the east. Pont 8 detail © NLS

Fig 50 Aerial view of Arbroath Abbey, now surrounded by an extensive burial ground and the town of Arbroath. The reputation of its orchards survived into the eighteenth century. SC798101

Tradition supported the reputation of monastic cultivation. Mr Ochterlonie of Guinde writing in the late seventeenth century related of **Arbroath Abbey** that the 'fyne gardines and orcheards (were) now converted to arable ground' (Macfarlane 1906–8, 2, 46), and Neill says of the Arbroath oslin (an apple then grown in Scotland) that, 'tradition uniformly ascribes its introduction to the monks' (Neill 1813, 2) (Fig 50). Although Neill reports that 'no regular orchards are to be found in Fife the remains of one are still to be seen at the ancient abbey of **Lindores**; and some varieties of apples still exist which are nearly unknown to modern horticulturalists' (Neill 1813, 131). In the later eighteenth century the fame of the horticultural skills of monastic houses seems to have been widespread. The subject forms part of several accounts of Scotland by inquiring visitors. Thomas Newte singles out Pluscarden for particular comment (Newte 1791, 156–7), and Pennant in his account of his tour in Scotland in 1769 describes the surroundings of Kinloss Abbey:

Near the abbey is an orchard of apple and pear trees, at least coeval with the last monks; numbers lie prostrate, their venerable branches seem to have taken fresh roots, and were laden with fruit beyond what could be expected from their antique look. (Pennant 2000, 98)

How much dependence can be placed on the authentication of fruit trees, dating from before 1560 and bearing fruit up until the later eighteenth century, is uncertain (Haldane 1934, 13–16), although Hayes (2007, 4) writes that fruit trees are long lived, with pear trees having the greatest longevity, typically surviving for two hundred years. A narrower gap can be advanced for the orchards of Midlothian and the Borders. In 1632 Sir Robert Kerr wrote to his son on the subject of major improvements to the family's house and estate at Ancrum near Jedburgh (Laing 1875, 62–76). In this formal letter, he recommends that his son should plant 'a fayr orchard of the best fruits yow can gett in the abbyes about yow'. The family of the Kerrs had acquired the monastic properties of Newbattle and Jedburgh Abbeys as well as Jedburgh Friary, and it was to these 'and other places of renown' that he was to look and plant or graft the best. This gives some substance to the claims for the survival and maintenance of orchards under lay ownership. Excavations at Jedburgh on the site of the friary, founded in the early sixteenth century and certainly by 1505, for the reformed Franciscan order of the Observantines (*TA*, 3, 58; Cowan and Easson 1976, 132), produced evidence of apple or pear pips which had been pulped probably in the process of the production of cider or perry (Dixon *et al* 2000, 72).

The area immediately around an abbey devoted to horticulture was intended to provide much of the food required for the monks and their servants, and vegetable gardens were of particular importance. There was a

Fig 51 Aerial view of Lindores Abbey with a working farm occupying part of its former gardens. SC496163

commercial market in vegetable seeds. Already in the early thirteenth century the garden of the Tironensian house of Lindores was being enlarged (Dowden 1903, 20), and seed was purchased for planting (Fig 51). The *Rentale Dunkeldense* relating to properties belonging to the Bishopric of Dunkeld records the purchase of vegetable seeds including beans, onions and cabbages. In 1509 seeds of onion and green stuff were delivered to Robert Skougal, in 1513 one and a half pounds of onion seed and three ounces of cabbage were received by Robert Gardiner and in 1558 'Unyun seid and uder dyvers kynd of seidis' at a cost of 52s 6d. In 1515 there was the purchase of five seed vessels at a cost of 10d (Hannay 1915, 68, 228, 292–3, 355).

Acquiring seed could involve long distance trade. There is evidence of the import of seed from England into Scotland in 1296–7. This is only known because a dispute between the partners involved was brought before the Fair Court of St Ives in Huntingdonshire in 1300 (Harvey 1990, 78). John Spicer of Godmanchester and Peter Chapman of St Ives entered into partnership to do business in various parts of Scotland in January 1296. Spicer loaded horses with leek seed bought with £3 from Chapman, and took it to Scotland. In April 1296 he returned from a second journey, and in February 1297 undertook a third journey with three horses loaded with leek seed. The dispute arose over

the division of the profit. These journeys took place at a time when Edward I was about to march into Scotland to establish his rule, or when his invasion was already under way. The market for vegetable seeds was presumably sufficiently established and profitable to make it worthwhile to travel in the winter with seed for spring sowing at a time of major disturbance, when from

Fig 52 Aerial view of Carse Grange, an outlying property in the Carse of Gowrie belonging to Coupar Angus Abbey, which provided fruit from its orchards and fish from its stanks or fish ponds for the monastery. DP039524

Fig 53 Aerial view of Coupar Grange, another property belonging to the abbey of Coupar Angus. The solid cropmarks, in adjacent fields of wheat and barley, are probably fish ponds with linking water channels, enclosed by a ditch which would be accompanied with a dyke and perhaps topped by a hedge. SC1237346

the evidence of the Plea Roll of the army in Scotland in 1296 theft, including theft from religious houses as well as travellers and residents, from Lindores to Inch was rife (Neville 1990, 75, 115, 121).

As well as the immediate precinct of the abbey providing ground for the cultivation of fruit and vegetables, there were various outlying estates or granges. **Carse** or **Kerse Grange**, near Errol in the Carse of Gowrie in Perthshire, belonged to the Abbey of **Coupar Angus** and lay about 17km to the south (Fig 52). The granges of Cistercian houses, such as Coupar, were supposed to be no more than one day's journey from the mother house, so that monks should be able to fulfil their spiritual duties. The granges were also used, particularly in the later medieval period, as temporary residences for the abbot and monks. In 1473 a grant was recorded in the *Rental Book of the Cistercian Abbey of Cupar-Angus* (Rogers 1879–80, 1, 189):

> our orchardis of our Kersgrange, togidder with four acrys of land, til our famyliar David Gardnar ... he sal put the sade orchardis til al possibil polici eftyr his pouar, that is to sa in biggyn of houses and hanyngis [enclosing of ground],

with castyn of waterstankis about of sic depnes that ged eyls and fyscis beand in tham ma be conseruyt and kepit bath swmyr and wyntir, and specialy with sykyr dykyn and hedgyn of the orchardis ... and rychtsua he sal hafe our doukat puttand it till all possibyl profit to the behufe of the Abbay ... wyth ympyn [grafting] and sauyng [sowing] with plantation of frote treis of the best kynd ma be gottyng.

This grant also includes two other important elements in the monastic diet: fresh water fish (including eels), which were raised and preserved in the stanks or fish ponds, and the keeping of domesticated fowl. In 1503 an orchard was to be established (or recreated) at Carse Grange (Rogers 1879–80, 1, 255):

> Heiratour the said Andro sal mak with awys of ws ane sufficiand orchard in al gudly hast he ma, with the best frut treis ma be gottin with sykkir dykin, hedgin and hangyng of the sammyn.

Similarly in 1549 a grant of Carse Grange was made to James Jackson, who had, in addition to 'castin the stankis' and planting young trees, to keep the orchard 'fra entres of ony bestiall or steling of our frucht, as ane gude trew gardener aucht to do to ws and our successoris and factouris, and sall serve the chapellane in our chapell' (Rogers 1879–80, 2, 239). **Coupar Grange**, which lies about 3 km to the north of the abbey, has the

Fig 54 Paisley Abbey as it appears on the manuscript map by Timothy Pont in the late sixteenth century, with its orchard among the other monastic gardens enclosed by an impressive wall. Pont 8 detail. © NLS

traces in cropmark form of what were probably fish ponds. The enclosures and pits that are visible may date from the period of the abbey grange (Fig 53).

The orchard at **Paisley Abbey** had an area of six acres and one perch with a dovecot nearby. A kaleyard (Lees 1878, 170) lay across the River White Cart. The monastery was prosperous, allowing not only the construction of a large church and a magnificent drain (Malden 1993, 13, 17), but also an impressive precinct wall, decorated with statues of saints in niches, enclosing the abbey and its orchard and yards. It is depicted by Timothy Pont on the manuscript map of the Barony of Renfrew (Pont MS 33) as an impressive square enclosure with trees and the commendator's house within it and the abbey church at the south-west corner (Fig 54). Patrick Neill reported that:

> At Paisley there is a very ancient orchard, which owing to the increase of the buildings, is now situated near the middle of the town. It formerly belonged to the noble family of Semple and is said to have been founded in the reign of James I of Scotland ... Some pear trees are here of a large size and venerable aspect: they are generally supposed to be the identical trees originally planted. (Neill 1813, 135)

During the excavation of the great drain of the monastery, apple pips and cores, as well as damson stones were recovered, probably dating from the fifteenth century (Dickson and Dickson 2000, 194–6) (Figs 55, 56).

The monastery of Kilwinning, a Tironensian house, is described by Timothy Pont in his account of the district of Cunningham in Ayrshire, written in the early years of the seventeenth century, where he records the layout of small two storey houses arranged around a cloister with a garden behind as having 'ye precinct enuironed with a faire stone vall, within vich ar goodly gardens and orchardes.' (Dobie 1876, 21).

The latest medieval monastic order to be established in Scotland was that of the Carthusians, who lived as hermits within a community, with lay brothers dealing with worldly matters. The best surviving British example of such a monastery is that at Mount Grace on the edge of the North York Moors where the layout of small two storey houses, arranged around two cloisters, with a garden behind, can be still appreciated (Coppack 1991). In 1429 James I established a house in Perth, known as *Vallis Virtutis* (vale of virtue), for twelve monks and a prior, who each had a small house with a garden behind, which he cultivated. A street known as Pomarium still survives in the south-west of the town, recalling the site of the orchard of the Charterhouse. The site of the Charterhouse was granted to the burgh of Perth in 1569 and a grant confirmed in 1600.

Elsewhere in **Perth** was the house of Dominican friars, known as Blackfriars and founded in the middle of the thirteenth century. It lay in the north-east of the town where names such as Blackfriars Street and Blackfriars Wynd recall its site. Like Holyrood and Cambuskenneth, it contained a royal lodging. James I was murdered there in 1437, and, according to tradition, Robert III watched the battle between Clan Chattan and Clan Kay, which took place on the North Inch in 1396, from what is known as the '**Gylten Herbar**' (Gilten Arbour) in the garden attached to the friary (NRS GD79/1/87; Fittis 1885, 157–8). According to Colvin's (1986, 13–14) discussion of the term, a *herbarium* formed part of a garden, which might often assume the character of a garden within a garden. Various references are made to benches of stone or turf within a *herbarium*. An English manuscript of about 1400 (Bodleian Library, MS. Bodley 264, fol. 258) shows a king and queen, seated on a turf bench playing chess in a walled garden planted with grass and flowers. These appear as low turf banks with sloping or straight sides, retained by wattle hurdles or a brick wall and planted with low-growing plants such as daisies or speedwell. Shade was provided by arbours or pergolas created from poles of willow or hazel arched across timber supports. Trellis panels would create a framework for training plants with 'windows' to view the wider world (Jennings 2005, 40–3). The gilded arbour in Perth might have been rather more elaborate, although the platform from which the king viewed the conflict from within the friary might be temporary. The ornaments of the ceiling of the later Monks' Tower were supposed to be copied from those of the Gilten Arbour.

Fig 55 View of the east section of the drain of Paisley Abbey. SC358176

Fig 56 The reconstructed cloister at Paisley Abbey DP012015

This decoration was carried out for the first Earl of Gowrie, who died in 1584, at the corner of whose garden the Monks' Tower stood (Fittis 1885, 158; Cooper 1999, 819) (Fig 276). The king's lodging in Perth was repaired and a new portal was built in 1531 (*MW* 1, 111).

The breadth of the scholarship of Dominican houses is exemplified by the works of one of the most eminent Dominicans of the Middle Ages, Albertus Magnus, who was born in Swabia in modern Germany about 1206, a noted theologian, who, among many other works, wrote a treatise *On Vegetables and Plants*, which contained a section on gardens designed for the pleasures of sight and smell (Harvey 1990, 6) (Fig 57).

> The lawn should be of such a size that about it in a square may be planted every sweet-smelling herb such as rue, sage and basil, and likewise all sorts of flowers, as the violet, columbine, lily, rose, iris and the like. So that between these herbs and the turf, at the edge of the lawn set square, let there be a higher bench of turf flowering and lovely; and somewhere in the middle provide seats so that men may sit down there to take their repose pleasurably when their senses need refreshment... Behind the lawn there may be a great diversity of medicinal and scented herbs, not only to delight the sense of smell by their perfume but to refresh the sight with the variety of their flowers, and to cause admiration at the many forms in those who look at them.

Works by Albertus Magnus were well represented in pre-Reformation Scottish libraries (Durkan and Ross, 1961, 34, 120, 159) (Fig 57). While the herb gardens associated with monastic houses may have contributed to the meals of the monks and their retainers, they will also have been used for medicinal purposes. Scent had its own medical uses; the perfume of both roses and violets were believed to be a prophylactic against the plague (Rawcliffe 2008, 10). The growing of garlic, marjoram, sage, rue and dill will have added much in the way of flavour to monastic meals and relieved their potential monotony. The selection of plants for medicine included leeks, celery, carrots, lupines and spinach, as well as coriander, fennel, hyssop, savory and anise (Stannard 1986, 76). Monks were not supposed to practise medicine, and surgery in particular was forbidden (Dingwall 2003, 43), but the care of health through suitable diet and the balancing of the four humours would be a constant underlying concern in a monastic community. Classical medical and botanical texts, most commonly the works of Pliny, Dioscurides

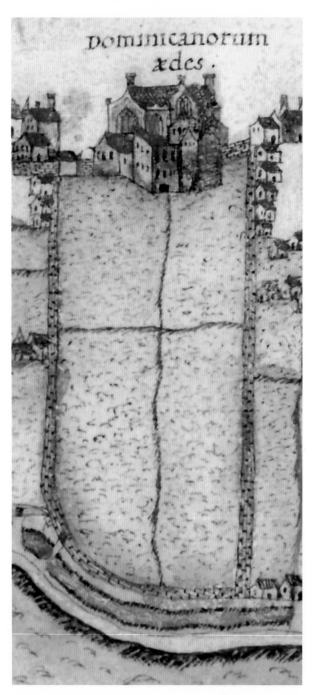

and Galen, often abridged or rewritten, were part of medieval libraries. Plant products were used both externally and internally. A paste of leeks could be laid on the skin for sores, a mustard plaster applied to the chest for colds. Leaves, especially millefoil or tansy, were used as dressings for wounds. Burdock leaves or the tough outer leaves of cabbage or beet were used as bandages. Dill and mint were used as carminatives for flatulence; squill was used as a diuretic in the case of dropsy; celandine and rue were used in eye salves.

Violet, rose, lily and borage petals were used in medicines (Stannard 1986, 87–9) (Figs 32, 33). In early medieval times there was a deliberate use of local remedies, as opposed to the exotics. Recipes favoured local wild and garden plants as cheaper substitutes. A list of plants described in herbals as growing in gardens, and plants described in gardening treatises as having medicinal uses, included many species that would be at home in Scotland (Opsomer-Halleux 1986, 105–12). In April 1500, for example, a friar was paid for bringing flowers which were to be included in a cordial given to Janet Kennedy, the king's mistress, at the time of the celebration for her rising from childbed (*TA* 2, 41).

Excavations at Jedburgh on the site of the friary produced evidence for the presence on the site of the eggs of maw worms and whipworms, parasites in the human intestine, which probably came from the remains of faeces; pollen from the plant tormentil, *potentilla*, which could be used against worm infestation, was also discovered on the site (Dixon *et al* 2000, 71–7). Dickson and Dickson (2000, 213) record botanical evidence from excavations in the towns of Aberdeen, Elgin and Perth, for opium poppy, hemlock, henbane and deadly nightshade, all powerful medicinal plants, which were not native to Scotland, but which can now be grown across the country. The frontispiece of the *Mirror of Phlebotomy and Practice of Surgery* by the most famous doctor of the later fourteenth century, John of Arderne, shows a physician with a medicine box and a ladle sitting within a herb garden, enclosed by a wooden paling fence (Fig 58). This late fourteenth or early fifteenth century manuscript, now in the Hunter Collection of the University of Glasgow (MS Hunter 112 (T.5.14)), is thought to be of provincial English origin (Gardham and Weston 2004).

Medieval hospitals were concerned with the care and maintenance of the aged and infirm and particularly their spiritual care, as well as that of travellers, pilgrims and the sick. As such, like monastic houses, they had their herb gardens. Almost two hundred medieval hospitals have been listed in Ian Cowan and David Easson's *Medieval Religious Houses in Scotland* (Cowan and Easson 1976, 162–200), although there are

Fig 57 The Dominican Friary in St Andrews before it was destroyed at the commencement of the Reformation in 1560 as depicted on a map of about 1580. S. Andre sive Andreapolis Scotiae Universitas Metropolitana MS.20996. © NLS

Fig 58 The doctor John of Arderne pictured in a manuscript copy of his work Mirror of Phlebotomy and Practice of Surgery. *The herb shown to the right of his head may be borage. MS Hunter 112 (T.5.14). © University of Glasgow Library, Department of Special Collections.*

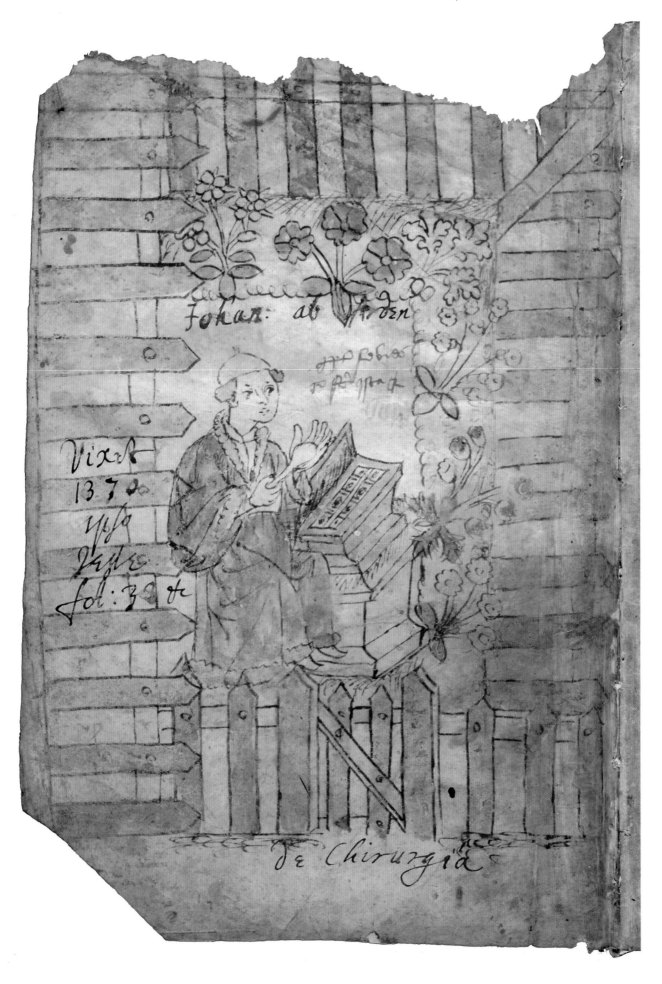

problems with the identification and location of many of them. Some were attached to religious houses, such as the Charterhouse in Perth and the Cistercian nunnery at North Berwick. Hospitals, close to but outside the boundaries of towns and cities, might be concerned with infectious diseases, particularly leprosy. Robert Henryson in the *Testament of Cresseid*, written in the late fifteenth century, describes Cresseid, made a leper by the gods, as passing to the 'Hospitall at the tounis end...Into ane village half ane myle thairby/Delyverit hir in at the Spittaill hous' (Wood 1968, 108). The hospital at Soutra, organised as a house of Augustinian canons, like Holyrood, is said, according to the *Scoticronicon*, to have been founded by Malcolm IV in 1164 for accommodating travellers, although in the later medieval period it seems to have become a lodging for three poor people (Cowan and Easson 1976, 192). Excavations at Soutra have recovered pollen of the opium poppy which, along with other evidence, might suggest a more medicinal regime was practised there (Moffat 1989, 3).

University Gardens

Herb gardens were not restricted to monastic houses. The universities founded in Scotland during the fifteenth century – St Andrews University established in 1425, Glasgow University, founded in 1451 and Aberdeen University founded in 1495 – were all established on the pattern of the University of Bologna. The typical medieval university had an Arts faculty through which all students progressed before entering one of the higher faculties of Divinity, Law or Medicine for professional training. The students studied the trivium of verbal arts consisting of grammar, rhetoric and logic and the quadrivium of numerate arts, mathematics, geometry, astronomy and music.

The **University of Aberdeen** was the first in Britain to appoint a professor of medicine in 1497 only two years after its foundation (Moir 1894, 95; Stevenson and Davidson 2009, 69). The manuscript map of Aberdeen by James Gordon of Rothiemay (Gordon 1661), produced

Fig 59 The Mediceners House and Precinct in Old Aberdeen with their gardens on the 1661 map of Aberdeen by James Gordon of Rothiemay. EMS.s.249. © NLS

in 1661, shows in Old Aberdeen the Mediceners House and next to it the Mediceners Precinct (Fig 59). The depiction of the garden is conventional but it does appear to have three separate plots, and, unlike the majority of gardens shown in Old Aberdeen, contains no trees. King's College had its garden to the south of its lodging range so that the students would benefit from its benign influences (Stevenson and Davidson 2009, 73) (Fig 272). The **University of Glasgow** or Glasgow College on the High Street founded in 1451 (Brown and Moss 1996, 4) had various gardens, a little meadow, an Old Pedagogy Yard, Paradise Yards, West Yards and a great orchard. The Old Pedagogy or Kitchen Yard was for growing vegetables and for supplying fowls for the kitchen and common table; a mudwall dyke was built in it in 1490. Paradise Yards lay between Blackfriars Kirk and the College (Fig 60). The Dominicans grew mustard and fruit trees there, referred to as 'pipanis' and 'ympis' or cuttings. There was a small physic garden nearby, the evidence for which lies in a copy of the *Historia Stirpium Commentarii Insignes* (Significant Notes on the History of Plants) by Leonhart Fuchs, published in 1549, which belonged to Mark Jameson, the Deputy Rector of the University in 1555. He annotates the volume with a list of twenty-two plants 'To be set and sawin in ye garding' (Boney 1988, 9–12). The list includes parsley, fennel, milfoil, celery, asparagus, betony, vervain, dropwort, valerian, black spleenwort, coriander, cumin, dill, anise, carrot, parsnip, fenugreek, hog's fennel, hart's tongue, savory, marigold and savin. This list is specialised; these plants had medicinal values for wound healing and fever reduction as well as diuretic and carminative qualities, and were in many instances good for cooking and eating, but it is considered that a disproportionate number of them were known abortifacients, and that other common plants of medicinal value were omitted (Boney 1988, 12).

The *Complaynt of Scotland* by Robert Wedderburn was a work with similar aims for the nation to that of David Lindsay's play *Ane Satyre of the Thrie Estates*, It was dedicated to Mary of Guise, widow of James V, who was addressed as the 'margareit ande perle of princessis'. It was written around 1550 and probably belongs to the time in the author's life when he was acting as chamberlain to the Knights of St John at Torphichen in West Lothian. In it is a list of plants which might appear in a herb garden in Scotland. Wedderburn describes 'al sortis of holisum flouris gyrsis [grasses] and eirbis maist conuenient for medycyn' and gives the plants and the condition for which they were a remedy (Wedderburn 1979, 53). Bettony was proposed for a sore head, beets dealt with constipation, borage comforted the heart, coriander was good for an old cough and celandine helped eyesight. Kirkliston, where an orchard and garden are recorded, was annexed to the Preceptory at Torphichen shortly before 1513 (*TA* 2, 370; Cowan and Easson 1976, 160).

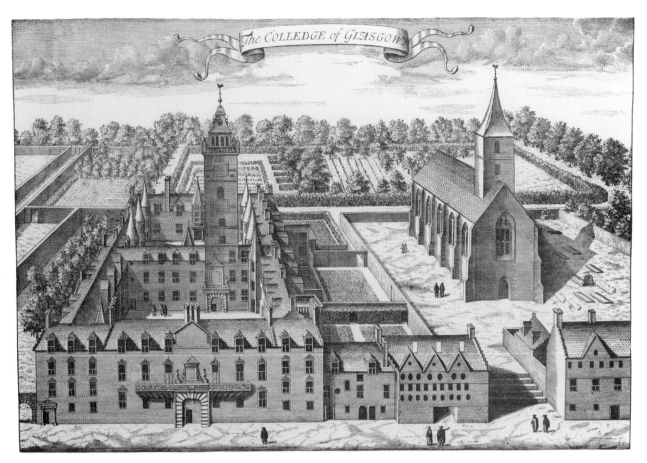

Fig 60 The University of Glasgow with its orchards and gardens as it appears on an engraving of the late seventeenth century by John Slezer for Theatrum Scotiae *in 1693. DP106452*

Andrew Boorde was a well known doctor and writer on medical and other subjects during the reign of Henry VIII. He began his career as an inmate of the Charterhouse in London, but after some twenty years there, gained a dispensation to study medicine abroad and travelled extensively, visiting Orleans, Poitiers, Toulouse, Montpellier and Wittenberg. His favourite university was Montpellier 'the most nobilist vniuersite of the world for phisicions and surgions' (Furnivall 1870, 194) (Fig 17). He spent about a year in Glasgow, writing in a letter to Thomas Cromwell on 1 April 1536 from Leith, 'I am now in skotland, in a lytle vnyuersyte or study namyd Glasco, wher I study & practyce physyk as I haue done in dyuerce regyons & prouynces, for the sustentacyon off my lyuyng.' He was also acting as an agent for Cromwell, reporting on foreign views of the actions of Henry VIII, and continues 'I resortt to the skotysh kynges howse, & to the erle of Aryn, namyd Hamylton, & to the lord evyndale, namyd stuerd, & to many lordes & lardes, as well spyrytuall as temporall, & truly I know ther myndes, for thei takyth me for a skotysh manes sone. for I name my self Karre, & so the Karres kallyth me cosyn, thorow the which I am in the more fauer' (Funivall 1870, 59).

Bishops and their Gardens

Gardens were one of the appurtenances of bishops' palaces, castles and manors. William Schevez, Archbishop of St Andrews from 1478, the best known and perhaps the most successful of early Scottish doctors, was born about 1428 and died in 1497 (Fig 62). He was a student at St Andrews and continued his studies at the University of Louvain with John Spernic, doctor of medicine and physic, a celebrated physician and astrologer. Shevez was appointed Master of the Hospital in Brechin and by 1471 had become a physician at the court of James III, supplying him with medicines and receiving an annuity of £20. He was employed on diplomatic missions to England, France and Rome. In the dedication to him of a work on astrology, which described the eclipse of 4 May 1491, he was referred to as proficient in every kind of literature, profound in learning, the founder of a library in St Andrews and the man who had brought from the darkness of obscurity the mathematical sciences, which, through the negligence of the Scots, had nearly been forgotten (Comrie 1932, 82–4). He purchased many books, and the *Ledger of Andrew Halyburton*, the Scottish agent at Middleburgh, records the sum of 500 gold crowns for books brought from the Low Countries for Schevez in 1493 (Innes 1867, 6). Several medical manuscripts which belonged to him survive: one in the British Library, one in the University of Edinburgh Library and one among the Hunter manuscripts in the University of

Fig 62 *Archbishop William Schevez on the obverse of a bronze medal designed by the Flemish artist Quintin Metsys in 1491 in the most fashonable Renaissance style.* © National Museums of Scotland. Licensor Scran

Glasgow. These are identifiable because Schevez had the useful habit of writing his name on various pages in his books. The first is a collection of four medical tracts translated into Latin from Greek, produced by teachers from the school of Salerno, containing accounts of remedies used by Schevez and others who practised in Scotland in the fifteenth century. Among the drugs described were opium and willow bark, used for pains of the liver, comforting defective eyes, for ears, for consolidating wounds, the prevention of conception and, in moderation, checking bleeding. The second, specially copied for Schevez, was a commentary on the 'Ninth Book of Almansor', an Arabic writer translated into Latin (Comrie 1932, 85–8). A late fourteenth century manuscript in the Hunterian collection which also belonged to Schevez includes *De Epidemia* by Raymond Chalin de Vinario, a physician who studied at Montpellier. An illustration in the volume depicts a red-capped physician, reading a book and holding some herbs with another basket of the same herbs behind him (Gardham, J and Weston, D 2004) (Fig 61).

Scottish students attended universities across Europe, even after the establishment of the Scottish foundations, with Paris, followed by Louvain and Cologne the most frequented (Dunlop 1942, 16). James IV sent his illegitimate son, Alexander, who was destined to occupy the archbishopric of St Andrews, to study in Padua with the most renowned scholar of the period, Erasmus, from

where he returned in 1510 (Macdougall 2006, 214). His exalted birth would have brought him into contact with the Renaissance culture of Italy at the highest levels, which included the design of gardens and their use as places for intellectual discussion. Foreign physicians visited Scotland to treat distinguished patients: in 1552 the Spanish doctor William Cassanate was assisted by the Italian Girolamo Cardono in treating John Hamilton, Archbishop of St Andrews. Cardano, who published several books on medical and mathematical matters, spent several months in Edinburgh and at the archbishop's castle at Monimail in Fife (Shaw 1983, 163), and achieved, according to his patient, a cure where the physicians to the French and Imperial courts had failed (Shaw 1983, 163–4).

Bishops and their retinues were among the most widely travelled people in Scotland and provided a means by which high culture and more transient fashions could reach Scotland and be made known widely. The need to visit Rome and receive confirmation of their see by the popes, as well as their despatch by the king on ambassadorial duties meant that they came into contact with those of the highest rank from across Europe, and would be invited to visit palaces and great houses and their gardens across Europe. Bishops had their own palaces and frequently castles, as at St Andrews, Glasgow and Aberdeen, usually in the towns of the cathedral of their dioceses, and in Scotland, like England, monastic houses, as at St Andrews and Whithorn, were attached to cathedrals and maintained the offices there. Elsewhere there were colleges of secular canons, forming a large resident group of clergy which served the cathedrals, either in person or through deputies. The bishops would also have manor houses elsewhere in their dioceses such as those belonging to the Bishop of Dunkeld at Clunie, east of the Tay, and Tibbermore, west of the Tay in Perthshire.

The survival of the accounts of the bishopric of Dunkeld between 1505 and 1517 allows the names of the gardeners belonging to the bishop's household to be known along with their wages in money and food. John Leslie was succeeded by John Broun (Hannay 1915, 96, 106,113 etc), while in 1513–14 Robert Howyson, who may be the same person as Robert Gardiner, was the gardener at the bishop's residence at **Clunie Castle** near Blairgowrie, where he had a croft of two acres in the south part of the orchard there (Hannay 1915, 74, 187). The bishop would have his residence on the small island in the loch; building was underway there at this time, and the site of the old castle on the mainland was quarried for building materials (Hannay 1915, 187). The terraces on the east and north sides of the earlier castle (see RCAHMS 1994, 105A) are likely to be garden features of a later date (Fig 63).

Something of the same culture is suggested in the west in Dean Monro's *Description of the Western Isles of Scotland*, written following a systematic route through

Fig 61 *A miniature of a red-capped physician with book and herbs in* De Epidemia *by Raymond Chalin de Vinario. The volume belonged to Archbishop William Schevez of St Andrews, whose signature appears at the top of the page. MS Hunter 35 18r (T.1.3).* © University of Glasgow Library.

Fig 63 Aerial view of Clunie Castle in the Loch of Clunie which was built for the Bishop Broun of Dunkeld in the early sixteenth century. The earthwork defences of the earlier royal castle on the shore were modified by later terracing. DP042065

the western islands of Scotland in 1549 (Martin 1999). The account of Raasay includes two castles, 'the castle of Killmorocht (Kilmaluig) and the castle of Brolokit (Brochel), with twa fair orchards at the saids twa castells ... pertaining to M'Gyllychallan of Raarsay be the sword, and to the bishope of the iles by heritage' (Martin 1999, 322; RCAHMS 1928, 178–80, 185).

The archbishops of **Glasgow** had a castle or tower house with courts and gardens attached, next to the cathedral where the Royal Infirmary now stands (Fig 64). In March 1553 Archbishop James Beaton received the newly created magistrates of the city in the inner flower garden next to the palace of the archbishop (*in interiore florum hortulo iuxta palatium Archiepiscopi Glasguensis*) (Innes 1843, vol 2, 580, no 523). The Bishop's Palace in **Aberdeen** was probably built about 1459 by Bishop Spence and demolished in 1655 for building materials for the construction of an artillery fortification on Castlehill. It was depicted on Gordon of Rothiemay's map (Gordon 1661) on the east side of Old Aberdeen to the east of St Machar's Cathedral and was described as 'Rwins of the Bishopps house' (Fig 65). It occupies two sides of a court to the north and east with a gatehouse and a fence on the south side, leading into what is called 'the Bishopps Garden'. 'The Chapellans Chambers', four ranges around a court with a tower at each corner built by the executors of Bishop Gavin Dunbar who died in 1532, formed the

southern boundary (Fig 65). Within the garden, which appears to have been enclosed to the west by a paling fence with a roofed entrance gate, is a rectangle of grass and a group of what are probably orchard trees. On this west side is depicted a remarkable three storey summer house, reached by steps from where there was 'a prospect of the whole town' (Robertson 1843, 152). To the east of the garden was the Bishops Green, with the ruins of a beehive doocot. Although the pictorial source is late, the layout is likely to reflect that of the sixteenth century. The bishop of Aberdeen had various principal residences on his estates including Fetternear and Old Rayne, of which little survive (RCAHMS 2007, 163). One of these residences was on a small island in

Fig 64 A print of the Archbishop's Castle in Glasgow from Joseph Swan's Select Views of Glasgow and its environs published in 1828. The ruins of the palace were removed in 1789 to make way for the Royal Infirmary. SC498287

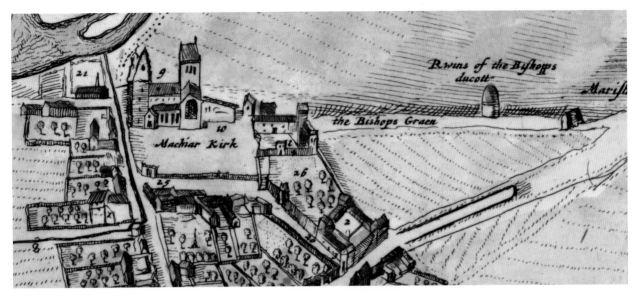

Fig 65 The bishop's palace next to St Machar's Cathedral on the 1661 map of Aberdeen by James Gordon of Rothiemay. EMS.s.249. © NLS

Bishop's Loch (RCAHMS 2007, 162, fig 8.26), where it is recorded that Bishop Benham died in 1282. Hector Boece said that the bishop 'found such delight in the pleasant groves adjoining the [loch] that he sought no other retreat' (Moir 1894, 15). As with the grants by the community of Coupar Angus, the bishop might specify certain conditions when granting a lease of the bishopric property; the lands of Terpersie in Tullynessle were let in 1428 by Bishop Henry de Lichton to John Clerk for a rent of eight merks and the requirement to build an honest house in which the bishop might lodge for one night each year. A further condition was the creation of a garden and the planting of trees (Innes 1845, 1, 229). These residences acted as centres for the organisation of the estates of the bishopric, and because of the partial survival of ecclesiastical records may provide some insight into the arrangements that might be appropriate for a lay landowner, where documentary evidence does not survive.

Fig 66 Pages from Dean Brown's Prayer Book showing the raising of Lazarus. The manuscript, made in Flanders for a Scottish churchman, James Brown, Dean of Aberdeen Cathedral, contains a memorandum of his mission to Rome in 1479 to seek the appointment of the Duke of Ross, James IV's younger brother, as Archbishop of St Andrews. The border decoration uncharacteristically includes thistles. © National Library of Scotland. Licensor Scran

Chapter 2: The Royal and Noble Garden 1100 to 1560

Ane gudlie grein garth, full of gay flouris,
Hegeit of ane huge hicht with hawthorne treis

'The Tretis of the tua Mariit Wemen and the Wedo' William Dunbar

Like the dignitaries of the Church, the kings of Scotland were linked to their peers elsewhere in Western Europe, as well as to Rome. They shared languages, French as well as Latin, as a means for the communication and for the transmission of a common courtly culture. This common cultural background applied to the creation of their gardens, as much as to their choice of music, literature or chivalric display, and gardening in Scotland in the medieval period can be seen as forming a part of a wider European practice, an element in the same nexus of trade and culture (Bawcutt and Hadley Williams 2010, 10–12). The majority of the surviving evidence is, in one way or another, documentary, and this favours knowledge of the gardens and gardeners of the king and the religious houses, those for which all expenditure must be accounted. The very partial survival of the records of even these institutions has been alluded to, but arguments for the non-existence of gardens and a low level of gardening skill, based on the absence of evidence, cannot be sustained. The pattern of the medieval garden, secular as well as religious, is one of enclosure, often by walls, sometimes by hedges and sometimes by a ditch, providing protection against theft and trespass, as well as shelter from the wind and weather. All these features are difficult to date in the

absence of excavation, and many of them would be appropriate to gardens of all periods. Once a garden has been established there is a strong tendency to continue to exploit the improved fertility of the soil, and most of the gardens referred to will have continued to be used in later centuries. The provision of food for the household would be the most important role of the gardens belonging to all ranks of society, but this does not prevent their perception as a source of leisure and an expression of status.

The records for the royal household, like those for monasteries and bishoprics, survive only in part, but do provide some glimpses of the existence of gardens and for their layout. These mainly relate to the later medieval period and may be illustrated, to some extent and with caution, by the writings of the poets who had specific relationships to the royal court, such as the author of *The Kingis Quair* and Gavin Douglas, author of *The Palice of Honour*. Writing about royal gardens in medieval England and drawing on the financial and administrative records relating to royal houses, Howard Colvin paid tribute to their survival, which was more complete than those in any other European state (Colvin 1986, 9); his discussion appeared in a volume concerned with gardens across Western Europe (Macdougall 1986, 30). He stressed that the monarchy was the least insular component of medieval English society, and noted the predominantly continental origins of the queens of England, pointing out that gardens were seen as the especial province of women. There is evidence of a Provencal gardener

Fig 67 Aerial view of Stirling Castle with James V's Palace, the King's Old Building of James IV and the site of the garden within the castle of James IV and V, furnished with turf benches and flowery knots for James V in 1532.

directing the royal garden at Windsor at a time when Eleanor of Provence was queen, in the earlier thirteenth century, and of Aragonese gardeners working for Eleanor of Castile at her manor of King's Langley, near London, in the later thirteenth century. Similarly in Scotland, the kings were connected by marriage and family relationships with the royal houses of Europe. Scottish kings from Malcolm Canmore in 1070 to Alexander II in 1285 married English and French princesses and noblewomen, closely related to ruling families. This custom continued in the later Middle Ages with David II marrying an English princess, James I, a cousin of Henry V, Jane Beaufort, James II, a daughter of the Duke of Guelders in the Holy Roman Empire, James III, a daughter of the king of Denmark, James IV, an English princess, and James V, a daughter of the king of France. The reasons for the marriages may have been for the political and, to a degree, financial benefits that they brought with them, but they also marked the status of the kings of Scotland, as did participation in an international culture that included the cultivation of gardens for recreation and display. Nobles holding land in Scotland belonged to families which held land in England and perhaps also in France, and married across what are now national boundaries; all the claimants to the throne following the death of the Maid of Norway in 1290 belonged to this milieu, with John Balliol, the king of Scotland initially recognised by Edward I, still owning a castle at Bailleul in Picardy (Nicholson 1974, 63).

Warfare provided a profession for many Scots, and might take the participants across Europe and beyond. The laird of Fast Castle served in the Turkish army, returning to Scotland from Cairo in 1509 (*TA*, 2, xxvii). Warfare might not lead to an appreciation of horticulture; there is an account of William of Scotland invading Northumberland in 1174 and besieging Prudhoe Castle on the Tyne when he 'destroyed its corn-fields and barked its apple-trees' (Anderson 1922, 2, 289), and in 1296 Edward I's army destroyed the orchard of the nunnery at Coldstream (Stevenson 1870, ii, 32). In Flanders in 1340, according to Froissart (1805, 1, 159), David II took the field alongside the kings of France, Bohemia and Navarre. Scottish troops fought against Henry V's forces at Beaugé in Anjou in 1421, winning honours and lands from the French dauphin (Dunlop 1942, 6). In the late fifteenth and earlier sixteenth centuries Scottish troops in French

service were present at all the major battles during the Italian wars. Members of the Garde Ecossaise, the personal bodyguard of the kings of France, took part in the battles of Fornovo (1495), Seminara (1503), Ravenna (1512), Marignano (1513), after which the bells of Edinburgh were rung in celebration of the French victory, and Pavia (1525). After the Duke of Albany gave up the regency in 1523/4, he went on to attack Naples for the French king, François I (Cooper 2008, 54). Albany held extensive French estates, and had many Italian connections: his second wife was the aunt of Catherine de Medici, who married François I's second son, later Henry II of France.

Scottish kings visited France and England, not always willingly. John Balliol and his son were imprisoned in England from 1296 and subsequently despatched to France. The ten year old son of Robert Bruce, David II, and his English queen took refuge in France from David Balliol after the defeat at Halidon Hill, staying at Chateau Gaillard above the River Seine in 1334, and David, following the battle of Neville's Cross, was an English prisoner from 1346 to 1357. James I was imprisoned in England by Henry IV in about 1406, having been captured by English sailors on his way to France, where he had been sent by his father, Robert II, for a safer upbringing than seemed to be available in Scotland. During the reign of Henry IV James was moved from the Tower of London to Nottingham Castle, Stratford Abbey, Evesham and Croydon. Henry V removed him back to the Tower and on to Windsor Castle; Pevensey and Pontefract, Raby Castle and London followed (Balfour-Melville 1936, 38). In 1418 he was at Kenilworth Castle, where Henry V had recently completed an enclosed pleasance across the lake from and just out of sight of the castle itself. The earthworks of a double-moated quadrilateral enclosure still survive. In the central area was a timber-framed banqueting house and gardens, which could be approached by boat (Thomson 1964, 222–3).

James I subsequently accompanied Henry to France in 1420 in an unsuccessful attempt by the English king to disengage Scottish troops from supporting the French king. When in Paris James was probably lodged at the Hotel de St Pol, which was surrounded by a pleasure garden, which had been laid out by Charles V of France and replanted by Charles VI in 1398. The garden contained a labyrinth, trellises, tunnels, arbours, ponds, orchards and ornamental plants (Cooper 1999, 832). It had a great circular pool with an encircling balustrade, and a lion spouting water in the middle (Colvin 1999, 8). James attended Henry's wedding to Katherine, the daughter of the King of France, and travelled back with the royal party to London for her coronation. He was in France again in 1421, returning to England after Henry's death in 1422, as a member of his funeral cortege, when, if not earlier, he would visit Hesdin.

Fig 68 The painting depicts the garden at Hesdin in Northern France in 1432 on the occasion of the marriage of the chamberlain of Philip the Good of Burgundy, André de Toulongeon. Hesdin, visited by James I in 1422, was a place to which important visitors were taken so that they might be impressed by the park with its hills, pastures and woods, hamlets, lodges, fish ponds, paddocks, mews, aviaries and menagerie. There were orchards of apple, cherry and plum trees and gardens of osiers, grapevines, roses and lilies. The garden is unenclosed, unlike many of the gardens depicted in Flemish manuscript paintings. Musée du Château, Versailles, copy of a fifteenth century painting or tapestry which has been attributed to Jan van Eyck. © Scala

The renowned garden at Hesdin in Northern France was a place to which important visitors were taken so that they might be impressed by the park with its hills, pastures and woods, hamlets, lodges, fish ponds, orchards, paddocks, mews, aviaries and a menagerie. There were orchards of apple, cherry and plum trees and gardens of osiers, grapevines, roses and lilies, including one called *li petit Paradis* (Hagopian van Buren 1986 120). Hesdin lay near the site of the Battle of Agincourt in the province of Artois, and it was on the route of the funeral procession of Henry V which took over six weeks to move from Bois de Vincennes near Paris via St Denis, Rouen, Boulogne and Calais to the burial at Westminster Abbey. The park was also renowned as the setting of the poem *Remède de Fortune* by the fourteenth century composer and poet Guillaume de Machaut, although the mechanical devices and moving statues in the park may have had a more immediate impact on the distinguished visitors (Woodbridge 1986, 16). A panel painting in the Musée du Chateau, Versailles, a copy of a fifteenth century painting or tapestry which has been attributed to Jan van Eyck, shows a *Jardin d'Amour* at the court of Philip the Good of Burgundy, set in the gardens at Hesdin in 1432 on the occasion of the marriage of his chamberlain, André de Toulongeon, with elaborate buildings in the park, fountains, feasting and music. The representation of Hesdin and the fete may be idealised, but it shows how such a courtly garden and an important wedding celebration should look (Fig 68).

James I has been convincingly credited with the writing of the poem *The Kingis Quair* (Mackenzie 1939, 13–26; McDiarmid 1973, 28–60), which records the poet's courtship, beginning with the lamenting of his imprisonment and his study of philosophy, before turning to his window and contemplating the garden outside, supposed to be based on that at Windsor Castle (Cooper 1999, 819). As in a dream vision in the poetic tradition of Chaucer and Gower, the scene is set in May and accompanied by the song of the nightingale.

> Now was there maid fast by the touris wall
> A gardyn faire, and in the cornere set
> Ane herbere grene, with wandis long and small
> Railit about; and so with treis set
> Was all the place, and hawthorn hegis knet,

And in the garden he saw:

> The fairest or the freschest yong floure
> That euer I sawe, me thought, before that houre;
> For quhich sodayne abate anone astert
> The blude of all my body to my hert.
> (McDiarmid 1973, 84–6)

Gardens had an important role in courtly culture throughout Europe, and an association with love and marriage as well as sensual and adulterous pleasures (McDiarmid 1973, 57). James I was married to Joan Beaufort in 1424 at Southwark Cathedral and eventually returned to Scotland, arriving at Melrose Abbey in April of that year. This account of James' courtship is believed to have been composed about 1435, many years after his return to Scotland.

James I's children were married across north and central Europe. His eldest daughter, Margaret, married the heir to the throne of France in 1436; her dowry contract included six thousand Scottish auxiliaries (Dunlop 1942, 6). Three of her sisters married into Brittany, Flanders and Austria, with two others, who had been sent to France to be provided with suitable husbands, returning to Scotland. Their brother, James II, married Mary of Gueldres, the niece of Duke Philip the Good of Burgundy, and the treaty which accompanied the marriage allowed Scottish merchants favourable status in all the Burgundian dominions (Nicholson 1974, 347–8).

There was a regular procession of churchmen, appointed to bishoprics, who would travel to Rome or Avignon, and even, briefly, Perpignan (Nicholson 1974, 244), to seek confirmation of their election and consecration. In 1428 an Act of Parliament ruled that no Scotsman might leave the country without letters of license issued for 'gude and honest cause' (Dunlop 1942, 9). When appointments (particularly to wealthy abbeys) were disputed, candidates would attempt to gain support at the papal court. Scottish clerics, including the abbot of Paisley, the warden of the Dominican friary at Ayr and a canon of Brechin Cathedral, attended the church council at Constance in 1415. The Scottish contingent at the Council of Florence in 1439, which saw the official reunion of the Greek and Roman Churches, was led by James I's nephew, Bishop Kennedy of Dunkeld and later of St Andrews, who was granted the abbacy of Scone by the pope (Dunlop 1942, 11). When John Hectoris Macgilleon was provided to the bishopric of the Isles by Pope Eugenius IV in 1441, he was accompanied by several petitioners from his diocese (Dunlop 1942, 9). Other examples of the visits of Scots to Italy survive because of their unfortunate outcome. Gilbert de Rerick, Archdeacon of Glasgow, travelled to Tivoli from Rome for the recovery of his health, but was waylaid, robbed and maltreated by the retainers of a local magnate (Dunlop 1942, 11).

Pilgrimage, a frequent motive for internal travel, was also a major reason, or excuse, for foreign journeys. The travels of nobles and bishops were more often recorded than those of less prominent Scots. In 1450, a year which had been proclaimed a jubilee by Pope Nicholas V, Bishop Kennedy of St Andrews set out for Rome as did the eighth Earl of Douglas, one returning via Flanders and the other through England (Nicholson 1974, 353–4). On his way to Rome the Earl of Douglas visited Philip the Good, Duke of Burgundy,

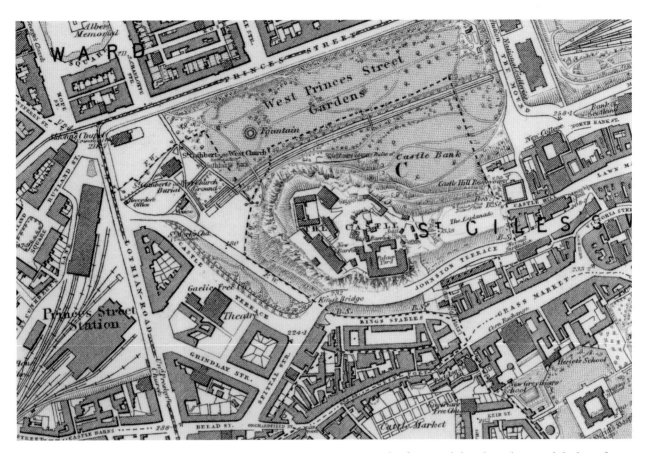

Fig 69 Map of Edinburgh in 1877 showing the area around the castle occupied by the early gardens lying between modern day Shandwick Place and West Maitland Street and Morrison Street and Bread Street. These gardens appear to have been concerned with food production, rather than more recreational pursuits. Bread Street was formerly known as Orchardfield Place and Orchardfield Street. Next to the King's Stables was the Barras, a defensive feature, which also provided a ground used for tournaments and tilting. Ordnance Survey First Edition 6-inch map Edinburghshire Sheet 2.

at Lille. He was accompanied by, among others, his brother James who succeeded him as Earl of Douglas, Sir James Hamilton, Sir John Ogilvy of Lintrathen, Sir Alexander Hume, Sir William Cranston and Sir Colin Campbell of Glenorchy, some of the most prominent figures in Scotland. The party continued to the court of Charles VII at Paris, from where they probably travelled to Chalon sur Saône to attend a tournament entitled 'The Fountain of Tears', organised by the renowned Burgundian exponent of chivalry, Jacques de Lalain (Stevenson 2006, 78–9).

In 1471 Robert Blackadder, the first archbishop of Glasgow, travelled to Rome on behalf of James III, and while he was there received the abbacy of Melrose *in commendam*; in 1483, he was in Rome for his consecration to the see of Glasgow; he undertook embassies to England, France and Spain, seeking a wife for James IV, visiting Ferdinand of Aragon and Isabella of Castile twice in 1495 and 1496. He died in 1508 at Jaffa on a pilgrimage to Jerusalem (Laing 1857, 222–6; Dunlop 1942, 12); 27 of the 36 pilgrims who set out with him from Venice did not return. The

opportunity for examining the culture and design of gardens of different countries of Europe at their highest levels was open to these travellers, as well as visits to the gardens of religious establishments and those within or adjacent to major towns and cities. The three most esteemed destinations for pilgrimage were Jerusalem, Rome and Compostella; the numbers of Scottish pilgrims visiting these places is extremely difficult to estimate. Not all would return; in 1326 a ship called the *Pelarym* was seized by English privateers and the Scots on board, pilgrims and women, were killed. Sir James Douglas, carrying the heart of Robert Bruce to the Holy Sepulchre, died in battle against the Moors of Granada in 1330 (Barrow 1976, 445–6). A century later the heart of James I was taken to Jerusalem, and then brought back to Scotland for burial with the rest of his body at the Charterhouse in Perth (Simpson 1999, 178). Andrew Boorde, who himself got as far as Jerusalem, met at Orleans in France nine English men and Scottish men on pilgrimage to Compostella (Furnivall 1870, 205–6), all of whom died on the return journey, according to Boorde 'by eatynge of frutes and drynkynge of water, the whych I dyd euer refrayne my selfe'.

While there was ample opportunity for Scots to view and absorb knowledge of garden design and planting in gardens across Europe, no precise instance of imitation has been recorded. An account of the gardens of **Edinburgh Castle** was written by Charles Malcolm in 1925 and begins with records from the reign of David I. The chartulary of Holyrood records a grant dated to

Fig 70 The gardens of the king at Haddington lay close to St Mary's Parish Church. SC1237407

between 1143 and 1147 of lands that had previously been given to the secular clergy of the 'Church of St Cuthbert next to the Castle of Edinburgh'. The area to be granted is described as 'all the land from the fountain (spring) that rises next the corner of the king's garden, on the way that leads to the same Church, and on the other side, below the castle, as far as a road below the castle towards the east' (Innes 1840, 4 no 1, 7–8 no 3). Malcolm identifies the well as St Margaret's Well and interprets its position in the corner of the king's garden as lying to the south below the castle close to the Grassmarket end of King's Stables Road (Malcolm 1925, 103–5). He believed that the original gardens extended west of the castle, occupying an area between modern day Shandwick Place and West Maitland Street and Morrison Street and Bread Street, and that they may have extended south to Tollcross and Lauriston Place (Fig 69). These gardens appear to have been concerned with food production, rather than more recreational pursuits. The area developed to supply the royal household and came to include stables and barns to hold such provisions as corn and malt and fodder for horses. Malcolm attributes the use of the Grassmarket for the sale of horses, cattle and sheep to the practice of sending animals from the royal lands in Bute, Carrick and Mar to Edinburgh and their sale beside the King's Stables (Malcolm 1925, 110). A reference to the *pomarium*

super montem prope castellum, 'the orchard on the hill next to the castle' (Malcolm 1925, 106) would indicate that the ridge to the south of the Grassmarket was in use as an orchard, although it may not have been part of the original royal garden. Bread Street was formerly known as Orchardfield Place and Orchardfield Street. Next to the King's Stables was the Barras, a defensive feature, which also provided a ground used for tournaments and tilting (RCAHMS 1951, 3; Dunbar 1999, 202–3). Tournaments are recorded in 1335 when Edinburgh Castle was occupied by the English; one, sponsored by Queen Annabella, wife of Robert II, took place in 1398, and another in 1500 during the reign of James IV when a Scottish champion fought with a Dutch or German knight (Stevenson 2006, 85). Tournament grounds were required for this high form of noble entertainment, and the patronage of tournaments was part of the creation of a chivalric image or icon of the king and his realm: James IV himself took part in elaborately conceived tournaments, harking back to Arthur and the Round Table and chivalric virtues (Fradenburg 1991, 154–5; Stevenson 2006). At Stirling, the Barras, an enclosure designed for judicial combats, duels, or tournaments, was on the low ground to the west of the castle (RCAHMS 1963, 183), but in the reign of James V may have lain beneath the south side of the castle in the vicinity of the royal garden and the King's Stables (Dunbar 1999, 204).

Following the English invasion of 1335, there was disruption to the gardens at Edinburgh Castle, for which

Fig 71 Doune Castle. Records indicate the presence of an orchard and a vegetable garden at the royal castle of Doune. DP051066

there is evidence from English records. The sheriff of Edinburgh, who was acting for Edward III, recorded that there was no rent from the kitchen garden below the castle, although it used to be worth twelve pence a year, and none from the orchard, which had been worth thirteen shillings and four pence a year. In the following year it was reported that both were worth five shillings and ten pence (Bain 1881, 3, 327, 376). The name of David II's gardener in 1363 was Malcolm Paganson (*RMS* App 2, 578, no 985), recorded only in a lost charter of which one line remains, an example of the relatively random survival of documentary information. In 1435, in the reign of James I, there was a payment for the late Walter Massoun and Nicolao Plummar for completing the garden of the king in the castle of Edinburgh, *complecione herbarii regis infra castrum de Edinburgh* (*ER*, 4, 623). This would seem to indicate a garden within the castle itself. The names of the tradesmen would imply that they were engaged in the making of a structure involving stone and water, perhaps a well or fountain. In 1493 and 1494, John Gardiner failed to provide the king with eight barrels of onions, but he was paid £5 6s 8d in 1496 (*ER*, 10, 589)

Elements of the royal demesne were frequently rented out (*Regesta*, 2, 51). One early example of this is the king's garden of **Carlisle Castle**, which was rented in 1130 for thirty shillings to William Fitzbaldwin

(Harvey 1990, 64). The Scottish kings had held Carlisle until 1085 and David I took possession of the castle again in 1135, dying there in 1153 (Summerson 1993, 1, 39; *Regesta* 1, 111). The other royal properties all appear to have had gardens attached to them, although often the only evidence for this is the references to the gardeners whose wages appear in the account books, in particular the *Accounts of the Lord High Treasurer of Scotland* (*TA*) and the *Exchequer Rolls* (*ER*).

In addition to the major palaces such as Linlithgow, Stirling and Falkland which survive to the present day, other properties were covered by the royal financial records at certain periods. These include Elgin, Traquair, Roxburgh, Jedburgh, Doune, Clackmannan, Forfar, Haddington, Kildrummy, Dunfermline and Cardross (Fig 71). In a case mentioned by Cox (1935, 19), the existence of the garden at **Elgin Castle** in 1261 is known because a crossbowman named Robert Spink claimed it on behalf of of his wife whose ancestors had held it as a hereditary right. Another garden known as the result of a family relationship is that at **Traquair** in 1288 where it is recorded that the gardener had taken flight because of the killing of his wife (*ER* 1, 46). Between 1189 and 1195 King William confirmed a grant by his grandfather, David I, which probably included the tithe of his orchard at **Roxburgh Castle** (*Regesta* 1, no 315, 326). In 1448 cabbage, scallion and onion seeds were sent to Doune for sowing, and in 1451 seeds of onions and scallions were recorded as sown in the garden at **Doune Castle** (*ER* 5, 304,479),

Fig 72 A floriated initial from the manuscript of The Romaunt of the Rose *by Geoffrey Chaucer set in an allegorical garden. Lines 22–23 on this page read,* The roser was, withoute doute, Closed with an hegge without, *setting the scene for a lover. MS Hunter 409. 57v (v.3.7) © University of Glasgow Library, Department of Special Collections.*

when it was in the charge of John Henryson. Against the yearly payment to the gardener at Doune Castle in 1456 is noted 'ill deserved'(*ER* 6, 285), and in 1460 the name of the gardener at Doune is again recorded as John Henryson (*ER* 6, 639). In 1329 seeds were bought for the gardens at **Clackmannan** (*ER* 1, 223), and in 1359 the orchard there was worth eight shillings and eleven pence each year. The gardener's wages at Forfar were five marks yearly and those of the gardener at Menmoreth (Menmuir) were one mark in 1264–6 (*ER* 1, 8). King William, at a date between 1178 and 1188, made a grant of a piece of land, which lay next to his garden and the burial ground of the church of St Mary and St Michael at Haddington, now St Mary's Parish Church (Fig 70). A hundred years later the gardener received eighteen shillings and four pence for his service in the garden there and for having the custody of food supplies (*ER* 1, 37), and in 1438 there was payment for work in the orchard (*ER* 5, 58). The orchard and doocot at **Ballencrieff** in East Lothian are recorded in 1486 and

1487, when they were in the hands of John Malynson, 'who pays no rent' (*ER* 9, 359, 475). The orchard at **Kildrummy Castle** is mentioned in 1438, (*ER* 5, 58), and again in 1503, when it was described as formerly belonging to the earl of Mar (*ER* 12 133). There was a Gardinarhill pertaining to the gardener, who looked after the gardens near the castle at Kildrummy, repairing ditches and dikes, and planting trees, flowers and herbs there. In 1501 the castle at Banff, with its 'mount' and garden, was in the possession of the king (*ER* 11, 374).

Cardross lies on the north side of the Firth of Clyde near Dumbarton Castle and the confluence of the River Leven. It was acquired by Robert Bruce in about 1326, in exchange for Old Montrose in Angus and lands at Leckie near Stirling, and it was there he died in 1329 (*ER* 1 4, 127). It would seem to have been intended as a place for domestic life and relaxation, although its closeness to Dumbarton Castle, one of only two castles in Scotland which the king had not ordered to be destroyed following the wars with the English, would provide some security. It was a *manerium* or manor house with a hall, chambers for the king and queen, a chapel, kitchen and larder. In the interior were plastered and painted walls and windows with window glass. A garden and a park were part of the complex, as well as a mews for hawking surrounded by a hedge (*ER* 1, cxx; Barrow 1976, 439–41). The Bolognese writer Pietro de' Crescenti wrote a book *Liber ruralium commodorum*, or the 'Book of country profits', in the late thirteenth century, much of it drawing on earlier writers, including Albertus Magnus (Whiteley 1999, 92–3; Calkins 1986, 157–73). This work was known in Scotland; a surviving copy, printed in Louvain, which belonged, in 1492, to Robert Kinman of Megginch, a follower of Archbishop Schevez, is now in the Radcliffe Library in Oxford (Durkan and Ross 1961, 121). It was translated into French in 1373 at the command of the French king, Charles V, as *Le Rustican*. While much of it was devoted to horticulture, there was a chapter on *Vergiers royaulx et des autres nobles puissans et riches*. Small private gardens, often situated beneath chamber windows, were a recognised amenity of princely houses, and were designed 'to give pleasure to people, and therefore preserve the health of the body as the state of the body affects the mind'. In 1329 the gardener at Cardross was called Gilbert, and in the same year various seeds (*diversis seminibus*) costing eighteen pence were purchased for the orchard, suggesting that the area around the fruit trees was cultivated, not with one crop (*ER* 1, 125–6), but with a variety, possibly for an ornamental effect. International contacts were not lacking: Bruce's chief physician was Patrick Beaton of the family of hereditary Gaelic doctors practising in Ireland and Scotland, but Maino de Maineri, who was born near Milan, taught at the University of Paris and was later court physician and astrologer to the Viscontis of Milan, was in attendance on the king during the

Fig 73 The rectangular medieval moated site of Hallyards in Perthshire emerging in cropmark form. The light mark indicating the line of the foundations of the stone enclosure wall is itself enclosed by the broad green line of the former water-filled moat, which was probably used for raising fish. Within the enclosure would have been the house and garden. The double lines of later water mains cross the site. SC1237396

1320s (Proctor 2007, 16–21). The king's son, David II, continued to live at Cardross as a child and the manor and park were maintained, with work recorded as carried out in 1362 (*ER* 1, 34).

Gardens had an important role in the literary and cultural life of the later Middle Ages. They had connotations which were both sacred and profane. The association with Virgin Mary reflected an image of the garden as a place of purity and innocence, separate from the evils of the world (Fig 96). The garden was also a place for earthly and sensual love, in its own way also apart from the wider world. One of the most famous poems of the medieval period was the *Roman de la Rose*, an allegorical dream vision, which explored the nature of *fin amour* or courtly love. Many manuscripts of the work survive, and it was extremely influential on the form of later poems; it appeared in English as *The Romaunt of the Rose* and the translation has been ascribed to Geoffrey Chaucer. The setting of the poem is a walled garden, where the poet learns how to woo his beloved (Fig 72). *The Kingis Quair* of James I was in the mainstream of this cultural phenomenon. The pattern of the medieval garden is one of enclosure, often by walls, sometimes by hedges and sometimes by a ditch. This might be a part of a wider garden landscape, linked to orchards and fish ponds, and, at the highest levels of medieval society, a park for deer (Woodbridge 1986, 17). The discovery of enclosures, including rectilinear examples, from

the air in the form of cropmarks is frequent, but their attribution to the medieval period and their identification as gardens is much less so. The moated site of Hallyards near Alyth in Perthshire, where traces of a stone wall can be seen inside the line of the broad moat, is of a size to enclose not only the hall and buildings appropriate to the centre of a major estate, but with an area some 75m by 50m, a substantial garden (RCAHMS 1994, 108–9) (Fig 73). It may be compared with the surviving earthwork of the Pleasance at Kenilworth

Fig 74 The cropmark of the site of a possible medieval garden near Rossie Priory in Perthshire. The light green line defines part of a walled rectangular enclosure which may have contained buildings as well as a garden. SC1237400

Castle and the earthwork evidence from Somersham in Cambridgeshire, where the Bishop of Ely had a palace (Taylor 1997, 22–3). The property of Hallyards is on record in 1506 (Hannay 1915, 76). Another site where the cropmarks are of a suitable form to be interpreted as a deserted garden of the medieval period was recorded near Rossie Priory, also in Perthshire; a small rectangle of ground is enclosed by a wall with some indications of what may be buildings nearby (Fig 74). Walled gardens might lie at some distance from the dwelling house, separate from it as a place of greater healthfulness, as well as peace and enchantment evoked by romances and manuscript illuminations (Whiteley, 1999, 94; Guillaume, 1999b, 105).

The Gardens of James IV

Expenditure on gardens was a minor part of the provision designed to maintain the role of the monarchy in Scotland and Europe. Major expenditure was on the most prestigious projects of military provision, such as ship building and the acquisition of ordnance, with tournaments providing a form of decorative display. The construction of palaces at Stirling, Falkland, Linlithgow and Edinburgh, along with their gardens, by the Stewart monarchs up to the reign of Mary was a claim to a cultural status on the European scale and a means of fulfilling their political aims through the creation of a court culture (Wormald 1988, 35–6). Although there is ample evidence for spending on the royal gardens,

Fig 75 James IV (1473–1513), oil painting by an unknown sixteenth century artist. © National Galleries of Scotland. Licensor Scran

this is put into proportion by the expenditure of, for example, James IV on buildings, ships, alchemy, horses, hunting, hawking, cards, apothecaries, tournaments, armour, music, dancers, golf, bowls and books. The kings of Scotland moved between their different properties throughout the year, the evidence for which often survives from the place of issue of the charters and grants. Edinburgh, Stirling, Perth, Dunfermline and Linlithgow were among the most popular. Sometimes particular seasons were associated with particular residences. Dunbar in his *Dirige to the King at Stirling*, addressed to James IV, contrasts the pleasures of Edinburgh with the pains of Stirling where Lent was being observed:

> The fader, the sone, the holie gaist,
> The blissit Marie, virgen chaist,
> Of angellis all the ordour nyne,
> And all the hewinlie court divyne,
> Sone bring yow fra the pyne and wo
> Of Striueling, everie court mans foo,
> Agane to Edinburchtis ioy and blys,
> Quhair wirschip, welthe, and weilfair is,
> Play, plesance eik and honestie
> Say ye amen, for chirritie.
> (Dunbar, 1998, 274–5)

A letter written in 1498 by Pedro de Ayala, another ambassador from Spain, was sent to Ferdinand and Isabella, following their request for a description of James IV and Scotland. He mentions that all kinds of garden fruits that a cold country can produce were to be found there and that they were very good, a statement echoed by Nicander Nucius, a native of Corfu in the service of Emperor Charles V, in 1545 (Brown 1978, 44, 61).

The Old Park of **Stirling Castle**, which was also known as the King's Park, was enclosed by William the Lion in the late twelfth or early thirteenth century (Fig 76). This park was repaired, and a new park was constructed in 1264 by Alexander III. These parks which lay to the south-west of the castle and would have been used for hunting continued to be referred to as the Old and New Parks up to the time of James IV in 1505 (*ER* 1, 49, no 179). The castle formed part of the jointure of the queens of Scotland from the time of Joan Beaufort, wife of James I, and it came to be used as the residence of their sons during their minorities. Some kings, such as James III, seem to have had a particular fondness for Stirling as a residence, and James IV and James V were responsible for the erection of the Great Hall and royal lodgings there (RCAHMS 1963, 182). While it is recorded that James IV was driven to return frequently to Stirling through remorse for the part he had played in the rebellion against his father, and that he 'daylie passit to the chapell Royall' and was 'ewer sade and dollorous in his mynd for the deid [death] of his father'

(Lindsay 1899–1911, 1, 218), he also enjoyed hunting in the nearby forest of Glenartney, a sport involving up to three hundred men. Tournaments were held there and minstrels entertained the royal court. In the year of James II's marriage to Mary of Gueldres a tournament was held in which Burgundian and Scottish knights took part. A new park was created, and wild white cattle, similar to those in the High Parks at Hamilton, as well as boar and deer, inhabited it (Richardson and Root 1948, 18) (Figs 76, 77). A cachepole or tennis court, like the contemporary and surviving example at Falkland, was erected in 1539 (*TA* 7 (1538–41), 168).

While the primary concern of this work is with what might conventionally be considered as gardens, associated with them in royal and noble castles and palaces were other features designed for entertainment and leisure. Parks adjacent to palaces and intended for hunting may have succeeded earlier royal castles and hunting lodges, favoured because of their nearness to good areas for hunting, such as Clunie Castle in Perthshire, Kincardine, both north of the Forth, and Traquair and Cadzow to the south (Gilbert 1979, 22). Parks existed next to Linlithgow, Stirling, Holyrood and Falkland, although judging by sixteenth century references to bringing deer to the parks at Stirling and Holyrood from Falkland (eg *TA* 3, 181, 362; *ER* 12, 389), only the last, the most remote from a town, may have had sufficient resources to support a herd (Fig 234). The gardens at Stirling and Holyrood were next to the park (at Linlithgow the park lay on the other side of Linlithgow Loch), and at Falkland there was a communicating gate between park and garden (Whiteley, 1999, 98). Hawking was a popular pastime and there are many payments throughout the Treasurers Accounts for hawks and for royal servants to travel to acquire hawks, as well as gifts to those who brought hawks to the king (*TA* 3, 131, 153, 167 etc). The association of the garden and the park brings together their use as places of open air entertainment. The lists used for tournaments were close to the gardens (*MW* 1, 112, 36); archery butts were at times placed in the gardens (*MW* 1, 112, 222), and tennis courts could also be constructed there (*MW* 1, 279–80). Precisely what is meant by 'great garden' and whether there was a contrast to privy garden at this period, in addition to an indication of size and contrast with smaller gardens, is unclear. They may have included orchards, and were a place for outdoor meetings and recreation.

As well as the two parks, there was more than one garden at Stirling Castle, although their precise sites are uncertain. One certainly lay within the castle, and is thought to be in the area which lies behind the present Chapel Royal, now entered through a vaulted passage. It was known as the King's Privy Garden (Richardson and Root 1948, 12) and later as the Nether Garden, the Chapel Garden and the Douglas Garden, from the tradition that the body of the eighth Earl of Douglas was

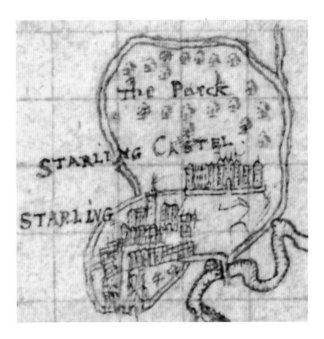

Fig 76 Stirling Castle and its hunting park as it appears on the manuscript map by Timothy Pont in the late sixteenth century. Pont 33 detail. © NLS

thrown down from a window into the garden after his murder at Stirling by James II in 1452 (Anon 1929, 223) (Figs 78, 79). It lay immediately to the north-west of the later King's Old Building. Payment of eighteen shillings, for the improvement of a presumably pre-existing garden and cleaning of the enclosure there, is recorded in the *Exchequer Rolls* in 1453 (*ER* 5, 597). Scott Cooper has associated the beginning of regular recording of payments for work on gardens with the influence of James II's queen, Mary of Gueldres, niece of the Duke of Burgundy, whose court was the most splendid in Europe. The personal device of the Duchess of Burgundy was the *hortus conclusus* or enclosed garden, a symbol of the Virgin Mary, and illustrations of gardens in Books of Hours and other religious paintings by artists of the fifteenth century patronised by the ducal court epitomise the garden of this period (Cooper 1999, 819–90). Maintenance of the gardens at Stirling continued during the reign of James III (*ER* 7, 59, 66, 188, 246, etc; *ER* 8, 50, 160, 243, 280, etc; *ER* 9, 249, 252, 325, 482, etc), when the gardener was paid in money and grain. James Wilsoun was the gardener in the castle of Stirling in 1461, receiving twenty shillings a year and continuing to at least 1476. He was paid for cleaning the ditches and for the care of the meadows at Stirling (*ER* 7, 69). He was also responsible at least at times for the granary there (*ER* 7, 69, 245; 8, 284) and for the building of the wall of the castle in 1467 (*ER* 7, 452), having more general duties at Stirling. In 1479 payments were made to Giles Macklehose (Gilleso Mackgilhoise) and Malcolm Maclary (Malcolmo Maklery) for the care of the garden and lawn of Stirling (*ER*, 8, 563). In 1480 and 1481 John Modane was paid twenty shillings for the care and repair of the garden (*ER*, 9, 3–4, 93).

Fig 77 Aerial view of Stirling with the castle near the centre of the photograph and the hunting park beyond. DP088846

Fig 78 Aerial view of Stirling Castle, showing relationship between the garden within the castle, the King's Old Building or King's House, the James V Palace and the Great Hall. DP079023

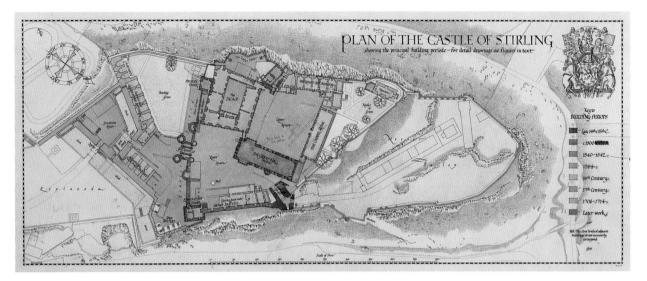

Fig 79 Plan of Stirling Castle from Stirlingshire: An Inventory of the Ancient Monuments *(RCAHMS 1963, Fig 86). SC800326*

The building of what was described as the King's House, immediately to the south of the garden, was completed in 1496 for James IV (Dunbar 1984, 19; Gifford and Walker 2002, 677) (Figs 78, 80). The association of the king's chamber and the garden was one commended by medieval authors (Whiteley 1999, 91–2). Another garden may have been created, or the existing garden extended to the north-west; in 1499 the *Exchequer Rolls* record a payment of eight bolls of oatmeal to Sir John Lundy for the custody of the ward of Stirling and the construction of ditches. The ward was changed by the command of the king into his garden in 1493. James IV may have used the garden within the castle for meetings: there is a reference in a letter from Ferdinand and Isabella of Spain to the two Spanish ambassadors in Scotland, in which the monarchs regretted their treatment by James IV during a meeting held in the garden of the castle in the winter of 1495. This was at a time when James had been seeking a wife from Spain, and the Spanish monarchs were using diplomacy to detach him from an alliance with France in favour of peace with England (Macdougall 1989, 122).

With the survival of some of the volumes of the *Accounts of the Lord High Treasurer of Scotland* from 1478 onwards, and their publication in the nineteenth and twentieth centuries, much more information about the royal gardens and parks becomes available during the reign of James IV. The regular payments to the gardener *infra castrum de Striveling* (within the castle of Stirling) of twenty shillings and a measure of grain continue from 1488, sometimes for his labours, sometimes for his service and sometimes for the repair of the garden (*ER* 10, 2, 4, 104, 108, 194, 264). Individual monks and friars were employed in the garden. In 1494 Friar Archibald Hamilton was awarded twenty shillings by the command of the king for the repair of the garden, as was Friar John Cauldwell in

1497 for his labours in the garden within the castle (*ER* 11, 18). Other payments were made in 1497, such as that on 27 October when a payment was made 'to the monk that castis (digs) the garden' (*TA* 1, 364). On 10 December £15 was paid to Dean Mathew Taket of Culross Abbey for the 'yard bigging' (*TA* I, 370). This may relate to an additional garden, and its preparation, construction and layout. On 19 February 1498 the gardener of Alloa brought trees to the garden of Stirling, and two days later Dean Matthew, now described as a monk of Stirling, was paid £10 to buy trees for the garden (*TA* I, 377–8). On 18 April he was responsible for the purchase of peas and beans for the garden at a cost of eighteen shillings (*TA* 1, 388). In 1499, when there seems to have been an exercise in catching up with in kind payments at Stirling, the gardener of the garden within the castle received for the repair of the garden eight measures of oatmeal for the previous eight years by the grace of the king (*ER* 11, 142).

An area at the north-east corner of the Old Park was set aside for another garden, and in 1499 seeds were purchased for the 'new garden' below the wall of the castle of Stirling (RCAHMS 1963, 219; *ER* 12, 76). These seeds were acquired from the garden belonging to the Church of St Mary in the Fields, known as Kirk o' Field, in Edinburgh, a garden that sixty years later would be the first in Scotland of which a detailed picture survives because it was the scene of the murder of Lord Darnley (RCAHMS 1951, 125).

The Treasurers Accounts for May 1498 to February 1500 do not survive, and the first clear distinction between payments for the old and new gardens of Stirling in these accounts comes on record in 1501, a year in which there seems to have been intensive activity in the gardens there. Payment of forty-five shillings was made to the gardener of the new garden below the wall of the Castle of Stirling (*ER* 11, 314), followed by payment to Master David Traile, provost of the newly erected college of priests of the Chapel Royal in the castle, for the repair of the garden within the castle, of

Fig 80 The 'garden within the castle' next to the King's Old Building in Stirling, James IV's Lodgings. DP073592

Fig 81 A line of trees including hawthorns along the boundary to the north of the later King's Knot, the garden below the castle. DP101946

twenty shillings and a measure of oatmeal (*ER* 11, 314), with an additional payment for the two previous years (*ER* 11, 315, 317–8). In the same year there were major purchases of fruit and other trees for planting in the new garden. The garden was protected by a thorn hedge; thorns for the hedge around the garden were purchased on 9 February 1501, some of which, or their successors, may still survive to the north-east of the King's Knot (Fig 81). Another four hundred thorns were bought at a cost of twenty-one shillings ten days later (*TA* 2, 82). The gardener at Scone was paid six shillings for osiers for the garden at Stirling on 21 February (*TA* 2, 98) and on 27 February carriage for nine horse loads of trees to be planted at Stirling cost twenty-seven shillings (*TA* 2, 98). Before this, on 17 January, Philpson of the Canongate in Edinburgh was paid forty shillings for sixteen pear trees to be sent to Stirling. They may have been carried in wickerwork baskets (Moorhouse 1991, 101). The payment for their transport to Stirling and for hay with which to bed the trees was five shillings and two pence (*TA* 2, 83). This may be an indication of an early retail market in fruit trees, which did not derive directly from a monastic source. George Campbell, who is recorded as playing at tables and at shooting with the king (*TA* 3, 179, 375), and who would die beside James at Flodden in 1513, was for the first time named gardener of Stirling, and was given fifty-six shillings to buy willows for the garden and to plant them (*TA* 2, 83). On 6 March seeds were purchased to be sown in the garden (*TA* 2, 82). On 7 March thirty-six trees for the garden were bought from William Carmichael at fourteen pence each (*TA* 2, 83), and these may have been the trees (possibly timber) brought to Stirling by boat for the loading of which, along with lead, nine shillings was paid (*TA* 2, 83). On 10 April 240 stakes were bought by George Campbell to be set about the loch in Stirling (*TA* 2, 84), and the same day the gardener of Scone brought herbs for planting in the garden (*TA* 2, 97).

April 11 brought a more exotic planting; the man who set the *wyne treis* or vines in Stirling received, by the king's command, fourteen shillings (*TA* 2, 102). On 24 April the French gardener received twenty-eight shillings, for going to Irvine for vines and for their carriage (*TA* 2, 104); it may be that the vines had been brought in by ship to Irvine. On 26 April the Frenchman, who set the *wyne treis* in Stirling, received fourteen shillings at the king's command, as did George Campbell and the workmen of the park dykes (*TA* 2, 105). The following year, on 11 February 1502, the French gardener was paid his wage of thirty-six shillings (*TA* 2, 136) and on 20 March George Campbell received twenty-eight shillings by the king's command (*TA* 2, 140). Some new planting was certainly taking place in this year for a man was paid four shillings for bringing rosemary from Bothwell to plant at Stirling (*TA* 2, 144). The gardens may have had other amenities: on 6 February 1501 sixteen pence was paid to a man who

Fig 82 James IV and Margaret Tudor as they are portrayed in the Seton Armorial *of 1591. Heraldry such as the arms depicted on Margaret's clothing may have been a feature of the design of knot gardens.* © *National Library of Scotland. Licensor Scran*

brought a peacock to the king, while the following year the man who brought peacocks from the Abbot of Scone received five shillings (*TA* 2, 96, 135). The peacocks may have been designed for culinary purposes, in addition to their decorative function. In July 1504 the master cook was repaid two shillings for the transport of the king's coffers and the white peacock to Stirling (*TA* 2, 445).

It was in 1503, the year in which James IV married Margaret Tudor, elder daughter of Henry VII, that another major planting scheme was recorded (Fig 82). Dande Doule brought nine horse loads of fruit trees from the Carse of Gowrie to Stirling at a cost of £6 13s 4d on 9 January, with expenses and carriage of forty shillings paid on 12 January. James IV had just travelled from Arbroath to Perth by way of Dundee, and it may be that an appropriate source of trees in the Carse was identified on the way. Unfortunately there is no mention of where in the Carse of Gowrie the trees came from, but on 26 January thirteen shillings was paid for the uplifting of certain trees in Hob Moncur's

Fig 83 Lindores Abbey as it appears on the manuscript map drawn by Timothy Pont in the late sixteenth century with no indication of the site of its orchard, although Yronsyde Wood is depicted to the east. Detail from Gordon 54b. © NLS

(Hobbe Mancuris) yard or garden (*TA* 2, 356). If the name 'Moncur' indicates a link to Moncur near Inchture, this may suggest the source of the trees, and may imply that they were the product of a lay rather than a monastic nursery. George Campbell was given twenty-eight shillings to buy trees on 17 January, and received fourteen shillings which he had laid down for carrying of 'certain treis' to the garden of Stirling (*TA* 2, 358). Sawyers were employed on the paling around the orchard at Stirling on 13 January, perhaps in anticipation of the need to protect the trees from deer, and the park pale also received work. Part payment on the pale of the garden was £4 4s. The sawyers on the orchard fence received fourteen shillings in drink silver, and the cost of the work on the park pale was £15 16s, followed by another £25 4s in March (*TA* 2, 354, 355, 358, 362). 'Divers seidis' for the garden at Stirling were bought from the master cook at the end of the month for fourteen shillings (*TA* 2, 356). Two items in the accounts reinforce the suggestion for a substantial expansion of the orchard: one on 10 February was fifty-six shillings to the gardener, George Campbell, to pay men to work in the garden, and the next, the following day, to Dean Matthew Taket, monk of Culross Abbey, for fifteen hundred plum trees for the garden at Stirling (*TA* 2, 358). Trees were lifted in 'Listoun', the Kirkliston or Newliston area between Edinburgh and Linlithgow, and brought to Stirling at a cost of forty-two shillings (*TA* 2, 370). A garden at Liston is mentioned in 1481, when it is recorded that lands were transferred from a mother to her son there in the presence of witnesses (NRS GD3/1/11/29/6). It was one of the possessions of the Knights Hospitallers, whose lands were controlled from the Preceptory at Torphichen. The garden was probably at Hallyards, as the 'yard' element in the name suggests,

the head of the barony of Liston, where earthworks still survive in part around the site of the now demolished later seventeenth century mansion house, which stood near the south-west end of the main runway at Edinburgh Airport.

George Campbell had forty-two shillings to make a pair of butts in the garden at Stirling in April (*TA* 2, 368), and evidence for what may be, at least in part, another amenity for the garden was the payment in February 1503 to the man who brought a swan to the king from the provost of Methven (*TA* 2, 358) followed by the provision of bere, a form of barley, for the swans in Stirling (*TA* 2, 394) at a cost of £8 0s 12d. In 1507 there was a payment to a man of the laird of Wemes (perhaps Castle Menzies) who brought three white deer to put in the park at Stirling (*TA* 4, 76).

The year 1504 saw further additions; in February George Campbell received £6 10s to buy more trees for Stirling (*TA* 2, 420), and at the end of March a man was sent to Lindores and to Coupar in Angus with twenty shillings for fruit trees for Stirling (*TA* 2, 425) (Figs 83, 84). On 26 March the gardener at Stirling was given three shillings to buy seeds for the garden (*TA* 2, 424). On 15 May the gardener of Stirling was to go to Culross for flowers to set, implying perhaps bedding plants, rather than seeds (*TA* 2, 433), on 19 May what were probably laurel trees were bought (*TA* 2, 434), and following this, in June, George Campbell received fifty-six shillings for the putting in order of the little garden (*TA* 2, 441). Planting continued in 1505, 1506, 1507 and 1508, with the purchase of seeds and trees for setting in the garden (*TA* 3, 129, 187, 367; *TA* 4, 101, 136).

The monastic houses of Culross, Lindores, Coupar Angus and Scone seem to have been in a position to supply the royal household with trees and plants, as well as men capable of supervising the layout and work of a garden. This may relate as much to their abilities as accountants as to their knowledge of horticulture. One of the longest serving of those with responsibility for royal gardens was John Sharp, usually described as Sir John Sharp, chaplain. His early career is not known, but he continued in the royal service until his death in 1538. John Sharp, whose title of 'Sir' indicates that he was not a graduate of any of the universities, had already been in charge of the creation of a garden in Edinburgh, presumably at Holyrood, in 1504 (*TA* 2, 329) and also seems to have acted as the king's agent in dispensing alms to various religious houses. In March 1505, he was paid twenty-eight shillings to pass from Dunfermline to Stirling to make the garden there (*TA* 3,132). He received a wage of forty-two shillings in May 1505, a further eighteen shillings later that month and twenty-eight shillings in June (*TA* 3, 137, 140, 146). He was provided with five ells of French tan (a tawny coloured cloth) for his clothing (*TA* 2, 329), a grant repeated in 1505 and 1506, which was the same cloth given to James' Danish cook, an indication of his

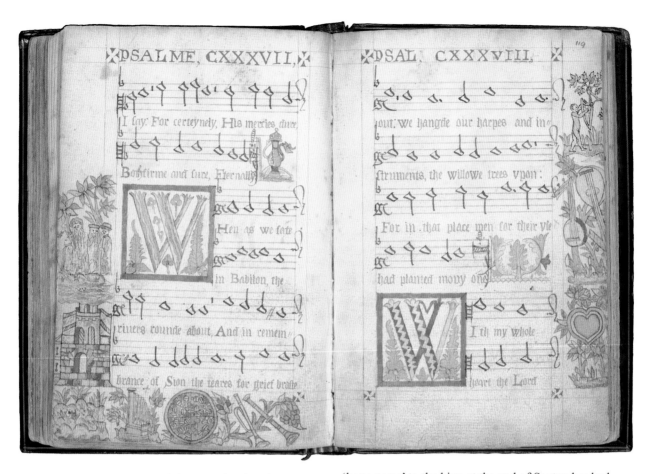

Fig 84 Psalm 137 'When as we sat in Babylon', a page from the Wode Partbooks. The partbooks were compiled by Thomas Wode, a former monk of Lindores Abbey. The abbey was well known for its horticultural skills and the Scottish kings used it as a source of plants for their gardens. University of Edinburgh Library Special Collections, Dk.5.14.118-19 © Edinburgh University Library

relative status. John Sharp's work at Stirling continued into 1507 when he received thirty-nine shillings and five pence for garden maintenance (*TA* 3, 407). The French gardener, presumably the one last mentioned in 1501, was paid ten French crowns, equal to £7, for his clothes for the three years past in March 1505 (*TA* 3, 130), with another twenty-eight shillings the following month (*TA* 3, 133). It is not known which of the gardens Sir John Sharp was to make at Stirling. George Campbell had been paid for putting the little garden (possibly the one within the castle) in order in 1504, and planting of the new garden below the castle had been going on since 1501. It may have been a third garden or a redesign of an existing garden. His later work on gardens took place at Holyrood.

As well as being paid their wages, gardeners might receive additional payments from the king, perhaps as tips for particular services; in 1506 fourteen shillings was given to the gardener who brought strawberries to James IV (*TA* 3, 199). The gardener and a woman who brought roses to the king each received five shillings (*TA* 3, 202). On 17 August 1507 the gardener at Stirling had nine shillings (*TA* 3, 334). A woman who brought

'bone peres' to the king at the end of September had ten shillings while the Stirling gardener only received three shillings for his pears in early October (*TA* 3, 346). After recording the payments to the minstrels at the christening of James IV's short-lived son, James, Duke of Rothesay, in February 1507 the Treasurers Accounts (*TA* 3, 370) contain the payment for a pound of onion seed, half a pound of cabbage seed and two ounces of pennet seed (possibly bennet or *herba benedicta*, which had medicinal uses). At the end of June of the same year, there was a payment to the gardener at Stirling, who presented strawberries to the king and received five shillings (*TA* 3, 398). This was a fairly regular event, and in the case of the pears presented to the king by the gardener of Stirling in October 1507 (*TA* 3, 346) and the cherries in July 1508 (*TA* 4, 136) may be an indication that the fruit trees purchased from 1501 onwards were bearing fruit.

Payments to people who brought fruit to the king were quite frequent, and may represent gifts of particularly early or out of season specimens or choice varieties. Payments or gratuities are recorded frequently in the Treasurers Accounts. Strawberries (*TA* 1, 288; *TA* 2, 111, 153, 380, 439, *TA* 3, 147) and cherries (*TA* 1, 179, 200; *TA* 2, 114, 153, 155, 380) seem to be the most frequently rewarded gifts, with apples, pears and plums (*TA* 1, 329; *TA* 2, 158, 361 376, 385, 386, 388) following. Some of these came from quite a distance as with the apples from Galloway and pears from Luss

Fig 85 The garden at Falkland Palace lay to the east of the palace (on the right side of the aerial photograph). There was direct access to the garden from the royal apartments by means of a stair. The real tennis court lay to the north of the palace at the top of the photograph. SC397113

(*TA* 1,180). Sometimes these were gifts from abbeys (*TA* 1, 288; *TA* 2, 376) and sometimes from nobles or bishops (*TA* 1, 301; *TA* 2, 154, 386, 388). In July 1491 two maidens who brought cherries to the king received eighteen shillings, but the payments were usually less (*TA* 1, 179).

The Treasurers Accounts and the Exchequer Rolls provide less information on the gardens of other Scottish palaces during the reign of James IV. The evidence for structures related to gardens at **Falkland Palace** after the death of James II in 1460, during the widowhood of Mary of Guelders, is considered by Scott Cooper (1999, 820) (Figs 85, 86). Falkland was, like Stirling and Linlithgow, part of the dower lands of the queens of Scotland (*RMS*, 2, 462). Following his return from captivity in England, it was seized by James I from the family of his uncle, the Albany Stewarts, and was granted by James II to his queen, Mary of Guelders. The castle lay to the north of the present palace and was sometimes referred to as Falkland Tower; the foundations are still visible (Dunbar 1999, 21). Mary survived her husband by only three years, but some works were carried out at her properties, including her gardens. In 1461 the gardener was paid for making a lawn (*viridarium*) near the chamber of the queen in

Falkland (*ER* 7, 75), which provides an early detail. In the same year a door was made in the chamber of the queen to allow her to go down to the lawn (*ER* 7, 78), presumably by a stair. Her other dower lands included Doune Castle, where there is a record of payment to the gardener in 1461, and Queenshaugh, in a meander of the River Forth near Stirling, where trees were planted in the same year (*ER* 7, 69). Seeds for onions and cabbages were bought for the garden at Falkland in 1448 (*ER* 5, 479) and in 1452 (*ER* 5, 502), and seeds for onions, vegetables and other herbs in 1465, 1466 and 1469 for planting in the garden of the king (*ER* 7, 33, 383, 664). The gardener's responsibilities often also included the maintenance of the meadows of Falkland and Auchtermuchty (*ER* 7, 454, 568).

Regular payments to the gardeners in money and grain, detailed in the *Exchequer Rolls* (*ER* 5–12 etc), for which there was a render of barrels of onions, continue from the later fifteenth century through the early years of the sixteenth century during the reign of James IV. In the *Exchequer Rolls* for 1487, the gardener William Thomson is recorded as dismissed for repeatedly failing to produce the onions. In 1496 the gardener is named John Gardiner (*ER* 10, 589) with the same name recurring in 1505 (*TA* 3, 156) and 1513. The king gave fourteen shillings to the gardener when he was at Falkland in August and October 1505, and again in January and October 1506 (*TA* 3, 156, 164, 179, 3 49), and pears were presented to the king in December 1506 and again on Christmas Eve (*TA* 3,

356, 359). Other payments of fourteen shillings were made in January 1506 (*TA* 3,179) and October 1506 (*TA* 3, 349). James Rook of Dundee sold 250 trees at a cost of three shillings and fourpence each, which were taken to Falkland via Lindores in late 1505. Another thirty-four trees were bought from Alexander Marshall and a hundred trees from Robert Beatson were purchased early in the next year (*TA* 3, 87). There is a mention of a new garden of Falkland in 1513 (*ER* 13, 504, 505) with a payment for the iron for making two gates for the garden there and the construction of a wall. This may have lain to the east of the palace with a walled garden adjacent to the 'new work', which probably contained the chambers of James and Margaret (*ER* 14, 174), allowing views into and access to and from the garden.

The connection between Lindores Abbey and the supply of fruit trees for the royal gardens has already been referred to, and in 1498 the abbot there was made keeper of **Linlithgow Palace** with the 'park, loch and garding of the samyn' with the power to appoint deputies (*RSS* 1, 88). Lindores was one of relatively few major abbeys which continued to be ruled by a monk, and did not have a layman as commendator (Cowan and Easson 1976, 70), at least until after 1560. It maintained its complement of monks and many of them went on to serve in the surrounding churches after the Reformation (Dilworth 1995, 81) including Thomas Wode who became Reader and Vicar of St Andrews, and was responsible for the manuscript of the psalter known as the Wode Partbooks which were extensively illustrated with plants and flowers (Ross 1993, 65) (Fig 87).

In 1461 Linlithgow Palace had been the subject of repairs in advance of the visit of the exiled king of England, Henry VI, with his wife and son (*ER* 7, 49) at the command of the widowed Mary of Gueldres. In 1496 it was employed as the residence of James IV's mistress, Margaret Drummond (*TA* 1, cxxxiv), and in July of that year the king gave two shillings to the gardener (*TA* 1 286) and nine shillings the following year (*TA* 1, 329). A payment to the gardener is recorded in 1488 (*TA* 1, 92) and gardeners were paid through the 1490s (*TA* 1, 92, 286, 329); ten shillings was spent on seeds for the garden there in 1491 (*TA* 1, 176). In 1498 and 1499 the gardener, as at Falkland, was called John Gardener (*ER* 11, 145, 146), but whether this was a generic surname, a member of the same family or the transfer of a gardener from one royal palace to another, is not known. The *Exchequer Rolls* also record regular payments in money and grain to gardeners at Linlithgow, but the form of the garden is unknown. In 1504 the palace gardens were looked after by John Morrison, as well as by a new gardener (*ER* 12, 573), and two dozen apple trees were purchased at a cost of forty-two shillings and seeds were to be sent to the gardener of Linlithgow (*TA* 2, 422). The following year (*ER* 12, 333), and again in 1512 (*ER* 13, 409), there were repairs to the garden and orchard. In February

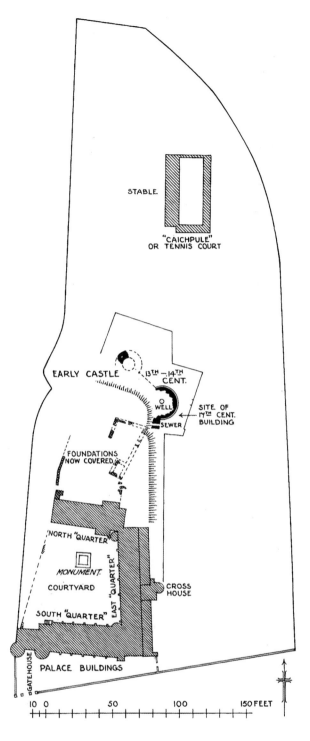

Fig 86 Plan of Falkland Palace from the Inventory of Monuments and Constructions in the Counties of Fife, Kinross and Clackmannan, *Fig 271 (RCAHMS 1933). SC397111*

1505 and 1506 a pound of onion and a pound of leek seeds were purchased, as well as a variety of other seeds (*TA* 3, 129, 367; 4,106). When the king was at Linlithgow in June 1505, the gardener received fourteen shillings and the same in June 1507 and August 1508, with twenty-eight shillings in January 1508 (*TA* 3, 140, 367; 4, 139, 98). Eight beehives were bought by the gardener in September of that year (*TA* 3, 159), and

Fig 87 The musician representing the tenor part and playing a shawm or sackbut has been identified with Thomas Wode, the compiler of the partbooks and a former monk of Lindores. University of Edinburgh Library Special Collections, La III.483.2.© Edinburgh University Library.

Fig 88 Aerial view of Linlithgow Palace and its former gardens. SC949581

Fig 89 A late seventeenth century view by Slezer of Dumbarton Castle, one of the strongholds of the kingdom of Scotland. James IV gave fourteen shillings to the gardener there when he visited in 1512. SC853661

in September 1511 the master cook paid the gardener of Linlithgow for fruit and honeycombs (*TA* 4, 310). The gardener brought strawberries and cherries to the king in July 1508, some of which were sent on to the queen in Edinburgh (*TA* 4, 132–3) about the time she gave birth to a stillborn daughter. In 1512 and 1513 the gardener at Linlithgow, Gilbert, had to supply onions and mustard (*ER* 13, 539, 540), and was given in each year fourteen shillings (*TA* 4, 350, 406). It is difficult to gain an impression of the gardens at Linlithgow. Unlike Stirling, there is no indication of major changes at any one period. It had an orchard and a vegetable garden, which included an area for strawberries. The garden or gardens may have lain to the west and north of the palace, from where it could be contemplated from the apartments of the king and queen (Dunbar 1999, 20–1). Viewed from the air following a period of drought, this ground seems to have the deepest soil, but the area around Linlithgow Palace, when seen from the air, shows evidence of multiple uses and many changes of use, from the castle demolished on the orders of Robert Bruce onwards to the present grassy park, so that interpretation of garden features of any period seems impossible without excavation (Fig 88).

Whether Margaret Tudor made any contribution to the design of the gardens of the royal palaces is not known. The garden of Richmond Palace, near London, which belonged to her father, Henry VII, is mentioned in 1501 on the occasion of the marriage of Margaret's brother Arthur, Prince of Wales, to Catherine of Aragon (Strong 1998, 23). Richmond was also the setting for Margaret's marriage by proxy to James, suggesting that this was the property selected for displaying the cultured nature of his court to important foreign visitors. Given Henry VII's reputation for careful attention to economy, expenditure on elaborate gardens seems unlikely, and Richmond may have been the most prominent example among the English royal palaces. Margaret's dowry was thirty thousand gold nobles, and with this additional income James was able to spend more on his court and his palaces.

A major poem dedicated to James IV was *The Palice of Honour* by Gavin Douglas, later translator of the *Aeneid*, and Bishop of Dunkeld. Written in the early years of the sixteenth century, it opens in May with the poet dreaming, *in a Gardyne of plesance with fragrant flouris blomand in their seis...And on the Laurers siluer droppis lyis* (Douglas 1827). The poem is a moral tale designed to draw a ruler to the right ways of ruling through the depiction of a royal progress and a description of a palace, peopled with legendary figures, Greek and Roman worthies and Old Testament heroes. It has the familiar form of the dream vision, as employed by James I in *The Kingis Quair*. This poem begins in the early morning with the poet rising to pay his due religious observance. The garden is described in terms of precious stones, ruby, topaz, pearl and emerald, and referred to as Nature's tapestry, a comparison of the natural with the unnatural that would be condemned by the Romantic poets, but which illustrates the way in which James' poetic contemporaries would view a garden. The flowers selected for particular mention are the daisy and the marigold. The poet awakes in a forest by a hideous

Fig 90 A view of Holyrood Palace with the hunting park beyond. SC1167611

flood and proceeds through a wilderness, in which Nature provided no comfort, towards the Palace of Honour. When the poet awoke again in the 'fair arbour' the poet thought it by comparison most like to hell, and took his solace from contemplation of the heavenly kingdom. By comparison with heaven the earthly garden, however rich, is a place of wickedness.

In his frequent and extensive travels around his kingdom James IV had the opportunity to see the gardens, both lay and secular, of his subjects. He visited Drummond Castle, the home of the family of his mistress, Margaret Drummond, where he gave five shillings to the gardener, as well as to the masons in 1496 (*TA* 1, 280). Lord Drummond was building a castle there at that time, which had probably been completed before 1509 when he received a new royal charter of lands in Strathearn including those of *Drummane, cum castro, fortalicio, manerio, pommeriis et ortis earundem* (Drummond, with the castle, fortalice, manor, orchards and gardens of the same) (*RMS* 2, 706–7 no 3306). In the anonymous poem *Tayis Bank*, which is believed to describe James' courtship of Margaret Drummond, the Tay at Stobhall is described thus:

About all blumet wes my bour,
With blosummes broun and blew,
Ofret with mony fair fresch flour
(Hazlitt 1895, 1, 171)

In June 1507 he visited **Craigbernard** (Craigbarnet) near Strathblane in Stirlingshire, the property of John Stirling, the comptroller of his household, where three shillings was given to the gardener (*TA* 3, 391); on 24 July in the same year he gave two shillings to the gardener of the provost of Dunbarton (*TA* 3, 405). In 1512 when the king was inspecting progress on the building of the 'New Werk' at the royal castle of Dumbarton on the Clyde, he gave fourteen shillings to the gardener there (Fig 89).

Until 1506 most evidence for interest in gardens and gardening had been focussed on Stirling, but attention moved to **Holyrood** following that date (Fig 90). The gardens there have been considered in detail by Fiona Jamieson (1994). The kings of Scotland had used the abbey at Holyrood as an occasional royal lodging throughout the medieval period, with the abbey employed for major ceremonies and the adjacent park for hunting, but the first reference to a permanent royal residence comes in 1473 with the glazing of a window in the queen's chamber (*TA* 1, 46). James held some notably elaborate jousts at Holyrood including the tournaments of the Wild Knight in 1507 and of the Wild Knight and the Black Lady in 1508. These were staged with an allegorical literary theme after the fashion of some well known continental contests, and James himself jousted as the Wild Knight (Fig 91). The 1508 event was at his invitation presided over by Bernard Stewart, Sire d'Aubigny, Captain of the King of France's Scottish guards, and veteran of the Spanish crusade and

Fig 91 The depiction of a joust is from a nineteenth century facsimile of a manuscript which records a series of tournaments held by Duke Wilhelm IV of Bavaria between 1510 and 1545. There are no illustrations of those held by James IV and in which he played a part, but they belonged to the same tradition of celebrating courtly and martial values and the magnificence of the monarch. © National Museums Scotland. Licensor Scran.

of the Italian wars, a knight with a European reputation for chivalry (Stevenson 2006, 94–7). One of the earliest references to a garden there, is that of 1 June 1506, when James IV gave five shillings to a Queen of May, as he walked to the garden of the abbot of Holyrood (*TA* 3, 197). Both the abbot and the prior had gardens within the abbey precincts, and James IV arranged to have his own garden created there. James was responsible for the renovation and construction of the royal palace which stood to the west of the abbey cloister, where all the principal rooms, including the royal lodging, were on the first floor (Dunbar 1999, 58). It is suggested that the immediate impulse for this decision was the king's wish to provide a suitable reception for Margaret Tudor, whom he married in August 1503 in the abbey church (Dunbar 1999, 56). In 1504 Sir John Sharp, *who makis the garding in Edinburgh*, was given cloth to the value of £4 10s as part of his fee (*TA* 2, 329). This garden probably lay to the west of the palace, and in 1505 he was paid to go to Stirling to make a garden there (*TA* 3, 132). Further works are recorded at Holyrood in 1507 with the draining of the loch beside the abbey 'for the gardyng to be maid' (*TA* 3, 299; *TA* 4, 44); these works came to a total of £33 6s 8d, and in August of the same year Sharp was paid thirty-nine shillings for putting the palace in order and making ready the garden, by which is probably meant the south garden (*TA* 3, 407). This was separated from the Abbey by a road running east and west leading to the monastic barns. In June the following year a lock and keys were made for the new garden, and there was a payment for the building of the new garden dykes (*TA* 4, 46). In 1511 a 'lione house' was constructed in the garden to accommodate this

Scottish royal and heraldic symbol (*TA* 4, 275). The lion had presumably been there for some four years since June 1506, when the man who brought a lion to the king received fourteen shillings, with another eight shillings and eight pence paid for the carrying of the lion in its cradle from Leith to Holyrood, followed by a payment to Andrew Broun 'that kepis the lioun in the Abbay' (*TA* 3, 200).

A reference to a payment in 1511 to a carter who brought necessaries to the queen's garden may relate to Holyrood (*TA* 4, 330). In the records of the earlier sixteenth century John Sharp emerges as the person charged with overseeing works in the palace as well as the garden (eg *TA* 4, 528; *TA* 5, 14; *TA* 6, 268), receiving twenty marks a year (£13 6s 8d) until his death in about 1538 (*ER* 17, 61). On 8 March 1529 he was granted an annual fee for his life, which was to be derived from the property of the Trinitarian Friary in Dunbar, an establishment which had supported only one friar maintaining divine service. This appears to be his only contact with the friary and there is no evidence to indicate that he was anything other than a secular cleric. However, a year later this grant was revoked and the income from the friary was transferred to the Trinitarian friars of Peebles. The employment of Sharp in the drainage of the area intended for the king's garden might suggest that he had some practical engineering and surveying skills, that he was concerned with the laying out of gardens, rather than the cultivation of plants and trees, and that this was taken forward into his oversight of building works. The abortive attempt to change the source of John Sharp's salary in 1528 may be one of the indications of James V's concern to rebuild and renovate the royal palaces.

James IV also encouraged the creation of gardens through the granting of feu charters to Crown lands. Although an extant example of a garden has yet to be identified, those who received grants from the king were encouraged to establish gardens as a suitable appurtenance of such landholding. A series of documents in the *Register of the Great Seal* belonging to his reign contain the provision that the grantee 'should build and maintain a sufficient house of stone and lime, with hall, chamber, barn, byre, stable, dovecot, orchards, gardens, beehives, with hedges and the planting of oaks' (*Necnon edificando et sustinendo sufficientem mansionem de lapide et calce, cum aula, camera, orreo, bostari, stabello, columbario, pommeriis, ortis, apium custodibus dictis le be-hivis, cum cepibus et plantatione quercuum &c.*) (*RMS*, 2, 730 No 3407 etc). This may have been the desired outcome of the grant, rather than what was actually achieved, but it does reveal to what the recipient of such a grant should aspire.

The Gardens of James V

Following the deaths of James IV, many of the nobility, and indeed his gardener, George Campbell, at Flodden in 1513, the records of gardening activity in the royal gardens virtually cease, until James V emerged from his minority and became effective ruler in 1528. James V continued the peripatetic life of his predecessors, usually staying no more than three or four days in one place and rarely more than three to four weeks. His usual movements encompassed Edinburgh, Linlithgow, Falkland and St Andrews, with visits to the Borders, Argyll and Angus and occasional excursions to the north-east of Scotland. He paid one visit to Orkney and the Hebrides (Thomas 2005, 50). Hunting took place in more remote parts of the country, as well as in the royal parks. Stirling, Linlithgow and nominally Falkland, which passed to Mary of Guise, were part of Margaret Tudor's dower properties, but were used by her son James V. The Palace of Holyrood was occupied while parliament was held in Edinburgh, as well as during major political and ceremonial events. Stirling was, perhaps, the most favoured residence, but the frequency of James' residence at any one royal property varied over time. The priory of St Andrews, which had been granted *in commendam* to the king's illegitimate son, was used by the king (Figs 93, 94). He married Mary of Guise there and the wedding was celebrated with dancing, feasts, music, plays, tournaments and hunting; she was met at the abbey gate with an entertainment by David Lindsay, which featured a cloud descending from heaven, from which an angel appeared presenting her with the keys of Scotland, followed by moral instructions (Thomas 2005, 192). James V's son and heir, James, who predeceased him, was born there. It is possible, if James V had reigned for longer, that a royal palace might have been developed there, as at Holyrood, another Augustinian house.

Gardeners continued to be paid, and sometimes named; after George Campbell's death Gillespy became the gardener of the great garden below the wall of Stirling Castle (*ER* 14, 37), but there is no further

Fig 92 James V. © National Galleries of Scotland. Licensor Scran

information on their achievements. The Duke of Albany, regent in the early part of James V's minority, but only intermittently present in Scotland, had strong French and Italian connections and brought in three thousand French troops (Cooper 2008, 54). In 1525 Walter Cunningham was given the office of forester and keeper of the King's Park of Stirling, and gardener of his garden there by the Earl of Angus. Angus, the head of the powerful Douglas family, was married to Margaret Tudor, James IV's widow, and with the thirteen year old James V in his custody was the dominant force in the government at that time (NRS GD 124/10/9). The *Accounts of the Masters of Work for Building and repairing Royal Palaces and Castles* begin in 1529 and supplement the *Accounts of the Lord High Treasurer of Scotland*, although there are also considerable gaps in these volumes.

James V's ambition to marry a daughter of the king of France, and the desire to present himself and his kingdom as a worthy suitor, has been given as a reason for the extensive building and renovation of the palaces of Stirling, Holyroodhouse, Linlithgow and Falkland. At Stirling, Holyroodhouse and Falkland there is also some evidence for the redesign and extension of the gardens. Like his father, James V was the recipient of poetic advice from his courtiers, in particular David Lindsay in *The Testament of the Papyngo*, which includes references to the palaces of Stirling (Snawdon), Linlithgow and Falkland. The poet falls asleep in his garth *Amang the flowreis fresche, fragrant and formose*. The papyngo or parrot bids farewell, characterising each place:

Adew fair Snawdoun, with thy touris hie,
Thy Chapell Royall, park and tabyll rounde!
May, June, and July walde I dwell in thee,
War I one man, to heir the birdis sounde,
Quhilk doith agane thy royall roche redounde.
Adew, Lythquo! quhose Palyce of plesance
Mycht be one patrone in Portingall or France
Fair weill, Falkland! the forterace of Fyfe
Thy polyte park under the Lowmound Law!
Sum tyme in thee I led ane lustye lyfe,
The fallow deir to see thame raik on raw
Court men to cum to thee, they stand gret awe,
Sayand, thy burgh bene, of all burrowis, bail
Because, in thee, thay never gat gude aill
(Lindsay 1879, 1, 84)

The earliest record which gives some idea of the
design of a garden refers to **Stirling Castle** (*MW* 1,
109–10), and suggests the creation of what might
be described as a medieval garden of classic form as
depicted in manuscript illuminations, such as Books
of Hours produced in Flemish workshops. Simon
Bening, one of the most eminent artists of the earlier
sixteenth century, whose workshop was responsible
for the *Hours* commissioned by James IV for Margaret
Tudor, was the brother in law of the merchant Andrew
Halyburton (Ditchburn 2001, 118–19, 124) (Fig 96).
The master gardener at Stirling was James Clement,
who was followed by Sir Walter Clement (*TA* 6, 102,
205). Maintenance of both gardens continued, and in
1531 a passage down from the castle to the park was
constructed (*TA* 5, 436). Between April and early June
1532 the garden inside the castle was redesigned. Turfs
were cut to make benches – an indication of scale is
given by the fact that four horses were required to bring
them into the castle – and the benches were constructed
by the gardeners. A shod spade, a wooden spade with
an iron blade fitted to it, was purchased for the gardener
at a cost of twelve pence. Flowers were planted and
flower seed sown. Seeds particularly mentioned, at a
cost of two shillings, were lettuce and thyme. Workmen
brought in new soil, and two gardeners, assisted by four
workmen, created 'knots', raised, usually square, beds,
often planted in geometric shapes (*MW* 1, 109–110).

The first written reference to a garden knot in
English occurs in 1496, according to the *Oxford
English Dictionary*, when a house is described as made
'lyke unto a knot in a garden called a mase'. A second,
dating from a few years later in 1502, cites details of an
account 'For diligence in making knottes in the Duke's
garden, Clypping of knottes and sweeping the said
garden.' The *Dictionary of the Scottish Language* gives
the *Palice of Honour*, written in the early years of the
sixteenth century, as containing the first Scottish usage
of the term. In the poem, the palace and towers are
described, in elaborate aureate language, as decorated
with gold and enamelled with pictures of birds, sweet

*Fig 93 The Pends, the entrance to the monastic precinct at St Andrews, where
Mary of Guise, James V's second wife, was welcomed by an angel seated on a
cloud and descending from heaven. SC1203874*

flowers, curious knots and high devises which 'to
behald war perfite Paradise' (Douglas 1827, 62). The
design of the knots at Stirling is not known, but they
may have been heraldic in form, as was the case at
Richmond Palace when it was fitted up for the arrival
of Catherine of Aragon in 1501 (Harvey 1990, 135),
perhaps bringing together the arms of Scotland and
France, or they might have taken a variety of geometric
forms. An early illustration of a knot appeared
in a volume published in Venice in 1499 called
Hypnerotomachia Poliphili attributed to a monk called
Francesco Colonna and written in Italian (Fig 97). This
work became very popular during the sixteenth century,
and was translated into French in 1546 and into English
in 1592 under the title *The Strife of Love in a Dream*.

*Fig 94 The Pends at St Andrews on the map by John Geddy dating from about
1580. S. Andre sive Andreapolis Scotiae Universitas Metropolitana MS.20996.
© NLS*

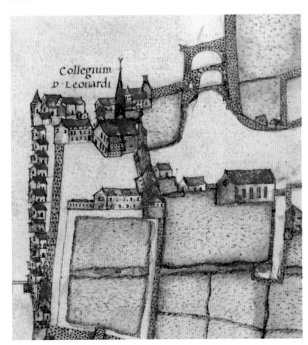

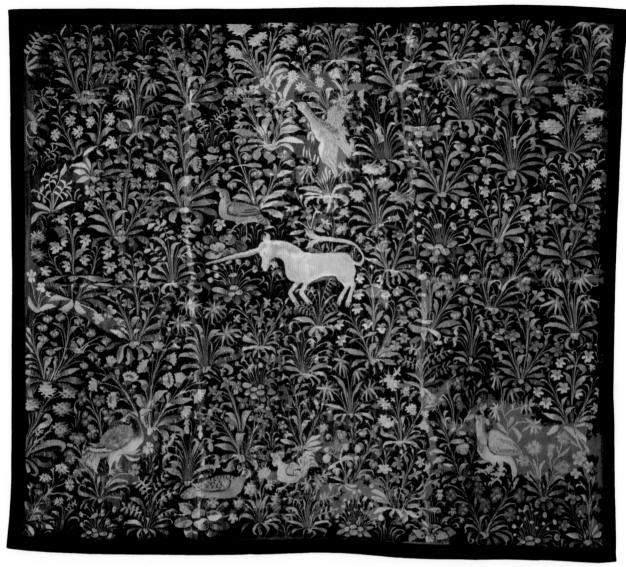

Fig 95 A fragment of a tapestry hanging of the type known as millefleurs, *a thousand flowers, a style popular in the late fifteenth and early sixteenth centuries. The tapestries were made in workshops in Flanders and Northern France and the kings of Scotland owned tapestries of this kind indicating an appreciation of flowers and plants.* © Victoria and Albert Museum, London

Like the *Roman de la Rose* and *The Kingis Quair*, the poem takes the form of a dream-vision, and tells of the search of Poliphilus for the beautiful nymph, Polia, through a classical landscape with ruins, to the circular garden of Cythera, which had an elaborate concentric plan. The book included designs for knots and proposals for their planting, and while there is no indication of the purchase of such a book, Scots in Italy moved in circles which would be familiar with the content of the work (Colonna 1499). Knot gardens relied on hedges laid out in geometric patterns. Box was not a popular choice at this time (Jennings 2005, 42–3), and the hedges may have been of lavender, hyssop, marjoram and thyme, plants which are referred to in the royal accounts (*MW*, 1, 110). The ground could be left bare or grassed, but coloured gravel, chalk, brick dust or crushed coal are known to have been used in the seventeenth century.

Simple plants like marigolds or violets might be planted within the enclosures (Jennings 2005, 42).

The location of this knot garden within the castle is uncertain, but the accounts for the garden are immediately followed by a payment for repairing and cleaning the turnpike stair that went up to the king's chamber (*MW* 1, 110), which might suggest that James was occupying the King's House or King's Old Building erected by his father, adjacent to the garden by the Chapel Royal. Direct access to a royal garden by means of a spiral staircase is recorded for various royal and princely gardens in France (Whiteley 1999, 95–6). Peacocks are again kept in Stirling in 1533 and 1534 (*TA* 6, 97, 206, 208), along with two cranes and two herons. The walls of the garden within the park were built or rebuilt in 1533 at a cost of £13 (*TA* 6, 154). Two gardeners of the great garden were paid in 1538 and 1540 (*ER* 17, 163, 277) for the guarding of the park at Stirling, and the cleaning of the park and meadow of Stirling.

The building of the new palace ('new work') at Stirling by James V, possibly under the supervision of

James Hamilton of Finnart, in the late 1530s, produced royal lodgings. The king's and queen's apartments were arranged around an internal court known as the Lion's Den, where the king's lion may at times have been kept (Fig 98). When a lion was presented to the king in 1539, the palace was then in the course of construction (Dunbar 1999, 209). As at Falkland, French influence is discernible, including that from buildings with which James V's second queen, Mary of Guise, was associated (Fig 99). These included Chateaudun, the residence of her first husband, the Duke of Longueville, and the palace of her uncle, the Duke of Lorraine, at Nancy (Dunbar 1999, 55). Neither of the two suites of rooms provides views of the gardens within the castle or those below the rock; it is possible that they may have been visible from the relatively public gallery that connected the two halls of the king and queen on the west. Excavations in the area known as the Ladies Hole have shown that there may have been a garden there accompanied by a terrace from which the garden below the castle could have been viewed (Ewart and Gallagher 2008, 15). A cachepole or tennis court, like the contemporary and surviving example at Falkland, was erected in 1539 in the town (*TA* 7, 168).

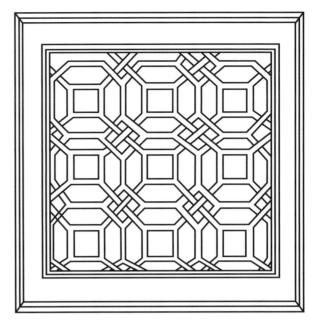

Fig 97 Design suitable for a knot garden based on an illustration in Hypnerotomachia Poliphili *published in Venice in 1499. GV004982*

Fig 96 The Virgin and Child seated next to a garden enclosed by a decorative timber fence. The image in watercolour on vellum was painted in Flanders about 1550 by Simon Bening, the artist responsible for the Book of Hours commissioned by James IV as a gift for Margaret Tudor. © Victoria and Albert Museum, London

James carried out considerable rebuilding at **Linlithgow Palace**, again under the supervision of James Hamilton of Finnart, completing the reconstruction of the palace initiated by his father. Payments continued to the gardener, but there is no evidence for a redesign of the garden there. One of his notable works, the elaborate fountain, was placed in the courtyard of the palace, a relatively public area, and not in the gardens.

At **Falkland Palace** the render from the gardener of barrels of onions continued. The gardener was named in 1516 as John (*ER* 14, 174), in 1525 as Dominus Thomas Kilgour chaplain, another of the men in holy orders who looked after the king's gardens, in this case a monk or friar (*ER* 15, 114), and in 1527 as John Strachan (*ER* 15, 350) who owed twenty-four barrels of onions when he was discharged (*ER* 16, 472). In 1535 the gardener was Thomas Melville (*ER* 16, 428, *TA* 6, 289, 417), who was paid £7 for procuring young trees for the king's garden at Falkland 'at his gracis command' (*TA* 7, 140).

The extensive rebuilding of the palace at Falkland by James V impinged on the garden design as well. The eastern range, which contained the royal lodgings, had an outward projection to the east known as the cross house, and was recent enough in 1516 to be referred to as 'new work'. This quarter of the palace was virtually rebuilt in 1537. The royal apartments had galleries on their east face, overlooking the gardens, and the cross house with its turnpike stair provided direct access to a terrace on the east and to the garden (RCAHMS 1933, 140) (Fig 102). James V visited France between September 1536 and May 1537 in pursuit of his marriage to Madeleine, the daughter of the king of France. On this journey, which included visits to many

Fig 98 Aerial view of the James V's new palace adjacent to the Great Hall and the King's Old Building, constructed under James IV, within Stirling Castle. The interior courtyard of the palace was known as the Lion's Den. DP043235

royal properties in Paris and across central France, he was accompanied by a French mason called Moyse (or Mogin) Martin (Dunbar 1991, 5). The east and south façades of Falkland Palace are decorated in an extremely sophisticated style, divided into bays with roundels containing portrait busts, and at least three master masons of French origin worked on the building (Figs 103, 104). Parallels with many French buildings of the earlier sixteenth century have been detected, in particular François I's chateaux of Fontainebleau and Villers Cotterets. Falkland is generally recognised as among the earliest examples of coherent Renaissance design in Britain (Dunbar 1999, 36). The buttresses of the east range bear the date 1537, which may suggest that it was being rebuilt for the reception of the new queen (Figs 100, 101). This east range, with formal rooms on the courtyard side and smaller rooms and galleries overlooking the gardens on the other, bears a close resemblance to that built by François I at the chateau of Blois, which was visited by James on two occasions in 1537 (Dunbar 1991, 6–7; 1999, 153). The

mother of Madeleine's successor as James' queen, Mary of Guise, sent a group of French masons and other artisans to Scotland in 1538, and the south range was rebuilt in 1539. Details of the garden are not known, and it probably remained in the same position, to the east of the royal lodgings, as in the time of James IV. To the north of the palace beyond the site of the old castle, a tennis court or 'caichpule' was begun in 1538. Later in the sixteenth century another building was attached on the west side, which may originally have been intended for other games, such as bowls or billiards (Dunbar 1999, 208). Other works at Falkland included the repairing of the garden dykes and gates in 1538 (*MW* 1, 219) and the plumbing for a fountain (*MW* 1, 261), which may have been in the court, as at Linlithgow, rather than in the garden, although the engraving of the palace and its surroundings in the late seventeenth century by Slezer (1693, pl 12) in *Theatrum Scotiae* shows no fountain there.

In addition to the major works at Stirling, Linlithgow and Falkland, James V was responsible for the surviving north-west tower at **Holyrood**. In June and July 1535, as part of the remaking and renovation of the palace, the walls of gardens by the main entrance work were built and repaired (*MW* 1, 132). In 1535 there are three references to the 'litill gardyng chalmer ... abone the peind' for its roofing by the slater, for iron work for the windows and for glass for the windows (*MW* 1, 187,188, 189); its whereabouts is not known. It may refer to a 'guarding chamber', but it might be one from which a garden or part of a garden could be viewed from above. It was constructed before Mary of Guise purchased the north garden from James Abercrombie, canon of Holyrood, in 1558 (*TA* 10, 394), and so it is unlikely, but not impossible, that the 'gardyng room' above the pend or vaulted gateway did relate to a garden on the north side of James V's tower, although it does not appear on the 'English Spy's map' of 1544 (BL Cotton Augustus I.ii.56). A structure above a pend would allow private access to a garden, as was the case with the one known to exist in the seventeenth century which led to the north garden above the way to the abbey church, or could provide access to the garden, avoiding those parts of Holyrood which were still in monastic use. The existence of a pend elsewhere in the royal/monastic complex of Holyrood is not known. The room in James V's tower from which the north garden would be most clearly visible was the closet on the north-west of the floor which was occupied by the queen. The element of the garden was that shown on Gordon of Rothiemay's map of 1647 as a compartment laid out in scrolling knots in the form of a *fleur de lys* (Fig 236). It is possible that this replaced a garden with a heraldic design recalling the French marriages of James V and Mary Queen of Scots, which are commemorated on the ceiling of the queen's apartments.

The gardens were mentioned by Alexander Alane, better known as the religious reformer Alesius, who was born in Edinburgh and studied at St Andrews. He fled to Germany in 1532 and it may be presumed that his first hand knowledge of Edinburgh dates from before this time. In Sebastian Munster's *Cosmography* published in Basle in 1550 Alesius provided a description of Edinburgh which included in the account of Holyrood a reference to its most pleasant gardens which were closed by a lake at the foot of Arthur's Seat (*amoenissimos hortos, quos cludit lacus ad fundum montis Cathedrae Arthuri*) (Scott and Laing 1827, 187).

In August 1535 the walls of the outer garden were repaired and the ponds were renovated. Two great double gates and a back door to the garden were fashioned by Tom Scoughall during a period of two weeks. These were hung on iron hinges and secured by three locks and a padlock (*MW* 1, 191–2). A French gardener, assisted by three workmen, was employed at Holyrood between September 1536 and February 1537 (*TA* 6, 302), possibly the one named as Bertrand Gallotre, formerly gardener to the king, in 1538 (*ER*, 17, 61), when he received £22 10s. The tools purchased for this garden work by the French gardener were

Fig 99 Detail of female figure decorating the north façade of James V's palace in Stirling Castle. It has been identified as Venus Armata, the Armed Venus, and like other figures on the palace exterior which are known to derive from engravings by the early sixteenth century Augsburg artist Hans Burkmair, it was probably based on a woodcut. © DB Gallagher

axes, spades or trowels, crowbars, hoes, mattocks, forks, dibbles and cutting knives, along with 'divers other instrumentis' (*MW* 1, 191). In 1537 two pairs of shooting butts were erected in the outer garden as part of the preparation of the palace for the entry of James V's first queen, Madeleine of France, who died at Holyrood in July of that year. Benches made of turf were constructed beside them. The little garden was laid with turf, and benches were also constructed there (*MW* 1, 222–5). The turf, or some of it, was carried from Liberton about 5km away (*MW* 1, 222), and the ponds around the garden were cleaned (*MW* 1, 223). The construction of stone benches is also mentioned (*MW* 1, 191). The gardener 'of the abbay' was given twenty shillings to buy pikes for the fish ponds in

Fig 100 *The courtyard of Falkland Palace in an engraving by John Slezer from the 1693 edition of* Theatrum Scotiae, *showing the sculpture and statuary surviving in a better state of preservation than at present. DP101768*

Fig 101 *The courtyard of Falkland Palace with its French-influenced sculptural decoration was probably rebuilt around 1537 for the reception of James V's successive queens. SC397095*

1539 (*TA* 7, 160). Repairs to a collapsed garden wall were made in 1541 when lists for jousting were being prepared as part of the celebrations at Holyrood at the time of the coronation of Mary of Guise, James' second wife, whom he had married in 1538 (*MW* 1, 288). In 1541 it is recorded that various large ash trees were removed from the abbot's garden and taken to Edinburgh Castle in connection with the preparation of the king's ordnance, probably for gun carriages (*TA* 8, 96).

The Minority of Mary Queen of Scots

In July 1542 John Ouchter was the gardener of Holyrood, receiving money for a gown of French black accompanied by a doublet, hose and a bonnet (*TA* 8, 96), and, when named gardener and keeper of the yards of Holyroodhouse for life in 1543, was paid fifty marks and twenty-six bolls of meal annually (*RSS* 3, 39 No 277). His successor John Morrison was granted the post of 'gardiner and keper of oure soverene ladeis yairdis on the south side of hir palice of Halirudhous for life' in February 1547 (*RSS* 5, 285). He was to retain two servants, who would roll and dress the gardens when necessary, and provide kale and herbs for the kitchen. It was probably in John Ouchter's time, or possibly that of his successor, that the first picture of the garden of Holyrood, and indeed any garden known to be in Scotland survives. Following the death of James V in December 1542 and the succession of Mary Queen of Scots at the age of a week, the Earl of Arran, the head of the Hamilton family and heir presumptive to the Scottish throne, became regent of Scotland. Mary's great uncle, Henry VIII, wished her to marry his son, the future Edward

Fig 102 The rebuilt cross house at Falkland which provided access to the east garden. SC397100

VI, and when the Treaty of Greenwich which set out this agreement was repudiated by the Scots, English invasions followed. These brought in French forces to oppose them, with twelve thousand troops, mostly French, but also Italian and German (Cooper 2008, 54). The diplomatic contacts which preceded this saw the gardens at Holyrood used for the meeting of the Earl of Arran with the English ambassador, Sir Ralph Sadler, who wrote to Henry VIII in March 1543: 'Upon my arrival I repaired forthwith to the governour whom I found in a garden at the palace of Holyrood-house and delivered unto him your majesty's letters ... There

Fig 103 A roundel with a male bust, perhaps a poet, from the interior façade of Falkland Palace. SC397181

Fig 104 A roundel with a female bust from the interior façade of Falkland Palace. SC397184

Fig 105 *James V built royal lodgings adjacent to Holyrood Abbey, which now form the north-west tower of the present palace. © Crown Copyright: Royal Collection*

was a great company of noblemen and gentlemen about him, which pressed so near him, as it seemed to me, that either he would fain have had me in some other place, where he might have secretly communed with me, or else intended to take counsel before he entred farther with me' (Sadler 1809, 65–6). His embassy did not progress well, with Arran inclining to the faction that favoured a marriage between Mary Queen of Scots and the Dauphin. In July of the same year, he wrote from Edinburgh 'as I walked here in a garden, and some of my folks with me, on the backside of my lodging, one (but I cannot tell who) shot a half-hag amongst us, and missed not one of my men, I dare say, four inches' (Sadler 1809, 237), incidental evidence for the recreational nature of the gardens in the town. The drawing of Edinburgh known as the 'English Spy's map' (BL Cotton Augustus I.ii.56), a bird's eye view of the town, shows Holyroodhouse, 'The King of Scots palace', from the north (Fig 107). At least nine enclosed areas are visible on the drawing and the buildings conceal the area to the south, where the royal garden was probably situated. The only features shown within the gardens and courtyards are trees, with no representations of butts, benches or indeed knot gardens. Depiction of gardens was not, of course, the point of the map, which seems to have been to

explain the campaign in Scotland, designed to secure the marriage of Mary and Edward, often referred to as 'The Rough Wooing'. Although this bird's eye view is taken from a different point, there is a considerable resemblance between the layout on the north side of Holyrood shown on the Gordon of Rothiemay plan of Edinburgh, produced about a century later, with its series of enclosed gardens. Even the pattern of tree planting along the northern edge seems to be reflected in the later drawing. Another English document, preserved in the Bodleian Library and dating from 1547, shows Holyroodhouse, mostly hidden by Calton Hill, but surrounded by trees (RCAHMS 1951, Plate 15).

The earlier royal gardens had been sited at some distance from the residential tower built by James V. In 1558 Mary of Guise extended the royal gardens at Holyrood by purchasing the north garden, paying Canon James Abercromby for 'his yeard lyand to the north-west side of the palice of Halierudehous' (*TA* 10, 394). She was already using it by 4 July in that year when a legal transaction took place 'in the garden of the Queen Regent on the west side of the palace of Holyrood' (Angus 1914, 34, no 161) (Fig 109).

Fig 106 *Mary Queen of Scots. SC1212805*

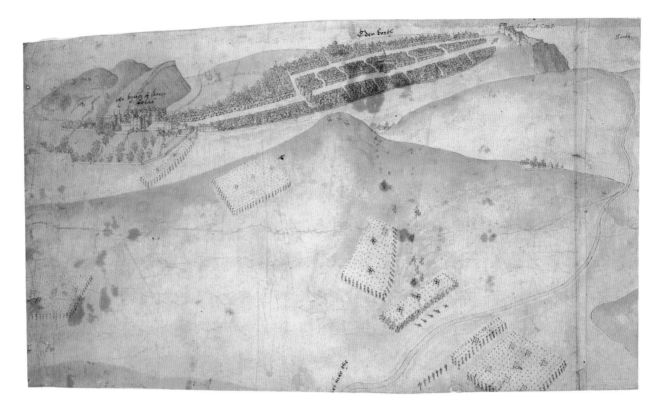

Fig 107 A coloured Plan or Bird's Eye View of the Town of Edinburgh possibly by Sir Richard Lee, also known as 'the English Spy's map'. It depicts the area between the Palace of Holyrood, which is annotated 'the kyng of skotes palas' and Edinburgh Castle. The plan was made by the English who attacked Edinburgh in 1544. English troops can be seen marching in formation with the English flag. The campaign was led by Edward Seymour, Earl of Hertford and first Duke of Somerset who was favoured by Henry VIII after his sister Jane married Henry in 1536. Cotton Augustus I.ii.56 © British Library

The Gardens of the Magnates

Most of the evidence for medieval gardens in Scotland comes from royal and monastic records, primarily because of the need to account for payments, and their subsequent preservation in national records. Although information about gardens of magnates and the gentry is less likely to be preserved, some information may survive in family collections; the detailed publication of such archives, which would be required to bring them to public notice, has rarely been carried out. Little has yet emerged from archaeological survey or been recognised. The re-interpretation of medieval designed landscapes around major castles and palaces as at Kenilworth and Bodiam in Sussex (Thomson 1964, 222–3; Everson 1991, 9; Everson 1996, 79–84; Taylor et al 1990, 155–7; Richardson 2010, 14–54) raises the question of the identification of such features in Scotland. One possible example is at **Caerlaverock Castle**, built about 1290, where the triangular building lies within a triangular moat in an area of earthworks and water currently obscured by trees (Figs 110, 111). An earlier moated castle lies to the south and both sites lie in a landscape of complex earthworks and water channels. In 1300 the

later castle was besieged by Edward I and described in a contemporary poem *Le Siege de Karlaverock* as occupying a beautiful situation 'for on one side, towards the west, could be seen the Irish Sea [the Solway], and to the north a fair country surrounded by an arm of the sea, so that on two sides no living creature could approach it without putting himself in danger of the sea. Nor is it easy to the south, for the many ways are made difficult by wood by marsh, and

Fig 108 Detail from the Bird's Eye View of the Town of Edinburgh showing an enclosed garden with a dovecot. It is sited on the slope of Calton Hill but may be a misplaced picture of Trinity Hospital founded by Mary of Gueldres in 1462 for the soul of her husband James II, which lay just beyond the town on the north side. Cotton Augustus I.ii.56 © British Library

Fig 109 Mary of Guise. © Scottish National Portrait Gallery. Licensor Scran

Fig 110 Aerial view of Caerlaverock Castle, a beautiful building in a beautiful setting. Its triangular form may have an emblematic significance. DP1156760

by trenches filled by the sea'. Its position saw the castle frequently involved in the Anglo-Scottish wars and it underwent considerable rebuilding in the fifteenth century (RCAHMS 1920, 23). Excavations on both sites, while primarily concerned with their occupation and defences, established the high status of their founders, the Maxwell family, and the importance of water management, although its decorative as opposed to its utilitarian nature was not discussed (MacIvor and Gallagher 1999; Brann 2004).

The example from the Kilravock family papers about the employment of a gardener and his assistant from Paisley at Kilravock near Inverness has been referred to in the previous chapter (Wilson 1839, xvi). It illustrates not only something of the geographical spread of gardens, but also of the movement of people and ideas within Scotland. Gardens were used as settings for poetry with a less elevated theme than the mirrors for princes or the pursuit of human and divine love, and the theme of Eve's betrayal of Adam is implicit in the use of the garden (Fig 112). Dunbar sets his *The Tretis of the Twa Mariit Wemen and the Wedo*, an account of women's experience of love and marriage, in a garden enclosed by hawthorns and hollies, prickly plants which might have been expected to repel the eavesdropper.

Apon the Midsummer Ewin, mirriest of nichtis,
I muvit furth allane in meid as midnicht wes past,
Besyd ane gudlie grein garth, full of gay flouris,
Hegeit of ane huge hicht with hawthorne treis;
Quhairon ane bird on ane bransche so birst out
hir notis
That neuer ane blythfullar bird was on the
beuche hard.
Quhat throw the sugarat sound of hir sang glaid,
And throw the savour sanative of the sueit flouris,
I drew in derne to the dyk to dirkin efter mirthis;
The dew donkit the daill and dynnit the feulis.
I hard, under ane holyn hewinlie grein hewit,
Ane hie speiche at my hand with hautand wourdis.
With that in haist to the hege so hard I inthrang
That I was heildit with hawthorne and with
heynd leveis.
Throw pykis of the plet thorne I presandlie luikit,
Gif ony persoun wald approche within that
pleasand garding.
I saw thre gay ladeis sit in ane grein arbeir,
All grathit in to garlandis of fresche gudlie flouris...
All full of flurist fairheid as flouris in Iune –
Quhyt, seimlie, and soft as the sweit lillies,
Now vpspred upon spray, as new spynist rose;
Arrayit ryallie about with mony riche wardour,
That Nature full nobillie annamalit with flouris,
Of alkin hewis under hewin that ony heynd knew,
Fragrant, all full of fresche odour, fynest of smell.
Ane cumlie tabil coverit wes befoir tha cleir ladeis,
With ryalle cowpis apon rawis, full of ryche wynis.
And of thir fair wlonkes (beauties) tua weddit war
with lordis,
Ane was ane widow, iwis, wantoun of laities.
And as thai talk at the tabill of mony tail sindry,
Thay wauchtit at the wicht wyne and waris
out wourdis,
And syn thai spak more spedelie and sparit no
matiris. (Dunbar 1998, 41–2)

What might be considered as a garden design or feature rather than a garden is the planting of thorn trees in the shape of James IV's ship the *Great Michael*, 'ane great scheip callit the greit Michell quhilk was the greattest scheip and maist of strength that ewer saillit in Ingland or France.' This was recorded by the chronicler Robert Lindsay of Pitscottie in his account of James IV's reign, written in the latter part of the sixteenth century. He describes the *Michael* as 12 score feet long and 35 feet broad within her walls, which were each 10 feet thick, and lest anyone should doubt his accuracy he writes, 'If ony man beleiffis that the descriptioun of the scheip be not of weritie as we haue writtin ... let him pase to the yeit of Tillebairne [**Tullibardine** in Perthshire] and their affoir the samin he will sie the length and breid of hir planttit witht hathorne againe be the wryghtis that helpit to mak hir' (Lindsay 1899–1911, 251–2). The

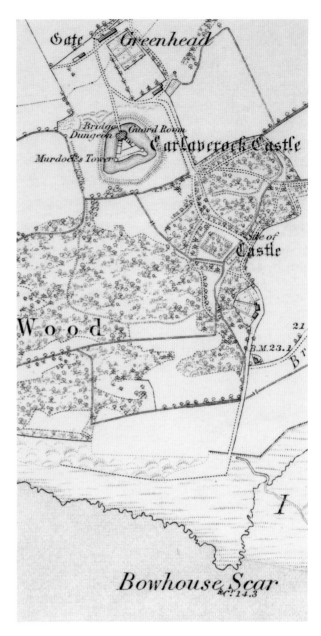

Fig 111 The earthworks around Caerlaverock Castle on the First Edition of the Ordnance Survey 6-inch map of Dumfriesshire surveyed in 1856. The earthworks, which do not appear to be defensive, may indicate the presence of a landscape around the castle designed for recreation.

availability of hawthorn for such a planting is known from James IV's gardens at Stirling. Tullibardine is shown by Timothy Pont enclosed by an extensive planting of trees rendered as bare branches on one map (NLS Pont 21(2)), and curving outlines, which might indicate trees or bushes in leaf on another (Figs 113, 114). One group of these in front of the entrance to the castle has a slightly crescentic form and might indicate the type of planting described by Pitscottie some twenty years before the likely date of the map. The remains of this feature were still visible when the writer of the *New Statistical Account* for the parish of Blackford recorded the site in 1837, saying that only three thorn trees had survived the encroachments of the plough (*NSA* 10, 299), and its site can be seen on aerial photographs about a hundred metres north of the site of the now demolished Tullibardine Castle. In the late 1850s the shape of the ship survived as 'an ornamental pond in which aquatic plants and birds luxuriated' (Macdougall 1991, 39). The *Michael* had been launched at Newhaven in 1511 with music and trumpet playing (*TA* 4, 252), and fitted out the following year. After the defeat at Flodden the ship was quickly sold to Louis XII of France by the governor during James V's minority. The construction of such a landscape feature presumably in the years shortly after its construction must have had a particular meaning for the owner of Tullibardine Castle, Sir William Murray, as well as to the shipwrights. It may represent a desire to memorialise in the landscape, particularly after the defeat at Flodden, a magnificent symbol of the reign of James IV which had become, very rapidly, a bygone age of national achievement.

During his minority James V spent part of his time at Dalkeith, then in the possession of the Douglas family, and there is a payment to the gardener of Dalkeith who brought pears to the king in 1525, as well as to a boy who brought him pears while he was staying there (*TA* 5, 258). Craigmillar Castle near Edinburgh, another place where James V was lodged as a child, is referred to as a castle and manor with dovecote, gardens, orchards and fish ponds (*ER* 14, 629). Royal accounts can show something of the gardens of great lords, when their lands were confiscated by the Crown following treason charges. In the later part of James V's minority, his mother, Margaret Tudor's second, recently

Fig 113 The depiction of Tullibardine Castle and the plantation of hawthorns representing James IV's ship, the Great Michael, *on the late sixteenth century manuscript map by Timothy Pont (Pont 22). © NLS*

Fig 112 Heads of women drawn on the last page of the manuscript of The Romaunt of the Rose *by an early reader. MS Hunter 409. 0151v © University of Glasgow Library, Department of Special Collections.*

divorced, husband Archibald Douglas, Earl of Angus, seized control of the king and ruled Scotland through him, while holding the office of chancellor. When James V, at the age of sixteen, began his personal rule in 1528, one of his early acts was to have Angus arraigned for treason, leading to the confiscation of his property and that of his supporters and relations (Cameron 1998, 19–27). One of these was his castle of Douglas, which was taken over by James, who paid the gardener for keeping the garden and the planting of trees and flowers, as had happened in the past (*ER* 17, 124, 222, 353). Another property which came into royal hands was Glamis, following the condemnation for treason in 1537 of Lady Glamis, the sister of the Earl of Angus, and her sons (Cameron 1998, 171–2). The gardener of Glamis, like other royal gardeners, was paid in money and oats (*ER* 17, 255, 285 etc), and in 1540 two men were paid for repairing the ditches of the gardens of Glamis and the fish ponds there (*ER* 17, 384). Other properties which appear in the Crown records, such as Banff in 1501 (*ER* 11, 374; 14, 607) and Bass of Inverurie in Aberdeenshire, include gardens in their description in 1520 (*ER* 14, 607, 629; RCAHMS 2007, 139). The orchard at **Kildrummy Castle** is mentioned in 1438 (*ER* 5, 58; RCAHMS 2007, 156–7), but its location in relation to the castle is unknown (Fig 115).

Chance is often involved in the survival of information about gardens. The existence of a 'great garden' at **Cassillis** in Ayrshire in the fifteenth century is only known because an agreement between different branches of the Kennedy family and witnessed by Bishop Kennedy of St Andrews was made near it in July 1444 (NRS GD25/1/34). In 1559 there is another reference to the garden at Cassillis, when it, along with

Fig 114 In the centre of the photograph are the surviving traces of the plantation of hawthorns representing James IV's ship, the Great Michael, *near the former site of Tullibardine Castle in Perthshire. PGA COMP 2005-04-21© NextPerspectives*

Fig 115 Aerial view of Kildrummy Castle where gardens were recorded from the fifteenth century. SC636463

Fig 116 Aerial view of the probably post-medieval earthworks of the gardens around Cassillis in Ayrshire. SC1237398

the place of Cassillis and its orchard, were assigned to the dowager countess of Cassillis by her son, the second earl (NRS GD 25/12/576). Although the outlines of earlier gardens at Cassillis, which precede the present layout, can be seen from the air, their rectilinear form reflects the portrayal on the seventeenth century maps of Blaeu, which were usually based on the surveys of Timothy Pont in the late sixteenth century, but they may incorporate an earlier layout (Fig 116).

Another Ayrshire garden of the mid sixteenth century is **Newton Castle** near Ayr, the description of which survives because of a legal case. Unfortunately the site was built over during the nineteenth century, although a large garden and dovecot, commemorated by the name 'Garden Street' were noted as late as 1723. Sir William Hamilton, who had married the first Earl of Cassillis' daughter, was provost of Ayr between 1539 and 1560. He had been a member of the household of James IV. He may have been a Glasgow graduate and, by 1526, during the minority of James V, was Depute Master of the Royal Household, a post he held until at least 1538. He travelled abroad on the

king's service, carrying a letter to Cardinal Wolsey and was part of an embassy to the Emperor Charles V to seek a wife for James V, both missions taking place during 1528. When the Earl of Arran, another Hamilton, became regent for Mary Queen of Scots, Sir William Hamilton was one of the ambassadors sent to negotiate with Henry VIII for Mary's marriage with the future Edward VI in 1543, and in 1553–4 was provost of Edinburgh. He inherited and was granted lands in Ayrshire, including Newton Castle, which was renamed 'the tower and place of Sanquhar-Hamilton'. The house is depicted by Slezer in his *Theatrum Scotiae*, printed in 1693, and may be of the fifteenth or sixteenth century, possibly with elements belonging to both periods (Fig 117). It appears to be an L-plan tower house with an enclosure adjacent and trees showing above the enclosure wall. In 1559 the castle was attacked and seized by John Wallace of Craigie with forty men, and damage was caused to his property, including his gardens. A result of this incursion was the compilation of an inventory of the contents and a description of the tower and its surrounding buildings, which was to be used by Sir William Hamilton as part of his case against Wallace in the Court of Session (Mackenzie 1990, 3–33; NRS

CS 7 20). The castle was well provided with furniture and household goods including silver plate, in addition to jewellery, clothing and stores of food. The two great orchards and gardens had three gates; they had hawthorn hedges and contained gooseberry bushes, red currant bushes, rose bushes, apple trees, plum trees, cherry trees, bullace (wild plum) trees, 'davr' trees, almond trees, plane, birch, ash, hawthorn and 'vtheris treis of pastyme'. The orchards were closed with two stanks or moats, and surrounded by a stone wall. In the gardens were kale and 'herbs' valued at £10. While Sir William Hamilton was obviously a wealthy man and a royal official, he was scarcely an exceptional member of his class, and information about his garden, which forms a very small part of the inventory, has survived only because of the attack and the subsequent attempt at a legal remedy.

The records of the Court of Session produce evidence for the making of 'ane knot of flouris' in the garden of the Tower of Auchenames in Renfrewshire before 1540; it was created by a servant who was not a gardener by profession (Sanderson 2002, 175). This house, which belonged to James Crawford, was described as 'a very high tour of 6 or 7 stories high' in the later seventeenth century (Macfarlane 1906–8, 2, 206). Although the site appears on Pont's map of Renfrewshire (Pont 33), it appears to be of relatively low status in relation to the neighbouring Castle Semple.

Evidence for the probable existence of a garden at **Castle Campbell** in Clackmannanshire comes from architectural survival, although the garden in its present form is unlikely to be of medieval date (Gifford and Walker 2002, 319). The south range at Castle Campbell has been compared to the King's Old Building within the castle of Stirling, referred to in contemporary accounts as the King's House, which was completed in 1496 (Dunbar 1984, 19; Gifford and Walker 2002, 677). At one end of the range, which may have been built about 1500 (Cruden 1999, 8), there was a vaulted transe or passageway which led through the building, and which would have provided access to the area to the south of the castle which is now a garden and may well have been a garden then (RCAHMS 1933, 324). Colin Campbell, first Earl of Argyll, acquired the property in the right of his wife, and, in 1490, had its name changed from 'Gloume' to Castle Campbell. His son Archibald, the second earl, served as James IV's chancellor and master of the household in the 1490s, and died alongside James at Flodden. The terraced garden at Castle Campbell has been associated with the erection of the south range, but it would indeed be remarkable if it belonged to this period, which would make it, arguably, the first garden of this type anywhere in Europe outside Italy, and it is more likely to belong in the later sixteenth or early seventeenth century (Figs 118, 124).

Fig 117 Newton Castle by Ayr by John Slezer from the 1693 edition of Theatrum Scotiae. *DP101799*

Another family with a tradition of serving the Stewarts was the Setons, whose main holdings were in East Lothian. *The History of the House of Seytoun to the year 1559* was written by Sir Richard Maitland of Lethington, a close relation of the Setons (Maitland 1829). The manuscript probably remained with the family until the estate was forfeited following the 1715 rising, and it was fortunately preserved in the Advocates Library in Edinburgh. Among their properties were **Seton** and Winton in East Lothian, Niddry near Winchburgh in West Lothian and Dalgetty in Fife. The first reference to a garden at Seton dates from the early fifteenth century, when it is related that Katherine Sinclair, the widow of William first Lord Seton, planted and made all the gardens there that were still surviving in 1560 (Maitland 1829, 29). She also extended the adjacent parish church of Seton, building an aisle on the south side, where she was later buried. The church was vaulted with walls of fine ashlar and a roof of stone. The account in Maitland's work gives a picture of the castle surrounded by a series of stone-walled enclosures, used as gardens. These would include a kitchen garden, a herb garden, a flower garden and an orchard. All would be suitable for recreation and the flower garden, would have contained benches of turf. The men of the family were well travelled; Katherine's grandson accompanied James I's daughter Margaret to France on the occasion of her marriage to the future Louis XI in 1436, and a later Lord Seton, whose second marriage was to one of Mary of Guise's attendants, was with Mary Queen of Scots when she went to France to be married to the future François II in 1548.

Fig 118 Castle Campbell in a late eighteenth century engraving showing the location of the transe leading through the south range to the garden. DP028201

Some of the family were learned, in particular George Seton, whose nephew was the writer of the *History*, and who was the son-in-law of the first Earl of Argyll. He was born in the middle of the fifteenth century, dying in 1508, a contemporary of James III and James IV. He studied at St Andrews and then in Paris. Astrology, theology and music were his particular interests; he was known as a great arranger of music and he had a reputation for extravagance. On a journey to France he was captured by Flemings, presumably pirates from Dunkirk, and robbed of his possessions. His response was to buy a ship and fill it with men of war and attack the Flemings in turn. His younger son fought for Louis XII of France, dying at Milan during the wars in Italy. George, in addition to establishing the college of priests at Seton and vaulting the choir, built what is described as the whole place of **Winton** with the garden. Richard Maitland of Lethington, born in 1496 (MacDonald 1972, 7), who wrote that he had seen the garden himself, said that it had a hundred carved ornamental wooden posts set about the knots of flowers, each of which was two cubits (about three foot) high with a double knob on top. The knobs were gilded and the wooden shafts were painted in various colours (Maitland 1829, 53). This is a most unusual, possibly unique, description of garden decoration, and would provide a colourful garden, even in winter with the painted posts setting off the green plants below. It may anticipate, in some ways, the design of the Privy Orchard of Henry VIII at Hampton Court in 1531, where heraldic beasts appropriate to the Tudor dynasty were set on painted posts with rails between the posts (Jennings 2005, 30). The beasts, which were painted in bright colours with much gilding, held a pennant with the royal arms or a Tudor rose (Figs 119, 120). This was a prelude to the extended use of beasts on posts in the Privy Garden and the Mount Garden, where the paths were flanked by king's beasts, and the Pond Garden bordered by beasts; the beasts were changed when there was a new queen (Strong 1998, 25–8; Symes 1996, 26–8). A drawing of Hampton Court and its gardens dating from about 1560 and preserved in the Ashmolean Museum in Oxford shows the Privy Garden consisting of two groups of square beds divided into quarters, surrounded by walks with a large number of free standing posts set in symmetrical plots. A clearer, if more restricted view, appears in the background to a picture of Henry VIII and his family in the Royal Collection painted about 1545, which may show the gardens at Whitehall Palace (Henderson 2005, 78), which was also drawn by Antonis van der Wyngaerde.

Seton was on the route from London traced by all the envoys from Henry VII and Henry VIII to James IV and James V, and by the late sixteenth century was a place to be visited and admired, however grudgingly, by travellers (Brown 1978, 82). A third Seton garden was at **Niddry Castle**, where a charter of 1506 refers to 'the orchart of Winchburgh' (*RMS* 2,637–8 no 2995) and one of 1548 records 'orchards, enclosed gardens within and outside, protected by the defences' (*RMS* 4, 54–5 no 222).

Fig 119 Hampton Court Palace *from the River by the Flemish artist Antonis van der Wyngaerde, drawn between 1558 and 1562, and showing near the centre the painted posts in Henry VIII's Privy Garden. There were payments 'for Cuttyng, making and karvyng of (159) of the Kynges and the quenys beestes stondyng in the Kynges new garden' in 1534. The design recalls the painted posts in the earlier garden at Seton Castle. WA.C.III.VII.504b © Ashmolean Museum, University of Oxford*

The English invasions of 1544 led by the Earl of Hertford saw the burning of the castle and place of Seton, the looting of the church and the burning of its wooden fittings (Maitland 1829, 42–3). It is recorded in despatches to Henry VIII that 'the same night we encamped at a town of Lord Seton's and burned Seton castle, and destroyed his orchards and gardens, the fairest in the country. We did him the more despite because he was the chief laborer to help their Cardinal out of prison, the only author of their calamity' (Gairdner and Brodie 1903, 332). Winton was also burnt during Hertford's invasion. Lord Seton took up residence at Culross, where he died and was buried in 1549; his body was removed to Seton after the English had left East Lothian. His son, who had spent much time in France, in turn, was sent as ambassador in 1558 to conclude the treaty and attend the marriage of Mary Queen of Scots to the dauphin (Maitland 1829, 44). The great tower and the house of Seton were repaired and a 'grit dyk and wall of stane about the yarde and grit orcheart of Seytoun' was constructed and a pretty house built on its garden side, making Seton more sumptuous than it was before. The author commends the improvements to the policy, as the 'maist tollerable kynd of prodigalitie and of sumptuous immoderate cost', because its benefits will pass to his descendants

and be an adornment to the country (Maitland 1829, 45). Seton was on the main road from London, and the house and gardens were favourably mentioned by travellers on the road from London in the late sixteenth and seventeenth centuries (Brown 1978, 82, 136).

Following the death of James V at Falkland, the Earl of Arran and later Duke of Chatelherault, head of the Hamilton family and James V's nearest surviving blood relative, became regent for Mary Queen of Scots. He had accompanied James on his visit to France in 1536 (Fig 121). Arran put his relatives and supporters in charge of much of the royal demesne, and used royal funds for his own and his family's benefit, even to the extent of paying for clothing for

Fig 120 A modern recreation of a garden decorated with painted wooden posts in the Chapel Court at Hampton Court. © DB Gallagher

Fig 121 James Hamilton, Earl of Arran and Duke of Chatelherault, Regent for Mary Queen of Scots between 1543 and 1554. © Scottish National Portrait Gallery. Licensor Scran

members of his family (*TA* 9, 10). As seems to have been customary, building and work on the royal palaces and gardens became less prominent and the Accounts of the Masters of Works (*MW*) are for the most part missing until well into the reign of James VI. Gardeners continued to be paid for working in the palace gardens (*TA* 10, 127). At Linlithgow in 1543 the gardener was Dominus Robert Akinhead, chaplain, another cleric, employed in this position (*ER* 18, 39). John Morrison remained as gardener at Holyrood and is recorded as receiving payment of thirty-two shillings in 1553 from the Treasurer for seeds bought by him and delivered to 'my lord governors gairdener in **Kinneil**' (*TA* 10, 174). Earlier in 1549–50 two pounds of onion seed, two ounces of lettuce seed and half an ounce of thyme seed were sent to Arran's residence at Hamilton (*TA* 9, 385). The deer park in the High Parks at Hamilton had been established in the mid fifteenth century, the period to which some of the trees there have been dated, although some are much older (Dougall and Dickson 1997, 78). 'Ane creill full of flowers was sent to Linlithgow' (*TA* 10, xxiv). Onion, leek, French lettuce seed, half a pound of parsley seed and ten ounces of bastard kale seed costing forty-two shillings was dispatched to Linlithgow for the lord governor's gardener along with the charges for a leather bag to transport them in and a boy to carry them there (*TA* 10, 83). It is interesting to see some details of a great lord's gardening, and it would seem that Arran was putting considerable effort into his own garden at Kinneil near Linlithgow in 1552. The provision is somewhat reminiscent of James IV's establishment of his garden at Stirling half a century

earlier. John Hamilton of Bothwell received £5 for his expenses for going to the Carse of Gowrie for trees, probably fruit trees, 'to my lord governor's house at Kinneil' in January 1552 (*TA* 10, 127). Two loads of thorns for enclosing and protecting the governor's 'yaird' of Kinneil (*TA* 10, 144) cost forty-eight shillings. The following January James Baxter was to visit various places in Fife and Strathearn for trees for Kinneil (*TA* 10, 155). Three horses were hired to bring trees from Holyrood 'to my lord governor's yaird in Kinneil', along with lettuce and marjoram seed, and John Morrison of Holyrood was sent to Dunfermline to look for flowers for the governor's garden. Others were engaged in the same task. A boy brought flowers from the curate of Stirling, who may have got them from the royal gardens there (*TA* 10, 174). Only additional expenses would be recorded in the accounts, and there may have been considerably more diversion of resources to his own personal properties. The form of the garden at Kinneil is not known at this period. The house was partly blown up by a later regent of Scotland, the Earl of Morton, in 1570, and the mansion was redesigned in the later seventeenth century. Arran was also reconstructing the house of Kirk o' Field, on what is now the site of the Old College of the University of Edinburgh, then just inside the town, from where seeds had come to Stirling half a century earlier, and where he paid fifty shillings to the gardener in compensation for the damage to his plants and trees caused by the works at Arran's lodgings there (*TA* 10, 109) in 1552.

Mary of Guise became regent for her daughter between 1554 and her death in 1560. The Treasurers Accounts are missing from October 1555 to January 1558, but there are payments of £7 to the gardener of 'hir grace garden in the abbay' in April 1555 to buy seeds with (*TA* 10, 275). The Master of Works Accounts have a few detached records for repairs at Stirling, including the repairing of the park gate (*MW* 1, 293) and **Holyroodhouse** for repairs to the park dyke (*MW* 1, 299). In 1558 John Morrison, here referred to as the gardener of the south yard of Holyroodhouse, was paid for cutting ditches to drain water from the south garden of Holyrood, which it has been suggested may mark the end of the use of the fish ponds (*TA* 10, 393; Jamieson 1994, 26). In March 1558 John Morrison had bought ten pounds worth of seeds for Holyrood (*TA* 10, 340). The shooting butts were repaired in the same year, and in October the sale by Dene James Murray, canon of the Holyroodhouse, of his yard lying to the north-west side of the 'palice of Halyrudhouse made in ane gardyng to hir grace', presumably Mary of Guise, was concluded (*TA* 10, 394). This would have been adjacent to the James V tower, refurbished at this time, which probably served as her lodging, as it would have done when she was married to James V, and as it did for Mary Queen of Scots.

Fig 122 A woodcut from Robert Henryson's Morall Fabillis of Esope the Phrygian, printed in Edinburgh by Thomas Bassandyne in 1571. It depicts a farmyard scene with a cock who finds a jasp (precious stone) on a dunghill, reflects upon its splendour, but leaves it on the ground as inappropriate for him and goes on his way to continue the search for food. © National Library of Scotland. Licensor Scran

Gardens in Towns and Villages

Gardens in towns and villages across Scotland are mentioned in numerous charters, sometimes in the form of 'tenement with garden' but often as part of the location of the property being gifted (NRS Catalogue *passim*). They will have been constantly reworked and subject to infilling by the building of workshops and extensions. Evidence from plant remains recovered during archaeological excavation suggest the presence in towns of most of the types of plants referred to in documentary sources, although some plants survive to be recognised by the palaeobotanist better than others. Traces of damsons, bullaces, wild or cultivated cherries and apples or crab apples have been recorded in towns. The powerful medicinal plants – opium poppy, henbane, hemlock and deadly nightshade – were grown, and while these might have come from the gardens of religious orders, they may have had a domestic source (Dickson and Dickson 2000, 213, 215) (Figs 122, 123).

Gardening in Scotland in the medieval period can be seen as forming a part of a wider European practice, part of the same nexus of trade, agriculture and culture. The majority of the surviving evidence is, in one way or another, documentary, and this favours knowledge of the gardens and gardeners of the king and the religious houses, those for which all expenditure must be accounted. The very partial

survival even of the records of these institutions has been alluded to, but arguments for the non-existence of gardens and a low level of gardening skill, based on the absence of evidence, cannot be sustained. Although an extant example of a garden has yet to be identified, those who were granted feu charters by the king were encouraged to establish gardens as a suitable appurtenance of such landholding and were required to build 'an adequate house of stone and lime, with a hall chamber, barn, cattle shed, stable, dovecot, garden, orchards and beehives etc' (*RMS* 2, 730, No 3407 passim).

Fig 123 Men cutting clover, a detail of an initial on the calendar page for June from the late twelfth century Hunterian Psalter. MS Hunterian 229 3v. © University of Glasgow Library, Department of Special Collections

Chapter 3: The Renaissance Garden 1560 to 1603

There he busied himself in making of walkes and alleys, in drawing of garden knots

James Melville of the Regent Morton at Lochleven Castle in 1580

Change and continuity mark Scottish society in the later sixteenth century. The most obvious change was the establishment of the beliefs and practice of the reformed Church as the official religion of Scotland. The Confession of Faith, which abrogated papal authority and forbade the celebration of mass, was ratified by Parliament in 1560, sounding a death knell for monasteries and other religious communities where the saying of the office was their central function. This either happened suddenly, as in the case of many friaries, or more gradually, in the case of some monasteries, such as Crossraguel, and even St Andrews. The effect of this legal settlement on landholding was considerable.

Gardens in Scotland also illustrate both change and continuity; the fashion for the enclosed garden within its protecting wall survives along with other courts and enclosures around the mansion, but grows in size. While food production to support the household remains central to their function, the relationship to the castle or country house becomes more explicit, with the garden arranged to complement the building. Although designs with a direct axial relationship between the two may belong to the following century, Castle Menzies, Muness Castle and Castle Campbell show recognition of this form of presentation, which may also have a practical, protective function (Figs 7, 124, 161). They become outward looking, taking in the land beyond the garden, exploiting the natural terrain and making

Fig 124 Aerial view of Castle Campbell with its terraced garden, perhaps the creation of Colin Campbell, sixth Earl of Argyll, an opponent of Regent Morton. DP061735

extensive use of water in the design. The house and the garden express their owners' changing perception of their country and society and their place in it. The Crown undertook little in the way of new gardens, as far as is known, although an argument from the absence of evidence is unreliable. After James VI received the English throne in 1603, his wife, Anne of Denmark, was notable for the establishment and redesign of gardens at her properties at Somerset House in London, Oatlands and Greenwich (Strong 1998, 87 etc). Dunfermline was Anne's favoured palace in Scotland. So little survives on the ground and in the documentary record that this site cannot be employed to produce a more balanced account of Scottish royal gardens at this period. As in England, in the reign of Elizabeth, the gardens of the nobility provide most of the evidence for developments in their design and its associated philosophy.

Gardens were recognised as contributing to health. Dr Andrew Boorde who visited Scotland in the 1530s and was a prolific writer on a wide range of subjects published *The boke for to learne a man to be wyse in buyldyng of his howse for the helth of body [and] to holde quyetnes for the helth of his soule, and body* in 1550, having incorporated material from his *Compendyous Regyment or Dyetary of Health* of 1542. In the first chapter he set out some desirable principles for the selection of the setting of a mansion, which, while they might not induce a landowner to build on a new site, might influence his choice for the development of a house and garden among a choice of existing properties. He favoured a site that was 'pleasaunt, fayre, and good to the iye, to beholde the woddes, the waters,

Fig 125 *The view from above Stirling Castle looking to the west towards Ben Lomond. The scenery visible from the castle and its encapsulation of the realm of Scotland were commended by the Master of Works in 1582, an early example of such appreciation of landscape. DP0790433*

the feldes, the vales, the hylles and the playne ground' (Boorde 1550, not paginated). This advice is echoed to some degree in the commendation of Stirling among the residences of James VI as having 'the maist plesand sitwatione off any of his hienes palayes be ressone it will have the maist plesand sycht of all the foure airthis [points of the compass]', mentioning the views along

the river valleys, up to Loch Lomond and down the Forth (*MW*, 1, 310) (Figs 125, 126).

The effect of the changes in landholding following the approval of the Confession of Faith by Parliament (*RPS*, A1560/8/3) was important and long lasting. The Church had held about a third of the agricultural land in Scotland. In the reign of James V, its possessions produced over £300,000 a year, compared with the yield from crown lands of £17,000; on the other hand the Church was liable for half the national tax in times of preparation for war. The Crown put considerable financial pressure on the Church from the time that

Fig 126 The view from above Stirling Castle looking to the east down the meanders of the River Forth. DP088742

James V took up power in 1528. The effects of his policy on individual monastic houses, such as Melrose, have been referred to in the first chapter, and many other monasteries had lay commendators, belonging to important landed families, who had a strong financial interest in their property. During James' reign the holders of the bishoprics agreed to grant the king £72,000 in four years, in addition to a permanent annual subsidy of £14,000 from their own benefices (Sanderson

1982, 67). The disposal of Church lands in feu, that is, a change from tenancy to a form of proprietorship (the nature of feudal tenure is described and discussed in Scottish Parliament Research Note 99/31), was to some extent a response to the need for money to pay these taxes, or, at least, that was the reason given. The granter of the feu charter received an initial payment, a grassum, followed by fixed annual payments.

The changes consequent on the ending of the role of monasteries continued and accelerated a process that had been underway since the late thirteenth century. Feuing has been described as one of the biggest changes

Fig 127 Figures in the lower margin of the later sixteenth century Wode Partbook. The figure on the right may be Thomas Wode, the former monk of Lindores Abbey, singing from a copy of his work. University of Edinburgh Library Special Collections, Dk 5.14.1. © Edinburgh University Library

affecting Scottish rural society in the sixteenth century, turning hundreds of tenants into proprietors, great and small (Sanderson 1982, 64). The move had been deliberately encouraged during the fifteenth century by an act of parliament of the reign of James II, which ordained that 'quhat prelate, barone or frehaldare that can accorde with his tenande apone setting of feuferme of his awin lande in all or in part, our soverane lorde sall ratify and appreif the said assedacioun ...' (*RPS*, 1458/3/16), and crown lands, particularly in Fife, Menteith and Ettrick Forest, were set in feu to the tenants. It would appear that more feu charters were granted after 1560, the year of the Reformation settlement, than earlier, but in the case of certain monasteries and bishoprics, feuing took place mainly before the Reformation; these included Coupar Angus, Kilwinning, Lindores and Holyrood. In the case of the Coupar Angus grant cited in the previous chapter, it can be seen that the abbey was attempting to protect its interests into an uncertain future, with the condition that there should be provision for the entertainment of members of the community on their property at Gallowraw (Rogers 1879–80, 2, 168–9). Gardens in the immediate vicinity of the monastic houses might remain in the possession of their previous beneficiaries (Dilworth 1995, 78). There are many enclosed plots within the precinct at St Andrews which represent the gardens of the canons. Although they appear on the Geddy map only as grass plots, they continued to be cultivated by the canons who remained after the dissolution of the monastery in 1560. The composer David Peebles, with his wife and sons, occupied a house within the Augustinian Priory at St Andrews where he had been a canon before the Reformation (Ross 1993, 66; Fleming 1910, 614). He was responsible for much of the music for the psalms in the Partbooks of Thomas Wode. The singing of the psalms was an important part of the services conducted by Wode, the first Reader at the Trinity Church at St Andrews and later Vicar of St Andrews, and himself a former monk at Lindores Abbey (Fig 127).

It is reckoned that much of the land, some 44 to 57 per cent according to one estimate, remained in the hands of the tenants who were already farming it, although the percentages varied from district to district (Sanderson 1982, 77); the other feuars were lairds and nobles, while, in about a quarter of cases, the lands fell to outsiders, lawyers, burgesses or crown officials. There was a highly active market in land in the late sixteenth century, driven not only by the process of feuing, but also by rising rents and the rising prices of foodstuffs, with general prices increasing fourfold between 1550 and 1625, and agricultural commodities rising at a much faster rate (Lynch 1991, 183). Because the annual feu duty was fixed, the new class of feuars were beneficiaries. They can be seen as a new and self confident group with claims to a greater role in establishing and appreciating the culture of Scotland, enjoying the poetry of Henryson, Gavin Douglas and David Lindsay, as well as the patriotic writings of Barbour, in their printed form. The establishments of many of these people appear on the maps of Timothy Pont, marked with one of his settlement symbols (Stone 2006, 50), but it is the houses of the nobility, sometimes with their gardens and parks, that are given the most prominence on the maps. The production of a survey of Scotland, in the form of a map and written descriptions, reveals how the country was perceived by Timothy Pont, a graduate of St Andrews, and himself a minister of the reformed kirk. This mirror of Scotland in the 1580s and 1590s records towns, villages, churches and mills, rivers and mountains, great houses, parks and gardens, and is of great value in the appreciation of the extent, and to some degree the nature, of gardens in late sixteenth century Scotland.

At the end of the fifteenth century, gardens across Europe were, for the most part, of the same type: an enclosed quadrangular space divided into squares or rectangles, perhaps with trees and plants trained into arbours, with or without a wickerwork frame, sometimes with a fountain or other central feature. This remained the most common form throughout the sixteenth century, even in Italy. There, other elements such as the exploitation of natural slopes and water sources were introduced; fountains, grottos and terraces, as well as a wider range of plants became part of the amenities of gardens. These features appeared first in

Tuscany and Rome in the later fifteenth century, and spread more widely across Italy during the first half of the sixteenth century. In France from the middle of the sixteenth century onwards there was a preference for the organisation of the gardens of major chateaux with a wide central alley on the axis of the house, around which were disposed lines of trees and square and rectangular stretches of calm water (Guillaume 1999a, 7–8).

A considerable range of plants was grown in Scottish gardens and orchards, although sometimes the range of planting seems to have been deliberately restricted. A contract, dated 7 June 1565, details an agreement between Mariota (Marion) Scott, Lady **Fordell**, and William Raa (Rea?), gardener, whereby it is:

> appointtit and aggreit betuix Marioun Scott, lady Fordell, on that ane parte, and William Raa, gardiner, on that uthir parte, that is to say the said William sall laubour, manuir and garne the yard of Fordell in all maner of behalffis as effeiris, and in dew tyme and sessoun; and at the tyme convenient sall plant and sett ... treis, ... the treis of the wards south and north, and sall saw na maner of cornes in the yardis except peis or benis, and sall laubour in to na uthir yard bot in it; for the quhilk caus the said Marioun sall content and pay to the said William sex bollis meill for this present yeir, viz., fra Witsonday 1565 quhill Witsonday in anno 1566 togidder with the proffett of the hall yardis, and to be payrit at four termes in the yeir, and the said William sall enter to the twa aiker of land and twa kyis gerss quhilk David Andersoun, gardiner, had of befoir, at the feist of Michaelmes nixtocum, and that the daid William sall craif no mair except the foirsaid meill for this yeir, and fra then furth the prottett of his land and yard; and as the said Wiliam is to haif the rig at the grene fute for uphalding of the parkis dyikis, and the gerss of Shonne to be keipit to the laird and ladyis horss.
> (NRAS Roxburgh Muniments 1100 Bundle 1938).

Vegetable and herb gardens, primarily planted for cooking and medicine, formed an important part of the surroundings of the house, as well as flower gardens. No book particularly concerned with plants grown in Scotland is known from this time, but Gerard's *Herbal* of 1597 is used by Robertson (2000) for an account of what would probably be grown in contemporary Scotland. New species were coming into Britain during the sixteenth century. A highly decorative depiction of flora appears in the miniature of 'A Young Daughter of the Picts' attributed to Jacques Le Moyne de Morgues and painted about 1585 (Frontispiece). It shows a girl carrying a spear and wearing a sword, and tattooed all over her body with symmetrically arranged flowers: peonies, hollyhocks, lilies, cornflowers, irises, horned poppies, columbines, rose campions, narcissus and tulips. Le Moyne de Morgues was a Huguenot refugee in London, who had taken part in a French expedition to establish a colony in Florida, which was overrun by the Spanish in 1565. His picture formed the basis for an engraving by Theodor de Bry, which appeared in Thomas Hariot's *A briefe and true report of the new found land of Virginia* (Hariot 1590). It formed one of a series of five ancient Britons, which appeared in a supplement intended to point out the similarities (and differences) between the native Americans and the earlier inhabitants of Britain. The anachronistic choice of flowers associates the Scots with the burgeoning flora of the period, whatever the intentions of the artist (and the author) might be.

Scotland was part of this European tradition, and particular aspects of it, especially the terraced garden and the design of the garden to provide selected distant views, were adopted with enthusiasm. Gardens whose remains survive recognisably today, whether on the ground or from the air, are those where there has been much reshaping of the ground, and this means that terraced gardens and water gardens are probably disproportionately represented in the perception of sixteenth and seventeenth century gardens. The eighteenth century desire to set the house in a more 'natural' landscape led to some very determined attempts at eradication, as is the case at **Monzie Castle** or **Drum Castle**, where only slight traces of the terraces remained at ground level. The enclosing garden walls may also escape demolition, allowing the existence of a garden of the same date as the wall to be recognised; **Edzell Castle** is perhaps the most notable example. Maps and plans reveal the wider distribution of gardens in the later sixteenth century. It is a cause of much regret that so many of Pont's manuscripts were lost, particularly those covering the south of Scotland and especially the area around Edinburgh where wealth and settlement were as dense as appeared in the extant maps of south-east Perthshire and Angus.

In 1558 Mary Queen of Scots had married the Dauphin, who succeeded to the throne as François II of France the next year, following the death of his father, Henri II, who died as a result of a wound gained during a joust against the captain of his Scottish Archers. Mary's mother and regent in Scotland, Mary of Guise, died in June 1560. Her husband, François II, died in December 1560, and Mary returned to Scotland in August 1561 at the age of eighteen. The parliament of 1560 had already forbidden the celebration of mass, and wide-ranging changes to the Church in Scotland were under way. Mary seems to have accepted these religious changes as a *fait accompli*, keeping her own Catholic chapel. Her own household was supported out of her income as a dowager queen of France and so

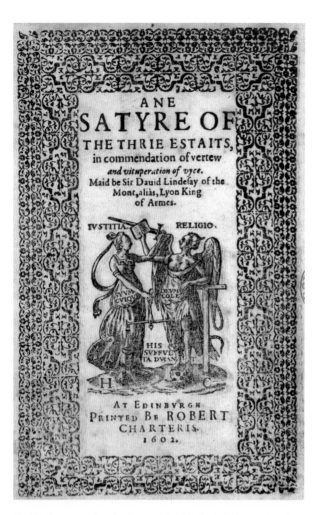

Fig 128 Frontispiece from Ane Satyre of the Thrie Estaits *by Sir David Lindsay. The play was acted in the presence of Mary of Guise in 1554 at Greenside, Edinburgh. This edition of the play was printed by Robert Charteris in Edinburgh in 1602. © Bodleian Library. Licensor Scran*

there is relatively little information in the Treasurer's Accounts relating to her servants. The early years after her return to Scotland saw her established at Holyrood, with Edinburgh the centre of her administration. The pastimes and pleasures of court life were employed as part of the proper behaviour of a ruling monarch in Scotland for the first time since the death of James V. Among these pursuits were music, dancing, needlework, cards and dice indoors, with hawking, hunting, shooting at the butts and golf outdoors, in all of which Mary participated enthusiastically.

The garden provided an outdoor extension to the palace or house, where certain activities could most properly take place; meetings with ambassadors and the granting of charters have already been mentioned. It provided a less formal space where the monarch could handle affairs, either privately, or in front of a deliberately large assembly. Masques, a kind of poetic drama with music and dancing, which were an important feature of court life in the sixteenth and seventeenth centuries, could be held indoors or outdoors. The commonest form was a dance by masked members of the court, sometimes including the ruler and close members of his family, in elaborate, matching costumes. In France they formed part of the celebrations of weddings and christenings, as well as major state occasions, and one of the most elaborate series of masques was that in 1558 celebrating the marriage of Mary and the Dauphin François. In 1554, during her regency, the play *The Three Estates* was acted in the open air in the presence of Mary of Guise, at Greenside on the lower slopes of Calton Hill in Edinburgh, as it had been two years earlier on the Castlehill in Cupar (Potter 1975, 81). An earlier version of the play had been written for performance before James V and Mary of Guise on Twelfth Night at Linlithgow in 1540. It was in the tradition, as were many later masques, of commentary on the state of the kingdom and advice to the ruler, which was also designed for the information and instruction of the audience, which would include the most influential members of the community, and might also convey a political message through reports to foreign rulers; it is from such reports that much of what is known of performances in Scotland derives (Fig 128).

The masques of the reign of Mary Queen of Scots seem to fall into two broad categories: those designed for public consumption with a more or less overt political message, and those designed for the enjoyment of the court and household and the queen herself. Again some of these were held in the open air; there was a 'running at the ring' on Leith sands (Carpenter 2003, 200) with the competing teams dressed as women and as 'strangers'. Twelfth Night and Shrovetide were two of the feasts often celebrated with masquing, neither of which fall at a time of year likely to encourage the use of gardens as settings, although the gardens at **Holyrood** were used for meetings with ambassadors even in February (Fraser 1969, 179). Mary's library contained a work called *Le Jardin de Plaisance et Fleur de Rhetorique*, a collection of courtly verse, which was designed for refined entertainment, and not a work on gardens (Sharman 1889, 53–4); one chapter provides information on the construction of moralities, mysteries and farces.

There is little information about changes to the gardens in Mary's reign. She stands apart from the earlier Stewart monarchs in not undertaking a building programme (Wormald 1988, 35), and there is no detail of additions to the garden apart from the repair of archery butts in 1567 in the south garden of Holyroodhouse (*TA* 12, 47, 49). It is recorded that she took part in a shooting match against her half-brother, James Stewart, Earl of Moray, and one of her ladies, and she herself was partnered by the Master of Lindsay (*CSP Scot* I, 621). The building and repairing of the butts could be a considerable undertaking; it took 17,000 turfs to repair the butts six years later, just after the fall of Edinburgh Castle to the king's party, when

Fig 129 A design for a tapestry by Antoine Caron depicting a water festival at Fontainebleau, created for Catherine de Medici and dating from about 1573. Such elaborate festivals were used to enhance the prestige and forward the diplomatic aims of the French court. Mary Queen of Scots would have been familiar with such events and organised masques after her return to Scotland. D767 © National Galleries of Scotland

James Douglas, Earl of Morton, was regent for the young James VI (*TA* 12, 351).

Responsibility for the gardens at Holyrood was divided in 1561; William Brown became the gardener of all the gardens and orchards on the north side of the palace (*RSS* V, 234), while in 1562 John Morrison was confirmed as keeper only of the gardens to the south of the palace (*RSS* V, 285). The Master of Works who had overall charge was William Macdougall in 1557 (*ER* 19, 130; *TA* 12, 47). These gardeners and their families continued as gardeners at Holyrood through the reign of James VI to the end of the century, and there were regular payments of £8 a year for seeds (*TA* 12, 58, 152, 216 etc; *ER* 20, 41, 120 etc). Animals were still kept at Holyrood, with the overall responsibility for the lion, lucerve (lynx), tiger and cocks of the game lying with Thomas Fenton, who was described as keeper of the garden at the end of the century (*ER* 23, 9, 46, 252).

One elaborate entertainment was held in May 1562 at Dunsapie Loch in Holyrood Park (Figs 129, 130). It celebrated the wedding of John, Lord Fleming, a relative and close supporter of the queen and brother of one of the four Maries. Among those present was the ambassador of the king of Sweden, one of the suitors for Mary's hand in marriage. The subject of this masque was the siege of Leith by the English in 1560, with galleys on the loch and the erection of a timber castle, and much shooting off of ordnance, presumably a firework display. Other evidence for the use of the park as a place for leisure and entertainment is an entry in the *Despences De La Maison Royale* (Household Accounts) for May 1565 when there is a payment to two men for 'acoustre ung lieu au parc present que la royne deult aller soupper' (for fitting up a place in the park at hand where the queen might go to have supper). As the previous reference was for payment to the same two men for cleaning the King's Chamber (Mary, like her mother, occupied the Queen's Chambers at Holyrood, even though she was the ruling monarch), presumably in preparation for their occupancy by Henry Stewart, Lord Darnley, it may be that the suppers were also with Darnley and close friends and household members, and that the place which had been prepared was a form of banqueting house (NRS E33/9/6) (Fig 132). Mary's wedding to Darnley took place at Holyrood at the end of July 1565 with a series of pageants of gods and goddesses, exotic visitors providing congratulations and the queen's four Maries performing a masque celebrating Salus, the goddess of life and health (Carpenter 2003, 216).

The structure known as Queen Mary's Bath House was originally built on the perimeter of the north garden

Fig 130 Aerial view of Dunsapie Loch in the Queen's Park, Holyrood, with the Palace of Holyroodhouse in the background. A masque, attended by Mary Queen of Scots celebrating the siege of Leith in 1560 was held on Dunsapie Loch on the occasion of the marriage of John, Lord Fleming, and Elizabeth Ross in 1562. SC577112

and could be viewed from the royal apartments in James V's tower, but is now isolated from the main palace gardens by a nineteenth century approach road. It is on the line of the precinct wall of the abbey and originally appears to have been designed as a fortification. There is structural evidence for a gunloop commanding the approach to the Watergate, the entrance to the burgh from the direction of Leith. Its original construction may relate to the abbey; comparable towers survive most notably at St Andrews. The front facing the palace was reconstructed with an external stair leading to a first floor chamber, but there is no surviving documentation relating to its building history. A dendrochronological sample of three exposed timbers from the exterior of the building, possibly part of the jettying for the first floor, gave a felling date of c1566, suggesting that the traditional association with Mary Queen of Scots may be correct (Ewart and Gallagher forthcoming). While the exact purpose of the building is not known (Cooper, 2000, 22–3) and will have changed through time, it may have been a banqueting house, the main activity for such garden buildings, designed for the refined partaking of wines and sweetmeats with intimates after leaving the main table, perhaps a successor in part to the 'place in the park' recorded in 1565 (Fig 131).

The most magnificent festivity of Mary's reign took place at Stirling Castle in December 1566 and celebrated the christening of her son, the future James VI. This included references to Arthur and the Round Table, foretelling Mary's and James' accession to the throne of the whole of Britain (Lynch 1990, 11–12). The verses by George Buchanan were spoken by maskers, dressed as Satyrs, Naiads and Northern Mountain nymphs, offering tribute from different parts of the realm. A fort of timber was constructed outside the castle, near Halyrude Church and again assaulted and defended by fireworks (Carpenter 2003, 221). The more domestic entertainments would involve music and dancing in which Mary herself might take part. It was to attend the wedding of Bastien Pages, one of her *valets de chambre*, who had been involved in the organisation of the masque at the baptism of the future James VI, that she left her second husband, Lord Darnley, at Kirk o' Field the evening before he was murdered.

After Holyrood, Stirling was the palace at which Mary spent most time, with Falkland visited for hunting, and Linlithgow used as an overnight stop on the way to Stirling. During the first four years of her reign, Mary, like her father and grandfather, spent much of her time travelling through her kingdom, establishing herself as queen through the suppression of rebellion and through presiding over the administration of justice, as well as attending more auspicious events such as weddings at Crichton Castle and Castle Campbell, and Holyrood. In 1562 she went to Inverness, travelling via Linlithgow, Stirling, Perth, Glamis Castle, Edzell Castle and Dunnotter Castle towards Aberdeen, moving on to Darnaway Castle, the property of her half-brother the earl of Moray and returning via Spynie, Aberdeen and Arbroath Abbey. In 1563 she visited Fife, and in July and August, Glasgow, Hamilton, Dumbarton Castle,

Fig 131 Queen Mary's Bath House, a possible garden building in the North Garden at Holyrood. DP108131

Fig 132 Portrait of Henry Stewart, Lord Darnley, Mary Queen of Scots' second husband. © Scottish National Portrait Gallery. Licensor Scran

Inverary, Glenluce Abbey and Whithorn Priory, before returning by way of Dumfries to Edinburgh. In 1564 she returned to Inverness, visiting Blair Atholl en route, where an elaborate hunt was staged, and going on to Dingwall and Beauly, returning by way of Aberdeen. Early in 1565 she was travelling from Edinburgh to St Andrews by way of Balmerino Abbey. September and October 1565, the year of her wedding, saw her travelling extensively in central and eastern Scotland, in reaction to a revolt led by nobles opposed to her marriage to Henry, Lord Darnley (Breeze 1987, 45–51). Many of the places where Mary stayed, particularly during the early years after her return to Scotland, were known to be the sites of gardens before 1560, or would appear on the maps of Timothy Pont in the 1580s and 1590s, associated with parks or, in some cases, gardens. The abbeys and priories where she stayed would still be inhabited by many of their monks, while the houses of the lay commendators, where she was probably lodged, would be maintained by their secular lords. Mary stayed at **Seton Castle**, the house of one of her principal supporters, where the house and garden had been reconstructed after English invasions. The gardens there were regarded as a place to be shown to visitors; in 1584 a German traveller, Lupold von Wedel, commented on the hedges there which had the height of two men (von Bülow 1895, 247).

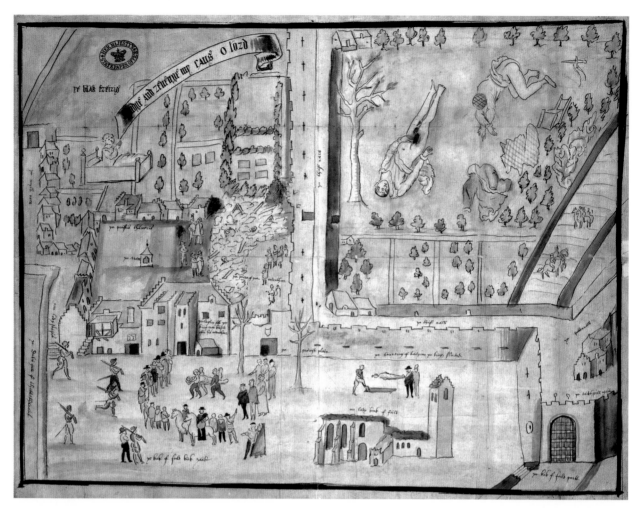

Fig 133 A complex drawing of the murder scene at Kirk o' Field combined with later events which was made for William Cecil, Lord Burghley, Queen Elizabeth's chief minister, in an attempt to explain the curious circumstances of Darnley's death in 1567. Darnley's body, along with that of his servant, was found outside the town wall of Edinburgh. The garden of Kirk o' Field lies within the wall. MPF1/366 © National Archives

The oldest detailed depiction of a garden in Scotland is that of the garden of **Kirk o' Field**, which lay on the present site of the Old College of the University of Edinburgh, just inside the town wall of Edinburgh which had been thrown up after the defeat at Flodden in 1513. The garden existed before then; it had been a source of seeds when James IV was reorganising the gardens at Stirling in 1499 (RCAHMS 1963, 219; *ER* 12, 76). The site of the Collegiate Church of St Mary in the Fields, which is on record about 1275, is now occupied by the Playfair Library and the adjacent section of the quadrangle. It was granted collegiate status before 1511 with a provost, ten prebendaries and two choristers. Its hospital was burnt by the English in 1544, and the Earl of Arran, while Lord Governor of Scotland for Mary Queen of Scots, built a mansion on the site, Hamilton House, which was noted for its gardens and its painted windows (RCAHMS 1951, 125) in 1552. Its construction caused damage to the adjacent garden belonging to the collegiate church, and compensation

was paid to the gardener (*TA* 10, 109). This building with its castellated wall head was the earliest part of Edinburgh University and became its library, surviving until 1798.

The drawing of the garden and its surroundings was made because the site was the scene of the murder on 10 February 1567 of Mary Queen of Scots' second husband, Henry, Lord Darnley (Figs 133, 149), an event which was almost immediately followed by her marriage to the Earl of Bothwell, and which led in a short time to the loss of her crown. The political importance of the event led to the need for a sketch plan of the 'murder scene'. It was made for Sir William Cecil, Lord Burghley, Elizabeth I's Secretary of State, in a not altogether successful attempt to clarify the extremely confusing circumstances of Darnley's death. It shows the garden adjacent to the house of the provost of the collegiate church, where Darnley was staying. The garden is enclosed by the city wall on the south, with stone enclosure walls to the north and east and the buildings of the college of priests to the west (Kerr 1932, 140). The garden is subdivided into five sections by a wall and lines of trees. The roughly square compartment nearest the priests' chambers and the provost's house, where Darnley was staying and where the queen had spent much of her time during the

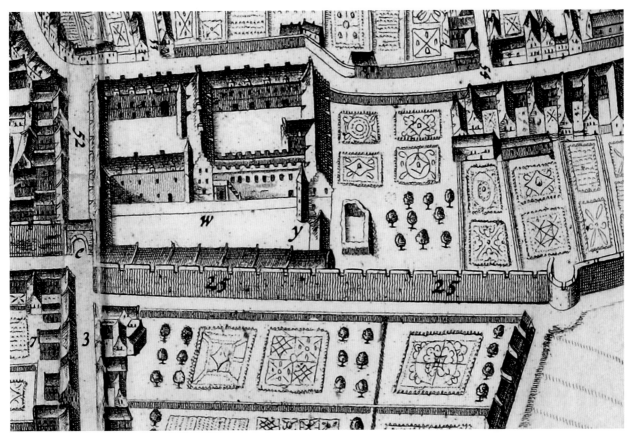

Fig 134 Detail of Kirk o' Field and its garden from the 1647 map of Edinburgh by James Gordon of Rothiemay in Theatrum Scotiae *by John Slezer (1693). DP101340*

week before the murder, was edged with trees with a path around and divided into four by paths forming four beds for grass or flowers. The next section to the north had two similar beds and some trees, drawn individually, possibly fruit trees. The next section to the east contained trees drawn in a similar fashion while the other two sections, defined by closely planted and larger trees, have no detail within them, and might have been grassed. The area outside the wall, where Darnley's body was found, was another enclosed garden, probably planted with fruit trees, and would have formed part of the Kirk o' Field gardens before the Flodden Wall was built (Mahon 1930, 41). There were still gardens laid out in four compartments in the same area on the map drawn by Gordon of Rothiemay eighty years later (Fig 134). Some of the gardens in the Canongate were managed as a commercial enterprise; James Kincaid, described in his will as a gardener, rented three yards there (Sanderson 2002, 66). In the absence of information on the maps of Timothy Pont, the dating of gardens tends to be aligned with the date of the building with which they are associated, if the design of the garden is congruent. The plan of Edinburgh published at Cologne in 1580 by Braun and Hogenberg provides little information about gardens in the city (NLS EMS.s.653).

Although this is the earliest detailed drawing of a specific Scottish garden, the illustrations in the Wode Partbooks, begun in the early 1560s and continued through the following decades, provide images of imaginary gardens populated by mythological monsters and astronomical symbols as well as by fantastical plants and flowers. Decorative thistles, a symbol of

Fig 135 A detail from Wode Partbooks, Cantus (Set 2), showing thistles, a symbol of Scotland. University of Edinburgh Library Special Collections Dk.5.14.152. © Edinburgh University Library

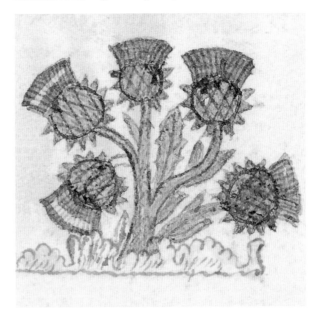

Fig 136 A garden populated by mythical monsters and astronomical symbols from the Wode Partbooks, a detail from the Cantus Partbook (Set 2). University of Edinburgh Library Special Collections Dk.5.14.13 © Edinburgh University Library

Scotland from at least the late fifteenth century, form an important part of the designs. Roses, gillyflowers (pinks) and violets, which have religious and scriptural connotations, adorn the opening initials to the psalms and canticles (Figs 135, 136).

If it is a reflection on Scottish culture that the earliest drawings of individual gardens, those at Holyroodhouse and Kirk o' Field, should be made because of an invasion and a highly political murder, it seems entirely appropriate that a third sixteenth century example arises out of a legal case. With the feuing of church property, lands which for centuries had only one owner were split, and disputes arose over the relative rights of the new multiple owners and their tenants (Omond 1887, 3–4). In an area to the south of Dalkeith in Midlothian, joint rights of pasturage, which had been enjoyed by the tenants of the barony of Ballintroddo, were questioned following the feuing of the estate. This had belonged to the order of Hospitallers, based at Torphichen, and was granted to the last head of the order in Scotland, James Sandilands, in 1564 (*RMS* 4, No 1499, 343–4). He split up the estate and feued lands on to, among others, George Dundas, who acquired **Arniston** (Harnestoun) in 1571, and Nicol Elphinstone, who bought **Shank** (Schank). This led to a law case between the new owners to settle their relative rights. To resolve this, a plan of the estate (NRS RHP 82800; Gibson 2007, 4–5) was drawn up in 1586, showing Shank Place (Fig 137). This appears

to have been a tower house with a single storey range attached and a small turret with a conical roof. In front of the buildings is a garden enclosed by a wall or paling and divided into three, with another enclosed area to the west of the buildings. There are conventionalised small bushes or trees in the enclosures, suggesting use as an orchard. A somewhat similar, but smaller, enclosure is shown in front of the smaller, single storey house of Birkenside to the south. Timothy Pont's manuscript maps of this area of Midlothian do not survive, and the much less detailed and smaller scale maps, based on his work and engraved by Henricus Hondius, published in 1630 and 1636, only show Shank as a minor settlement as it also appears on the map published by Blaeu in Amsterdam in 1654. However, John Adair's manuscript map of about 1682 shows Shank in its enclosed garden surrounded by a park with an avenue leading to the turreted mansion. John Reid, the author of the first book specifically intended for gardening in Scotland, was gardener here from 1680 to 1683. On the Roy map of 1747–1755 the policies are laid out in symmetrical avenues reflecting those illustrated in Reid's book (Reid 1988, 53 facing) (Figs 333, 334). The estate then was owned by Sir George Mackenzie of Rosehaugh, often referred to as 'Bloody Mackenzie', the jurist, statesman and notorious persecutor of the covenanters. The garden of the 1580s is not responsive to aerial survey, and maps from the nineteenth century show a very different layout.

Few surviving gardens can be securely dated, and the indication of some form of a garden on the maps of Timothy Pont usually only provides (most welcome) evidence for its existence with few clues to the design. The most prominent feature of most gardens and orchards would be a stone wall or strong fence intended to keep out animals, domesticated and wild, that would raid the garden plants for food. This is the main symbol used for a garden on Pont, and on occasion it may indicate a small park. Pont's maps generally represent settlements with one of a variety of symbols (Cunningham 2006, 49–54). An unusually detailed example is the depiction of **Castle Menzies**, then known as Weem, in the upper valley of the River Tay in Perthshire. The castle is shown as a substantial building standing four storeys high and four bays across with a tower to the east and to the west (Pont 23) (Fig 138).

The mansion is surrounded on west and north by a series of enclosures, shown in plan form, with tree symbols appropriate for deciduous trees within them, probably indicating orchards. On the east side immediately next to the building are a series of five rectilinear enclosures (Brown 2005b, 248). Their depiction resembles features in the garden at Kirk o' Field. Four of the rectangles are of much the same

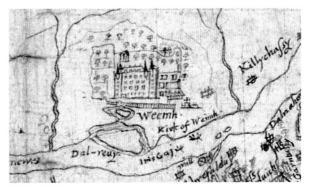

Fig 138 Castle Menzies as it appears on the late sixteenth century manuscript map by Timothy Pont (Pont 23). It is one of the most detailed depictions of a building and garden on the Pont maps. © NLS

Fig 137 A detail of NRS RHP82800 showing Shank Place in Midlothian with its tower house and walled garden in 1586. © NRS

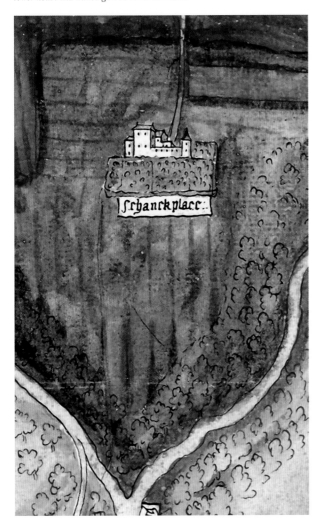

size, with the fifth at least twice as large. They may be parterres with paths between them, but the largest rectangle has some indication of a roof at its east end, a red mark, which may, on analogy with the castle and the building to its north, represent a roof. A single line encloses these features to north and east, while to the south is a fence-like marking, similar to that along the south side of the castle. When viewed from the air in a dry summer when the field to the east of the castle is planted with barley, a cropmark is formed, indicating a quadripartite division of the area (Fig 7). The marks show an almost square enclosure to the east of the castle, divided into four sections, each measuring about 25m each way. The cropmarks appear with different details visible in different years according to the crop and soil moisture deficit, so that the transcription incorporates features from different photographs. These may show garden details that did not exist contemporaneously. The enclosure appears in some photographs as a light mark, indicating a wall footing or a stone or gravel path. There are slight indications of elaboration at the two corners on the east side, possibly marking a small turret or other decorative feature. The two parallel light lines which divide the enclosure, north and south, could mark the sides of a broad walk some 4m across, but could also be the foundations of a building. Its position would correspond with the large rectangular mark on the Pont depiction. At right angles to this feature, running north, are what appear to be the foundations of two buildings, but which may indicate the position of some slighter structure. Two other probable building foundations, running east and west, lie to the north. These markings could well represent successive occupation, rather than suggesting part of a garden design. Closer to the castle the markings are partly overlain by a modern track (Fig 139).

It would seem likely that the four large rectangles represent a four fold division of a walled garden by paths. The size of the possible parterres is comparable with examples at Holyrood on the Gordon of Rothiemay drawing of 1647. On the Pont map other less formal enclosures containing trees, perhaps orchards, are shown

Fig 139 Castle Menzies, the sixteenth century mansion of the Menzies family in Strathtay. It can be related to the depiction on the Pont manuscript map (Pont 23). SC1029162

Fig 140 The panel above the original entrance to Castle Menzies bearing the initials and impaled arms of James Menzies and his wife Barbara Stewart, with the date 1571. SC1237641.

to the north and west. These enclosures, which would fall within the area of later building activity, have not been detected as cropmarks. The garden lay to the east of the castle, with its centre point aligned with the building, and would be overlooked from the chamber on the first floor, a formal reception room used for the entertaining of distinguished guests and by the family, as well as from the upper chamber and bedrooms above and in the north-east jamb. The elaborate corbelled turrets to the north and south at this end of the house, with their conical caphouses, would also provide an elevated position from which the garden could be viewed and the prospect down the valley enjoyed.

A certain amount is known, and more conjectured, about the building of Castle Menzies. Above the original entrance to the house is a panel bearing the initials and impaled arms of James Menzies and his wife, Barbara Stewart, and the lintel is carved with the date 1571 (Fig 140). The family had previously been based at Comrie Castle, but when it was destroyed by fire in 1487, they moved down to Weem on the River Tay and erected a house, which was called Place of Weem. It was scarcely built before a rival family, the Stewarts of Garth, seized and demolished it (MacGibbon and Ross 1887–92 4, 37–8). The building of what is now known as Castle Menzies followed the marriage of James Menzies and Barbara Stewart, the daughter of the Earl of Atholl, and this union marked the reconciliation of the Stewarts and the Menzies. The third floor windows have pediments in the form of semicircles and triangles, one of which bears the initials IM and BS for James Menzies and Barbara Stewart and the date 1577, possibly that of the completion of the house. The creation of the garden to the east of the house may have followed. James Menzies died in 1585 and his wife two years later, when their son was a minor. How long the garden remained in anything like the form it appears on the Pont map is unknown, but it may have survived up until the time of the 1745 rebellion. A high wall to the east of Castle Menzies, probably that of the formal garden, was demolished when the castle was occupied by the troops of the Duke of Cumberland in 1746, because it limited the defensive capabilities of the building. Although the owner of Castle Menzies supported the Hanoverian government, considerable damage was caused to the house and gardens, destroying part of the orchard and a large number of fruit trees (NRS GD 50/128). The picture presented on William Roy's Military Map of Scotland of 1747–55, which must have been prepared only a few years after the destruction caused by the garrison, shows lawns extending up to the mansion, with a formal garden laid out some distance to the east in the position where the gardens appear on the First Edition of the Ordnance Survey map surveyed in 1862 (Brown 2005b, 248).

The portrayal of this considerable mansion in its Highland setting was only one of the images of substantial and architecturally sophisticated buildings, shown on Pont's map along the upper reaches of the River Tay. Balloch Castle and Grandtully, surrounded

by trees and enclosed by an elaborate paling similar to that at Castle Menzies, also appear, but neither is shown in the detail that marks the drawing of Castle Menzies. There is no obvious reason for this; the house and family were not of exceptional importance. It has been suggested that the cartographer might have been entertained there during his work in the region. Where the site appears on the margin of another map centred on Loch Tay (NLS Pont 18), there are three representations of Weem, two of which have been crossed out because the course of the River Tay has been drawn in the wrong place. Each one of them is slightly different, and in none of them is the garden shown clearly. Jeffrey Stone uses this example (Cunningham 2006, 50) to suggest that the prominent pictographic representation of buildings, as opposed to abstract or ideographic images, was as much a function of the social status of the occupiers as of the dimensions of the building, and that 'what Pont was mapping was a "landscape of power"' (Goodare 1999, 251). However, the detail of the garden at Castle Menzies is supported by the physical evidence of the aerial photographs, and while it would be unwise to argue from the absence of the depiction of a garden that no garden was present, it is possible, when enclosed parks and gardens are shown adjacent to a pictograph of a building, to presume that such a feature existed there.

The pictogram on the Pont manuscript maps that is closest to the image of Castle Menzies is that of the castle at **Blair Atholl**, where what appears to be a knot garden lies to the west of a magnificently turreted mansion (Pont 19) (Fig 141). The garden is square and surrounded by a wall, shown as a double line to the north and west, but as a single line to the south

Fig 141 The castle of Blair Atholl as it appears on the late sixteenth century manuscript map by Timothy Pont (Pont 19). What may be a knot garden lies next to the castle. © NLS

Fig 142 Darnaway (Tarnwa) Castle in Moray with its enclosed garden on the late sixteenth century manuscript map by Timothy Pont (Pont 8). © NLS

Fig 143 Aerial view of Ballinbreich Castle on the north coast of Fife with the cropmarks of its enclosed gardens in front of the castle, probably belonging to more than one period, and lying within a broad curving ditch. SC1037626

and directly adjoining the castle on the east. Trees were planted around the garden outside the wall. The significance of the double line, which contrasts with the single line at Castle Menzies, is uncertain. The garden at **Darnaway Castle** in Moray is enclosed in this way, as is the castle park at Stirling (Figs 76, 142). It may imply a substantial stone wall; it might also indicate a wall on which it was possible to walk and look down into the garden. Within the garden are four rectangular features, presumably flower beds, and on the line of the front wall is a building, with two marks perhaps indicating windows and two storeys, and a gap between it and the mansion, where there might be an entrance. This might be a garden building, providing a place for post-dinner refreshment. It is unlikely to be a gatehouse being set, like the garden, away from the usual approach to the castle. Like Castle Menzies, **Blair Castle** appears on several of the Pont manuscripts, four in this case (Pont 19, 20, 23 and 25), looking different in each case, but only on Pont 19 are there clear indications of a formal garden. The gardens at Blair underwent extensive replanning in the eighteenth century and the mansion was extended over part of the area occupied by the sixteenth century garden (Cruft 1984, 287; Dingwall 1992, 153–72).

The less well-known **Ballinbreich Castle** in Fife and its garden or park are also shown on the Pont manuscript maps. The castle stands on the summit of long ridge overlooking the Firth of Tay and its garden appears as a cropmark on aerial photographs (Fig 143). Often known and pronounced as Balmbreich (RCAHMS 1933, 146), the castle was largely rebuilt

Fig 144 Ballinbreich (Bambrich) Castle as it appears on the late sixteenth century manuscript map by Timothy Pont (Gordon 54b). © NLS

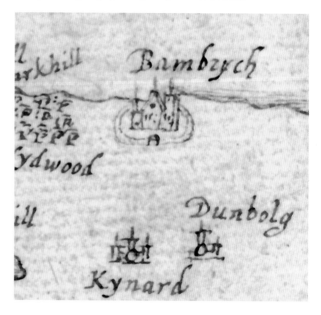

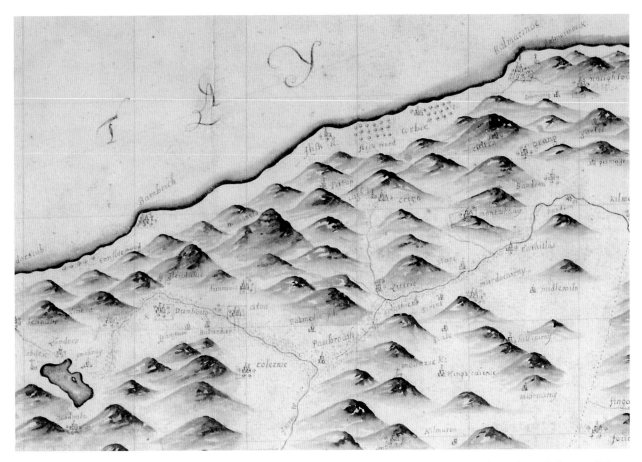

Fig 145 Ballinbreich Castle as it appears on the late seventeenth century manuscript map by John Adair (NLS Adv.MS.70.2.11 (Adair 7)). Other houses with parks and gardens in North Fife on the map are Flisk and Dunbog © NLS

and extended in the later sixteenth century. MacGibbon and Ross comment that the workmanship of the masonry was not surpassed in Scotland in buildings of a similar date (MacGibbon and Ross 1887–92, 4, 416), suggesting that the owner, the Earl of Rothes, considered it to be a major residence, although **Leslie House** near Glenrothes in central Fife, where the later seventeenth century terraced gardens survive, subsequently became their principal seat. Ballinbreich is depicted on the manuscript map of north-west Fife, referred to as Gordon 54b, which was glued on to a map by Robert Gordon, covering the north of Fife; the reason for this is uncertain (Stone 1989, 198) (Fig 144). The castle is enclosed by what seems to be a curving wall or bank with a central gate. No tree symbols appear within it. Aerial photographs show the cropmark of a curving ditch to the south of the castle, which probably lay on the outside of the wall or bank, and from which much of the material that would be required for a bank might have been excavated. This probably reflects the images on Pont's maps, but there are other cropmarks evident, closer to the castle, including an inner curvilinear ditch, which is linked with the surviving bank that surrounds the castle on the north. This could be the feature indicated on the map, where individual

features are not drawn to scale, and would be small for a garden. Rectilinear markings within the outer ditch may well indicate garden features of a later date, perhaps reflecting the overall rectilinear layout depicted on the Roy Survey, although the Adair manuscript map of around 1684 still shows the castle surrounded by trees within a curvilinear enclosure (NLS Adv.MS.70.2.11 (Adair 7)) (Fig 145). Other houses, which appear on the same small surviving sheet, with parks and gardens attached, are Flisk to the east of Ballinbreich and Dunbog to the south. Much of the mapping of the rest of Fife has not survived, and in its absence it is difficult to assign the remains of gardens, such as **Balvaird** or **Balcomie**, whose style suggests a date in the later sixteenth or earlier seventeenth century, to the earlier of the two periods in the absence of other evidence. When the Englishman Fynes Morrison paid his brief visit to Scotland in 1598, he travelled from the ferry at Kinghorn to Falkland to see James VI and noted that 'the gentlemen's dwellings were shadowed with some little Groves, pleasant to the view' (Brown 1978, 86).

However, one example where evidence from excavation suggests a date prior to 1600 is **Aberdour Castle**, which was the property of the Earl of Morton, regent of Scotland for James VI from 1572 to 1578 (Hynd and Ewart 1983). This castle was not established on a new site, but was already old when it came into Morton's possession, with the earliest surviving part, the tower, dating from the fourteenth century. The date

Fig 146 Aerial view of Aberdour Castle, a property in the care of Historic Scotland, showing the restored terrace garden and the late sixteenth century dovecot. DP016777

of James Douglas' birth is unknown and suggestions range from 1516 to 1525. He succeeded to the title of Earl of Morton, and to the lands of Aberdour, through his wife in 1553 (Hewitt 1982, 1–2). Through other family connections he had responsibility for the castle of Tantallon in East Lothian, and was involved with gardens at Loch Leven. Dalkeith was the most prestigious house belonging to his branch of the Douglas family. Mid eighteenth century estate maps and some surviving surface evidence indicate the former presence of a terraced garden adjacent to the sixteenth century circular dovecot. The original form of the site of the garden had been a natural amphitheatre, part of the geological feature known as the raised beach. The designer of the garden had taken this natural shape and cut deep into the subsoil at the internal angle and used the spoil to build up the terraces on the west, formalising it into an L-shaped structure. Excavation revealed the remains of the vertical stone walls supporting the front edges of four descending terraces.

These were set at right angles to each other, running east and west and north and south, ending on the south with the late sixteenth century dovecot (Fig 146). There is evidence for stairways between the terraces, set at the internal angles of the terraces, to allow access between them. Two short fluted stone pilasters found on the site may have been part of the stairway construction (Hynd and Ewart 1983, 105). The area in the angle, bounded to the south-west by the mill lades and what is suggested might be mill ponds, is identified as an orchard on the mid eighteenth century estate map. Analysis of the soils to discover what plants might have grown in the terrace garden proved to be unrewarding because the chemical conditions had produced rapid organic disintegration, but pollen from a water lily was one of the few survivals, raising the question of whether the mill ponds might have had an ornamental function. Alleys, arbours and decorative planting in knots would probably have occupied the terraces, with an ornamental orchard below. Although the finds from the excavation did not come from a stratified context because the terraces were constructed of redeposited material, and consequently do not offer positive dating evidence for the gardens, the pottery sherds retrieved reflect late sixteenth and early

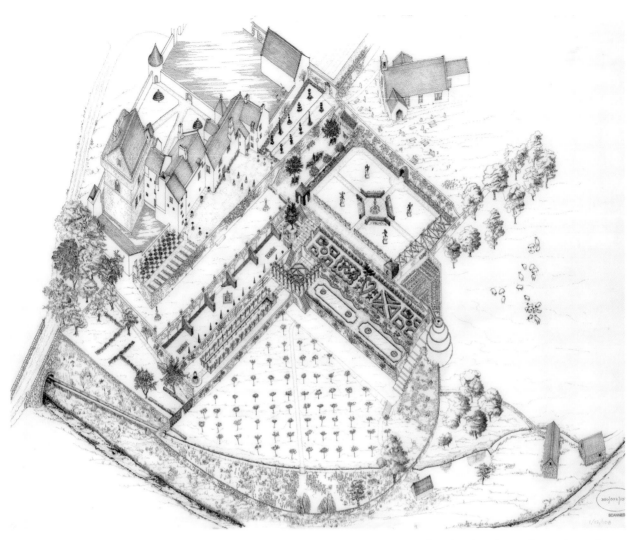

Fig 147 Reconstruction drawing of the gardens at Aberdour Castle in the mid seventeenth century by John Knight and Historic Scotland surveyors showing decorative parterres and paths on the terraces, with an orchard below. 356-002-107 © Historic Scotland

seventeenth century dates, suggesting that the terraces were the result of the activities of Regent Morton and his immediate successors. The terrace garden lay to the south of Aberdour Castle, away from the entrance front, so that the inhabitants could look down on the gardens and across the Forth towards Edinburgh. The south range, a building of the sixteenth century which provided residential accommodation on the first floor, had a staircase leading down to the upper terrace (RCAHMS 1933, 17–21). The garden is bounded on the east by the parish church and burial ground. The area to the north of the church and east of the castle is now occupied by a walled garden, which could be entered from the terrace on the west and on the east from the kirk lane. Both doorways into this garden were elaborately decorated and recorded the initials of the builders; the eastern gate bears the date 1632, contemporary with the extension of the castle to the east by the seventh Earl of Morton (RCAHMS 1933,

18). A reconstruction drawing shows the garden as it may have looked in 1650 (Apted 1985, 20–1) (Fig 147).

James Douglas visited England frequently, initially as a prisoner in the aftermath of the battle of Pinkie, and met Elizabeth's Secretary of State Sir William Cecil, later Lord Burghley, when he was in Scotland in 1560 in support of the Lords of Congregation, the protestant opponents of Mary of Guise. Morton visited England the same year to propose a marriage between Elizabeth and the Earl of Arran. He became a member of Mary's Privy Council and Lord Chancellor in 1563, supporting her marriage with Darnley and serving as carver at the banquet following the wedding ceremony. He was one of the murderers of David Rizzio and subsequently fled to England and Flanders, and, at least according to his own statement, knew of the plot to murder Darnley at Kirk o' Field, although he was not a party to the conspiracy. This knowledge was the immediate cause of his execution in 1581. He was approached about becoming a party to the murder while in the garden of another Douglas property, Whittinghame Tower in East Lothian (Hewitt 1982, 7). He was one of the Scottish commissioners at York in 1568 at the enquiry into the conduct of the Earl of Moray, then regent

Fig 148 An initial M from the second Cantus set of the Wode Partbooks decorated with hearts, the Douglas symbol, which recalled the mission of the earlier James Douglas who set out from Scotland to take Robert Bruce's heart to the Holy Land. University of Edinburgh Library Special Collections, Dk.5.14.80. © Edinburgh University Library

for the infant James VI, and the deposition of Mary Queen of Scots, and was again in London in 1571 in connection with Mary's continuing imprisonment in England. His frequent travels would have allowed him to see recent developments in architecture and garden design in eastern England, as well as being in a position to see and discuss garden designs in Europe (Hewitt 1982, 3–7, 11). He was also a patron of music, commissioning Andro Blakhall, the minister of Musselburgh, to compose for the king a setting of Psalm 43 which was included in the Wode psalter, which begins 'Judge and defend my cause, O Lord', the psalm which was put in the mouth of the infant James VI following the murder of his father, Darnley, and those of his regents, the earls of Moray and Lennox (Ross 1993, 90–2) (Figs 148, 149).

When James Douglas became regent in 1572, he assumed the responsibilities of the monarch for the royal castles and palaces and their gardens; there are no records, however, as there were when the Earl of Arran was regent during the minority of Mary Queen of Scots, of the appropriation of gardeners, trees and plants from the royal domain for his own estates. His methods of raising money from the post of regent are more difficult to trace, but contemporary opinion considered him to have profited considerably during this time (*TA* 13, viii–xix). **Dalkeith**, a Douglas property, was often used by the regent for hunting and fishing. After he was deprived of the regency, he withdrew to **Lochleven**, the property of his cousin William Douglas, where it is recorded 'There he busied

himself in making of walks and alleys, in drawing of garden plots or knots, little minding any State affaires in appearance' (Hume 1644, 342) (Fig 151). Another contemporary historian of Fife origins, Sir James Melville, writes that Morton was at Lochleven 'making the walks of his garden even' (Melville 1929, 233), and John Colville (1825, 165) records that Morton made his residence in the island castle of Lochleven 'devysing the situation of a fayre gardene with allayis, to remove all suspicion of his consavit treason'. It is not known whether these plans were for Lochleven Castle, where, before the partial draining of the loch, the surface area of the island would have been even smaller than it is at present (RCAHMS 1933, 296), or for the adjacent New House of Lochleven on the mainland near Kinross, or for Aberdour Castle or yet another of his properties.

Around this time, a portrait of Morton was painted by Arnold Bronckhorst, an artist of Netherlandish origin (Fig 152). He came to Scotland via England in order to search for gold, a quest for which he had been given a commission by two other painters working in England, Nicholas Hilliard and Cornelius Devosse. In 1581 he was granted the office of 'court painter' for life with a yearly pension of £100, but had already been painting portraits for and of the king for more than a year before this (Thomson 1974, 44–7). His portrait of James Douglas, now in the Scottish National Portrait Gallery, shows the earl standing in an open gallery with classical architectural features and a view of a pale green landscape and an elaborate castle beside the sea, reached across a bridge. The details do not match any of the properties with which Morton is associated, but it may be a fanciful portrayal of Tantallon, where

Fig 149 The infant James VI pictured calling out for vengeance for the murder of his father, Lord Darnley, a detail from Fig 133, the depiction of the murder of Darnley sent to Lord Burghley. MPF1/366 © National Archives

Morton's wife was kept while she was insane, or of Aberdour, or even of Lochleven, where Morton, according to the chroniclers, spent much of his time after he lost the regency, the period when the portrait must have been commissioned; the bridge might be a misunderstanding by the artist of the means of access to the castle. Portraits with houses and gardens forming an element in the background became more common in the earlier seventeenth century, when the sitters wished to emphasise this aspect of their possessions and of their taste. It was relatively unusual in the 1580s to select an architectural or garden theme. A portrait of the young James VI by Arnold Bronckhorst showed the king with a sparrow hawk on his left hand (Fig 150), an early indication of his love of hunting, and the portrait of James' tutor, the poet and scholar of European reputation, George Buchanan, probably by Adrian Vanson, depicts him reading a book. About 1618, James VI's wife, Anne of Denmark, chose to be painted beside the palace and garden building at Oatlands near London which she had commissioned from Inigo Jones. More usually, the choice of dress indicated what elements of his status the sitter wished to be recorded, and the armorial bearings of the family were perhaps the most usual addition in Scottish portraits, with marshal attributes becoming more common for male portraits during the seventeenth century. Anne Erskine, Countess of Rothes, whose husband owned Ballinbreich, was shown about 1626 with her children in a detailed picture of a room within what was presumably one of her own houses. Morton's choice of a castle in a landscape for inclusion in his portrait is an indication of the status he awarded to these aspects of design.

Aberdour, with its wide outlook, is the earliest terrace garden in Scotland for which there is an indication of a probable date. It may belong to the 1570s, although any time is possible from the 1550s, following the death of Morton's mother-in-law, who occupied the castle during her widowhood, to the year of his own death in 1581. This form of garden may be seen as a product of Italian Renaissance thought. Architectural theorists, in particular Leon Battista Alberti, looked to classical precedents, particularly the descriptions of his own villas in the letters of Pliny the Younger. Study of the classics and particularly Latin authors was a major element of the education system in Scotland, and these writers enjoyed an immense prestige. Publication and printing of editions of the texts went on rapidly during the fifteenth and sixteenth centuries, with editions of Pliny's *Letters* first produced in Bologna in 1498, followed by an edition from Aldus Manutius in Venice in 1498, and by numerous others during the following century. His words, in this extensive quotation, seem relevant to the aspirations of various gardens in Scotland during the sixteenth and seventeenth centuries:

Fig 150 Portrait of the young James VI with a hawk by Arnold Bronckhorst.
© Scottish National Portrait Gallery. Licensor Scran

The house for the most part faces south, and in the summer entices the sun from midday, and in winter from a little earlier, into a colonnade which is broad and correspondingly long ... In front of the colonnade is a terrace divided into several sections of different shapes which are separated by hedges of box. From it a raised platform slopes downward, on which there are shapes of animals, facing each other, fashioned from box. On the level below there is acanthus, soft and virtually transparent. There is a walkway round it enclosed by compact bushes cut into various shapes; close by there is a circular drive which encloses box in different shapes, and shrubs kept low by being cut back. The whole area is protected by a wall, which is hidden from view by a tiered hedge of box. Outside the wall there is a meadow: nature has made it as much worth seeing as the garden just described, which was devised by human skill. Beyond it there are fields and many other meadows and plantations... At the side (of the villa) there is a covered gallery for summer use, which is set on an eminence, and which seems not so much to look out on the vineyard as to touch it

Fig 151 Aerial view of Lochleven Castle where the Earl of Morton was supposed to have spent his time after he gave up the regency 'devysing the situation of a fayre gardene with allayis, to remove all suspicion of his consavit treason'. SC800125

... The straight edge of the riding circuit is broken at its end by a semi-circular curve, which changes its appearance. It is encircled and shaded by the thicker shade, but in the inner circuits, of which there are several, it gets the most translucent daylight. In that area roses grow as well. And the cool in the shadows is moderated by shafts of not unwelcome sunlight.

At the far end of this curved sector, with its varied and manifold twists and turns, a return is made to a straight lateral stretch, though there is not just this one, but several separated by box hedges lying between them. At some points they are divided by lawns, and at others by box shrubs fashioned in a thousand shapes. Here and there these form letters which spell out the names now of the owner, and now of the specialist gardener (topiarist). Miniature obelisks rise upward, alternating with fruit trees planted there. Amidst this creative work, most characteristic of city life, you suddenly confront the imitation of an imported country scene.

At the head of the colonnade a dining room juts out. Through its folding doors it surveys the end of the terrace and immediately beyond it the meadow and the expanse of countryside. From the windows on one side it looks out onto the side of the terrace

... and on the other the grove and its foliage, which lie within the exercise ground for horses close by. ... In one place there is a little meadow; in another the box is displayed in groups and cut into a thousand forms; sometimes into letters spelling the name of the master or the signature of the topiarist; whilst here and there arise little obelisks intermixed alternately with apple trees. (Pliny 2006, 114–7)

The owner looked beyond the intensively ordered garden to hills and woods, the haunt of wild animals, allowing the garden to take in the natural world. This concept was adopted in the villas of fifteenth and sixteenth century Italy. To Pliny the views were crucial, facilitated by the placement of terraces and garden buildings, as well as by large windows and open porticoes.

Works by Pliny, Vitruvius and Alberti were found in the libraries of Scotland, and an Edinburgh lawyer, John Marjoribanks, for example, had books by all three on his shelves by the 1550s (Durkan and Ross 1961, 128). Alberti composed his book *De Re Aedificatoria*, in ten parts, on the model of the Roman writer Vitruvius' *De Architectura*, and it was to a considerable extent dependent on it. The work was composed between 1443 and 1452, and it circulated in manuscript – Lorenzo the Magnificent had a copy – before being printed in 1485. Alberti belonged to the circle of scholars around Pius II, who became pope in 1458 and died in 1464. His name before becoming pope was Aeneas Sylvius Piccolomini, and in his early years he had visited Scotland on an ecclesiastical mission. He chronicled his life in his thirteen volume autobiography, *Commentarii*, in which he records his plans for the reconstruction of his native village, Corsignano near Siena. Work began in about 1460 on what was to be an ideal Renaissance city called Pienza after himself. Alberti was not himself a practising architect, and the detailed planning was carried out by Bernardo Rossellini (Woodbridge 1986, 34). The site of Pius II's birthplace became the site of the Palazzo Piccolomini. A garden was constructed attached to the extremely impressive palace. The nature of the terrain on the edge of a steep hill required massive foundations, to ensure that the garden would be on a level with the ground floor portico of the palace; it was overlooked by galleries at first and second floor levels. The garden faces south-west with the wall at the end of the garden pierced to allow views across the Tuscan countryside to Monte Amiato. This allowed the interpenetration of art and nature as advocated by Alberti, although still preserving, with walls to north-west and south-east, the enclosure and privacy of a medieval garden, as was also approved by Alberti (1988, 300). In the foundations under the garden are stables and storerooms. The garden is seen in architectural terms as an extension of the house, both being conceived in terms of harmony and proportion expressed by means of geometry. The planting was also to be symmetrical, with trees and shrubs arranged in lines, circles and semi-circles.

Another medium through which classical and Italian ideas about the design of gardens spread across Europe was an allegorical romance by the Venetian Francesco Colonna *Hypnerotomachia Poliphili*. Translated into English in 1592 as *The Strife of Love in a Dream*, and in 1546 into French as *Le Songe de Poliphile*, the book was mentioned in the previous chapter as providing the first engravings of designs for knot gardens to be printed (Fig 97). Poliphilus dreams of his search for the nymph Polia; his quest begins in a wilderness and continues through classical landscapes to the circular garden of Cythera. The book is particularly remarkable for its woodcut illustrations, which include galleries, porticos, obelisks, statues and fountains, tunnel arbours and peristyles. It also includes four quite complicated designs that could be used for garden compartments or knots (Colonna 1499, not paginated). This combination of romantic, classical and geometric landscape proved a popular ideal from which elements could be borrowed. *Hypnerotomachia* and Alberti's *De Re Aedificatoria* became more widely known following their translation into French in 1546 and 1553 (Woodbridge 1986, 33). Later writings on architecture and design carefully engaged with earlier texts and an awareness of these writings spread throughout Europe, becoming a necessary part of the knowledge of those with claims to culture and status (Howard 2007, 96–100).

The Medici villas in Tuscany, which were much visited by foreign diplomats and tourists, provided an early and admired model (Fig 153). The sites of twenty-four examples from the fifteenth and sixteenth centuries are known in Tuscany, as well those erected by the family in Rome. Their uses were multiple; they were used for the practical purposes of farming, but also as a retreat from the city, as a place to engage in philosophical conversation and as a base for hunting, but also as a means of establishing and presenting the role and status of the Medici family. One of these properties, the Villa Medici in Fiesole, became the focal point for a group of humanists, patronised by Lorenzo the Magnificent. It lies on a hillside and the garden is formed by a series of terraces, revetted with vertical stone walls, with sheltered loggias overlooking the garden and Florence beyond. Unlike the garden at Pienza, which still retained a strong sense of enclosure, with the view across the valley of the Orcia only visible through the deliberate openings in the wall, the view at Fiesole across the Arno valley was unconfined.

The invasions of Italy by the French kings Charles VIII, Louis XII and François I from 1494 in pursuit of French claims to the kingdom of Naples brought the rulers into direct contact with Italian culture and Italian gardens. The armies passed through Florence and Rome and took Naples. Near Naples the garden at Poggio Reale, which has not survived, was much admired, and a Neapolitan engineer returned with the

Fig 152 Portrait of James Douglas, Earl of Morton and Regent of Scotland, by Arnold Bronckhorst. Scottish National Portrait Gallery. Licensor Scran

Fig 153 The Medici Villa dell'Ambrogiana was built for the Grand Duke of Tuscany, Francesco I, in 1587 on a site beside the River Arno and was one of the villas most visited by the Medici court. It was an example of a villa-fortress and, as well as being on the most important river in Tuscany, it was adjacent to the ducal hunting reserve on Monte Albano. The gardens were laid out on a strict geometrical pattern with paths and covered walks around parterres. Museo di Firenze com'era, Florence © 2011 Photo Scala

king to France and worked on the gardens at Amboise, Blois and Gaillon (Woodbridge 1986, 35; Guillaume 1999b, 107–8). Louis XII laid claim to the Duchy of Milan and led another army into Italy in 1499. His successor François I continued to pursue these claims, invading Italy in 1515, and showing a marked interest in importing Italian artists into France. His work at Fontainebleau during the 1530s, with its employment of large areas of water as well as fountains, resulted in the most important garden to survive, in part, from the first half of the sixteenth century (Androuet du Cerceau 1988, 187–9).

Most of the gardens in France during this period, which were influenced by the gardens of Italy, have been changed or built over. As in Scotland, the gardens constructed on terraces and water gardens are, to a degree, an exception to this, and, as in Scotland, royal gardens provide the majority of evidence, at least in the first half of the century (Boudon 1999, 137–8). Changes in taste in garden design and more profound developments of the areas around the palaces and chateaux have meant that much of the evidence for these gardens comes from *Les plus excellents bastiments de France* of 1576 and 1579. This work, dedicated to Catherine de Medici, mother of three successive kings

of France and Mary Queen of Scots' one time mother-in-law, was written by the architect Jacques Androuet du Cerceau. The integral treatment of gardens and architecture, and the lavish illustration of the volumes make both these works brilliant sources of information. In his earlier *Livre d'architecture contenant les plans et desseings de cinquante bastiments tous differens* of 1559 and a second volume concentrating on chimney pieces, dormer windows, doorways, fountains, pavilions and burial monuments in 1561, he presented ideas to readers who wished to build, dividing his designs between those intended for princes and great lords and those intended for people of medium and small estates.

The use of water and the construction of gardens on terraces have been particularly distinguished as influences from Italy, albeit selectively employed by French designers (Guillaume 1999a, 113). From the 1550s interest in the development of garden designs can be seen to increase among French nobles with close connections to the court (Boudon 1999, 140). These included Mary Queen of Scots' uncle, Charles de Guise, Cardinal of Lorraine, who acquired the estate at Dampierre to the south-west of Paris in 1552 and had gardens constructed there which included a canal and extensive water gardens, reminiscent of a later design published by du Cerceau (Boudon 1999, 143–4). In the same year he acquired the chateau of Meudon which now lies in the south-west suburbs of Paris, from a mistress of François I. The cardinal had spent much of the late 1540s in Rome, receiving his cardinal's hat and attending the conclave for the election of Pope Julius III, and had the opportunity to view the major garden designs of Rome, central and northern Italy. He was the first patron in France to set out to create a garden on a slope, and exploit the distant views. The chateau at Meudon overlooked the valley of the Seine, and the plan was to build a grotto linked to the house by two terraces, although this was not completed in his lifetime. The architect was the Italian Primaticcio, who worked for François I and his successors at Fontainebleau. Meudon was celebrated by the poet Ronsard, who had known Mary at the court of Henri II. The number of chateaux with elaborate gardens increased during the second half of the sixteenth century and again in the earlier seventeenth century. Water gardens were more popular than terraced gardens in France; a reason suggested for this was the greater expense of shifting earth, compared with digging canals (Boudon 1999, 151). Even given all the chances of survival, it would seem that terraced gardens were the more popular form in Scotland, possibly to a greater extent than in England.

Morton's ambitions for his garden at Aberdour, and his personal involvement in garden design, can be compared, on a smaller scale, to that of his contemporary, the English statesman Lord Burghley, whose gardens at Theobalds and London are the best recorded of any in Britain at this period. Gardening may be considered as a proper and prestigious activity for powerful, cultured men with a dominant role in the governments of their countries. Good government and good gardening were often treated metaphorically, as in Shakespeare's *Richard II*, where the proper cultivation of a garden and the maintenance of good order in the realm were compared. William Cecil, Lord Burghley, had a house on the north side of the Strand in London, and his gardens, set away from the street, included in the mid 1560s a quadripartite central garden, a spiral mount enclosed in a square by a wall with a tree at each corner and a rectangular orchard with tennis courts to one side. Cecil worked on the plan himself (it is annotated in his handwriting), and it is particularly interesting that he considered the house and garden together. He purchased a moated manor house at Theobalds in Hertfordshire in 1564, which he decided needed enlargement to make it suitable for visits by Queen Elizabeth.

In his youth William Cecil had served in the household of the Duke of Somerset, the Lord Protector for Edward VI of England, alongside Dr William Turner, known as 'the father of English botany', and he displayed in his letters a lifelong interest in plants and gardens. A sketch of the gardens at Theobalds showing the great garden divided into nine square compartments, with provision for a fountain at the centre, the moat converted into a canal crossed by a bridge, was made by Burghley himself. His biographer noted that his 'greatest greatness and only happiness' was 'riding in his garden walks, upon his little muile' and Burghley had himself painted riding on the mule (Henderson 2005, 24–6; 83–7). Descriptions of the garden come

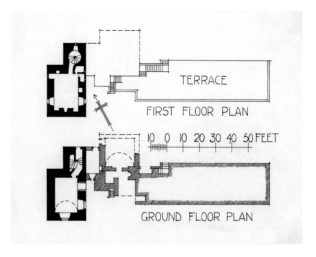

Fig 154 Plan of Whittinghame Tower in East Lothian with its garden terrace, from the Inventory of East Lothian *of 1924 (RCAHMS 1924, 132). The garden at Whittinghame was one of the sites where the murder of Lord Darnley was plotted. ELD 106/1*

from the 1590s and 1600s when foreign travellers were recording in their diaries the most remarkable sights of the country.

Another garden associated with Regent Morton was at **Whittinghame Tower** in East Lothian, a building of late fifteenth or early sixteenth century date. It was there he was approached by the Earl of Bothwell and Maitland of Lethington about becoming a party to the murder of Darnley in 1566 (Bannatyne 1836, 317–18). A north-east facing garden terrace, approached by two sets of stairs, lay between the tower house and the ravine through which the Whittinghame Water flows, and was visible there until the early twentieth century (RCAHMS 1924, 132–3) (Fig 154). It overlooked a level area and a still surviving ancient yew tree, and may have dated from the later sixteenth century or the first half of the seventeenth century when there was another earl of Morton with a strong interest in gardening. A supporter of Regent Morton until his fall was Mark Kerr, who had been Abbot of Newbattle Abbey before the Reformation and retained much of its property. His house at Monktonhall near Edinburgh had a ceiling painted in 1581 with elaborate mythological scenes and emblems (Fig 155).

Among those responsible for Morton's fall was Colin Campbell, sixth earl of Argyll, the head of the conspiracy which forced Morton to resign his position as regent in 1578. It was probably this chief of the Campbells who was responsible for the construction of the terraced gardens at **Castle Campbell** in Clackmannanshire, but they may have been the work of his successor who succeeded to the title as a child of eight in 1583 (Fig 124). Castle Campbell was part of the lands inherited by the first earl of Argyll through his marriage to an heiress of John, Lord of Lorn, in about 1470. He obtained an Act of Parliament to change 'the name of the castelle and place quhilk wes callit the

Fig 155 *Detail of a painted ceiling of 1581 formerly at Prestongrange in East Lothian, which belonged to Mark Kerr, Abbot of Newbattle Abbey before the Reformation, and later a supporter of Regent Morton. It shows gardening tools and the image is derived from an engraving by the Hans Vredeman de Vries* Grottesco in diversche manieren *published in Antwerp in the later 1560s. It is now in Merchiston Tower in Edinburgh. SC1051521*

Gloume' (*RPS* 1490/2/28) to Castle Campbell, setting out his family's claim to this strategic site in central Scotland, close to the royal centres of Stirling and Edinburgh. The castle is spectacularly positioned on the edge of the Ochils above Dollar, with a panoramic view over the valley of the Forth. The first earl erected a tower there, but, perhaps at the beginning of the sixteenth century, a residential range with hall and chamber was built to the south across the width of the promontory. This has been likened to the King's Old Building in Stirling Castle, which was completed in 1496 (Dunbar 1984, 19; Gifford and Walker 2002, 317). A passage at the west end of the range linked the courtyard and the garden. It consists of two descending terraces with revetting walls linked by a stair. If the terraced garden were to be dated to about 1500 (Gifford and Walker 2002, 319) it would be unprecedented in Europe outside Italy. It more probably belongs to a period in the latter part of the sixteenth century. It may be noted that the windows on the first floor in the south range which overlook the garden were enlarged, allowing a better view over the gardens and across the valley of the Forth. Three of the openings have been taken down to floor level, and the central one may have served as a door with a stair, possibly of timber, leading down to the garden. Mary Queen of Scots was entertained here in January 1563 when she attended the wedding of the sister of the sixth Earl of Argyll. The festivities included banquets and masques, including one where the guests dressed as shepherds. James VI was also a guest at Castle Campbell, when, in August 1580, an order was issued for the repair of the royal castle at Doune, so that it could be used as a pleasant summer residence for the king (*MW*, 1, 307). In an inventory of 1595 there is a reference to the 'new work' at Castle Campbell (Campbell 1913, 303), which may be the building in the east range entered from the loggia on the courtyard side, adjacent to the south range. The building of this 'sophisticated piece of design' (Cruden 1999, 11) seems to have led to some changes in the layout of the hall and chamber, and it may be contemporary with the changes to the fenestration, which might be linked to the construction of the garden in its present form. Unfortunately no details of the design of the garden survive, but it would presumably have been laid out in knots, and excavation might reveal something of their form, since the garden does not seem to have been disturbed since the burning of the castle in 1654. In 1663 the Earl of Argyll bought the town house of the Earl of Stirling, near the castle in Stirling, which became known as Argyll's Lodging, and Castle Campbell ceased to be a residence of the Campbell family (Cruden 1999, 29).

Another magnate who petitioned for his house to be renamed, to accord, on this occasion, with his title rather than his family name of Gordon, was George, fourth Earl of Huntly. In 1544 he sought confirmation of a charter granted by James IV to his father in 1506,

Fig 156 Huntly Castle: the medieval motte to the left of the circular tower probably served as a mount within the later gardens which could also be viewed from the large upper windows. The inscriptions above and below the windows commemorate the first Marquess of Huntly and his wife. DP008972

changing the name of his castle from Strathbogie to Castle of Huntlie, when it became his principal residence (*RMS* II, No 2909, 618; Simpson 1960, 7). George Gordon became chancellor of Scotland during the minority of Mary Queen of Scots, and accompanied her mother, Mary of Guise, on her visit to France in 1551, providing him with plentiful opportunities to see chateaux and gardens at the highest level. It is suggested that his reconstruction of his 'palace' at **Huntly Castle** was connected with the visit by Mary of Guise in 1556 (McKean 2001, 107–10). Its major feature was a large round tower on the south-west with a viewing platform at the top which would allow a wide panorama over the gardens and park. His grandson, similarly George, the sixth Earl and first Marquis of Huntly, also made major contributions to the palace, erecting a first floor loggia and adding a row of oriel windows on the south front and one to the round tower to allow the viewing of the garden and park in the years following his return from exile in France in 1597 (Fig 156). These magnificent additions to the building were an affirmation of the owner's status and presence in the country (Brown 2011, 63). The only feature surviving which relates to the garden of this period is the truncated twelfth century motte on the west side of the present castle,

which probably served as a mount from which the garden could also be viewed. Timothy Pont's manuscript map of this area of Aberdeenshire does not survive, although it appears on Gordon 26 (NLS Adv.MS.70.2.10 (Gordon 26)), but the maps of the region around the Huntly family's other major house in the north, **Bog of**

Fig 157 Bog of Gight (Gordon Castle) with its enclosed park planted with what may be evergreen trees as it is depicted on the late sixteenth century manuscript map by Timothy Pont (Gordon 23). © NLS

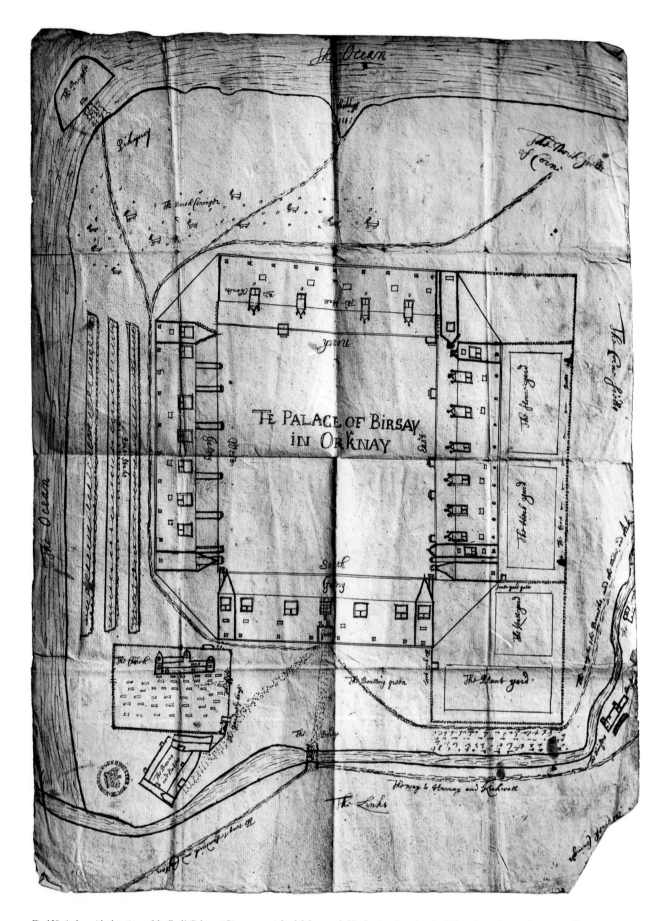

Fig 158 A plan with elevations of the Earl's Palace at Birsay on mainland Orkney probably showing the palace in the late sixteenth or early seventeenth century. The herb garden and the flower garden are in the position most sheltered from the effects of the wind. RHP35836. SC1038662

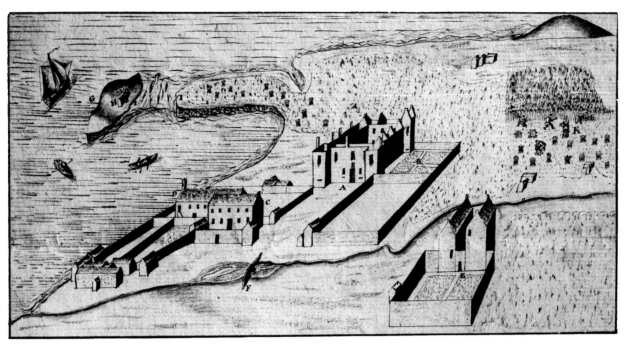

Fig 159 A plan of the Earl's Palace at Birsay on mainland Orkney probably showing the palace in the late seventeenth century after the roofs had fallen in. From a drawing in Edinburgh University Library. SC1038661

Gight, later **Gordon Castle**, near Fochabers, show the towered structure surrounded by a large enclosure or park occupied by trees (Pont 9 and Gordon 23). This is similar to the depiction of the area around Huntly Castle on the mid seventeenth century map by Robert Gordon, but gives no indication of the form of the garden (Gordon 26) (Fig 157).

The houses and associated gardens of important nobles, landowners and ministers of the Crown were not restricted to mainland Scotland or even to islands with a benign climate. Robert Stewart was an illegitimate son of James V and half-brother to Mary Queen of Scots (Manson 1983, 209). He was an enemy of Regent Morton and following Morton's execution in 1581 he was created Earl of Orkney. Even before that date he had begun to build himself a large palace near the shore of **Birsay** Bay in the north of mainland Orkney (Fig 160). The window above the entrance gateway on the south is dated 1574; the palace was completed by his son, Patrick, who succeeded his father in 1592 (RCAHMS 1946, 9). The building was constructed on four sides of a rectangular court, two storeys high with cellars below, and was described in 1633 as 'a sumptuous and stately dwelling' (Monteith 1845, 4). The ceilings of the hall and chamber were decorated with paintings, mostly depicting scenes from scripture. The seventeenth century plan of the building preserved in the National Records of Scotland (NRS RHP 35836) shows a building with rows of tall chimney stacks, reminiscent of those at Pinkie House near Edinburgh, and three long peat stacks on the western seaward side, running the length of the palace. On the eastern side

are shown the Herb Yard and the Flower Yard, with the archery butts to their east, sheltered by the building from the westerly winds. The kale yard and the 'Plante' Yard lay to their south, with a bowling green beside the entrance gate. With the exception of the bowling green, these were all walled and had a central rectangular area surrounded by a path. Beyond the palace to the north was a coney garth or rabbit warren (Fig 158). A later view, taken after the palace had lost its roof, and perhaps dating to the eighteenth century, shows the garden to the east of the palace divided into four compartments by paths (Fig 159). While walls provide much in the way of protection from the wind (McKean 2003, 142), it is likely that low-growing species would thrive best in this environment and the effects of salt spray would also have to be considered. What this plan does indicate is that, even in a relatively harsh environment, gardens for both food and recreation were considered obvious and necessary parts of the house of a great noble.

Information on gardens at the palace at Kirkwall is lacking, but it would have enjoyed a more favourable climate, and the site is, at the present day, one of the small number of locations on the islands to support sizeable trees. The garden there had belonged to the palace of the bishops of Orkney before it was taken over by the Stewart earls. The most recent bishops had been Robert Reid, whose connections with Pluscarden and Kinloss and gardens there have been discussed in an earlier chapter, and Adam Bothwell who succeeded Reid in 1559, and like Reid had Europe-wide connections. Bothwell played a major part in the political affairs of Mary Queen of Scots' reign, and was the bishop who married Mary and the Earl of Bothwell. The catalogue of his library has survived and demonstrates the breadth of his intellectual interests.

Fig 160 Aerial view of the Earl's Palace at Birsay which dates from the 1570s. The site of the herb garden and flower garden was on the east side of the building now occupied by the roadway edged with posts and a field. SC1038663

Fig 161 Aerial view of Muness Castle on the island of Unst, the most northerly of the Shetlands, and the surviving earthworks of its garden. It was enclosed by a broad bank and descended by at least three terraces to the former freshwater loch. What may be a garden mount, possibly with a small building on its summit, lies outside the bank to the south-east. The layout is confused by later structures connected with farming. SC1237402

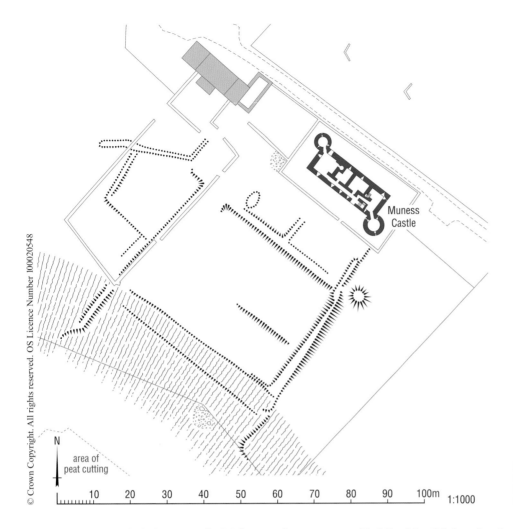

N

area of
peat cutting

| 10 | 20 | 30 | 40 | 50 | 60 | 70 | 80 | 90 | 100m | 1:1000 |

Fig 162 Plan of Muness Castle and its garden showing the relationship between the castle and the design of the garden. GV004975

His collection included Crescentius' *Liber ruralium commodorum*, written in Latin and dating from the end of the thirteenth century, which concerned itself with the management of a country estate, and included a section on pleasure gardens, as well as other volumes on agriculture. This book's influence during the later Middle Ages and Renaissance was considerable (Calkins 1986, 157–73). Books on the medicinal uses of plants, as well as those with a more descriptive botanical approach, written by contemporary writers as well as classical sources, formed part of Bothwell's collection (Shaw 1983, 158, 162).

The creation of gardens extended to Shetland, and even to the north isles of Shetland. **Muness Castle** is situated on a low ridge, aligned north-east and south-west, on a promontory on the eastern side of the island of Unst, overlooking a small harbour at a distance of about half a mile (Fig 161). It was begun on a new site by Laurence Bruce of Cultmalindie in Perthshire, who was the half-brother of Robert Stewart, Earl of Orkney, the builder of the palace at Birsay. The castle is characterised by WD Simpson as 'a most finished and scholarly piece of architecture' (Simpson 1959, 1). It is thought to be the work of the same architect, probably Andrew Crawford, who was responsible for

Earl Patrick of Orkney's palace at Kirkwall, his castle at Scalloway and the remodelling of Noltland Castle on Westray, Orkney. Laurence Bruce came to the Northern Isles in the train of his half-brother, probably in 1569; Robert granted him the offices of Foud or Sheriff in 1573 and Admiral-depute of Shetland in 1577, and Laurence gained a reputation for oppression in Shetland through exploitation of his position (Anderson 1982, 1678). Disputes with Robert's son, Patrick, may have contributed to his decision to build himself a fortified residence at Muness. While the Z-plan tower house, with its opposed cylindrical towers and corbelled turrets on the other corners was designed for defence, providing flanking fire on all four sides, it is also a very decorative structure with elaborately carved corbels and shot holes in a variety of forms. Above the entrance, which is on the south, was a horizontal panel within a moulded border with the following inscription:

LIST ZE TO KNAW YIS BULDING QUHQ
BEGAN LAURENCE THE BRUCE HE WAS
THAT WORTHY MAN QUHA ERNESTLY HIS
AIRIS AND OFSPRING PRAYIS TO HELP AND
NOT HURT THIS VARK ALUAYIS THE YEAR
OF GOD 1598

Fig 163 The terraced garden at Busta House on mainland Shetland seen from the gate leading out towards the Busta Voe. M. Brown

A scale and platt stair, a marker for architecturally ambitious buildings at this date, led up to the first floor (Glendinning *et al*. 1996, 41). This was occupied by a hall with a chamber at one end and a study in the circular tower. The bedrooms above could only be reached through the chamber, providing a measure of privacy and security for Bruce and his family (RCAHMS 1946, 129–31). Two windows in the hall and one in the chamber provide views to the south-west.

The building of a lairdly residence was accompanied by the construction of an appropriate garden in the most up to date style. A terraced garden was laid out to the south-west on the axis of the castle, extending down to what was formerly a freshwater loch. A flat area close to the tower on the south occupies a similar position to the bowling green on the plan of the palace at Birsay. It is bounded on the north-east by a low bank, possibly the remains of a path, with a sunken area beyond. The whole area has been much affected by the building of later walls associated with agriculture, which are now ruinous. However, the stone and turf banks which enclosed the garden to the south-east and three terraces extending from the castle for about 50m survive; the lowest of these may have served as a garden wall. The original width of the upper terrace may have been 50m and the terrace below may have been 75m across but later agricultural activities make certainty difficult (Fig 162).

The terraces stand about 0.6m and 0.4m high, with a slight depression in the upper terrace in line with the possible path, which might indicate the site of steps or a ramp leading down to the lower terrace. Below the second terrace the ground falls more steeply to a low wall or possibly a third low terrace, bounding the garden on the south-west. The bank on the north-west side of the garden is much obscured by later drystone walls and it is difficult to discern its original form. The bank on the south-east stands about 0.75m high and may have been sufficiently broad to support a path from which the garden could be viewed. Just outside this bank is a flat-topped, turf-covered mound made up of earth and small shattered stones, standing up to 1.6m high on the south-west. MacGibbon and Ross (1887–92, 2, 258) identify the grass-covered ruins of a square tower in about this position. The present remains do not suggest such a structure, but there may have been a feature here providing a view over the garden, with some form of small building providing shelter and a place where the owner might refresh himself with wines and sweets at the conclusion of dinner (Quest-Ritson 2003, 21). The best preserved and best dated of these structures is that in the garden of Edzell Castle, where the banqueting house is built on a corner of the garden walls of 1604 (Fig 184) (Simpson 1952, 12).

The garden is now covered in turf and grazed by sheep. Even enclosed by higher banks and walls than now survive, it is difficult to conceive of a more improbable site for a garden than this one, and difficult to imagine anything growing successfully in this exposed position more than a short distance away from the shelter of a wall or bank especially at a time when the climate may have been colder than at present. Its creation is evidence for the importance attached to a garden, particularly one laid out on a formal pattern, as part of the culture of the well-connected gentry at the turn of the sixteenth and seventeenth centuries. It can never have been productive and can only have been a place for pleasant resort for a small part of the year. The laying out of a garden, like the building of a well ordered and decorative tower house, was a claim to status and the possession of refined manners and taste across Scotland.

The garden of **Busta House** near Brae in Shetland is constructed in a similar style and may also belong to this period, but may date to later in the seventeenth century or even the early eighteenth century, like parts of the mansion. Unlike Muness it occupies a sheltered position, which has allowed trees to survive. It faces east and overlooks the stretch of water known as Busta Voe. Until additions were made to form a hotel in the 1980s, the house was thought to date, for the most part, to 1714, the date above the principal entrance. It does seem to incorporate an earlier house, possibly built by the Giffords, who acquired the property in the late sixteenth century, and were, like Laurence Bruce, incomers to Shetland. The first Gifford was the Reader in North Maven in 1567, a Protestant divine of a lower status than a minister (Tudor 1883, 412). The plan of the garden best emerges from the First Edition of the Ordnance Survey 6-inch map, surveyed in 1887–8, which shows a rectangular garden, enclosed by stone walls up to 3m in height (Figs 163, 164). To the south an area delineated by scarped slopes served, during the nineteenth and earlier twentieth centuries, as a kitchen garden. The house stands on a terrace above the walled area of the garden, which is divided by a central path leading down to the harbour, and laterally by two other lower terraces. What may be interpreted as a garden mount stands at its south-east corner (Henderson 2005, 169). This circular mound, which has the name Olwell Knowe and may be partly natural in origin, would provide a view over the garden and over Busta Voe. There is no direct dating for the garden. A visitor to Shetland in 1818, Samuel Hibbert, who had a particular interest in geology, commented that the garden was laid out 'in regular parterres, that shews much of the formal taste of the last century' (Hibbert 1931, 207). While a date similar to that at which the house had been rebuilt would be the most obvious one for the design of a contemporary garden, this is not conclusive (Fig 165).

In the absence of information on the maps of Timothy Pont, the dating of gardens tends to be aligned with the date of the building with which it is associated, if the design of the garden is congruent. The absence of maps for the area around Edinburgh, the Lothians

Fig 164 Busta House as it was depicted on the First Edition of the Ordnance Survey 6-inch map of Shetland surveyed in 1877–8.

Fig 165 Vertical aerial view of Busta House and its terraced gardens surrounded by high stone walls. PGA_HU3466_2008-05-08 © NextPerspectives

and much of Fife, some of the most populous areas of Scotland, has reduced the amount of information available about gardens of the later sixteenth century. Where there are surviving remains of garden features, as at **Duntarvie Castle** near Kirkliston in West Lothian, the principle of associating the garden with the building and its patron applies (Fig 166). Duntarvie is dated to the late sixteenth century and seems to have been built on a new site; its symmetrical layout and its central straight stair anticipate developments in the next century (Glendinning *et al* 1996, 46). The building is rectangular, four storeys in height, with square towers of five storeys attached to its northern angles. Within these, circular stair turrets were corbelled out and rose above the main roof to give access to the balustraded lookouts formed on the flat roofs of the towers (RCAHMS 1929, 186–7). The entrance lies in the centre of the south front, and the ground floor is vaulted and lit by small windows, with the kitchen at the east end having, unusually for the period, a separate scullery and back door, leading out to the north side of the house. The principal public

Fig 166 Aerial view of Duntarvie Castle showing the earthworks of the garden and the fish ponds. The foundations of later buildings, possibly belonging to the use of the site as a farm, are visible in front of the fish ponds. SC1110462

rooms are on the first floor on each side of the stair, with four large windows overlooking the ground to the south of the mansion. The balustraded area on the tops of the towers would serve as the equivalent of the mounts in other contemporary gardens, allowing a bird's eye view, and providing a private space for the concluding course of a meal. The house may have been built for James Durham of Duntarvie, who was described in 1588, in a charter under the great seal (*RMS* 5, 1578, 538–9), as the king's familiar servant and banker (*argentarius*). The garden is mentioned by MacGibbon and Ross (1887–92, 2, 518):

> On all sides there are remains of carefully arranged pleasure-gardens, with fine trees and shady walks, but they are now entirely abandoned, and the house, having passed through the stage of occupation by farm servants, is fast falling into decay.

The trees which survive are a mixture of oak, ash, sycamore and fir.

It is improbable that all the features that appear on the plan and the aerial photograph belong to the late sixteenth or early seventeenth century (Fig 167). A drawing of the house in 1835 by Alexander Archer shows it surrounded by mature trees and a curving drive in the taste of the period to which the artist belonged. An aerial photograph, taken in 1990, shows the full extent of the garden, in part in cropmark form, before a road was put through it, and before clearance from the area around the castle was dumped across the eastern part of the enclosure. The garden is divided into two roughly equal parts. The more westerly has the mansion house near its centre with a series of low banks and scarps defining enclosed areas around the house, which would correspond to different courts and gardens. The pleasure garden would lie to the south of the house. Two narrow banks, some 2m apart, which survive for a length of about 90m, lie at a distance of about 75m from the mansion parallel to its long axis, just inside the present fence which encloses the property. Another similar set of banks lies about 3m to their north. There is a gap in the line of the inner bank, which would allow access to the ground between the two features. The more easterly section of these banks forms a narrow enclosure whose purpose is uncertain. The banks are high enough and broad enough to provide a raised walk, but the area enclosed, some 50m in length, is only between 1m and 2m in width. It does not seem to have held water, and it may be that the banks were built for the planting and protection of saplings along the edge of the garden, a fashion favoured in both France and Italy (Guillaume 1999b, 105). The area to the south of the house is divided into three sections by low scarps; the largest of these is adjacent to the approach from the south-east

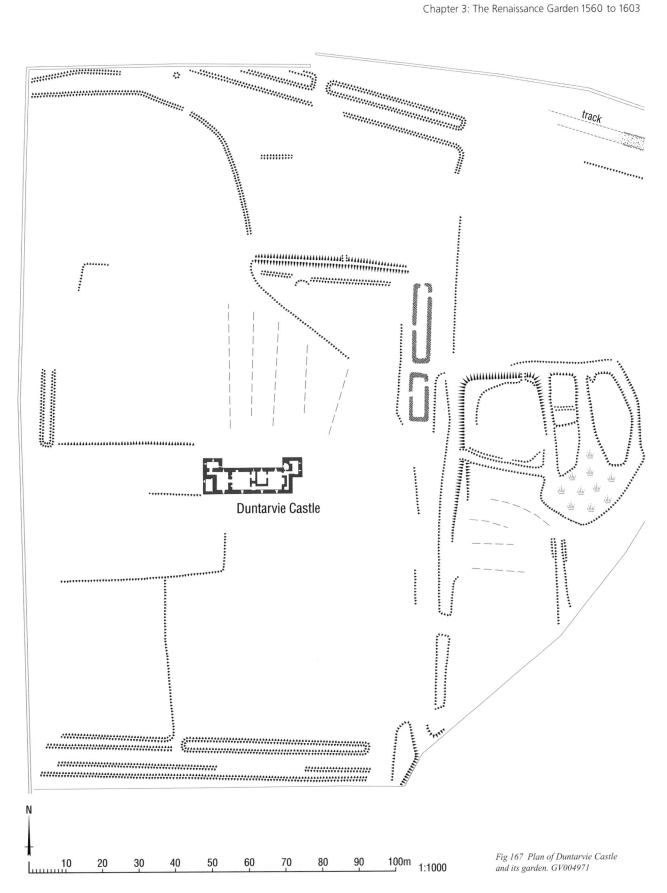

Fig 167 *Plan of Duntarvie Castle and its garden. GV004971*

from the direction of Edinburgh; the other two divisions would be more private.

The ground to the north of the mansion has the remains of further double banks, one on the same alignment as the house at a distance of about 45m and others on a slightly different alignment, close to the northern boundary, but very similar in form to those on the south with the same type of gap as though for

Fig 168 Duntarvie as it appears on the Military Survey of 1747–1755 showing the garden divided into four sections to the west of the house. © British Library. Licensor Scran

an entrance. A short length of a similar double bank can be traced to the west, again close to the modern boundary, suggesting that these banks marked the earlier division between the policies and the farming landscape. A curving bank indicates another enclosure. This northern area is more likely to be used for the more practical needs of the household, perhaps barns, stores and stables, poultry yards, vegetable gardens and orchards. The Military Survey of 1747 to 1755 shows the garden around the house divided into four slightly unequal areas, which may represent the slight surviving earthworks, and surrounded by a rectilinear arrangement of trees (Fig 168). It certainly gives a more symmetrical picture than the survey of the surface features.

There is a marked division between the east and west sections of the garden, which lies on the same alignment as the road which approaches Duntarvie from the south. Two later rectangular structures, which probably belong to the use of the site as a farm in the eighteenth and nineteenth centuries, are found adjacent to this boundary. The more easterly part of the garden has at its centre an arrangement of three raised islands, one roughly square and two rectangular, surrounded by channels which would have been filled with water. The area to the south of this is still waterlogged. There is some variation in the surface features of the islands, which probably relates to their functions. Such islands, really enclosures surrounded by water, might have multiple uses: a haven encouraging the breeding of waterfowl, fishing, growing plants on a protected site, a little banqueting house or a place for philosophical retirement (Henderson 2005, 128–37). The channels, however small, could be used for boating (Henderson

2005, 129). Freshwater fish from fish ponds were considered a luxury food (Currie 1990, 24).

This interest in water gardens derived in part from medieval fish ponds and in part from French and Italian theory and models. One of the most remarkable examples of the use of water in a garden is at **Craigmillar Castle**, which lies about 3 miles south of Edinburgh (Fig 169). Its owners, the Preston family, began the building of the castle in the later fourteenth or early fifteenth century with a large tower to which other surviving ranges were added in the fifteenth and sixteenth centuries (RCAHMS 1929, 120–6). One interesting feature of the merlons of the enclosing defensive wall on the east is the placing there of the initials SP for Simon Preston (RCAHMS 1929, 124), while GP, probably for George Preston, appears on the north curtain wall (Simpson 1954, 9). There is extensive use of coats of arms and the rebus (a press and a tun) of the Preston family (MacGibbon and Ross 1887–92, 1, 195). The most notable fifteenth century lord was Sir William Preston, the second laird of Craigmillar, who obtained the relic of the arm bone of St Giles and presented it to the church in Edinburgh. The castle, when in the ownership of his grandson Simon, was employed for the confinement of the younger brother of James III, the Earl of Mar, in 1479 when he was suspected of threatening the king's position. This Simon may have been responsible for some of the outer walls surrounding the castle; the gate to the west garden at Craigmillar now has the Preston coat of arms and the Preston rebus above it accompanied by the date 15(1)0 (Pringle 1990, 7). Craigmillar is referred to in 1520 as a castle and manor with dovecote, gardens, orchards and fish ponds (*ER* 14, 629), and it was regarded as a suitable residence for James V during his childhood, at times when Edinburgh was judged to be unhealthy (*TA* 5, 130, 148).

Simon, George and William were the most common Christian names used in the family. Another Simon Preston was provost of Edinburgh in 1538–43 and 1544–5. Following the capture of the castle by the English during the invasion of 1544, he was taken prisoner and had to walk to London before being released (Pringle 1990, 9). There was considerable reconstruction work at Craigmillar following his return to Scotland. Simon Preston was present in Paris at the marriage of Mary Queen of Scots to the Dauphin in 1558. He was much involved in affairs of state during her personal reign, and she nominated him for the post of provost of Edinburgh, which he held between 1565 and 1568. Mary stayed at Craigmillar Castle on several occasions, the most significant of which was in 1566, when she came there to convalesce following a serious illness. While she was resident, certain of the nobles including the earls of Argyll, Huntly and Bothwell, made an agreement for the assassination of Lord Darnley, subsequently known as the Craigmillar Bond, and it was there that Mary suggested that Darnley, who had also

Fig 169 Aerial view of Craigmillar Castle with its gardens from the north-west showing the site of the former orchard and its fish pond to the right of the photograph. SC1237403

been ill, should stay following his return to Edinburgh early in 1567. He chose rather to lodge at Kirk o' Field, where he was murdered. It was to Simon Preston's town house in Edinburgh, on the site of the present City Chambers, that Mary was brought following the defeat at Carberry Hill, before her imprisonment in the island castle of Lochleven.

Again in 1589 the next laird, David Preston, was entertaining James VI at Craigmillar, when his scheme to travel to Norway in person to marry Anne of Denmark was formed. James did travel within Scotland, staying with members of the nobility and gentry, but there is no information about his appreciation of their gardens. One garden he is known to have visited in Denmark was that belonging to Tycho Brahe, Uraniborg, the castle of the heavens, on the island of Hven in the straits between what are now Denmark and Sweden. His visit took place in 1590, when he was staying at the Danish court following his marriage. There was a banquet with musicians, entertainers and plenty of wine; the company spoke in Latin. James' interest was in Brahe's scholarship, which was particularly concerned with astronomy; they discussed the Copernican system and James left a Latin epigraph on the door (Stewart 2003, 115–16); Tycho Brahe's post was that of Royal Astrologer, providing prognostications to the court.

The house was surrounded by a garden, which in its use of geometry epitomised the garden of the scholar. It was square, divided into four, with a circle at its centre in which the house stood. In its later form, probably the one which James saw, four exedra were added, each enclosing a small circular pavilion. The numbers expressed the harmony of the world. James was accompanied by a number of Scots nobles, some of whom visited Uraniborg again before their return to Scotland at the beginning of May that year (Parrott 2010, 66–77). A retinue of some three hundred accompanied James to Norway, but this decreased to about fifty, when he travelled to Denmark; firsthand experience of an important philosophical garden may have influenced gardens in Scotland. David Lindsay's garden at Edzell of 1604 shows evidence, through its surviving sculpture, of an elaborate intellectual framework underlying its design.

Craigmillar was perhaps the foremost of major houses or castles around Edinburgh (Dalkeith was another), where the owners and their guests could participate in the political life of the capital while enjoying the pleasures of the surrounding countryside and living in a healthier location. The appurtenances of the castle in 1520 included dovecots, gardens, orchards and fish ponds (ER 14, 629) and these may have been conventional attributes listed in the grant, but the quality of the buildings of the castle and its choice for entertaining royal guests in peacetime would suggest that it was provided with a garden from at least the early

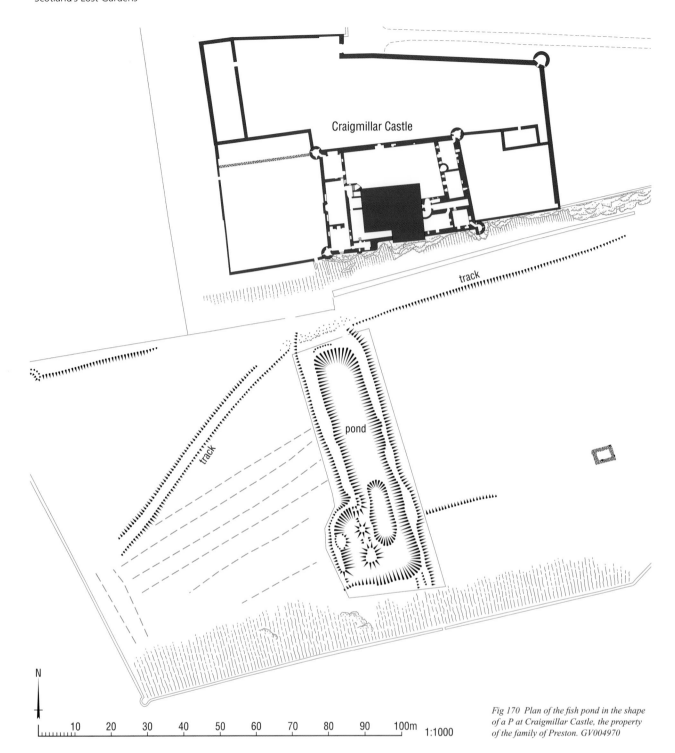

Craigmillar Castle

pond

track

track

N

10   20   30   40   50   60   70   80   90   100m   1:1000

Fig 170 Plan of the fish pond in the shape of a P at Craigmillar Castle, the property of the family of Preston. GV004970

sixteenth century. There are walled gardens to the east and west of the castle between the mid fifteenth century inner curtain wall of the castle, which encloses the tower, accommodation and service ranges and courtyard, and the mid sixteenth century perimeter wall. It is possible that gardens in these positions date from the period when Sir Simon Preston returned from England and carried out repairs to the castle following its capture by the English. The east garden is adjacent to the chapel, and the west garden was probably later redesigned around a sundial of 1660, the date the property was sold to the Gilmour family. This was removed to Inch House when

the Gilmours left Craigmillar in the eighteenth century (Somerville 1990, 261). Below the castle to the south is an area identified in later descriptive sources as the orchard (Whyte 1792, 329; NRS RHP 140422), and in the orchard is the remarkable fish pond in the shape of the letter P, associating its creation with the Preston family, whose fondness for putting their initials on their property has already been noted. This is a most unusual form of fish pond, and while there may have been parallels to it, they have not been noted (Fig 170).

The forming of fish ponds in particular shapes for symbolic reasons is known. During Queen Elizabeth's

Progress of 1591, Edward Seymour, Earl of Hertford, created an entire landscape to stage an entertainment for the queen at Elvetham in Hampshire. This included the excavation of a crescent-shaped lake with three islands in it, a tribute to Elizabeth as Diana, the virgin goddess, on which a *naumachia* or sea battle was staged. The site of the entertainments was identified through aerial survey (Wilson 1982, 46–7). Other elaborate water features are known (Henderson 2005, 127–37), but none that celebrate the family and its ownership in this way, although it has been suggested that the earthworks of fish ponds adjacent to a garden at Kettleby in Lincolnshire may incorporate the initials of Robert Tyrwhitt who died in 1617 (Everson *et al* 1991, 13). The Grand Duke of Tuscany, Ferdinando de Medici, had his name in capitals spelled out in flowers and plants in the garden of the Villa dell'Ambrogiana near Florence, a former fishing lodge acquired by the Medici in 1574 (Lazzaro 1990, 36), and illustrated in one of the series of lunettes painted by Giusto Utens between 1599 and 1602; in the later 1590s there were frequent contacts between James VI and Ferdinando (Mackie 1924, 279). Pliny had mentioned the spelling out of the owner's name by means of topiary (Pliny 2006, 117) (Fig 171).

In Scotland, the first Marquess of Huntly commemorated his marriage and the rebuilding of Huntly Castle with a huge inscription containing both his and his wife's names (Fig 156), but the Prestons' presentation of their name was on an even larger scale, with the pond and its surrounding bank measuring some 75m in length overall by 20m, giving a width within the banks of between 10m and 12m. The bank has been constructed so that it provides a pathway around the P with two small platforms opposite each other on the inner edge of the stem of the P, which could be used for angling or provide a stance for a seat; there are two other similar platforms on the head of the P. Within the pond itself are two small circular islands in the head of the P, measuring just 1.5m and 3m in diameter, which could provide a nesting place for waterfowl. In the late eighteenth century the islands are described as each having a hawthorn planted on it, while the pond was bordered by a row of trees. The orchard of some two acres then contained only a few old fruit trees (Whyte 1792, 329). The bottom of the pond is now about 1.5m below the top of the surrounding bank, with a deliberately deeper area to the east of the two little islands. The depth to which the pond was filled with water is not known, but it would be capable of taking a small boat. In the later seventeenth century the access to the fish pond and orchard was from the west garden by means of a handsome balustraded stair, probably the work of the Gilmours, who rebuilt the west wing of the castle to provide accommodation suitable for the family of that time (MacGibbon and Ross 1887–92, 1, 196). Because of the absence of close parallels, it would only be possible to date the fish pond to the later

Fig 171 Detail from the painting dating from between 1599 and 1602 by Giusto Utens of the Villa dell'Ambrogiana showing how the name of Grand Duke Ferdinand of Tuscany was spelled out in flowers along the edge of the parterres. Museo di Firenze com'era, Florence © 2011 Photo Scala

sixteenth or the early seventeenth century. The history of the Preston family would suggest that such a bold statement of family pride would be more likely to belong to the earlier period, possibly during the time of David Preston between 1569 and 1593, who entertained James VI there. The family played a less prominent role in Scotland after this time, although the commissioning of a sundial dated to the earlier seventeenth century bearing the Preston arms, which was also removed to **Inch House** when the Gilmours left Craigmillar, suggests the development of the gardens in this period (MacGibbon and Ross 1887–92, 5, 496). The garden and the form of the letter P would be best seen from an elevated viewpoint. On the first floor chamber at the south end of the west range a now blocked doorway led out to a projecting timber gallery with a pentice roof from which the area to the south of the castle, where the orchard and fish pond lay, could have been viewed in some comfort (Pringle 1990, 29). The stone-flagged roof of the tower, then as now, would provide wide views all around.

The castle of **Tolquhon** in Aberdeenshire was reconstructed by William Forbes between 1584 and 1589, and was visited by James VI in July of that year (Simpson 1948, 1–2) (Fig 172). This property had belonged to the Prestons of Craigmillar until the early fifteenth century, and when William created his new works around a rectangular inner court, he preserved the historic Preston Tower, and placed his own coat

Fig 172 Aerial view of Tolquhon Castle in Aberdeenshire with its gardens enclosed by stone walls. SC1237404

of arms with the date 1586, surmounted by those of the king, over the entrance to the inner court; in the same year he made the legal arrangements to secure his estate, including his new buildings, to his son. He later recorded on a panel to the right of the gatehouse: AL THIS WARKE EXCEP THE AULD TOUR WAS BEGVN BE WILLIAM FORBES 15 APRIL 1584 AND ENDIT BE HIM 20 OCTOBER 1589. The builder was Thomas Leiper, a member of a family of Aberdeenshire masons who may also have carried out work on the summer house in the garden of Edzell Castle in Angus (MacKean 2001, 147). Forbes' new works included a long gallery on the west side of the building adjacent to a round tower with the laird's private room in it, from both of which the garden could be contemplated. William Forbes' library, some books from which can still be identified, was kept in an arched book press in the west wall of the long gallery (Simpson 1938, 252–6; Simpson 1948, 7). Twelve bee boles or recesses for containing beehives were constructed along the

wall which separates the garden from the outer court. A cruciform arrangement of yews and hollies formed two intersecting avenues (Simpson 1938, 264). Simpson says (1938, 268) that, following the taking into care of Tolquhon by the Commissioners of Works, a small lake was created where there was formerly 'an ugsome swamp'. It may be that there had been some form of water feature in William Forbes' extensive and carefully laid out garden.

The presence of a date stone on a newly erected house often indicates the date of the house and, by extension, a garden which is directly related to the building. **Torwoodlee Tower**, erected for George Pringle, is dated to 1601. The garden which accompanies it is probably the first surviving example of a remarkable series of seventeenth century gardens in the Tweed valley and its tributaries, whose existence was first indicated in the *Inventories* for Selkirkshire and Peeblesshire (RCAHMS 1957; RCAHMS 1967) (Figs 173, 174). Although it is called Torwoodlee Tower, it is actually a long rectangular building of two storeys and an attic. It is dignified on the east, the entrance front, by a higher projecting tower, semicircular on plan up to

Fig 173 Torwoodlee Tower. SC1161172

the main wall head, where it is corbelled out to form a square tower. This contains the entrance, leading to the scale and platt stair up to the first floor, and, beyond this, a turnpike stair (RCAHMS 1957, 39). On the first floor there was probably a hall and two chambers from which windows looked to the west over a walled garden of about half an acre in extent. A door in its west wall may have communicated with an orchard or other gardens. The construction of the house required extensive terracing to provide a level site for the mansion and the broad courtyard which precedes it. On the north side of the court is a range of vaulted cellars which support a terrace, distantly reminiscent of the arrangement at the Palazzo Piccolomini in the blend of usefulness and recreation. On the south side there are two terraces with a retaining wall at the back of the second and lower terrace, aligned with the south gable wall of the house and topped with a low loopholed parapet. While there is some suggestion of defence, the primary aim would seem to be to provide walks with views over the surrounding countryside and the Gala Water.

Many tower houses would formerly have had gardens attached which have been built over during conversion of the property to a farm when the owners moved to more comfortable or spacious accommodation. Gardens which lack distinctive features such as terraces, fish ponds, or a depiction on the maps of Timothy Pont, may be tentatively assigned to a

similar period to the building to which they are attached unless there is stylistic or documentary evidence to the contrary. The tower and a garden associated with it at **Plunton** near Borgue in Kirkcudbrightshire were recorded by RCAHMS in 1911 (RCAHMS 1914, 38–9) (Figs 175, 176). The building of the tower may be attributed to the second half of the sixteenth century, at the time when the Lennox family of Cally were expanding their influence in the area (M'Kerlie 1877, 3, 198). The entrance to the L-plan tower is situated at the angle between the main block and the stair tower. It was approached from the north-east, across a waterlogged

Fig 174 Plan of Torwoodlee Tower where there were terraced gardens constructed above vaulted cellarage. DP071191

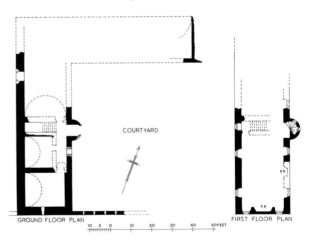

GROUND FLOOR PLAN

COURTYARD

FIRST FLOOR PLAN

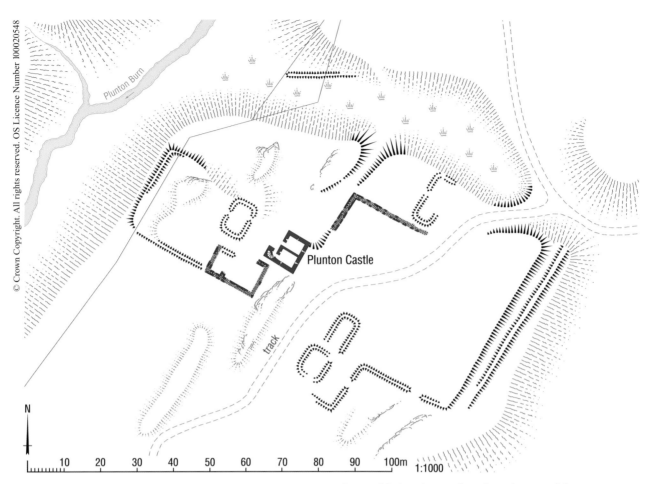

Plunton Castle

N

10 20 30 40 50 60 70 80 90 100m   1:1000

Fig 175 Plan of Plunton Tower and the gardens around it. On the south-east of Plunton Tower the earthworks of the former enclosed gardens can be identified, with a terrace beyond at a lower level. The foundations of the buildings close to the tower may also be sixteenth century in date and form part of an inner court. The other foundations may belong to a later period when the Tower had ceased to be the principal residence of the family. GV004976

ditch and around the north-east side of the tower, to a small court flanked by service buildings. The garden lies to the south-east, sheltered from the access road by a stone wall. It is overlooked by windows in the hall on the first floor and the two chambers on the second floor, as well as providing a view from the decorative turrets corbelled out at both ends of the east wall. Walls and banks define an area for the garden of about 50m by 38m. Plunton is a fairly typical small tower house of the later sixteenth century, and the survival of the garden enclosure may be related to the desertion of the tower house, as a principal residence, by the late seventeenth century, after which it became part of the property of the Murrays of Broughton and Cally (M'Kerlie 1877, 3, 201–2; NRS GD 10/993, 1016).

One L-shaped tower house with a garden attached is **Balvaird Castle** in Perthshire. This tower house, probably dating from the earlier sixteenth century, received extensive additions in 1567, at which time a gatehouse range was added, bearing a dated panel, leading in to the inner court (Lewis 1992, 365). The walled garden and orchard and kitchen garden may have

been added to the south and north-east of the court at this time. The garden measured about 25m by 22m, and the orchard was about 130m by 78m, the whole totalling some 3 acres (Fig 177). The Murrays who owned the tower left Balvaird for Scone in 1658, and the tower, while remaining in their possession, ceased to be the residence of a major family (Lewis 1992, 382).

Another example of a tower house with a walled garden and orchard attached is **Balcomie Castle** in the East Neuk of Fife, where Mary of Guise had landed in 1538. The mansion dates from the late sixteenth century and has, like Balvaird, a gatehouse range. The garden and orchard lie to the south-east of the castle enclosure, not immediately adjacent to the house. The entrance to the garden dates from the late sixteenth or early seventeenth century and may be associated with the work on the gatehouse which is attributed by a panel to 1602 (RCAHMS 1933, 62–3). Sir James Learmonth of Balcomie was one of James VI's Fife Adventurers, who tried to colonise the savage island of Lewis. When he died there in 1598, the estate passed to his brother, John. The orchard and garden together have an area of almost three acres (Fig 178).

The problems involved with the depiction by Timothy Pont of houses and gardens, in particular the partial surviving coverage of Scotland and the different way in which detail is presented on different manuscript maps, have already been outlined. The importance

Fig 176 Aerial view of Plunton Tower from the north. The shadows pick out the form of the banks which formerly enclosed the gardens, as well as those defining the court on the north-east entrance side of the Tower. SC1237406

of this loss in terms of lack of information may be illustrated by the remark of Henri, Duc de Rohan, who visited Scotland in 1600, and says of Edinburgh that 'more than a hundred country-seats are to be found within a radius of two leagues of the town' (Brown 1978, 93). However these maps do provide evidence for the existence of certain gardens in the late sixteenth century, which can in some cases be confirmed by surviving remains as earthworks, stone enclosures and cropmarks. Although much of the coverage of Scotland is missing, and this includes some of the richest and most densely inhabited areas, the maps of quite extensive areas of the north-west of Scotland do survive, and reveal an absence of anything that could be interpreted as a garden, although woodland does appear. Gardens designed to produce foodstuffs must have been present, and in the 1540s Dean Munro makes reference to two orchards in the Hebrides (Martin 1999, 322; RCAHMS 1928, 178–80, 185). Gardens are recognised in the Northern Isles as the work of recent incomers from mainland Scotland, and it may be that their apparent absence in the north-western parts of Scotland is a true reflection of the absence of an element in the cultural life of the sixteenth century that flourished across southern Scotland and the north-east of the country.

Royal gardens would seem to have received little attention during the reigns of Mary Queen of Scots and James VI. It is difficult to judge how far this reflects lack of the laying out of new gardens and the redesigning of existing ones, and how far it is the result of the absence of documentation. Both the Master of

Fig 177 Aerial view of Balvaird Castle with its walled garden and large orchard and probable kitchen garden. SC1237405

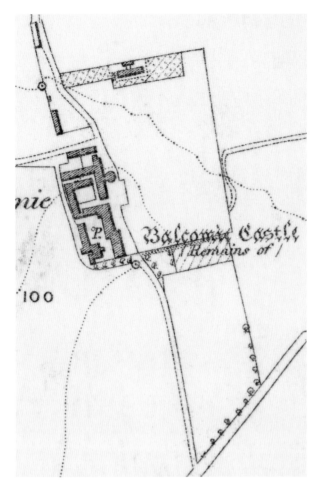

Fig 178 Balcomie Castle with its walled gardens as it was depicted on the First Edition of the Ordnance Survey 6-inch map of Fife in 1854.

Works Accounts and the Treasurers Accounts are sparse during these years. There is no record or tradition of James refurbishing gardens before his marriage to Anne of Denmark, like his grandfather and great grandfather before their marriages, but the royal gardeners continued to be paid, and it may be that the gardens there remained much the same.

Alexander Montgomerie presented a poem of praise and advice to the young James VI called *The Navigatioun*. He wrote in the character of a traveller such as Fynes Moryson or Lupold von Wedel, and compared the king to a rose in the bud, set in a garden surrounded by his kindred, his council and true preachers of the word of God:

> Haill! Bravest burgeoun brekking to the rose
> The deu of grace thy leivis mot unclose;
> The stalk of treuth mot grant thy nourishing:
> Thy noble counsel, lyk trees about thy grace,
> Mot plantit be, ilk ane into his place:
> Quhais ruiting sure and toppis reaching he
> Mot brek the storme, befor it come to the.
> They of thy bluid mot grow about thy bordour,
> To hold thy hedge into ane perfyt ordour,

> As fragrant flouris of ane helthsome smell,
> All venomous beistis from the to expel.
> Thy preachers true mot ay thy gardners b[e]
> To clense thy root from weeds of heresie.
> Thy gardene wall mak the Neu Testament:
> So sall thou grow without impediment;
> (Montgomerie 1887, 205)

When Anne of Denmark became Queen of England, she evinced a lively appreciation of the arts, and her patronage of Ben Jonson and the court masque is well recorded. These, as has already been noted, were frequently associated with and took place in gardens. Anne had the gardens at Somerset House in the Strand in London redesigned by the Frenchman Salomon de Caus and a huge grotto fountain depicting Mount Parnassus installed there fed by water raised from the River Thames, which provides some parallels for the form of the King's Knot at Stirling. Another palace granted to Anne was that at Greenwich, which although not completed before her death, shows a garden of similarly elaborate design. Several of Anne's portraits show her in the setting of a garden (Strong 1998, 87–97). No traces of the gardens at what seems to have been Anne's favourite residence in Scotland, **Dunfermline Abbey**, survive, and Slezer's late seventeenth century engraving gives no indication of its earlier form (Slezer 1718). The records from James VI's reign are lacking, but a private act of Parliament by Anne in 1606 granting the keepership of the Palace of Dunfermline to Alexander Seton shows a concern with preserving what is there, which included her gardens:

> We, considering how necessary it is that the foresaid palace of ours of Dunfermline and all the buildings pertaining to it should be kept patched and roofed, and that the orchards and gardens within the bounds and walls of our said palace should be carefully looked after, lest by negligence and the passage of time they deteriorate (which often happens with this kind of palace unless diligent care is taken, and unless a careful and prudent keeper is found and put in place for the same palace buildings and gardens ...)
> (*RPS* 1605/5/121)

John Taylor, the Water-Poet, on his visit to Scotland in 1618 records seeing the ruins of the 'Queenes palace (a delicate and princely mansion ... with faire gardens, orchards, meadows belonging to the palace' (Brown 1978, 115) (Fig 179).

At the time when Gordon of Rothiemay produced his map of Edinburgh in 1647, the pattern of enclosures, at any rate on the north side of the **Palace of Holyroodhouse**, was similar to that of the English

Fig 179 Dunfermline Abbey as depicted by John Slezer in the 1693 edition of Theatrum Scotiae when no indication of the form of the gardens of the time of Anne of Denmark are recorded. DP102161

Spy's map of 1544. One feature mentioned during James' reign is not referred to earlier; in 1582 a charter was granted to Lord Ruthven, giving him the New Frater or refectory of the monastery and the monastic kitchen, which had been granted to his grandfather by Mary Queen of Scots in 1564 (Gallagher 1998, 1088–90; *RMS* 5, 142 no 456; NRS E14/2.f179). This property was located between the monks' dormitory on the west, and the commendator's house and the yard called the 'seage of troy' on the east. This reference to a yard or garden known as the 'Siege of Troy' may go back to a period when entertainments, whether tournaments or masques, were held there, or it may indicate the site of a maze. Both topiary and turf mazes were called by this title and one formerly existed at Hampton Court near the surviving maze. There is no other reference to this yard, but, particularly if it were a turf maze, it may have required little in the way of construction and less in the way of demolition. A well-connected German traveller, Lupold von Wedel, who came to Scotland in 1584 visited Holyrood during James' absence. He commented that while the building was of mean appearance, it was surrounded by fine gardens with beautifully planted hedges (von Bülow 1895, 254). The gardens of Linlithgow, Falkland and Stirling also seem to have been maintained (*ER* 22, 153, 231, 298 etc), but again there is no evidence for their extension or redesign. New butts were constructed at Stirling in 1577, and the gate of the garden below the castle was repaired in 1579 (*TA* 13, 163, 281). In 1583, when James was almost seventeen, an estimate was prepared for the repairs necessary to put the royal palaces in order. Reference to this estimate for **Stirling Castle** has already been made, but it is worth stressing the emphasis placed on the views around the palace and the importance attached to the landscape around (Figs 125, 126).

> Quhilk qwarter off the said paleys is the best and maist plesand sitwatioune off ony of his hienes palayes be ressone it will have the maist plesand sycht of all the foure airthis, in speciall perk and gairdin, deir thairin, up the rawerais of Forthe, Teyth, Allone, and Gwddy to Lochlomwnd, ane sycht rownd about in all pairtis and downe the rewear of Forthe quhair their standis many greit stane howssis. (*MW* 1, 310)

Chapter 4: The Union Garden 1603 to 1660

See, read, think and attend. View and with grateful eyes enjoy these hours and the garden

Inscription in the garden of Dundas Castle

The year 1603 saw a major change in the social fabric of Scotland with the departure of the king and court to England. Despite James' promises of frequent and regular visits, he was to return to Scotland only once, in 1617. In the meantime the government of Scotland was carried out by the office holders he appointed. Scots were able to visit England and travel freely through it to Europe, unlike the owners of Aberdour and Craigmillar in the mid sixteenth century, who first visited the country as prisoners of war. Scots held prominent positions at the royal court. Lawlessness on the Borders was gradually suppressed, and, if the outcomes were less clear cut in the Highland north and west, efforts were made to encourage a more uniform culture across the country, at least with regard to those who held land. The number of gardens which survive in a form that allows a visitor to gain a more immediate impression of their original appearance is much greater in this period.

Descriptions and depictions of gardens have also survived in greater numbers than in earlier centuries to be preserved in public and private collections in Scotland. The style of gardens remained broadly the same: there might be a walled garden or series of walled enclosures, terracing or water features, sundials, fountains, sculpture; and the outlook from the garden remained important. Classical references underlay the choice of decoration, although their meaning to the owner of the garden might have changed. The walls

which surrounded these gardens still survive adjacent to houses of the same period, and have been recorded in the county inventories, particularly those covering the Lothians and Fife (RCAHMS 1924, 1929, 1933). Many of these houses belonged to royal officials, successful lawyers and minor landholders, some of whom had benefited from grants of former church lands. Examples are Crichton House near Pathhead (RCAHMS 1929, 51), Royston House near Granton (RCAHMS 1929, 31), The Inch now in south Edinburgh (RCAHMS 1929, 118), Fountainhall near Wester Pencaitland and Northfield House near Prestonpans (RCAHMS 1924, 86, 104).

The best known garden of this period is probably that at **Edzell Castle** in Angus (Fig 181). This was the property of the Lindsay family and occupied a strategic position in relation to the passes from Angus to the region of Mar to the north, across the mountains. The castle was built at various times during the sixteenth century; a tower house was constructed to which ranges around a courtyard for domestic occupation and services were later added. Both Mary Queen of Scots and James VI visited the castle when it was the residence of Sir David Lindsay, the creator of the garden which adjoins to the castle on the south-east. This is the most well preserved of the surviving gardens of the early seventeenth century, and provides, through its sculpture, evidence for the elaborate intellectual framework, which lay behind its design, and may have extended to the choice of plants (Parrott 2010, 75–7) (Fig 182).

Sir David Lindsay was one of the more remarkable characters in Scotland in the late sixteenth and early seventeenth centuries. He was educated in France at

Fig 180 Aerial view of the King's Knot below Stirling Castle, arguably the most remarkable survival of an early seventeenth century garden in Europe. SC101862

Fig 181 Aerial view of Edzell Castle showing the walled garden immediately adjacent to the castle. SC674819

Paris and later at Cambridge, and had legal training, becoming a Lord of Session with the title Lord Edzell in 1593 and a member of the Privy Council in 1598 (Lindsay 1849, 1, 331–3, 372 etc). There was already a garden at Edzell in the time of his father, the evidence for which is a document of 1552, concerning the resolution of a feud there in the '*viridarium* or garden ... at his fortress of Edzell, at the eleventh hour before noon' (Lindsay 1849, 1, 346). James VI visited the castle in June 1580 and again in 1589. It was there that he heard the news of the assassination of the French king, Henry III, his mother's first husband's last surviving brother. Pont's depiction of the castle (NLS Pont 30 (6)) shows what may be enclosures, but no indication of a garden or a park, as appears, for example, at nearby Arnhall. In 1588, in correspondence with a legal colleague from his Edinburgh home, Lindsay related how the chirping of birds brought to mind the northern mountains 'albeit presentlie environit with their quhyte winter robbes, yit befoir I visie thame sall be deckit with their grene fragrant May garmentis', reflecting descriptions of nature in contemporary verse (Brown 2004, 209). There is evidence in family letters for a policy of tree planting in the late sixteenth century on his own estate and on those of his brothers, which may indicate that this practice was more widespread in Scotland at this period than has been realised. He

sent a thousand young birch trees to his half-brother, Lord Ogilvie. His brother Lord Menmuir, the owner of Balcarres and President of the Court of Session, wrote to him asking for firs and hollies, and dispatching elm seeds to Edzell in his turn. David Lindsay also sent Lord Menmuir a copy of a work of the Roman writer Columella and *La Maison Rustique*, presumably the book by Charles Estienne and Jean Liebault, published in Paris in 1578. Both were concerned with agriculture

Fig 182 The walled garden at Edzell with its twentieth century planting and elaborate sculptural decoration of the early seventeenth century. SC798692

(Lindsay 1849, 345–6). He intended to rebuild the village of Edzell (Lindsay 1849, 345–6, 348) and in 1592 plans for a symmetrical design including a cross and market place were prepared (Bardgett 1989, 152). Lord Menmuir lived at Balcarres in Fife, but the modern form of the garden there is that of an early Victorian recreation of a seventeenth century garden.

David Lindsay was also intent on the exploitation of minerals from the estate. In 1592 Lord Menmuir was appointed 'Master of the Metals' with responsibility for regulating all mining of ore and manufacture of metals, and was involved in leasing the gold mining rights at Crawfordmuir. He was already known to have sought out mining specialists in England, Denmark and Germany, and his knowledge was applied to lead mining in Glenesk near Edzell and the extraction of alabaster for lime (Lindsay 1849, 352–3, 343–5). This anticipation of increased wealth may have been a factor leading to his creation of the extensive and elaborate landscape around the castle, which originally extended beyond the surviving walled garden.

This is placed immediately next to the castle, and a doorway leads into it from the courtyard, with another entrance on the wall lying to the east (Fig 183). While the castle and garden do not lie due north and south, but rather north-west and south-east, the directions adopted here are those given by W D Simpson, and the description of the panels and other sculpture is derived from his work (Simpson 1952, 7–14). There are identical heraldic panels on both sides of this door, which bear the arms and initials of Sir David Lindsay, Lord Edzell, and his second wife Dame Isobel Forbes, with his family motto *'DUM SPIRO SPERO – while I live I hope'* and the date 1604. The arms are: dexter quarterly, first and fourth, a fess chequy for Lindsay; second and third, a lion rampant debruised of a bendlet for Abernethy (the family which held Edzell before the Lindsays), impaled with sinister, three bears' heads muzzled couped, for Forbes (Simpson 1952, 7). The inner face of the garden wall was divided into compartments by a series of pilasters, each made of two long stones, with bases, caps and bands variously decorated. The pilaster stones have disappeared, but the bases, caps and bands remain. The wall head is finished by a moulded coping into which are set a series of semicircular headed niches, probably intended to display busts. The pediments of these niches are carved with scrolls on the garden side, while on the exterior they bear the shamrock, thistle, rose and fleur de lys for Ireland, England, Scotland and France, the countries ruled or claimed by James VI following the Union of the Crowns in 1603. There are no niches on the west side of the garden, and the wall is finished with a plain cornice, leading to the suggestion that the design was never completed.

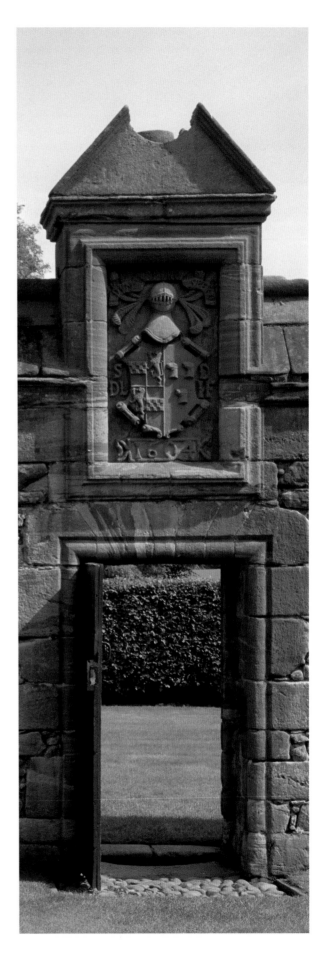

Fig 183 The inner side of the east doorway into the walled garden of Edzell with Sir David Lindsay's arms and the date 1604 above. SC1239299

Fig 184 The banqueting house at the south-east corner of the garden at Edzell. The window over the doorway is surmounted by Sir David Lindsay's initials. SC798693

On the east side of the garden, sixteen compartments are defined by the pilasters, with a further thirteen on the south and fourteen on the west. There are two different ways of handling these compartments. In the first the central part of the wall space is taken up by a representation of the arms of the Lindsays, the fess chequy, created by constructing three rows of four stone recesses arranged like squares on a chess board. The recesses are dished so they can take flower containers. The sandstone wall must be imagined as the red (gules) of the coat of arms, the solid squares would be painted blue (azure), and the flowers in the recesses would provide the white (argent), or these last two might be reversed. Above this are carved in relief the seven-rayed

stars or mullets, which the Edzell Lindsays adopted from the earlier owners, the Stirlings of Glenesk. The centre of each star is pierced to provide a nesting place for birds (Simpson 1931, 140), or, according to MacGibbon and Ross (1887–92, 2, 366), for shot holes (Fig 189). Alternating with these in the second scheme there is one rectangular recess dished to take flowers, with a sculptured panel above. On the east side the panels are vesica-shaped, like an almond, and display relief sculptures of the Planetary Deities. On the south side they are arched and bear the Liberal Arts and on the west side they are square-headed with the Cardinal Virtues.

There are eight panels on the eastern wall of which the most northerly is blank, with what were popularly considered to be the planets in the early seventeenth century: Saturn, Jupiter, Mars, the Sun, Venus, Mercury and the Moon. The order is based on

Fig 185 The image of Saturn, one of the Planetary Deities. Relief sculptures of the planetary deities are set into the east wall of the garden. Saturn's attributes include a goat and a baby. SC1144507

Fig 186 The image of Luna, another of the Planetary Deities, based on an engraving by Georg Pencz, a pupil of Albrecht Dürer. SC1144509

the medieval theories of the cosmos, in which the earth was considered to be the centre of the universe, enclosed by nine concentric revolving crystal spheres or heavens, and has more in common with astrology than astronomy. The first seven were each the seat of a planet, so towards the north outwards from Earth, the Moon, Mercury, Venus, the Sun, Mars, Jupiter and Saturn. Beyond Saturn was the heaven of fixed stars, the blank panel presumably painted with silver stars on a blue ground, reflecting the Lindsay coat of arms, and beyond all these revolved the ninth or imperial heaven, the throne of God. The sculptures used as models are copies of a series of copperplate engravings which were made in 1528–9, by a Nuremberg artist called Georg Pencz, who was a pupil of Albrecht Dürer. The sculptor of the panels has made a very faithful copy, even including the initials IB (Iorg Bentz) on the halberd carried by Mars, which bore this signature of the artist on the original engraving (Simpson 1931, 141–5). The image of Saturn is the only one not drawn from this source (Fig 185). The engravings of Georg Pencz were used as sources for paintings and sculptures across Europe, occurring as far east as the castle of Telc in Moravia.

The apparent paths pursued by the planets across the heavens all cross the twelve signs of the Zodiac. The astrologers awarded two of these signs to each planet as its Day and Night Houses, with the exception, logically, of the Sun, which has only a day sign and the Moon, which has only a night sign. The Night House is omitted from Saturn and the Day House from Mars and Venus, possibly because of lack of space. The twelve signs of the Zodiac were distributed into 'houses of heaven', and each planet, when in its own house, was believed to exert a particular influence on human affairs. Below each figure is its astronomical sign (Fig 186).

The arched-headed panels on the south side of the garden representing the Liberal Arts are seven in number. The first three are Grammar, Rhetoric and Dialectic, which formed the first part of the medieval university curriculum, the Trivium. Grammar, the art of construing words correctly, was followed by Rhetoric, the art of connected discourse, and succeeded by the art of argument. The four higher studies formed the Quadrivium – Arithmetic, Music, Geometry and Astronomy. The panel depicting Astronomy has disappeared (and was already absent in 1838 when the garden was described by Hutcheon (1838). The name

Fig 187 Musica, one of the personifications of the Seven Liberal Arts set into the south wall of the garden, is playing a lute, surrounded by musical instruments. SC1237416

Fig 188 Geometria, another of the Liberal Arts, places calipers against a sphere.Other instruments connected with measurement and building lie at her feet. SC671957

of Grammatica has been broken off, and Educator has been inscribed at the side by someone who did not know the sequence of the Seven Liberal Arts. The source for these representations is not known but is likely, as with those for the Planetary Deities, to be German in origin. The figures are female and are engaged in practising the art each embodies. Grammatica, wearing a teacher's gown, is instructing a boy who is reading a book. A hen and chick, an image of instruction, appears at the boy's feet. Rhetorica is seated in the act of declaiming with a scroll in one hand and the caduceus, a short herald's staff entwined with serpents, in the other. Dialectica emphasises her argument by striking her palm with her fist. On her head perches a swallow while round her arm is a serpent and at her feet two frogs, alluding to aspects of argument. Behind Dialecta are little figures representing Aristotle and Zeno, although the left hand figure has almost completely vanished. Arithmetica is calculating, flanked by Pythagoras and Boethius. The headless Musica is playing on a lute with five strings, flanked by a harp, viol, a small lute or possibly a mandora, all stringed instruments, and a music book (Fig 187). Geometria, the best preserved of the group, is shown placing callipers against a sphere entwined by a serpent, a symbol of endlessness. Near her feet are placed a protractor, a set-square and a measure or straight edge. She wears a city wall-type crown and has, behind

her, buildings, suggesting that the aspect of geometry celebrated is that related to architecture (Fig 188).

On the west side, in rectangular frames, are the Cardinal Virtues, which consist of the three Christian Virtues, Faith, Hope and Charity, and the four Moral Virtues, Prudence, Temperance, Fortitude and Justice. Each Virtue, named at the bottom of the panel, is personified by a female figure, whose image stands proud of the frame. The order in which they are placed is not conventional. Fides holds up a chalice and would have held a cross or possibly a crucifix. Like so many images of the crucifix of the seventeenth century or earlier in Scotland, the cross has been broken off because of its association with Catholic reverential practices. Beneath her feet is a serpent. Spes is shown with an anchor and a spade. Justitia appears with a sword and scales. Caritas cradles two babies in her arms, with two young children clutching her skirts. Prudentia looks into a hand mirror, a symbol of self-knowledge, the foundation of prudence. A serpent twines around her arm. Fortitudo is shown with the column from which she has broken the capital, and Temperantia is depicted pouring water from a jug into a shallow wine glass. Near her feet are distinctively shaped containers for wine and water.

Simpson comments that the sculptures on the three walls were carved by three different sculptors, and that they were based on drawings, or rather woodcuts, and not sculptural models. He was looking for German sources, and noted Sir David Lindsay's involvement with German mining contractors, particularly Bernard Fechtenburg and Hans Ziegler from Nuremberg, in his bid to exploit the mineral resources of his estate. He speculates that the source of the designs may have been included in an Album Amicorum, a cross between an autograph book and a travel record in which the owner got his friends to write their names or depict their coat of arms. One such is that kept by Michael Balfour of Burley, now in the National Library of Scotland (NLS MS 16000). It includes many elaborate depictions of Central European coats of arms, as well as the autographs of people he met, including Scots, on his travels for education or for diplomacy. The volume also includes pictures of the places he visited; he had a particular interest in the dress of the different Italian cities, particularly Padua and Venice. One picture is from the journey from Padua to Venice by the horse-drawn passenger boat, the Burchiello, which shows a Venetian villa, with its garden behind a wall (NLS MS 16000 103r).

At the south-east corner of the garden at Edzell, and projecting beyond it, is an elaborate banqueting house of two storeys. The design of the interior walls of the garden is continued across its façade. Over the window on the first floor on the garden side is a panel with Sir David Lindsay's monogram, SDL (Fig 184). In appearance it resembles a miniature domestic house of the earlier seventeenth century, with its crow-stepped gables and its decorative panels above the windows, its chimneys and its turnpike stair housed in a circular stair tower; there is another monogram over the window on the outside. Simpson likened it to Muchalls Castle in Kincardineshire (Simpson 1931, 167). There are two rooms on the ground floor; the one towards the garden has a ribbed and groined vault with an ornate boss, and a stone bench around the wall, and the other, entered from outside the garden, has a plain vault. The spiral stair can be entered from the room towards the garden as well as from the exterior. The upper room has a closet off it in a round turret corbelled out on the south-east; there is a fireplace at the east end with a cupboard next to it. Beneath the windows facing out from the garden are ornate triple gun loops, which have been compared to those at Tolquhon Castle where the mason was probably Thomas Leiper (McKean 2001, 147).

At the south-west corner of the gardens are the remains of a bath house, which had been subjected to extensive stone robbing, and which was excavated in 1855 (Jervise 1857, 226–9). The building was rectangular and consisted of three rooms with an entrance from the garden, and probably a door from the exterior. There was a bathing room with a well, a dressing room and a sitting room with a fireplace.

The walled garden was part of a larger scheme for the policies around Edzell Castle. There are no contemporary descriptions of this outstanding ensemble, but the Reverend Mr Ouchterlonie, minister of Guinde, writing towards the end of the seventeenth century, relates that in addition to the 'delicate garden' with pictures and coats of arms in the walls and the fine summer house and bath house, there was an excellent kitchen garden and orchard with 'diverse kinds of most excellent fruits and most delicate' and a new park with fallow deer (Macfarlane 1906–8, 2, 39). Evidence for the boundary of the park was noted by Simpson (1931, 171). The outer court was large and level, and near the present farm of Mains of Edzell is an early seventeenth century dovecot of rectangular form with crow stepped gables. It originally had round turrets resting on continuous corbelling at its north-west and south-east corners, which would have had conical cap roofs like that on the summer house; similar turrets were probably also present on the bath house. The boundary walls which are shown on the First Edition of the Ordnance Survey 6-inch map, surveyed in 1862–3, probably indicate the areas of these other gardens.

This is a remarkable ensemble and it should be noted that there is no surviving reference to it for about a hundred years after its creation. The survival of the garden is probably owing to the history of its owners. The Lindsays of Edzell were short of money. Sir David Lindsay had to pay out substantial sums as a result of the involvement of his son and heir in contemporary feuds. During the Civil War, a later David Lindsay was a supporter of the Covenant and his lands were harried by the royalist Marquis of Montrose, while Cromwell's soldiers occupied the castle in 1651 and, following the revolution of 1689, the then laird did not accept the Presbyterian settlement and was involved in a series of disputes with the government. By 1715 it was found necessary to sell the estate to the Earl of Panmure, a cousin of the Lindsays of Edzell. The earl forfeited his estates following his participation in the Jacobite rebellion of that same year. The property passed to the York Buildings Company, and suffered neglect and some active stone robbing. Because the family was relatively impoverished, there were no major changes to the house and garden during the later seventeenth century, and its lack of a proprietor during the eighteenth century precluded the change to an informal landscape garden. Following the bankruptcy of the York Buildings Company in 1764, the roofs and floors were stripped out and sold for the benefit of their creditors (Simpson 1931, 118–9). By the time restoration and preservation took place during the middle of the nineteenth century, the architectural elements of the garden were recognised as a remarkable survival from the seventeenth century and cared for accordingly (Jervise 1857, 229). Such gardens had again become fashionable, and it is at this period that the gardens at Balcarres were redesigned.

The present planting of the parterres at Edzell dates back to the 1930s and, and was centred on a yew tree, reflecting the subjects of the sculptures around the walls in a planting of modern species. Excavations in 2004 uncovered a central circular pit filled with a mass of red sandstone boulders which may have formed the base for a structure in this position (Stewart 2004, 19) (Fig 182).

The intellectual position behind the creation of the garden at Edzell has been set out by David Allan (Allan 1997, 59–80). He singles out the resurgence of interest in classical Stoicism across Europe in the later sixteenth century, led by scholars intent on the recovery, publication and reinterpretation of the major texts of ancient Stoicism. Zeno, Cicero, Seneca, Epictetus, Marcus Aurelius, Pliny, Tacitus and Boethius were the subjects of a scholarly movement centred in France, but with offshoots in the Low Countries. Central to this study was a critique of the unpredictability and viciousness of the public sphere. In the Roman world it was seen by the Stoics as the moral duty of citizens to engage in public life, and where a retreat to the garden, while it might be evidence for distaste for corruption and dissimulation in the world of affairs, could be seen as a form of self-indulgent Epicureanism. The Neo-Stoics on the other hand, inspired by the writings of Justus Lipsius, considered that the garden was the most appropriate venue for the effective Stoical cultivation of *prudentia* (prudence). Lipsius was teaching at the University of Leiden during the wars between Hapsburg Spain and the Dutch. Literary pastoralism was cultivated by the circle around Sir Philip Sidney's sister, the Countess of Pembroke, and was a common theme in contemporary Scottish poetry and prose, with William Drummond of Hawthornden as a major Scottish exponent in the early seventeenth century. The garden walls and leafy groves shut out the warring world:

> Where thickest Shades me from all Rayes
> did hide
> Into a shut-up place, some Sylvans chamber,
> Whose seeling spred was with the lockes
> of Amber
> Of new-bloomed Sicamors, Floore wrought
> with Flowres
> (Drummond 1976, 15)

> The world is full of Horrours, Troubles, Slights
> Woods harmelesse Shades have only true
> Delightes
> (Drummond 1976, 111)

Sir David Lindsay's garden is, perhaps, too much of a piece of self-assertion and a tribute to himself, his family and his king, who had recently ascended the throne of England, to match fully with this vision of the garden as a place outside the competitive world of early seventeenth century Scotland. A more practical scientific philosophy was derived from Renaissance hermeticism, a tradition which was developed from a work supposedly written by an ancient Egyptian priest, Hermes Trismegistus, a contemporary of Moses. Through knowledge Man could control natural forces, and this led to an interest in the development of technology. John Dee, the Elizabethan magician and mathematician, wrote a preface to a translation of Euclid, published in 1570. In it he outlined the whole state of science as it was then known, moving from a discussion of number and its mystical implications, to the sciences dealing with number, arithmetic, algebra and geometry. Among the sciences dependent on number were law, the military arts, surveying, geography, astronomy, astrology and music. These were directed, among many other applications, to the making of machines, the management of water, mining, architecture, navigation and map making (Strong 1986, 213–15).

An even more distinguished creator of gardens was Alexander Seton, Earl of Dunfermline. He was a member of the family which owned Seton, Winton and Niddry, where gardens of considerable elaboration are known to have been established in the fifteenth and sixteenth century. Born about 1555, he was educated at the College of Jesuits in Rome, going on to study law in France. In 1571 he was presented to Pope Gregory XIII and made an oration before him; the records of the college list the books he brought with him to Rome (Maitland 1829, 63). In 1565 Mary Queen of Scots, his godmother, had granted him Pluscarden Priory of which his father, the fifth Lord Seton, had been commissioner since 1561. It was later given to the illegitimate sons of the Regent Morton, but restored to Alexander Seton after Morton's execution. It was, with Urquhart, erected into a barony in 1587, which he sold in 1595 for £40,000 (*RMS* 6, no 410, 139). This enabled him to buy Fyvie Castle the following year, when he was also made heritable bailie of Dunfermline (Paul 1906, 3, 369–70). He accompanied his father on an embassy to Henry III of France in 1583 to re-establish and reorganise the appointments to the king's royal bodyguard, the Scottish Archers. Another member of this embassy was William Shaw, who was appointed the royal Master of Works at the end of the same year. It has been suggested that Shaw may have been involved with the design of Fyvie (Glendinning *et al* 1996, 41–2). When he died in 1602, a Latin elegiac couplet in his memory composed by Alexander Seton appeared on his tomb (RCAHMS 1933, 112). In 1586 Seton became, like Sir David Lindsay and his brother Lord Menmuir, a Lord of Session. Then in 1593 he was appointed Lord President, a political advisor of the king and one of the auditors of the exchequer, responsible for the royal finances, known as the Octavians.

By 1599 he had carried out extensive works at **Fyvie Castle** (Fig 190). One of these was the reconstruction

Fig 189 The Lindsay fess chequy represented in different colours of lobelia against a red sandstone wall. Above are the seven-rayed stars or mullets, which were adopted from the arms of the earlier owners of Edzell, the Stirlings of Glenesk. SC1237425

of the south range as a show front with its circular towers flanking a doorway, which does not seem of practical use as the main entrance to the castle because it leads only to corridors and stairs, and provides no direct access to the courtyard. Above were large living rooms (Simpson 1938, 45). The façade is, however, remarkable for its symmetry. The area to the south of it was known as the 'Barras Green'. The west range was the residential wing. On the first floor were a dining room and a chamber served by the grand newel stair

and with a side door leading out to the garden. The area to the west was known as the 'Old Garden' and the 'Bowling Green' on a plan by John Innes of 1822. In the mid eighteenth century, under new owners, there were gardens to the north, south and west, which were later transformed to an informal arrangement of grass and trees around the castle. Until recently it was not possible to date the slight traces of features beneath the lawns, which appear on aerial photographs, but recent excavation there for the National Trust for Scotland has revealed the presence of a walled garden with internal paths (Cameron 2011).

Sculpture commemorating the builder of Fyvie and his first wife decorated the buildings he erected and transformed, but only a few pieces of this period

Fig 190 Aerial view of Fyvie Castle from the south now set in an informal landscape, but formerly with the Barras Green to the south of the building and the 'Old Garden' and 'Bowling Green' to the west of the mansion. SC1237511

at Fyvie suggest a programme which might be likened to that at Edzell, and their significance has not been identified; it is possible that the sculptures were inserted at a later period. They are plaques built into the later eighteenth century western buttress, into the Meldrum Tower and into the Seton Tower, depicting a nude figure of a woman in a conventional classical attitude of modesty, a bearded and turbaned oriental with the inscription ARIADNUS BARBARUS and the figure of a man with the inscription PETRUS LADUS DUX VENETIE, identified as Pietro Lando, Doge of Venice from 1539–45. Little figures in what seems to be sixteenth or early seventeenth century dress may have decorated the roof lines of the towers.

Seton was Provost of Edinburgh for ten years between 1598 and 1608. His official residence was in the Cowgate, and in 1597, the English envoy, Sir Robert Bowes, in a letter to Lord Burghley, wrote:

> Albeit I expected audience of the king on the next day he was so entertained with great affairs as it was deferred until Friday last in the afternoon. That day in the Lord President's garden in Edinburgh the King declared to me how greatly he had been (and was) grieved and tired with these accidents fallen at the late meeting ... (Allan 1997, 68)

Alexander Seton was entrusted with the guardianship of Charles, James VI's second son, who was born in 1600. He was a sickly child and stayed in Scotland, travelling to England with Seton in 1604. Here Seton was involved in the negotiations for a union of Scotland and England and the creation of the kingdom of Great Britain, one of James' dearest projects (Maitland 1829, 66). Seton became chancellor, representing the king in the Scottish Parliament, and was created Earl of Dunfermline in 1605 (Paul 1906, 3, 370). He was also Keeper of Holyroodhouse and responsible for Anne of Denmark's properties in Scotland. The writer of his obituary wrote of his wide travels for knowledge, which 'bee-like' he brought back for the good of his country (Allan 1997, 67).

Pinkie House is situated about five miles from Edinburgh; a tower, which had belonged to Dunfermline Abbey, formed the core of Seton's 'suburban' house (Fig 191). In 1613 he was able to regard his house there as completed, according to the inscription recorded on the front of the house:

DOMINUS ALEXANDER SETONIUS HANC DOMUM AEDIFICAVIT NON AD ANIMI SED FORTUNARUM ET AGELLI MODUM 1613 (Alexander, Lord Seton, built this house in 1613, not as he would have wished, but according to the measure of his means and estate (RCAHMS 1929, 81).

Fig 191 Aerial view of Pinkie House and the 'most sweit' walled garden, which formerly contained a knot '200 foot square'. SC1237432

Fig 192 A nineteenth century engraving showing the elaborate well in front of the house in what was probably originally intended to be a courtyard (Billings 1845-52, 4, plate section 30). SC1212072

This may be a reference to the intention, as at Fyvie, to erect a house around a courtyard, when in practice only two ranges were built. An elaborate draw well with an open crown was constructed in front of the house in what would have been the courtyard, with, in addition to the initials AS, ED and MH for Alexander Seton, Earl of Dunfermline and Margaret Hay (his third wife) and their coats of arms, the elegiac couplet: (Fig 192).

> FONTE HOC FRIGIDIOR QVO NON VEL
> PVRIOR ALTER
> ET CAPITI ET MEMBRIS VTILIS VNDA FLVIT
> (From this fountain, unsurpassed for coolness
> and purity, there flows water benign alike for
> heads and for limbs) (RCAHMS 1929, 81)

There were gardens to the north, south and east of the house, enclosed by massive walls. Those around the north and east gardens had moulded copings with doorways, two of which bear the initials of Alexander Seton and his countess and their ages, giving a date of 1612 for their setting up. In 1884 two slabs, which 'had long been lying detached and exposed to the weather' were built into the garden wall. They may originally have been placed at the entrance to the garden over the outer gate (Lauder 1900, 190), and

Fig 193 The Latin inscription in the garden of Alexander Seton's villa *at Pinkie celebrating his gardens laid out 'for the honourable delight of body and soul'. SC1235235*

recall Italian and ancient Roman examples. One panel bears a coronet with the initials AS and MH and reads:

D O M
SIBI POSTERIS BONIS OMNIBVS HVMANIS
VRBANISQUE
HOMINIBVS VRBANITATIS OMNIS
HVMANITATISQVE
AMANTISSIMVS ALEXANDER SETONIUS
VILLAM
HORTOS ET HAEC SVBVRBANA AEDIFICIA
FVNDAVIT
EXTRVXIT ORNAVIT NIHIL HIC HOSTILE NE
ARCENDIS
QVIDEM HOSTIBVS NON FOSSA NON VALLVM
VERVM
AD HOSPITES BENIGNE EXCIPIENDOS
BENEVOLE

TRACTANDOS FONS AQVAE VIRGINIS
VIRIDARIA
PISCINAE AVIARIA PER AMOENITATEM OMNIA
AD CORPVS
ANIMVMQUE HONESTE OBLECTANDVM
COMPOSVIT
QVISQVIS IGITVR IN HAEC FVRTO FERRO
FLAMMA
SEV QVOMODOLIBET HOSTILITER SE
GESSERIT
IS SE OMNIS CARITATIS VRBANITATISQVE
EXPERTEM IMMO HVMANITATIS OMNIS
HVMANIQVE
GENERIS HOSTEM PROFITEATVR LAPIDES
SANCTI
LOQVENTVR ET PROMVLGABVNT
(To God the best and greatest. For his own benefit, for the benefit of his descendants, and for that of all men of cultivation and urbanity, Alexander Seton, most loving of culture and humanity, has founded, erected and decorated a *villa*, the gardens and these suburban buildings. Nothing here to do with hostility, not a ditch

or rampart against enemies, but a fountain of pure water, lawns, fish ponds and aviaries for the kindly welcome of guests. In the ways of pleasantness he has laid these out for the honourable delight of body and soul. Therefore he declares that whoever faces these as an enemy in any way, whether by theft, sword, or fire, let that man declare himself devoid of charity and urbanity, and an enemy of all culture and the human race. The sacred stones will speak and proclaim it.) (Fig 193) (RCAHMS 1929, 85)

The other panel bears, beneath a coronet and the initials ASED, a more religious message:

[DEO] [O]PTIMO MAXIMO
[RE]RVM [OMNIVM] AVTHOR[I]
LARGITORI CONSERVATORI
IEJOVAE STATORI
CVIVS NVTV BENEFICIO
STANT BONA OMNIA C[ERTA]
HONOR OMNIS GLOR[IA]
(To God the best and greatest, the author, the giver, the preserver of all, Jehovah, who is my strength by whose will and loving kindness all good things are assured, all honour and glory.) (RCAHMS 1929, 85)

The words, in Greek capitals, *Eulogia kai Eucharistia*, Praise and Thankfulness, follow.

This is a garden furnished with inscriptions. What survives in the house is an elaborate pictorial scheme. The top floor in the eastern part of this house is formed by a long gallery with a coved timber ceiling. It is filled with coats of arms, Latin and Greek inscriptions and emblematic panels of classical and mythological subjects. At the centre of the ceiling is a remarkable *trompe l'oeil* cupola, offering the illusion of a glimpse of the sky, harking back to the playing with perspective of the late fifteenth century ceiling in the ducal palace at Mantua, by means of a design from one of the most advanced European pattern books, concerned with mathematics and the theory of perspective. Seton was the dedicatee of Napier of Merchiston's treatise of 1617 that explained the invention of the system of calculating rods known as Napier's Bones. The scheme of the decoration has been discussed in detail by Michael Bath (Bath 2003, 79–103) who stresses, as at Edzell, the neo-Stoic philosophy behind the paintings (Fig 194).

Seton's inscriptions make clear the important part to be played by the gardens in his 'suburban' house, and Allan (1997, 69) notes the reference to the peace and joy to be realised in a cottage. The gardens could be viewed from the upper floors of the house, as well as from the oriel windows to the south. There was a walled garden in this position to the south of the house on Roy's map of Pinkie, but walls of the same massive nature as those to

Fig 194 Panel from the ceiling of the Long Gallery at Pinkie House showing an emblem of Temperance derived from Horace's Epistles *and* Satires. *The bearded man filling his pitcher at the fountain has been identified with Alexander Seton (Bath 2003, 81–2) and this personification echoes the modest nature of the inscription on the front of the house.*

the north and east did not survive here to be recorded in the earlier twentieth century (RCAHMS 1929, 85).

The house and garden were known as places to be visited and admired. A description of the garden by Sir John Lauder, who visited Pinkie in September 1668, mentions:

A most sweit garden, the knot much larger than that at Hamilton and in better order. The rest of the yeard nether so great nor in so good order nor so well planted as is in Hamilton yeard. The knot heir will be 200 foot square, a mighty long grein walk. Saw figs at a verie great perfection. Above the utter gait as ye enter into the place ther is an inscription in golden letters telling the founder therof, and assuring them that shall ever attempt to destroy that fabric by sword, fyre, demolishment or other ways that the very stones and beams ut of the wall shall exclaim against them as destitute of all humanity and common courtesie. 18 plots in the garden with summer houses and sundrie parks.
(Lauder 1900, 189–90)

A knot 200 feet across would fit within the walled garden immediately to the east of the house.

Fig 195 The water parterre at Brunston Castle adjacent to the sixteenth century castle and the modern farmhouse. SC1128191

A mound is depicted in the grounds of Loretto School on the First Edition of the 6-inch Ordnance Survey map of 1853, in line with the long axis of the north garden at Pinkie. The site of the mound has been associated with the Chapel and Hermitage of Our Lady of Loretto, which was ruinous by 1590, and may have later been in use as an icehouse. Whatever its origins and subsequent history, it may have been adapted to act as a prospect mound providing views over the gardens at Pinkie (*Stat Acct*, 16, 5; *NSA* 1, 274; Robertson 1953, 132–3).

John Preston of Penicuik, Lord Fentonbarns, was another royal official who served James VI and I. He held various administrative posts, and was a Lord of Session, a member of the Privy Council as well as one of the commission, appointed in 1611 to manage the royal finances. His pensions amounted to more than

£1000 Scots, mainly drawn from various former abbey lands, including Jedburgh, Holywood, North Berwick and Haddington. He had acquired Brunston Castle in Midlothian by 1613. The castle at **Brunston** (also known as Brunstane) is described in the *Inventory of Midlothian and West Lothian* as a fair-sized mansion, built on a courtyard plan (RCAHMS 1929, 154–5). It had belonged to the Crichton family from the late fourteenth century, and, in 1493, a charter of the lands of Brunston was granted to Edward Crichton and his spouse, Agnes Cockburn, for a redendo or rent of a red rose yearly on the ground at Brunston on the feast of the nativity of St John the Baptist. This implied the presence of a garden there in the late fifteenth century. A date stone above the main door carries the date 1568, probably the date when the castle was rebuilt. There is a tower on the north entrance side of at least two habitable storeys with a gate lodge attached; the dwelling house proper was on the southern side and was three storeys in

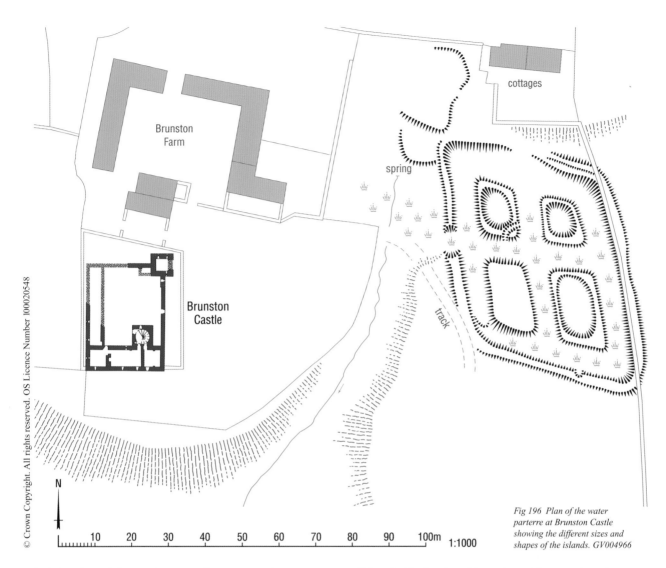

N

10 20 30 40 50 60 70 80 90 100m

1:1000

Fig 196 Plan of the water parterre at Brunston Castle showing the different sizes and shapes of the islands. GV004966

height. The Crichtons also owned property at Brunstane to the east of Edinburgh, which was acquired by the Maitland family about the beginning of the seventeenth century, where the design of the garden will be discussed in the next chapter. The difference in the spelling of the name of the two properties is a modern convenience.

About 80m to the north-east of the castle is a water garden, which might also be referred to as a water parterre or a series of fish ponds (Fig 195). This is rhomboidal or diamond-shaped and measures about 50m north and south by 80m west-north-west and east-south-east (Brown 2009, 20–1). Four diamond-shaped islands occupy the interior of the site, each surrounded by broad channels, now full of water and rushes. They create the shape of an uneven St Andrew's cross within an enclosing bank, which again forms a raised path around the water feature. Although each island differs in shape, form and profile, they all reflect the diamond shape of the overall site. Three of the islands have a diamond-shaped sunken area within them, forming an internal pond. A bank surrounds each pond also forming a raised path. The fourth island is a low mound (Fig 196). While the channels and internal ponds could support

fish suitable for the table and provide a nesting place for water fowl, it is clear that recreational, symbolic and aesthetic reasons lie behind the creation of this complex. From the towers of the castle there would have been a bird's eye view of the water garden. A round-headed gateway about a metre in width leads out from the courtyard of the castle onto a level area which would probably have been a garden, and on across the burn to the water garden (Fig 197).

Fishing and the pleasures of looking at fish and water are well documented in the seventeenth century in books such as *Cheape and good husbandry for the well-ordering of all beasts, and fowles, and the general cure of their diseases* by Gervase Markham (1568?–1637), first published in 1614. It contained a section on the making of fish ponds. Markham was a prolific author, who wrote books on a considerable variety of topics including archery, horsemanship, hawking, fowling and hunting, land improvement, military exercises, various plays and poems, letter writing guides and the duties of the husbandman and the housewife. His books were reprinted throughout the seventeenth century, and in the 1623 edition of *Cheape and good husbandry* he describes how to construct a fish pond, how to stock it and how to extract the fish (Markham 1623, 174–9). In this edition the publisher, Robert Jackson, inserted a plan of a complex of ponds which strongly resembled an actual example found at Tackley in Oxfordshire, which belonged to his friend, John Harborne (Whittle and Taylor, 1992, 37–63). The plate on page 174 showed four islands of two different shapes with small internal ponds surrounded by channels and walks. Fish ponds form part of many gardens of this period where earthwork remains survive, but perhaps the closest parallel to the water features at Brunston is at Raglan Castle in Gwent in South Wales. In a plan of Raglan of 1652 two formal water gardens are shown (Whittle 1989, 89–90; 1992, 23). One consists of four rectangular islands surrounded by water channels. The other more elaborate example is a rectangular area divided into diamond-shaped and triangular islands by narrow channels. Both now survive, like Brunston, in pasture. Italian water gardens frequently embellished with fountains, such as the outstanding example at the Villa Lante near Viterbo, were a constant source of inspiration. John Preston died in 1616, and it may be

Fig 197 Brunston Castle as drawn by Alexander Archer in 1836. The gate out into the garden has been closed. DP066910

that the water garden was the work of his son, another John, a lawyer like his father, who became a Member of Parliament and Solicitor General. The garden might be the work of their wives. Preston's third wife, who survived him, was Margaret Collace, widow of John Sharp of Houston, another lawyer, who certainly employed a gardener at Houston House in West Lothian. A simple garden with parterres was recorded there on an estate plan of 1759 (Sanderson 1987, 29; NRS GD30/1675; RHP 10659). Brunston ceased to be the

Fig 198 The busts of George Foulis, the King's Master of the Mint, and his wife, Janet Bannatyne, on their tomb in Greyfriars Kirkyard. Greyfriars was the most prestigious of the early seventeenth century burial grounds in Edinburgh. Like the sculptures in their garden it emphasises their marital union. DP110106

principal residence of its owners and the castle had fallen into ruin when it was drawn by Alexander Archer in 1836 (RCAHMS MLD/178/4) (Fig 197).

Evidence for the construction of a garden by another royal official survived at **Ravelston House**, the home of George Foulis, who was the 'king's moneyer' or Master of the Mint. George Foulis and his wife Janet Bannatyne bought Ravelston in 1620 (Fig 198), and their seventeenth century house, with a date stone of 1622 above a door decorated with stylised flowers, was destroyed by fire, probably in the following century (Fig 199). The site is now occupied by the Mary Erskine School. The fountain was situated in the walled garden. It stood 11 feet 6 inches (3.3m) high and consisted of an octagonal shaft and base on which a circular basin was set. Within the basin the octagonal shaft was enriched with lion masks and, above, on each face was a dolphin with a lead tongue fashioned like a tortoise head, from which a stream of water flowed. The shaft then tapered and terminated with a unicorn holding a shield, on which there was a crowned thistle. On one facet, just above the lion masks, the fountain was dated 1630, while on the opposite side were the initials GF and IB linked by a lovers' knot. There was another fountain, possibly of similar date, and a lectern dovecot stood

Fig 199 Garden doorway of 1622 belonging to Old Ravelston House decorated with stylised flowers and the initials of the owners. SC1243591

Fig 200 The fountain of 1630 at Old Ravelston House was surmounted by a unicorn bearing a shield with a crowned thistle. Water flowed from the mouths of fantastic beasts. SC1243589

Fig 201 Detail of the fountain at Old Ravelston House. The initials of the owners were linked by a lovers knot. SC1243590

Fig 202 *Aerial view of Elibank Castle and its terraced gardens high above the River Tweed. DP060998*

outside the walled garden (RCAHMS 1929, xli, 24–5) (Figs 200, 201). Ravelston was one of a large number of gardens clustered around Edinburgh, and their contents were of value. In 1625 John Rait and Alexander Dean were hanged for stealing various herbs and bee hives from the gardens of Barnton, Pilton and other places (Chalmers 1807–24, 2, 94).

Other gardens belonging to the royal servants who governed Scotland after James had gained the English throne adopted different patterns. One of the most impressive is that at **Elibank Castle** in Selkirkshire on the south side of the River Tweed between Traquair and Ashiestiel. Here the use of a steep hillside results in one of the most Italianate gardens in Scotland belonging to this period (Fig 202). It was the house of Sir Gideon Murray who, after a markedly violent early career, acquired the lands of Elibank in 1595; the neighbouring lands of Glenpoit had been granted to him as a child. In 1603 he was appointed a border commissioner and was knighted for his services in 1605. Five years later he became a member of the Privy Council, and was appointed a commissioner for the exchequer, receiving an annual pension of £1200. In 1612 he took his seat in Parliament as shire commissioner for Selkirkshire. He became one of the lords of the articles, a member of the committee that received petitions and drafted legislation. The same year he received the offices of treasurer depute, comptroller and collector depute of the new ecclesiastical lands with a salary of £1500. His cousin Robert Kerr or Carr, the Lord High Treasurer and favourite of James VI, was resident in England

and treated his post as a sinecure. Elibank became the acting royal treasurer in Scotland. As such he was responsible for the repair and refurbishment of a number of royal properties in Scotland, in particular in 1617 the rebuilding of the north range at Linlithgow after its collapse, and, in the same year, the financing of James' 'hamecoming' which required work at Holyrood,

Fig 203 *This vertical aerial photograph taken in 1948 before forestry planting shows how the rock on the hillside above and to the south-west of Elibank Castle has been cut back to ensure a level site for the upper gardens. RAF 541_A_438_3024*

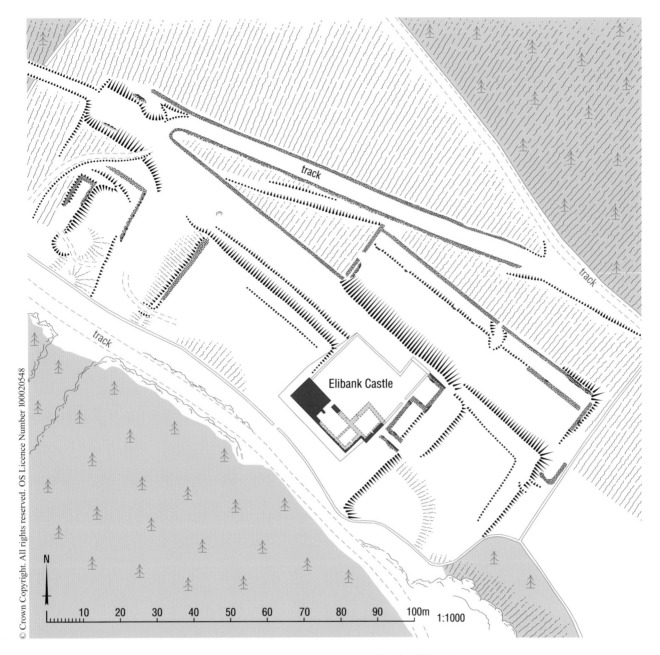

N

| 10 | 20 | 30 | 40 | 50 | 60 | 70 | 80 | 90 | 100m | 1:1000 |

Fig 204 Plan of Elibank Castle and its gardens with the carefully graded approach from the valley below. GV004972

Stirling and Falkland. He was appointed in 1613, like John Preston, Alexander Seton and Sir David Lindsay, an Ordinary (that is salaried) Lord of Session with the judicial title Lord Elibank. His annual pension from 1616 was £2400 and the right for his life and for that of his sons to import thirty tuns of wine duty free (*DNB* 2004). His family held the house of **Black Barony** or Darnhall near Eddleston, which descended to his nephew. Black Barony was described in 1649 as having been repaired by Sir Archibald Murray. 'The Park here is an Ornament to the House, being well stored with Forrest trees in a place where there are so few' (Macfarlane 1906–8, 3, 151). Sir Archibald had died in 1634. The house has been in continuous occupation and the garden is still well wooded. A surviving feature on the south side of

the Dean Burn is a mound, perhaps of seventeenth century date, which is likely to have served as a prospect mount, but its relationship to a contemporary garden is unknown (RCAHMS 1967 2, 286).

The castle at Elibank, which lies at a height of about 210m above sea level, is much ruined (Fig 204). It formerly stood at least four storeys high and comprised a rectangular main block about 21m in length by 7m with a wing on the north-east some 8m square and an entrance at the centre of the north-east side of the main block. The entrance opened into a forecourt which may have had a gatehouse at its north-east corner. The castle occupies a platform that has been terraced on all four sides with the ground cut back and built up to allow the layout of three surviving rectilinear gardens.

Fig 205 Aerial view of the ruined Langshaw Tower. At present there is a single terrace in front of the tower within the walled garden, but a series of terraces which formerly lay within a tree-lined enclosure survive on one side. SC1161174

When the land had been set in feu ferm by James IV in 1511, a condition of the grant was that the recipient was required to build 'an adequate house of stone and lime, with a hall, chamber, barn, cattle-shed, stable, dovecot, garden, orchards and beehives' (*RMS* 2, 779 No 3617).

The access to the castle is by means of a straight, well-engineered road which leads up from the modern road to the south-east, turning sharply back on itself to the north-west from where the terraces of the garden can be viewed from below. The road, which is cut into the slope and walled, continues past a junction where the surviving traces of buildings may indicate the site of what may have been an outer court with stables and farm buildings, before continuing along a near-level way to the inner court in front of the castle, where entrance may have been through a gatehouse (RCAHMS 1957, 35–6). There are slight traces of what may have been an earlier track with a steeper gradient above the road.

A rectangular garden, measuring about 45m by 30m, lies to the north-west immediately next to the castle where the ground on the south-west side has been cut back to provide a more level platform. Vertical air photographs, taken by the Royal Air Force in 1948 (RAF541/A/438:29 July 48), show the original extent of this garden, which has been obscured by the subsequent construction of a track connected with afforestation (Fig 203). There are the remains of a stone wall on the north-west above an artificial slope towards what may have been the outer court. A slight scarp on the north-east lies above two terraces running down to the entrance road to the castle. This area is overlooked from the first floor of the castle by a room where there are surviving indications of a fireplace.

On the other side of the castle is a rectangular garden also measuring about 45m by 30m with its long axis running north-east and south-west. It is on two

levels, the higher part lying to the west, where it has been obscured by the construction of later walls. There is a scarp on the north-east and south-east creating a slight terrace above the most impressive of the three gardens, which faces north-east. This has terraces on two levels, enclosed by stone walls, and measures about 75m north-west and south-east by 20m, with stone walls surviving to north-west and south-east. The upper terrace has a stone revetment, which appears to continue above ground level as a wall. A hollow between these two gardens may mark the site of a stair, leading to the garden below. Opposite this is a break in the wall of the lower terrace, leading beyond the enclosed garden on to the steep natural bank above the approach road.

What the different gardens were employed for is not known, but it is likely that they included a garden decorated with knots, an orchard and a garden for vegetables. All of the gardens can be viewed from different parts of the castle. Only some of the windows in the castle survive, and the function of the apartments within the castle is uncertain. The chamber may have overlooked the garden to the north-west of the building, beyond which lies what may have been the outer court. This may have been the site of the vegetable garden or orchard. The more secluded garden to the south-east of the tower might have been a knot garden or an orchard and the long garden with its two terraces would be particularly suitable for walking.

Sir Gideon Murray, the owner of Elibank, had at least three other houses. One was on the north side of the High Street in Edinburgh near the Luckenbooths by St Giles Kirk, and another was the tower at **Langshaw** in Roxburghshire (Fig 205). This had been the property of Melrose Abbey and in 1586 was held in

Fig 206 Langshaw Tower as it appears on the Military Survey of 1747–55 (08/3A) flanked by two symmetrical enclosures. © British Library. Licensor Scran

Fig 207 *Vertical aerial photograph of the site of Posso Tower and its gardens showing the fish pond with its island and the terraces in relation to the buildings. PGA_NT2033_2007-10-05 © NextPerspectives*

Fig 208 *A ground view of the pond at Posso with its island, from the terrace to the west looking towards the nineteenth century house. DSCN0094*

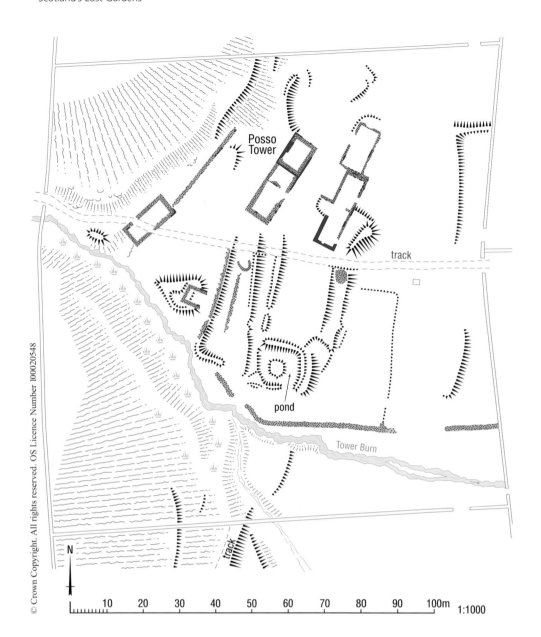

Posso
Tower

track

pond

Tower Burn

track

N

10 20 30 40 50 60 70 80 90 100m 1:1000

Fig 209 Plan of the earthworks of the garden at Posso. The building to the east of Posso Tower may have been the principal residence of the owners, the Naismiths of Posso, in the earlier seventeenth century. A level area, possibly the site of a parterre, lies to the south between the building and the pond, with lines of terraces and a possible viewing point to the west. GV004977

feu by George Hoppringle or Pringle, who also owned Whytbank Tower. His son and grandson, both called James, sold it to Murray in 1606. The Pringle family, whose gardens along the Tweed will be discussed later, were probably responsible for the construction of the earlier part of the tower, with a later wing added by the Murrays. Which family was responsible for the creation of the gardens there is uncertain, particularly as the house continued in use up to the eighteenth century, when it served as a village school (RCAHMS 1956, 292–3). At present in front of the tower there is a walled garden with a single terrace. To the south are a series of low terraces, visible on aerial photographs, which lay, according to the Military Survey of 1747–55, in a tree-lined enclosure with another similar and parallel enclosure to the north (Fig 206).

A third Murray garden was at **Ballencrieff Castle** near Aberlady in East Lothian. This had been part of the royal domain, and there are references to the orchard

and dovecot there from the fifteenth century onwards in the *Exchequer Rolls* (*ER* 9, 359, 475, 580). Part of the payment for Ballencrieff was a render of a thousand cherries each year (RPS 1617/5/64). The restored house and its present garden now lie in an area of arable cultivation, but no evidence for the earlier form of the garden has emerged.

Some 3.5 km to the west of Elibank Castle is the ruinous tower at Plora Burn, another tower where there is evidence for gardens with a series of terraces below the tower and its inner court. This belonged to the family of Lowis of Plora, who received the feu of the property in the sixteenth century (RCAHMS 1967, 263–5).

The Manor Valley to the south-west of Peebles has three sites where, it has been suggested, the remains of gardens, associated with tower houses of sixteenth century date, survive (RCAHMS 1967, 237–8, 265–7, 268–9), all of which appear on maps prepared during the earlier seventeenth century (Blaeu 1654, *Atlas*

Fig 210 The garden terraces at Posso looking to the south.

7m, this could be the mansion house of the owner of the garden. What survives of the garden is a series of enclosures whose walls would protect the gardens and orchard from incursions by livestock. Five terraces of varying width are its most outstanding feature (Fig 210). Between the upper three and the two lower terraces and immediately to the south of the possible mansion house is a flat rectangular expanse of turf measuring some 25m by 14m which may have been the site of a decorative parterre, directly overlooked from the mansion house. To the south of this garden is a sunken rectangular feature about 10m square with a central island, a fish pond similar to one quarter of the fish ponds at Brunston (Fig 208). A feature in the upper part of the garden may mark the site of a stair leading up to other garden areas. It may also have been designed to provide a position from which the garden could be viewed. There are a number of aged sycamores surviving on the site, which were probably contemporary with one of the phases of the garden. A terraced track or walk lies to the south of the main complex, possibly, as is suggested at Whytbank, providing level ground for exercise for recreation and health.

The owners of Posso in the late sixteenth and seventeenth centuries were the Naesmyth family. James Naesmyth was heir to his grandfather, Michael Naesmyth, inheriting the property in 1611. It is likely that he was the creator of the garden remains which survive at Posso. He was Sheriff Depute of Peebles, a Member of Parliament in the reign of Charles I, and in 1649 he was referred to as Falconer Royal and Chief of the Name (Macfarlane 1906–8, 3, 150). His uncle, John, was surgeon to James VI (NLS Acc.8522). A sundial

Fig 211 The sundial at Posso which bears the date 1649.

Major Tweedale). The earthworks at Newholm Hope are difficult to interpret satisfactorily, and the terraces at Langhaugh lie within a forestry plantation, but the garden at **Posso Tower** which lies at a height of about 270m above sea level, brings together the features of a terraced garden and of a decorative fish pond. It provides the closest surviving parallel in Scotland to Brunston, though on a smaller scale, with its single pool and island.

The old tower at Posso probably dates from the earlier sixteenth century (Figs 207, 209). What are described in the *Peeblesshire Inventory* (RCAHMS 1967, 265) as outbuildings may actually be the remains of later residential buildings, probably contemporary with the remains of the garden. This is particularly likely in the case of the building to the east of the tower where traces of fireplaces on the ground and first floors could be seen, with a staircase in a stair tower connecting the two floors. Measuring about 11m by

Fig 212 *Aerial view of Monzie Castle in dry conditions showing the grass-covered terraces. SC505291*

Fig 213 *An engraving of 1822 showing Monzie Castle with level lawns surrounding the later house. DP097567*

inscribed with the date of 1649 survives at Posso near a later house, but the terraced garden, and particularly the fish pond, is more likely on stylistic grounds to belong to a date in the 1620s (Fig 211).

A Perthshire mansion where terraces were introduced was **Monzie Castle** near Crieff (Figs 213, 214), but here the terraces were almost obliterated when the lawns were extended right up to the house, probably at the same time the Adam-style castellated mansion was added between 1797 and 1800 (Gifford 2007, 540);

the remains were initially identified from the air (Fig 212). The earlier house, dated to 1634 on the lintel over the main door and on the pediments of the second floor windows, was built by James Graham and his wife, and it is likely that the terraced gardens should be associated with it. James Graham, a relative of Montrose, died at the battle of Philiphaugh in 1645. The ground on which the house stands (an earlier tower is shown on Pont (Pont 21)) is now relatively level and some considerable effort must have been employed to achieve the desired effect. There are three terraces to the south-east and at least one to the south-west, where a garden was created or recreated in the twentieth century. To the north-west of the house is a natural mound which has been turned

Fig 214 *Plan of the terraced garden at Monzie Castle, which may have related to the early seventeenth century building. GV004974*

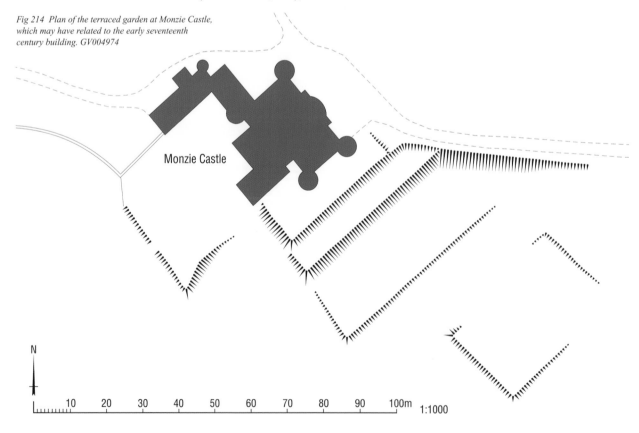

Monzie Castle

N

10 20 30 40 50 60 70 80 90 100m 1:1000

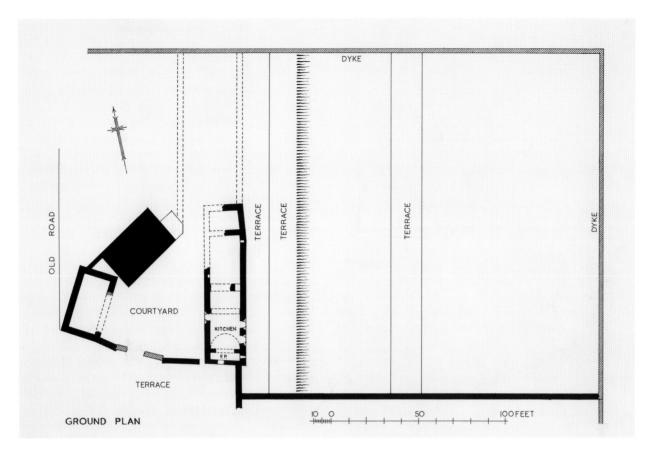

Fig 215 Plan of the buildings of Whytbank set around a court and its gardens, taken from the Inventory of Selkirkshire. *The plan of the terraces is based on the First Edition of the Ordnance Survey 6-inch map of Selkirkshire surveyed in 1858, when the terraces were already planted with trees. RCAHMS (1957), Fig 7.*

into a square terraced mount. Its date is unknown but, according to the *Old Statistical Account* for the parish of Monzie written in 1793, there was a summer house in the form of a Chinese temple, hexagonal in plan with a pointed roof and a balcony on top (*Stat Acct*, 15, 254), presumably a reuse of an existing feature.

The survival of these early seventeenth century gardens owes much to their desertion at an early date in their history, when their owners adopted another estate as a permanent residence, while still retaining the land and in some cases deriving their principal title from that particular property, as the Lords Elibank did. The height at which they were situated would always render the cultivation of many garden plants difficult. The presumption is that such gardens, as at Torwoodlee, existed at a lower level, but that most were swept away following changes in style and ownership. One garden that is known about only from a chance visit and the survival of a manuscript is that at Gala House, now called **Old Gala House** in Galashiels. The house lies in a suburban setting at a height of about 110m with much of the former garden covered by housing, and even on nineteenth century maps there is little to match the description in the manuscript. This was written by Christopher Lowther, a younger son of the Cumberland

family, who died in 1644, and who was probably about twenty at the time of his travels in Scotland in 1629. A meeting at Langholm in Dumfriesshire with Robert Pringle led to a recommendation to Sir James Pringle of Galashiels, at whose house Lowther and his two companions stayed on their journey to Edinburgh and on their return. James Pringle was, according to Christopher Lowther, encouraging the cultivation of trees by his tenants who were to plant six fruit trees or twelve other trees, or face a fine. He had 'a very pretty park with many natural walks in it, artificial ponds and arbours now a making, he hath neat gardens and orchards, and all his tenants through his care, he hath abundance of cherry trees, bearing a black cherry, some of which I see to be about 30 yards high and a fathom thick, great store of sycamores, trees he calleth silk trees, and fir trees' (Lowther 1894, 18). The morning of their departure, they walked abroad into park, gardens and other places.

Christopher Lowther also comments on the number of houses belonging to other members of the Pringle family living along the Tweed and Gala Water, 'gentlemen all of pretty seats and buildings' (Lowther 1894, 17), and later, in the 1649 'Description of the Shirefdom of Selkirk by Wm Eliot of Stobbs & Walter Scot of Arkiltoun' (Macfarlane 1906–8, 3, 138–9), these properties are, among many others, described as the principal houses of the shire. One of these, which has already been described, was Torwoodlee, which was built for George Pringle in 1601, and which incorporated garden features in its design. Another Pringle house

Fig 216 *Aerial view of the reconstructed Whytbank Tower and its gardens from the north. PGA_NT4337_2007-10-05. © NextPerspectives*

where something of the garden survives is that at **Whytbank Tower** near Clovenfords (Figs 215, 216). It stands at a height of about 260m, which must have produced some gardening challenges. The tower is dated to the sixteenth century; it was reconstructed between 1987 and 1992, along with the garden. As at Posso, there is across the courtyard from the tower a rectangular building, which measures about 27m by 7m. It contains a kitchen and three other apartments on the ground floor and was probably used as a residence in the seventeenth century, possibly by the James Pringle who died in 1622 or by his grandson and heir, another James (Fig 217). It is on the same alignment as the gardens, which measure about 62m east-south-east by 58m. It may have been planned to overlook this extensive terraced garden with its four terraces, alternately broad and narrow, which had retaining walls of stone laid in clay. In the revetment of one terrace are two small recesses which were probably bee boles to hold skeps (Fig 218). On the south side of the garden is an L-shaped enclosure, measuring 62m by a maximum of 40m, which may have been the orchard. The tower is approached from the south by a road which runs along a terrace parallel to the contour, flanked by a second lower terrace. Both terraces, which extend for at least 300m, are revetted by drystone walling (Fig 219). These

would have been designed to allow gentle and civilised walking out from the house, perhaps particularly for the women of the family. It is possible that the gardens and the mansion house were constructed or improved by the younger James Pringle, who had served for some years in France as an officer of the Scots Guards, and who in 1622 married Sophia Schoner, a Danish woman, who had been a maid of honour to Anne of Denmark, and who died in 1626. Like James Naesmyth of Posso he was a Member of Parliament in 1633 (Craig-Brown 1886, 471–3). The Earl of Ancram refers to him as his 'cousin Whytbank, a very politique man and a great pond maker' (Laing 1875, 72).

Sir Robert Kerr, Earl of Ancram, has provided in a letter to his son his beliefs about the creation of a suitable house and garden for a principal landowner. This is the major practical guide available for the layout of a garden before the publication of *The Scots Gard'ner* by John Reid in 1683, although despite its formal tone, it was a private document. Kerr was married to a niece of Gideon Murray of Elibank, and became a groom of the bedchamber to Prince Henry, eldest son of James VI and I, and later to his second son, the future Charles I. He travelled to France in 1607, and was later in Spain in 1623 with Charles on his unsuccessful attempt to marry the daughter of the king of Spain. He also accompanied Charles on his visit to Scotland for his coronation in 1633, on which occasion he was granted the earldom of Ancram. He had inherited the estate of **Ancrum** in 1590 following the murder of his father. Like William

Fig 217 *Whytbank Tower, the probable seventeenth century range and the upper terrace in 2010. DSCN0115*

Fig 218 The bee boles set into the lower terrace wall at Whytbank. DSCN0116

Drummond of Hawthorden, to whom he sent his verses, he wrote in praise of the solitary life (Laing 1875, 522). In 1631 his eldest son William married Anna Kerr, his cousin, who was Countess of Lothian in her own right and the heiress of Newbattle; and his father wrote to his son as William, third Earl of Lothian, in 1632. Robert Kerr would appear to have passed over management of the estate of Ancrum to him at this time, and in his letter suggested improvements to the house and policies there, saying that as he was paying for the improvements, his son should accept his advice or reply with reasons to the contrary (Laing 1875, 62).

Whether his son actually carried out these proposals is not known, although he certainly carried out works in the garden at **Newbattle Abbey**, the inheritance of his wife. The tower at Ancrum, which probably dated from 1558, was completely rebuilt following a fire in 1885. The Kerrs had been granted the land in feu ferm in 1542 by Jedburgh Abbey (*RMS* 3, 628–9, no 2720) so that the payment could be spent on the restoration of the monastery after it had been burnt by the English. What may have been an indication of a garden adjacent to the tower appears on the Timothy Pont manuscript map of the area (Pont 35(2)) (Fig 220). Roy's Military Survey depicts only avenues of trees around the mansion, and, although a survey of the estate in 1796 (NRS RHP 47938) showed what appear to be a series of parterres within a walled garden, they do not, as Robert Kerr had recommended, lie near the tower. His advice is contained in a letter written in December 1632 (Laing 1875, 64–74). His concerns cover architecture, garden design and estate management, and aim to reconcile the establishment and maintenance of the status of their family with an increase in the financial return. He writes that now his son has neighbours of some standing, 'yow

must disporte your business in another manner, and make Ancram and that which belonged to it the prime place and example to the rest, as it is the cheeff, and yields so many different occasions of ornament and polishing, which our people call policy', and that 'yow must make all things of bewty and ornament and vse, not only for your self but other folk'. He adds, 'Now for your vtter court and the approaches to your house, which are most materiall; yow must have a speciall regard to them to make them fayre and easye and noble and plesand as the ground will afford, for yow must not contract them now, but rather extend them to a forme suttable to your quality.' His advice, as he said, threatened to amount to the volume of a book. When he was writing in 1632, the garden lay next to the laigh hall, and he proposed that it should be replaced by a back court for the storage of fuel, peat, wood and coal and the hen houses. The front or entrance court on the other side should be paved. He suggested the building up of the foregate with lodgings and a gallery over it, 'because all the bewty of the garden must be cast that waye, and it lyes to the sunne, which in Scotland

Fig 219 A section of the terraced walk to the south of Whytbank Tower. DSCN0124

Fig 220 The mansion of Ancrum as it is depicted on late sixteenth century manuscript map by Timothy Pont (Pont 35 (2)) about the time that Robert Kerr inherited the estate following the murder of his father. There is an indication of an enclosure with trees in it. © NLS

is a mayne consideration'. This was to be 'your fayre building' and Sir Robert recommended building 'the principall fyre rooms' there, and considered that the building should 'be kept sweet for interteyning my frends at solemne tymes ... and easy lodgings to lodge a great man'. It was to be a separate structure from the tower to which it was to be joined by a 'balcon or ship gallery', preserving the defensible nature of the tower. His proposal might be paralleled in the ruinous buildings surviving at Whytbank and Posso, which have a similar relationship to the garden.

What Robert Kerr refers to in his plan as the 'very garden', is to be enclosed by walls, and it would lie towards the town. This would be the settlement of Over Ancrum, which would seem from the Pont map to lie to the east of the tower. The removal of various buildings there was recommended in the letter, and, by the time of the Military Survey, the settlement seems to have disappeared. 'Now for that which is the very garden, which consists of knotts, it will lye best and evenest round about the tower, and on the backside next to the towne will be on[e] of the best pairts of it when your wall is built crosse from the nooke of the tower to the towne green.' He emphasises the need for walls and a gate for the garden. 'Yett take away presently these high trees which grow so neere the tower ... and there yow must make your garden, with walks from it to the doucat (dovecot) alleye, and so along to your park, which is your cheeff garden and bewty.'

The orchard was considered as both recreational and productive. It was to be surrounded by high walls, and the recommendation was to plant 'a fayre orchard

of the best fruits yow can gett in the abbyes about yow'. The site was the 'fittest for fruit of all the places about Ancram, as lyeing wele to the sunn and vnder the north wynd'. His son was to create a walk in the orchard bordered by 'on eyther side a fayr rowe of good fruit trees, with a gate at eyther end' so that he could walk from the house through and into the park. 'Where fruit trees will grow, plant them, but never plant a fruit tree where it will not grow wele ... Never plant it where the north wynd cums to it – it is lost labour.' He continues 'your aples and plooms and sum choyse peares will grow best on the orchard ye are to make in the brae ... peare trees will grow wele, wheroff seek out the best within Newbattle and Jedburgh and other places of renowne, and eyther plant or graft the best ... and when it cums to the even of the orchard along towards the park, make long walks planted with trees, and in the sight, in the midst of it, plaic arbors or what yow will, variously as your fancy leads yow, or as yow are counseld by such as have skill'. In another part of the orchard he recommended to 'plant it with cherrye trees; for I have seen excellent cherryes growing there with little caire, so as I know it will be an excellent cherry garden, which in Scotland is one of your best fruits where they are choysed, and plant abbondance of grosers (gooseberries) and risors (raspberries) and strauberryes, and roses and all flowers all over your orchard, for they will grow well in Ancram'. He favoured keeping the orchard concealed from passersby, and to achieve this he recommended that 'next to the dyke within the orchard plant rowes of playne trees in walkes, to keep the sight of these that stand at the crosse to looke into the orchard, or men as they ride doun the toun gate', (presumably that of Over Ancrum). The productive side of cultivation in the orchard was not to be neglected: 'and in your orchard wher you may have mowing grasse or sherring grasse among the trees, never want it'.

Another practical concern in the creation of the garden and policies around the house was the provision of walks. Sir Robert Kerr suggests: 'make a walk vnder the doucot yarde dyke to walk vnder the north wynde within the orchard, and then on eyther syde a fayr rowe of good fruit trees, with a gate at eyther end to go into it, and out to the rest of the parke; and from it, as also from the long alley, and above it, extend that walk all along the bankhead to the little bank, and on the topp off it too, till yow cum to the even ground that goeth to the kirk, and planting all the steep of the killing-brae with birkes and ony other sortes of trees, be tymes it will be a pleasant walk for both sight and smell, and keep the hasells of the little bank undestroyed, for theye are the best and ayrlyest nuttes of all the countreye'. This reference to the planting of trees is supplemented by the injunction to remove the tall trees which were around the tower, and the trees which Kerr's own brother had unadvisedly planted. The walks could range more widely: he suggests the construction of steps 'to goe vpp to walk sometimes on Gregly Law and there, iff you make a bonfire at any tyme, sett it on there; for from thence it will be seen over all the country, and yow will see into your park ... and all over the gardens and orchard'. It would have something of the function of a prospect mount.

He wished to extend the park and policies by demolishing and removing various houses and crofts, first satisfying the tenants with alternative accommodation, and proposing that, by agreement with the minister, he should take 'his kirkland into your parke, with a high wall round about it, it would compare then with an Englishe parke'.

Other features included fish ponds, which he considered 'a most necessary thing, especially in a place so farr from the sea'. On their land was 'a great lake very deepe, which yow may eyther putt pearches and other fishes to nourishe in it, or iff they will not live their, drayne it and make a meadow of it'. Currently it could not even be used for curling. In addition, within the park was 'wett ground or marshe, which, cast into fine ponds, and separated, one at the end of another by sluces ... the partitions between the ponds will serve as bridges to bring away the hay, and it will be a very fine prospect when the sheep bank above it is all planted with trees promiscuously of all kinds, especially birks for smell'.

There is a clear association of gardens with organised communal sport and recreation, although this may well be an association with the castle, tower or house rather than directly with the garden. Sir Robert Kerr proposed to have an outer green for football beyond his outer court. In this same area from which various houses would have to be removed, there would also be provision for running at the ring or glove, which could be watched from the bank above. There was also reference to the 'bowbutts'. The space between the goals or refuges, marked by trees (dealtres), in the old balgreen (ball green) was to be planted with pear trees. Football had been played in the outer court, an area in a similar position to that at Edzell, where the four great growing trees marked the dobts (Macfarlane 1906–8, 2, 39) and, before the late seventeenth century reorganisation, also at Glamis (Millar 1890, 41).

Travellers dwell at length on the lack of woodland in Scotland, except around the houses of proprietors. Fynes Morrison, who visited Scotland briefly in 1598, writes 'onely the gentlemens dwellings were shaddowed with some little Groves, pleasant to the view' (Brown 1978, 86). It is a little curious in the light of these comments to find that the Earl of Mar, the owner of Alloa, as well as estates in the Highlands, was in 1621 requested to send four or five thousand young fir trees and a quantity of seed to James' favourite, George Villiers, then Marquess of Buckingham, to beautify his house at Burleigh on the Hill in Rutlandshire (Lee 1980, 210); Buckingham had accompanied James on his visit to Scotland in

1617. Kerr spoke with approval of the planting of trees around Ancram, and it had been a subject of the correspondence between David Lindsay of Edzell and his brother (Lindsay 1849, 345–6) in the 1580s. Anna, Marchioness of Hamilton, had purchased young trees from the Laird of Pollock in 1626 (Marshall 1973, 56) and, in an undated letter to Sir Colin Campbell of Glenurquey thanking him for fir seed, wrote that 'I think moir of them nor ye can imagin, for I love them moir than I dou al the fruit tris in the wordil. I haue alrady ane four or fayf houndir of my auin planting, that is pratti treis, and deid dereckly weith them as ye set doune in your lettir; bot my sonne louis them no les nor I dou, and he hes wilit me to plant a greit manay meie, quhich meid me trobbil you for this year.' Her son-in-law, Lord Lindsay, was she said, 'ane warie grit planter of his eig as euir I kneue anay, and I am glaid to cherich him to it. He will send ane hors and man for ane leid of them within ten or tual dayis...He hes takin in ane greit baunis for them. He can win the seid himselue, as he hes sein me dou, so ye wil only neid to send him the noutis' (Innes 1855, 439–40). This reveals a very personal attitude to the improvement of an estate. Colin Campbell was also requested to supply seed by the first Earl of Lauderdale in 1637, whether for his house at Lauder or for Lethington, later Lennoxlove, is not known. His own gardeners would extract the seed (Innes 1855, 438).

Later English travellers continued to comment on the absence of woodland in Scotland in contrast to England. Such remarks need to be considered carefully. Some could be attributed in part to the habit of repeating what previous travellers had written and some to a certain parochialism with regard to England where there were many parts in which trees were not a conspicuous feature of the landscape, while others seem to exhibit an automatic prejudice. In 1650 Anne Halkett, a woman of Scottish parentage but brought up in England, wrote in her journal about her visit to Aberdour, 'I was lead in through the garden which was so delightful and fragrant that I thought I was still in England'. This general prejudice against Scotland related to people as well. In Edinburgh she writes, 'I was mett in the outtward roome by my Lady Anne Campbell [Argyle's eldest daughter], a sight that I must confese did so much surprise mee that I could hardly beleeve I was in Scottland, for shee was very handsome, extreamely obleiging, and her behavier and dress was equall to any that I had seene in the Court of England' (Halkett 1875, 58). Such views, though verging on the comic, do indicate that accounts of English travellers require some interpretation and knowledge of their literary antecedents. The perception that more tree planting was required emerges in the writings of William Lithgow, a native Scot, who had travelled extensively across Europe, the Near East and North Africa, and must command greater attention. He wrote in his verse *Scotland's Welcome to her native sonne and soveraigne lord, King Charles ...*

Fig 221 Kenmure Castle with terracing on the natural mound on which it is built. (Grose 1789-91). DP103538

Ah! What makes now my countrey looke so bare?
Thus voyd of planting, Woods and Forrests fayre:
Hedges, and Ditches, Parks, and closed grounds,
Trees, Strips, and Shaws in many fertile bounds:
But onely that the Land-Lords, set their Land,
From yeare to yeare, and so from hand to hand;
They change and flit their Tennants as they please,
And will not giue them lease, Taks, Tymes, nor ease,
To prosper and to thryve ...
This is the cause, my Commons, liue so poore,
And so the Peasants, can not set nor plant
Woods, Trees and orchards, which my valleys want,
But leaue Mee halfe deformd ... (Lithgow 1633, 12)

This work was in the tradition of David Lindsay's *Ane Satyre of the Thrie Estaits* or the *Testament of the Papingo*, with the personification of Scotland pointing out to the monarch the need for reform. The more secure tenure provided by the setting of land in feu ferm encouraged the long term investment in land. A more widespread cultivation of gardens, along with the building of houses, became a symbol of wealth and status. At a lower level, as Lithgow writes, this security did not exist, and planting would require putting out effort for a future from which neither the tenant nor his heirs would benefit. Sir James Pringle of Gala House encouraged his tenants to plant fruit trees from which he as the landlord, rather than the present tenants, would benefit in terms of increased rents in the future.

The gardens where the physical form has survived are usually those where conditions were unsuitable for cultivation or where the owners have made their principal residence elsewhere. Gardens were widespread across Scotland. Henri, Duc de Rohan, who visited Scotland in 1600 as part of an extensive tour of Europe, which included Italy, Germany, the Low Countries and England, recorded that there were more than a hundred country seats within two leagues of Edinburgh (Brown 1978, 93), but descriptions are few. A most unusual survival is Timothy Pont's account of Cunningham, *Cuninghame Topographized* (Dobie 1876). This is an example of the writing of chorography, the contemporary term for the art and science of presenting a part of a country, as opposed to geography, the description of whole countries and larger areas. It was a qualitative art and was intended to present the true form, rather than correspondence or measure of the region with the whole of the world (Withers 2006, 141–2). It was probably compiled between 1604 and 1608, and lists the towns, settlements and houses in that district, describing many of the dwellings there as well planted, or with gardens and orchards adjoining or 'decored vith pleasant gardens and orchards'. This account would suggest that these were the usual appurtenances of any gentleman's house, and were there similar descriptions by Pont of other well-inhabited areas of Scotland, it is probable that they would indicate at least a similar density of gardens and orchards around mansions. Another writer, Robert Gordon of Straloch, who provided the description of Fife as part of the *Atlas Major* of Blaeu, writes that 'this province is everywhere most splendidly provided with innumerable villas, castles and seats of the nobility, to set down a list of them would take much labour, and this short chorography would scarcely contain it; but certainly this practice of country life makes a great contribution to the attractiveness and culture of the kingdom, as each takes pains to adorn and cultivate his estate in rivalry'. The manuscripts maps of the region of Cunningham have not survived. Pont's description of **Blair Castle** was 'ane ancient castell and strong dounioun veill beutified vith gardens, orchards and partiers seated one the brinke of ye Riuer Garnock it is the ancient patrimony and heritage of ye Lairds of Blare' (Dobie 1876, 11). It contains the first known use of the term 'parterre' in Scots. The *Oxford English Dictionary* only notes its earliest use in English in 1639, giving a reference in England. Kelburn Castle appears as 'a goodly building veil planted hauing werey beutifull orchards and gardens and in one of them a spatious Rome adorned with a christalin fontane cutte all out of the liuing rocke'. This would suggest the creation of a grotto, a picturesque cave or cave-like chamber, or at least the use of an earlier structure as grotto. Whether the crystalline fountain was a natural spring or owed its form to piped water is not known (Dobie 1876, 18).

One of the earliest examples of a grotto was in the Boboli Gardens in Florence, constructed about 1554–5, where water and statuary combined with hydraulic engineering produced (and produces) a remarkable effect on the visitor whom it was intended to impress. Like the gardens of the Medici villa at Pratolino, where there were a series of grottoes, this was a sight on the circuit of all foreign travellers of the late sixteenth and early seventeenth century seeking to extend their cultural education (Strong 1998, 78–83). While there was a room known as a grotto at Lord Burghley's mansion at Theobalds in 1600, it would seem to have been part of the main house (Henderson 2005, 164–5). There are records of other grottoes designed in England for James and Anne of Denmark and, before his death in 1612, for Henry, Prince of Wales. In 1598 Henri IV of France had sent for garden designers from Florence with knowledge of the creation of water features to work on the gardens at Fontainebleau. Salomon de Caus, a French engineer, who had visited Pratolino and other Italian gardens, was in London between 1607 and 1612. Henry employed him as a tutor in the science of

Fig 222 Kenmure Castle and its gardens as depicted on the mid eighteenth century Military Survey (04/3b). There are two walled gardens with what may be parterres and vegetable plots within them. © The British Library. Licensor Scran

perspective, and de Caus dedicated *La Perspective, avec la raison des ombres et miroirs* to him. This extensively illustrated work included instructions on how to depict a garden in perspective which would double the apparent length of the plot. Grand Duke Cosimo de Medici of Tuscany sent to London, at Henry's request, an Italian architect and engineer, Constantino de' Servi. He prepared a plan for extensions to Richmond Palace and its gardens in 1611, which included the grotto already begun by de Caus beside the River Thames (Henderson 2005, 103–6).

Members of Scottish landowning families were part of the intimate circle around James VI and his sons, and would be fully acquainted with the gardens which were being developed around the royal palaces in England. The description of Galloway, which was prepared by John Mclellan, the minister of Kirkcudbright between 1638 and 1650, was written for the publication of Blaeu's *Atlas Major*. Mclellan did not have the interest in gardens and policies of the region shown by Timothy Pont, and gathering information about this area is a matter of inference. **Kenmure Castle**, the property of one of the Gentlemen of the King's Bedchamber, is described as 'pleasantly scituated on a mount, having a wood of great overgrown oakes on one side' (Macfarlane 1906–8, 2, 63). In Francis Grose's *Antiquities of Scotland* (1789–91) one of the many illustrations shows Kenmure Castle standing on a terraced mound (Fig 221). The mound is natural, and the terraces were later considerably obscured by the construction of a carriage road to the castle in 1817 (MacGibbon and Ross 1887–92, 4, 256). Two walled gardens are depicted on Roy's Military Survey; one contained a walk edged with small

Fig 223 Kenmure Castle and its gardens as depicted on the First Edition of the Ordnance Survey 6-inch map of Kirkcudbrightshire surveyed in 1849–50. The elaborate arrangement of parterres had been swept away by the date of the next survey in 1894.

trees, a large plot and a series of six small plots, which might be parterres or vegetable plots (Fig 222). The First Edition of the Ordnance Survey 6-inch map of 1849–50 depicts three terraces in this area, which still survive. To the west, on the other side of the road to New Galloway, is the second walled garden laid out with cross walks and again planted with what appear to be small trees. This is a very elaborate garden, which in style belongs to the seventeenth century (Fig 223). The history of its owners would suggest that its creator might be Sir Robert Gordon of Glen, who succeeded in 1604, or his son Sir John Gordon of Lochinvar, who inherited the estate in 1628 and died in 1634. The latter was probably responsible for much reconstruction of the sixteenth century castle. Sir Robert was a Gentleman of the King's Bedchamber, and his son is recorded as having travelled on the Continent. Sir John was a very active landowner, the founder of the burgh of New Galloway, and in 1633 was granted the titles of Viscount Kenmure and Lord Lochinvar by Charles I. What may suggest the earlier date for the design of the garden is the sundial from Kenmure, now in Dumfries Museum, which is dated to 1623. This is one of the two oldest surviving dials in Scotland which can be dated with certainty (Somerville 1990, 21) (Fig 224). After the first viscount's death and

for the rest of the seventeenth century and the eighteenth century the estate was heavily encumbered by debts (Maxwell-Irving 1997, 41–54). The bones of this garden survive, with its terraces and avenues still visible.

One of the more northerly gardens known from the earlier seventeenth century is that at **Dunrobin Castle**. Jean Gordon, Countess of Sutherland, was the wife whom Bothwell divorced in 1566 in order to marry Mary Queen of Scots. She married the Earl of

Fig 224 The summer face of the dial from Kenmure Castle of 1623, one of the two oldest dials in Scotland which can be dated with certainty. It is now in Dumfries Museum. SC1238462

Sutherland in 1573, and, during her husband's lifetime directed the management of his estates (Fig 225). The gardener employed at Dunrobin was James Rynd who, in 1616, was paid £22 13s 4d a year and supplied with working clothes. In 1630, the year after Jane Gordon's death, Dunrobin was described as a house 'well seated on a mote hard by the sea, with fair orchards, where there be pleasant gardens planted with all kynd of fruitts, hearbs and flowres used in this kingdom, and abundance of good saffron, tobacco and rosemarie, the froot being excellent and cheeflie the pears and cherries' (Sanderson 1987, 50). Robert Gordon of Gordonstoun, a son of Jane Gordon, described the gardens of his own early home, Dunrobin Castle, in his account of Sutherland in Blaeu's *Atlas Major*. He wrote that it was 'most commodious for its situation, gardens and orchards, full of varied flowers and trees, excellent saffron, a very deep fountain of sweet water built from squared stone, and an enclosure stretching three miles in length and well stocked with rabbits ... Proof of the goodness of the soil is that in the Earl's garden at Dunrobin Castle on the Ocean shore, saffron grows and ripens well, although that plant is late-ripening and dislikes cold soil.'

Another northern garden was that of the Sutherlands' rivals, the earls of Caithness, at the **Castle of Mey**. It is a name that the traveller William Lithgow played on in his poem of thanks for his entertainment there:

Sir! Sighting now thy Selfe and Pallace Faire,
I found a novelty, and that most rare,
The time though cold and stormy, sharper Sun,
And far to Summer, scarce the spring begun,
Yet with good lucke, in Februar, Saturnes prey
Have I not sought, and found out fruitfull May,
Flank'd with the Marine coast, prospective
stands,
Right opposite, to the Orcade Iles and Lands:
Where I for floures, ingorg'd strong grapes of
Spaine,
And liquor'd French, both Red and white amain:
Which palace doth contain two foure-squar'd
Courts,
Graft with brave works where th'Art drawne
pensile sports
On Hals, high Chambers, Galleries, office,
Bowres,
Cells, Rooms, and Turrets, Plat-formes, stately
Towers:
Where green-fac'd gardens, set at Flora's feet,
Make Natures beauty, quicke Apelles greet:
(Lithgow 1640, 508)

A mansion was added to the thirteenth century tower at **Drum Castle** in Aberdeenshire in about 1619 and the gardens at Drum Castle in the early seventeenth century appear to have consisted of a walled garden immediately

Fig 225 *Jean Gordon, Countess of Sutherland. © Scottish National Portrait Gallery. Licensor Scran*

to the south of the house, with a series of descending terraces beyond (Murray and Murray 2008, 18–19). Excavations in 2008 on the south side of the mansion revealed the series of garden terraces which had been suggested during geophysical survey in 1988 (Fig 226). One terrace was depicted on the First Edition of the Ordnance Survey 6-inch map, which was prepared in 1865–7. The terraces are laid out axially to the mansion and are likely to be of a similar period, a date supported by the finds from the excavation. The part nearer the mansion was walled and traces of what may have been

Fig 226 *Drum Castle where excavations have revealed the seventeenth century terraced garden. DP020751*

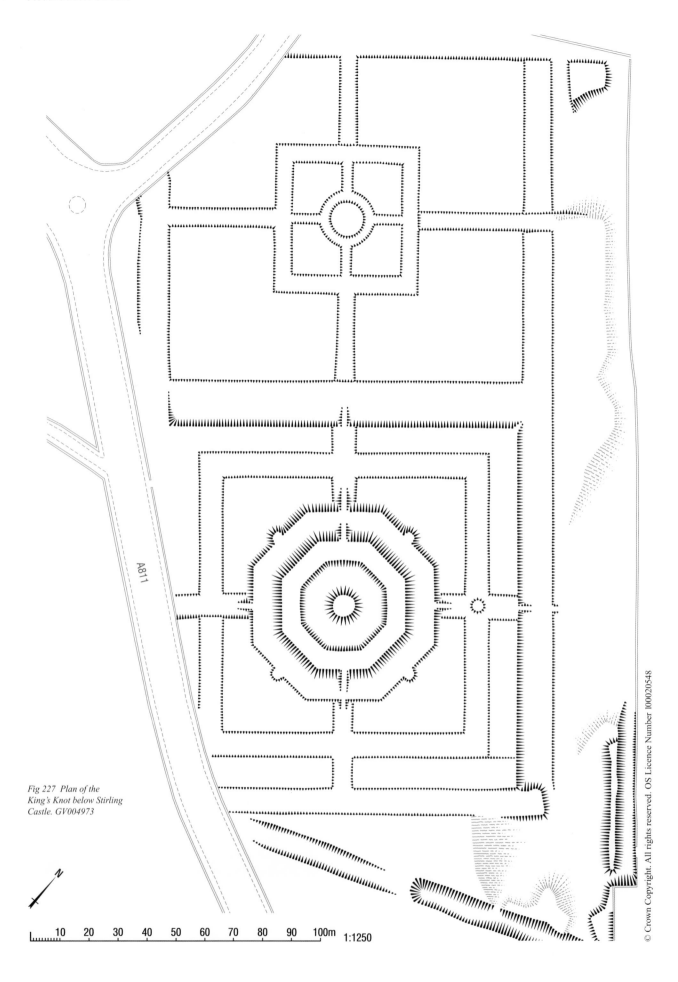

*Fig 227 Plan of the
King's Knot below Stirling
Castle. GV004973*

A811

N

10   20   30   40   50   60   70   80   90   100m   1:1250

Fig 228 Aerial view of the King's Knot at Stirling with the detail of the earthworks emphasised by the light frost. The Knot would have been planted with low growing plants and hedging with a fountain perhaps intended for the centre of the mount. SC1018862

geometrical parterres were found. Further south there were revetting walls, garden beds and stone paths. In the material used to level up parts of the site to form the terraces, the excavators found medieval pottery and tile, presumably brought from elsewhere around the castle (Murray and Murray 2008, 18–19). It is described in Blaeu's *Atlas Major* as 'excellently equipped with buildings and gardens' (Macfarlane 1906–8, 2, 284), and Spalding describes how the 'pleasant garden-planting' was cut down to make huts by the Marquess of Argyll's forces in 1644 (Spalding 1829, 455). The garden and policies at nearby Crathes were seen by Robert Gordon of Straloch as the creation of the first baronet, Sir Thomas Burnett (1619–1653), who 'has by care and skill subdued the genius of the place, for by planting firs and other trees of many kinds he has covered the forbidding crags, laid it out with gardens, and clothed it with pleasance' (Macfarlane 1906–8, 2, 284).

Gardens were widely distributed across Scotland during the earlier seventeenth century but evidence is lacking for the West Highlands, with little in the way of clues on the maps of Timothy Pont or those in Blaeu's *Atlas* or from the accounts of travellers. The examination of estate papers may go some way towards filling this gap.

While James VI and his family had moved south, following his accession to the throne of England, Stirling, Linlithgow, Holyroodhouse and Falkland were still royal palaces, and Edinburgh and Dumbarton royal castles, while Dunfermline was the property of Queen Anne. In 1603 James had promised in the speech he delivered after the sermon in St Giles, Edinburgh, to return to Scotland at least every three years. His palaces were maintained, or in the case of the north range at Linlithgow, not maintained, so that, despite many warnings, the building collapsed in 1607. It was, however, rebuilt under the supervision of the King's Master of Works, Sir James Murray of Kilbaberton with the finances coming through Sir Gideon Murray of Elibank, after James VI's visit to Scotland in 1617. In his manual of advice on kingship, *Basilikon Doron*, intended for his son Prince Henry, James recommended him to visit Scotland at three yearly intervals and to know his subjects when, as he hoped, Henry might rule England as well (James VI 1599, 64–5). Although James did not return to Scotland until 1617, there were various false alarms which stimulated activity in the intervening years (*MW* 2, xx–xxi), so that, while his visit and that of Charles I in 1633 provided most of the occasions for work on the royal palaces and gardens, not all developments should be attributed to the preparations for their advent. A poem by William Drummond of Hawthornden, entitled 'Forth Feasting A panegyric to the kings most excellent Maiestie', pictures Scotland after James' departure as 'a garden of its Beautie

Fig 229 Aerial view of the King's Knot with the cropmarks of the ditches of an earlier, probably prehistoric, enclosure beneath, which perhaps led to the identification of the site in the Middle Ages with King Arthur's Round Table. SC1018860

spoil'd' and on his return 'Let Mother Earth now deckt with flowrs be seene' (Drummond 1617). Cultivation was employed as one of the motifs of the country's celebration of the king's return.

The most remarkable earthwork survival of all gardens in Scotland is that known as the **King's Knot**, which lies below and to the south-west of **Stirling Castle** (Figs 180, 227, 228). It has no close parallels surviving elsewhere in Europe. Its date is not known, but consideration of the remaining documentation and its stylistic affinities would suggest a date in the earlier seventeenth century. The Master of Works Accounts for 1617 for the Castle and Park of Stirling are incomplete and frequently indecipherable. This is the period immediately before James VI returned 'salmon-like' to Scotland, and when a great deal of preparation was going on to present both James and his English courtiers with a positive view of Scotland, although the diatribe, produced probably by Anthony Weldon, a member of James' household, provides a picture which highlights all of the prejudices he chose to cultivate (Brown 1978, 96–103). What does survive in the Master of Works Accounts is the record of a payment to the gardener, Richie Buckam, of £3 for six days' work, and a payment of £5 16s 8d for seventy loads of green turf to the alleys

in the garden, but work on the park dyke and gates came to more than £1900, perhaps reflecting James' well-known fondness of hunting (*MW* 2, 25, 27, 31). Flowers for the garden were also paid for and Alexander Quhitbrow, a gardener presumably at Stirling, was paid for ferns, thyme and lavender for the king's chamber 'at the first coming' (*MW* 2, 444). James visited Stirling on 30 June 1617 and left for Perth on 5 July, having heard a speech on the Roman antecedents of the ancient town (Adamson 1618). The work on the park dykes continued in 1618 (*MW* 2,108–9) and locks for the garden were paid for in that year (*MW* 2,108–9).

The next set of accounts for Stirling date from 1625, shortly after Charles I succeeded to the throne, and they are similarly damaged by damp. The stanks or ponds were cast (dug out) between 16 May and 22 August, and Richie Buckham was paid for supervising the work, as well as receiving drink on the occasion of an inspection visit by the Master of Works, James Murray of Kilbaberton (*MW* 2, 163–72). The clearance of the stanks required 'coal rakes', perhaps for removing coal or stones, which had been used to make decorative patterns, as well as axes to cut the roots of bushes, which may also have been ornamental. Fifteen workmen are mentioned in the accounts which, over some four months, amounts to a very considerable degree of clearance. The cost for labour was in the region of £500, based on the detailed list of 6 June 1625 (*MW* 2, 165), which suggests a large undertaking. This would seem excessive for clearing fish ponds, and might indicate the construction of new water features. There is also the question of what happened to the earth and other material removed from the stanks. A new timber gate incorporating some ironwork was put up in the park, and there were repairs to the dovecot, which may have been in the Nether Garden beyond the Chapel Royal (*MW* 2, 169, 178). In 1629 a bolt was put on the gate 'at the head of the plaine treis' (*MW* 2, 243)

The accounts for 1628–9 survive in better order. They include sums for the planning and contriving of a new orchard and garden in Stirling, with reference back to garden work in 1627. William Watts, His Majesty's Master Gardener at Stirling, was repaid £375 12s 0d, for the wages of workmen for twenty-two weeks and for various materials used (*MW* 2, 230). William Watts had been recruited as a result of a warrant from Charles I to the Earl of Mar as Royal Treasurer to choose a 'skilfull and well experimented' gardener in England to go and reside at Stirling for reparation of 'the orchard adjoining his Majestys Park of Stirline' which, the king is informed, has 'for lack of attendance become wild and overgrown with bushes and brambles, and which state of matters 'being an imputatioun to that whole kingdome' he thinks should be remedied'. The gardener should receive £30 sterling yearly and should provide advice on other royal gardens and orchards (*Hist MSS Comm* 1904, 131). The creation of the gardens, whose earthwork remains, generally known as the King's Knot, has most reasonably been associated with the payment for the planning and creation of a new orchard and garden there under the direction of William Watts (RCAHMS 1963, 219). There is, however, no proof that this is the case, but William Watts received a further £478 3s 6d for workmen's wages and other provisions for twenty-six weeks disbursed between May and November 1628 and between January and August 1629, again for the 'platting and contriving his majesties gairdein warkis at the park of Stirling' (*MW* 2, 242, 243, 257). In a rental of 1642 there is a reference to the orchard of the king known as *lie gairdine*, next to the garden of the great edifice known as the Newark (Mar's Wark) in Stirling *ad pomarium regis lie gairdine, contiguam ad hortum magni edificii lie Newark in Stirling* (*RMS* 9, 403 no 1072).

The gardens below the castle were first specifically mentioned in 1499 (*ER* 12, 76) when, in the reign of James IV, there was considerable expenditure on trees and plants. They had probably been part of the royal park which they adjoined, but there may have been another and earlier feature there. Aerial survey in 1975 and subsequent years revealed the cropmarks of up to three lines of ditches suggesting an oval enclosure beneath the Knot, which might be of prehistoric date, although any periods preceding the construction of the Knot are possible (Fig 229). Recent geophysical investigation has extended the known area of this earlier feature. Medieval tradition associated Stirling

with the Arthurian city of Snowdon or Snawdon (Loomis 1956, 17). This reference first appeared in Froissart's *Chronicles*, and in his *The Bruce*, written in the later fourteenth century, Barbour describes how, after the Battle of Bannockburn, the defeated Edward II escaped around the Park of Stirling, 'close by the Round Table' (Barbour 1996, 226). In the mid sixteenth century David Lindsay referred to the 'Tabyll Round' at Snawdon (Stirling) in his *Complaint of the Papingo* (Lindsay 1879, 75). The conclusion is that there was some feature close to but below the castle, which was identified with the Arthurian Round Table. Throughout Britain various monuments were associated with King Arthur, one of which, 'King Arthurs Round Table' near Penrith, is a prehistoric hengiform earthwork with a passing resemblance to the King's Knot. It would be a well known sight to anyone travelling to Scotland by a western route. 'Arthur's O'on' near Falkirk, which was probably of Roman date, was another monument attached to Arthur's name. What the site near Stirling was is unknown. There is no indication of a particular feature on Pont's map of Stirling, which clearly shows the Park beside the castle (Fig 76). The Arthurian Legend was invoked by Scottish and English kings in their entertainments and in their patronage of writers. In 1509 James IV gave the name of Arthur to one of his sons, who did not survive infancy, and who was, at the time of his birth, the presumptive heir to the English as well as the Scottish throne. In James VI's reign there were Arthurian references in masques, in particular that written by Ben Jonson for Prince Henry, the *Barriers* of Twelfth Night 1610. King Arthur's Round Table was specifically suggested as a device or emblem for Prince Henry (Strong 1986, 141–5).

The King's Knot takes the form of an octagonal stepped mount which, although not very high, some 3m, would allow the surrounding parterres to be viewed from above. The mount lies within a double-ditched almost square enclosure measuring about 129m by 127m, the south-west angle of which was destroyed by the building of the turnpike road to Dumbarton about 1813. The two stepped platforms are eight-sided, surmounted by a sunken octagonal compartment with a circular flat-topped mound at its centre. To its north-west was a garden of similar size, with a double quadrilateral design of raised parterres, defined by paths, around a central circular bed.

Perhaps the nearest parallel to the King's Knot in Scotland is at **Lincluden College** near Dumfries, a medieval nunnery which was suppressed in 1389 and replaced by a college of secular canons (Fig 230). The surviving buildings are those of the collegiate church and the house of the provost, which overlooks the garden. This is enclosed by a raised walk and decorated with a low grass-covered mound on two levels; the lower part has twenty sides and the higher mount at its centre has eight. The garden here was first clearly noted when

Fig 230 The earthworks of the garden at Lincluden College were noted by late eighteenth century travellers but, with this style of garden having passed out of fashion, they were attributed to the medieval period. SC1020630

Thomas Pennant visited in 1769: 'Behind the house are vestiges of a flower garden, with parterres and scrolls very visible; and near that a great artificial mount with a spiral walk to the top, which is hollowed, and has a turf seat around to command the beautiful views.' He presumed, with a moralising remark, that the garden was the creation of the provost and bedesmen before the Reformation (Pennant 1776, 105). It is, however, more likely the creation of the lay provost of the college in the earlier seventeenth century. The last clerical provost, Robert Douglas, celebrated mass there until at least 1585. He held his office into the 1590s and may have lived until about 1609 (M'Dowall 1886, 153–4; Hume

1985). His nephew and successor, William Douglas of Drumlanrig, held the property up to the time it was granted in 1617 to Sir Robert Gordon of Lochinvar, the owner of Kenmure who was probably responsible for the garden there, and to John Murray of Lochmaben, later Earl of Annandale, who was a groom of the bedchamber to James VI (NRS RPS 1617/5/70), and subsequently to Robert, Lord Maxwell and first Earl of Nithsdale (RCAHMS 1914, 252). The 'indwellar in the Colledge' in 1627 was one John Bowie, presumably a tenant (M'Dowall 1886, 158). James is reputed to have visited Lincluden on his visit to Scotland in 1617 after his stay at Drumlanrig on his way to Dumfries (M'Dowall 1886, 157; McNeill 1996, 45).

Traces of the garden survived into the nineteenth century and it was recalled, in the Imperial Gazetteer of 1854, that there 'were not long ago, distinct vestiges of a bowling green, flower garden and parterres' (Wilson 1854, 335). The remains of the garden emerged when the site was in the process of being put in order by the Office of Works after it came into state care in 1922. One autumn morning a workman on the motte looked down on to bare earth covered in frost and noticed a pattern was visible. He pegged out the pattern and a subsequent excavation revealed the matching features beneath (Reid 1931, 9). It was put into repair on the instructions of Sir Charles Peers, the Chief Inspector (NRS *MW* 1/651). The garden is overlooked by a motte of Anglo-Norman date based on a natural ridge (RCAHMS 1914, 255), which has been transformed into a terraced garden mount, and which survived at least until the later eighteenth century (Pennant 1776, 105). This garden was probably laid out for an owner close to the court of James VI.

Octagonal designs appear in garden settings in Androuet du Cerceau's *Les plus excellents bastiments de France*, but are more common for architectural or sculptural features, such as the pavillion at Gaillon and the fountain at Blois (Androuet du Cerceau 1988, not paginated). A plan dated 1609 by Robert Smythson for Ham House, near London, then the property of Sir Thomas Vavasour, the king's Knight Marshall, showed an octagonal stepped sunken garden, measuring about 85m by 66m and centred on an oval parterre which could be viewed from the raised gravel paths around it. Perhaps the closest parallel in England appears on Smythson's plan of the gardens at Somerset House on the Strand in London showing the changes considered by James' queen, Anne of Denmark. The plan of the King's Knot, if not the elevation, provides a parallel. The private garden, designed to be adjacent to the proposed extension of Somerset House, then renamed Denmark House, consisted of two shallow terraces linked by short flights of steps. Below, towards the River Thames, was a square garden with paths paved with black and white stone around the perimeter, linked to a circular walk within which was an octagonal setting designed for a mount, in this case intended to represent Mount Parnassus, the home of Apollo and the Nine Muses. This was a popular Renaissance subject for sculpture, representing poetry, music and all the arts, and the account of King James' return to Scotland plays on this theme (Adamson 1618). In 1613 the Parnassus Mount at Somerset House was described by a foreign visitor as surmounted by a Pegasus, a gilded horse with wings, accompanied by various statues including one of black marble representing the Thames. The Parnassus Mount was the work of Salomon de Caus, a French Huguenot engineer who had visited various gardens in Italy, including Pratolino, before working for the Archdukes Albert and Isabella in Brussels (Henderson 2005, 99–104). A hundred years later the gardens at Somerset House had been flattened. Those at Stirling survived because written into the later

Fig 231 The lower and less elaborate of the gardens below Stirling Castle. SC1018862

rentals for the area of the King's Knot was the provision that the land should be used only for grazing and must not be ploughed (NRS, SC67/49/17, p.439).

There has been some discussion about the authenticity of the current state of the garden below Stirling Castle. Earthworks appear on a painting of the 'Burgh and Castle of Stirling' by Vorsterman and on a plan of Stirling dated 1725 (RCAHMS 1963, Plates 120, 121). They do not greatly resemble the present appearance of the site which has led to the suggestion that the King's Knot might have been considerably altered, to the extent of originally having been on a different alignment (RCAHMS 1963, 219). This change was supposed to have taken place about 1867. Queen Victoria and Prince Albert had remarked on the neglected appearance of the King's Knot during a visit to Stirling, and after some time had elapsed, a 'thorough restoration and renewal was accomplished ... under the care and supervision of the late Provost Rankin and Mr Mathieson of Her Majesty's Office of Works, the original well-defined plan scrupulously adhered to and the main part of the work consisted in repairing the ravages effected by frost and rain during centuries of neglect and having the whole surface re-sown with grass and re-turfed where necessary' (Shirra 1889, 34). Comparison between the Ordnance Survey

Fig 232 The engraving by John Slezer of Linlithgow Palace in the 1693 edition of Theatrum Scotiae *shows the terracing of the knoll on which the palace stands. DP101766*

large scale plan of Stirling, surveyed in 1858, with a recent digital plan reveals that there has been little change over the last century and a half. Less detailed plans from earlier in the nineteenth century, such as that by Loudon in the *Gardeners' Magazine* of 1842, show an earthwork of essentially the same form. The lower area of the garden was referred to as the Queen's Knot (Fig 231); part of it was included by Loudon on his plan (Loudon 1842, 596–606).

During the eighteenth century various historians and travellers mention the gardens. Sibbald, writing in 1707, refers to 'an Orchard and the vestiges of a large and spacious Garden' (Sibbald 1892, 46). Defoe refers

to the gardens as 'very old fashion'd' but adds that the 'Figure of the Walks and Grass-Plats remains plain to be seen' (Defoe 1727, 753–4). Pennant refers to the King's Knot 'where according to the taste of the times, the flowers had been disposed in beds and curious knots, at this time very easily to be traced in the fantastic form of the turf' (Pennant 1776, 225). Nimmo, who composed his *History* prior to 1777, says that 'in the garden is a mound of earth in the form of a table known as 'The Knot' where, according to tradition, the court sometimes held fêtes champêtres.' His editor continues 'Around the garden in Mr Nimmo's day were the vestiges of a canal on which the royal family and the court arrived in barges', which was destroyed by the construction of a public road (Nimmo 1880, 1, 82). This story was continued by later writers. There is now no surviving evidence for such a structure, although the creation of a canal would be entirely in keeping with seventeenth century garden design, and examples of water gardens elsewhere in Scotland at this period have already been described. There is also no trace of the fish ponds which undoubtedly existed during the sixteenth and certainly the earlier seventeenth centuries according to the many references in the Master of Works Accounts. The considerable amount of paid work on the 'casting of the stanks' in 1616 (*MW* 2, 163–72) may actually relate to a water garden of which there is no other surviving evidence than late and romantic tradition.

It is not known how the gardens were planted or otherwise decorated, but low evergreen hedges delineating beds, areas marked out in different colours, whether derived from plants or from brick or coal or gravel, would be usual. The projecting lobes on the

Fig 233 The engraving by John Slezer of Falkland Palace from the East in the 1693 edition of Theatrum Scotia, *showing a balustraded terrace overlooking a walled garden. DP101767*

middle terrace may have been intended to carry arbours and seats. It is now approached up turf ramps, but steps may have been planned and there may have been other architectural features in stone, such as balustrades. Balustrades were being quarried in 1617 (*MW* 2, 25, 27, 28), in 1628 (*MW* 2, 241, 242, 244), in 1629, when some of them were destined for the tops of the low towers (*MW* 2, 247, 255), and in 1633 (*MW* 2, 323, 358). There is no mention in the accounts of the site for which they were intended. The garden gates were themselves decorative features for which six wooden knobs were produced in 1629 (*MW* 2, 255). An account in 1628 gives the payment for the transport of seventy loads of sand with a similar amount in 1629 from the garden to an unstated destination, possibly the castle (*MW* 2, 236, 243). Such a garden would be expected to boast elaborate fountains and a collection of statuary, but nothing is known of any work or purchases to support this presumption.

Work was also taking place in the Nether Garden beyond the King's Old Building. New boards and some new ironwork were provided in 1629 for a latticed gate, as well as a lock and two keys (*MW* 2, 249, 252). The inner door to the garden was also reinforced and provided with a lock and key, along with a lock and key for the dovecot there. The dovecot in the park had been repaired in 1625 (*MW* 2, 178). The construction of two wheelbarrows for the low garden suggests some more horticultural activity there (*MW* 2, 253–4).

The gardener's men were also responsible for the preparation of the bowling green, which was constructed to the west of the sixteenth century entrance to the castle and from which the gardens below could be viewed. They received drink for spreading refuse, presumably to create a level surface (*MW* 2, 233, 245). There is an account for payment for the demolition by fire of an 'upstanding craig at the greine' followed by the carrying of turf to cover the fire (*MW* 2, 244, 245). Some of the baluster shafts recorded in the Master of Works Accounts survive here (RCAHMS 1963, 187, 193). Bowling greens formed part of the gardens of gentry families as well as noblemen, becoming increasingly popular during the seventeenth century.

There were repairs to the park dyke as a result of flooding from the Raploch in 1633 (*MW* 2, 358,359, 360). The 'plaine trees gate' required mending and the locks replacing (*MW* 2, 360), and the king's gardener William Watts was paid for the cutting and carrying of bulrushes from the bog in the park to the new garden and orchard, and for digging and carrying of turf to mend and fence the garden against the incursions of the deer (*MW* 2, 370).

Works were taking place in the gardens of other royal properties in Scotland in the earlier seventeenth century. Little is known of changes at Linlithgow, although the 'great caitchepule' or tennis court there

Fig 234 Detail from the manuscript map by John Adair of the 'East Part of Fife' of 1684 showing the garden of Falkland Palace in the form of a parterre divided into four parts with trees, perhaps an orchard beyond. (Adv.MS.70.2.11 (Adair 7)). © NLS

was repaired in 1626 (*MW* 2, 204). However, depiction of Linlithgow in *Theatrum Scotiae* by Slezer, published in 1693, shows that in the area around the palace two large terraces had been created which may belong to this period, although they might equally belong to the period after the Restoration of Charles II. Robert Sibbald, who as a child during the civil wars had lived in Linlithgow, refers to the terrace walks on the west side of the palace in a work published in 1710 (Sibbald 1710a, 15) (Fig 232).

At **Falkland Palace**, as at Stirling, there were payments in 1628 to 1629 for designing and making 'his Majesties gairdein anew' (*MW* 2, 275), presumably under the direction of William Watts. There were repairs to the 'yaird dyikis', but more remarkably £33 6s 8d was paid to a mason, John Patterson, for a sundial and a pillar to set it on. The price included the gilding and colouring as well as 'all materiallis thereto', presumably the various pointers necessary. John Patterson was also responsible for the painting of two globes on top of the four circular turrets there. The tennis court was repaired, and locks provided for it and for the orchard and garden gates (*MW* 2, 289–90). There was a gate from the tennis court into the orchard. Further construction at Falkland had been carried out earlier than this. One feature that was completed in June 1622 was the building and making watertight of two great terraces. There is a terrace on the east side of the eastern wing at Falkland above the garden, but on Slezer's view of Falkland from the east, there is also a terrace with a balustrade at first floor level overlooking a walled garden with grass and trees. It is here that waterproofing would be important (Fig 233). The manuscript map of the east

Fig 235 A view of Falkland Place painted by Alexander Keirincx about 1639. Keirincx was of Flemish origin but worked in Holland and England. He painted a series of castles, palaces and towns for Charles I of which Falkland and Seton are the only examples in Scotland to survive and be recognised. © National Trust for Scotland. Licensor Scran

part of Fife by John Adair, dated to about 1684 (NLS Adv.MS.70.2.11 (Adair 7)), also appears to show a walled garden with perhaps an orchard to the north and beyond that the enclosed park (Fig 234). About 1639 Charles I commissioned the Flemish artist Alexander Keirincx to produce landscapes with various castles and towns in England and Scotland. When Charles' collection was dispersed under the Commonwealth, most of these were lost, and with regard to Scottish sites only Falkland and Seton Palace have been recognised. Falkland is depicted in a distant view, but the painting shows the gardens in two compartments to the east of the palace, enclosed by a wall (Fig 235). Charles II stayed at Falkland in 1650 when he was twenty-one, where he appears to have been much preached at, although there is some mention of dancing and playing at cards (Paterson 2003, 109).

As is also the case with the accounts relating to the other royal palaces before the visit of James VI, there are few surviving references to work at Holyrood, but a store for beer, made of timber, was constructed in the garden, perhaps required because of the expected influx of guests, and 'the two rooms toward the garding higher and lower to be plaistred and whyted and glassed' (*MW* 2, 442). More information is available

about the gardens at **Holyroodhouse** on the map of Edinburgh and the Canongate by James Gordon of Rothiemay printed about 1647 but it can only be used with caution in relation to Holyroodhouse thirty years earlier (Fig 236). It shows the gardens of the palace in considerable detail. Given the different viewpoints – the English Spy's map (BL Cotton Augustus I.ii.56) (Fig 107) takes a bird's eye view from the north-west and Gordon of Rothiemay from the south – there is considerable congruence in the layout of boundaries. The gardens are depicted as enclosed by stone walls and the table describes the whole area as 'the palace of holy-rude-hous with the south and north gardiens'. Within these irregular outlines, square and rectangular knots and parterres have been laid out, mostly on a quatrefoil plan. In the most north-westerly of the gardens, trees have been placed in the remaining space, and to the east of this enclosure, north of the abbey burial ground, is a possible orchard. There are buildings set in the south-west and south-east corners of this enclosure. Gordon's map provides evidence for the construction of a building on the north side of James V's tower which provided access to the north gardens across and above the public entrance to the abbey church and the burial ground. This may be 'the galrie that gois to the north gairding' for which the fittings for seven windows were provided in 1633, with the stair 'that gois doun to the gairdin', for which brackets were paid for in the same account (*MW* 2, 331). The engraving of the west front of the palace shows what appears to be a two storey

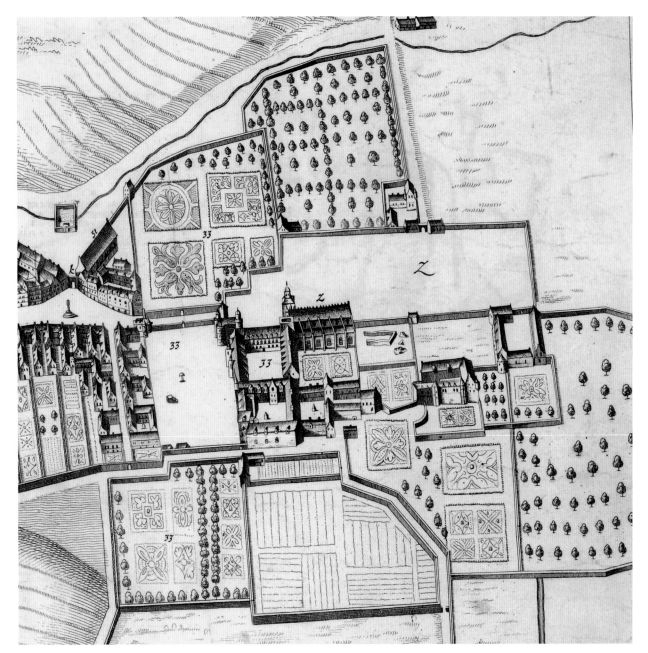

Fig 236 A detail from Gordon of Rothiemay's 1647 plan of Edinburgh
Edinodunensis Tabulam *printed in Amsterdam, showing the layout of the gardens*
around Holyroodhouse. DP101340

timber-framed building, which would allow a private
route to the gardens (Figs 237, 238). This may be the
gallery of the garden whose lock required mending in
1633 (*MW* 2, 327). The former cloister garth had been
laid out in knots. The area to the east of the palace, now,
for the most part, incorporated in the park, is occupied
by buildings and walled gardens associated with the
offices of the bishops and deans of Edinburgh. These
are also depicted as decorated with knots, with the most
easterly part planted with trees. There are also walled
enclosures to the south of the palace, a small rectangular
area with a building in one corner, which was later the
house of the gardener, with a larger polygonal area to

the south from which it appears to have been divided.
The layout of the beds in both these areas suggests the
growing of vegetables, while the gardens immediately
to the west are laid out with a design of four larger
parterres, with trees around the west and south sides,
divided by a tree-lined avenue from four smaller
parterres arranged north to south. The detail of the
layout may belong to a somewhat later date.

What plants were used in the knots is unknown,
but a bill presented by Andrew Carwall in April 1622
records the purchase of thirty wicker spars at a cost
of £4 10s 0d (*MW* 2, 151). These were to be used to
separate grey valleys (or sunken areas) from red valleys
in the south garden, presumably different sections of
the colouring in the knots. The materials used may be
brick dust and coal dust. At the same time three locks
were fitted to the garden gates, and a lock and two

Fig 237 A detail from Gordon of Rothiemay's 1647 plan of Edinburgh showing the gallery on the north side of the James V tower at Holyrood which provided direct access to the gardens from the palace. DP101340

keys were provided for the privy garden (*MW* 2, 143). According to the plan prepared by Robert Mylne after the Restoration of Charles II, the privy garden was the most westerly of the north gardens (Mylne 1893, np). In 1626 butts were constructed in the privy garden and the walls of the north gardens were repaired (*MW* 2, 195).

Fig 238 Engraving of the west front of the Palace of Holyroodhouse by James Gordon of Rothiemay with the James V tower and the gallery leading to the garden on the left. DP106455

In April 1633 the *Accounts of the Masters of Works* lists twelve gardeners 'at the north yaird and close' (*MW* 2, 317, 318). This included William Watts, who was paid £4 for six days' work, twice as much as the others. In May 1633 seven gardeners were employed in the south garden (*MW* 2, 322). This was in the period before Charles I visited Scotland for his coronation. Again the garden gate was repaired and reinforced, and 144 great bell nails were purchased for it, presumably producing quite a formidable effect (*MW* 2, 320). Keys, locks and repairs were again required for the various doors which gave access to the garden (*MW* 2, 327) and a new garden entry was made (*MW* 2, 319). James Jonston, who was gardener to Lord Ross, received £10 for flowers delivered to Andrew Caldwell for the king's garden (*MW* 2, 326). The butts were rebuilt in the yard where the lion had been kept, still known as the 'lyon yaird', and the 3360 turfs were required for their construction or refurbishment, while another 460 turves went to the north garden (*MW* 2, 330).

As at Falkland, a sundial formed part of the decoration of the gardens at Holyroodhouse, but this was a far more costly and imposing piece of sculpture, and, unlike the one at Falkland, it has survived (MacGibbon and Ross, 1887–92, 5, 441–3) (Figs 239, 240). It was made by John Mylne, the King's Master Mason, assisted by his sons, John and Alexander. The first reference to the dial in the accounts is in April 1633 when payments were made for a pound of white wax, turpentine and for the sharpening of a file (*MW* 2, 316). John Barton was responsible for making, engraving and gilding the dial itself (*MW* 2,

328), and two and a half rose nobles were allotted for the gilding at a cost of £26 11s 8d (*MW* 2, 319). These coins presumably came from some form of collection or hoard, as they were issued in the fifteenth century and would have been perceived in the seventeenth century as bullion. Six iron bars were required for the dial (*MW* 2, 331). John Sharp, described as a worker in brass and copper, was paid £30 for the 'steilhouse' of the dial, which weighed twenty-six pounds, including the provision of the copper and the workmanship. By 8 July the work was finished and John Anderson was paid £280 10s 0d for painting the dial and the council house (*MW* 2, 334). The main cost of the sundial, paid at the same time, was for the work of John Mylne and his team, amounting to £408 15s 6d. It included the stone and its cutting and carving, the foundations, the steps, the pillar and the 'degries' (*MW* 2, 336). The sundial, of the obelisk type, was erected in the north garden. Its octagonal pedestal stands 10 feet high (3.3m) on a base 10 feet 3 inches wide consisting of three octagonal steps. It bears the initials of Charles I and his queen, Henrietta Maria, and the arms of the United Kingdoms, displayed within the garter. The facetted head is a polyhedron with each of the twenty-nine faces presenting a dial. The undersides display devices relating to the kingdoms and the royal family, such as the rose, the thistle, the Prince of Wales feathers and the Scottish crest (RCAHMS 1951, 152–3).

Fig 239 The sundial made by the King's Master Mason, John Mylne, and his sons along with John Barton, John Sharp and John Anderson for the North Garden at Holyrood in 1633. Crown copyright: Royal Collection.

Such elaborate sundials would appear to have been a particularly Scottish aspect of garden design in the seventeenth and early eighteenth centuries (Somerville 1990, 234), although Charles I had an example in the garden at St James Palace in London which was, according to a foreign visitor in 1640, 'not very big and has nothing remarkable, except that in the middle we see in a large square stone with a hollow in the middle containing a hundred and seventeen dials' (Pattacini 1998, 4). The popularity in Scotland of sundials with

Fig 240 The sundial in the North Garden at Holyroodhouse in an aquatint from a drawing by Edward Blore of 1826. The gallery leading to the garden has been converted into a house attached to the north side of the James V tower. SC932469

Fig 241 The winter face of the earliest dated free-standing dial from Kenmure Castle set up in 1623 by John Bonar, Schoolmaster of Ayr. It is a sun, moon and tide dial and lists ports in Scotland, Ireland, the Low Countries and France. SC1238452

polyhedral heads is unparalleled across Europe, and the obelisk form is not known elsewhere. They are concentrated, as with gardens of that date, in the more fertile and populous areas of Scotland. The strong interest in mathematics, of which Napier of Merchiston was the outstanding proponent, seems to have encouraged this development, and dialling was taught in schools (Somerville 1986, 240).

What may be the earliest dated free-standing dial (as opposed to one attached to a building) in Scotland is one from Kenmure Castle, now in Dumfries Museum (Fig 241). Its original position is not known, but it probably occupied a central position in an enclosed garden below the castle. It is a sun, moon and tidal dial, and is one of four made by John Bonar of Ayr between 1623 and 1634. It consists of a heavy slate slab, rectangular below and semicircular above, with a summer face and a winter face, and was set up on 11 December 1623. There is a list of names of ports all around Britain, the North Sea and the Channel (the port establishments), with a concentration on Scotland, indicating the appropriate high tides in relation to the moon. There are Latin tags all around the edge and on the upper summer face which mainly relate to time. The longest verse describes the progress of the sun through the Zodiac, illustrating the association of astrology and astronomy, particularly evident at Edzell. It runs:

QUHAIR MENNOCK MONTANE MOUNTES
FRA THE WOLD
A LAPIDICE DID RAISE ME FRA THE RUITE
TWICE NINE THOWSAND OF MILES
PHOEBUS IS ROLD
THE NATURALL DAY TO RINE ON ME BUT
BUITE

QUHEN HE WALD FEED ON VENISON AS
FRUITE
THEN CAPRICORN WITH HORNS DOES HIM
EFFRAYE
HE HAISTES SYNE TO LEIFF ON
LAMPETTES RUIDE
OUT THROUGH THE SIGNS WITH CANCER
FOR TO STAYE
QHHEN ARIES AND LIBRA MAKS DERAYE
IN SABLE WEED FOR PHAETON HIM
CLEEDS
ENDYMIONS SPOUS THAT LIQUID FEELDS
ARAYS
PORTUMNUS
SOJURS TEACHES HEER THAIR MEEDS
LET ALL ESTAITS MY MUISSINGS HEERON
SKANCE
LEARN BY MY SHADE OF WARDLIE GLEE
THE GLANCE
LAUS HONO IMPERIUM DOMINO AMEN
(Somerville 1986, 235)

The reference to Mennock Hill may be an error for The Merrick in Kirkcudbrightshire. Two other dials in the same group have a reference to The Merrick. (See also Fig 224.)

John Bonar was Schoolmaster in Ayr between 1612 and 1638. His next dial known is from Bangor in Northern Ireland and was made in December 1630. James Hamilton was created Lord Claneboye in 1622 as a reward for services for James VI, and was granted Bangor Abbey in 1630. He was born in Ayrshire, the son of the minister of Dunlop, and one of his brothers was the master of Ayr Grammar School in the 1640s. John Bonar may have set up the dial at Bangor himself for there is a record of him travelling to Ireland (Somerville 1986, 235–40). The verses on this dial also relate to the sun and the Zodiac and refer to the origin of its stone in south-west Scotland.

THE OREADES THAT HANTS ON
MEAROCKS MOTE
AND SATYRES TRIPPING AYE FROM HILL
TO HILL
ADMIRING PHOEBUS COURS AND
PHOEBUS LOTE
THE EDUB CALD QUHAIROFE THEY HAD
NO SKILL
THEN ALL AGREEING WITH TEARES YAT
DID DISTILL
OUT OF THAIRE CHEEKS TO MAK A
BULS(LE) RAND STRAND
THE EARTHE TO BREAK AS THEY WAR
WARNEDED TILL
BE ARLADGE VOICE AT KEYLOCH BROOK
ME FAND

Fig 242 The elaborately carved and inscribed fountain and sundial at Dundas Castle erected by Sir Walter Dundas in 1623. It bore the admonition 'See, read, think and attend' and was to serve as 'a future memorial for his posterity, as also an amusing recreation for friends, guests and visitors'. SC1237551

OUT THRROWE MY CENTER A GNOMON
THEY MADE STAND
AT MORNING NOON AND EVEN OF AN
LENGHTE
THE ZODIACK SIGNS WEELL TILL UN STAND
WITH AEQUINOX AND SOLSTICES THE
STRENGHTE
SEN PHOEBUS HEER BRINGS TROUBLE
CAIRE & TOYLL
PRAY UNTO GOD TO SEND A BETTER SOYLL
TO GOD ONLY WISE BE GLORY THROUGH
JESUS CHRIST FOR EVER AMEN

Another similar dial with a similar verse, now in the National Museums of Scotland, was engraved on 22 September 1632 and first recorded in a garden at Whithorn. It may have belonged to a member of the family of the earls of Wigtown, which was connected by marriage to the Campbells of Loudon in Ayrshire, the recipients of John Bonar's fourth dial of 1634. The sundial stood in the gardens there until the 1950s.

A fifth example, now in the garden of Broughton House in Kirkcudbright, probably came from MacLellans Castle in the town, which was the house of a family linked with those of the other owners of this particular form of dial (Fig 16). It bears the arms of Sir Robert MacLellan of Bombie with the motto 'Think On', which came from the family of his wife, Dame Grissel Maxwell. The dial was made by James Broun in September 1636 (Somerville 1986, 233–42). Its inscription is more concerned with astronomy than astrological description, and gives the relative sizes of the planets and the length of their rotation, still

reflecting pre-Copernican astronomy with mention of the crystal sphere. It reads:

Ye moone in a month and is less 42 tymes.
Mercury in a year and is less nor the earth 19 tymes.
Venus in a yeare and is less nor the earth 6 tymes.
The sunne in 365 days 5 hours 49 minutes he is bigger nor the earth 140 tymes.
Mars in 2 yeares he is less nor the earth 13 tymes.
Jupiter in 12 yeares his cor(por)ation or bignes exceeding the earth 14 tymes.
Saturn performs his cours in 30 yeares his corpulancie exceeding the earth 22 tymes.
The starrie firmament in 7000 yeares.
The crystalline spheir performs his motion in 49000 yeares. (Somerville 1986, 237)

Another possible dial of this form was found in the moat at Caerlaverock Castle (Somerville 1990, 78). While the sundials and moon dials would have a practical function in allowing the correction of the contemporary unreliable time keeping of clocks and watches, the more elaborate predictions of tides at a wide variety of ports could only be of scientific and cultural interest.

When free-standing dials with complex polyhedral heads were reviewed by Andrew Somerville in 1990, he dated them to between 1623 and 1731. He was able to identify forty-seven surviving examples as belonging to the period before 1700, with many more, while not specifically dated, belonging to the same period (Somerville 1990, 234). They often provide an indication of a garden of this period, although sundials in the form of obelisks were also used as the centre

Fig 243 Detail of the fountain at Dundas Castle. SC1237542

Fig 244 *The walled garden of Dundas Castle in 1794 drawn while the early seventeenth century mansion was still standing next to the fifteenth century tower. The sundial and fountain may occupy the central point of the garden. The parterres have been reduced to an expanse of grass. DP102247*

pieces for markets. The elaborate dials, many with complicated inscriptions, were an important element in the design of a garden in Scotland.

Contemporary with the dial from Kenmure Castle was that from **Dundas Castle** in West Lothian (Figs 242, 243). This is an unusual and elaborate construction, which seems to have combined a dial and a fountain. It was erected by Sir Walter Dundas in 1623, and his initials and arms and those of his wife appear on it (RCAHMS 1929, 205–6). It seems to have been erected to complement the seventeenth century mansion which was built beside the still surviving fifteenth century tower. This mansion was demolished prior to the building of the present house of 1818. A pen and wash drawing of 1794 (Fig 244) shows it surrounded by lawn at that date. The fountain originally formed the centrepiece of a walled garden with a banqueting house at each corner (MacGibbon and Ross 1887–92, 1, 332–5). All this had been swept away and there may have been alterations to the structure when it was moved to its present position subsequent to the First Edition of the Ordnance Survey 6-inch map of 1854–5.

Steps forming an open arch led up to the lectern dial on its platform which was decorated with cherubs and masks. Jets of water would spring from the mouths of grotesque masks below. On each of the four faces are two panels with a Latin inscription, which may be translated as follows:

Fig 245 *The sundial of 1630 in the garden of Drummond Castle. It was carved by John Mylne and his sons and bears the initials of the Earl and Countess of Perth. The inscription refers to the inhabitants of different parts of the world. SC757631*

Sir Walter Dundas in the year of our lord 1623 and 61st of his own age erected and adorned as an ornament of his country and family, sacred to the memory of himself, and as a future memorial for his posterity, as also an amusing recreation for friends, guests, and visitors, this fountain in the form of a castle, this dial with its retinue of goddesses, and this garden with its buildings, walls and quadrangular walks, surrounded with stones, piled on high, rocks having been on all sides deeply cut out, which inconveniently covered the ground. Whosoever thou art who comest hither, we, so many half-fiendish spectres, are placed here lately by order, expressly for bugbears to the bad, so that the hideous show their visages, lest any meddling evil-disposed person, should put forth his hand on the dial or garden. We warn robbers to depart, burglars to desist, nothing here is prey for plunderers. For the pleasure and enjoyment of spectators are all these placed here; but we, who rather laugh with joyous front, to a free sight, we bid frankly the kind and welcome friends of the host. Boldly use every freedom with the Master, the dial, the garden, and with garden-beds and couches – him for friendship and conversation, them for recreation of mind and thought. With ordinary things to content us here, is to be even with others – we envy not their better things.

The other panel declares:

See, read, think and attend. Through rocks and crags by pipes we lead these streams That the parched garden may be moistened by the spring water. Forbear to do harm, therefore, to the fountain and garden which thou see'st. Nor yet shoulds't thou incline to injure the signs of the dial. View and with grateful eyes enjoy these hours and the garden, And to the flowers may eager thirst be allayed by the fountain.
In the year of human salvation 1623.
(Fyfe 1852 189–90)

This elaborate construction, with its retinue of goddesses, may have had a philosophical theme on the order of that incorporated in the scheme for the garden of Edzell Castle, or, more simply, have been designed for the recreation of mind and thought, as at Pinkie House. As at Edzell there is a strong emphasis on the family's arms and their noble status. The mention of the need to cut out rock to achieve a suitable setting for the garden indicates the importance of achieving a suitable setting for the house.

The building or remodelling of a house and the creation or recreation of a garden are frequently linked. One of the best known dials in Scotland is that at **Drummond Castle** in Perthshire which was made by

Fig 246 The multiple gnoma *on the sundial at Drummond Castle, indicating the time in different places. SC1124367*

John Mylne in 1630, three years before his sundial was erected at Holyroodhouse (Figs 245, 246). There had been a garden there for over a century (Fig 247). James IV had visited Drummond Castle in 1496 and given the gardener five shillings (*TA* 1, 280). The dial, which now occupies a central position in the formal gardens, bears the names of the Earl and Countess of Perth and the date 1630. John Mylne and his two sons were paid £32 18s 0d for work on the dial in

Fig 247 The sundial standing at the centre of the formal garden at Drummond Castle. SC757628

Fig 248 The natural mound next to Lincluden College was converted into a motte in the medieval period. It was terraced and became a garden mount in the seventeenth century with a path leading to the summit and a turf seat from which the walled garden and the surrounding countryside might be contemplated. SC373093

Fig 249 Aerial view of Newbattle Abbey with the twin sundials set at the corners of the later formal garden. SC798486

October 1629 (Mylne 1893, 114), when they were
also carrying out other works at Drummond Castle.
The inscription reads:

> We are the hours on the pillar you see
> Marked by the shadows that ever flee,
> And move with the sun in its course on high,
> Noting the time passing swiftly by.
> Sisters are we, then why are we clad
> In joyful robes and robes that are sad.
> We who have rays from the sun at morn
> Are servants to those in the East who are born
> Who live in those regions far remote,
> Where the Medes and the Persians round Babylon
> fought.
> We whose robes are red and bright
> Have our names from the sun's retreating light,
> Italians, Bohemians, all are we,
> And the bright tints of the West you see.
> We who are dark and dusky in hue
> Mark out the hours on the zodiac blue,
> To the people of France and the people of Spain,
> Who live by the side of the weltering main.
> (Ross 1890, 205)

The verses describe the hours as sisters. The reference to
them as clad in differently coloured robes may indicate
some painting of the dial to match the different times of
day or times in different places. The painting of rays on
the multiple dials is described in a contemporary work
along with a description of how to make the various
calculations (Gunter 1624, 3–9, 17–59). The date of
the construction of the terraces at Drummond is not
known. They were certainly in place by 1685 when they
appear on the manuscript map by John Adair of about
that date (NLS Adv.MS.70.2.11 (Adair 2)). The Earl
of Perth erected another dial at his house at Stobhall,
north of Perth.

Free-standing sundials were a popular feature of
seventeenth century gardens in Scotland. Their appeal
may lie less in their ability to provide the local time than
in the complexity of their sculpture and the mathematics
which lay behind it. The setting out of the hour lines is
an exercise in trigonometry, aided by the publications of
Napier and others. Symbolic meanings relating to love,
truth and constancy are likely to have been associated
with the dials by their seventeenth century owners. The
carving of hearts on the dials is common as well as
the initials of married couples. Other examples which
belong to the first half of the century were in gardens at
Newbattle, where two facet-headed dials were erected
in 1635 by Robert Kerr's son, the Earl of Lothian (the
recipient of the letter about the planning of a house and
garden), at Inveresk Lodge dated 1644, at Neidpath Castle
dated to 1650, and at Kirkforthar House in Fife dated
1645, as well as similar undated dials which probably
belong to this period (Somerville 1987) (Figs 249, 250).

Fig 250 Detail of the carving, showing the arms and initials of the Countess of Lothian on the sundial at Newbattle Abbey. SC774351

Sundials were also a potent symbol of the power of
time. In the later sixteenth and seventeenth centuries
the consciousness of the fleeting life of man in the face
of eternity and the need for him to be able to account
to God for the proper use of his life on earth was a
common poetic theme. Alexander Montgomerie, the
leader of James VI's Castalian band, was a Scottish
poet concerned with this theme and its association with
the cultivation of Melancholy. Shakespeare's *Sonnet 77*
begins: 'Thy glass will show thee how thy beauties wear,
The dial how thy precious minutes waste, ... Thou by thy
dial's shady stealth mayst know Time's thievish progress
to eternity'. The perception of this aspect of moral and
intellectual life was one of the associations of the garden
during the reign of James VI and later. The prominent
presence of sundials among a blooming garden would
have something of the effect of a reminder of death,
'Et in Arcadia Ego', and the production of a delicious
melancholy (Strong 1998, 214–19).

Gardens were, for the most part, designed to be
viewed from the house or the terrace on the opposing
side to the entrance front, but garden mounts were
created or adapted from natural features to provide
an alternative viewpoint. The existence or possible
existence of garden mounts in and adjacent to gardens
of the seventeenth century has already been alluded
to at Lincluden (Fig 248), Muness, Busta, Kenmure
Castle, Black Barony, Monzie and Pinkie, as well as
their relationship to a creation such as the King's Knot
at Stirling. Their dating may be associated with the
design of the individual gardens, but some examples lie
beyond the gardens. Mounts continued to be erected into
the eighteenth century; the example at Hopetoun was
formed in 1730, when it is described as 'A Mount with

Fig 251 The medieval motte at Lochwood Castle which has been terraced to form a garden feature. SC381741

a Bank and Ever Green Wilderness round From whence a Prospect of the whole River and Country as far as the Eye can serve: This Mount is formed out of the Rubbish of the Old Castle of Abercorn – Ane Obeliske on the Mount 90 feet high' (RCAHMS A33042P). A few years later and the castle would have become in itself a feature in the park.

Another garden where a mound was altered to provide a feature was that at **Lochwood Castle** in Dumfriesshire where an earlier defensive work, a motte, in part of natural origin, was terraced (Figs 251, 252). Known as the Mount, it stood to the north of the long range of buildings of seventeenth century date and their associated courts, and the earlier tower, which received additions in 1603. To the west was a walled garden with a central mount about 9 feet (2.76m) high; its summit had a diameter of about 10 feet (3.07m) It still survived in 1912 when the site was visited by RCAHMS staff. Around its base was a shallow trench with a width of 12 feet (3.7m), perhaps suggesting a water feature. On top of the mound were four wild cherry trees (RCAHMS 1920, 114–17). It was compared to a similar mound which occupied the centre of the garden at **Logan House** in Galloway (RCAHMS 1912, 61). At **Dunninald Castle** in Angus, the site of the former seventeenth century mansion of the Erskines of Dun, a mount is placed in line with the long axis of the formal garden. One mound, demolished in 1964, was at Tyrie in Aberdeenshire where, in the early eighteenth century, a large formal garden was recorded (MacFarlane 1, 53). Cromwell's Mount in the grounds of Broxmouth House in East Lothian was in a position which overlooked the site of the Battle of Dunbar in 1650 (*Stat Acct*, 5, 485). This mound, which stands up to 2.5m in height, would have overlooked the gardens from the west.

A mound in **Banff** known as Pennant's Mount, in the area of the yards of the former Carmelite Friary, was excavated in 1989. In the seventeenth century the property was in the possession of the Ogilvy family. Sir George Ogilvy was a royalist, and his garden was 'inclosed with excellent Stone-walls and planted with the best Fruit-trees then could be had' (Cramond 1891, 41). The mound stood 2.3m high and was roughly oval, measuring about 16m by 12m at its base (Greig 1989, 19–20). This may have overlooked the garden destroyed in 1640 by the covenanting troops of General Munro: 'Who no sooner he came thither, but he set down his quarter in the laird of Banfe his beautifull garden, which was a great ornament to the towne of Banfe, and being gallantly planted and walled, overshadowd and enclosd the east syde of that towne. The souldiours were no sooner sett downe there, but they fell too to make havocke of all the fruict and other trees which stood there in great aboundance; leaving not so much as one standing tree, younge nor olde, and cutting upp all the hedges to the rootes, in which deformed condition it is yet to be seen as they left it' (Cramond 1891, 94).

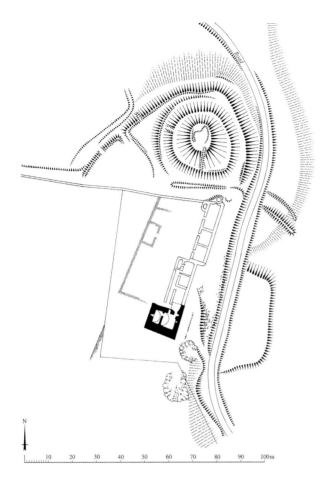

*Fig 252 Plan of the site of Lochwood Castle with the motte on the north.
A garden mount formerly stood at the centre of a walled garden to the west.
SC382040*

Gardens, already referred to in earlier chapters, dating to the sixteenth century or earlier, continued in use and were extended and modernised to accord with contemporary taste. **Aberdour Castle** saw the creation of a rectangular walled garden to the east of the terraced garden of about half a hectare in extent, which is dated from an inscription on a gateway to 1632 (Figs 253, 254). The garden was entered from the terraced garden through a gate decorated with the Douglas heart. A summer house was built which projected above the south-east angle of the garden and beneath it there was a bridge connecting the walled garden with the kitchen garden on the other side of the lane to the parish church (Hynd and Ewart 1983, fig 6). William, Earl of Morton, was Lord Treasurer of Scotland between 1630 and 1636 (Apted 1985, 1, 16, 28). A pedestal sundial bearing the Douglas arms and the insignia of a knight of the Order of the Garter was recorded at the nearby Aberdour House in 1928, but probably came from Aberdour Castle (RCAHMS 1933, 17); the Earl of Morton became a knight of the Garter in 1633 (Fig 255).

Seton Palace continued to be admired by passing travellers, and provided lodgings for James VI in 1617 and Charles I in 1633 on their visits to Scotland. The

seventeenth century garden walls with their rounds or lookouts at four corners still survive (RCAHMS 1924, 125). James VI rested at the south-west round on the first stage of his journey to England in 1603 (Maitland 1829, 60). The garden's apple trees, walnut trees, sycamores and other fruit trees flourished despite the proximity of the sea (Brown 1978, 136). It is the subject of one of the two surviving pictures of Scottish buildings painted by Alexander Keirincx for Charles I, which shows the building from a distance, environed in trees (Figs 256, 257).

According to the description by Richard Maitland (Maitland 1829, 35) there had been an important garden at **Winton** in the early sixteenth century. In 1620 George, tenth Lord Seton and third Earl of Winton, 'built the house of Wintone, being burned of the English of old, and the policy thereof destroyed, in anno 1620: He founded and built the great house from the foundation, with all the lairge stone dykes about the precinct, park, orchard and gardens thereof (Maitland 1828, 74). The house was built by William Wallace, the King's Master Mason and the person responsible for the early phases of Heriot's Hospital in Edinburgh which is extremely rich in decorative detail. The entrance was on the north. The gardens on the south fall towards the Tyne Water in four terraces. The three upper terraces are supported by high retaining walls while the lowest is formed by above a sloping grass bank. In the top

Fig 253 A re-creation of the walled garden at Aberdour Castle, which is dated to 1632 by an inscription on a gateway. © Historic Scotland

Fig 254 A garden doorway of 1632 at Aberdour Castle from a drawing by H H Dalrymple of 1902. DP057854

Castle in West Lothian would indicate that the gardens there were being, at the very least, maintained during the first half of the seventeenth century. The walled garden was laid out on a south-facing slope at some distance from the castle, and was entered from the north. The stone used in its construction has been compared to that used in the extension upwards of the tower. This, it has been suggested, may be dated to the seventeenth century (RCAHMS 1929, 211). A walled orchard lay to the east. It has been suggested that the enlargement of a window in the south wall at second floor level was to allow a view along an avenue (Proudfoot and Aliaga-Kelly 1997, 838) (Fig 260).

The gardens of **Bog of Gight** or **Gordon Castle** were recalled by John Spalding in his *History of the Troubles* when he wrote of the departure of Henrietta, Marchioness of Huntly, who was forced into exile because of her religious beliefs, and 'leaves with woe heart her staitly building of the Bog, beautified with many yards, parks and pleasures' (Spalding 1829, 328). On Pont's map, Bog of Gight had been depicted with a park planted with what were probably fir trees. Henrietta's husband, the first Marquess of Huntly, was

Fig 255 The sundial with the Douglas arms and the insignia of the Order of the Garter which probably came from Aberdour Castle. The Earl of Morton became a Knight of the Garter in 1633. SC1110918

revetting wall are two seventeenth century pediments enriched with vine scroll. They flank a panel bearing a shield charged with the royal arms, which were probably inserted here following the enlargement of the house in the early nineteenth century. The inscription below the shield reads IACOBUS-S-BRIT-FRANCE-ET HIBER celebrating the Union of the Crowns. To the east of the house is a level garden above a terrace created by two high sloping banks above a small stream. The house and gardens appear on the manuscript map of East Lothian by John Adair, which is dated to 1682 (NLS Adv.MS.70.2.11 (Adair 10)) (Figs 258, 259). It shows the terraces to the east and south, below which trees are planted. It might be the orchard referred to by Viscount Kingston, who wrote the continuation of the *History of the House of Seytoun* in 1687. There were four gardens around the house, which may have been grass plots.

The statement by John Reid, the author of *The Scots Gard'ner* published in 1683 (Bartow 1879, 243), that his father and grandfather had been gardeners at **Niddry**

Fig 256 Seton Palace about 1640 by Alexander Keirincx. The emphasis is on the surrounding landscape. © Scottish National Portrait Gallery.

'fully set to building and planting of all curious devices' (Spalding 1829, 38). An arcaded loggia ran round the outer wall of the house at *piano nobile* level, allowing wide views over the surrounding gardens and parks (Glendinning *et al* 1996, 46) (Fig 261).

Scottish clients, when commissioning their portraits, had always included reference to aspects of their lives and position they considered most important: coats of arms, weapons, books, jewellery, hunting dogs or heirs. During the earlier seventeenth century their houses in their landscapes begin to be included. The artist George Jamesone, born in Aberdeen about 1590, was apprenticed to John Anderson, an Edinburgh painter, who was responsible for the decoration of the room at Edinburgh Castle where James VI had been born, on the occasion of James' return to Scotland in 1617. Jamesone began painting portraits in the 1620s and after 1633 had studios in both Aberdeen and Edinburgh (Thomson 1974, 13–43). Paintings attributed to George Jamesone which included buildings set in a landscape are a portrait of William Ramsay, Earl of Dalhousie, for which a date of 1635 is suggested (Thomson 1974, 113–14, fig 100), and one of the family of Thomas Hamilton, Earl of Haddington, set in a landscape with a fountain (Thomson 1974, 122–3, fig 101).

The well-known map of Edinburgh and the Canongate, dated to 1647, was produced by James

Gordon of Rothiemay, the fifth son of Robert Gordon of Straloch and the inheritor of his interests in cartography and of his manuscripts (Fig 262). It provides a record of the earlier seventeenth century Palace of

Fig 257 Seton Castle with its gardens as they were depicted on the manuscript map of 1682 by John Adair (Adv.MS.70.2.11 (Adair 10)). © NLS

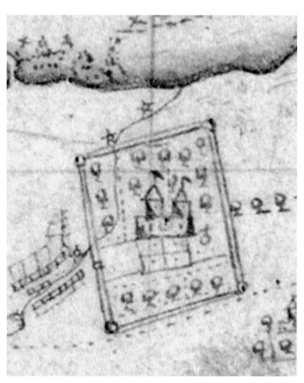

Holyroodhouse and its extensive gardens with their elaborate parterres (NLS EMS.s. 52). The details may or may not be accurate (the sundial erected in 1633 is not depicted), but the plan does indicate the design of the gardens and forms of knots adopted there. The layout of the south-west and north-east parterres in the north garden with their looser scrolling designs contrasts with those of the other parterres with their more obvious geometrical forms. The choice of a design incorporating the *fleur de lys* may be a compliment to Charles I's French queen, Henrietta Maria, from whose rooms, had she ever occupied them, it would have been most visible. They recall those illustrated by André Mollet in his book *Le Jardin de Plaisir*, a work dedicated to Queen Christina of Sweden and published in 1651. André Mollet was one of a dynasty of French gardeners; his grandfather, Jacques Mollet, had worked for a cousin of Mary Queen of Scots at the Chateau of Anet; his father had been gardener to Henri IV of France with responsibility for gardens at the Louvre and the Tuileries Palace in Paris, as well as those of Saint-Germain-en-Laye and Fontainebleau. Earlier in his career in 1629, André Mollet had been summoned to England by Henri IV's daughter, Henrietta Maria, who had married Charles I four years earlier. He may have worked on the gardens at St James Palace, in London, which were described as consisting of 'two grand gardens, one with parterres of different figures, bordered on every side by a hedge

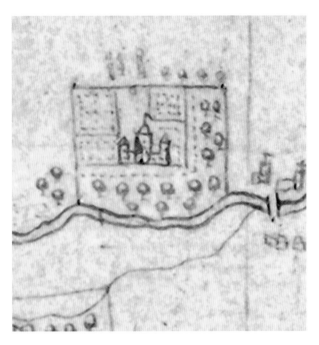

Fig 258 Winton Castle and its gardens on the manuscript map of 1682 by John Adair (Adv.MS.70.2.11 (Adair 10)). © NLS

of box, carefully cultivated by the hands of a skilful gardener: and in order to render the walls on both sides which enclosed it appear the more agreeable, all sorts of fine flowers were there sowed ... The other garden ... of the same extent, had divers walks, some sanded and others of grass, but both bordered on both sides with an infinity of fruit trees, which rendered walking so

Fig 259 Aerial view of Winton Castle with its terraces to the south and east. SC1031186

agreeable that one could never be tired' (Strong 1998, 188). André Mollet went on to work for the Prince of Orange in 1633, and later returned to France, before being recalled in 1642 to lay out the queen's garden at Wimbledon (Pattacini 1998, 4–8). There were a series of gardens there, including parterres with four knots, 'fitted for the growth of choyse flowers; bordered with box in the points, angles, squares and roundles and handsomely turfed in the Intervalles or little walkes thereof' and a maze 'of young trees wood and sprayes of a good growth and height ... the walkes or intervals whereof are all grass plotts' (Strong 1998, 191–4). The royal gardeners at Holyrood were in a position to know of the works of their counterparts in England; Mollet and his nephew Gabriel were to return to England in 1661 to keep the gardens at St James' Palace (Pattacini 1998, 10) (Fig 263).

While the surroundings of houses in the country provided greater opportunities for the laying out of gardens, these were also a feature of the towns. Much of the evidence for this in the middle of the seventeenth century comes from the town plans of James Gordon of Rothiemay. In his depiction of Edinburgh, the houses on both sides of the Canongate are shown with gardens running, for the most part, between the rear of the houses and the town wall (Fig 262). The gardens are shown laid out in small parterres, not as elaborate as

Fig 261 Bog of Gight (Gordon Castle) showing the walls around the garden in an engraving by John Slezer. The image captioned 'Invero' or Inverary first appeared in Theatrum Scotiae *in 1719. The statues are unlikely to have been present in the earlier seventeenth century. DP101793*

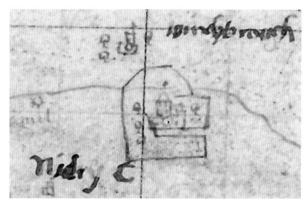

Fig 260 Niddry Castle with its walled orchard and avenue on the manuscript map of 1684 by John Adair (Adv.MS.70.2.11 (Adair 8)). © NLS

those at Holyrood, but such as would require regular maintenance. George Heriot, a goldsmith to James VI and Anne of Denmark and the founder of Heriot's Hospital, is reported to have built a 'Square of Free-stone with a good garden behind' near the foot of the Canongate (Macky 1729). The garden parterres are interspersed with groups of up to five trees, often laid out geometrically, some of which may be orchard trees, and with plots indicated with rows of lines, which are probably vegetable or herb plots. How much imagination went into the depictions of these gardens is unknown and it is difficult to believe that all the proprietors maintained their gardens to a similar standard, but it may be pointed out that the topography of Edinburgh with high ground to the north, east and south of the Canongate, would

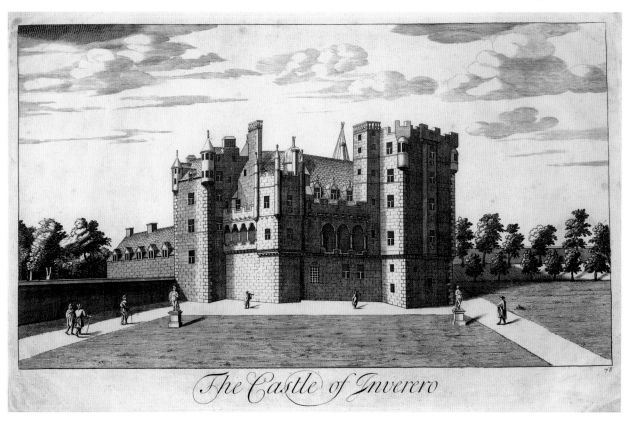

The Castle of Inverero

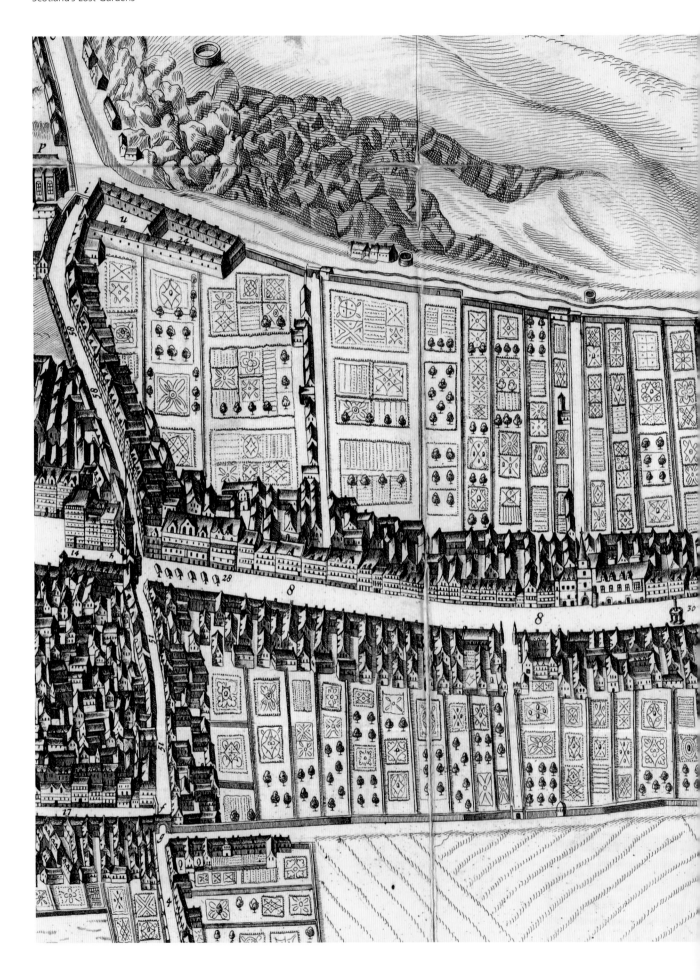

Fig 263 *A detail from the 1647 plan of Edinburgh by James Gordon of Rothiemay showing the design of the parterres in the North Garden of Holyrood. The scrolling design of the south-west section with its fleur de lys motif recalls the work of the French gardener André Mollet who worked for Henrietta Maria, Charles I's queen. DP101340*

Fig 262 *(Previous pages) The gardens of the Canongate in the 1647 plan of Edinburgh by James Gordon of Rothiemay. DP101340*

allow some view into most of these enclosures. Moray House, the town house of Margaret, Countess of Moray, clearly identifiable by the pyramidal gate posts on the Canongate side, is laid out around a courtyard with the garden to the rear. Immediately behind the buildings are two small parterres with two larger ones to the south, all surrounded by paths. At the bottom of the garden are nine trees laid out symmetrically. The garden is enclosed by walls to east, west and south, with the wall to the west separating the garden from a close leading down to a private gate opening on to the Cowgate. There is a banqueting house with an ogee roof built on or against the rear wall of the garden, which would have provided a view up and across the parterres (Fig 264). In the description of Edinburgh, written by David Buchanan to accompany Gordon of Rothiemay's plan, he says of the gardens of Moray House, 'These gardens are cultivated with so much taste and such care that they easily challenge comparison with those of warmer tracts, and even almost of England itself. And here you see how much human art and industry avail in supplying the defects even of nature. Hardly any one could believe that in cold countries so much amenity could be secured in gardens' (Macfarlane 1906–8, 2, 639).

Fig 264 *Moray House and its gardens. The pyramidal gate posts are visible on the Canongate and there is an ogee-roofed banqueting house built at the foot of the garden. DP101340*

Fig 265 Trinity Hospital and its garden and dovecot on the 1647 plan of Edinburgh by James Gordon of Rothiemay. DP101340

In Edinburgh proper, rather than the suburb of the Canongate, the gardens are far more limited in extent. Gardens are depicted on the north side next to Trinity Hospital and its almshouses whose walls enclose, in addition to a series of small parterres, a dovecot and rows of trees (Fig 265). On the south side of the Cowgate, behind the buildings and with a wall to the rear, are another series of gardens laid out in a similar fashion to those in the Canongate, with others around the Old High School and to the east and west of the Old College. The houses on both sides of the Grassmarket are depicted with gardens to the rear. Beyond the wall the suburbs of the Pleasance, St Mary's Wynd, the Potterrow, Bristo, the Society and the West Port are shown with gardens behind the houses.

The most elaborate, and probably the most recent garden depicted by James Gordon is that surrounding **Heriot's Hospital** (Fig 266). George Heriot died in 1623, leaving provision in his will for the erection of a hospital for the upbringing and education of fatherless boys. The site selected lay just outside the Flodden Wall, and the town council surrounded the area with the Telfer Wall. This was built between 1628 and 1636 at the same time as the building of the earlier stages of the Hospital, and named for the mason responsible for its construction. The first builder responsible for

the Hospital was the King's Master Mason, William Wallace. After his death the work was continued by his assistant, William Aytoun. What influence they may have had on the design of the garden is unknown. The foundation stone was laid in 1628, and progress was initially rapid, but slowed in the 1630s because all payments were made from the revenue from Heriot's bequest, part of which consisted of debts owed him by the Crown. Work ceased at the time of the Bishops' Wars in 1639, but resumed in 1642 and was almost finished in 1650 when the Hospital was taken over by Oliver Cromwell for his injured soldiers. It remained in their occupation until 1658 (MacGibbon and Ross, 1887–92, 4, 138–9), when they were removed to a house in the Canongate, known as the New Hospital, at the Town's expense. In addition to work on the house, the garden was to be prepared and planted, and the appointment of the gardener was to approved by the Hospital's physician and officers (NRS GD421/1/7/66), suggesting that its contents were to be of medicinal use.

The Hospital was approached from the north up a steep narrow street, the opposite side from the principal entrance today. The entry, through a gatehouse, led into a garden which surrounded the building on all four sides. In 1647, the year before the building was completed and before the first inmates arrived, the garden is shown as laid out in eight parterres to the west and as uncultivated ground to the east. Each parterre was enclosed by what appears to be a low hedge. To the

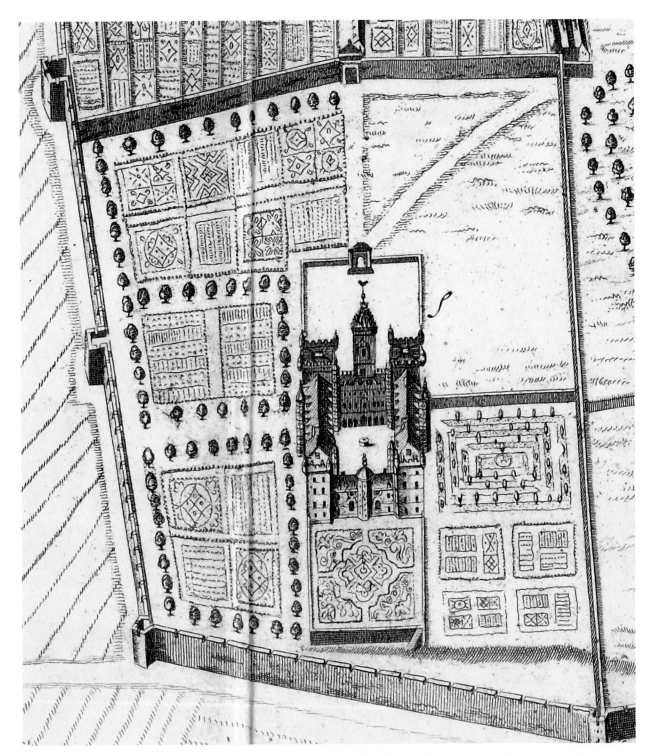

Fig 266 Heriot's Hospital surrounded by its partly completed garden on the 1647 plan of Edinburgh by James Gordon of Rothiemay. The scrolling design of the parterres to the south of the building, as at Holyrood Palace, recalls those of André Mollet. The trees planted in the pattern of a maze to the east of the Hospital may be young fruit trees. DP101340

south of these parterres on the west side of the building is a rectangular section divided by a broad walk running north and south and containing plants in rows, possibly a kitchen or herb garden, the alternating sections seeming to contain low shrub-like plants and smaller plants possibly in planted rows with furrows in between. John

Reid, writing in the later part of the seventeenth century, advises that a kitchen garden should be divided into ridges (Reid 1988, 20). To the south of this was a garden divided into four sections surrounded by low hedges with walks around. Two were laid out as decorative parterres and the other two, with plants similar to those immediately to the north, set out in rows. These gardens were surrounded by single rows of trees and walks.

The garden to the south of the hospital building was precisely aligned with the building and enclosed by a wall. There was a single small doorway leading into it

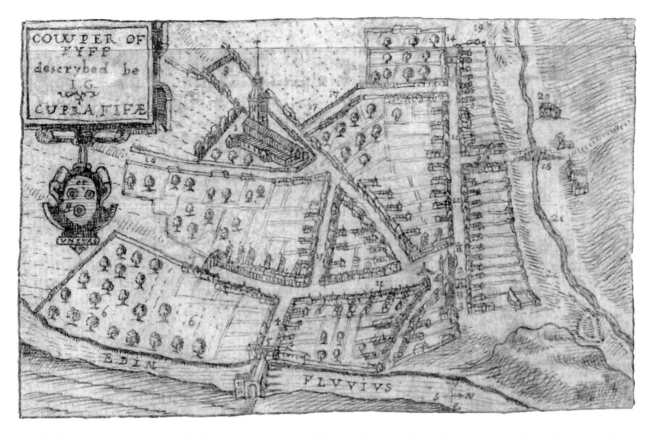

Fig 267 Manuscript plan of Cupar by James Gordon of Rothiemay prepared in 1642 as part of the project for the publication of an atlas of Scotland by Johannes Blaeu in Amsterdam. (Adv.MS.70.2.10 (Gordon 53). © NLS

Fig 268 Manuscript plan of St Andrews by James Gordon of Rothiemay prepared in 1642 as part of the project for the Blaeu atlas of Scotland. *(Adv.MS.70.2.10 (Gordon 53)). © NLS*

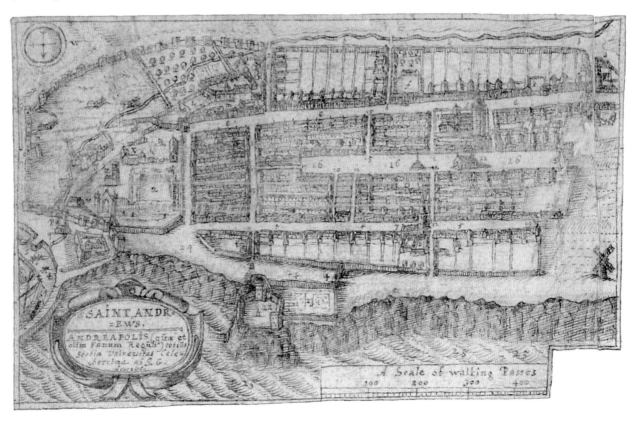

Fig 269 Detail of St Andrews Castle, viewed from the north, on the manuscript plan of St Andrews prepared in 1642 showing what appear to be parterres in the garden beside the castle. (Adv.MS.70.2.10 (Gordon 53). © NLS

from the Council Room of the Hospital, which could be used by the governors of the institution, and it was overlooked from the Master's apartments (MacGibbon and Ross, 1887–92, 4, 145, 149 figs 722, 726). The principal entry to the gardens visible on Gordon's engraving seems to be by means of a stair built against its south-east corner, which would be somewhat inconvenient for gardeners. There was an entry in the west wall by the time Slezer produced his engraving of the building, which, although it was not published until

1719, shows the building at an earlier date, possibly in the 1680s (Slezer 1719) (Fig 318). This garden is laid out in a direct relationship to the building and is centred on the projecting bay of the chapel. It contains the most elaborate series of parterres, set around a central feature which might be a sundial, a fountain, or, less probably, a small tree. Its design of scrolls and flowers again recalls the work of André Mollet, and the complexity of the paths might be compared with the description of Henrietta Maria's garden at Wimbledon where a fountain formed the centrepiece.

To the east of this walled garden is a plot with four parterres, two smaller to the south and two larger to the north, all of which are laid out in a mixture of knots and other linear plots, and enclosed by a low hedge. To the north of this is a rectangular maze of a simple symmetrical design in which it is unlikely that anyone would become lost. It is obvious from the engraving that it had been recently planted and that space had been allowed for the trees, which resemble a cypress in shape, although yews would be a more likely choice for a maze, to grow and close up the gaps. Its centrepiece, in a circular setting, is a tree. Mazes, as well as being decorative, were symbolic of the difficulties faced in life. The maze is closed off by a wall from the uncultivated ground to the north, which may, at the time the engraving was made, have served as a yard for the masons who were working on the completion of the building.

From the elaborate layout and sophisticated design of the gardens around Heriot's, it seems clear that they were not designed primarily for the use of the orphans for whom the hospital was supposedly built, but were

Fig 270 The garden beside St Andrews Castle as it appears on the Geddy map of about 1580, but which may reflect its appearance at a period before 1560. S. Andre sive Andreapolis Scotiae Universitas Metropolitana MS.20996. © NLS

rather intended as an ornament for the city and a resort for the citizens, and perhaps to provide a more direct benefit for the trustees and members of the town council, who had a supervisory role, and in the later seventeenth and eighteenth century the gardens certainly fulfilled that role. Even in its unfinished state, the Hospital was shown to visitors such as Sir William Brereton in 1636 (Brown 1978, 141). While there was a considerable amount of sculpture, including sundials, associated with the building, it does not appear to have been extended to the gardens. The parterres in the gardens of the Town's College in Edinburgh (Fig 134) do not show the influence of the latest fashions in design, unlike some of those at both Holyrood and Heriot's Hospital, but retain a strongly quadripartite design.

Two other town plans produced by Gordon of Rothiemay are of those of St Andrews and Cupar in Fife, both of which appear as insets on a manuscript map of Fife (NLS Adv.MS.70.2.10 (Gordon 53)). It was prepared in 1642, as part of the project for the publication of an atlas of Scotland by Blaeu in Amsterdam in 1654. The plan of Cupar (Fig 267) shows the burgage plots to the rear of the houses of the town, most of which are empty of any indication of cultivation. Walled enclosures by the West Port contain trees which may be fruit trees, as do the less well populated areas of the town near the church and the enclosure to the south known as the Barony. **St Andrews** provides something of a contrast (Fig 268).

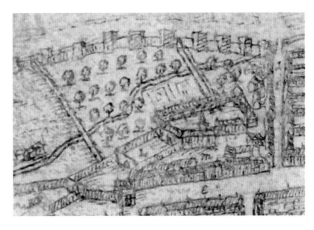

Fig 271 St Leonard's College in St Andrews with its orchard and its gardens laid out in parterres. (Adv.MS.70.2.10 (Gordon 53). © NLS

The walled garden next to the castle of the archbishop, which on the map of 1580, attributed to John Geddy, but probably surveyed at an earlier date, appears as an empty enclosure, as it would probably have been after the siege of the castle in 1546–7 (Figs 268, 270). In 1642 there are indications on the map of parterres within the garden and the castle yard. The colleges of St Salvator and St Mary are depicted with trees, perhaps orchards, in their yards, while St Leonard's has what appear to be parterres laid out behind the college buildings towards the Kinness Burn, with trees planted in rows behind. The houses in the centre of the town are densely packed; those on North Street and South Street have plots behind them, but no evidence for cultivation is shown (Fig 271).

Fig 272 King's College on the plan of Aberdeen by James Gordon of Rothiemay printed in 1661. The garden is depicted with simple parterres and edged with trees. Description of new and of old Aberdeens, with the places neerest adjacent (EMS.s.249). © NLS

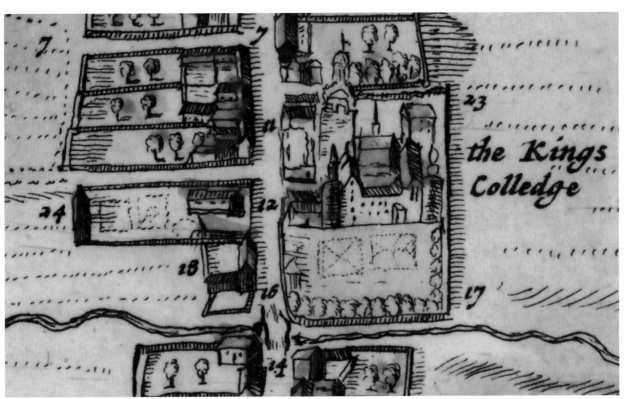

Marísh

the Keátle
Hill.

The Loch
of Old Aberdeen

Cluyns Garden

The
Broom
Hill

Powies Burne

Sunny syde

THE

SPIT:

TALL.

HILL.

R.

Machar Kirk

the Bishops Green

Rvins of the Bishops
ducott

Marish

ay to the Bridge of D

Marish called
Balliffs Bog

ABREDONIA
VETUS
The Old towne of
Aberdone

the Kings
Colledge

Rvins of the
Snow Kirk

Rvins of the
Spittall Kirk

Marish

THE

HI

The latest of James Gordon's town plans is of that of **Aberdeen** which he presented to the town council in 1661 (NLS EMS.s.249) and depicts both Old and New Aberdeen; it shows gardens lying behind the majority of the houses, most of which are planted with trees and some of which have simple parterres (Fig 273). Singled out for more detailed depiction is **King's College** garden, which lies to the south of the college buildings, surrounded by a palisade or wall, with a line of trees to east and south and an indication of a simple parterre (Fig 272). The Marquis of Huntly's garden appears to have a free-standing sundial in it; and Gordon of Cluny's walled garden has parterres and an orderly orchard behind, running down to the Old Aberdeen Loch (Fig 10). Of the **Bishop's Palace** only the garden wall survived (Innes 1842, 23). The garden adjacent to the Tradesmen's Hospital also has indications of walks and parterres within it. Aberdeen is presented on Gordon's plan as a garden city, and in the contemporary translation of his Latin description of the town, he writes, 'Many houses have their gardings and orcheyards adjoining; every garding hes its postern, and thes are planted with all sorts of trees which the climat will suffer to grow; so that the quholl toune, to such as draw neer it upon some syds of it, looks as if it stood in a garding or little wood' (Innes 1842, 9). In 1635 the artist George Jameson acquired a plot of land outside the city, which was also described in the translation of Gordon's description of Aberdeen. 'Next to the well of Spaa, hard by it, ther is a four squair feild, which of old served for a theatre, since made a gardyne for plesur by the industrie and expense of George Jameson, ane ingenious painter quho did sett up therin ane timber hous paynted all over with own hand'. He was granted tolerance 'to mak sic building, policie, and planting within and about the said plot of ground ... to the effect the same may redound to the public wse and benefit of the toune' (Innes 1842, 10) (Fig 274). The garden was supposed to revert to the city on his death. This was recognition by the town council of gardens as an ornament to a city and a public benefit. By the time Gordon prepared his plan the enclosure was bare, but the little banqueting or summer house was still depicted (Fig 275).

No plan of **Glasgow** is known from the early seventeenth century, but an account written in 1658 provides a very enthusiastic description in which the author praises the 'pleasant and fragrant Flowers that so sweetly refresh'd me, and to admiration, sweetened our present Entertainments' (Franck 1694, 91). The Incorporation of Gardeners of Glasgow is thought to go back to the very early years of the seventeenth century. Its charter was re-issued in 1691, indicating the presence there of a number of gardeners and the need to regulate their craft and apprenticeships, as well as maintaining

Fig 274 A self portrait of George Jameson. © Scottish National Portrait Gallery. Licensor Scran

and protecting their privileges (Robertson 2000, 174). The university gardens continued to be cultivated; the Great Garden extended to the banks of the Molendinar Burn and Principal Strang is credited with laying out a large and stately orchard probably within it. Access was restricted to the Principal and Masters, and the students were specifically excluded (Fig 60).

A new walled garden, known as the Little Yard or Blackfriars Yard in the 1630s, was established with a gardener's lodge adjacent. In 1614–15 John Govane, 'gairdner' was paid £5 for thorn trees for a hedge along the paths in the garden, and W Seller and his man were paid £7 for seven days' work 'setting and building' the hedge. At the same period another hedge and the building of a 'fale dyke, a wall coped with turf' were paid for. In 1637–8, Robert Hutchisone received £10 'for binding and dressing of the Garden hedges'. 'Parcells of Flowers for the gardene, tulips, anemonies and ranunculus' cost £1 14s 0d in 1656, and in the same year payments for two rolling stones for the garden suggest the presence of grass plots. In 1643 and 1644 fruit from the orchard was sold for £26 13s 4d, presumably after the College had kept what it required (Boney 1988, 134).

The dating of the creation and elaboration of specific gardens to the period of the civil war and Commonwealth in Scotland, roughly between 1650 and 1660, the time of the first statutory union with England, is difficult to document. Many gardens seem to have been damaged during the civil wars; Glamis Castle was occupied by an English garrison (Millar 1890,

Fig 273 Aberdeen depicted by Gordon of Rothiemay as a city of gardens. (EMS.s.249). © NLS

Fig 275 The garden of pleasure on the site of the play field which belonged to George Jameson, the artist and citizen of Aberdeen. His timber house 'painted allover with his own hand' stood at the centre. (EMS.s.249). © NLS

39); Fyvie Castle was also garrisoned, and the Earl of Dunfermline subsequently petitioned Parliament for relief from paying a levy for support of the army because 'it being too manifest and well-known that not only was his house and planting of Fyvie defaced and destroyed by the enemy, but likewise his said house for a long time was kept as a garrison for the use and defence of the country, by which occasions his whole lands of Fyvie and tenants thereof were ruined and destroyed' (RPS A1649/1/36). Drum Castle was attacked and the gardens damaged in 1640 and 1644 when the Earl of Argyll's foot army 'cuttit doun the pleasant gardyne planting to be huttis' (Spalding 1829, 1, 220, 2, 274), and Edzell was garrisoned by a detachment of Cromwell's soldiers in 1651 (Simpson 1931, 118). In 1640 Huntly or Strathbogie Castle also saw soldiers 'hewing down the pleasant planting about Strathbogie to be huts for the souldiers to sleip within upon the night; whereby the haill camp was well provydit of huts to the destroying of goodlie countrie policy' (Spalding 1829, 1, 222). The walled garden and other enclosures and buildings around the castle were used as part of the defences by the occupying troops (Spalding 1829, 1, 281). When Charles II came to Scotland in 1650, after the execution of his father, he spent his first night at Bog of Gight or Gordon Castle (Keay 2008, 54). Access to the young king was under the control of the covenanting party led by the Marquess of Argyll, and when Charles was staying in **Perth** he resorted to receiving his supporters in a summer house by the river in a continuation of the use of gardens as a venue for unofficial diplomacy (Balfour 1824, 4, 128–9) (Fig 276). He was probably lodged in

the King's House. This was the former property of the earls of Gowrie which had been forfeited to the Crown following the Gowrie Conspiracy in 1600.

Linlithgow Palace was fortified by Cromwell in 1650 by building a wall from the parish church to Linlithgow Loch, turning the gardens around the palace into a stronghold. Many of the buildings in the Kirkgate were demolished, including the town house and the burgh hospital, providing stone for the defences and a clear field of fire. The church was used as a stable for his horses (Ferguson 1910, 209; Waldie 1894, 79). In such conditions it is not surprising that there are few surviving traces of the gardens, and that the engraving by Slezer, published in 1693, shows the surroundings of the palace almost stripped of vegetation (Fig 232).

In the case of the **Holyrood** gardens it may be that the situation changed to a more commercial form of gardening, rather than seeing a phase of destruction. When the first Duke of Hamilton was invested as hereditary keeper of the palace in 1646 it was *cum eius hortis, pomariis et sphaeristeriis lie bouling-greens'* – with its gardens, orchards and bowling greens. He had to pay wages in money and grain to the gardeners of the north garden, the south garden and the little garden within the palace, perhaps the former cloister garth (*RMS* 9, 644 no 1710). The absence of royal authority in the 1640s allowed the gardeners at Holyrood to take on a more independent role there, although already in 1633 an area at Holyrood was referred to as Andrew Caldwell's yard (*MW* 2, 331) and in 1639 payment for three 'pairs of great bandes for the gate that goes in to Androw Caldwales yaird' appear in the accounts of the Master of Works (*MW* 2, 397). In 1644 Andrew Caldwell acquired land and property in the south garden of which he was already in occupation, *domus antiquas edificatas et vastas (per dictum Andrew occupant) ad lie north-eist neuk australis hortis de Halyruidhous* 'the old houses, built and waste, which the said Andrew occupies, in the north-east corner of the south garden of Holyroodhouse' (*RMS* 9, 578–9 no 1524). A later acquisition of land by Andrew and his son Thomas in 1655 indicates that the 'ancient buildings in the north east corner of the south garden' had been the monastic brewhouse and barn, which had been demolished and replaced by a house and other buildings (NRS RS26/3 ff313r-315r). The wills of the gardeners show their sense of identification with their role as gardeners of particular areas at Holyrood and also the way that the occupation of gardening ran in their families. The testament of Thomas Caldwell, 'gardener in the abbey', was registered in 1671 (Edinburgh Commissary Court CC8/8/74); the will of Hendry Caldwell, 'gardener in Quhythouse', now a suburb on the south side of Edinburgh, was recorded in 1646; the will of Elizabeth Hamilton, spouse of John Caldwell gardener and burgess of Paisley, was recorded in the Glasgow Commissary Court in 1651 (CC9/7/31). The will of

Fig 276 Detail from John Slezer's engraving 'The Prospect of ye Town of Perth' from Theatrum Scotiae *of 1693, showing the garden of the King's House by the River Tay which Charles II used for private meetings with supporters. DP102160*

John Brown, 'gardener of His Majesty's North Yards', was registered in 1649 (CC8/8/64), that of Robert Sympsone, 'gardener at Lord Holyroodhouse yairds', in 1652 (CC8/8/66) and that of Margaret Beattie 'spouse to Andrew Mitchell, gardener of the abbey yards' in 1656 (CC8/8/68).

For others the wars may have encouraged the pursuit of gardening. Sir Walter Stewart was the owner of **Coltness House** in Lanarkshire, where, after his marriage in 1654 at a time when Cromwell had united the government of Scotland with that of England, he put in order and extended the house his family had acquired, and turned to the garden:

He sett himself to planting and inclosing, and so to embellish the place ... The gardens were to the south of the house, much improven and inlarged, and the nursery-garden was a small square inclosure to the west of the house. The slope of the grounds to the west made the south garden, next the house, fall into three cross tarresses. The tarras fronting the south of the house was a square parterre, or flour-garden, and the easter and wester, or the higher and lower

plots of ground, were for cherry and nut gardens, and walnut and chestnut trees [were] planted upon the head of the upper bank, towards the parterre, and the slope bank on the east syde the parterre was a strawberry border.

These three tarrases had a high stone wall on the south, for ripening and improving finer fruits, and to the south of this wall was a good orchard and kitchen garden, with broad grass walks, all inclosed with a good thorn hedge; and without this a ditch and dry fence, inclosing severall rows of timber trees for shelter; to the west of the house, and beyond the square nursery garden, was a large square timber tree park, [with] birches, towards the house, and on the other three sydes, rowes of ash and plain, and in the middle a goodly thicket of firs. To the north of the barn court, and north from the house, was a grass inclosure of four akers, with a fish pond in the comer for pikes and perches. All was inclosed with a strong wall and hedge-rowes of trees: so the whole of this policy might consist of ane oblong square, of seven or eight akers of ground, and the house near middle of the square, and the longer syde of the square fronted to the south; the ordinary enteries to the house were from east and west, but the main access from the easte. (Dennistoun 1841, 55–7)

Chapter 5: The Restoration Garden 1660 to 1714

*Make all the Buildings and Plantings ly so about the House,
as that the House may be the Centre; all the Walks, Trees
and Hedges running to the House*

'The Scots Gard'ner Publish'd for the Climate of Scotland' by John Reid Gard'ner

After the peaceful return of Charles II as king, Scotland, which had endured much disruption as the consequence of the battles of the civil wars on its territory, appeared to resume the pattern of social life of the earlier part of the century. The country was ruled from London through Scottish nominees of the king, men who had for the most part been his supporters during the 1650s. Many of those who had not been imprisoned under the Commonwealth had spent time in exile in Holland and France. The estates of some landowners had been confiscated and many more had been heavily fined for their adherence to the royalist cause. The royal palaces in Scotland suffered during the wars. There was a fire at Holyrood in 1650 while it was occupied by Cromwell's soldiers and, although some rebuilding took place, this was subsequently removed at the order of Charles II. The timber in the park at Falkland was felled by the English. Linlithgow was garrisoned. Charles stayed in Stirling Castle in 1650, and Cromwell besieged it the following year. Charles II never returned to Scotland after the Restoration, but there was a determination among his influential followers that the Palace of Holyroodhouse should be rebuilt, for it would serve as a symbol of the re-establishment of the Kingdom of Scotland. Charles himself took a keen interest in the plans, and also wished to see works carried out at his castle of Stirling.

Fig 277 Leslie House with its well-preserved terraced gardens was built in the late 1660s. It belonged to the Duke of Rothes, a supporter of Charles II and Chancellor of Scotland, and was one of the first houses and gardens to be constructed after the Restoration of the king. DP036611

The dominance of the landed gentry in this period was epitomised by the construction of country houses and their gardens. The re-establishment of a hierarchical system of government, which derived its authority from the monarchy and in which the nobles saw themselves as possessing a major and recognised role, led to the formation of factions which sought to influence the king and gain offices and patronage in Scotland. Many of the great houses and gardens rebuilt at this time belonged to those who enjoyed royal favour. Classical models, with the status and authority that attached to them, were perceived to be the appropriate medium for expressing the culture of such a society with its desire for stability after the upheavals of the mid-century, but the prestige of the French court and its gardens was increasing, and symmetry was perceived as an attribute of order (Fig 278). The increasing size of gardens and parks led to the taking in of land which had been used for arable cultivation, as at Lethington (Lennoxlove) and Kinnaird, and the restriction of the use of the land and access to it.

This was the first period when it was considered that modern gardens had surpassed their classical predecessors. According to John Evelyn, the moderns excelled the ancients in their cultivation and care of a wide variety of plants (Sieveking 1908, 190–2).

André Mollet, whose earlier work appears to have influenced the design of Scottish parterres in the 1640s, published *Le Jardin de Plaisir* in 1651 when he was working for Queen Christina of Sweden in

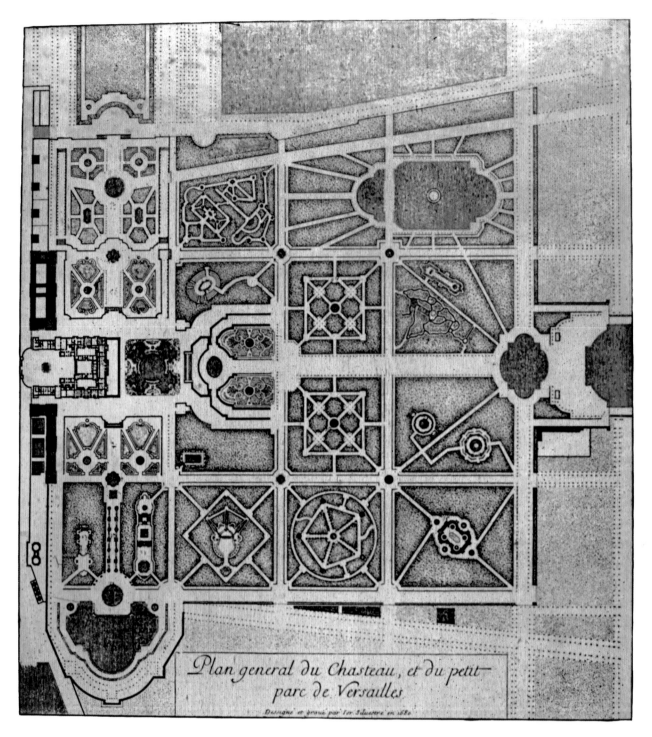

Fig 278 Plan general du Chasteau, et du petit parc de Versailles *by Israël Silvestre, 1680. This engraving of the gardens between the palace and the Grand Canal illustrates the strongly geometric nature of the layout of Versailles with the alignment of the gardens responding to that of the palace, the seat of the Sun King, Louis XIV. © W A Brogden / The Robert Gordon University. Licensor Scran*

Stockholm. The book was published in three editions with Swedish, French and German texts, and an English edition appeared in London in 1670 as *The Pleasure Garden* (Mollet 1670). In it Mollet set out the classic French concept of the design of the garden as a whole (Woodbridge 1986, 179):

In the first place, we say, That the Royal and Lordly House ought to be situated in an advantagious place, thereby to be supply'd with all the requisite things for its Embellishment, of which the Water has the first place, be it of Spring or otherwise; for it is with a great deal of reason that Water is said to be the Soul of Gardens, since that without it they seem always to be dying.

The second thing requisite to the decoration of Houses of Pleasure, is to have the conveniency to plant before them a great Walk of double or treble rank, either of female Elms, or of Lime Trees, which are the two sorts of Trees which we esteem the fittest for this purpose; which Walk ought to be drawn by a Perpendicular Line to the Front of the House, and of a convenient and proportionable breadth to the House; and for the Basis of the said Walk, may be made a large Demy-circle, or Square; and in case the place will allow it, there may be also drawn large Walks on the Right and Left of the said Front, which must be Parallel to the said House. As also at the end of the Garden another Walk in a direct Line to the great Walk, in the midst whereof there may be with conveniency a Door of Railes or Palisado's, through which, when the doors of the House are open'd, one may see from one end to the other, as far as our sight will extend. Such outward Works are most necessary to the Adorning of Houses; and as I put them here in the Front, and before the In-works; it is also by them, that one ought to begin to Plant even before the Building of the House, that the Trees may be come to half-growth when the House shall be built.

Let us come to the inward embellishments, which we commonly call Garden; which ought to be composed of Imbroider'd Ground-works, knots of Grass, Wildernesses, fine Alleys in Terrasses, and flat Walks, so ordered, that they may still end at some Fountain or Statue, and at some of the extremities of these Alleys, ought to be set up some fine Perspectives painted on Cloth, that they may be removed at will, to preserve them from the injuries of the Weather. In fine, to finish our Work, the Statues ought to be erected upon their Piedestals, and the Grotto's built in the most convenient places; as also the Fountains, Spurts, Ponds, Falls of Water, Bird-cages, and such like Ornament, which being well order'd and placed, will give the last Perfection to the Garden of Pleasure.

First we should say that the royal house must be sited to best advantage, in order to ornament it with all things necessary to its embellishment: of which the first is to be able to plant a big avenue with double or triple rows of female elms or lime trees (which are the two species of tree we esteem most suited to this effect) which must be placed in line at right angles to the front of the chateau ... Then facing the rear of the house must be constructed the *parterres en broderie*, near to it so as to be easily seen from the windows, and gazed upon without obstacles such as trees, *palissades* or any other elevated thing which can prevent the eye from embracing its full extent. Following the said *parterres en broderie* will be placed the parterres or compartments of turf,

as well as the *bosquets, allées* and high and low *palissades* in their proper place: made in such a way that most of the said *allées* lead to something and always terminate in a statue or the centre of a fountain; and at the extremities of these *allées* put fine perspectives of painted canvas, so as to be able to remove them from damage by weather when one wishes to. And to perfect the work, statues should be placed on pedestals, and grottoes built in the most suitable places. Then raise terrace walks according to the convenience of the place, without forgetting aviaries, fountains, water jets, canals, and such ornaments which duly being carried out, each in their place, form the perfect pleasure garden. (Mollet 1670, 1–2)

Mollet subsequently made his way to England where work began on St James's Park shortly after the Restoration, and he and his nephew Gabriel were formally employed there from 1661. Mollet died in London in 1665, probably from the plague.

Classical learning and an appreciation of the prestige of the culture of France was allied to a recognition and knowledge of Scottish history and antiquity, and the particular nature of its culture. When proposals were made for the unification of England and Scotland in the late 1660s and early 1670s, they were opposed by landowning and commercial classes (Paterson 2003,

Fig 279 The keystone over the gate to the garden at Carnassserie Castle in Argyll erected in 1681 and bearing the initials of Sir Duncan Campbell of Ardbreck and his wife Lady Henrietta Lindsay. SC359836

Fig 280 Aerial view of Balcaskie House, the home of Sir William Bruce between 1668 and 1684. DP050894

177, 188). The evidence for gardens begins to survive in areas such as Argyll, where they have not been recognised at an earlier period. Carnassery Castle was built between 1565 and 1572 by John Carswell, Bishop of the Isles and a close associate of Archibald Campbell, fifth earl of Argyll. Whether there was a garden attached to this architecturally distinguished tower, probably built by masons from the Stirling area, is not known. When it was partly remodelled in 1681, a garden gateway surmounted by the initials of the then owner and his wife, Sir Duncan Campbell of Auchenbreck and Lady Henrietta Lindsay, was created which leads into an enclosure measuring about 60m by 40m (RCAHMS 1992, 224–5) (Fig 279).

The building or rebuilding of great houses, and probably of the gardens which accompanied them, would seem to have been delayed until the middle or later part of the 1660s. Many landowners required time while they recovered from debts arising from fines imposed by the previous regime, and while they sought to have debts owing to them repaid (Lee 2010, 6, 40). Sir William Bruce, who was to become the most influential architect of the period, purchased **Balcaskie** in Fife in 1665 (Fig 280). He built the house there on the site of an earlier structure between 1668 and 1674 (Gifford 1988, 84–6). The house, situated on ground which slopes down to the sea, consisted of a central

block of three storeys with projecting pavilions at the four corners. Terraced gardens were laid out to the south of the house with their central axis aligned on the Bass Rock, with its historically important castle.

Fig 281 The architect Sir William Bruce © Scottish National Portrait Gallery. Licensor Scran

Fig 282 Bird's eye view of Balcaskie from Inigo Triggs' 1902 volume, Formal Gardens in England and Scotland. *SC1020854*

This alignment of gardens and avenues, on sites and monuments which recalled the history of Scotland, was to continue and become a notable feature of gardens

designed by Bruce and by his successors. The source of this predilection is not known, but it echoes the urban planning of Pope Sixtus V (1585–90). He laid out long

Fig 283 Balcaskie House as it was depicted on the manuscript map of Fife by John Adair in 1684. Adv.MS.70.2.11 (Adair 7). © NLS

straight avenues in Rome and erected fountains and obelisks, recalling the city's ancient origins, as focusing points for the long vistas (Wittkower 1958, 6).

In 1674 Sir William Bruce had been sent twenty-two pear trees at his lodging at Holyrood by Hew Wood, the gardener at Hamilton, which may have been for his own garden at Balcaskie. The accompanying letter refers to:

> 8 swan-eggs, 8 english bergamots, 2 Carnocks – 2 pear dangerous, as for the rest of the trees I could get non except 2 of the keeping pund pear of Cambusnathen [Cambusnethan] for there is hardly any nurseries here beside our own, and also those few they have hardly know their names, so that if one should buy them they can not be sure of the kinds they call for. (Robertson 2000, 126–7)

The upper terrace lies to the south of the house, with two terraces below. The drawing of the house and policies on Adair's map of 1684 shows a quadripartite design for the garden immediately in front of the mansion, with enclosed gardens on both sides, and a terrace falling to another enclosed garden below; an avenue runs on the same axis to the north of the house

(NLS Adv.MS.70.2.11 (Adair 7)) (Fig 283). It appears in a similar, although simplified, form on Roy's Military Survey of 1747–55. Although Sir William Bruce sold Balcaskie in 1684, the gardens, which were in the most modern taste, have survived to a large extent. In about 1710, it was described by Sir Robert Sibbald as 'a pretty new house with all modern conveniences of terraces, gardens, parks and planting' (Sibbald 1803, 338). The garden was restored in the early nineteenth century, when it attracted favourable comment from Sir Walter Scott in his diary for 17 June 1827: 'Balcaskie is much dilapidated; but they are restoring it in the good old style with its terrace and yew-hedge. The beastly fashion of bringing a bare ill-kept park up to your very doors seems going down' (Scott 198, 358). The garden was selected for illustration in the early twentieth century volume on formal gardens in England and Scotland (Triggs 1902, 170) (Fig 282).

Another house of a similar date was that at Panmure in Angus which, according to Mr Auchterlonie of Guinde in the later seventeenth century, was thought to be 'by many, except Halyruidhous, the best hous in the Kingdome of Scotland, with delicait gairdins with high stone walls, extraordinare much planting young and old, many great parks about the new and old house, with a great deal of planting about the old house, brave hay meadows well ditched and hedged and in a word, is a most excellent sweet and delicat place' (Macfarlane 1906–8, 2, 48). Patrick, Earl of Panmure, had accompanied James VI to England as a page, became a Gentleman of the Bedchamber to Charles I and had attended the king until his imprisonment at Carisbrooke, when 'bloodie traitors ... thrust him from his attendance'. The estate was 'robbed and spoylt by the usurpers forces, here, and fyned in a vast soume of money whereby he was forced to redeem his estate from forfaultre' (Macfarlane 1906–8, 2, 48). In 1666

Fig 284 Panmure House with its terraces as depicted on the First Edition of the Ordnance Survey 6-inch map of Angus surveyed in 1859.

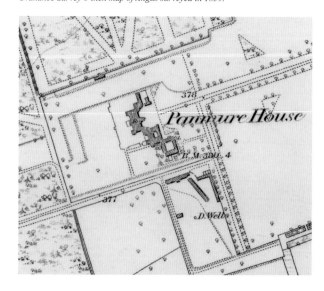

Fig 285 Panmure House and its terrace before its demolition in 1955. SC971359

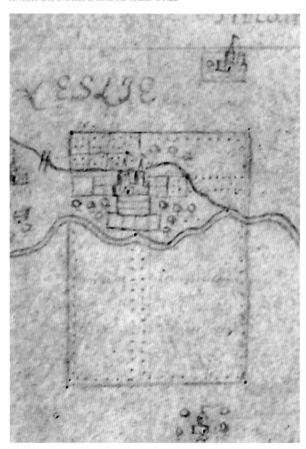

Fig 286 Leslie House as it was depicted on the manuscript map of Fife by John Adair in 1684. Adv.MS.70.2.11 (Adair 7) showing the gardens, including the terraces and avenues around the house. © NLS

Pattrick's son agreed with John Mylne, the Master Mason to the Crown, for the rebuilding of his house at Panmure. It is believed that Sir William Bruce may have been responsible for the design of the entrance court, and the general similarity of this house, demolished in 1953, to his own work at Balcaskie suggests that he played a part in the overall plan (McKean 2001, 252). A photograph of the house in its latter years shows it standing on a terrace from which a centrally placed staircase led down to gardens at a lower level, and the First Edition of the 6-inch Ordnance Survey map of 1858 depicts the extensive terraces surviving in an informal garden of lawns and a few trees (Figs 285, 284).

Leslie House was another mansion with extensive gardens, built for an important supporter of Charles II, the Earl and later Duke of Rothes (Fig 277). He carried the sword of state at the king's coronation at Scone in 1651 and spent some years after the Battle of Worcester imprisoned in the Tower of London and in Edinburgh Castle, as well as suffering the sequestration of his estates and being heavily fined. His family also owned Ballinbreich Castle, where the gardens may have become neglected lacking necessary maintenance, when attention became focused on Leslie. After the Restoration he was rewarded with a large pension and a number of high offices of state. Again William Bruce, whose son later married the earl's younger daughter, would appear to have participated in the design of Leslie House, which

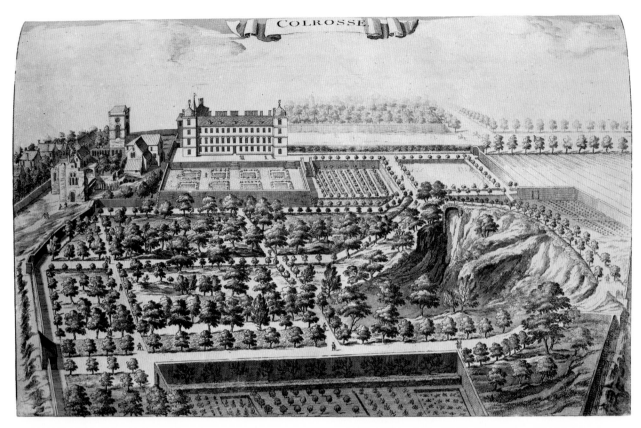

Fig 287 Culross House from Theatrum Scotiae *by John Slezer. The engraving was published in the edition of 1719, two years after Slezer's death. SC1129171*

was built on four sides of a courtyard with gardens all around. Bruce was a cousin of the Countess of Dysart, who had helped Leslie under the Commonwealth. The mansion was under construction when Sir John Lauder visited it in 1669 and wrote that 'a most magnificent house is a building' (Lauder 1900, 197). About 1680 Thomas Kirke on a tour through Scotland described the gardens:

> On one side of the house are gardens with little statues; in the middle of the fountain stands Apollo. On another side of the house are good gravel alleys, and walls with fruit-trees. At the foot of these is a square level piece, not finished, wherein is intended to be a fountain, and this piece is to be moated round. On the other side are two large courts with broad gravel walks, which lead to the house. On the fourth side is a bank with trees, which goes steep down to a brook, and on the further side of the brook are large gardens. (Kirke and Thoresby 1892, 17)

The manuscript map of Fife of about 1684 by Adair (NLS Adv.MS.70.2.11 (Adair 7)) shows in miniature the gardens at this period (Fig 286). The series of terraces facing south, on which fruit trees would thrive, are supported by vertical stone walls 'in the middle, and round which the present Earl designs to carry the River' (Macky 1729, 164).

By the time of the First Edition 6-inch map, the area was informally planted with trees. On the Adair drawing an avenue continues to the south beyond the River Leven, on the axis of the house. The garden with little statues would have lain to the east of the mansion where there are now a series of shallow terraces divided by paths. Another avenue is shown running east. To the north of Leslie House, where the ground falls steeply to the Camby Burn, the gardens beyond are now occupied by modern housing, while to the west, the entrance front, were courts, but these have not survived the changes in fashion.

In 1747 instructions for the gardener, one Andrew Brown, stated:

> he was to keep both the gardens and the courts in order and to finish the bowling green in the court. In addition, he was to raise a sufficient number of fruit trees of the best kinds for supplying the place of the old and decayed ones; he was to propagate fig trees, apricots, peaches, nectarines for the garden walls and to graft some of the best kinds from the old trees; he was to graft some filberts to supply the place of the old ones when they should be cut. Furthermore, was to lay new gravel upon the parterre and long walk, and employ his men when they could not work in the garden in assisting Robert Greig to prune the barren [non fruit-bearing] planting' (RCAHMS typescript MS D4.3)

Fig 288 Aerial view of Culross House with the site of the abbey on the left of the photograph. DP014180

It is unknown whether the old trees dated from the time of the Duke of Rothes or from that of his daughter. She succeeded him in 1681 and went to live at Leslie House, leaving her husband's house at Tyninghame to tenants (she died in 1700) (Chalmers 1887–1902, 3, 489).The document does, however, provide some evidence for what was cultivated in the garden.

Fife was well provided with notable gardens. Among them was **Culross** House which was erected on the site of **Culross Abbey**. The monastery had been known for its horticultural expertise and the area of the gardens had presumably been under cultivation for centuries. The mansion was built in 1608, probably on the site of the house of the abbot, and has been described as a piece of proto-classicism unparalleled in Britain (Gifford 1988, 157). It was depicted in an engraving by Slezer for *Theatrum Scotiae*, although the image was not published until the edition of 1719 (Figs 287, 288). A broad terrace, supported by a vertical wall, lies in front of the house. Below the terrace is a walled garden, approached down three sets of stairs and divided by gravel paths into eight grass plots, each surrounded by a flower border. What appears to be a walled orchard, with the trees planted in eight lines and grass growing below, lies to its east and another walled garden is shown beyond where a number of figures appear to be engaged in planting the ground, the upper part of which is shown as ridged while the lower part may still be in grass. The ground

further to the south, where it falls steeply, is divided by parallel walks into rectangular areas planted with trees of different sizes, shapes and probably ages. A walled vegetable garden lies to the east above an abandoned quarry. To the south again is another walled kitchen garden containing a variety of vegetables, including some growing in sunken beds, and fan-trained fruit trees growing against the south-facing wall. A second floor was added to the mansion about 1670 and this may have been the occasion for the laying out of the gardens on the lines depicted by Slezer. The garden house, a vaulted recess at the east end of the upper terrace, is dated 1674 (Gifford 1988, 157–8) (Fig 289).

In the later seventeenth century Culross belonged to Alexander Bruce, Earl of Kincardine, and his Dutch

Fig 289 The vaulted garden house at the east end of the terrace at Culross House. SC1129157

Fig 290 Aerial view of the garden at Pitmedden terraced on two levels linked by a double stair. SC972046

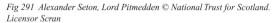

Fig 291 Alexander Seton, Lord Pitmedden © National Trust for Scotland. Licensor Scran

wife, Veronica van Sommelsdyke, whom he married at The Hague in 1659. He was a cousin of Sir William Bruce and one of the group who supported Charles II's policies in Scotland, initially as an ally of the Duke of Lauderdale. Alexander Bruce became Chancellor of Scotland and an Extraordinary Lord of Session in 1667. He was also a founder member of the Royal Society. Macky's description of Culross comments on the extensive prospects across the River Forth and to the mountains above Stirling:

> One cannot imagine a nobler Palace: It's built all of Free-stone; the Front to the South, is above two hundred Foot, with a Tower, three Stories high at each Corner: and under this Front is a Terras, as long and as broad as that at *Windsor*, with a Pavilion at each End; and below the Terras run hanging Gardens for half a Mile, down to the *Frith*; The Design of these gardens was vast; but as they are, you can only judge of what they were to be, and might be. When my Lord Mar was laying out his fine gardens at Allaway, I am told, that when he saw these, he thanked God that Culross was not his, for the Expence of keeping it up would ruin him. (Macky 1729, 176–7)

The placing of a large garden below the terrace on which the house sits is exemplified by **Pitmedden** in Aberdeenshire where the house was, unfortunately, demolished after a fire in 1807, but where the gardens have been colourfully restored by the National Trust for Scotland (Fig 290). The garden was the creation of Sir Alexander Seton. Following his father's death in the service of Charles I, he was, along with his brother, brought up in the guardianship of their cousin, the third Earl of Winton, a member of a family with a documented strong interest in the creation of gardens over many generations (Fig 291). Seton was admitted as an advocate in 1661 and became an Ordinary Lord of the Court of Session, as Lord Pitmedden, in 1677. He was Member of Parliament for the County of Aberdeen in 1681, 1685 and 1686 and was dismissed from office in 1686 following his opposition to James II and VII's attempts to repeal the acts against dissenters in religion, and subsequently refused to sit as a judge under William and Mary because of his earlier allegiance to James. The foundation inscription for the garden bears the initials of Alexander Seton and his wife, Margaret Lauder, as well as the date of May 1675 (Fig 292). The rectangular garden, which faces east and lies on two levels divided by a 4m high terrace wall, measures 190 yards by 160 yards (61m by 51m). Terraces to the north and south of the lower garden, as well as to the west, allow it to be viewed from above (Shepherd 2006, 205). On the upper terrace is a contemporary fountain, and water flows to a font recess in the stairway leading to the lower garden, which is entered by a double flight of steps through a gateway with pinecone-topped gate piers. These gates were probably moved from the original entrance to the mansion on the west. Two pavilions with ogee roofs were built at the junction between the lower and upper gardens; the upper room in the north one has panelling dating to 1686. It has been suggested that the close resemblance between these pavilions and those at Hatton House in Midlothian make it probable that the same architect or master mason was involved. The garden lies at the centre of an extensive network of drystone enclosure walls, laid out on a rectangular grid and related to the wider organisation of the estate (Addyman and McGowan 2005, 19).

The most influential of Charles' Scottish ministers was John Maitland, first Duke of Lauderdale. His mother was the daughter of Alexander Seton, Earl of Dunfermline, the owner of Pinkie and Fyvie. In his earlier career during the civil wars Lauderdale had been involved with the 'Engagement' or Treaty of Carisbrooke, presented to Charles I in 1647. One of the conditions of this, in return for the support of the Scots against Cromwell, was for the frequent residence of future kings and princes of Wales in Scotland (Airey 1884–5, 3). John Maitland's father, the first Earl of Lauderdale, had been interested in planting and had requested fir seed from Sir Colin Campbell of Glenorchy in 1637. His reference in this context to 'his awin gardinars' may indicate something of the establishment at either Lethington (Lennoxlove) or Thirlestane, his principal properties (Innes 1855,

Fig 292 The gate into the garden at Pitmedden recording its foundation. SC1238212

438). Lauderdale's brother, Charles Maitland, became an Extraordinary Lord of Session in 1669, with the title Lord Hatton from the estate in Midlothian which he inherited in the right of his wife. He served as Lauderdale's agent in Scotland in building as well as in political activities.

Charles II began work on the gardens at Hampton Court early in his reign, apparently inspired by the gardens of Louis XIV, which were characterised by their grandeur, their integrated planning, their size, their broad straight vistas, their axial views, their symmetry, their sculptures and their water features. The gardens at Versailles became a vehicle for demonstrating to all of Europe the superiority of France and of French gardening (Woodbridge 1986, 213). Their influence and that of Louis' principal gardener, André Le Nôtre, affected the design of gardens in Scotland and across the rest of Europe. While many Scots had for centuries sent their sons to France with the aim of ensuring

Fig 293 John Maitland, Duke of Lauderdale. © Lennoxlove House Ltd. Licensor Scran

Fig 294 Elizabeth Murray, Countess of Dysart and Duchess of Lauderdale. © Lennoxlove House Ltd. Licensor Scran

a good education, as well as an acquaintance with a wider world, such a visit was becoming an expected element in the life of a nobleman. The *grand tour* across Europe to Italy was seen as a finishing school for all the young nobility and gentry whose families could afford the cost, while the *petit tour* to France and the Low Countries was undertaken by members of gentry families of more limited means. The visit to Versailles and the contemplation of the French grand manner of gardening formed a strand in their common experience of European culture (Fig 278). Its absorption into the Scottish concept of gardens, whether in approval or disapproval, is borne out in the nature of the designs adopted by Scots during the later seventeenth century and into the eighteenth century.

In 1671 Sir William Bruce of Balcaskie was appointed Surveyor General of the Royal Works in Scotland with an annual salary of £3600 Scots (about £300 sterling), a post in effect granted by Lauderdale. His appointment included the unstated assumption that Bruce would also supervise Lauderdale's own building works at Thirlestane, Brunstane and Lethington, and take advantage of his official position in forwarding these private commissions (Fenwick 1970, 26–7). **Thirlestane Castle** was to become a more dignified residence; therefore, the offices were removed from the ground floor to a formal courtyard, and an impressive approach from the west was planned. Thirlestane stands on a hill, overlooking the town of Lauder, and plans of the gardens around the mansion show that they were closely linked to the house by walls and pavilions and flights of steps, so that the gardens were an integral part of the whole design (Fig 295). A new terrace raised on vaults was required to achieve this. Lauderdale wrote frequently from London enquiring about progress and suggesting changes like an additional pair of pavilions on the east to balance those on the west, ensuring that 'the house will look uniformie to both gardens'. The builder was John Mylne, the King's Master Mason, who was employed at the same time at Leslie House. (Dunbar 1975, 203–6).

The duke and duchess visited Scotland in 1672 when Lauderdale decided to have the western pavilions raised by one storey. The old parish church of Lauder, which stood to the west of Thirlestane, was demolished in 1673 to allow the regular layout of the policies. A new church was built in the burgh and some of the tombstones were

The Duke of Lauderdale does not seem to have exhibited much interest in refashioning his houses and gardens before 1670. About this time, he became close to Elizabeth, Countess of Dysart, the owner of Ham House near London and daughter of the first Earl of Dysart, who had died in 1655. She, like her father, had supported the Restoration of Charles II. They were married in 1672, seven weeks after the death of his first wife (Baird 2003, 90, 97). All three of his properties near Edinburgh, Thirlestane, Lethington (Lennoxlove) and Brunstane, as well as the Countess of Dysart's Ham House, were the subject of extensive building projects employing many of the same architects, masons and other craftsmen.

Fig 295 Aerial view of Thirlestane Castle showing its relationship to the town of Lauder. SC987737

removed there. Between the demolition of the old parish church and the erection of the new one in the centre of Lauder, the duke had his own chapel in the north-west pavilion of the castle fitted out with benches to allow continuity of worship for the people of Lauder. The gardens to the south were to be laid out the following year, as the duchess had decided.

Thirlestane Castle was drawn by John Slezer, the author of *Theatrum Scotiae*, the book of engravings which forms one of the main sources for Scottish castles, mansions and their gardens in the later seventeenth century. Slezer, who came of a German speaking family, first visited Scotland in 1669 and returned to Scotland in 1671 when he secured the

office of Chief Engineer in Scotland and Surveyor of His Majesties Stores and Magazines. In a letter of recommendation from the Earl of Kincardine to the Duke of Lauderdale, the hope was expressed that Slezer 'shall do you some satisfaction as to your house of Thirlestain Castle' (Dunbar 1975, 211). In addition to the detailed plans of the castle, there is a coloured plan of the gardens and surrounding policies which was attributed to John Slezer and Jan Wyck (Fig 296). Wyck was a Dutch artist who had settled in England after the Restoration of Charles II. In later life he was known for his battle scenes, distinguished by their bird's eye viewpoint and his depiction of individual soldiers. The similar plan of the gardens at Ham House, attributed to the same surveyor and artist, is dated to 1671. It seems probable that the Thirlestane plan belongs either to this period or to a period later in the 1670s. The

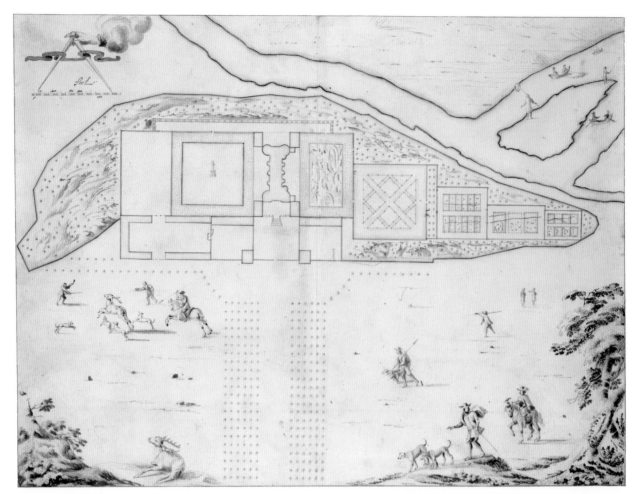

Fig 296 Plan for Thirlestane Castle and its gardens by John Slezer and Jan Wyck. The area of the gardens is limited by the nature of the ground and each individual compartment has its own design. SC372553

ground plan of the building is thought to be by Slezer, while Jan Wyck is believed to have been responsible for the drawings of the figures in the gardens and park and also to have supplied the figures for Slezer's other depictions of Scottish buildings for a payment of ten shillings sterling a sheet (Dunbar 1975, 212). The park at Thirlestane is occupied by figures hunting stags, while the Leader Water is favoured by fishing parties (RCAHMS BWD/43/13).

A new avenue was designed, leading directly from the burgh of Lauder to the castle forecourt, and various people who owned properties through which the avenue was to pass had been persuaded to sell. Trees were to be ordered from Holland and Lord Hatton was told to purchase 'als many and what sorts you please. Whenever you give occasion I shall never wearie to send answers, for I am fond of this work' (Dunbar 1975, 205–6). The straight avenue was planted with six rows of trees, mainly ash and elm, on each side aligned on a walled central court from which a flight of steps led up to a terrace in front of the main entrance. This was known as the Great Terrace; it was fronted with a balustrade and was laid with different coloured flag

stones in a chequer pattern (Fig 297). On one side was the chapel and on the other the buttery. Two walled courts, with a walled garden behind, lay immediately to the north of the mansion. This garden consisted of a broad gravel walk within the wall which surrounded a grass plot with a statue placed centrally; the identity of the statue cannot be ascertained from the drawing. A gate on the east opened on to a long terrace, edged with small trees or shrubs from where there would be an extensive view. Immediately to the south of the mansion was a walled rectangular garden, which also opened on to the long terrace. Within it, a broad gravelled walk surrounded what appears to be a grass parterre of asymmetrical design. This would be a grass lawn where differential mowing would leave a design in the longer grass. The French term for this, presumably derived from English, was *boulingrin*, and they were popular in the later seventeenth century. The flowing curves of the design are in the tradition of Mollet and Le Nôtre, but the overall lack of symmetrical pattern is unusual. When the south side of Thirlestane was depicted by Slezer, it was shown as a series of grassy rectangles with two statues in the classical style and so the original design may never have been realised. One of the statues is a female shown running while clutching a piece of drapery; the other, apparently unclothed, stretches out an arm towards her (Fig 298). The gardens

Fig 297 The entrance front of Thirlestane Castle. From the Great Terrace there were wide views across Lauder and Lauderdale. The engraving by John Slezer first appeared in the 1719 edition of Theatrum Scotiae. *DP106451*

Fig 298 Thirlestane Castle from the south with statues at the centre of the parterres. There is extensive provision for looking at the gardens from roof level. This view appears in the 1718 edition of Theatrum Scotiae. *DP102174*

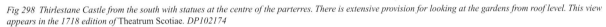

Fig 299 Aerial view of Thirlestane Castle from the south-east showing the modern garden. SC1238192

Fig 300 Thirlestane Castle: detail of the roof terrace and projecting windows overlooking the gardens. SC1238213

could be viewed from balustraded walks at roof level, while at ground level in the south garden there were arcaded loggias on each side (Figs 299, 300). Although the dedication of the Thirlestane engravings was to Charles, Earl of Lauderdale, the duke's brother who inherited Thirlestane in 1682 and died in 1691, the detail given of the plan of the ground floor might suggest that Slezer was involved at an earlier date, particularly given Lauderdale's habit of employing crown officials on his own building projects.

The next enclosed garden to the south, later described as the Flower Garden, is paralleled in the design at Ham House. The walled garden has a broad grass walk surrounding narrower grass walks in the form of a St Andrews Cross with additional smaller walks in a diamond pattern. These are edged with small trees or shrubs. The triangular and lozenge-shaped areas in between would be planted with flowers. The garden opens to the south into a narrow enclosure planted with small trees, possibly orchard trees, and was probably designed as a secluded walk. No communication is shown with the three gardens further south, which decrease in width according to the contours of the ridge on which Thirlestane stands. They are marked out in small plots and may have been intended as kitchen gardens. The gardens are laid out to fit the relatively small summit area, and it is likely that some levelling took place there in the course of the creation of the gardens. Trees are shown scattered down the steep slopes. By the time of the First Edition of the 6-inch Ordnance Survey map of 1857, and probably considerably earlier, the landscape had been informalised, but traces of the positions of some of the gardens can be seen in the depiction of the hachures on the summit of the ridge.

Lauderdale's second building project was undertaken concurrently with the reconstruction of Thirlestane. It was the rebuilding of his mansion at **Brunstane**, the closest of his houses to Edinburgh, and work which was underway there by 1672 included the construction of bridges to improve the approach to the house. Again the architect was Sir William Bruce. Lauderdale saw it as a lodge rather than 'a house of much receipte' for he already had official lodgings at Holyroodhouse. The avenue leading to the house seems to have been one of the earliest features. The duke wrote to William Bruce in October 1672 about the planting of this avenue, which lay to the north-west on the main approach to the house. The gardens lay to the south, overlooked by the private apartments of their owners. Pavilions were placed at each end of this side of the house. The building work seems to have been completed by the summer of 1674, but the layout of the gardens and policies continued into 1675 when the gardener, William Sheill, was paid for planting and watering lime trees that had been sent from London (Dunbar 1975, 215–17). The layout of the approach and grounds is depicted in a plan prepared by Bruce which shows that the avenue was planted with three rows of trees on each side. A subsidiary approach from the west was lined with only one row of trees on each side (Fig 301). The house was enclosed on three sides by walled courts and gardens. Although there have been many changes to the building and its surroundings, the outline of the garden on the north-east was detected as a cropmark during aerial survey (Fig 302). The walls were surrounded inside and out by regularly planted trees set out in parallel rows.

The most important house belonging to the Maitland family, the one where Lauderdale himself had been born, was **Lethington** or **Lennoxlove** in East Lothian, about two miles north of Haddington (Fig 303).

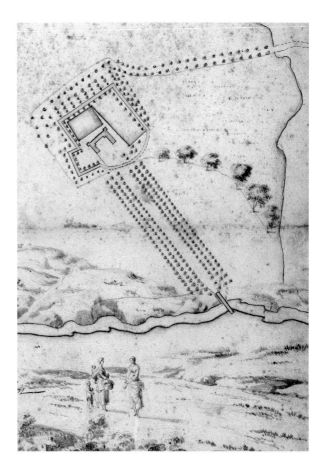

Fig 301 Plan of Brunstane with its triple-planted avenue by William Bruce. Lime trees were sent from London in 1675. SC1212694

According to an inscription of 1626 the fifteenth century tower had been improved and extended by the duke's father (RCAHMS 1924, 45), and this was probably accompanied by a redesign of the garden. While Bruce was responsible for the building of additional accommodation, much of the work of the 1670s was

Fig 302 Aerial view of Brunstane from the south-east showing the boundary of the garden in cropmark form. SC1110452

Fig 303 Aerial view of Lennoxlove (Lethington). The gardens are for the most part creations of the nineteenth and twentieth centuries. SC1031178

Fig 304 Plan of the park and garden of Lethington within its enclosing wall by John Slezer and Jan Wyck. Trees were transplanted from the earlier garden to the east and north walks. SC1239916 © Courtauld Institute

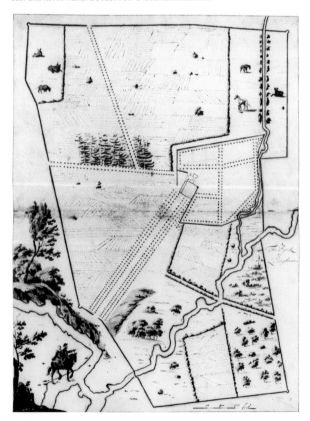

designed to modernise the mansion, including the insertion of the first sash windows installed in Scotland (Dunbar 1975, 219). New kitchens, pavilions and stables were constructed with the apparent intent of forming the sides of a courtyard in front of the earlier tower house. This would be approached by an avenue similar to those at Thirlestane and Brunstane.

The first work by the Duke of Lauderdale relating to the garden appears to have been the enclosure of the park by a stone wall and the planting of copses within the park. The great gates of the park and the inner gates were painted grey, and the duke's arms were erected at the west gate (Baird 1930, 17). In April 1674 the avenue was already 'inclosed, planted and hedged' and 'two copses or inclosed ground alreadie planted and finished, the on whereof lyeth upon the south west corner of the said park, and the other at the old quarrell (quarry) holles beneath the hillhead, and siclyk the other ffyve copses to be planted, ffour whereof ar to be of ffirr on top of the hilhead and the fyff with other tries at the old quarrel holles above the longsyde' (Baird 1930, 17; Dunbar 1975, 218). Plans by John Slezer and Jan Wyck show a broad tree-lined avenue with three rows of trees on each side leading from the north-west with a garden on a rectilinear plan laid out behind and to the south of the mansion divided by smaller avenues lined with trees (Fig 304). The quarrier's account in 1673–4 records 'for fiftie days work for pulling up of trees in the yeard and laying of them in the cairts and helping for to set them in the East and North Walks

£17-18-00', showing that trees were transplanted from the garden to furnish the avenues. The same account reveals the presence of a bowling green; it is referred to because of a plan to take down the wall surrounding it and to put in a drain on its east side. The bowling green, however, remained since another account records that one Robert Grant was paid five shillings for cutting it in 1677. There was also an orchard to the east of the mansion (Baird 1930, 18–19).

The earlier layout of ploughed fields and rig and furrow is depicted within the park wall, and the fields were being cultivated with oats, bere and peas as well as grass in 1674. There were enclosures for cattle, possibly wild cattle, at the north-east and south-east corners of the park, and for horses, separated from the cattle by the Bolton Water. The fir trees are carefully distinguished from the deciduous trees on the plan. The contract for the walling of the park was completed in 1677. A gardener called Alexander Sheill is recorded in 1673, and the names of the gardeners there in 1674 were Philantus ('lover of flowers') Lindores, George Hunter, George Fleming and John Hume, all of whom were burgesses of Haddington. A French gardener, possibly the Philantus Lindores mentioned above, apparently required an interpreter (Baird 1930, 22).

A second plan of the house and garden of Lethington by Slezer and Wyck shows the area around the house in more detail. Laid out on a very regular grid, it differed markedly from that given on the plan of the park (Fig 305). This depicts an avenue with six trees on each side and appears to cut across the design indicated on the other plan. It may be of a later date or it may be an alternative design for this area. A walled garden, possibly the flower garden, with walks on a diamond pattern, as at Thirlestane and Ham House, lies immediately behind the house to the east. What appears to be a rectangular pond or short canal lies to the south of it. Another larger walled garden, divided into four sections by broad paths, lies to the south of the water feature, with a rectangular garden to its west divided by paths in the form of a St Andrews cross with curvilinear paths between the arms and the space between the paths grassed. This may have been a wilderness and is a simpler version of that which appears on a plan for Ham House (Dunbar 1975, Pl XXV). Further to the east was a grassed area edged with trees or bushes. Beyond it was a rectangular area laid out with paths, again very similar to an area of the garden at Ham.

The depiction of Lethington on Adair's manuscript map of East Lothian of 1682 (NLS Adv.MS.70.2.11 (Adair 10)) shows the park as a neat pentagon enclosed by a double line which indicated the stone wall; at the angles are what are presumably the little turrets depicted on the plan of the park. There is an avenue running to the house from the north-west. A series of gardens enclosed by a wall lie to the east of the mansion, confirming that the design on the plans by Slezer and

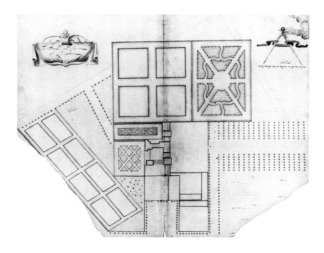

Fig 305 Plan of the house and gardens of Lethington by John Slezer and Jan Wyck. This may be an alternative or later design for the area around the mansion. It shares various features such as the intersecting walks on a diamond pattern with Thirlestane and Ham House, the property of the Duchess of Lauderdale near London. SC1239903 © Courtauld Institute

Wyck had, at least in outline, been carried out. The park and gardens were, apart from the line of the avenues, much altered during the nineteenth century. A sunken garden to the east of the mansion designed by Lorimer was laid out on the site of an earlier bowling green, and the seventeenth century sundial now occupying a central position on the lawn to the east of the present mansion belongs to the early twentieth century revival of interest in period gardens (Fig 306).

The Duke of Lauderdale's younger brother, Charles, succeeded him in the earldom of Lauderdale. He had acquired the tower of **Hatton**, which lies about ten miles

Fig 306 Lethington as it was depicted on the manuscript map of East Lothian by John Adair in 1682 showing the enclosure wall, the tree planting and the gardens around the house. Adv.MS.70.2.11 (Adair 10) © NLS

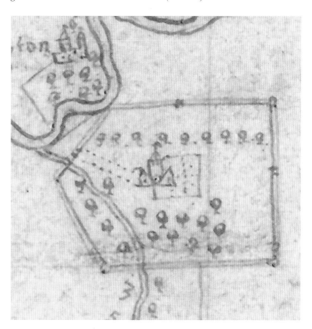

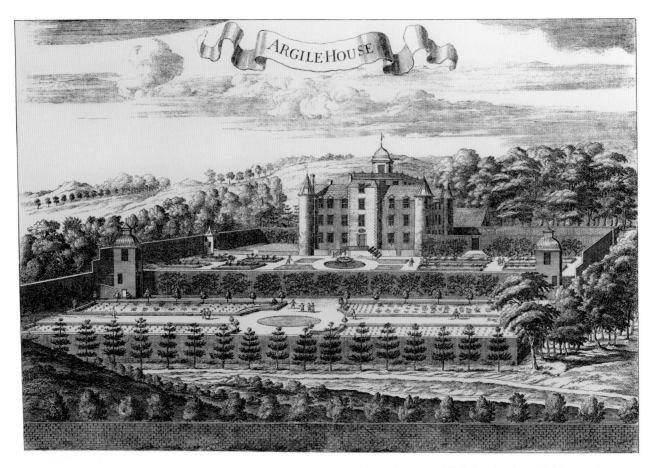

Fig 307 Hatton House in Theatrum Scotiae *by John Slezer. The engraving was published in the edition of 1719, two years after Slezer's death. It shows the gardeners employed in the garden on the terrace beside the centrally placed fountain. SC712215*

Fig 308 Detail of the lower garden with its espaliered fruit trees trained against the terrace wall from the Slezer engraving. SC712215

to the south-west of Edinburgh, through his marriage to its heiress, Elizabeth Lauder, in 1652. The garden at Hatton, as it is depicted in the engraving by Slezer for *Theatrum Scotiae*, unfortunately wrongly entitled Argile House, is one of the gardens in Scotland in this period to emerge most forcefully from the pages of that work (Fig 307). Charles Maitland benefited from his brother's position as Charles II's favoured minister in Scotland (Paterson 2003, 195). He was appointed Treasurer Depute and Master of the Mint and was involved with the restoration of the Palace of Holyroodhouse, becoming in 1679 Surveyor of the Royal Palaces and Castles in Scotland. The building of Hatton and the construction of its gardens took place between 1664 and 1691, the year of his death, but work there was continued by his sons, Richard and John, the fourth and fifth Earls of Lauderdale. When work began on the gardens, which appear in the Slezer engraving, is unclear, but Sir John Lauder writes in his journal for 1668 following his visit to Hatton:

> All the ground about it the Laird is taking just now in to a park ... The garden that lies to the west of the dungeon [the tower of Hatton] would have bein better placed to the southe of the house wheir the bowling greine is, tho I confesse that by reason of the precipice of the bray hard at hand it would have bein to narrow. Hes its ponds. (Lauder 1900, 193)

Because the gardens depicted by Slezer lie to the south of the house, it would seem that Lauder's opinion came to be shared by Charles Maitland. It presumably required a very considerable amount of excavation and levelling to achieve the terraces and garden buildings which Slezer depicts and which still survive in part.

By 1683, in his manuscript account of Scotland, Sibbald was able to describe it as 'the noble dwelling of Haltoune where are fine gardens and a large park with a high wall about it' (Findlay 1875a, 4). Slezer's engraving shows a view from the south with the mansion surrounded by formal gardens. The garden closest to the house is enclosed by walls. It might be entered from the door on the south side by means of two symmetrically disposed flights of steps or from a gate leading from the court to the north of the house, presumably the entrance used by the gardeners, who are depicted in the garden. On the upper terrace in the centre is a fountain framed by two grass plots on each side, with four rectangular flower beds contained within low walls or fences arranged symmetrically on both sides. Espaliered fruit trees are trained along the walls and there is a two storey pavilion with a pitched roof set against the west wall. On the lower terrace, which was reached by flights of stairs at each end, were two two storey pavilions with ogee roofs (Fig 309). They had doors opening on to the lower terrace and may have been entered from the upper terrace as well. The central feature on the lower terrace was a circle, probably of grass, around which were four beds with symmetrically arranged plants. The vertical wall, standing some 19 feet (5.79m) high, which supported the upper terrace, and the enclosing walls were planted with espaliered fruit trees, with regularly planted trees to the south (Simpson 1945, 24) (Fig 308). The house and garden are depicted in a well-wooded landscape. The gardens were added to by Charles Maitland's successors with statues, urns, a stone arbour by the bowling green, gateways, avenues and a bath house inserted into the upper terrace, furnished with statues and decorated with shells like a grotto. The bath house contained a basin 10 feet (3.05m) in diameter, filled from the overflow on the terrace above (Simpson 1945, 25). Although Hatton House was damaged by fire in 1952 and demolished in 1955, the structures of the terraced gardens survive.

In 1666 the Duke of Lauderdale's only daughter, Mary, married John Hay, Lord Yester, who became second Marquess of Tweeddale on the death of his father in 1697 (Fig 310). The first Marquess of Tweeddale, also John Hay, was the owner of **Yester House** in East Lothian, which was the subject of five paintings of the house, gardens and surrounding estate by a Dutch artist, possibly Jacob de Wet the Younger, the painter of the line of Scottish kings, real and imaginary, for the Palace of Holyroodhouse. Jacob de Wet, who also worked for Patrick Earl of Strathmore, the owner of Glamis, was active in Scotland in the mid 1680s and

Fig 309 The east garden pavilion at Hatton House. DP100259

Fig 310 John Hay second Marquess of Tweeddale, Lord Chancellor of Scotland, supporter of the Union and owner of Yester House. © Glasgow Museums. Licensor Scran

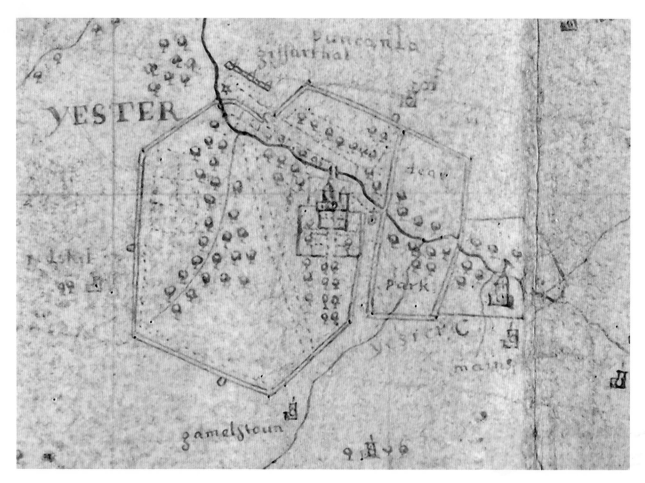

Fig 311 Yester as it was depicted on the manuscript map of East Lothian by John Adair in 1682. The enclosing stone wall is emphasised and it may be noted that the access to the parish church of St Cuthbert beside the mansion house is left open from the south (Adair Adv.MS.70.2.11 (Adair 10)). © NLS

died in Amsterdam in 1697. Both the first and second marquesses were painted, by Peter Lely and Gerard Soest respectively, in a landscape setting with trees. The first Marquess was the grandson of Alexander Seton, first Earl of Dunfermline, whose gardens at Fyvie and Pinkie have already been discussed in Chapter 4. He also owned Neidpath Castle near Peebles, the site of another important garden of the later seventeenth century, which he sold in 1686 because of financial difficulties. After initially opposing the king, he fought for Charles I after his surrender to the Covenanters in 1646 and, like Lauderdale, favoured the Engagement. After the Restoration he became President of the Privy Council and an Extraordinary Lord of Session, and was until the early 1670s a political ally of Lauderdale. It had been intended that Lauderdale's estates would pass to his daughter's descendants, but this legal settlement was revoked following his marriage to the Countess of Dysart (Paterson 2003, 194).

A catalogue of books in the possession of the second Marquess of Tweeddale, made in 1704 which included those of his father, contained many books dealing with horticulture as well as architectural treatises. His library

was for the most part kept at **Pinkie**, which he had acquired as a result of debts owed to him by the fourth Earl of Dunfermline, whose estates were forfeited in 1690 following his adherence to the cause of James VII and II (RCAHMS 1929, 83). Pinkie appears to have been in Tweeddale's possession by the 1670s when Thomas Kirke visited, describing the gardens as being in good order, although the house was unfurnished (Kirke 1677, 12). In 1668, when Sir John Lauder of Fountainhall visited Pinkie, he recorded in his diary that it was: 'A most sweit garden, the knot much larger than that at Hamilton and in better order. The rest of the yeard nether so great nor in so good order nor so well planted as is in Hamilton yeards ... Saw figs at a verie great perfection ... 18 plots in the garden, with summer houses and sundry pondes' (Lauder 1900, 189–90). In 1697 a decorative niche, flanked by garden doors, was inserted in the east wall of Pinkie House at ground level, facing the garden. It bears the coronet and initials of the second Marquess of Tweeddale (RCAHMS 1929, 81–2) and provides evidence for the further embellishment and appreciation of the garden there, at the time when the rebuilding of Yester House had begun.

The Hay family house at Yester (also known as Bothans) was a four storey tower, probably built in 1582 by William, fifth Lord Yester. By the late seventeenth century, wings had been added on each side of the tower, with a forecourt and entrance gate on the north.

To the south of the house were the gardens. Adair's manuscript map of 1682 (NLS Adv.MS.70.2.11 (Adair 10)) (Fig 311) shows the policies enclosed by stone walls with two gaps to allow access to the church from Gifford and from Long Yester to the south. A separate near-rectangular enclosure is labelled 'dear park'. A series of enclosed gardens lie to the south of the house, the one closest to the house divided into compartments with other gardens to east and west. Further to the south is another quadripartite garden, possibly marked out by trees or bushes, again with other gardens on each side. An avenue continues the centre line of the garden to the south. On the north side of the Gifford Water, an avenue, terraced on its north side, defines the approach from the village of Gifford, which is still marked by the remains of a lime avenue, and there is also terracing on the south side of the river. The line of an avenue (perhaps not yet planted) extends from near the village of Gifford right across the park, dividing it into two unequal parts.

Like other major royal officials such as Rothes and Lauderdale, Lord Tweeddale, who was also a member of the Royal Society, would seem to have considered building a new house at Yester, and in 1670 consulted Sir William Bruce, who was involved with the design of several major houses at this date. However, he would appear to have decided to confine his works to the refurbishment of the principal rooms and to the redesign of his gardens. This included the walling of his park, an expensive undertaking, which was completed in 1671 shortly before that at Lethington. The next year he wrote to his son, Lord Yester, who was living in London with his wife and his mother-in-law, the Countess of Lauderdale: 'my parke will be closed within this month and I am designing som long walks in it, if you pleas to send me the breadths of the walks in St James Park, both the largest as that be the Pell mel, and that we walked in beyond the cannal, and also of the narrower, it will help me much'. Three weeks later he reported that he was laying out a walk 900 paces in length and 50 feet broad, and proposed during the following year to add flanking walks of lesser breadth: the trees in all three walks were to be planted at 25 feet intervals. Payments for various garden works and for the purchase of seeds, trees and shrubs appear in the Yester accounts during the next two decades. The suppliers included Henry Fergusson and John Falconer in Edinburgh and London and Wise in London, while trees and shrubs were also obtained from Holland and from the royal garden in Paris (Dunbar 1973, 39, n7). In 1686 James Smith, who was later to be responsible for the rebuilding of Yester House, supplied four stone bases for lead statues at a cost of £54 16s 0d Scots (Dunbar 1973, 22).

A series of five late seventeenth century paintings depict the garden, enclosed by a wall, laid out symmetrically in front of the house to the south, divided by paths into four grass plots (Fig 313) with

Fig 312 A statue of Lucretia from the parterre on the right hand side nearer the mansion of Yester. The lead statue is of Dutch origin and may stand on a base supplied by James Smith in 1686. DP109185

Fig 313 Yester House had a tower at its core and was extended at different times during the seventeenth century. The house was depicted in a landscape setting with tree-planted hills. In front of the house is a fountain with symmetrically designed parterres around it, divided by paths and planted with grass or flowers; each has a classically inspired statue at its centre. DP109185

a tree planted at each of their corners, and a statue in the centre of each compartment (Fig 312). The paths meet in a central circular basin with a fountain, but the central path continues through the other compartments to end at the gate at the south end of the garden. Two other gardens lie to left and right, with a statue centrally placed in each one and a complex design of flower parterres. At the inner corner of the flower parterres, nearest to the house, stand twin domed arbours. To the south are square grass plots planted with small trees and bushes, the more westerly of which has a statue at its centre. To right and left are hedged compartments, possibly kitchen gardens. Further to the south on the same axis, beyond a well-spaced line of trees, the outer two of which appear to be deciduous and the inner four evergreens, are a further eight compartments. The more northerly gardens on each side of the central path have a symmetrical layout of flower parterres; those to the south are planted with a grouping of trees. Two men stroll across the garden, while a woman with a dog walks down the central path (Fig 19). To the west is a hedged maze with a mount at its south-west corner, crowned with a domed arbour (Fig 314). This has been compared with the combined mount and maze at Sorgvliet near The Hague, the garden of William Bentinck, Earl of

Portland. He was an important supporter of William III, who became Surveyor of the Royal Gardens – although Yester may well predate Sorgvliet (Steele and Cooper 1998). The wall is closed by a graceful gate, leading out to a double avenue of firs through an area of woodland to a plantation on the skyline.

The cascade at Yester, the earliest one known in Scotland, is perhaps the outstanding feature of the garden, and appears on two of the paintings, depicted from different angles. It lies to the west of the avenue and at right angles to it (Figs 314, 315). A *château d'eau* consisting of a triumphal arch with niches to left and right is set above five domed and recessed compartments; the water falls into an octagonal basin in which there is a *jet d'eau*. It ran downhill in channels, passing over a stepped weir into a rectangular lake or wide canal, linked to other water features. White openwork fencing surrounds the cascade and the eastern end of the lake. A boat is shown on the water in which there are two people, one playing a bowed instrument, possibly a bass viol. A line of trees is planted along the south side of the lake, reflected in the water, with two small circular structures at the corners. The selection of the site may be due to the topography and the supply of water. There is no indication of the cascade on the Adair map other than the line of the stream, which may later have been channelled to feed it. The groups of brightly dressed people in the painting, centred on the cascade, suggest a rather scattered *fête champêtre*. Italian gardens provide the best surviving examples of such water

Fig 314 The mount at Yester enclosed by a maze with hedges and a garden house at the summit. It is depicted as partly enclosed by trees and its origins may lie earlier in the seventeenth century. DP109180

stairways. The Villa Lante at Bagnaia near Viterbo exemplifies the type, and the cascade at the Villa Farnese at Caprarola, also near Viterbo is, like Yester, situated on an axis different from that of the principal house and its surrounding gardens. The Villa Doria Pamphili on the Janiculan Hill in Rome, where the gardens were laid out in the mid seventeenth century was provided with a cascade, leading to a short canal situated away from the main house, the Casino del Bel Respiro. It was an example readily visible to those taking part in the grand tour, and appeared in publications on the buildings of Rome (Blunt 1982, 218–19, 265–6 etc; Atlee 2006, 153 etc). When the Marquess of Tullibardine was at The Hague in 1706, he wrote to the Earl of Mar, 'I could get nothing yt. was entire of plans & views of gardens worth sending but versailes, villa Pamphillia & some other places in Italie which no doubt you have being very common ...' (Gifford 1989, 67), indicating how familiar the layout of the Villa Doria Pamphili might be to Scottish connoisseurs. For those whose time or means extended only to the *petit tour*, examples in the neighbourhood of Paris included St Cloud and Sceaux (Woodbridge 1986, 255–60).

The pictures also show the park walls and the landscape divided up into rectilinear grass parks, separated by lines of trees, as well as the broad avenue depicted on Adair's map. The regularly planned village of Gifford is included on one of the paintings (Fig 1). The road and bridge by the village is populated by a horse-drawn carriage, and by several riders and pedestrians. To the south of the village, a stretch of the Yester Water is shown to have been canalised. It runs below what appears to be a broad walled terrace; a bridge across the canal leads to a garden divided in four by lines of trees. It is uncertain what is growing in these compartments which appear to be only partly cultivated.

The building of a new house at Yester began shortly after the succession of the second Marquess in 1697. It was undertaken by Alexander Macgill and James Smith, both architects and masons, and the influence of Sir William Bruce's work on the design has been noted. The old house is believed to have been demolished by 1705–6. Work was also done in the gardens at this time; new walls and terraces were laid out, the grotto rebuilt, while in 1710 a new fountain, a cascade and a stair to the bowling green were under construction (Dunbar 1973, 22). The policies were much admired by visitors. Macky writes:

> The Palace of Yester ... stands in the middle of the best planted Park I ever saw: The Park Walls are about eight Miles in Circumference; and I dare venture to say, there is a Million of full grown Trees in it. In short, it's larger, as well walled, and more regularly planted than Richmond in Surrey... The Parterre and Garden behind the House is very

spacious and fine, rising up by an easy Ascent into
the Park, as those of my Lord Rochester's does
near Richmond. There is a handsome Basin, with
a jett d'eau in the middle of the Parterre, with four
good Statues upon Pedestals at each Corner. There
are abundance of Evergreens, and green Slopes,
regularly disposed; and to the West of the Garden
on an artificial Mount, is a pleasant Summer-
House. At the upper End of the Garden, fronting
the Salon, are a pair of Iron Gates, which open into
the park. The Green-house joins the Pavilion to the
West as does a Laundry to the East. The great Area
before the Gate is not laid out yet, but according
to the Disposition design'd, it will be very noble,
with Visto's from it cut through the Wood, and
Statues at the end of every Visto to terminate the
view. There is a pretty rapid stream runs by the
House, and by its rustling through the trees as it
runs through the Park, makes the whole very rural.
There is a pretty Bowling-green by this River Side:
and the Stables, hen-house, and Coach-houses
are at a Distance in the park, as is the Custom in
all the great Houses I have yet seen in Scotland.
Every Nobleman's House hath what they call the
Mains, where their Land-Labourers, Grooms, and
every body belonging to the Stable and Poultry,
reside. (Macky 1729, 30–3)

Defoe concentrated his comments on the extent and the
value of the planting at Yester, as well as at Pinkie and at
another Tweeddale property at Aberdour. A survey of the
gardens to the south of the new house and a new design
for them by Charles Bridgeman, dated to about 1720, has
survived. It shows the garden plan to be similar to that
which appears in the late seventeenth century paintings,
although the parterres are differently laid out. There
appear to be fewer trees actually in the garden, and a
circular pond lies outside the garden gate. Bridgeman's
plans were not implemented (Steele and Cooper 1998).

A few years later, *Retirement: a poem, occasioned
by seeing the palace and park of Yester* was published
in Edinburgh in 1735. It was dedicated to the fourth
Marquess of Tweeddale and describes a garden which
resembles that depicted on the series of paintings, but
which demonstrates a rather different attitude towards
the garden at a period when its owner was out of
political office:

In Solitude sweet YESTER lies conceal'd ...
Thy Palace, TWEEDDALE, represents thy Soul
Its Disposition shews the Owner's State,
Where all is finish'd, chaste, correct, and great!
Full, in the Front, an ample Circle lies,
Where Trees on Trees in soft Succession rise!

*Fig 315 The view of the cascade and canal at Yester enclosed by white-painted
fences and relatively newly planted trees. © Scottish National Portrait Gallery*

A blooming Round! – where Verdure ever new
Spreads the fair Amphitheatre to view
While in the intermediate Space below,
The Brook's clear Waves in calm Procession flow,
High o'er the Banks, their lovely fragrant Shade
The native Rose and twining Woodbind spread;
Beneath a Bowling-green, laid out, appears
And with its Square, the bounded Prospect chears.
Behind the fair-dispose'd Parterre is seen
With Flow'r adorn'd, and Slopes of lively Green,
A chrystal Fountain in the Center plays
And mitigates the Sun's intemp'rate Rays.
Four Statues, equal, rise on every Hand,
Divide the Circuit, and the Space command;
... A Neighb'ring Structure's well-intended Care
Invites those Plants that shun our Northern Air;
Protected, here the tender buds may bloom,
Or the fair Orange shed its rich Perfume...
Below, the Brook in Mazes wanders round
And sports delightful thro' the flow'ry Ground.
Here the bleak Hills, irregular, and rough,
Appear, as Foil, to set those Beauties off...
A winding path, with thickest Umbrage spread,
Does to the Centre of the Forest lead:
Here num'rous Vistas croud upon the Sigh,
And every Termination gives Delight;
Some rural Object still presents to View,
A Grove, a Village or the Mountain blue!
But now descending from the pleasing Scene,
With easy Steps the AVENUE I gain
Where to the left, the Brook its Passage steals,
And in its rocky bed its stream conceals;
Now gently purling, forms a soft Cascade,
Now glides involv'd beneath the happy Shade.
(Boyse 1735)

Rather than seeing the park, garden and plantations as
the centre of its owner's power and influence and as
playing an important role in improvement of the whole
nation, they have become a retreat, rather like the kind
of garden praised by writers of the earlier seventeenth
century. At this period in the 1730s, however, the
enclosed garden has become an entire landscape, a
concept, looking forward to 'laying out ground in a
natural way' which was actually to begin at Yester in
the 1750s. By 1760 the formal gardens had been swept
away, with Bishop Pococke recording that 'the lawn
behind the house is fine with large trees interspersed
where the sheep feed and there is a terrace round it,
on one side is a hermitage and on the other a summer
house in a little island, beyond this the park' (Pococke
1887, 316).

Both the Duke of Lauderdale and his brother
were involved in the rebuilding of the **Palace of
Holyroodhouse**, under the superintendence of the
Master of the Works, Sir William Bruce, with its
construction undertaken by Robert Mylne, the King's

239

Master Mason. His warrant was revoked in 1678 on the ground that the reconstruction of Holyrood was complete, but it may have been withdrawn because of political differences between Bruce and Lauderdale (Colvin 1995, 173). In 1671 sketch plans were submitted to Charles II, which placed the new Privy Garden adjacent to the king's great apartments. The palace was to become a building on a symmetrical plan, which retained some features of historic interest, particularly the great tower of James V. Charles was familiar with the royal gardens in France and with those in Holland, where he had been in exile, and took an interest in the planning of both the palace and the garden (Hunt 1886, 143; Fenwick 1970, 31). While the principal palace gardens had lain to the north and south during the sixteenth and earlier seventeenth centuries, with the new royal apartments forming the east wing of Bruce's work, greater priority was to be given to the gardens to the east where the new privy garden was placed. By 1674 the buildings which lay to the east of the palace, belonging to the Bishop and the Dean of Edinburgh, had been acquired and compensation paid; the demolition of the Dean's house took place by the end of 1676 (Mylne 1893, 193). This allowed the opening of a vista to the east. Some work had taken place by the end of February 1676 when a payment was made 'For levelling the gardens, gravell and grass works and bring in the wattr to the hous ...' (NRS E7/2/137). On 26 July 1676 the king expressed somewhat premature approval 'of the finishing of the newly designed privy garden in a square betwixt the church on the north syd and the design'd King's offices on the south syd green gravel plots and walkes' (Mylne 1893, 193). Payment was made in March 1681 'for levelling the garden and parter (parterre) without it' (NRS E7/2/389) and 'laying the alleys thereof with gravel' (NRS E6/3/389). In July 1682 an estimate was prepared of work that needed completion (NRS E27/24). It was noted that the wall of the Privy Garden on the east side of the palace had been built, being 200 feet (60m) square and 4 ells (3.76m) high 'with a fyn hewen cope round about'. The garden still needed the basin 'in the middle of the s[ai]d garden of sixtin foot sq[uai]r and clos pavemented' with its 'fyn pedestal I the middle thereof'. The parterre outside the garden, referred to in March 1681, was probably the garden of St Anne's Yards, immediately to the south of the new Privy Garden. In 1674 Sir William Bruce had been sent twenty-two pear trees at his lodging at Holyrood by Hew Wood, the gardener at Hamilton, but these may have been for his own garden at Balcaskie (Robertson 2000, 126–7).

James, Duke of York, Charles II's brother and later James II and VII, was sent to Scotland in 1679 as High Commissioner, replacing Lauderdale. He was lodged in Holyrood Palace with his wife, Mary of Modena, and after 1681, with his younger daughter, Anne, who became queen in 1703. While this appointment served to keep him out of England, where his conversion to the Church of Rome rendered him unpopular and a threat to the stability of the government, his residence in Edinburgh was initially well received and the palace and its gardens served something of their intended purpose, with a variety of social functions, including the performance of a masque, *Mithridates, King of Pontus*, by Nathaniel Lee. James also visited the palace at Linlithgow and Stirling Castle. He cultivated the Scottish gentry of Episcopal and Catholic sympathies, including Robert Sibbald, Geographer Royal and Royal Physician. In this way his presence served as a focus for various cultural and intellectual institutions, which had been lacking in Scotland since James VI succeeded to the English throne. The Royal College of Physicians, the Advocates' Library and the Order of the Thistle were instituted at this time, and encouragement given to the Physic Garden and the Royal Company of Archers. Edinburgh and its university received new charters, and patronage was extended to surgery, cartography, mathematics and engineering (Cherry 1987, 98–102).

Charles II's gardens at Holyrood were never completed according to plan, and there is no evidence that the basin designed to stand at its centre was ever made. A description of the palace in 1745 commented that 'eastward from the palace is St Anne's yard, designed to be laid out into long garden walks adorned with statues; but the revolution coming on, attended with a long and expensive war, and afterwards the union with England prevented this' (*Gentleman's Magazine* 15, December 1745, 682). A description of 1710 relates how 'the palace is bounded with lovely Gardens. On the south-side lies the Queen's Park, which is stored with a great variety of Medicinal plants. Here also is an admirable Fountain, which thro' conduits serves the whole House' (Chamberlayne 1710, 460). The area of the garden extended beyond the present grounds at Holyrood. The planting may have taken place because the area to the east was described as covered with large oaks in the later eighteenth century (Arnot 1779, 309). The area was associated with James, Duke of York, later James VII and II, during his stay in Scotland between 1679 and 1682, and it became known as the Duke's Walk. Slezer's engraving of the north side of Edinburgh (the Queen Anne View), probably drawn about 1690, shows the buildings and gardens in a rather jumbled fashion because of the angle of view, making it difficult to make sense of the palace and its gardens. The north garden with the sundial is clearly shown, as is the long range of the tennis court. The engraving, however, cuts off the area to the east of the palace and the new Privy Garden and conceals it behind buildings, although there appear to be trees planted in this area. The ground immediately to the east of the palace was later developed as a bowling green, and the name survived through the eighteenth century (Fig 316):

Fig 316 A view of the gardens at Holyrood from 'The North Prospect of the City of Edenburgh' engraved around 1710. SC1245640

Behind, or to the eastward of the Palace, was a bowling green, inclosed, upon the north, by the church-wall, upon the south by the laundry, long since allowed to go to ruin, and, in its place, a stone wall has been erected. The field E from this is called St Anne's yard. (Kincaid 1787, 115)

Some royal officials had lodgings in the palace; when Lauderdale was in Edinburgh in 1670, John Broun and Grisel Bruce, gardeners at Holyroodhouse, were paid fifteen shillings sterling 'for furnishing the kitchen with turnips, carrots, cabbages, spinach, beets, summer savory, winter savory, rosemary, thyme, sweet marjoram, mint, balm, purslane, lettuce, sorrel, parsley, laurel and bay leaves' (Marshall 1973, 52). The dukes of Hamilton had been appointed to the heritable office of Keeper of the Palace and of the north and south gardens in 1646 (*RMS* 9, 644 no 1710). In 1693 this grant was expanded to include St Anne's Yards. The Hamiltons later exploited their office, letting land there, which eventually resulted in the creation of a small suburb. In 1689 William Miller, formerly under-gardener at Hamilton Palace, was granted the position of gardener at Holyrood. He, like John Reid and a number of other gardeners, was a member of the Society of Friends or Quakers. He rented houses and yards in the south yards from Anne, Duchess of Hamilton, in 1701, paying £100

Scots a year (NRAS 332/F/1/735). In 1716 William Miller rented (or renewed the rental of) several houses at Holyrood and constructed a new house there around that date (NRAS 332/E/2/10). William lived on until 1743, and several of his children continued as gardeners and plant and seed merchants. George Miller, his son, was the gardener of the Duke of Hamilton's garden at Kinneil (NRAS 332/L/1/304), while in 1695 James Miller wished to resign as gardener at Kinneil (NRS GD406/1/4007).

The Physic Garden for the cultivation of medicinal plants was instituted in St Anne's Yards in 1670 by Sir Robert Sibbald and Andrew Balfour. This name was applied to the general area to the south and east of the palace and its application varied through time. The area measured only 40 by 40 feet (12m). Both physicians had travelled extensively in Europe during their studies of medicine. Sibbald had stayed in Paris for nine months where, as he wrote, 'I studied the plants under Junquet in the King's Garden' (Sibbald 1833, 17). It is known that Sibbald met and stayed with the great Scottish gardener Morison in Blois at the garden of the Duke of Orleans, whose physician he was. Sibbald described this study in his autobiography and went on to put it into practice in Edinburgh:

Doctor Balfour and I first resolved upon it, and obtained of John Brown, gardener of the North Yardes in the Holyrood Abby, ane inclosure of some 400 foot of measure every way. By what we

Fig 317 A plot adjacent to Trinity Hospital was leased to James Sutherland for a Physic Garden in 1676 as it was depicted by John Slezer in the engraving of around 1710. SC1245640

procured from Livingstone and other gardens, we made a collection of eight or nyne hundred plants ther. (Sibbald 1833, 21)

The North Garden at Holyrood was depicted by Slezer about 1690. Sibbald described the 'curious Garden' of Patrick Murray, Laird of Livingstone, a keen gardener who exchanged seeds and information with other gardeners throughout Europe. Sibbald admired his collection of nearly a thousand plants, many of which were to find a home in the Physic Garden (Sibbald 1710, 21). The purpose of the garden was to supply fresh plants for medical prescriptions and to teach medical botany to students, and Balfour and Sibbald were appointed Visitors to the Garden. 'By Dr Balfour's procurement, considerable pacquets of seeds and plants were yearly sent hither from abroad and the students of medicine got directions to send them from all the places they travelled to' (Sibbald 1833, 22).

The preparation of remedies derived from plants formed a major part of medical practice at this time as in earlier periods. Many new plants had been introduced to Europe and their study was becoming regularised. The Surgeon Apothecaries Company in Edinburgh had a garden planted with medicinal plants from 1656, and at Heriot's Hospital, ground was set aside in 1661 for

the planting of 'all sorts of physical, medicinal and other herbs such as the country can afford' and set down that it should be open to anyone who wished to study the plants (Robertson 2000, 129).

By 1676, it was obvious that the Physic Garden was too small for its purpose, and a plot adjacent to the **Trinity Hospital** was added that year, leased to James Sutherland for nineteen years by the Town Council and placed in his charge. This was a much larger area, measuring 300 feet by 190 feet (90m by 58m). In 1695 he took over part of the King's garden at Holyrood where he grew vegetables and medicinal herbs. James Sutherland later became the Professor of Botany in the Town's College and was, in 1699, appointed as Regius Keeper by William III (Fig 317).

In 1683 Sutherland had published the *Hortus Medicus Edinburgensis: or, A catalogue of the plants in the Physical Garden; : containing their most proper Latin and English names; with an English alphabetical index*. This was to be sold at the shop of an Edinburgh seed merchant and at the Physic Garden itself, indicating that this garden was already a place of public resort. The garden was supported by the City of Edinburgh and the Catalogue was dedicated to the Lord Provost, George Drummond. Sutherland considered the garden in relation to other gardens in Europe and reckoned that it was on a level with most of them for the number and the rarity of its plants. He had for the previous seven years used his foreign correspondents to acquire seeds and plants from the Levant, Italy,

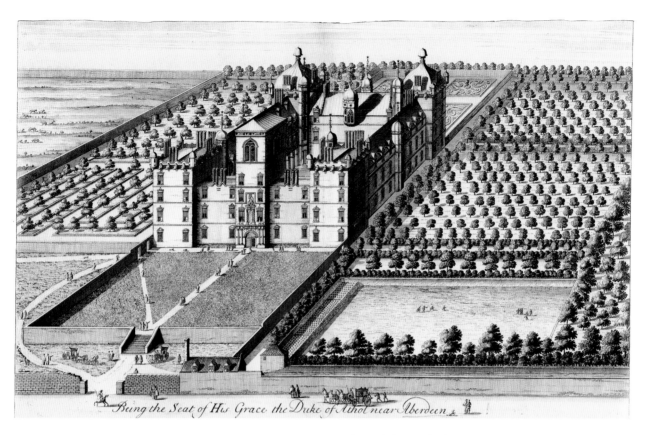

Fig 318 Heriot's Hospital and its gardens, which became a place of resort for citizens and visitors, in an engraving from John Slezer's Theatrum Scotiae *of 1719. It is misidentified on the plate as 'Bogengight' or Gordon Castle DP106457*

Spain, France, Holland, England and the East and West Indies, as well as collecting them through his own travels in Scotland. He stressed the importance of the garden for the teaching of apothecaries' apprentices. His disposition of the plants 'was according to the most natural and rational Method, and according to the best and latest authors of Botanie, and particularly our most Learned and Incomparable Countreyman Doctor Morison' (Sutherland 1683, Epistle Dedicatory). Robert Morison, a native of Aberdeen, had been appointed royal physician and professor of botany by Charles II. The Physic Garden also served as a nursery from which plants could be purchased. In August 1691 the Earl of Morton, who owned Aberdour, bought from James Sutherland a collection of fruit trees, roses and shrubs at a cost of £47 0s 0d Scots. North America was the ultimate source for many of the shrubs (Robertson 2000, 91–2). Part of the north garden was granted as a physic garden in 1704 and put in the charge of James Sutherland, who was also to put in order the palace gardens in general (NRAS GD/220/6/1742/3). Various grants of ground at Holyrood may in fact confirm an existing situation. In 1716 the Duchess appointed Charles Alston to be keeper of the physic and flower garden at Holyrood, 'with power to improve the same to the best advantage with herbs, plants, flours, hedges, walks and other decorments for phisicall uses as well

as beautfieing and adorning the said palace, and to doe every other thing for the improvement of Bottany and others within the said garden' (NRAS 332/E/2/10). The Physic Garden moved to Leith Walk in 1763.

The gardens of Holyroodhouse became a place, in some sense, of public resort. In 1691 regulations on the proper conduct of visitors were imposed when it was forbidden to walk on the grass or exercise dogs except on leads, while the playing of 'Goulfe, putting stone or at Nyne holles' was only allowed to the residents of the palace (NRS E7/6/220).

The use of royal gardens or parts of them as a place of resort for the better sort of citizen had grown up in France where the Tuileries on the edge of Paris during the seventeenth century remained open to the

Fig 319 Detail from the engraving of Heriot's Hospital showing the parterres on the north side which were laid out in a scrolling design. DP106457

public in spite of opposition by Louis XIV's finance minister, Colbert (Coffin 1982, 209; Woodbridge 1986, 242–5). Charles II opened the replanted St James's Park in London to the public and it was much visited, according to various references in Pepys' Diaries. There was recognition of the desirability of public gardens as an adornment to Edinburgh by the Town Council. The gardens in Edinburgh which received favourable mention from visitors were those attached to **George Heriot's Hospital** (Chamberlayne 1710, 3, 465). These are depicted on Slezer's view of Heriot's Hospital, unfortunately entitled 'the Seat of his Grace the Duke of Atholl near Aberdeen or Bog of Gight', which was drawn before the steeple was erected, probably in 1693 (Fenwick 1970, 74) (Fig 318). The gardens are less elaborate than those which appear on Gordon of Rothiemay's bird's eye view of Edinburgh of 1647 (NLS EMS.s.52) (Fig 266). The engraving shows coaches arriving at a gate on the north side of the garden and a stream of people approaching on foot. The only depiction of the boys who lived in the Hospital may be in the enclosed grassy garden to the west or right hand side of the engraving, where there are some running figures inserted by Jan Wyck. Most of the enclosures around the building are occupied by trees set out in a quincunx arrangement; those arranged in straight lines may be orchard trees. To the south of the Hospital, facing the original entrance front, are scrolling parterres in the manner of Mollet, perhaps executed in box or the dwarf juniper recommended by John Reid in the *The Scots Gard'ner* (Reid 1988, 26) (Fig 319). In 1728 Agnes Steven, the widow of John Weir, who had been gardener to Heriot's Hospital, wrote in her petition to the Council that she would continue to care for the wilderness and flower garden there, as well as furnishing the Hospital 'with roots and others' as was formerly done by her husband (NRS GD421/10/60). Kirke, Macky and Defoe all describe visits to the gardens and their enjoyment by the citizens.

Stirling too saw a move to more general use of gardens by the public. In 1661 the Masters of Cowane's Hospital in Stirling, an almshouse founded in 1637 for twelve 'decayed gild breither', ordered 'caus level the yaird of the said hospital and make a walking green thereof and plant it about with plain trees and the like, and to pavement the close and outwalke (terrace) with hewin stones'. A gardener, William Stevenson, was appointed in 1667 when flowers were also bought. A hedge of '300 thornes' was planted in 1670 on the north and east sides, and a sundial was set up in 1673. In 1701 the 'ballasters in the high walk' were set up, and trees and plants, including apricots and peaches, double yellow roses, jasmine and gillyflowers, were imported from Holland. In the early eighteenth century few people were applying to take up places as guild brothers at Cowane's Hospital and it was proposed that part of the garden should be laid out as a bowling green. Thomas

Harlaw, the gardener of the Earl of Mar at nearby Alloa, was approached to produce a plan for which, in 1712, he was paid £25 16s 0d, and the sundial was resited in the same year. In 1713 Harlaw came to Stirling to direct the levelling of the garden for a bowling green, and flowers were bought for the borders. The parterre, which still survives, may date back to this time (NADFAS Garden History Group 2000, 10, 37, 65, 89–90) (Fig 320).

Works on Stirling Castle had been ordered by the king at the same time that building was to be undertaken at Holyrood. Sir William Bruce was to carry out repairs to the Castle of Stirling and its park dykes in 1671 (Marshall, 1881, 328), although this may have been to the detriment of the garden. In 1681 a powder magazine was constructed in the garden within the castle (RCAHMS 1963, 188). With no visits being made to Scotland by rulers until the nineteenth century, the royal palaces fell into decay or were occupied by royal officials and their families, sometimes on a hereditary basis. The earls of Mar were governors of Stirling Castle. At Stirling Daniel Defoe describes 'a very pretty little Flower-Garden, upon the Body of one of the Bastions, or Towers of the Castle, the Ambrusiers serving for a Dwarf wall around the most Part of it; and they walk'd to it from her Ladyship's Apartment upon a Level along the Castle-Wall' (Defoe 1968, 754).

Little is known of any developments at **Falkland Palace** in the later seventeenth century. Two engravings appear in *Theatrum Scotiae*. One depicts the courtyard of the palace with groups of people, troops, drummers, coaches and dogs, as well as the bearer of what appears to be a large flag with the cross of St George, possibly a historical scene. The other, a view from the east, shows a walled garden planted with trees, with another walled garden to its north (Slezer 1718, Pl 11) (Fig 321). While the garden appears to be cared for, it has none of the orderly symmetry of other major gardens of this period. Sibbald recounts that the timber in the park at Falkland had been felled by the English in Cromwell's Usurpation 'under pretence of needing the timber for building the Citadel of St Johnstown (Perth) and allowed almost all of it to be cut and the deer to be destroyed' and the 'East part of it [was] casually burnt in Charles 2nd time' (Sibbald 1710, 151). He also records that the 'King's Park and a Wood are adjacent to it (the palace), into which, as also into the Plain towards the East, it hath a most pleasant Prospect. The Marquess of Athol is Hereditary Keeper of this Palace, and hath a considerable Rent by the neighbouring Lands and Stewardry' (Slezer 1718, 5). In 1699 the first Marquess of Atholl commissioned Alexander Edward, who frequently worked with William Bruce on garden design, to draw plans of the palace (Lowrey 1987, 25).

Fig 320 The garden of Cowane's Hospital in Stirling in a drawing from Inigo Triggs' 1902 volume, Formal Gardens in England and Scotland *(Plate 85), showing the bowling green and the winding walks.*

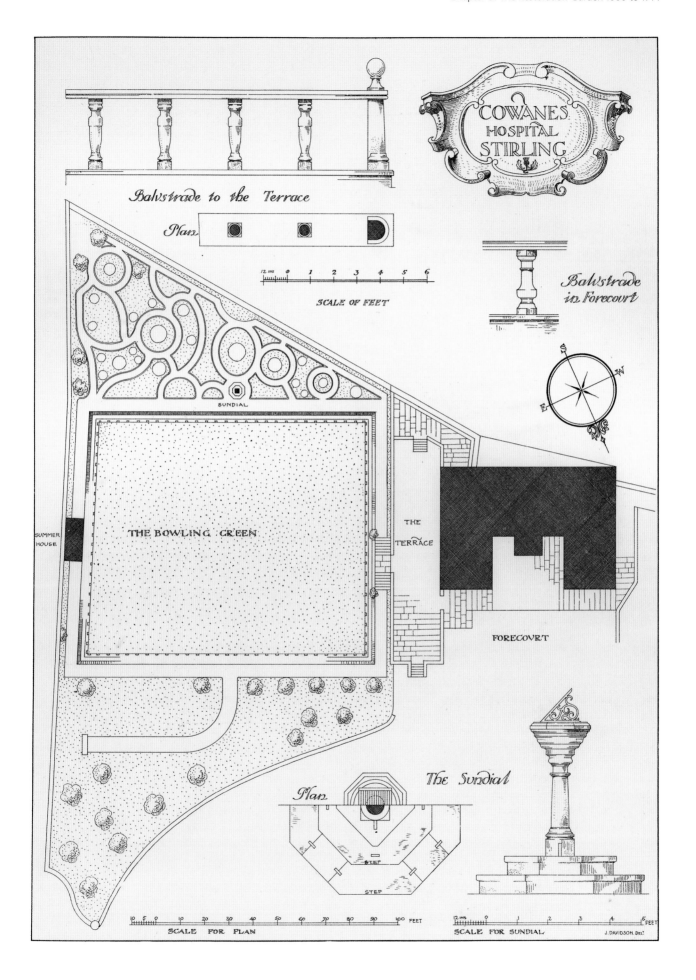

Balvstrade to the Terrace

Plan

SCALE OF FEET

COWANES HOSPITAL STIRLING

Balvstrade in Forecourt

SUNDIAL

SUMMER HOUSE

THE BOWLING GREEN

THE TERRACE

FORECOVRT

Plan   The Sundial

STEP

STEP

SCALE FOR PLAN   FEET

SCALE FOR SUNDIAL   FEET

J. DAVIDSON. DELT.

Fig 321 A detail from John Slezer's engraving of 'The Prospect of Falkland from the East'. It first appeared in the 1693 edition of Theatrum Scotiae. *DP101767*

In 1683 *The Scots Gard'ner* was printed in Edinburgh. This book was written by John Reid, a gardener of some experience, who had at the time of the book's publication already left Scotland for New Jersey in pursuit of land of his own and an opportunity to employ his skills and talents in a wider landscape, resulting in uncorrected proofs and a list of corrigenda at the end of the text (Reid 1988, 125). Its full title is *The Scots Gard'ner in two parts The First of Contriving and Planting Gardens, Orchards, Avenues: With new and profitable ways of Levelling; and how to Measure and Divide Land. The Second of the Propagation & Improvement of Forrest, and Fruit-Trees, Kitchen-Hearbes, Roots and Fruits: With some Physick Hearbs, Shrubs and Flowers. Appendix shewing how to use the Fruits of the Garden: Whereunto is annexed The Gard'ners Kalendar. Published for the Climate of Scotland* (Fig 18). This extended title encapsulates the range of subjects included within the responsibilities of a gardener at this period in Scotland. According to a memorandum written by Reid in the year of his death in 1723, he was born in 1656 at Niddry Castle, where his father and grandfather had served as gardeners to the Seton family (Bartow 1879, 245–7). Reid attended school until the age of nine when his father died. The following year he went to work for an Edinburgh printer, but his apprenticeship lapsed on the death of his employer, and he returned to Niddry and took up work as a gardener there in 1673, when he was persuaded 'to learn the old but pleasant art of Gard'nery'. After

a year Reid had decided upon horticulture as a career and moved to Hamilton Palace in 1674, where he 'dived into that noble science' for a year before going to Drummond Castle in 1675. He then took up a post in 1676 at Lawers in Perthshire, where he remained for four years. It was at Lawers that he wrote *The Scots Gard'ner*. He had become a Quaker while he was at Hamilton, and at the age of twenty-two married another Quaker ten years his senior. In 1680 he moved to Shank near Dalkeith. In 1683 he or a namesake published a work in Edinburgh entitled *A brief account of the province of East:New:Jarsey in America* encouraging emigration from Scotland (Anon 1683). Reid's will, probably made before he left Scotland, describes him as 'gardener in the Shank', and it was not registered until 1693 (Edinburgh Commissary Court CC8/8/64). Others of the same surname were also recorded as gardeners. James Reid was referred to as gardener at Priestfield, Edinburgh, in 1663 (Edinburgh Commissary Court CC8/8/74); there was an Alexander Reid, 'gardener in Weyme' (Castle Menzies) in the 1670s (NRS GD1/449/166, GD1/449/207) and a William Reid, gardener in the Grange on the south side of Edinburgh, in 1700 (NRS GD118/186).

John Reid left from Leith on the *Exchange* with his family in August 1683. On the same ship was another gardener, John Hampton, from East Lothian, who was also a Quaker and travelling to New Jersey. They became the surveyors for the new settlement; their skills in laying out settlements and land holdings were much esteemed, and in 1702 John Reid became the Surveyor General of New Jersey (Bartow 1879, 244). John Reid and his family prospered in New Jersey and he acquired an estate which he named Hortensia. His interest in gardening and botany was maintained; in a letter to Scotland he writes, 'There are a great store of garden Herbs here. I have not had time to inquire into them all, neither to send some of the very pleasant, (tho' to me unknown) plants of this country, to James Sutherland, physic gardener at Edinburgh, but tell him, I will not forget him when opportunity offers' (Reid 1988, viii). Mathematics and surveying remained an important concern and in 1709 he had plans to make a map of Canada along with observations on the soils and the settlements there. Shortly before his death he wrote a memorandum of his life which serves as the main source for what is known of his personal history (Bartow 1879, 182–3, 243–8).

John Reid's book was the first to be designed specifically for gardeners in Scotland. It drew on earlier works on gardening, particularly those which were especially concerned with the growing of fruit trees, and notably on *The French Gardiner* by Nicholas de Bonnefons, translated into English by John Evelyn in 1658. His book is written, he says, 'for the good of my Country'. He referred to 'learned Evelen and ingenious Cook' (Reid 1988, 77) and Evelyn's volume on trees, *Sylva*, and Moses Cook's *The manner of raising ordering and improving forrest-trees* are both works with a strong scientific bent. According to Reid, many books on gardening were for other countries and climates and many were less than practical in their approach; his was designed to produce both profit and pleasure. It concludes with a Gardeners' Calendar on the lines of that written by John Evelyn as the *Kalendarium Hortense or the gard'ners almanac directing what he is to do monethly throughout the year, and what fruits and flowers are in prime* which appeared in *Sylva* (Evelyn 1679). Reid's particular interest was surveying, and he provided instruction in how to undertake this. He assumed a fair knowledge of mathematics in his readers and presumed they had some academic training, so that the contexts were understood.

Reid begins his book on gardening with a section on the construction of the house. He links his house directly to the garden by means of a stair, descending from the hall or dining room to a parterre of grass and gravel, with two pavilions at the corners away from the house set outside the line of the parterre (Reid 1988, Fig 1) (Fig 322). His descriptions allow a picture of the garden to be built up:

> Pleasure-Gardens useth to be divided into walkes and plots, with a Bordure round each plot, and at the corner of each, may be a holly or some such train'd up, some Pyramidal, others Spherical, the Trees and Shrubs at the Wall well plyed and prun'd, the Green thereon cut in several Figures, the walkes layed with Gravel, and the plots within with Grass, (in several places whereof

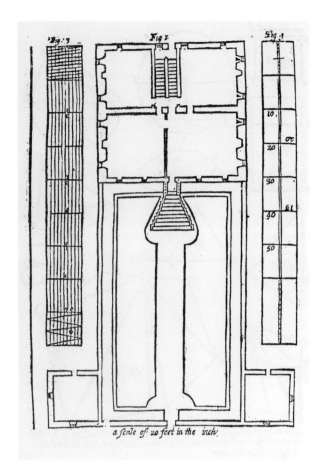

Fig 322 Illustration from The Scots Gard'ner *showing the relationship between the house and garden (Reid 1988, Fig 1).*

> may be Flower pots) the Bordures boxed, and planted with variety of Fine Flowers orderly Intermixt, Weeded, Mow'd, Rolled, and kept all clean and handsome. (Reid 1988, 26)

He advocated plain straight paths and borders running from the house door. Borders and paths should be the same width. The borders should be 'boxed', and his favourite plant for this, rather than box, was the dwarf juniper, and planted with flowers. The boxing could also be formed from timber or stone. There were, in his view, three different ways of planting borders. Borders should be planted in five rows and the different kinds of plants should be mixed so that no two of the same kind or colour should be placed together without other kinds or colours intervening. When gaps appeared because their flowering season was over, annuals raised in pots could be put in to fill the vacancy. His second method was to set out the borders with plants in five rows of five, so that they formed a square; a square each of tulips, of boars ears (possibly bears ears (Robertson 2000, 53)), of crocuses, of July flowers (stocks), of anemones and of cowslips were planted and the pattern repeated according to the space. The colours of each kind of plant should be intermixed and so should different categories of plants, so that similar plants are not adjacent, providing interest all year. His third method was to plant flowers of the same kind in thickets by themselves in beds or ridges, whether annuals or perennials. The border would be divided in six or eight ridges according to the size of the plants. Symmetry should be maintained so that the borders on each side should have the same kind of plants.

The paths should be gravelled and the enclosing walls planted with a mixture of fruit and flower bearing trees. The outer court was to have a central path with a long grass plot on each side and a border against the walls planted with laurels or other leafy shrubs. Detailed instructions are given on how to construct walks and borders and of their relative heights. The more scientific aspects of gardening are given greater emphasis, in particular the grafting of fruit trees and the preparation of seeds for tree planting. Reid is emphatic on the need for enclosure, whether by brick or stone walls or by hedges of holly or hawthorn (Reid 1988, 83–4), concluding his work with the words: 'There is no way under the Sun so probable for improving our Land as Inclosing and Planting the same: Therefore I wish it were effectually put in practice' (Reid 1988, 125).

John Reid had already worked in some of the major gardens of Scotland at this period, several of which have already been referred to or described. The garden at **Hamilton Palace** seems to have been recognised as a centre where those who foresaw a career in horticulture might gain experience and a reference which would stand them in good stead. The head gardener was Hew Wood and he had six under-gardeners there. He was a Quaker who appears to have played a part in the conversion of many to the sect in Scotland, holding Quaker meetings at his house in Hamilton. He was in post by 1662 (NRAS332/F/1/232) and died in 1702, when he was buried in his garden. A remarkably large number of gardeners in Scotland in the later seventeenth and eighteenth centuries were Quakers, although there were only a few hundred members of the sect in Scotland. They were seen as a threat to the social fabric of Scotland, with their pacifism and their refusal to swear oaths in courts of law being singled out as a menace, and they suffered from various forms of persecution (Lee 2010, 169). Their employers seem to have borne with their religious practices, and many proved to be successful businessmen. Hew Wood's elder son, James Wood, married the daughter of another Quaker gardener at Kelso, and later worked for the first Duke of Queensberry at Drumlanrig. His younger son succeeded him at Hamilton.

William Miller, a sub-gardener at Hamilton, had married Margaret Cassie at Hew Wood's house in Hamilton in 1680; he had moved to Newark by 1684 and on to Holyrood by 1689. Two of his sons became gardeners; the eldest, George, ran a nursery garden at Holyrood, and later became gardener at Kinneil, and his second son went into partnership with his father,

providing seeds, trees and shrubs across Scotland (Marshall 1973, 71–3; Robertson 2000, 196). In the 'Appendix Shewing how to use the fruits of the Garden' in the *The Scots Gard'ner* Reid writes: 'Its to be noted, that the ingenious and most industrious, Hugh Wood Gard'ner at Hamiltoun can accommodate you with the above mentioned Fruits, together with multitudes of other sorts, whither English, Dutch, or Scots' (Reid 1988, 124). Hew Wood, with his wife, also held land in the burgh of Hamilton outside the palace gardens, where he may have raised the plants he sold (NRS GD85/266). By 1693 the Duke of Hamilton was writing from London to his wife, saying that he had sent trees to Hew Wood, but that he wished he could replace him with a better gardener (NRS GD406/1/7324). It is perhaps an indication of the development in gardening skills since Wood began at Hamilton more than thirty years before, or perhaps a feeling that his commercial operations were occupying too much of his attention.

Much of the information about the content of the gardens at Hamilton Palace comes from Rosalind Marshall's 1973 study of the household of Anne, Duchess of Hamilton, between 1656 and 1716 (Marshall 1973). The Palace of Hamilton had been rebuilt in 1591 following a fire (Macaulay 1989, 17), on a courtyard plan on the site of a previous house which had been known as the Orchard (Marshall 1973, 37). Its gardens were subsequently extended following an exchange of property in 1601 (NRAS2177/Bundle 513). The gardener in the early seventeenth century was Robert Hutchinson, who was given £10 Scots a year to spend on seeds, visiting East Lothian to buy them and travelling as far as Fife 'to see a garden'. Anna, Marchioness of Hamilton, had shown considerable interest in planting, purchasing young trees from the Laird of Pollock in 1626, and her undated letter to Sir Colin Campbell of Glenorchy, thanking him for fir seed, has already been quoted (Marshall 1973, 50–1, 56; NRS GD112/560b). Documentary evidence indicates the presence of a painted sundial carved by Ralph Rawlinson for which 'orologe stone' he was paid in 1648 (Marshall 1973, 51).

In about 1677 Isaac Miller produced a series of drawings showing the façade of the palace and its plan, as well as the collegiate church of Hamilton which stood immediately to the east. The drawings of the gardens and the park are in plan form with measurements attached. Little is known of the career and connections of the draughtsman, Isaac Miller, who was employed as a carpenter, but may have had more overall responsibility for building works. He may have been related to William Miller, recorded as under-gardener at Hamilton in 1680. Various people of this surname worked for the Hamilton family during this period. The palace had a courtyard plan with entrances from the south, from the west through the stables and

Fig 323 Drawing by Isaac Miller of the façade of Hamilton Palace made about 1677, showing the balcony and the balustraded corner towers from which the garden could be viewed. SC750308

offices, and from the garden to the north. What was probably the north façade of the palace has a doorway slightly off centre with what appears to have been a large, possibly timber, balcony above it, decorated with what may be carved upright posts and knobs. This would allow a view over the garden, as would the corner towers on this face with their balustrades around the roofs (Fig 323).

The plans (Figs 324, 325) depict a series of enclosed gardens surrounded by stone walls. Immediately to the north of the palace, between the two projecting towers, and in front of the entrance passage, was a level garden with paths crossing at right angles, from which steps descended to a parterre. This may be where a new bowling green had been laid out in 1666 near the south gate or more probably it may have near the main public entrance to the palace (Marshall 1973, 51). The drawing may indicate schematic trees and trellising on both sides of the steps, set against a vertical wall supporting the upper terrace. Among the series of walled enclosures around the house was one known as the Statue Garden, containing painted statues

with a painted sundial at its centre. This sundial may have been the one referred to earlier, carved in 1648 by Ralph Rawlinson. It is possible that this was the garden reached by steps which lay below the one immediately in front of the house, although no statues or sundials appear on Isaac Miller's plans. This garden was slightly rhomboidal in shape measuring 60 yards (55m) at the south end and 70 yards (64m) at the north end with walls 99 yards (90m) long to east and west. It was laid out with broad paths in a cross design with paths along the walls and a circle at the centre, presumably around some particular feature, such as the sundial, and half circles to the north and south. According to Reid's ideal plans, this would be the Flower Garden. There were two small rectangular exedra or niches at the centre points of the east and west walls which probably contained seats, but may have housed statues. Two garden pavilions or banqueting houses with an upper floor were built against, or onto, the east wall. The more northerly of these allowed access to the steps which led down to what may have been the vegetable garden, and was close to the entrance leading into the orchard.

The orchard lay to the east of the Flower Garden and could also have been viewed from the garden pavilions. The orchard was planted in the pattern Reid

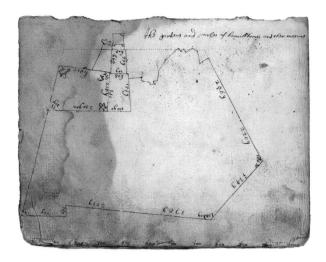

Fig 324 Plan of the gardens and Low Parks of Hamilton Palace by Isaac Miller from about 1677 with the palace and church towards the top. SC1245365

refers to as square and which is shown in his Fig 5 (Reid 1988). It was already in existence during the lifetime of the first duke, when a hundred small nails had been bought 'for trees nailing to the brick walls', and, given the name of the house to which the Hamilton family had moved during the sixteenth century, 'The Orchard', had flourished before then. Brick makers were hired to produce bricks for extending the orchard wall, against which peaches, apricots and cherries were grown. Part of the orchard was in use as a cherry yard and this fruit would seem to have been a particular favourite of the duke. The source of some of the trees was Scottish: cherry trees had been obtained from the garden of the laird of Ormiston in East Lothian; pear trees had come from Struthers near Paisley. Peaches and apricots, vines, mulberries and nut trees were bought from London, and grafts on other types of fruit tree, as described by John Reid, were much favoured, with '5 peaches upon apricots, 4 peaches upon plums and 2 apricots being brought by a Bo'ness ship from Holland' (Marshall 1973, 55).

A flight of steps placed centrally in the north wall led down to another walled garden, again slightly rhomboidal, measuring 80 yards on the south, 100 yards on the north and 153 yards to east and west. This may be the Pond Garden, where there were fish ponds and fountains. It is divided in four by broad paths that are set at right angles with rectangular ponds in the two northerly sections. These are described as 'much admired and where there were fountains' (Marshall 1973, 51).

The largest garden lay to the east. It appears to have had the most elaborate layout with a pavilion near its south-east corner opposite the one leading from the Flower Garden, and a rectangular exedra at the centre of its south wall. The beds were rectangular, each with an arc in place of the outside corner. Like the other gardens, it was divided into four parts each of which

seems to have been divided in two. Each section seems to be edged or walled, perhaps as Reid describes it 'boxed'. The more northerly sections have rectangular ponds and as these would conflict with the layout of paths, it may be that what was being depicted was a change of plan. This was probably the Kitchen Garden, an important and appreciated part of the surroundings of the palace; a gilded sundial stood at the centre and there was an avenue of alternating horse chestnut and cherry trees across it (Marshall 1973, 52; Robertson 2000, 194). This garden was quadrilateral, but judging from the angles given on the Isaac Miller plan, which contrive not to add up to 360 degrees, somewhat irregular. Hew Wood wrote letters to David Crawford, the Hamiltons' secretary, about progress on the gardens and what was required to plant them. In 1693 thorn hedges were planted there, beginning at the east gate and 'came westward with the holey-hedge and if this present storm had not hindered we had by this gotten the lenth of both gravell walks planted, for I have already got ten hundred thorns. The aller (alder) trees are planted: ... I hope not to forget the straw-berrys, when tyme of planting them comes' (Robertson 2000, 194).

There were yearly orders for garden seed from Henry Fergusson, the seed merchant, whose shop was 'a little above the head of the Blackfriars Wynd' and where James Sutherland's *Catalogue of the plants in the Physical Garden at Edinburgh* was for sale (NRAS 332/F/1/265 etc; Marshall 1973, 52). The seeds included Strasbourg onion seed, often supplemented with French, Flanders and Spanish onion seed; seeds for leeks, both French and London, French cucumbers, Dutch parsnips, Italian celery, turnips, beetroot and radishes were bought regularly. Young cabbage plants were bought a thousand at a time, with a considerable variety of types being available and the accounts mention English, Scots, Dutch and Russian cabbage. Lettuce, which had been grown at Hamilton since the 1620s, spinach and endives, peas and beans were all cultivated. There were special hotbeds for the rearing of asparagus, and frames for 'tender herbs' and for bringing on melons and gourds (Marshall 1973, 52–3). Reid thought that melons 'are not worth the while', creating as they did, a considerable amount of work for the gardeners:

for you must raise them on the early Hot-bed
(the making whereof is in Chap. 2 Sect. 7) which
(when fit for feed) prick 4 or 5 in together, at 3
Inches distance, through the bed, setting drinking
Glasses on them at first, and cover on the matts
over the whole carefully, to preserve from
Snow, Rains and Winds: taking off the matts in
temperate days, but keep on the Glasses, except
in a warme space; that you acquaint them a little
with the Air, by raising the edg of the Glasses,
with a little Straw on the laun side, closing it at
night again. (Reid 1988, 95)

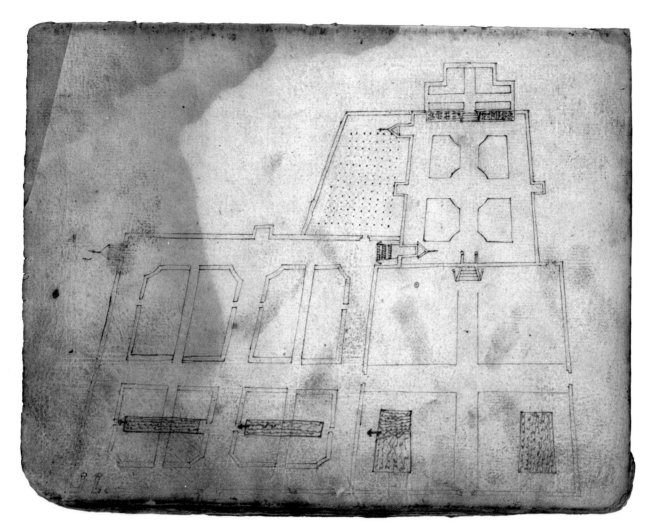

Fig 325 Plan of the gardens of Hamilton Palace by Isaac Miller from about 1677 showing a series of walled enclosures around the mansion which was sited at the top of the drawing. They were approached from a terrace in front of the house leading to walks through the gardens. These included a flower garden, a vegetable garden, an orchard and a pond garden. SC1245364

Beyond the garden was the park. The area shown on Isaac Miller's plan was the Low Parks, where there was an avenue for which Hugh Miller wrote to David Crawford requesting 'a considerable number of those elms at Paisley to help our north avenue in the little park for many of the elms planted there are but insufficient but I think it is late now in the year to transplant them' (Robertson 2000, 194). To the south, towards Cadzow, lay the High Parks or, as John Lauder, the future Lord Fountainhall, described the scene, 'the wood which is of wast bounds: much wood of it is felled: there be many great oaks in it yet: rode through the length of it, it is thought to be 5 miles about. Saw great droves of hart and hind with the young roes and fawns in companies of 100 and 60 together' (Lauder 1900, 186). This park, which had medieval origins, had been stocked by the first Duke of Hamilton, who had acquired red deer and roe deer from Sir Colin Campbell of Glenorchy, as well as fir seed. The deer created problems with the planting

of young trees, as well as providing a tempting target for the local poachers (Marshall 1973, 56). Slezer's engraving of the town of Hamilton shows a deer hunt in the foreground, but the garden is unfortunately concealed by buildings (Fig 326).

The gardens at Hamilton Palace became a popular attraction for visitors who were making a tour of Scotland. In addition to the impression made on him by the deer park, Lord Fountainhall, who had received part of his education in France and the Low Countries, commented:

> Went and saw the yards: great abundance of as good wines (vines), peaches, apricoats, figs, walnuts, chaistins (chestnuts), philberts etc in it as in any part of France; excellent bon Crestien pears, brave palissades of firs, sundry fisch ponds. The wals are built of brick, which conduces much to the ripening of the fruits; their be 20 ackers of land within the yeards. Their's a fair bouling graine before the palace gate. (Lauder 1900, 186)

When he visited Pinkie later in 1668, he commented in his journal that the knot at Pinkie was much larger than

Fig 326 Detail from 'The Prospect of the Town of Hamilton' from John Slezer's Theatrum Scotiae *of 1693 showing the environs of Hamilton Palace. DP101775*

that at Hamilton and in better order (Lauder 1900, 189). Thomas Kirke, who visited Scotland in 1677, wrote that:

> We rode up the river Clyde, a most pleasant stream. Eight miles above Glasgow, a most pleasant place, where is the palace of the Duke Hamilton. We waited on him, and he ordered his gentleman to show us his yards. Here is a great plot of ground for gardens &c., not yet finished; but the design promises a good product. He was going to his Park with some company, and gave us a slender invitation and left us. (Kirke 1892, 46)

William Lindsay, Earl of Crawford, was another visitor to the gardens, and more particularly to the orchards of Scotland, including Hamilton. In 1692 he drew up a list of fruit, 'The Earl of Crawford's Judgment of fruits in order set down as I esteem them according to their Goodness'. It included twenty-two kinds of apples, forty pears, thirty-six plums, eighteen cherries, eight peaches, two nectarines, six apricots, eight gooseberries, four currants, four strawberries, two raspberries, two filberts and three artichokes. He recorded where he had found them across the south of Scotland, listing some sixty orchards including the former monastic sites at Lindores, Kilwinning and Paisley (NRS GD45/18/746;

Robertson 2000, 108–43). Hamilton produced for him Nonsuch and Malcotton pears, Duchess damsons, orange apricots, white globe gooseberries and great bright redcurrants (Marshall 1973, 54). In 1693 Robert Sibbald wrote in *Theatrum Scotiae*, giving somewhat skewed directions:

> Its chief Ornament is the Palace of the Duke of Hamilton, the Court whereof is on all Quarters adorned with most noble Buildings; especially the Frontispiece looking toward the East, is of excellent Workman-ship; and has a majnificent Avenue: Upon the One Hand of this Avenue, there is a Hedge, and on the other, fair large Gardens, abundantly furnished with Fruit-Trees, and pleasant Flowers of all Sorts. Upon the West side of the Town there is a large Park, surrounded with a very high Stone Wall, which is about Seven Miles in Circuit; the Brook Aven running through it. This Park is also famous for its Forest of Tall Oaks, and for the great Number of Harts and Buffles it abounds with. (Slezer 1693, 8–9)

The rebuilding of Hamilton Palace did not begin until 1693, although it had long been contemplated. Recovery from the losses of the interregnum, the payments for reclaiming the lands and the achievement of political stability must have been factors in this delay, and a redesign of the garden in a rather different style followed. In 1696, after the death of Duchess Anne's husband, her son wrote to his elder brother, the Earl of Arran, asking whether their mother should employ one of Hew Wood's sons as a gardener, and mentioning in the same letter that the foundations of the new house were being laid (NRS GD406/1/6945).

The other major house belonging to the Hamilton family in Scotland was **Kinneil** near Bo'ness, where a garden is known to have been laid out in the 1550s, although it had undergone much in the way of destruction and change since then. The duke and duchess were not often resident at Kinneil and indeed spent more time at Holyrood, because the duke attended Parliament and meetings of the Privy Council in Edinburgh. Coal mining and other industrial activities provided a source of revenue. The house took on much of its present form in the last quarter of the seventeenth century when extensive alterations were undertaken by the third Duke and Duchess Anne, whose arms appear on the panel in front of the north-east pavilion (RCAHMS 1929, 190–2; Marshall 1973, 57–60). The gardens are shown in miniature in schematic form on John Adair's map of West Lothian of about 1684, with what appears to be a rectangular walled garden in front of the house and a parterre divided into four, surrounded by paths. Beyond this is another rectangular walled enclosure depicted with two trees inside, possibly the orchard, and beyond that a much larger walled rectangular enclosure with the trees planted in squares. What is probably a tree-lined avenue runs to the east (NLS Adv.MS.70.2.11 (Adair 8)) (Fig 327).

As at Hamilton there were flower gardens, kitchen gardens and an orchard, and as at Hamilton, though not on the same scale, a deer park. Among the seeds bought for Kinneil in 1703–4 were beans, carrots, parsnips, radishes, celery and cauliflower (NRAS 2177/ Bundle 2816). Both fruit trees and seeds were sent by sea (NRAS 332/M/2/21). The Earl of Crawford wrote of the Murray pears and the Brethern pears which flourished there; there were also cherry trees, apricots and peaches around the walls of the kitchen garden. Some of the fruit was sent to Hamilton for the family, but the remainder was sold and formed part of the estate revenues. A note of 17 July 1696 records that Henry Anderson, gardener in Grange, Edinburgh, and William Pinkerton, gardener in Linlithgow, summoned by Daniel Hamilton, chamberlain of Kinneil, as expert witnesses 'to comprise and value the whole pears, apples, plums, cherries, gooseberries and currantberries of the yards of Kinneil, do find the same, (excepting those in the north yard which are reserved for her Grace the Duchess her use) to be worth only £20 Scots money' (Marshall 1973, 59). This inquiry may be the result of low yields associated with the successive years of poor weather at the end of the seventeenth century (Morrison 1995, 11–12). Several of the gardeners at Kinneil are known by name. One was George Miller, the son of William Miller, gardener at Holyrood (NRAS332/L/1/304). In

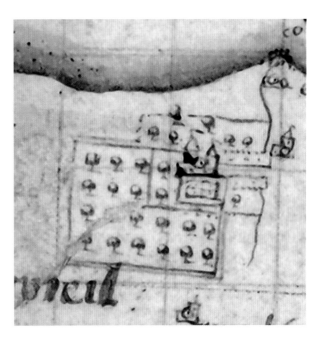

Fig 327 Kinneil House and its gardens as depicted on John Adair's manuscript map of West Lothian in 1684 (Adv.MS.70.2.11 (Adair 8)). © NLS

1695 a gardener called James Miller wished to resign from his post there (GD406/1/4002); it was written of his successor that, 'although the new gardener does not write well, he draws better and has much more mathematicks as ever H. Wood had' (GD406/1/4009). Another gardener at Kinneil was John Cocks whose widow, Margaret Maxwell, petitioned the Duchess of Hamilton for payment of wages of £90 owing to her husband at his death in 1706 (NRAS332/C3/81).

John Reid's next home was at **Drummond Castle** in Perthshire where he went in 1675, the property of the Earl of Perth, and the garden there has already been referred to in Chapters 2 and 3. One of its most striking features is the series of terraces that descend from the ridge on which the castle sits, to the large formally planted walled garden, which lies to the south (Fig 328). While these terraces may belong to the earlier seventeenth century, perhaps around 1630 when the sundial was carved by John Mylne and his sons, the first evidence for their existence occurs on John Adair's manuscript map of about 1683 (NLS Adv.MS.70.2.11 (Adair 2)) (Fig 329). The garden is depicted with two terraces leading down to a rectangular parterre which was divided in four, in a Latin cross rather than the St Andrews cross, which was adopted when the gardens were redesigned in the earlier nineteenth century (Fig 330). This was probably the flower garden. The position of the sundial is not indicated. To the east and west are rectangular walled enclosures planted with trees in squares, perhaps the orchards. To the south of the flower garden are a series of walled enclosures which follow the rectilinear layout of the garden, perhaps the kitchen gardens. Further to the south lies what is probably another walled orchard. The whole

Fig 328 Aerial view of Drummond Castle and its gardens under snow. SC9494575

Fig 329 Drummond Castle and its gardens as depicted on John Adair's manuscript map of 'Straithern, Stormont, & Cars of Gourie with the rivers Tay and Ern' in Perthshire in 1683 (Adv.MS.70.2.11 (Adair 2)). © NLS

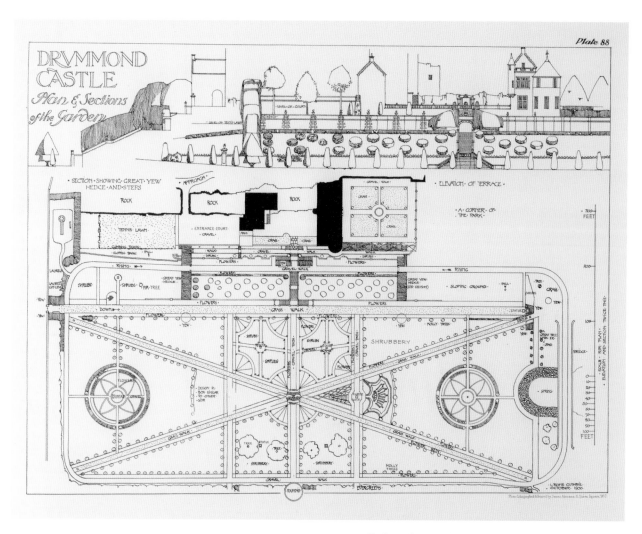

Fig 330 The garden at Drummond Castle in a drawing from Inigo Triggs' 1902 volume, Formal Gardens in England and Scotland *Plate 88.*

area surrounding the castle and gardens is enclosed by a wall, creating an extremely geometric and orderly plan, as depicted by Adair. This area beyond the gardens is planted with larger trees and may be identified as the park. Directly to the south and on a line with the central axis of the castle is a broad avenue, with others running east and west.

After only a year at Drummond, Reid moved on to a neighbouring estate, that of **Lawers** or Fordie, which belonged to Sir James Campbell. Here he stayed for four years and, while he was resident there, married another Quaker, Margaret Miller from Kirkintilloch in 1678 (Bartow 1879, 245). The present mansion of Lawers was designed by William Adam. It was built between 1724 and 1726 as a reconstruction of the previous house, when the north became the principal front, with changes and additions made in the later eighteenth and nineteenth centuries (Adam 1980, 29, Pl 158). Little is known of the form of the mansion in the late 1670s. The manuscript map by Adair of about 1683 (NLS Adv.MS.70.2.11 (Adair 2)) shows the earlier house set centrally within its gardens (Fig 332). There

are walled gardens on both sides, with another walled garden beyond, and two larger walled gardens to the south. In front of the mansion is a garden without the usual paths marked on it, possibly a reflection of Reid's dislike of such arrangements (Reid 1988, 26, Fig 2). Beyond the garden is an avenue, of which some trees, or their successors, still survive. Running to the south and terminating to the north of the River Earn, it is closed by a line of trees at both ends. The Ordnance Survey First Edition 6-inch map, surveyed in 1863, reveals that the area of the gardens had been considerably reduced and most of it changed to lawns and fields. The offices occupied the area immediately to the west of the mansion with a bowling green marked to the west, and the avenue, while it had been cleared near the house, continued beyond the road between Comrie and Crieff.

Aerial survey during the dry summer of 1989 revealed, in the parched grass surrounding the present house, an arrangement of enclosures, reminiscent of that depicted in the map of 1683 (Fig 331). In the absence of excavation, the features cannot be dated and may well belong to more than one period of development. In front of the mansion, to the south, is a parterre divided into four by paths set at right angles. This was not a layout favoured by Reid, although he describes it as frequently

Fig 331 *Aerial view of Lawers House where the parchmarks reflect the layout of the gardens as depicted on the Adair map of 1683. SC1110455*

Fig 332 *Lawers House and its gardens as depicted on John Adair's manuscript map of 'Straithern, Stormont, & Cars of Gourie with the rivers Tay and Ern' in Perthshire in 1683 (Adv.MS.70.2.11 (Adair 2)). © NLS*

employed. He preferred to see all the paths running in the same direction away from the house, parallel to each other, and as this arrangement does not appear on Adair's map, it may be of an earlier or later date (Fig 332). The central path leads to what may have been a paved terrace from which there are indications of a flight of steps leading to a lower garden. Similar, but larger, gardens lie on both sides, with traces of one garden surviving to the east of the house in a design reminiscent of Sir William Bruce's own garden at Balcaskie in Fife. The larger enclosures to the east and the west may be reflected in the elaborate arrangement of walls and paths which emerge as parchmarks through the turf on the west side, although these may have belonged to a later walled kitchen garden. To the rear of the present house are traces of a series of buildings of unknown date, arranged around a courtyard. Whether the gardens of Lawers depicted in the

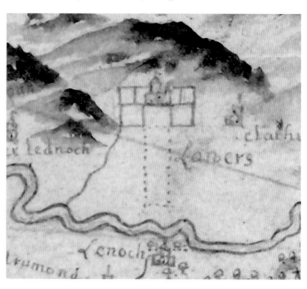

1680s were laid out by John Reid, who wrote the *Scots Gard'ner* there, is unknown, but he was employed there from 1676 to 1680 immediately prior to the production of the map, and his eldest daughter was born there.

In 1680 he moved with his family to **Shank House** in Midlothian, one of the earliest gardens to survive in pictorial form in Scotland (Fig 137) because the estate was the subject of a court case in 1586 (NRS RHP 82800). The gardens at Shank do not survive and there is little detail, except for an avenue, on the manuscript map by John Adair (NLS Adv.MS.70.2.11 (Adair 9)) (Fig 333). The Roy Survey of 1747–53 (BL Maps K.Top.48.25-1.a-f.) shows a large formal garden laid out in the form of a St Andrews cross, intersected by a central path (Fig 334). Shank was the estate of Sir George Mackenzie, Lord Advocate and member of the Privy Council of Scotland during the reigns of Charles II and James II and VII. In his youth Mackenzie was the author of *A Moral Essay preferring Solitude to Public Employment*, which appeared in 1665. It was dedicated to the seventeenth Earl of Crawford, who had resigned office within two years of the Restoration in the face of the increasing anti-Presbyterian stance of Charles II's administration. Mackenzie was usually in opposition to the party of Lauderdale, but reached an accommodation with it in 1674, when he became Lord Advocate. He wrote in 1663 that 'every private Christian should be tolerated by his fellow-subjects to worship God inwardly according to his conscience', although man should 'conspire in that exterior uniformity of worship which the laws of his Country injoins' (Allan 1999, 261), and in the early 1680s he played a notoriously active role in the suppression of convenanting activity. Like William Drummond of Hawthornden before him, he praised the retired country life in *Caelia's Country-house and Closet*:

> O happy Country Life, pure like their Air;
> Free from the rage of Pride, the pangs of care:
> Here happy Souls lye bath'd in soft content,
> And are at once secure and innocent.
> (Allan 1999, 269)

Reid's ability to move around Scotland as a gardener for different estates would suggest a recognition for his skills that went beyond his immediate neighbourhood and was appreciated in spite of his adherence to Quakerism. His move to New Jersey would also suggest a belief in his own abilities that proved to be justified by his success there (Fig 335).

Reid's statement near the beginning of his work sets out the principles of his garden designs:

> Make all the Buildings and Plantings ly so about
> the House, as that the House may be the Centre;
> all the Walks, Trees and Hedges running to
> the House.

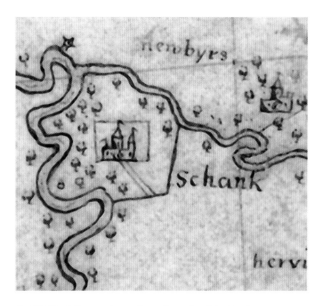

Fig 333 Shank House and its garden as depicted on John Adair's manuscript map of Midothian about 1682 (Adv.MS.70.2.11 (Adair 9)). © NLS

As the Sun is the Centre of this World: as the Heart of the man is the Centre of the man: as the nose the Centre of the face: and as it is unseemly to see a man wanting a leg, ane arm &c. or his nose standing at one side the face, or not streight, or wanting a cheek, ane eye, ane eare, or with one (or all of them) great at one side and small on the other; Just so with the house-courts, Avenues, Gardens, Orchards, &c. where regularity and uniformity is not observed. Therefore whatever you have on the one hand, make as much, and of the same forme in the same place, on the other.' (Reid 1988, 2)

Fig 334 Shank House as it appears on Roy's Military Survey of 1747 to 1755. © British Library Licensor Scran

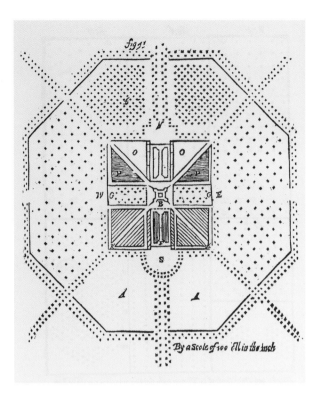

Fig 335 Figure 9 from John Reid's The Scots Gard'ner *illustrating his advice, 'Make all the Buildings and Plantings ly so about the House, as that the House may be the Centre; all the Walks, Trees and Hedges running to the House' (Reid 1988).*

Something of Reid's interest in surveying in the garden appears at **Saltoun Hall** in East Lothian. This was the property of Andrew Fletcher, an opponent of the Union with England and a well-known political theorist, who succeeded his father in 1665. He spent much of his time in France and Holland, as well as London, and the care of the estate was left to his brother Henry, who inherited Saltoun in 1716 and lived to 1733. A plan of the gardens there was attributed to Henry by his grandson, and the design may be dated to the period around 1700 (RCAHMS Collection ELD\110\93; Brogden Drawings Inventory 10). It shows the ground plan of the hall which incorporated a tower and apartments labelled hall, dining room, drawing room chamber, gallery, chapel and library arranged on three sides of a court with a central pond or basin. The back court lay beyond the road to the barns. There were four gardens enclosed by walls, each with a pool at its centre. These were designed to be intervisible with each other, and the walls were pierced by doors or grates to permit this. The garden closest to the house was known as the Flower or Summer Garden and was laid out with eight symmetrically arranged paths which met at the fountain. The one beyond it was the Physick or Spring Garden with concentric beds centred on the fountain. There was a view from the house to both fountains. To one side was the largest enclosure, the Fruit or Harvest Garden laid out in sixteen rectangular plots and, adjoining one side of the house, the Evergreen or

Winter Garden arranged in long narrow rectangular beds around the fountain (Fig 336).

The gardens designed by Earl Patrick of Strathmore and Kinghorn, who inherited Glamis and Castle Lyon (now known by its earlier name of **Castle Lyon**) in Angus, as a child in 1646, exemplify Reid's view of garden design and the centrality of the mansion. The effort involved to shape the landscape around these towers or mansions in order to achieve what the earl considered appropriate for their gardens was considerable and expensive. Earl Patrick kept an account of his activities in *The Book of Record* (Millar 1890). He intended it to be a 'Book of Record of all my transactions as debtor or creditor and with my Tenants & the effects of my estate And in a word of all my proceedings Beginning in the month of Januarie 1684'. In this work the earl describes the desolate condition of Glamis Castle and Castle Lyon, as a result of his minority, the debts left by his father and the mismanagement of his estates, as well as of the effects of the civil wars. In 1660, when he was seventeen, he confronted his difficult financial situation: 'inflam'd stronglie with a great desyre to continue the memorie of my familie, I looked upon nothing as too hard hopeing still to doe it ... I did deny myselfe the satisfactione which the most pairt of youth of that aige desyre, of goeing abroad and travelling' (Millar 1890, 19, 24). After finishing at the University of St Andrews, he settled at Castle Lyon near Dundee. This house stood upon a rock, and much effort was expended on creating the gardens there. Earl Patrick writes in 1684:

> The whole bounds of the kitchean yeard and nouricerie below the house and upon the west syde thereof is formed out of a declining rock which came out that farr, and the whole falling walks are cutt out of rock upon the East halfe of them and all filled up and carried ground upon the west halfe. And this I mention the more particularly because all levellings when done are so under cover disguise that it's scarce to be beleeved what work or labour there hes been att the doing of it, besyds the Litle garden, which is before the gate where the statues are, was nothing but a litle piece of ground without forme declining to the east, an ugly rock standing up in some places as high as the top of the statu's are upon the west syde. The bowling green no better and the plott upon the south side of the house worst of all, the utter court beat doune by force of quarry mells and peiks to render it accessable, the north and middle greens clouts of corn land. The south green a piece of my father's planting and oarchard. The great low gardine A marrish, stuborn clay raised to the hight its now of with carried ground. (Millar 1890, 34)

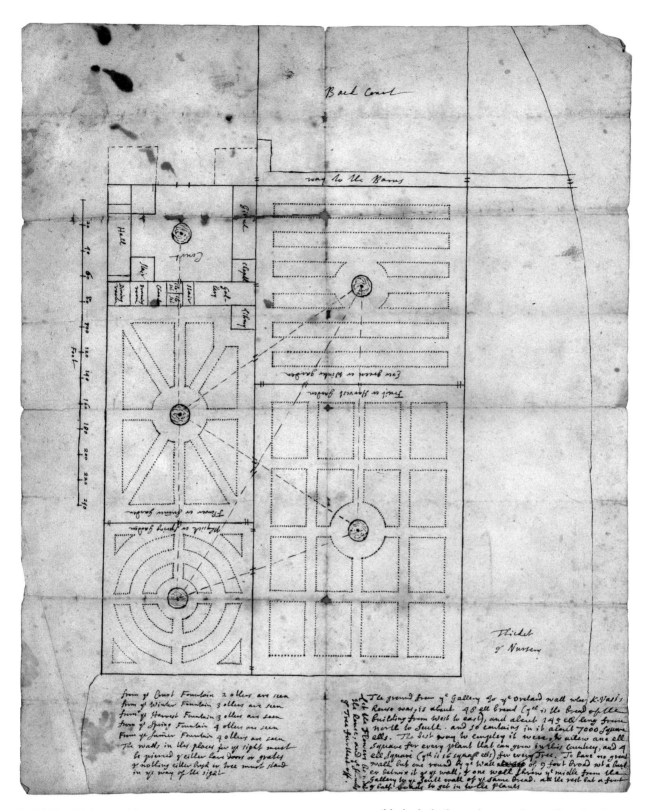

Fig 336 Plan of the house and the seasonal gardens at Saltoun Hall with dashed lines indicating the intervisibility of selected features. ELD\110\93

As Earl Patrick writes, it is difficult to envisage that the castle, now a prison, was so defensively situated, and Roy's Military Survey emphasises the regularity of its layout (Figs 337, 338). Adair's depiction shows Castle Lyon surrounded by a series of walled enclosures which

presumably include the various gardens referred to in the *Book of Record* (NLS Adv.MS.70.2.11 (Adair 2)) (Fig 339). The drawing of Castle Lyon made in the late 1740s by John Elphinstone shows some of the walled gardens and terraces with the garden on the entrance front adorned with a line of trees, an example of the topiarist's art. The parterre divided by cross walks was possibly that shown on Roy's map. Smooth grass (a

Fig 337 Aerial view of Castle Huntly (Castle Lyon) and its terraced gardens. DP075677

gardener is on hand with a rake and a garden roller) with a path around, it provides a suitable surface for the recreation of the well-dressed figures depicted (BL K.Top.50.62).

Earl Patrick envisioned Castle Lyon as the summer residence of his family, with Glamis designed for the winter, but it was not until 1670 that he felt able to turn his attention to the latter. His desire to achieve a symmetrical dwelling applied also to his plans for the gardens, for which a considerable amount of evidence survives (Brown 2005a, 19–39). He writes: 'Yet I did covet extremely to order my building so that the frontispiece might have resemblance on both sides' (Millar 1890, 41). His aims for both house and garden faced considerable problems because of the existing buildings and gardens on the site.

The gardens at **Glamis Castle** have been on record from the earlier sixteenth century following the confiscation of the estates by James V, when work on the ditches and on the fish ponds was paid for from the king's resources (*ER* 17, 384; Brown 2005b, 251). Two of the manuscript maps of Timothy Pont show Glamis from what appear to be different angles; both may depict gardens (NLS Pont 26 and 29) (Fig 340). Glamis Castle is now surrounded by lawns and parkland, with a straight tree-lined avenue providing the approach from a southerly direction (Fig 341). An aerial survey in August of 1989 provides the first clear indication of the nature of the remains of earlier gardens at Glamis, with photography from August 1994 supplementing the earlier evidence, and geophysical survey confirming much of the detail (Aspinall and Pocock 1995, 61–84). For the most part, the outline indications of formal gardens emerge as lighter markings in the turf around

the castle. Here the roots of the grass were unable to acquire sufficient moisture to sustain growth because of underlying stone, gravel or packed clay banks. The lines have been drawn out and rectified and the features set against the Ordnance Survey map surveyed between 1920 and 1923. Most of the parchmarks seem to relate to the layout of the policies of Glamis carried out by Earl Patrick (Brown 2005a, 25).

When the earl first came to Glamis in 1680, the only approach to the castle was from the south-east. An examination of the aerial photographs from 1989 reveals three lines of parchmarking to the south-east of the castle, on a north-west to south-east alignment. One of these on plan appears as two near-parallel lines, some 7m apart, running from the more westerly of the two yew trees south-east towards the sundial and on towards the avenue running east and west (Fig 343). Its northern edge is slightly darker and might indicate the line of a narrow ditch. There is also a less certain and darker southern margin. The more northerly line appears on the geophysical survey as a low resistance feature which, it is suggested, may mark the course of the approach referred to above from the south-east (Aspinall and Pocock 1995, 63). It may terminate on the north-west in line with the door depicted on Pont 26. Only part of the line of the suggested approach to the

Fig 338 Castle Huntly (Castle Lyon) and its gardens as they appear on Roy's Military Survey of 1747 to 1755. © British Library Licensor Scran

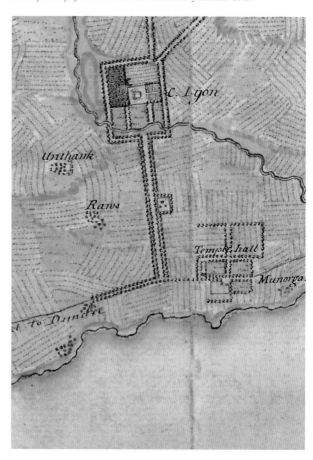

Fig 339 Castle Huntly (Castle Lyon) and its gardens as depicted on John Adair's manuscript map 'Straithern, Stormont, & Cars of Gourie with the rivers Tay and Ern' in 1683 (Adv.MS.70.2.11 (Adair 2)). © NLS

castle is visible on the geophysical survey as a line of low resistance. It might be expected that the main access road to the castle might have been more prominent in both the aerial photographic and geophysical survey; the masking effects of later garden works and their subsequent demolition may explain the lack of detail. The evidence from aerial survey and geophysical survey is, for the most part, complementary, although the aerial photograph suggests a broader track than the interpretative plot of the geophysical survey does (Aspinall and Pocock 1995, 65).

The aerial photographs show evidence from more than one period. The parchmarks (Fig 342) would indicate that the quadripartite garden on the east side may have extended further to the west, making a design of at least six parts. The line on the aerial photograph would seem to indicate that the path on the south continued to the west and what might be a continuation of the central path is visible within the court. This suggests that there may have been an earlier garden on the site. However the relationship between the paths and the wall around the garden and the court is unclear, and the nature of the material that would produce the markings – gravel or stone – may have obscured earlier features.

The date of this earlier garden is unknown, but it would probably have been later than that of the survey by Timothy Pont, whose work seems to have been concluded by about 1596 (Stone 1989, 5). Harry Gordon Slade describes with enthusiasm the building works of the period 1600 to 1626 (Slade 2000, 28–35), and the form of the garden, walled with plots divided by paths, would be appropriate for that time (Anthony 1991, 25–56), although a rather earlier or later date cannot be

ruled out. The garden, of which six sections are visible, may have been larger than the surviving traces indicate.

Earl Patrick certainly saw himself as starting afresh. *The Book of Record* recounts how his first task was to remove the 'old chattered and decayed trees, which surrounded the house, yet there were not many, and the most of these that were, were to the southward, a common mistake of our ancestors whereas reasonably any thickets or planting that are about any man's house ought rather to be on the north, northeast, and northwest'. He records that 'The whole planted ground [was] not exceeding four aikers att most' (Millar 1890, 38). While the acre of the time differed somewhat from the statute acre used by the Ordnance Survey, the approximate area occupied by the parchmarks of the bowling green, outer court and garden is somewhat less than four acres. With the suggestion that there may have been an earlier garden in this area, it may be that the planting cleared was an element in an overgrown garden, although, as Earl Patrick received the not inconsiderable sum of a thousand pounds Scots for the timber, the trees may have covered a more extensive area. The removal of some of the earlier buildings seems to have caused problems and he underwent 'great censure in the cuntrie' for pulling down that which he had not built, despite the fact, as he writes, that he had to remove the trees and some buildings to carry out improvements. He writes that he did preserve one of the 'dooll trees where they played of old att the foot ball upon the green att the burne syde', another example of the earlier provision for sport close to the mansion, and that the commons did not complain about the destruction of the trees, because they had a natural aversion to all forms of planting. He reckoned that he was only able to preserve

Fig 340 Glamis Castle with its elaborate roofline as it appears on the manuscript map by Timothy Pont in the late sixteenth century. There is some indication of an enclosed garden. Pont 26. © NLS

Fig 341 Glamis Castle in its semi-informal grounds approached by the replanted avenue from the south. SC969737

Fig 342 Aerial view showing the outlines of the gardens and inner court to the south of Glamis Castle emerging as parchmarks. Even the foundations of two of the statue bases can be detected as light marks in the corners of the inner court despite the destruction of the formal gardens in 1773 as a prelude to the creation of a proposed landscape garden. SC516722

his own young plantations because of the punishments he imposed on those he caught deterred other offenders. The deep and broad ditch that enclosed the castle has completely disappeared, as have the other ditches, perhaps including the sixteenth century fish ponds, under the forecourt and gardens. The pends which he put across these ditches were still visible when he was writing in the 1680s (Millar 1890, 39–41).

Earl Patrick described the approaches to Glamis and its immediate surroundings in the following way:

> There be now an entrie from the four severall airths and my house invyroned with a regular planting, the ground on both syds being of a like bigness and the figure the same with a way upon either syd of the utter [outer] court to the back court where the offices are att the north gate the gardners house is apon the on side and the washing and bleatching house on the other with a fair green lying thereto to bleach upon and a walk there is planted which goes round the whole intake, wherein when you are walking you'l behold the water runing in both syds of the planting. And upon the west syd where the river is to make the way accessible from the west I have built a bridge and have cut downe a little hill of sand which I caused carrie to such places as were weat and marish. The utter Court is a spacious green and forenent [to the front] the midle therof is the principal entrie to the south with a gate and gate house besyde two rounds upon each corner, the on is appointed for a Dayrie house and the other for a Still house, and the gate house consists of on roume to the gardine and another to the bouling green, the walls are lined, the roof plaistered, the floor lay'd with black and whyt stone and are verie convenient and refreshful roumes to goe in to from the gardine and Bouling green. Ther is in the gardin a fine dyal erected and howsoon the walk and green plots are layed there will be statu's put into it, and there is a designe for a fountain in the Bouling green and on great gate from the gardine and another from the bouling green to the utter court att the southend of which directlie forenent the gate of the inner court, there is another great gate adorned with two gladiators, from which the avenue goes with an enclosure on each syd holdne with a plantation of fir trees. (Millar 1890, 44) (Fig 344)

The rounds or small towers still survive roofless and the sundial stands at the centre of the paths in the garden as revealed in the parchmarks. The statues, in addition to the gladiators, included four lead figures of Stewart kings by the sculptor Arnold Quellin (Apted 1984), as well as a bust of the earl himself. These were probably originally painted 'after the manner of brass'. The choice of statuary reflects the claims and concerns of

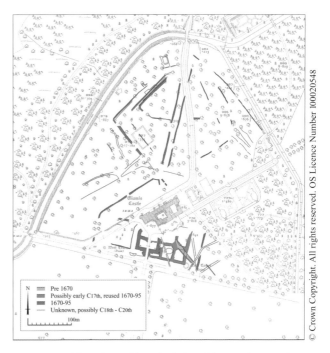

Fig 343 Plan of the gardens at Glamis Castle derived from aerial survey. Most of the visible features belong to the later seventeenth century and Earl Patrick's restoration of his estates. The OS 1:2500 map forms the base for the drawing.

the garden designer, Earl Patrick, and excited comment from travellers visiting Scotland (Stewart 2002, 243). What are probably the bases for two of the statues have been identified on the aerial photographs taken in the summer of 1989 and their form and position are indicated on the RCAHMS plan. Macky describes the balustrades of stone finely adorned with statues (Macky 1729, 140). The picture of the south of the castle from about 1750 by John Elphinstone, preserved in the British Library, shows six statues in the inner court (BL K.top 49, 23.a.5).

The aerial photographs reveal the outlines of the earl's central inner court with what is probably the bowling green to the west and the garden to the east. According to the plan by Thomas Winter of 1746, it was divided into four sections by presumably gravel paths that enclosed what may have been decorated parterres or grass plats (Symes 2000, 93). These were surrounded by walls (McKean 2003, 142). The form of the divisions is simple. The sundial (Somerville 1990, 45) stands in the centre of the garden with what are now two large yew trees in the northern divisions (Robertson 2000, 149), possibly a survival from the planting of the late seventeenth century. It is similar to the arrangement of the yew trees at Prestonfield House in Edinburgh (Tait 1989, 361). The detail of Glamis in the portrait by Jacob de Wet also allows the walls around the inner court and the two flanking gardens to be seen (Fig 347). At both the south-east corner of the garden and at the south-west corner of the bowling green are the rounds which Earl Patrick referred to. They seem to have been designed, as he preferred, to combine use and ornament. The present

Fig 344 The 'fyn dial' purchased by Earl Patrick and set at the centre of his garden to the east of the inner court of Glamis, where it still stands. SC358183

the reuse of the stone might contribute to the absence of evidence; excavation might reveal more in this area. The form of the garden on the east side is considerably clearer with a pattern of four compartments divided by paths on both the aerial photographs and the geophysical plot. The detail which emerged in the reprocessing of the data (Aspinall and Pocock 1995, 63) of what are interpreted as linear dividers in the two southern quarters of the eastern garden cannot be identified from the aerial photographs, where the strong marks resulting from the grass mowing run parallel to the east–west axial avenue and consequently to the cropmarks of the earlier garden.

The elaboration of the entrance to the court, as it appears in the background to the portrait by Jacob de Wet of the earl and his sons (Slade 2000, 40), painted in 1683, can also be detected (Fig 347). This shows a projecting pavilion with a central arch surmounted by a balustrade and a statue of Hercules. This structure is reflected by the triangular parchmarks on the aerial photographs on both sides of the present entrance drive, but not by the interpretation of the geophysical plot. The central section of the parchmark on the entrance wall is broader. The de Wet painting shows a higher section of walling here, again surmounted by a balustrade, and set behind the line of the wall of the court. By 1746, the time of the plan by Thomas Winter and the drawing by Thomas Sandby, the entrance wall was of uniform height, only raised immediately over the arch; the projecting front wall had been removed so that the entrance was inset, presumably resulting in the removal of the wash house and the gardener's house, when it had become unfashionable to have such useful offices on the main approach to the mansion. The line of the path around three sides of the court can be picked out on the aerial photographs as a broad light band, less prominent on the east, where the geophysical evidence is very indistinct.

This creation of a grand and imposing approach to the castle employing order and symmetry to illustrate the owner's domination of the landscape is a feature of late seventeenth century landscape gardening, Versailles being the supreme example. The earl's emphasis on his own personal role in the layout, allied to the perception that his works might have benefited from a professional input, is less usual (Williamson 2000). He stresses the confusion of the earlier layout to the south of the castle.

> All this before mentioned was within the bounds
> of that which you now see is the forecourt where
> the two greens are on each syde of the pav'd walk
> a strange confused unmodel'd piece of business
> and was to me a great eye sore. (Millar 1890, 39)

When he was deciding on the improvements he would make at Glamis, the first step taken by the Earl of Strathmore was the making of a 'skame and draught

structures do not lie at the corners of the parterres as they are visible on the aerial photographs or on the geophysical survey, and it is suggested that they may have been rebuilt at a later date (Aspinall and Pocock 1995, 65).

In the plan of 1746 by Thomas Winter (Figs 345, 346) the east enclosure was referred to as 'The Flower Garden Grass and Gravell' and the western enclosure as 'A sunk Plot of Grass and Boxwork' (Apted 1986, 106). The enclosure to the west, intended for a bowling green, and also referred to as the Fountain Garden, is less distinct than the garden on the east, both on the aerial photographs and on the plot of the geophysical survey, despite the plan showing a similar pattern of paths. This may be due to its original sunken form and the need for a greater depth of material to create a level surface, or, in part, because of the possible presence of infilled ditches in this area (Millar 1890, 39–40). The demolition of the walls of the gardens in 1773 (Apted 1986, 107) and

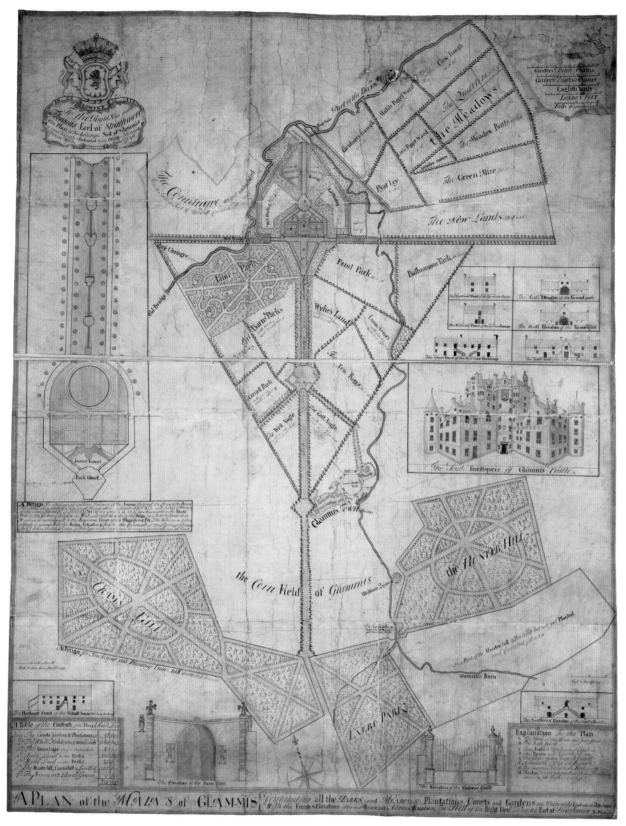

Fig 345 Plan by Thomas Winter of the Mains of Glamis of 1746 demonstrating the strong geometrical layout adopted by Earl Patrick. SC672953 Reproduced by kind permission of the Earl of Strathmore

of my whole project for unless men so doe they will infallibly fall into some mistake, doe that which they will repent ymselves aftr, and be obleidged to pull their own work downe againe. Therefore necessarie it is for a man to desyne all at once (chalk is no sheers, and the desyning hereof does not impose any necessity upon the projector but that he may verie well prosecut his designe by pecemale as he can)' (Millar 1890, 40). He continues:

I confess I am to blame that designing so great a
matter as those reformnes putt all together comes
to, I did not call such as in this age were known
and reput to be the best judges and contrivers, for
I never bestowed neither gold nor mony upon this
head, and I look upon advyce as verie necessarie to
the most part of undertakers, and the not seeking
and taking counsel is commonly the cause why
things are found amiss in the most parte of designs
that way, nor have I the vanity to consider my owne
judgement as another cannot better, yet being
resolved to performe what I have done with little
noice and by degrees, and more to pleas and divert
my selfe then out of any ostentatione, for I thank
God I am as litle envious as any man and am verie
glad to behold things weell ordered and contrived
att other mens dwellings and never Judged anything
of my owne small endeavours worthie to make
so much noice as to call for or invit to either of
my houses skilled publick Architecturs My work
and projects lykways being complexed things and
hardly on man being found fitt to give advyce in all
I never Judged it worth the trouble of a convocation
of the severall artists such as masones who's tallent
commonly lyes within the four walls of a house,
wrights, for the right ordering of a roofe and the
finishing the timber work within, gairdners for
gardens, orchards etc. (Millar 1890, 42)

This might be read as something of an indirect boast
on the earl's part, but it does indicate that, in addition
to the general recognition of the professional skills
of the architect Sir William Bruce, the Mylnes and
Tobias Bauchope, who worked on many of the houses
previously described, gardeners were also seen as
specialists in their field, although an enlightened amateur
such as Earl Patrick could replace them in the design
stages. Because he frequently fell into disputes with his
workmen, he may have been wise to employ as few as
possible. Earl Patrick was not so modest that he did not
take steps to immortalise his achievements, bringing in
Slezer to make a record of his building, possibly in the
late 1670s (Dunbar 2000, 111):

I have indeed been att the charge to imploy on who
is to make a book of the figure of the draughts and
frontispiece in Talyduce [*Tailledouce*, French term
for etching on copper] of all the Kings Castles,
Pallaces, towns, and other notable places in the
Kingdome belonging to privat subjects who's desire
it was att first to me, and who himself passing by
deemed this place worthie of the taking notice
of. And to this man (Mr Sletcher by name) I gave
liberall money because I was Loath that he should
doe it att his owne charge and that I knew the cuts
and ingraving would stand him mony. (Millar
1890, 42)

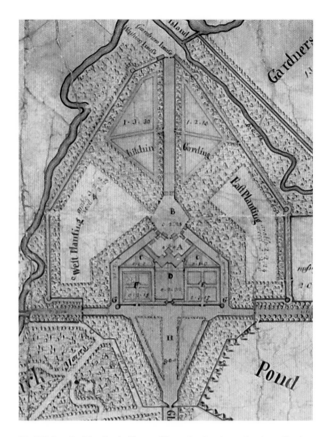

Fig 346 *Detail of the plan by Thomas Winter showing the gardens immediately
around Glamis Castle. SC672953 Reproduced by kind permission of the Earl of
Strathmore*

In 1683 the earl also employed the Dutch artist Jacob
de Wet the Younger, who had produced the portraits of
all Charles II's predecessors as king of Scotland, which
hang in the Palace of Holyroodhouse, to paint himself
and his three sons. Earl Patrick is set against a large
urn and the lower part of a classical pillar, swathed in
drapery, and he points to a depiction of Glamis set in
its courts and gardens in the background (Fig 347). The
image of the castle bears a close resemblance to that
produced by Slezer. This sense of satisfaction with the
results of his work on Castle Lyon and particularly on
Glamis 'inflam'd stronglie with a great desire to continue
the memorie of my familie', emerges from what is an
account of his life in the *Book of Record*. While his
works on the castle resulted in a building which is very
similar to that depicted on the Pont manuscript maps of
the late sixteenth century, his gardens were designed in a
contemporary, classical mode.

Earl Patrick's garden works epitomise some of
the themes which first come clearly into view in later
seventeenth century Scotland. The introduction of
statues into the garden was first noted at Leslie House,
with their inclusion at Thirlestane following soon after.
Hamilton also had statues. At Yester in East Lothian
four stone pedestals for lead statues were purchased
in 1686 from James Smith, who was the overseer of
the Royal Works from 1683, at a cost of £54 16s Scots

(Dunbar 1973, 22). Later in the period, Sibbald, Defoe and Macky record the frequent presence of statues in the gardens of mansions in Scotland (Sibbald 1710a; Macky 1729; Defoe 1968). While the making of dials and their placing in gardens was carried out in Scotland in the earlier seventeenth century, free-standing statues do not appear to have formed part of the ornamentation of gardens. Even in 1708 the presence of statuary could cause adverse and prurient comment. Sir David Dalrymple visited the gardens belonging to the Earl of Mar at Alloa and wrote in a letter to his absent host that he had visited with 'a squadron of pretty women who were no fools and they spok with delight of everything but the filthy naked statues yet I think they must have seen them so near as to know they were naked tho on my conscience they tasted no forbidden fruit' (NRS GD 124/15/897/2). Scottish masons could produce sculpture in the round; the statue of George Heriot, for example, above the entrance to the quadrangle of George Heriot's Hospital was carved by Robert Mylne. Relief sculpture in stone, however, such as is present at Edzell, and often employed for burial monuments, was much more common. Whether there was some specific prejudice against graven images is uncertain.

Daniel Defoe wrote of Glamis:

Glames is, indeed, one of the finest old built Palaces in *Scotland* and by far the largest ... The great Avenue is a full half Mile, planted on either Side with several Rows of Trees; when you come to the outer Gate you are surpris'd with the Beauty and the Variety of the Statues, Busts, some of Stone, some of Brass, some gilded, some plain. The Statues in Brass are four, one of King *James* VI. one of King *Charles* I. booted and spurr'd as if going to take Horse at the Head of his Army: one of Charles II. habited *à la Héro*, which the World knows he had nothing of about him and one of *James* VII. after the Pattern of those at *Whitehall*. (Defoe 1968, 799)

Earl Patrick arranged the purchase of his statues in London, on a visit he made with his eldest son in the autumn of 1685, the year in which James II and VII became king. The earl had travelled to London to seek relief from debts due as a result of his father's actions, but found his six months stay in London yielded no great improvement in his finances, except for an appointment as an Extraordinary Lord of Session with a pension of £300 sterling per year. His account of his costs in London indicates an amount spent of £1500 sterling, but this included the purchase of 'a grate dale of furniture, plate, and statues' (Millar 1890, 91). An agreement was concluded between Earl Patrick and Arnold Quellin, 'Carver', to provide four lead statues of the Stewart kings, each in different dress and posture, and a bust of the earl 'in Clay to the Life'. These were

Fig 347 Detail from the painting of 1683 by Jacob de Wet of Earl Patrick and his three sons showing Glamis Castle, with its inner court flanked to the east by the garden and to the west by the bowling green. Reproduced by kind permission of the Earl of Strathmore

all to be cast in lead and coloured; they were to be packed up and sent by sea, and the total cost was to be £160 sterling (Apted 1984, 53–61). The statues of James VI and Charles I survive at Glamis and the bust of the earl is mounted in a circular recess above the front entrance (Fig 348). Quellin was born in Antwerp in 1653 and was a pupil of Grinling Gibbons. He was esteemed as a sculptor, and the statues for Glamis must have been some of his (or his workshop's) last works for he died in 1686. He was succeeded by John van Nost, his foreman, who married his widow. Van Nost was later a noted producer of garden sculpture, and his works survive widely in England (Symes 1996, 34). The subjects usually chosen for statues at this period would appear to have had either classical or historical significance. The reference to Greco-Roman themes reflects a common culture across Europe, familiar to all visitors. The historical statues would have a more national and personal significance. No major scheme echoing the iconography of Apollo and its reflection of the Sun King, Louis XIV, has been recognised in Scotland, but Earl Patrick's choice of statues of the later Stewart monarchs would declare his family's history of loyalty to the Crown.

To the north of Glamis Castle, beyond the service courts, an elaborate and geometrical layout of kitchen gardens was established, as well as plantations to the east and west of the south avenue. Traces of the boundaries of the kitchen gardens and plantations can be detected from the air at different times of year as parchmarks and as ditches under conditions of low sunlight (Fig 349). The 'Plan of the Mains of Glamis', made by Thomas Winter in 1746 with proposals for additions to the earlier garden, shows, particularly in the area around the castle, the formal landscape as envisioned by Earl Patrick, although not all the details of his plan were achieved before his death in 1695 (Figs 345, 346). The avenues by means of which the mansion would be approached can be seen to north, south, east

Fig 348 Glamis Castle from the south surrounded by lawns with the formal arrangement of inner court and gardens swept away. Two of the statues of the Stewart Kings stand at the beginning of the avenue. SC1018916

Fig 349 Aerial view of the elaborate layout of the kitchen gardens to the north of Glamis Castle. Although the grounds have been informalised, the avenue and the geometrically designed gardens can still be seen as parchmarks. SC969735

and west. This extremely geometric layout was removed in the later eighteenth century. However, the avenue to the south was replanted, probably between 1835 and 1846, when tastes changed yet again (Brown 2005a, 36–7). The avenue to the north emerged in the form of a parchmark in 1989, and, while the avenue running east and west survives in part above ground, the section further to the east can be seen as a cropmark in what are now open fields.

Avenues were one of the most conspicuous features in the policies around country houses, and must have served as a major symbol not only of the extent of the land owned by the proprietor, but, in the light of Earl Patrick's account of the problems he faced in preserving his young trees from the ravages of the commons, of the social control which could be exerted by the landowner (Millar 1890, 41). Earl Patrick wrote with pleasure about the planting of his avenues and his desire to extend them as far as he could (Millar 1890, 46). John Reid's third chapter is devoted to the laying out of avenues and walks; he prefers that the end of an avenue should be out of sight of its beginning, a feature more easily achieved across 'a Brae, then to the eye it appears Infinitum, and where that cannot be had, it doth very well where the sight terminates in a grove or circle of Firrs' (Reid 1988, 15). John Adair's manuscript

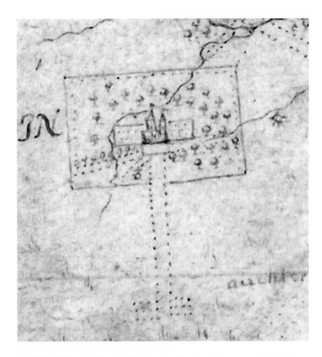

Fig 351 Tullibardine Castle with its enclosed park and avenues as depicted on John Adair's manuscript map of 'Straithern, Stormont, & Cars of Gourie with the rivers Tay and Ern' in Perthshire in 1683 (Adv.MS.70.2.11 (Adair 2)). © NLS

maps of the first half of the 1680s show the spread of avenues around major houses in the areas covered by his more detailed surveys. Kinneil and The Binns in West Lothian, Yester and Lochend in East Lothian, Leuchars and West Wemyss in Fife, and Megginch and

Fig 350 Aerial view of Moncur Castle with the ditches which protected the planting of the trees of the avenues appearing as dark green cropmarks running to the castle. SC672951

Fig 352 Aerial view of the cropmarks of the holes dug for tree planting for the avenue of the demolished House of Nairne. SC1238209

Tullibardine in Perthshire, all of which were houses of nobles and gentry prominent in late Stewart Scotland, display this development, although the numbers of examples on Adair's maps (Figs 286, 306, 351 etc) are a fraction of those depicted on the Military Survey of the mid eighteenth century. Drummond Castle, the home of the Lord Chancellor of Scotland, had long avenues extending from the policies on three sides (Fig 329). Others of lesser status might adopt the fashion: **Moncur Castle** was abandoned after a fire in the early eighteenth century; the cropmarks in the arable fields around it show the lines of the ditches for the avenues radiating from the house (Fig 350). The avenues at Mertoun

Fig 353 Biel with its terraced gardens above the Biel Water as it was depicted on the manuscript map of East Lothian by John Adair in 1682 showing the enclosure wall, the tree planting and the gardens around the house. Adv. MS.70.2.11 (Adair 10) © NLS

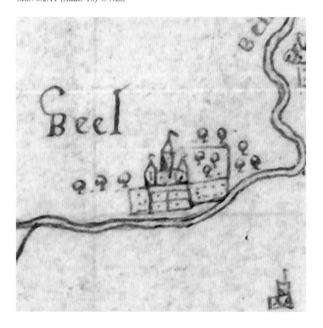

House in Berwickshire can be seen in what is now an informal landscape in front of the present mansion. Some of the actual pits dug for the planting of the trees may be visible from the air, for example at Taymouth Castle and House of Nairne in Perthshire (Fig 352).

As in the later sixteenth and earlier seventeenth centuries, terraces formed an important element in garden design, and many of them are difficult to date with precision. Reid mentions two forms of terrace: those which are supported or retained by vertical walls and those formed by sloping banks. Each would have a walk along its length. The planting he favoured for the former was to have trees grown against the wall and low bushes, such as laurels, on the other side of the path. For the other type, borders would be planted on both sides of the walk; cherries would be appropriate there; on the sloping banks themselves violets, strawberries and grass should be grown (Reid 1988, 30–31). The late seventeenth century examples are, on the whole, steeper and higher than those created earlier.

The gardens at Leslie, Drummond and Hatton with their elaborate terraces have already been referred to. The terraces at **Biel** in East Lothian exemplify a type of terraced garden which was favoured in the later seventeenth century (Fig 354). Adair's map of East Lothian of 1682 (NLS Adv.MS.70.2.11 (Adair 10)) shows the terraced and other gardens there, and they appear with more accuracy on the estate plans of about 1700, which are some of the earliest in Scotland (Figs 353, 355). The inset detail of the house and garden shows the terraces below and to the south of the house, edged by conical trees. There is an enclosure below the terraces which is also planted with conical trees set out in squares. The form of these trees on the estate plan might suggest that they have been cut into shape, perhaps an example of topiary, although an orchard might have been expected in this position. Between the terraces and this area of tree planting was a narrow canal with two bridges providing access. To the south of the area of tree planting the Biel Water had been straightened into a channel running east and west. To the east and west of the terraced garden were grassed walks bordered with trees. The presence of the Biel Water encouraged the incorporation of water features into the garden; There was, for instance, a circular pond to the west, surrounded by grass and perhaps shrubs. A canal was constructed running east and west through the garden, with parallel walks beside it. On the eastern side of the garden it first narrowed and then widened to form a more ornamental water feature, bordered with grass walks and plantations of trees closely set out in a quincunx pattern. An avenue still leads to the house from the north, and rectangular fields, or rather enclosed parks for grazing cattle, were laid out parallel to this avenue to the north and south of the house. This created a contrast with the earlier irregular field patterns to the south.

Fig 354 Aerial view of the long terraces at Biel House. SC1246148

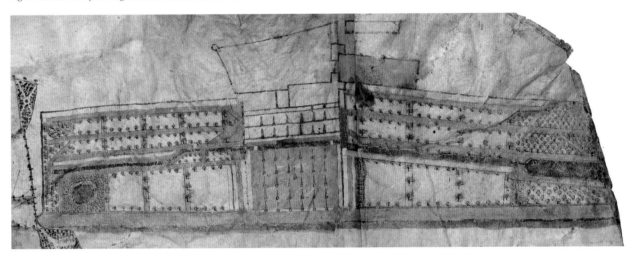

Fig 355 Detail of the house and garden of Biel from a manuscript plan of about 1700 of the estate of Biel showing the terraces, water features and planting. SC1217467

Fig 356 Presmennan with its enclosed park and gardens as it appears on the manuscript map of East Lothian by John Adair in 1682 showing the enclosure wall, the tree planting and the gardens around the house. Adv.MS.70.2.11 (Adair 10) © NLS

The owner of Biel at this time was John Hamilton, who had married the granddaughter of another John Hamilton, first Lord Belhaven and Stenton. He was the eldest son of Robert Hamilton, Lord Presmennan, a judge in the Court of Session, and grandson of James Hamilton of Barncluith in Lanarkshire. This John Hamilton's house at Presmennan, with its twin towers, is given considerable prominence on Adair's map, where it is shown surrounded by parterres and walks as well as by one of the largest woods in the county. Robert Hamilton died in 1695 and, by the time the estate plan was surveyed, his house had lost its prominence, since it was no longer occupied by the landowner, although the plantations had increased considerably and the formal arrangement of trees to the north of the house had survived (Fig 356). Both of these Hamiltons were connected with the dukes of Hamilton and the wider network of related Hamilton families. Biel House with its terraces, clipped trees and the canal was painted by James Norie in grisaille probably in the 1740s (Holloway 1989, 65).

At some time before 1685 another John Hamilton was owner of **Barncluith**, a small estate described about 1710 as 'belonging to Hamilton of Barncluth; situate upon the water of Aven, very near to the entrie of the great parks of Hamilton; a pleasant place with

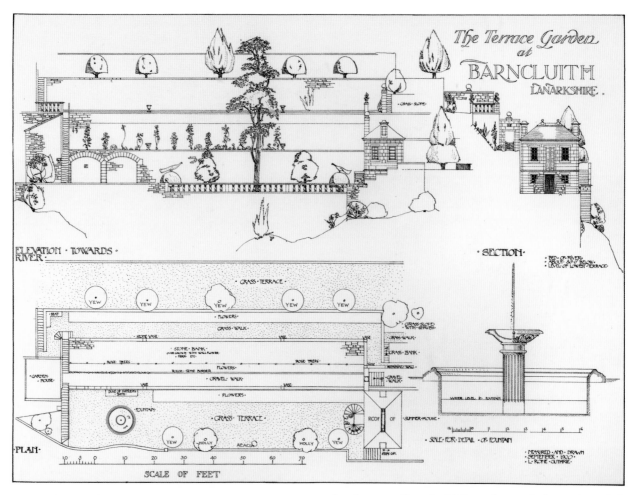

Fig 357 A plan, section and elevation of the terraced gardens at Barncluith in 1900. The garden was the subject of interest to travellers and tourists from the eighteenth to the twentieth century and, while the planting has changed and various items from Hamilton Palace sales have been incorporated, the garden would seem always to have been valued (Triggs 1900, 174).

Fig 358 A much magnified detail from the large plan of the parks and gardens of Hamilton Palace surveyed by Alexander Edward in 1708 showing the buildings, gardens and terraces at Barncluith. It was described as 'very Romantick' by Macky in the early eighteenth century (Macky 1729, 281). SC750221

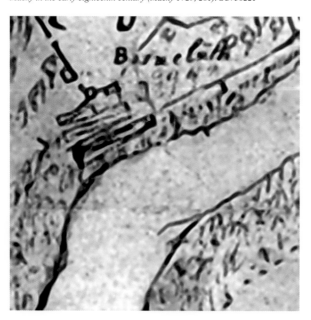

fine terras walkes, fruitfull gardens and pleasant woods' (Hamilton 1831, 17). This is the first known reference to the gardens there which came to be a regular stop on the circuit for travellers visiting Scotland from the early eighteenth to the twentieth century (Macpherson 1862, 64) (Fig 357). These gardens are dramatically placed on the steep bank of the River Avon. Below the level of the tower, which has been dated to the sixteenth century, and the mainly nineteenth century house are now five narrow terraces. These are linked by staircases, and there is an elaborate summer house and a garden house at the ends of two of the terraces (Figs 358, 359). The level garden which lies adjacent to and at an angle to both house and tower, is distinguished by yew trees that are cut into elaborate shapes. Macky probably visited the area in the early eighteenth century, and certainly prior to 1723, and describes Barncluith as a kind of appendage to Hamilton Palace:

> Joining to the great Park is a very Romantick garden, call'd Baroncleuh, which consists of seven hanging Terras-Walks, down to a River Side, with a wild Wood full of Birds on the opposite Side of the River: In some of those Walks, are Banquetting-Houses, with Walks and Grotto's, and all of them fill'd with large Ever-greens, in the Shapes of Beasts and Birds. (Macky 1729, 281)

Fig 359 A view along the terraces and one of the garden buildings at Barncluith taken about 1900 illustrating their narrow but substantial nature. The yew trees in the upper garden may survive from the seventeenth century (Triggs 1902, 175).

John Hamilton of Barncluith held various offices in Lanarkshire in the Hamilton interest (RPS 1685/4/128 etc) including Sheriff Depute of the Lower Ward of Clydesdale (Hamilton 1831, 2), and in 1692 was godfather to Lord Basil Hamilton's son William at the parish church of Hamilton (Marshall 1973, 121). There have been several restorations and some reshaping of the garden over the centuries, but it still retains its basic plan. Visitors included Sir Walter Scott, William and Dorothy Wordsworth, and William Cobbett, all of whom were enthusiastic and valued the garden for its 'old world charm'. The garden at Barncluith is a remarkable creation. Its survival may be owing to the non-residence of its owners during the later eighteenth century and the occupation of the house by tenants, which may have led to repair and maintenance, but not to a full scale redesign. Macky's reference to the garden as 'very Romantick', as though it were not in

the current taste, might suggest an earlier date than the later seventeenth century. James Hamilton, who died in 1632, might in that case have been its creator. It might also have been established by his son, Quentin Hamilton, who held the castle of Avondale for Charles II in 1651 and lost more than £10,000 in payments for the garrison, which his widow and children sought to recover after the Restoration. As a result of his actions on behalf of the king, his estate is said to be 'much crazed' (RPS 1661/1/394). In the absence of accounts of the gardens before 1710, or more details of the individuals who owned the property, it would be difficult to assign Barncluith with its late seventeenth pavilions to the same period as Elibank or Whytbank, although the origins of the garden may lie in the earlier seventeenth or even the late sixteenth century.

There are other examples of gardens that have utilised terraces above steep grass slopes and these seem more likely to belong to the later seventeenth century, not only from the association with the building or reconstruction of the house to which the garden belongs, but also from the presence of potential

Fig 360 Aerial view of the terraced garden at Neidpath Castle in drought conditions. Between 1682 and 1686 Robert Inglis and Thomas Boyd were employed to construct terraced walks linked by steps. SC937339

patrons and from documentary evidence. However, the division is far from clear-cut. The terraces at **Neidpath Castle** above the River Tweed near Peebles provide a well-preserved example of this type (Figs 360, 361). The gardens lie to the east and south of the castle; on the east side there are three broad terraces, the middle one of which is now occupied by the track to the castle from the Peebles to Lanark road. This terrace widens to the south as it approaches the castle and there are the remains of a small building, which may have been a garden house or dovecot, perched on a rocky bank. A further series of four narrower terraces extends down the slope below this terrace and the forecourt of the castle; these were formerly enclosed by a wall on three sides. The 'gairdene of neidpath' was recorded in 1581 (RCAHMS 1967, 259) but it seems more likely that the surviving earthworks belong to a later date. The gardens are noted in the

early eighteenth century as 'a sloping Parterre in good order, and three or four pretty Terraces, betwixt the house and the water' (Pennicuik 1815, 271). Building work was being carried out there from the later 1660s until about 1686 when John Hay, second Earl of Tweeddale and owner of Yester, sold the estate to the Duke of Queensberry who passed it to his second son, the Earl of March. Neidpath had never been the main residence of the Hay family. Between 1682 and 1686 Robert Inglis and Thomas Boyd were employed to construct terraced walks linked by steps, together with a summer house (Cruft *et al* 2006, 581). The work was under the direction of James Bain, Principal Master-Wright to the Crown, who was at the same time engaged on the building of Panmure House in Angus and Holyrood (RCAHMS 1967, 261). The head of a lectern sundial, incorporating numerous individual dials, some of which are of sunk geometric form, is preserved within the castle. There were extensive plantations of poplar, beech and fir around Neidpath, which were the work of the Earl of Tweeddale and the Earl of March.

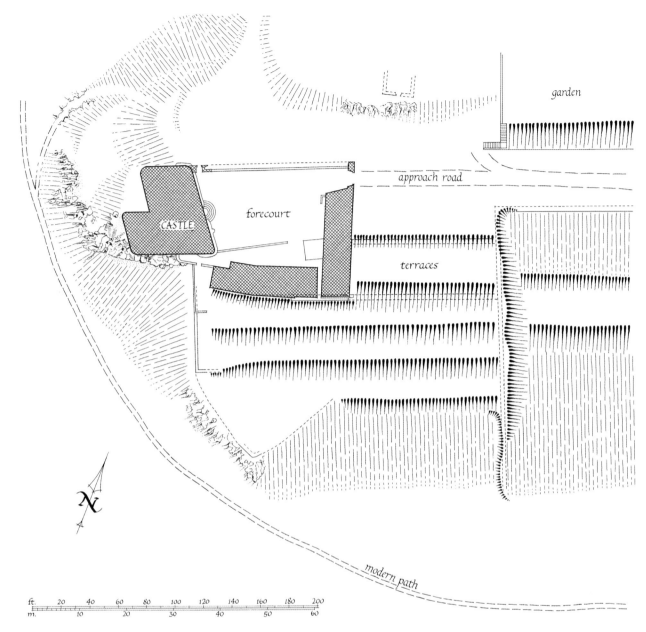

Fig 361 Plan of Neidpath Castle and its terraced garden from Peeblesshire.
An Inventory of the Ancient Monuments *Fig 256 (RCAHMS 1967). DP071193*

Another terraced garden, probably belonging to
the same period, is that at **Hangingshaw** in Yarrow.
From a broad terrace in front and to the south of the
earlier house, a staircase descends into the walled
garden where there are two further narrower terrace
walks running parallel above a level rectangular garden,
probably set out with flower beds where there is now a
central pool. Holly and yew trees were planted along
the terraces. In the early eighteenth century when
Hangingshaw belonged to John Murray, the heritable
sheriff of Selkirkshire, it was described as 'a very good
house with orchards parks and planting' (Macfarlane
1906–08, 1, 359). The Military Survey of 1747 to 1755
shows the mansion centrally placed above the terraced
gardens with plantations to the north intersected by

geometrically planned avenues. What may have been an
orchard and a kitchen garden, judging from the pattern
of planting, lay on either side of the central garden.
Long avenues ran to the north and south. The garden
appears to have been restored and extended before the
survey carried out for the Ordnance Survey First Edition
map in 1858 (Figs 362, 363).

Clackmannan Tower stands on a prominent
ridge overlooking the burgh of Clackmannan and the
upper reaches of the Firth of Forth from the summit of
King's Seat Hill (Fig 365). It dates from the fourteenth
century and was formerly in the possession of the kings
of Scotland, when the Exchequer Rolls record the
produce of the apple orchard (*ER* 1, 223, 571). During
the seventeenth century (and earlier) there were many
modifications to the tower, but the principal residence
of the family until 1791 was the adjoining mansion,
which has now been completely demolished (*Stat Acct*

1791–97, 14, 635). It is depicted standing to the west of the tower in a drawing by David Allan of 1782 (Fig 366). The house, with its crow stepped gables, was probably built in the seventeenth century. This would be an appropriate date for the gardens, which survive as earthworks (Fig 364). Immediately to the south of the tower is a level platform, probably a bowling green (RCAHMS 1933, 316), from which a scarp descends to a level enclosed garden. It is defined by banks to east and west and by a scarp slope to the south, which measures about 50m north and south by 40m and a path leads down from the level of the tower. Immediately to the west of the tower, and including the place where the mansion house formerly stood, is a level terrace some 125m east and west by up to 55m, defined by scarp slopes. Traces of stonework at its north-east corner suggest some form of building there. Below this garden, to the south, are three terraces extending down the hill, two broad with a narrow walk between. The terraces are now linked by a path at their west end. This whole area, with the exception of the fenced portion around the tower, has been in agricultural use for the last two centuries. To the west of the tower are a series of four walled rectangular enclosures which, on the Ordnance Survey First Edition 6-inch map surveyed in 1861–3, were labelled 'Nursery' and planted with small trees. The 'Nursery' may have been an orchard belonging to the tower.

Fig 362 The formal garden at Hangingshaw with its terraces to the north on the First Edition of the Ordnance Survey 6-inch map of Selkirkshire surveyed in 1858.

Fig 363 Hangingshaw with its terraced gardens on Roy's Military Survey of 1747 to 1755. © British Library Licensor Scran

Like Clackmannan, **Airth Castle** in Stirlingshire on the south side of the Forth belonged to a branch of the Bruce family from the middle of the fifteenth until the late seventeenth century (Fig 367). The property passed through the female line before being sold in 1717 to James Graham, Judge-Admiral of Scotland. Four years later he commissioned a survey of the policies, along with plans for their embellishment in a more modern

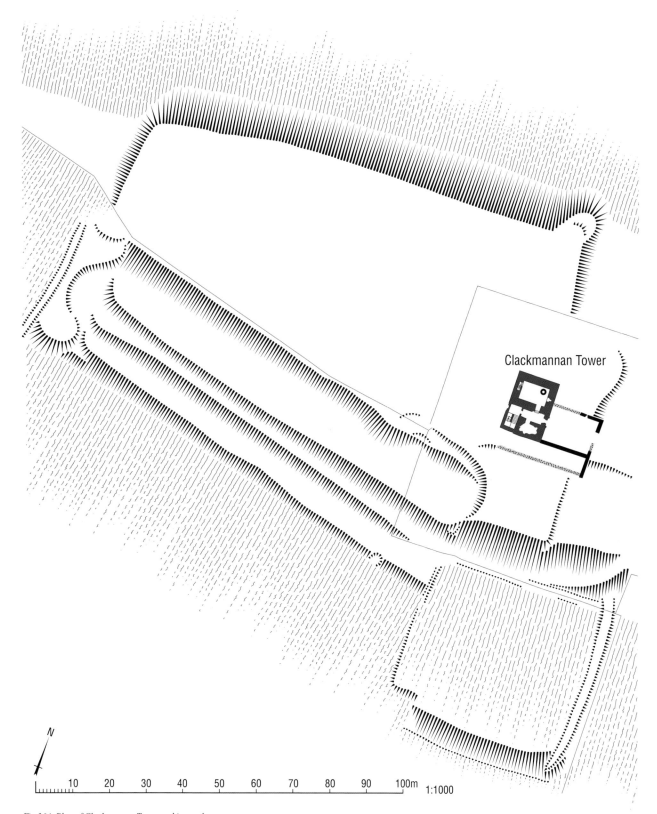

Clackmannan Tower

N

10 20 30 40 50 60 70 80 90 100m 1:1000

Fig 364 Plan of Clackmannan Tower and its garden terraces

taste from William Boutcher (Fig 368), and a plan and elevation of Airth House was prepared by William Adam (RCAHMS 1963, 230–7). The survey purports to be 'exact' and shows three terraces, supported by vertical walls, edged with alternating trees and shrubs, lying to

the south of the castle. A bowling green may have lain to the east of the upper terrace. These terraces, or their replacements, survive today. To the west of the lowest terrace and on the same alignment is a small rectangular walled enclosure with trees planted within the walls, labelled 'kitchen ground for early peas'. Below this is

Fig 365 Aerial view of Clackmannan Tower from the east looking along the terraces below and beyond the castle. SC732202

a long canal with semi-circular ends and an exedra on the south side in alignment with the centre of the house and with the avenue to the south. It runs through a plantation laid out partly in a strongly geometric design and partly in wilderness fashion, that is with curving paths through the trees. To the north-west of the house is a walled garden divided into four by grass paths edged with trees, which meet in a circle at its centre. This would be an appropriate site for the facet-headed sundial dated to 1690 (RCAHMS 1963, 237), whose present whereabouts is not known. In front of the castle were symmetrically arranged lawns, while immediately to the east of the castle is the ruin of the church which, on the plan, is set in a rectilinear enclosure edged with trees, as it still survives. Geometrically designed avenues and enclosures with geometrically planted trees extend to north, south and west. The castle sits on a hill and, apart from the area immediately round the house, the garden has been converted to farmland. The more elaborate design, with its obelisk, bastions, its fire walls for vines and other early fruit, and curving water features, was put forward in 1721 and was probably never carried out (see Fig 428).

The importance of the planting of trees was recognised in the later seventeenth century, as in earlier periods, both as an adornment to an estate and as a source of future income. It was also seen to be a

contribution to the good of Scotland as a nation. Reid devoted a considerable part of his book to the subject of the planting of forest trees, and considered the subject as lying within the province of the gardener (Reid 1988, 74) (Fig 369). An estate which was recognised as one of the most prominent examples of the practice of making plantations was **Tyninghame House** in East Lothian,

Fig 366 Drawing of Clackmannan Tower in 1782 by David Allan with the seventeenth century house to which the terraces were probably related visible beyond the tower. SC723818

Fig 367 Aerial view of Airth Castle, its terraces and the site of the former gardens from the north. DP032621

which belonged to the Hamiltons, earls of Haddington, and distant relatives of the ducal family. The estate was purchased in 1628 by the first Earl of Haddington who had been one of the Octavians and later President of the Court of Session and Secretary of State. These posts required regular visits to James VI's court in London. The earliest conversation piece known to be painted in Scotland and showing a family, was by George Jamesone. It was commissioned for the second Earl and

may have been painted in 1637, the year in which he succeeded to the earldom (Thomson 1974, 123–4). The background shows a garden with trees and a fountain and while it is improbable that it portrays any actual scene, it does provide a pointer to the interests of the artist's patron. The mother of the sixth Earl was Lady Margaret Leslie, daughter and heiress of the Duke of Rothes. The sixth Earl married his cousin, Helen Hope, the daughter of John Hope of Hopetoun and sister of Charles, first Earl of Hopetoun. Helen Hope's interest in planting is believed to have strongly influenced developments on the estate of Tyninghame.

After his mother inherited the Rothes earldom
in 1680, the family moved to Leslie in Fife and the
Tyninghame estates were let for nineteen years, leading
to their neglect. The garden, which may have been
terraced, was damaged. The sixth earl's handbook *Forest
trees: some directions about raising forest trees* (dated
from Tyninghame in 1733) was published posthumously
in 1761 as *Treatise on the manner of Raising Forest
Trees* and in it he describes the scene at Tyninghame
(Hamilton 1954):

> They pulled up the hedges, plowed down the
> banks and let the drains fill up ... my wife was a
> great lover of planting, she did what she could
> to engage me to it, but in vain. At last she asked
> leave to go about it, which she did; and I was
> much pleased with some little things that were
> both well laid and executed, though none of them
> are now to be seen; for when the designs grew
> more extensive, we were forced to take away
> what was first done.

He comments that:

> The first marquis of Tweeddale, my Lord
> Rankeilor, Sir William Bruce and my father,
> with some others, had planted a great deal;
> yet I will be bold to say, that planting was not
> well understood in this country till this century
> began. I think it was the late Earl of Mar that
> first introduced the wilderness way of planting
> amongst us, and very much improved the tastes
> of our gentlemen, who very soon followed his
> example. (Chalmers 1824, 3, 489–90)

Adair's manuscript map of 1682 (NLS Adv.MS.70.2.11
(Adair 10)) shows the garden lying to the west of the
house, divided into four sections by paths, with what
is probably an orchard to the north and another walled
garden to the south (Fig 370). These were all enclosed
within a rectangular walled park, edged with trees.
Macky describes the 'great Additions and Improvements
made by this present Earl. Many Millions of Trees hath
he planted in a sandy Down or Links, as they call them
here, between his House and the Sea, and they thrive
mightily. He hath also laid out several Avenues through
his Park, which when full grown, will be as noble as
any in Britain' (Macky 1729, 26). The Military Survey
of 1747 to 1755 shows the layout of the avenues and
plantations, which have subsequently been replanted on
several occasions, but the design can still, for the most
part, be recognised at the present day (Figs 371, 372).

The most prominent architect in post-Restoration
Scotland was as previously discussed Sir William Bruce.

*Fig 368 A survey made by William Boutcher in 1721 of Airth with its parterres,
terraces, canal, plantations and winding wilderness walks. DP090704*

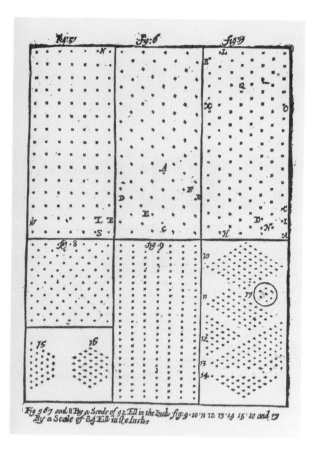

Fig 369 A variety of patterns for tree plantations from John Reid's The Scots
Gard'ner *(Reid 1988).*

His position in the 1670s as Overseer of the Royal
Works was the only official recognition of his skills,
but his designs and his influence affected the creation
and rebuilding of many of the foremost buildings in
Scotland between the 1660s and his death in 1710 and
beyond. His early career in the years leading up to the
Restoration took him abroad. He is said to have played

*Fig 370 Tyninghame House in its walled park before the creation of the
extensive plantations as it appears on the manuscript map of East Lothian by
John Adair in 1682. Adv.MS.70.2.11 (Adair 10) © NLS*

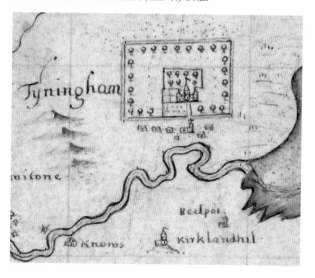

Fig 372 Tyninghame House with its plantations as depicted on Roy's Military Survey of 1747 to 1755. © British Library Licensor Scran

a part in bringing General Monk over to the Royalist cause in 1659, and the existence of a passport for Bruce signed by Monk certainly suggests that he may have been concerned in the negotiations which preceded the Restoration; it permitted Bruce 'to passé about his occasions on this side the Fryth (of Forth) & other parts of Scotland', but also refers to his impending 'returne to Holland' where Charles II was living in exile (Walker 1990, 74). Shortly after the Restoration he was knighted, and under the patronage of Lauderdale received various offices, such as commissioner of excise in Fife, that gave him a regular income, which enabled him to buy the estate of Balcaskie and in 1675 that of **Kinross** (Fenwick 1970, 26) (Fig 373). He saw himself as an architect and his portrait of 1664 by John Michael Wright (Stevenson and Thompson 1982, 66–7) shows him in this guise (Fig 281). With the death of Charles II he fell out of favour and lost his public employments. Despite the fact that he had lost his offices under James II, he was believed to be a Jacobite sympathiser, and during subsequent reigns spent time in prison. From 1686 he was able to turn his attention to his estates and to the completion of his house and gardens at Kinross, although with the loss of his salaries and pensions he was always straitened for money for his works and their upkeep. Numerous accounts of his personal expenditure indicate his interests in gardening, music and painting, and he owned books published in French and Italian, as well as in Latin and Greek; he appears also to have had a reading knowledge of German and Dutch (Colvin 1995, 173–4).

Three contemporary plans of the house, garden and estate at Kinross have been attributed to the hand of Alexander Edward, because of the similarity to that

employed on a design for the gardens and policies at Hamilton dated to 1708 where he includes his name in the dedication (see Fig 397). Alexander Edward was born in 1651, the eldest son of Robert Edward, the minister of Murroes in Angus, who enjoyed the patronage of the earls of Panmure, owners of Panmure House, where the influence of William Bruce has been detected (McKean, 2001, 252). Robert Edward was interested in astronomy, dialling and cartography. Alexander Edward became minister of Kemback, situated between Cupar and St Andrews, in 1682 and was dispossessed in 1689 as a result of the 'Glorious Revolution' of 1688 and the subsequent establishment of Presbyterianism in Scotland, although he seems to have kept possession of the manse until 1694. In 1677 he had listed the books he had purchased since 1670. Although much of his reading was theology, he had also purchased Leonard Meager's *The English Gardener* and Charles Etienne's *Libellus de re Hortensi* in 1674, and in 1678 he bought Evelyn's *The French Gardener* bound with John Rose's *The English Vineyard Vindicated*. In the same notebook were notes on the making of a sundial and, in the hand of his brother John, notes on a surveying instrument called the Graphometer. Another notebook from this period includes detailed practical notes on painting. There was a long gap between Edward's graduation from St Andrews University in 1670 and his ordination to the ministry in 1679, and it may be that he was considering an alternative career, perhaps in architecture, rather than the family involvement in the Church. He was in contact with Sir Robert Sibbald and was to be one of the contributors to his proposed descriptive atlas of Scotland. He seems to have become friendly with Sibbald, and through him met James Sutherland, Intendant of the Physic Garden (Lowrey 1987, 17–18).

In 1685 Edward was involved with Bruce in the drawing of plans of the house, the gardens and the wider estate at Kinross, the first evidence of his concern with

Fig 373 An aerial view of Kinross House from the north-west illustrating its relationship to Lochleven Castle. SC702473

the layout of gardens, undertaken at a time when he was in possession of a parish with financial security (Lowrey 1987, 4–8). Bruce chose the site for his mansion at Kinross on land to the south of the old house of the Douglases, where he himself stayed during the building works. It was one of relatively few projects where he had the opportunity to design a new building, and to a degree select the site for the garden. The surviving plans allow much of the detail of the garden to be described, and they were followed, to a large extent, when the gardens were recreated between 1902 and 1908 (Triggs 1902, 177; RCAHMS 1933, 299) (Figs 374, 375). Bruce laid out the house and garden in a strict axial relationship aligned on the castle of Loch Leven, where Mary

Queen of Scots had been imprisoned. On the plan of the grounds 'points the castle' is written at the harbour for the barge in front of the Fish Gate which was placed on the centre line of the house, and on the plan of the gardens '2000 foots to the Castle in the Loch'. This recalls Bruce's focusing of the gardens at Balcaskie on the Bass Rock, and it was followed by the incorporation of historic sites and notable natural features in the layout of gardens in Scotland. The whole house and garden was tied into the landscape. Bruce had one of the turrets of Loch Leven Castle repaired in 1690, enhancing the prospect (Walker 1990, 11). The house stands at the centre of the garden, approximately a double square, which was approached from the burgh of Kinross to the west by means of an avenue 1434 feet long, lined with rows of trees. What is marked as the 'new kitchen garden' lies near the west end of the avenue, an early

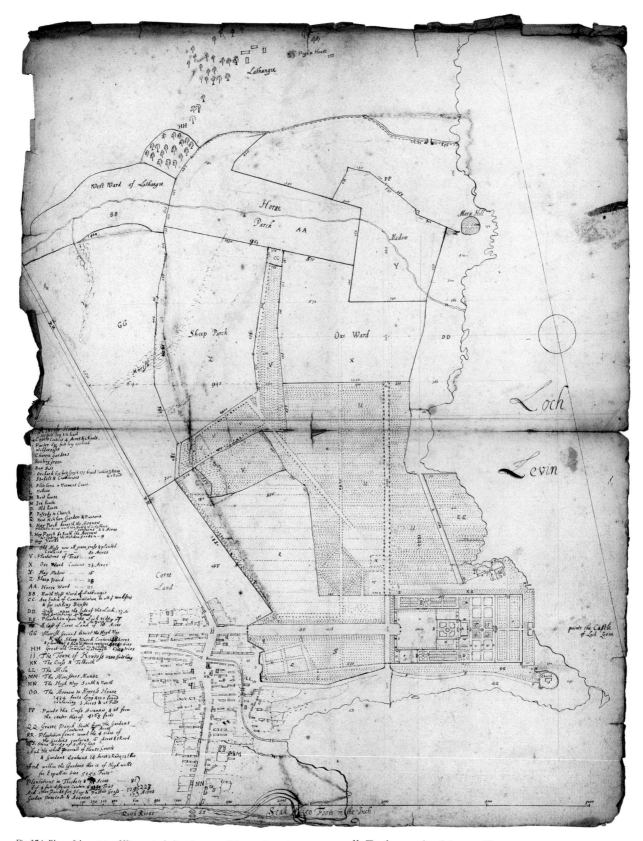

Fig 374 Plan of the estate of Kinross including the town of Kinross drawn by Alexander Edward. © Sir Robert Clerk, Penicuik House. SC1238201

example of the separation of the more workaday garden from the house. A gate opened into a large outer court with stables and coach houses immediately inside the

wall. To the south of these offices were 'bow butts', a feature frequently a part of gardens in the sixteenth and early seventeenth centuries, especially in royal palaces, but uncommon at this time. Its inclusion may reflect the revival of interest in archery, with the establishment of the Royal Archers in 1676 with its stress on loyalty and

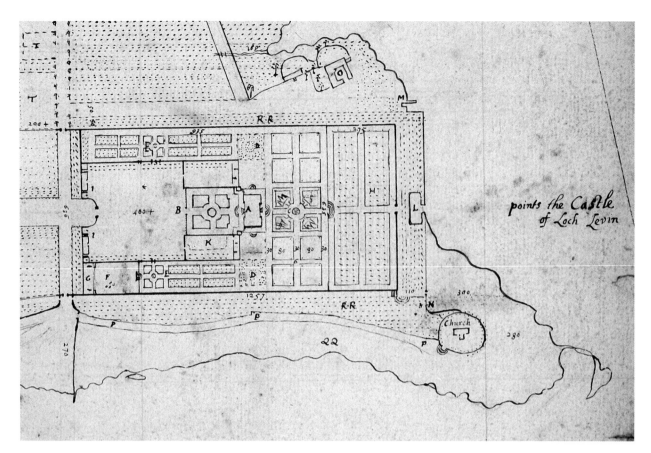

Fig 375 Detail from the plan of Kinross showing the house, court and garden. © Sir Robert Clerk, Penicuik House. SC1238201

patriotism (Cherry 1987, 100). A bowling green, entered through an arch in its east wall, lay next to it. On both sides of the court along its north and south sides were double rows of trees shielding the walls of the 'cherrie garden plotts' with 'litle flour plots' dividing them on their long axis and broad walks all around. Immediately in front of the house was the inner court, with broad cross walks separated by walls from the kitchen and women's courts on either side. Little flower gardens lay to north and south of the house with what are described as wildernesses beyond. The flower gardens are marked out with twelve beds, each row of three set at right angles to its neighbour. The wildernesses, the same size as the flower plots, have a more elaborate design, possibly formed from gravel paths, which if planted with trees rather than bushes between them, would have rapidly become overgrown.

The house was surrounded by a terrace from which semi-circular steps led down to the parterres to the east, the more private part of the gardens. The main entrance to the house on the first floor opens into a panelled entrance hall: behind lies the drawing room, originally the 'Garden Hall', from which there is access to the garden (RCAHMS 1933, 301. The central feature was a basin with a 'jaddo', *jet d'eau*, or fountain surrounded by grass parterres in an unusual design. The parterres on both sides were of grass with a tree planted at each

corner, the whole surrounded by broad straight walks (Fig 376). At the terminations of the central cross walks were two seats 'with Dorik pillars' or summer houses. A further set of steps leads down to the four orchard plots set on either side of the central walk leading from the house to the elaborate Fish Gate and the harbour for the barge. The owners of Kinross could enjoy the delights of a much larger sheet of water than was available in the most extensive gardens, as well as the fish for which the shallow Loch Leven was famous. The whole garden is protected by stone walls, and serried ranks of trees lie outside these on all sides, providing an external framework, and perhaps reflecting contemporary French practice. The high walls, suitable for espalier trees, extended to 5,150 feet. Just beyond the south-east corner of the garden in the direction of the old church was the 'amphitheater banck' with its three tiers, an unidentified lozenge-shaped garden and the ice house. Further plantations lay on the north and east sides of the garden, with parks for sheep and horses and meadows beyond. The stone for the two Doric seats or summer houses set against the north and south walls of the 'grass garden' was quarried in 1683 (Walker 1990, 23). The ice house, along with the 'lettel fouls house that stands in the orchard', was roofed with turf in 1686 (Walker 1990, 27).

The garden at Kinross both epitomised and transcended the Scottish gardens of the later seventeenth century. It was 'Admyred by everie bodie' even before its completion (Dunbar 1970, 65). A letter to Bruce dated October 1687 concludes, 'I hear Lady Lauderdale's

Fig 376 Kinross House from the east. The pool was the site of the 'jaddo' or fountain. SC1029102

gardens at Ham, are but a wilderness to be compared to yours at Kinross', and Sibbald described the house as 'a stately building which for situation, contrivance, prospects, avenues, courts, gardens, gravel-walks and terraces, and all hortulane ornaments, parks and plantings is surpassed by few in this country' (Sibbald 1803, 275). The garden was begun certainly before the house. In 1683 Tobias Bauchop contracted to build the garden and orchard dykes, and Mungo Wallace was working on the two summer houses against the north and south walls of the garden (Walker 1990, 23). The establishment of a garden of this scale required considerable understanding of the existing soil conditions, and a radical approach, removing soil and bringing in more fertile earth, was adopted.

Letters, quoted by Walker (1990), provide useful information on the way in which the contents of a garden designed to impress might be acquired, and what arrangements were in place to ensure their survival. Plans had already been made to stock the garden. When William Bruce's son, John, travelled to France in 1681 to study in Paris, he was accompanied by a well-educated relative of his mother, Dr James Halkett, and they were charged to buy and send back materials for the garden at Kinross. Letters relating to this *petit tour* give an impression of the buildings and gardens, as well as the studies, considered to be worthwhile for the

heir to a Scottish estate. Study in Paris was followed by a visit to Belgium and Holland and a return in 1683 via London, where he was to 'kiss the King's and Prince's hands'. Fortification and design were included in his education; he wrote to his father in 1682, 'I have sent you a piece of design such as it is, for I have left it off now more than these two months, because I have no spare time for it and that is a thing I may come to by myself ...' He visited Versailles as well as the chateaux of Chantilly and Liancourt, and travelled to Angers, Blois, La Rochelle, Poitiers, Chatellerault, Richelieu, Tours, Orleans and Chambéry, a list that gives an idea of what was considered an appropriate experience. Among the letters from his tutor are references to the seeds and trees which William Bruce had requested them to acquire. In November Halkett wrote:

Your son has provided some shrubs, roots, seeds and horse chestnuts which I am to get next week and shall send for Scotland with a ship that is daylie expected at Roanne [Rouen]... The roots, seeds, etc, I wrote of I cannot possiblie get till next week. I believe they will come to 10 crowns.

John Bruce himself wrote from Paris:

Therefore we went to Monsieur Marcian, Intendant of the Physic Garden with whom Dr Halket was acquainted before, who is a very discreet man and knows where such things are to be had ... for Horse Chestnuts you may have both the trees and the nuts, but he advises you to take none of the nuts for they are very ready to go back. He says for Juliflowers you can have no sets, for it is a flower that doth not grow very well here. But you may have the seed, but he says he will not be answerable that they will produce the right flower. He says you may have the Cardinal's flower, but that it is very hard to be brought up. For ever-green trees I cannot give you an account as yet, for I have not been in many of the fine gardens yet, but in my next letter I shall write you a particular account of the prices ...' 'I have sent you a parcel of the prettiest plants I could find and what I judged most proper for our country. There is anemones here at the rate of 4 pistoles apiece, but they are so delicat that they would do no good with us.

On his journey into Holland he visited Chantilly, Cambray, Valenciennes and Engien, the property of the prince of Aremberg, where he noted 'the walks and hedges which are the prettiestly cut and in the best order that can be' (Walker 1990, 62–8).

James Shanks was principal gardener at Kinross and was resident there from 1675 when Sir William Bruce bought the estate. He received £62 Scots plus six bolls and two firlots of meal a year; his assistants, of which there were three or four, had twenty merks the half year, a similar quantity of meal, and a pair of shoes; weeders in the gardens, usually boys, were paid from two pence to four pence per day (Walker 1990, 18). It was most likely James Shanks who planted out the various special shrubs and flowers despatched from Paris. Dr Halkett sent instructions, writing probably late in 1681:

In the box there are first two bundles of ane evergreen shrub the roots bound up in two pieces of cloath with earth about them; each bundle contains 3 plants which so soon as they come to your hand you must separate neatly ane from another ... and set them in six earthen pots with good earth about them. When it is very cold cause take them into the house. They will begin to flower so soon as they are planted, there must be nothing also done to them till next harvest. The Latin name of the shrub is Laurus Sylvestris Soho Minore. The French name is Lauride Fin. It is very much esteemed in France because when it has once taken well with the earth it flowers all the year.
The other six roots bound up within six pieces of cloath must be planted in well-made earth in six of the best places of your parterre so soon as they arrive and covered with halfe a foot thick of straw because of the cold. It is a tall plant and

carries tufts of pretty scarlet flowers. The Latin name is Lychnis Hirsuta flore coccinea pleno. The French name, 'Croix de Jerusalem.'
There is a paper of roots written on the back Jonquilles Doubles; must be set in well-made earth so soon as they come to your hand and covered with a foot thick of straw against the cold. The Latin name is Narcissus Juncifolius flore rotundo roseo ...
The horse chestnuts you wrote for (besides that they are verie dear) cannot be transported, for when they come to a man's height they spread immediatelie and grow bushier at the top; the nuts are verie scarce this year, but I shall endeavour to get what quantitie you desire ...
There are three papers with ranunculus roots, upon ane is writ 'Geant de Rome'. The Latin name is Ranunculus Romanis. Upon the 2nd is writ Ranunculus Plucho?. The Latin name is Ranunculus Asphodelis ...
You might set them in February and cover them with half a foot of strawy dung.
There are 3 pounds of single anemone roots in 3 or 4 papers writ on the backs 'Anemones Simples'. You must plant some of them when they arrive; another parcel in February, another in Aprill, another in June that you may have them always in flower. Cause take care to gather the seed for it is from the small ones they have those fine anemones whereof one root here costs sometimes 4 pistoles. There are other three papers with seeds. That which is marked Amaranthus Cristatus etc. must be sowed in a hot bed in the beginning of March exposed to the sun; when the plants are pretty big if you please you may take them up and put them in pots which must be exposed to the sun as much as you can; they use to be very pretty ...
There is a paper with some double poppy seed which must be sowed presentlie up and down your parterre, one or two ... it will produce very fair double poppies of pretty colours. There are in the little barrel 300 horse chestnuts put up with sand. They must be presentlie set in the places where you have a mind to have them grow; they take best with a hot sandy soil.

In January 1682 he wrote:

The 4th instant My Lord Kincardin parted from Paris homewards; I sent along with Dr Ezit(?) a pound of anemone roots. They are verie good of all colours and all double; they cost two crownes (listed as £7:4:0) and thought verie cheap; I sent also 2 dozen ranunculus roots at a pennie the piece; when you sow them if it be frost you must cover them with half a foot of dung, which take

of(f) when the cold is over, but carefully that
you break no little bud; if the weather is warm
cover them not with dung but mix a little with the
prepared earth ...

This was followed in August of the same year

... In one of your letters you desire to know
what to doe with anemone roots in the summer;
You must immediately after this comes to your
hand cause take them up and keep them in a box
without earth or sand till the end of November
or thereabouts and then plant them again (but
not in times of frost) in good earth which covers
the earth a foot thick to preserve them from
the snow, and in March the leaves will begin to
come forth...

The laurels may have been those mentioned on the plan
at N: 'Lowrall tries upon the Tarris walk around the
Great House & stone pilasters between them.'

There is a record of Sir William's wife, Mary
Halkett's involvement with the garden, along with James
Shanks, in her letters to her husband. At the end of
December 1685 she was writing:

James Shanks just now showed me a paper of
orders from you to him ... you had caused ship
some seeds and trees of which there is no word
of their arrival as yet, and it seems (some)one
should have been sent to the Ely [Elie on the
south coast of Fife] to have enquired for the ship
there, ... it shall be no longer delayed, I never
heard of it till just now. James says he can get no
acorns in this country.
The earth in the Church Gate [a field] is very
good and the carts is busy bringing it to the
places you appoint it to be laid in, but the hired
carts is given over their work in carrying the soil
out of the cherry garden where the good earth is
to be laid, pretending it is so hard they cannot get
it wrought, but I have ordered James Shanks to
go to them and get them to work again.

Early the next year:

Your acorns which you sent came here two days
since and the other seeds that was with them,
only the Gillyflower (pinks or wallflowers) seed is
missing. The poke had been opened and was not
full by a great deal. If you could get more of them
it would be well done to send them, for none can be
got in this country. And there is no fir-seed gotten
as yet, though James Shanks says he has taken
many ways to provide it ... There is one of the seeds
that you have sent that he does not know. You must
send word home, and when it must be sown.

... I have received the draft of the wilderness you
sent and both I and James Shanks understands
it well, but there is a difficulty that hinders, that
nothing can be done in order to it, for the ground
differs much from what you expect, for it wants
two foot off a hundred South and North and is a
hundred and eleven foot East and West including
the two borders in which the holly hedges is
set which I wonder you say nothing of. So you
must write new directions before anything can
be done, tho' the weather were seasonable as it is
frost and snow and since yesternight the Loch is
all frozen over, but the snow is but little.
James Shanks has the whole 7000 alders upon
his hand and very busy setting them. All the
trees from England and Holland is come safe
home and is as well cared for as can be. I read
your letter to James Shanks and he says your
orders will be exactly performed, only he fears
that firs will not be got from Craighall ... it shall
be tried. (Walker 1990, 19–21)

William Bruce had earlier designed houses at
Moncreiffe and Dunkeld, neither of which survive
(Dunbar 1970, 63). The Slezer engraving of Dunkeld
House gives little idea of the design of the garden
there, and the details which emerge in cropmark form
recorded during aerial survey may belong to a layout
dating to the earlier eighteenth century and later
(Walker 2002, 22–36).

Some of the buildings for which Sir William Bruce
prepared designs were probably never constructed. An
example is **Kinnaird Castle** in Angus, the house of
the Earl of Southesk (Fig 377). Earlier drawings for
the house and gardens had been made by John Slezer
(RCAHMS Collection AND\37\25–7). Shortly after
Alexander Edward had been expelled from his parish
of Kemback he began to appear as a collaborator
with William Bruce and as an architect and landscape
architect in his own right. A series of plans for the
house and garden at Kinnaird drawn by Alexander
Edward, some dated to 1695 and 1696, survive, some
of which would appear to be alternatives. How far the
design belongs to Bruce or to Edward or is the result
of cooperation is unclear. They all show an elaborate
layout of gardens, orchards and avenues. In front of the
house in one plan (RCAHMS Collection AND\37\31)
there were to be parterres which could be looked at
from terraces above on all sides and which could be
reached by stairs; one of these was supported on a
grass slope. From the terrace was a grand view of the
country. In the centre was a court with small trees
planted in rows down each side. One of the rectangular
enclosures was described as a wilderness, perhaps the
parterre to the left of the facade of the house which
had a spiral mount in each of the four corners, each
with a tree on top. In the centre was an oval pond with

Fig 377 An aerial view of Kinnaird Castle with the lines of the planting ditches for the trees of the avenue emerging as darker lines in dry conditions. SC1248914

two smaller hexagonal ponds and two circular ponds set between the mounts; all the features were linked by paths with the spaces between planted with closely set shrubs or plants. On the other side was a parterre with a layout of paths combining a rectangle, an oval, a square and a circle. The most remarkable features were two parterres with elaborate 'compartments with little embroydery' very much in the style of the *Jardin de Plaisir* (Mollet 1670), one with a fountain at its centre (Figs 379, 380). The orchard with its sixty apple trees, sixty pear trees, eighty-two cherry trees and fifty plum tree arranged in rows lay on either side of a garden of grass and parterres planted with evergreens and horse chestnuts (RCAHMS Collection AND\37\35). A bowling green 150 feet square (45m) was planned to one side of the house. It was to be surrounded by a gravel walk and an inner smaller path 'whitend with

shells' (RCAHMS Collection AND\37\37), all enclosed by a hedge. Statues were to be placed on either side next to the house.

Another plan (RCAHMS Collection AND\37\ 33) shows an oval water-filled 'ring stanck' crossed by a bridge to an unidentified building, perhaps ruinous or only partly built, with gravel walks, greens and projecting arbours (Fig 381). Kirke describes plans for a moated garden at Leslie House (Kirke 1892, 17). This design may reflect the layout of the Maritime Theatre in Hadrian's Villa at Tivoli, which was only accessible by draw-bridges across its water-filled moat and is thought to be a place of private retirement for the emperor. It is also reminiscent of the arrangement at **Rothesay Castle** where the moat, dug out in the 1870s at the instigation of the third Marquess of Bute and presumably reflecting what the excavators discovered,

Fig 378 Plan of Kinnaird Castle and its policies by Alexander Edward. The avenue forms a major feature of the geometric design and was planned in detail. Reproduced by kind permission of Earl of Southesk. SC1238200

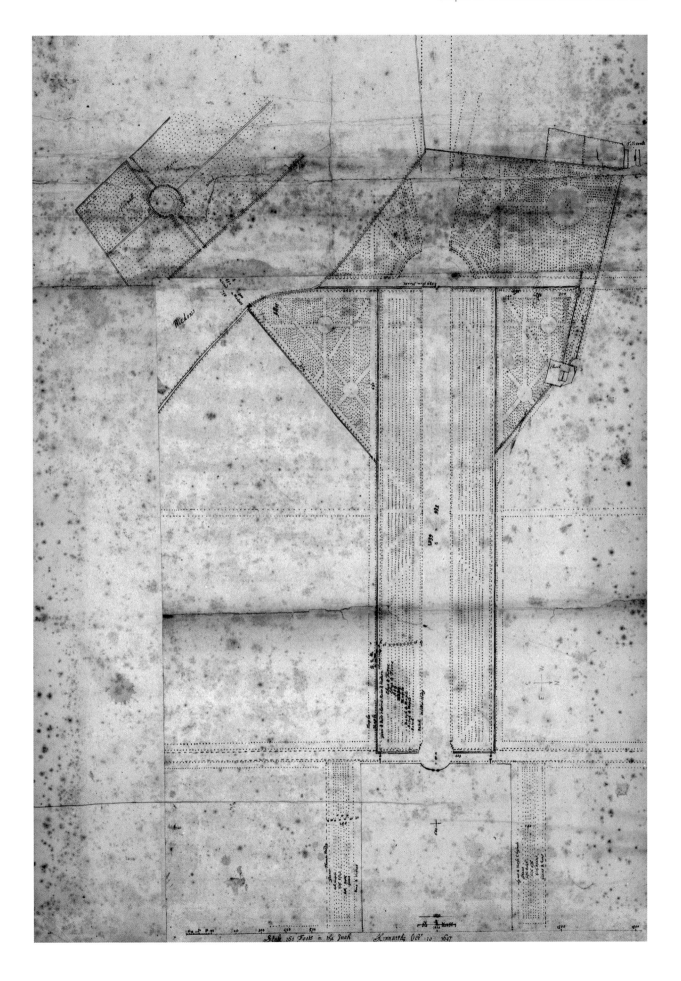

Fig 379 Detail of a design probably never carried out for the elaborate parterres in front of Kinnaird Castle including 'compartments with little embroydery'. The spiral mounts stand at the corners of one parterre possibly the one referred to as a wilderness. Reproduced by kind permission of Earl of Southesk. SC1238195

has, as well as small islands, circular features projecting into the moat, a design which may go back to the period of the abandonment of the castle, which had been ruined in the 1685 invasion by the Campbells when Sir James Stewart, the hereditary keeper, took up residence in the Mansion House in Rothesay High Street. This was constructed facing the castle, and a garden may have been created at the same period (Pringle 1995, 10–11) (Figs 382, 383). This use of islands in gardens has also been recorded at Sanquhar Castle, where the first Duke of Queensberry chose to live both while he was rebuilding Drumlanrig and after its completion about 1690. The formal gardens lay to the west of the castle and included a fish pond and an island (RCAHMS 1920, 190; Maxwell-Irving 2000, 230), which was described by Grose towards the end of the eighteenth century:

> Here formerly the Queensberry family kept their
> deer in a large park, now converted into a farm.
> Upon the bottom that lies beneath the west side
> of the castle were formerly the gardens, where
> the remains of a fish pond with a square island in

the middle is still visible. On the south side of the castle was the bowling green, pretty near entire.
(Grose 1789–91, 148)

The Earl of South Esk died in 1699, without any of the building works at Kinnaird having been carried out. The scheme which does seem to have been realised was that for the west avenue, one of several geometrically related examples which were aligned on a variety of landscape features including churches and mansions (RCAHMS Collection AND\37\41). Aerial survey has recorded the eight rows which were dug to receive the trees within two outer trenches (Figs 377, 378). The avenue was laid out over former arable land and the marks of the earlier ploughing can be seen running roughly at right angles to it. The planting trenches and the young trees were enclosed by hedges of a mixture of holly and hawthorn planted six inches (0.15m) apart. This was presumably designed to protect the young trees as they grew and may not have been intended as a permanent feature. The difficulty of preserving plantations was noted at Glamis. The innermost row was of beech planted 6 and a half feet (2m) apart. There was a gap of 26 feet (8m) before the eight inner rows, which were planted 10 feet (3.05m) apart with 13 feet (3.96m) between them. The trees selected were beech and maple, beech and maple, maple, ash fir, and fir and gean. The outer row was a

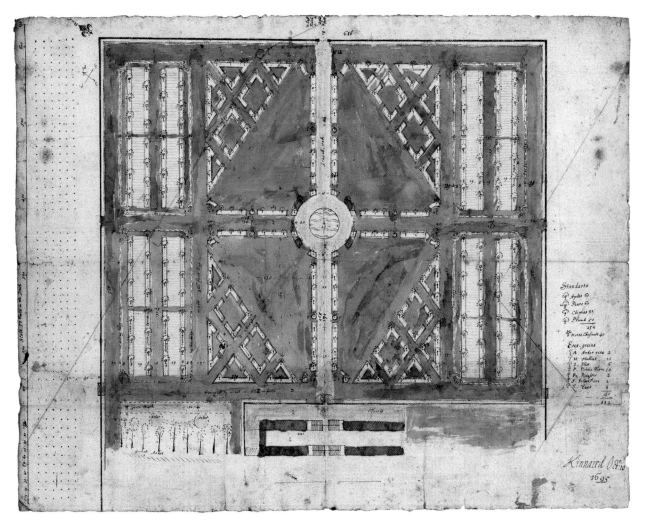

Fig 380 Plan for the elaborate layout of the orchard at Kinnaird Castle. Reproduced by kind permission of Earl of Southesk. SC1238197

mixture of geans, cherries, rowans and laburnum. The avenue had rides across it; ditches with steep grass-covered slopes enclosed the avenue and may also have been intended to protect the trees. The aerial photograph on which the line of the avenue was revealed also shows how the policies were informalised in the late eighteenth and nineteenth centuries with scattered trees and turf.

At much the same time as he was working on Kinnaird, Alexander Edward was commissioned to produce designs for the house and the policies at the nearby **Brechin Castle**, the secondary residence of his father's patrons, the earls of Panmure. The layout which appears on the Military Survey of 1747–55 shows terracing above the steep bank of the River South Esk, a six part division of the garden to the north of the castle and a long west avenue bordered with rows of trees, which is still visible (Figs 384, 385). Further work was carried out there following Edward's journey to England, France and the Low Countries in 1701.

While the majority of Edward's and Bruce's clients appear to have been sympathetic to the exiled James II and VII, the owner of **Melville House** in central Fife,

was a supporter of the 'Glorious Revolution' of 1688. The first Earl of Melville had been in exile in the Low Countries between 1683 and the accession of William and Mary to the throne. He was granted the rank of earl and held major public offices, including those of President of the Privy Council and President of the Committee for the Security of the Kingdom in 1696. Melville House was laid out and lavishly furnished as a demonstration of his authority and wealth. The family moved there from the nearby sixteenth century Monimail Tower, a building which still survives in the garden, and may have been retained as a banqueting house. The state bed is now in the Victoria & Albert Museum and is one of the most important examples of its type in Britain. Sibbald described the mansion as 'a great noble and regular new House richly furnish'd with office houses without, large gardens, vast enclosures for pasture and barren planting built by the late George, Earl of Melvill Secretary of State and High Commissioner to the Parliament and afterward Lord Privy Seal to King William and Queen Mary' (Sibbald 1710, 153). Alexander Edward was working on the design at the same time as or shortly after those for Kinnaird and Brechin Castles. His labours are referred to in a letter from William Bruce to the Earl

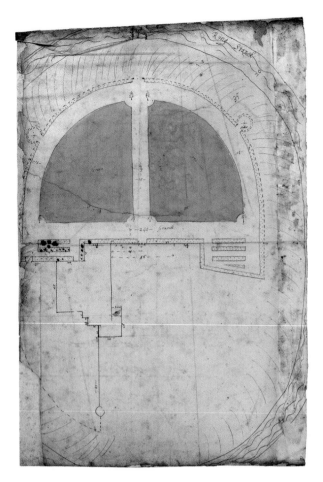

Fig 381 Plan for a garden set within a moat with gravel walks, greens and projecting arbours by Alexander Edward. Reproduced by kind permission of Earl of Southesk. SC1238196

of Melville in April 1697 in which he wrote: 'I have painfully improven the draught for your los. House and kept the bearer from morning till night close to extend the whole stories & elevation of the fronts of ye whole, we were but ended this night late ...' (Lowrey 1987, 10) (Figs 386, 387).

The house was approached from the south-east by a straight length of beech avenue half a mile long, which led to the forecourt. This was flanked by two garden houses, small square buildings with slated ogival roofs, surmounted by weather vanes pierced to form the legend 'M 1697'; the garden houses were linked by a low wall which terminates in two pedestals on which are lead statues of Mercury and Fame, and two yew trees were planted to form an appropriate background (RCAHMS 1933, 211–12). The contractor and probably the principal architect was James Smith, who had married a daughter of Robert Mylne and had been responsible for building the new gateway at Holyroodhouse. He had been appointed as Royal Surveyor in 1683. Following Bruce's political problems, he was the architect favoured for the construction of several important country houses, including Drumlanrig, Yester, Hamilton Palace and Dalkeith Palace. Little is known of his involvement with the design of the gardens that surrounded them.

The Slezer engraving of **Dalkeith** with the title 'Glamms House' shows the house which existed before Smith's work there, still retaining much of its fifteenth and sixteenth century appearance (Fig 388). A free-standing sundial stands in front of the main gate and there is a large orchard to the east enclosed by a wall, but no indication of other gardens close to the castle. Adair's manuscript map of about 1682 (NLS Adv. MS.70.2.11 (Adair 9)) presents a similar picture, with the extensive walled park to the north. A plan in the collections of the Duke of Buccleuch (Cox 1935, fig VII) from about the same period, which may indicate what was proposed rather than what was carried out, shows part of the orchard converted to a parterre with a geometric design and four arbours lying to one side of a short avenue; the sundial has disappeared and another parterre with an interlocking arrangement of paths and planting has been inserted on the other side of the avenue, a wall for fruit against the south wall of the stables and a kitchen garden lies to the east. Three short radiating avenues recall the plan of Versailles. James Smith's new mansion, which incorporated and concealed part of the old castle, does not appear to have been accompanied by a flower garden. The contemporary design for the grounds appears to be very severe. There is a grass plot in front of the new mansion from which the eye would pass to an avenue 1873 feet (571m) in length, cut into the ground and the earth removed, so as to ensure a view to the south-east. Towards the mansion the sloping banks on both sides stood 28 feet (8.5m) above the level of the avenue, diminishing to the south-east. Five trees were planted on each side near the house, increasing to seven in the middle and diminishing to six at the far end. An orchard was planned to the east

Fig 382 Rothesay Castle on the Second Edition of the Ordnance Survey 6-inch map of Buteshire revised in 1897 showing the layout of the moat after the excavations carried out by the third Marquess of Bute.

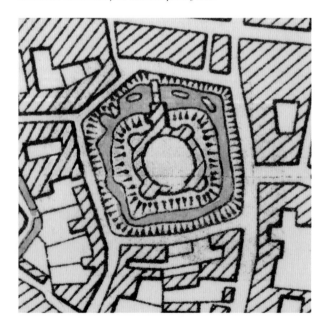

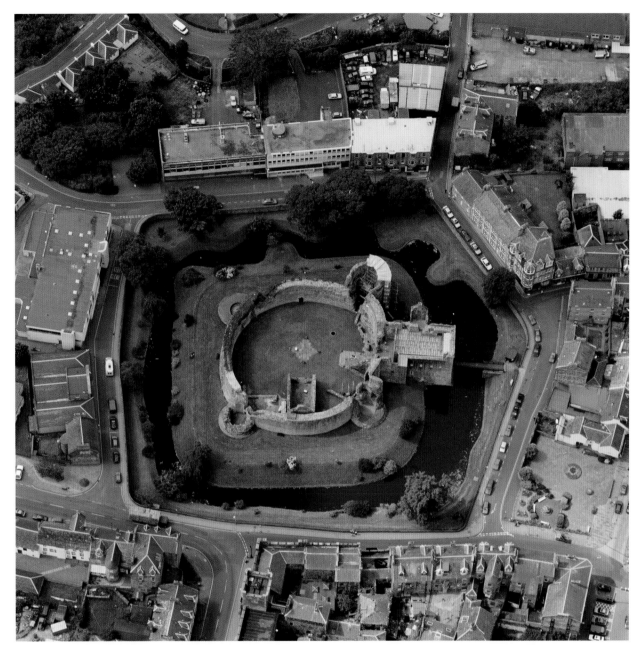

Fig 383 Aerial view of Rothesay Castle. The surviving features projecting into the moat recall those on the plan for a garden set within an oval moat at Kinnaird Castle. They probably date from after the abandonment of the castle following the invasion of 1685 when the earls of Bute took up residence in a town house in Rothesay. SC972833

of the avenue (Buccleuch Drawings 197: RCAHMS Collection MLD\24\65). This was a major exercise in levelling. The work presumably took some time; Daniel Defoe wrote, 'The park is very large, and there are fine Avenues, some already planted, others design'd, but not yet finish'd, also there are to be Water-Works, *Jette D'eaus*, and a Canal, but these are not yet laid out; nor are the Gardens finish'd, or the Terraces, which will be very spacious, if done according to the Design' (Defoe 1968, 771). Documents in the National Records of Scotland (NRS GD224/217/3) refer to payments for cutting and keeping up the terrace banks, in making a

new kitchen garden and in making up the wilderness, which appears with its straight, radiating walks on the Military Survey, probably drawn about 1754, and on drawings in the collection of the Duke of Buccleuch (Buccleuch Drawings Inventory193, 226 and 227; RCAHMS Collection MLD\24\63, 95–6).

In 1701 Alexander Edward set out on a journey through England to the Low Countries and France. This was financed by various patrons who each contributed £10 sterling; his contract required him 'to make draughts of the most curious and remarkable houses, edifices, gardings, orchards, parks, plantations, land improvements, coall works, mines, waterworks and other curiosities of nature and art' and there was specific mention of the coal and lead mines around Newcastle. He was to report every month to the Earl of Mar, and, on his return, he was to produce a full written

Fig 384 Brechin Castle with its gardens, policies and west avenue as depicted on Roy's Military Survey of 1747 to 1755. © British Library Licensor Scran

account of his travels for each of the subscribers, and to give them a choice of any three drawings of houses and gardens. In addition he was bound to visit the houses of each of these patrons for three days in each of the next three years (NRS GD124/16/24). This was presumably so that they could draw upon his experience for the benefit of their estates. On his journey south he met Sir Hans Sloane, secretary of the Royal Society, physician and botanist, to whom he conveyed a book as a gift from Sibbald and a letter of introduction in which Alexander Edward was referred to as 'a man of excellent parts'. His excursions in England were much concerned with ancient monuments, from Holy Island in the north-east to Stonehenge in the south-west. Many houses and gardens are mentioned in his notebook, including Castle Howard, Chatsworth, Belvoir Castle and Burghley House. When he was in London he arranged for Robert Balfour, a gardener in Tottenham presumably of Scottish descent, to buy seeds and plants from nurseries and private gardens there to send back to his patrons in Scotland. The Earl of Mar's order was the largest, reflecting the planting going on in his garden at Alloa at the time; his kitchen garden was to be stocked with plants ranging from carrots to tobacco. In London Edward visited Whitehall, the Tower and Hampton Court, and he made a rough sketch of St James's Park, as well as John Evelyn's garden at Sayes Court.

He left London in March 1702 and returned from France in July of the same year. He visited most of the major towns in Holland and at least three houses with notable gardens including Sorgvliet, the house of Hans William Bentinck, Earl of Portland, William

III's minister and ambassador to France, who also had oversight of the royal gardens, and that of Arnold Joost van Keppel, Earl of Albemarle, courtier and army commander. One of his duties on his tour was to take a ciphered letter from the fourth Duke of Hamilton, a Jacobite sympathiser, to the court of the exiled James II at Saint-Germain-en-Laye. In Paris, as well as visiting notable palaces and houses, he purchased more than five hundred plans and perspectives of houses and gardens and dozens of prints of architectural details, paintings and tombs, maps, mathematical instruments, seeds, paper and books, including a description of Versailles and of the palace which Louis XIV favoured later in his life, Marly, the gardens of which greatly impressed him. His report to the Earl of Mar stresses practical features at Marly such as paths and steps, but he also admired the water features at Versailles and noted the long hunting rides through the plantations, a feature he was already familiar with at Panmure. He pursued his interest in early Scottish history, visiting the Scots College where he transcribed two twelfth century charters. He had been recommended to see the chateaux of Chantilly, Sceaux and Saint-Cloud, as well as Richelieu, south of the Loire, and he returned to Scotland following a voyage down the Seine to Le Havre (Lowrey 1987, 19–23). He wrote from there to the Earl of Mar;

> I have toiled for sight as much as I could & out
> wearied all I could ever ingadge & have searched
> for draughts both chops & Libraries & have spent
> almost 200 livers that way & purchased all the
> plangs of Houses gardens Ports Tombs doors
> Chimneys yea not omitting Pulpits Churches &
> their Doms that my purse could reach or was to be
> sold & a good many perspectives & some pictures
> ... I have bought a double of some good draughts of
> houses & diverse choise Gardens for your L[ordshi]
> p which exceed all thats to be got at Lundon &
> I have purchased origenall draughts illuminat &
> drawen be the choisest designers of Gardens ...
> (Gifford 1989, 66–7; NRS GD124/15/219)

Experience from visiting gardens in France was pursued by practising gardeners, who might also be in contact with the Jacobite court at Saint-Germaine. A letter from Versailles to the Earl of Breadalbane from Duncan Foster, who had hoped to be employed at Taymouth, describes his travels to France and his experience there:

> Had remained 12 weeks at London expecting
> recipient's answer to letter writer sent with
> the Duke of Beaufort's letter; having regretted
> that Breadalbane was not then to employ him
> he decided it was not worth his while to stay
> in England, and hearing of the extraordinary
> gardens in France and Holland, he decided to
> improve himself to be more capable for recipient's

service later; leaving Lady Glenorchy on 16 March, he set off on 19 March and reached Dieppe on 26th of that month; he spent 8 days at Rouen and then went to St Germin where he met several acquantances with the Earl of Perth, who was kind to writer on account of recipient and Beaufort; Perth promised to get the Prince of Wales to recommend writer as his own gardener, for there were two gardeners recommended to learn management of flowers and waterworks; on 2 May writer entered with the 'floranger' and has improved himself more in a month there than in a year in England, on flowers and greens of all kinds of arburs, heges, wilderness waterworks, and walks, our flour garden is foull of flours the year round, so sun as on flour feads thair is another put in his place; our heges in the winter is of al sorts of hardi grens as lorell, yeus, junipers of all sorts, siprys, bayes, sederss, lorell-stinous which flours all winter; in the summer all thos is moved eals where, and in thair roum thair is put pomgranets, olives, oleanders, mirttels, oranges & limons tres. All this I hope your lordship will have at Taymouth in a short tym; it will be no great charges except the building of a grenhouse in the corner of the old chirey gardin. We have on flour garden of inbrothered [embroidered] works planted with bothe the borders 3 foote and a halfe, others we have 16 fote gravell, nixt to that 3 foot of grase, nixt a border of 3 foot, within the border 3 foot of gravell the midell all gress, all this look mighty fine, they have not this way in England as yet of gras and gravell, if your Lordshipe his not finest your flour garden I wish you to take this meathod and I shall send drafts from hence. (NRS GD112/39/178/12)

Duncan Foster was later employed as gardener at Taymouth and he is recorded as paying for garden equipment there in 1707 (NRS GD112/29/57). In 1717 he was writing to the Earl of Breadalbane about developments in the garden there when the wall of the inner court was demolished and the level of the bowling green raised (NRS GD112/20/1/31; 112/39/275/15).

The Breadalbane estates were still regarded as a source for the supply of fir seed while he was gardener there and a quantity was requested by the Duke of Kent (NRS GD112/39/281/22).

Following his return to Scotland Edward took up several projects on which he had previously been employed with Sir William Bruce. One of these was the building works on **Craigiehall House** in West Lothian, which belonged to the third Earl, later first Marquess of Annandale, whose daughter married the first Earl of Hopetoun. Annandale had approached Bruce in the summer of 1694 on the subject of Craigiehall, and consequently the cartographer John Adair was

Fig 385 Aerial view of Brechin Castle and its long west avenue. SC1238194

approached to 'make a verie exacte mappe of the ground' (Lowrey 1989a, 2). This would be used by Bruce to plan the house courts and parterres before the house itself was designed. The reference to Edward's employment there comes in a letter to the Earl of Mar (Lowrey 1987, 25) who himself was to provide garden designs for Craigiehall in 1708. It also refers to Edward's presence at a house in England belonging to the second wife of the Duke of Hamilton, son of Duchess Anne, at Ashton near Lancaster. The inner court at Craigiehall was divided into four with a statue provided by Mar at the centre of each quarter, with garden seats at each end of the transverse walk. There are records of payments to workmen in the garden the same year, as well as the purchase of bell glasses from Leith to protect delicate plants (NRAS2171/Bundle 664). The gardens were much changed in the latter part of the eighteenth century, but the Military Survey shows the careful distribution of the policies within a geometrical plan (Fig 389).

Fig 386 Aerial view of Melville House with its ogee-roofed garden pavilions from the north-west. William Bruce and Alexander Edward were concerned in its design. SC1238214

Edward was also concerned with the construction of **Hopetoun House** for the first earl on a new site to the west of South Queensferry, where work began in 1696 (RCAHMS 1929, 186). In his *History of the Sheriffdoms of Linlithgowshire and Stirling* Sibbald records that the Earl of Hopetoun:

> By the advice of his Cousin the Lord Rankilor, Sir William Bruce and Mr Alexander Edward, Great Masters in Architecture and contrivance of Avenues, Gardens and Orchards, has raised a stately house with avenues in all Quarters. The principal Avenue openeth from the East, with Large Office houses and regular planting upon each side; this, when the Gates are all open, gives a Prospect through the Inclosures near a Mile long. The House stands in the Center; a large double house with Wings on the South and North side of it, the Rooms are stately and well contrived, and are suteably furnished: there is a fine Scale-Stair under the Cupula; the Courts are large, and there are fine Gardens and Orchards about the House, embellished with Waterworks and Jettoes: the great Avenue opens to the West towards the Church, to which the Earl has added a Chapel for a Burial place. (Sibbald 1710a, 20–1)

The date for the first construction of the garden is uncertain, but payment for the gardener for Hopetoun, James Stevenson, is recorded from 1703/4. Vegetable seeds had already been purchased in March 1702 and trees were also sent to Hopetoun from London by Alexander Edward in the same year (Robertson 1995, 9, 13, 78). A model of the garden existed in 1710, when payment was made for its transport to Edinburgh (Robertson 1995, 17), and its construction may have preceded this date by some years. While no drawings survive before those made by William Adam in about 1725, which were connected with the reconstruction and modernisation of the house and garden, these plans do illustrate the general layout adopted by Bruce and Edward, and further information about their design and appearance has emerged as a result of aerial survey. The lawns to the west of the mansion would appear to have been turfed since at least the time of William Adam's survey of about 1725 (NRS RHP 6800), which shows the overall layout of the policies.

A series of aerial sorties in both summer and winter have led to the revelation of the narrow trenches dug to take the low hedges which formed the basis of the design of the parterres to the rear of the house (Figs 390, 391). In dry summers the greater depth of topsoil has allowed the grass to flourish over the trenches when that surrounding them has become parched. Survey under snow revealed that the lawn is still not absolutely level after some three centuries, with the planting trenches still slightly lower than the areas around. A

Fig 387 Melville House with its gardens, policies, avenue and barren (non-fruit) planting as depicted on Roy's Military Survey of 1747 to 1755. © British Library Licensor Scran

design of scrolls and shells of the type depicted in the plans for Kinnaird Castle can be seen. The designs appear to be rather less delicate than those depicted by André Mollet and bear more resemblance to certain of those engraved in *La théorie et la pratique du jardinage* by Antoine-Joseph Dézallier d'Argenville, a work first published in Paris in 1709. The plate illustrating the *Parterre de Broderie meslee de massifs de gazon* (lawn) has a particular resemblance to the surviving evidence, although utilising a palmette rather than a shell, and, like the parterre at Hopetoun, is designed to accommodate a circular or oval basin (Dézallier d'Argenville 1712, Pl 1B), while the *Parterre de*

Compartiment (Dézallier d'Argenville 1712, Pl 2B) has a similarly bold use of scrolls. The parterre may well have been laid out after Edward's return from France with his large collection of engravings. A volume of forty-nine engravings, formerly at Hopetoun and later at Dalmeny, includes seventeen views of Versailles, mostly of the garden layout, including a parterre design with shell motifs. Other volumes of French engravings have been dispersed (Macaulay 2009, 8–9). A double line of square features is visible in the grass on the west side of the building along and parallel to the offices which lie on both sides of the mansion. These markings may have been created as planting holes, and trees in this position would give greater privacy to those walking in the garden. It is possible that they could mark the foundations for some architectural feature, perhaps a colonnade, or be the foundations for plinths for statues.

Fig 388 Dalkeith House in Theatrum Scotiae *by John Slezer. The engraving was published (and misidentified) in the edition of 1719, two years after Slezer's death. The sundial protected by railings is a notable feature of the approach. SC570928*

Macky comments that, 'The parterre fronting the saloon is longer than that at Canons and like it has a large bason of water at the bottom' (Macky 1729, 202). The oval basin, with its fountain on the west side of the parterre, was under construction in the period 1701 to 1705 when there are references to mason and plumber work, for 'pipes laid at and above ye funtain head', 'a hunder and nyntie ffootts of pethment [pavement] in the botom of the basson' and 'cast and laid into the bason of great pip – 102 yairds – £5-12-0' and 'for casting 40 yards of great pipe and laying them with lies from ye bason to ye sea' (Hogg 1975, 82). The western half of the fountain basin was surrounded by a wilderness and there was a reference to the pointing of the 'bason in the willdernes' in 1704, although this may relate to another fountain (Hogg 1975, 84). In 1709 an estimate was produced for the centrepiece of the fountain. 'A flying horse and Fame as big as the Life' at a cost of £200. 'Ffour statues about the fountain ... six foots high at 30£ per piece or if 5 1/2 foots 25£ each' (Robertson 1995, 5). The choice of the statue of Fame may be due to a quotation by Sophocles referring to Fame as 'the immortal daughter of golden Hope'. In 1705/6 the sculptor John van Nost supplied a 'Pegasus and fame' to Sir Nicholas Shireburn of Stoneyhurst in Lancashire. Andries Charpentiere or Andrew Carpenter is presumed to have used the same mould for 'Fame borne aloft by the winged horse Pegasus' for the fountain at Powis Castle. The design derived from a composition made in marble for Louis XIV's chateau at Marly, which was being made when Alexander Edward visited Paris.

Four further statues, 'Cain and Abel, Diana and a Buck, a Gladiator and a Hercules and Club', each 6 feet high and of metal were ordered from John van Nost in London, at a cost of £86 sterling, including delivery by sea. A month later there was an order for an 'Adonis with a grayhound att his feet, a hunting horn in on hand and a hunting in the oyr. Venus with Cupid att his foot. A Venus coming out of the bath and a Phaon playing on a pipe' at a price of £56. A list of statues and vases and their suggested sites was prepared in 1709; as well as the fountain statues, there were Hercules and his Mistress, or as an alternative, Venus and Adonis, for the two large plots of the parterre, Bacchus and Ceres for the Inner Court, urns for the terrace on the west side of the house; covered flower pots on the terrace in front of the house and two vases on the terraces on each of the sides; two figures of Hope were suggested for the stone pillars between the two courts (Robertson 1995, 4–5, fig 2). By 1728 there were nine large statues and six small ones in the parterre, although, before the works by William Adam in the 1720s, there were also some statues in the front court (Robertson 1995). The

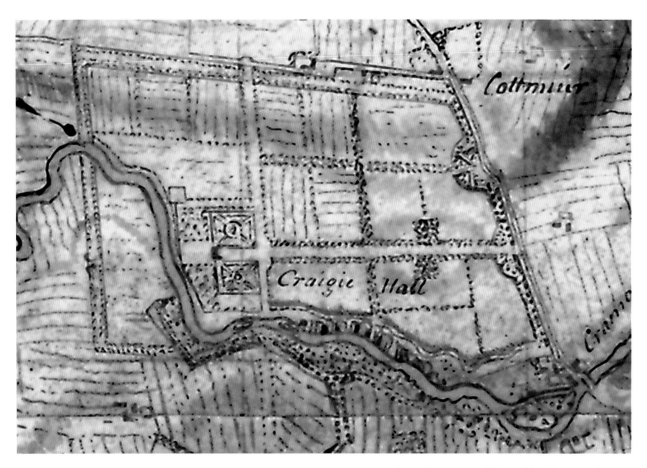

Fig 389 Craigiehall as it appears on Roy's Military Survey of 1747 to 1755.
William Bruce and Alexander Edward were involved with the design of the house
and policies, which are organised within a geometrical plan. © British Library
Licensor Scran

Sea Walk was probably built by the mason Thomas
Bauchope whose accounts in 1704–5 refer to 'the
taras (which) mesurs in all 2114 ffootts at fyve shilling
Scots per foot is £528' (Hogg 1975, 83). Two 'Summer
seats' were built of stone in the court to the front of the
house, and a joiner made 'on bige half round Chare for
the garding' as well as 'too Chares to ye garding bing
square' (Robertson 1995, 14).

The kitchen garden was an important element in
the design of the policies. A large order of peaches,
cherries and apricots came by sea in 1704. Bricks were
made for the north wall of the kitchen garden in 1705
and the other walls were built soon after. The Edinburgh
seed merchants George Mowbray, Mrs Duncan, Arthur
Clephane and Charles Crokatt were early suppliers for
the kitchen garden, but after 1707 William Miller from
Holyrood seemed to be favoured as the provider of an
extensive range of vegetables. Accounts from 1706
refer to barren trees and flowering shrubs and continue
through 1709. The north and south cherry gardens may
have been stocked with trees for which 'ane guinie of
gold' was given in January 1706 (Robertson 1995, 14).

Plants came from a wide variety of sources: Sir
William Bruce's garden at Kinross provided roses, 450
hollies, jonquils and crocuses, and Lord Rankeillour

sent several consignments of firs, with others coming
from Blair Drummond, Castle Lyon (Castle Huntly) and
Doune. Dwarf box came from Alva, 1800 hollies from
Culross, and payment was made to Drummond Castle
for yews. Orange trees came from London. Closer to
hand, 12,000 thorns came from Gogar, hollies and
beeches from Colinton, and William Miller provided
5100 dwarf box, 850 Dutch alders, 6000 beeches, 3000
hornbeams, 300 apple stocks and nine gilded hollies.
Turf for the walks and parterres was cut at Newliston
and West Kers, and grass seed arrived from Tyninghame,
the home of the Earl of Hopetoun's sister. Trees,
including beech, elm, fir, hawthorn and holly were
also planted from seed, and the gardens of other Hope
properties such as Niddrie and Midhope were being
used as nurseries (Robertson 1995, 14–16).

John Macky visited Hopetoun at the time when the
Earl of Hopetoun had recently begun to make alterations
to the east or entrance front of the house, according
to designs by William Adam, and so must have been
making notes on the mansion about 1721 (Macaulay
2009, 1) (Fig 406). He writes:

The courtyard is callonaded, and adorn'd with
Statues and Vases; ... The Parterre fronting the
Salloon is longer than that at Cannons, and like
it, hath a large Bason of Water at Bottom: It's also
adorned with a multitude of Statues on Pedestals,
as at Cannons; but the Views here are prodigiously

Fig 390 *Vertical aerial view of Hopetoun showing the layout of the gardens around the house dating from around 1700. William Bruce and Alexander Edward were both involved in the design of the house and gardens. PGA COMP 2005-04-21 © NextPerspectives*

Fig 391 *Vertical aerial view of Hopetoun showing the trenches dug for the elaborate parterres, with scrolls and shell motifs emerging from the turf in dry conditions to the west of the mansion. The design of the parterres is very close to French models. A line of square marks, perhaps planting holes or perhaps the foundations for statue bases, can be seen parallel to the wings. PGA COMP 2005-04-21 © NextPerspectives*

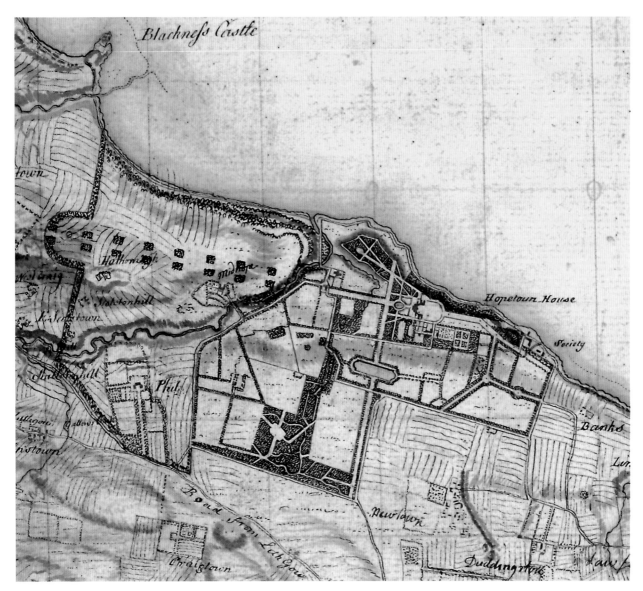

Fig 392 Hopetoun as it appears on Roy's Military Survey of 1747 to 1755. The house and gardens of Willian Bruce and Alexander Edward were modified after 1720 by William Adam. The gardens around the mansion formed part of a much larger design. © British Library Licensor Scran

more extensive. From the Terras to the North of this Parterre is the finest View I ever saw any where; far beyond Frescati near Rome or St Michael del Bosco, near Bolognia, for Variety. Looking to the East you see all the Islands of the Frith to its Mouth; all the Towns on the Coasts of Fife and Lothian as far as St Andrews one way, and North-Berwick the other; looking to the West you see all the rest of the Frith, Stirling and its Castle, with the Mountains of Perthshire and Argyleshire; and looking North you have Dunfermling, and all the Country round it, full in View; the Frith lying under you like a Pond, which is here about two Miles broad. There are also several Visto's from each of the many Walks that run from this Parterre; some of them ending in a Parish-Church, some in an old

Tower. And through the great Avenue fronting the Palace, your View terminates on North-Berwick Law, near the Bass, at thirty Miles Distance, appearing like a Sugar-Loaf.

This fine Palace and Garden, lies in the middle of a spacious Park, well stock'd with Deer, and environ'd with a Stone Wall.

To the South of the great Avenue lies the Kitchen-Garden; and joining to it a House and Walk for Pheasants, and a Plantation for other Fowls and Beasts; and under his great Terras there is a Bed of Oysters, from whence his Kitchen is supplied all the Year round, in the greatest Quantities. (Macky 1729, 201–3)

The overall design of the garden shows the interest in incorporating distant features into the garden, as was the case at Bruce's houses at Balcaskie and Kinross. William Adam recorded on his plan the eastern avenue 'carrying your eye over two miles of the River Forth to the island and ruins of Inchgarvie and from thence

Fig 393 William Bruce and Alexander Edward were also involved in the plans for the (demolished) House of Nairne. SC1238193

forward along the River 22 miles or more to North Berwick Law' with, as noted by Sibbald, a secondary vista north-west to Blackness Castle. The Military Survey of 1747 to 1755 shows the extension of the line of the avenue to the west by means of double lines of square plantations (Fig 392).

Another house and garden with which Bruce and Edward were involved was **House of Nairne** in Perthshire, which was built for William, second Lord Nairne, a son of the Marquess of Atholl, for whom William Bruce had worked at Dunkeld House (Fig 393). A letter from Lady Nairne to the Countess of Panmure refers to his presence at House of Nairne in January 1705. Following a fire there the house was rebuilt, starting in 1706 and completed in 1710, the year of Bruce's death and two years after that of Alexander Edward. A drawing of the house by James Nairne, grandson of the second Baron Nairne, has an inscription which reads 'The House of Nairne – of Strathord built by William Lord Nairne and destroyed by his nephew James Duke of Atholl'. The site of the house cannot now be recognised on the ground (Fenwick 1970, 103–6), but aerial survey has revealed the lines of the avenue and some of the plantations around the house, which provides evidence for the carrying out of a plan for the gardens (Figs 394, 395).

Alexander Edward's work extended to properties of Scottish landowners resident in England. In June 1706 he was reported to be going 'to take care of the D. of Hamilton's Gardens at Ashton' (Lowrey 1989, 25). Ashton Hall near Lancaster had been acquired by the fourth duke as part of his wife's inheritance, and a letter

to him from Ashton in July 1708 reported on progress of masonry and joiners' work there (Lowrey 1989, 25). He had already, along with the Earl of Mar, provided advice to another of her sons, the Earl of Orkney, for his house at Cliveden in Buckinghamshire (Lowrey 1989a, 26). Alexander Edward's last garden design is that for the gardens and parks attached to **Hamilton Palace**. It is dated to 1708, the year of his death. The plan is entitled 'A map with some Alterations to the gardens, Courts, Aveneues, Plantations, & Inclosures of Hamilton Humblie overfared be Alex: Edward Aug 31 1708 according to a Scale of 500 foots in the Inch' (Figs 396, 397). The gardens at Hamilton were already well developed, and Edward would seem to have built on the strong north and south axis already determined. The north avenue had been laid out about 1693 and a south avenue had been proposed and partly planted by 1708. Edward brought the Low Parks and the High Parks together by means of an avenue which ran from the River Clyde on the north to the south edge of the High Parks and Patrickholm House, a distance of about three miles (Lowrey 1987, 26). To the west and parallel with this he proposed a great vista focusing on Bothwell Bridge and the steeple of Bothwell Kirk to the north and beyond the High Church and Steeple of Glasgow (Lowrey 1989, 25). A complex and geometric series of belvederes, etoiles and radiating rides at different angles linked the palace and its gardens and the various parts of the parks, as well as the major natural features of the Rivers Avon and Clyde. One belvedere was called the Selkirk Belvedere after the title of Duchess Anne's husband, a title which passed to their second son, and a planting was created imitating the thirty-two rays of the Order of the Garter, which had been granted to the late Duke of Hamilton.

Fig 394 House of Nairne with its avenue and plantations on Roy's Military Survey of 1747 to 1755. © British Library Licensor Scran

According to the key to the plan the gardens which lay to the north of the palace were changed from terraces supported by breast walls to terraces above green slopes, with four statues placed in 'embroidered plots', while the lower parterres were partly decorated with cut grass and a little embroidery with a large jaddo or *jet d'eau* in the middle. Upon the east side of the high parterres would be a grotto walk planted with a mixture of Dutch and wych elms, while the limes in the lower parterre might easily be shaped into superb colonnades or arched pillars. Upon the other sides might be four little bosco wildernesses or groves with hornbeam and holly hedges. This would reduce the size of the old kitchen gardens, which could then be extended into the former orchard, which might be moved to the east of the churchyard. Elements of the Pond Garden were changed into a small canal. The entrance to the churchyard, which lay immediately to the east of the palace, had to be maintained and should, like the churchyard, be planted with evergreens, but a strip garden should be planted with hedges for orange trees between it and the forecourt. Alternative uses for the neighbouring plot were a pear orchard, a regular grove of limes or walnut hedges or a labyrinth wilderness, which might easily have a jaddo in the middle (Fig 398).

The plan for Hamilton is the grandest and most extensive of Alexander Edward's designs and shows how his studies of the great gardens of France at the beginning of the eighteenth century were absorbed into his vision for the most prestigious garden in Scotland. It takes in the natural topography of the lower Clyde valley and marries the concern with associating the designed landscape with memorials of the Scottish past, with an appreciation of the wider landscape. The last item (Z) – 'the highest gleame' – on the key to the 'Map' records the position in the south avenue where the River Clyde is visible over the palace (Fig 399). While Alexander

Fig 395 The cropmarks of the planting holes for a plantation at House of Nairne in a pattern illustrated in John Reid's Scots Gard'ner *(Reid 1988). SC1238208*

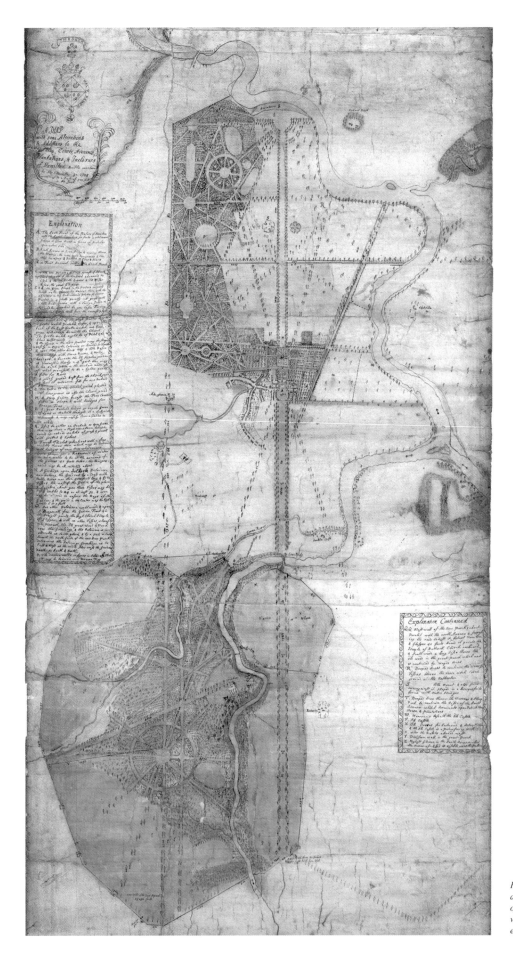

Fig 396 The plan of the gardens at Hamilton, which had a length of more than three miles, managed within a strongly geometric and emblematic framework. SC750026

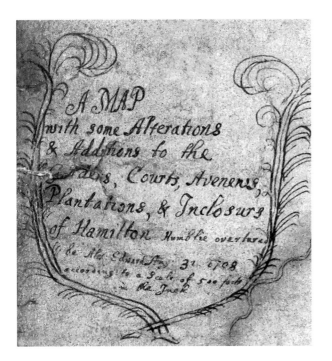

Fig 397 *The title of the plan of Hamilton Palace and its policies in the handwriting of Alexander Edward. SC750026*

Edward died less than three months after the completion of his plan and can never have seen its fulfilment, it formed the blueprint for the development of the gardens there. Macky wrote some years later: 'The Palace of Hamilton lieth in a fertile fine Plain, between a great Park of six and seven Miles in Circumference, walled round, and a lesser Park behind the Gardens, both well wooded and water'd the great Park having a River running through its Middle, and extremely well stock'd with Deer' (Macky 1729, 278–9). After Edward's death the prints he had collected of houses and gardens were

of interest to architects and collectors in Scotland, particularly those who had sponsored his expedition to England and France. The Earl of Panmure wrote to the Earl of Mar saying that he had attempted to secure and preserve his plans (GD124/15), while Alexander McGill, the architect and mason, also wrote to Mar about his 'desiring a share of the booty, if there be any pilfering about Mr Edwards sketches or draughts' (NRS GD124/15/938).

However, at Hamilton, as at Hopetoun, only a relatively short time elapsed before William Adam was called in to make changes to the landscape designed by Alexander Edward. Adam's work did away with the complex formal gardens around the palace, and a rectangular canal was inserted into the north avenue. Chatelherault, the hunting lodge or dog kennel, built between 1732 and 1743, was placed across Edward's south avenue, and gardens were laid out around it. It served as an eyecatcher from the palace, and became the termination of the avenue, for which a much greater length had been proposed by Edward. Its relationship to the natural and informal valley of the Avon may be seen as marking a development in appreciation of gardens and their surrounding landscape differing from that of the late seventeenth and early eighteenth centuries.

The most prominent and active patron of the design of gardens and the wider landscape at this period was John Erskine, sixth Earl of Mar, one of the sponsors of Alexander Edward's visit to England, the Low Countries and France in 1702. Margaret Stewart's article on Lord Mar's Gardens at **Alloa** c1700–1732 illuminates the developments in garden and estate planning in the earlier eighteenth century and their economic basis (Stewart 1989, 33–40). The purchases made on Mar's behalf when Alexander Edward was in London have

Fig 398 *Detail of the gardens to the north of Hamilton Palace. Wildernesses were introduced and the Pond Garden was converted to a small canal. SC750221*

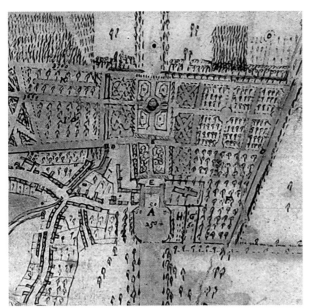

Fig 399 *Section of the plan of Hamilton showing the position of Z, the most southerly point from which the River Clyde could be seen. SC750026*

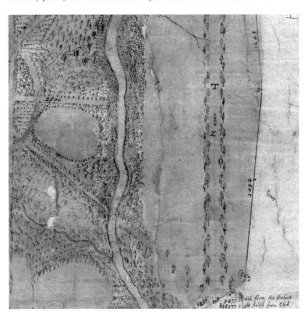

Fig 400 Alloa as it appears on Roy's Military Survey of 1747 to 1755 illustrating the close relationship between the town and Alloa House. © British Library Licensor Scran

already been referred to, and, when he was in France, Edward wrote to Mar mentioning the little diamond-shaped parterres on the garden side of the house at Alloa, which were presumably in existence prior to his departure (Fig 401). Following his return, plans were prepared for Alloa, drawing on the materials Edward had acquired abroad. The first mention of garden plans occurs in a letter of 1703; there were three broad avenues meeting at the south of the house, modelled on the entrance front at Versailles, with a kidney-shaped moat deriving from that at the Grand Trianon. Mar's plans for Alloa of 1710 show avenues radiating out from the mansion, which was built around the old tower, with vistas terminated by Sauchie Tower, Clackmannan Tower, Old Stirling Bridge and Elphinstone House in the manner of Kinross and Hopetoun (NRS RHP 13258/1). The dramatic peaks of the Ochills and the wide view of the Firth of Forth also served as a landscape setting for the garden. The sites recalled not only the long and distinguished history of the Erskine family, but the history of Scotland. As at Hopetoun there was a statue group of Cain slaying Abel, which stood in the basin between the diamond-shaped ponds in the centre of the avenue between the inner gardens and the house, and a statue of a gladiator was placed at the centre of the entrance court. The plan also shows kitchen gardens, orangeries, wildernesses, orchards, bosquets and ornamental parterres.

The design of the garden at Alloa was linked to the planning of the town and of Mar's industrial ventures there (Fig 400). The plan of 1710 incorporated the construction Lion of the Gartmorn Dam, the largest artificial reservoir in Scotland before the late nineteenth century,

which provided a head of water to drain the coal workings at Park Miln, a water supply for the town, and a power source for snuff mills and a rope works, before passing through the garden where it fed the fountains, basins and fresh and salt water fish ponds, while at the foreshore the flow was controlled by a sluice for cleansing the harbour (Stewart 1998, 17–18) (Figs 401, 402). Mar was often absent from Alloa but would write to his brother, James Erskine, Lord Grange, with instructions about his plans for the house and garden. His head gardener was Thomas Harlaw (NADFAS 2000, 84), who had to carry out the plans, as well as order more practical gardening matters. Harlaw was far from unlettered. Lord Grange wrote to him in 1711:

Thomas, I here send you a supplement to the Art of Husbandry which you have the loan of from me. I likewise send you Mr Evelyn's translation of Rapin's poem of Gardens, which will divert you in the winter nights. There is another thing I would suppose would be no trouble to you, but rather a Divertisement in the winter evenings when darkness confines you to the house, and I should be glad if you would try it. Nobody, I think, can contrive or dispose a garden to advantage except he know exactly at what seasons the several plants that ought to be in it are in perfection – and at what different seasons these plants make their several appearances ... Whoever knows this ... may almost perpetuate spring and summer by a constant appearance of plants ... We have an example of this in the Art of Husbandry ... but this being calculated for the climate and soil of England, does not, I suppose, hold in Scotland. Therefore I wish you would adjust such a list to our clime and soil ... Did we but see many flower gardens thus ordered that the dazzling beauties of everyone of these glorious plants were courting our admiring eyes, and that through their various successions all the seasons and months of the year, ... None who has sight could be so dull as not to love your art and esteem your employment ... There is no diversion and recreation upon earth that pleases one more, than to wander in a complete garden, where flowers and herbs, water, trees and shrubs combine to make a little paradise. ... But good Thomas, I must use one argument with you for the doing of it. As the performance of it will be easy for one of your experience in gardening and agreeable to one who takes pleasure in his art, so none but one of your experience can do it to purpose. (NRS GD 124/15/1039).

Fig 401 Detail of 'Plan of Alloa The Seat of The Lord Mar &c, In The Shire of Clackmannan In Scotland ...' 1710 and 1728, showing the elaborate formal gardens aligned on the harbour and Alloa House RHP 13258/000/1 © Mar and Kellie Muniments, GD124. National Records of Scotland

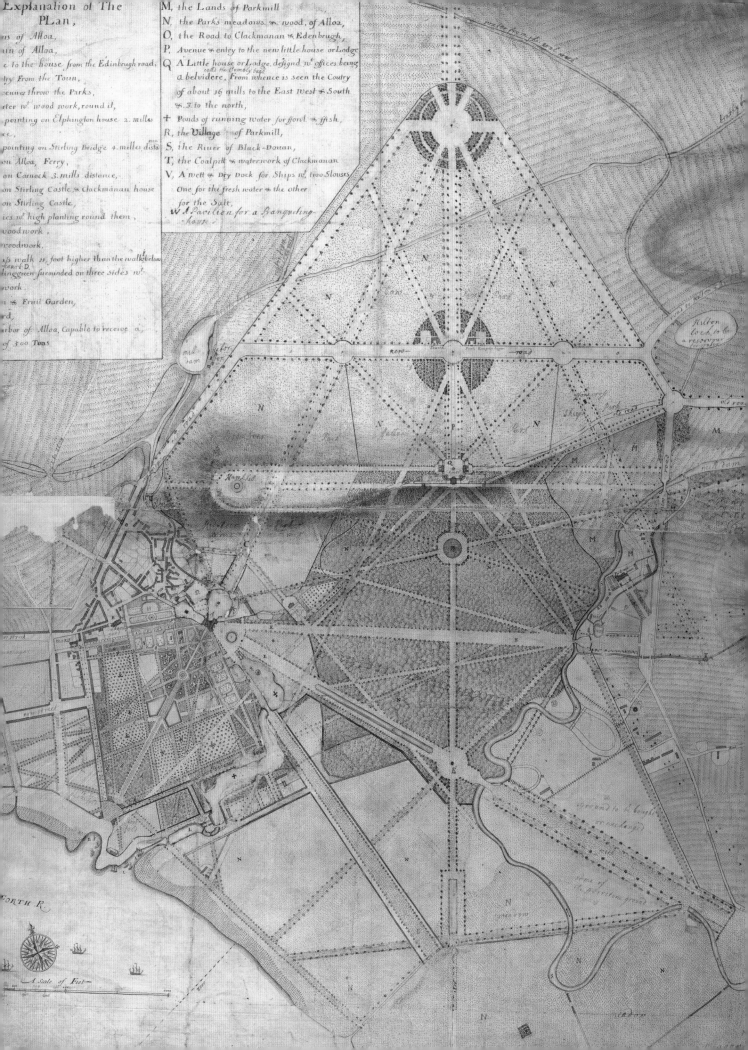

Explanation of The
PLAN,

... of Alloa,
... of Alloa,
... to the house from the Edinbrugh road,
... From the Toun,
... venues throw the Parks,
... ter w.d wood work, round it,
... pointing on Elphinston house 2. milles
...,
... pointing on Stirling Bridge 4. milles dista.
... on Alloa, Ferry,
... on Carnock 3. milles distance,
... on Stirling Castle & Clackmanan house
... on Stirling Castle,
... ies w.t high planting round them,
... woodwork,
... woodwork.
... ss walk 11 foot higher than the walk below
... lingreen surounded on three sides w.t
... work.
... & Fruit Garden,
... rd,
... rbor of Alloa, Capable to receive a
... of 800 Tons

M, the Lands of Parkmill
N, the Parks meadows & wood, of Alloa,
O, the Road to Clackmanan & Edenbrugh,
P, Avenue & entry to the new little house or Lodge
Q, A Little house or Lodge, design'd w.t offices being
a belvidere, From whence is seen the Coutry
of about 16 mills to the East West & South
& 3. to the north,
+ Ponds of running water for fforil & ffish,
R, the Village of Parkmill,
S, the River of Black-Douan,
T, the Coalpitt & waterwork of Clackmanan
V, A wett & Dry Dock for Ships w.t two Slouses
One for the fresh water & the other
for the Salt,
W, A Pavilion for a Banqueting-
house.

FORTH R.

A scale of Feet

Fig 402 The wheel for raising water to a tank on the top floor at Alloa House for the laundry and other purposes as projected by the Earl of Mar in 1728 during his exile from Scotland. RHP132581/000/19 © Mar and Kellie Muniments, GD124. National Records of Scotland

In 1714 Harlaw produced a plan with a key showing which plants should be selected to produce this effect (NRS GD 124/15/1114) (Fig 403). He kept a diary of work in the garden, in which he noted the gardeners' and workmen's progress with mowing and weeding the parterre and flower borders, shearing hedges, digging and moving earth and sand. In January 1703 Mar writes:

Tell Thomas Harlaw I had a draught of the gardens. I'm sending down some fruit trees which he must plant in a nurserie. He must send to Nithrie [Niddry] to get from Hopton's gardener some grafts of the duke chirrie which he promist me.

In April 1708: 'I hear my trees are arrived at last, I hope Tom Harlaw was immediately sent for and that they are gone to Alloa, though I am afraid most of them are lost.'

Harlaw wrote to Mar in May 1706: 'My Lord, I have cut out the shrub wilderness on the south east side of the garden leaving the walks ... and shall endeavour to be as busy at the High Wilderness as possible ... the grand

Allee is pretty well swarded. I cut a melon yesterday and sent it to Stirling with a few ripe plums ... The hedge along the Coalgate advances very well along with your lordship's new planted nurserie ...'

In May 1708 Harlaw wrote to Lord Grange 'I have got a Hee swan from Menstrie to put in the ponds at Alloa. I am afraid he will wander for want of a neighbour. May it please your Lordship to procure a she one out of the north loch or where your lordship pleaseth and send it with the bearer which will not be unacceptable to my Lord your brother ...'

In the same year Mar wrote to his brother 'I have sent some statues in a ship ... They are very hevie so great cair must be taken in removing them from the shipe to the bark that cairies them to Alloa, and in taking them out of the bark again' (NADFAS 2000, 77–9).

Macky, who may well have visited Alloa some years before the first publication of his book in 1723, described the gardens there in hyperbolic terms:

The plantation around the House of Allaway is the largest, and finest, (laid out by the unhappy Earl that commanded in the Rebellion,) of any in Britain; it far exceeds either Hampton-court or Kensington; the Gardens consisting of two and forty Acres, and the Wood, with Visto's cut through it, of one hundred and fifty Acres. The Entry from the Town is from the West, by a pair of fine Stone Gates, through a spacious Avenue, which leads you to an Area fronting the House on that side, in the middle of which is a Gladiator, after the manner of that at Hampton-court, and on the right hand of this Area is a spacious Garden, with a fine Terras, and Bowling-green, adorn'd with the largest Evergreens you can see any where. To the South of the House is the Parterre, spacious and finely adorn'd with Statues and Vases; and from this Parterre ... you have thirty two different Visto's, each ending on some remarkable Seat or Mountain at some Miles Distance; one of them shews you Sterling-Castle, at four Miles Distance; another the Palace of Elphingston, on the other Side of the River; a third the Castle of Clacmaning; and so the rest: In the middle of this long Terras, is a Bason of Water, like that of the Duke of Chandois, at Cannons, in the middle of which is the Statue of Cain slaying of Abel; and at the End to the River, are a Pair of pyramidical Gates, where a ship of three hundred Tuns may unload. The Avenue to the East through the Wood, is prodigiously long and large; and between each Visto, from the Parterre, are Wildernesses of Trees for Birds and little Grotto's: The House was not yet quite finished; but by the great Stair-cases from every Front, one can guess at its Grandeur. (Macky 1729, 177–9)

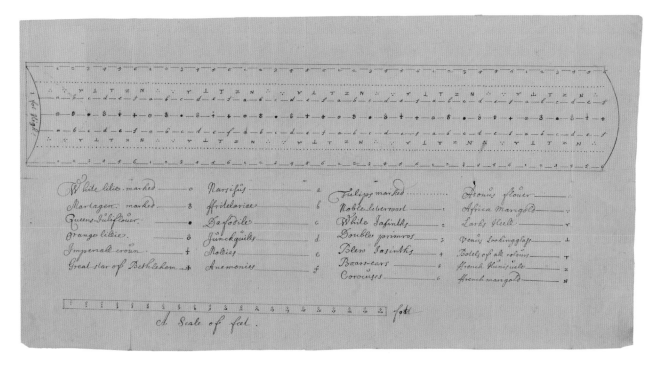

Fig 403 *Plan for a garden with a list of flowers to accompany the letter sent by Lord Grange to the head gardener Thomas Harlow. © Mar and Kellie Muniments, GD124. National Records of Scotland*

Mar was Secretary of State for Scotland from 1705 to the accession of George I, but his leadership of the 1715 rebellion led to his exile in France and Italy, which lasted for the rest of his life. His brother Lord Grange acquired his forfeited estate, and held it in trust for the family. Mar's plans for Alloa were worked and reworked in accordance with his own ideas and with developing fashions in garden design (Fig 404). The old embroidery parterres were replaced, in plan, with flat lawns and flower borders with statues, and the kitchen gardens were removed to the rear of the house. Ponds with topiary borders were introduced and 'Green rooms' of various shapes formed. Margaret Stewart identified an increasing modification in favour of contemporary French gardens of which Mar would be acquiring a deeper knowledge. She also mentioned that the incorporation of utility within the garden and the engagement with the wider landscape was giving way to a sense of dense enclosure, in which the monuments which embody the Scottish past are fixed tableaux at the ends of thick high foliage walls (Stewart 1988, 39). In some senses the gardens at Alloa mark the culmination of a way of thinking about gardens. New ideas about nature and its relation to gardens were beginning to make themselves felt in England and Scotland.

Fig 404 *A drawing made by the Earl of Mar in 1731 during his exile from Scotland showing the view he envisaged from the front of Alloa House. © Mar and Kellie Muniments, GD124. National Records of Scotland*

Chapter 6: Evolution and Innovation 1714 to 1750

Too formed for Nature – yet too wild for Art

'Loch Rian' by Samuel Boyse

The form of gardens in Scotland did not change with the accession of George I to the throne of the United Kingdom, but the death of William Bruce in 1710 and the death of Alexander Edward in 1708 and the exile of the Earl of Mar following the 1715 rising saw the departure of the most influential of the architects and designers of the late seventeenth and eighteenth centuries. William Adam was to become the favoured architect for the next generation who wished to build or extend their country houses and redesign their gardens. By 1721 he was working at Hopetoun and his design for the landscape around the house showed none of the parterres on the French pattern which had lain to the west of the mansion and extended as far as the oval basin in the time of William Bruce. While their outline was preserved, a smooth expanse of turf interrupted only by paths laid out at right angles ran up to the mansion. The entrance court to the east of the house was raised and separated by a sunk fence from the oval drive, which was flanked by small plantations. Adam's plan does not indicate that this court was, as it is at present, laid down to grass, although its dimensions, 774 by 360 feet (235m by 110m), would make paving or gravel an expensive choice (Jacques 2000, 31; Williamson 2000, 12). This development cannot be seen as a decisive break with the elaboration of the gardens of Bruce and Edward, but its greater simplicity does represent the continuing evolution of the appreciation of classicism

in Scotland. Not only William Adam but the owner of the house, the Earl of Hopetoun, was closely concerned with the reworking of the building (Rowan 1984, 189, 192), and he may have had an equivalent voice in the changes to the garden design (Fig 406).

However, even a cursory examination of the Roy Military Survey, the map prepared between 1747 and 1755 in the aftermath of the 1745 Jacobite rebellion, reveals a country studded with formal gardens and landscapes that stand out against a background of agricultural use. While these occur far more frequently in the Lowlands and Aberdeenshire than elsewhere, a glance at the coastal areas of the West Highlands shows, even there, the adoption on a small scale of a regular plan for the surroundings of the dwellings of local land holders; this may be noted especially in Argyll, extending up the coast into Ross and Cromarty (Figs 407, 408). The Hebrides, Orkney and Shetland were not included in Roy's Survey. Many of these estates had been newly laid out in the first half of the eighteenth century, and indicate the continuing adoption and desirability of the formal plan. They are portrayed in remarkable, and as far as can be ascertained, accurate detail, raising the possibility that at times existing estate plans may have been utilised, providing a shortcut, although such features as walls, avenues and buildings had a military significance; it is thought that Roy himself was responsible for the detail, while Paul Sandby undertook the subtle relief shading of the mountains (Bonehill and Daniels 2009, 86–7).

One of Adam's early clients was John Dalrymple, field marshal and second Earl of Stair. He followed a military career from an early age and took part in an

Fig 405 The gardens of Castle Kennedy on the isthmus between the White Loch and the Black Loch were the long-running project of Field Marshal Stair and his gardener, Thomas McCalla, during his retirement from diplomacy, warfare and political office between 1720 and 1740. DP052060

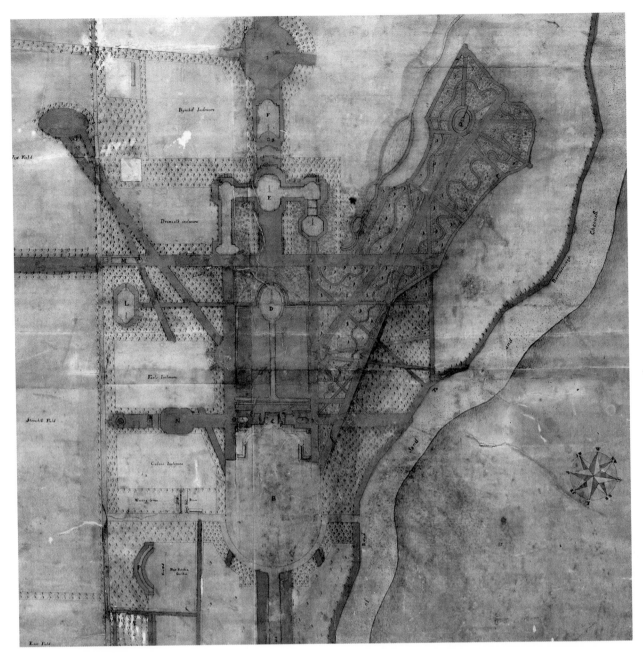

Fig 406 Plan of Hopetoun by William Adam. The elaborate parterres have disappeared and the forecourt has been raised but the overall layout is similar to the design of William Bruce and Alexander Edward. SC1238191 © Hopetoun House Preservation Trust

embassy to Vienna in 1700. He was engaged in the European wars of the early eighteenth century, fighting in the battles of Blenheim, Oudenarde and Malplaquet. After the accession of George I and following the Treaty of Utrecht, he was appointed minister-plenipotentiary at Paris becoming ambassador to France in 1719, where his lavish spending in support of his position contributed to his later financial problems. An important part of his duties was the detection of Jacobite intrigues and the dissuading of France from supporting the Old Pretender, and in pursuit of this aim he corresponded with Jacobite sympathisers including the Earl of Mar. Stair was a

founding member of the Society of Improvers in the Knowledge of Agriculture and introduced many new developments on his estates, including the large-scale cultivation of turnips and cabbages. While he held no military or diplomatic posts for more than twenty years following 1720, he spent time, when not engaged in political intrigues, at his estates at Castle Kennedy in Wigtownshire and at Newliston near Edinburgh, which he had inherited from his mother. In the 1740s he was back on campaign in Europe, fighting the Battle of Dettingen under the command of George II (Brown 1991, 149; *DNB* 2004, 14, 1000–4).

The gardens at **Castle Kennedy** had been briefly described in the late seventeenth century by Mr Andrew Symson, the minister of the parish, in response to Sir Robert Sibbald's request for information towards the compilation of his proposed 'Scotish Atlas, or the

Fig 407 Flowerdale or Gairloch House on the north-west coast of Ross and Cromarty with its formal laid out plantions as they are depicted on Roy's Military Survey of 1747 to 1755. © British Library Licensor Scran

Description of Scotland'. He writes about the gardens and orchards, environed with a freshwater loch, noting that the property had formerly belonged to the earls of Cassillis. On a small island in the loch the late Earl of Cassillis had erected a little house to which he was rowed between sermons at the parish church (Macfarlane 1906–8, 2, 91). The tower house at Castle Kennedy, which burnt down in 1716 and was never rebuilt, was situated on an isthmus between the Black Loch and the White Loch. Despite this destruction (and it may always have been the intention to construct a modern mansion there) elaborate works on the gardens, which covered some 70 acres (28ha), were undertaken by the field marshal and his chief gardener, Thomas McCalla, for over twenty years. When he was in Galloway the earl lived at Culhorn near Stranraer, where he also undertook work on the garden and the landscape surrounding the house; his regiment was also based at Culhorn, and some of the soldiers carried out earth moving at Castle Kennedy, while the horse dung was used for the garden (Dalrymple 1908, 25). Both the garden designer and nurseryman William Boutcher and William Adam were consulted about the gardens at Castle Kennedy. Boutcher was certainly involved about 1722 and provided a garden plan (Tait 1980, 10), but the plan which was adopted is thought to be the work of Adam modified by the Earl of Stair and his gardener (Tait 1980, 12).

The very distinctive natural setting of Castle Kennedy with its twin lochs and confined site, would seem to have been both a challenge and a stimulus, while the absence of a house and the presence of a ruin seem to have presented no hindrance to the design of long vistas and walks (Fig 409). There are various references to

Adam visiting Castle Kennedy in subsequent years (Tait 1980, 40), and in 1727 Stair was to recommend Adam for the post of Surveyor of the King's Works in Scotland (Gifford 1989, 107). At least two copies of the plan of the gardens for Castle Kennedy were made; one remained with the owner and one with the gardener (Dalrymple 1908, 19). A version of the plan was found in a cottage on the estate about 1840, when the garden had become overgrown (Maxwell 1908, 79); Sir Thomas Dick Lauder, who saw the plan, commented that there had been considerable deviation from it in the grounds as they had survived, noting that 'while formality is strictly observed throughout every part of it, yet it is replete with these great charms – intricacy and variety. These would be sufficient of themselves to save the whole from condemnation' (Dalrymple 1908, 37–8).

Fig 408 Applecross House with its parterres and formally designed policies as they appear on Roy's Military Survey of 1747 to 1755. © British Library Licensor Scran

Fig 409 Castle Kennedy and its geometric layout of plantations as it appears on Roy's Military Survey of 1747 to 1755. © British Library Licensor Scran

John Claudius Loudon, garden designer and theorist, was asked to undertake its restoration in the 1840s (Fig 411).

Aerial survey during a period of drought has revealed a series of features in the turf which belong to several periods, but which include the outlines of the layout of the 1720s and 1730s. The gardens run between the irregular shores of the Black Loch and the White Loch to the north of the castle, with a surviving walled garden to the south and an avenue, known as Dettingen Avenue, beyond it, running to the edge of the White Loch. The traces of the walled enclosure to the west of the ruined tower house and some other features may have come through from the seventeenth century garden (Fig 410).

The most obvious feature is a broad avenue, which is not centred on the house, but very slightly to its west. It does not relate to the garden constructions carried out in the time of the second earl; it is on the same alignment, but set a few metres to the west. It would appear to be earlier than this design and may indicate an intention at some time to rebuild the mansion on a larger scale on a slightly different site, a plan that was subsequently abandoned; excavation would establish the relative sequence of the designs. A canal was constructed between the two lochs by 1732 (Dalrymple 1908, 18).

In front of the mansion to the north was an enclosed garden consisting of a wide terrace through which ran three paths, one central and one at each side. It was divided in two laterally by a line indicating the foundation of a wall; this whole area may have been formed of grass parterres enclosed by hedges. The

Fig 410 Aerial view of Castle Kennedy with the parchmarks of garden features, probably narrow planting trenches for low hedges, in front of the ruined tower house. These may predate the second earl's designs. SC1018855

paths led down by means of turf steps to a narrow lower terrace, and down again onto slightly lower ground. Both central sets of steps were in the form of a shallow ellipse. Some walks were gravelled and some sown with grass. At the north end of the area was a lower central semi-circular feature. This area of the garden was protected from the inroads of cattle and sheep by the construction of a sunk fence. Beyond it to one side on the north-west was the large circular pond referred to as the Basin, and on the north-east the stepped mount or Belvedere, Mount Marlborough; the head gardener wrote to Lord Stair in 1733, 'From the belluadair the bason apers lik a great glas' (Dalrymple 1908, 19) (Fig 405). The pond

was created by cutting off a small bay in the White Loch and raising the ground around it (Dalrymple 1908, 20). There is mention of a bowling green for which William Adam designed a Temple and published the design as a plate in *Vitruvius Scoticus* (Plate 121) (Fig 412).

The published correspondence between the Earl and Thomas McCalla throws considerable light on proceedings in the gardens at both Castle Kennedy and **Culhorn House** and provides evidence that changes were made in the process of working on the gardens (Dalrymple 1908, 17–29). McCalla wrote that he was waiting for a letter from Stair with instructions, but put forward his own view as to what could be done with the land, reporting on the soil conditions and what could be done to remedy them, in addition to making alterations to the plans on his judgement of what looked well (Dalrymple 1908, 18). As with the designs of William

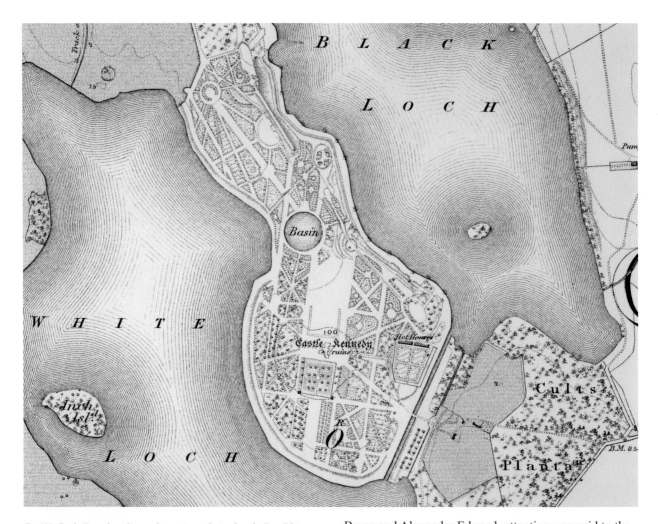

Fig 411 Castle Kennedy and its gardens as it was depicted on the First Edition of the Ordnance Survey 6-inch map of Wigtownshire surveyed in 1847 before the building of Lochinch Castle in 1864–8.

Fig 412 The Temple designed by William Adam for a site by the bowling green at Castle Kennedy (Vitruvius Scoticus Plate 121). SC1238228

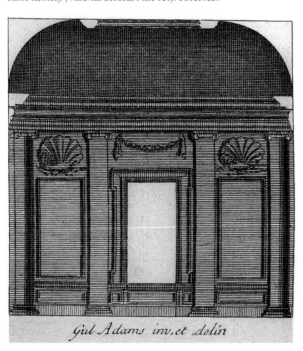

Bruce and Alexander Edward, attention was paid to the laying out of walks related to monuments of antiquarian significance. One walk was aligned on Cairn Macneilie to the north-west beyond the White Loch (Dalrymple 1908, 19). The construction of views was preceded by an experiment to see how effective they might prove. There was a considerable amount of earth moving involved, which included the formation of the ridge of hills above the Black Loch, where there was no suitable soil. Earth had to be brought up in barrows (Dalrymple 1908, 17). An oval bowling green which was already in place in some form lay on the east side of the garden and was cleared of ash trees and enclosed by a holly hedge; it also had a 'dimond bank', possibly one cut at sharp angles (Dalrymple 1908, 14, 18, 24). One notable undertaking was the excavation of a canal between the Black Loch and the White Loch and the creation of a great walk alongside it planted with dwarf clover seeds (Dalrymple 1908, 18, 22) (Fig 405).

Fruit trees were brought from Stair's other estate at Newliston; various types of vine were also planted and a fig tree which had stood in the previous garden had cuttings taken from it (Dalrymple 1908, 17). Melons were cultivated, protected by melon glasses (Dalrymple 1908, 25, 26, 27). The old brick walled garden near the tower house was cleared and the walls were rough cast

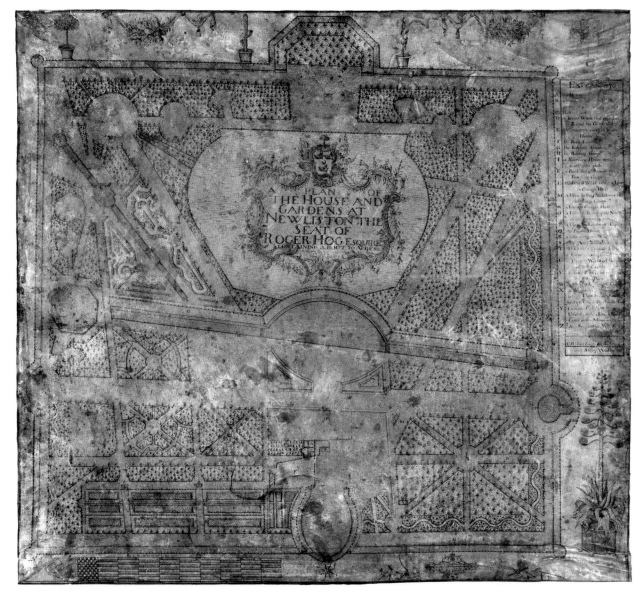

Fig 413 Plan of the house and gardens at Newliston with its strongly geometrical but slightly asymmetric design, a copy of the plan made by William Adam for Field Marshal Stair. DP097618

preventing (to some degree) the snails attacking the fruit trees there (Dalrymple 1908, 17, 24). The nearby Stair property at Carscreuch was used as a nursery for the gardens at Castle Kennedy and Culhorn. Yews and shrubs came from Ireland and it was planned that the walks should be planted with pyramid hollies and yews (Dalrymple 1908, 17–18). Wildernesses were planted with flowering shrubs such as rosemary, bay and laurustinus, although they suffered in cold winters (Dalrymple 1908, 29). Seeds for beech and holly were collected and fir seed promised from Campbell estates. Requests were made by Lord Stair for a supply of these, as well as yew berries, clover and grass seed (Dalrymple 1908, 17–18, 21, 23, 27). Trees were raised in nurseries and often required watering immediately after they were planted, for which a form of water pump ('the

Ingin') proved extremely useful (Dalrymple 1908, 17, 23). There was tree planting in avenues and plantations mixed with the cultivation of recently introduced crops such as turnips, as well as cabbage and carrots sown on a large scale (Dalrymple 1908, 28).

Some of the labour required for the construction of the gardens was supplied by the soldiers and horses of Lord Stair's own regiment but the gardener complained about the difficulty of getting them to work long and hard enough, as well as difficulties with receiving the money to pay them and others working on the gardens (Dalrymple 1908, 17–20, 25, 26).

Castle Kennedy had become a recognised place to visit by 1733. McCalla wrote to Lord Stair about the compliment paid by the owner of Leslie House, who belonged to a family noted for their encouragement of plantations, 'My lord Rothes was hir and commended this plais aboue any plas euer he had sen.' Lord Grange's son, the nephew of the Earl of Mar came, 'who veued the gardens very sharply and went along the ridge nir

Fig 414 Aerial view of Newliston from the north with its walls, bastion and corner towers.

to the draw bridge and then went up the wallk that uas cot thro the uhins to the top and along the ridge to Kern McNilli, and then bak to the gardens, and went thro them a second tim' (Dalrymple 1908, 21, 28). The gardens were celebrated in verse by Samuel Boyse who wrote in a work addressed to Lord Stair in 1734:

Fig 415 Newliston with its plantations and walks as they appear on Roy's Military Survey of 1747 to 1755. © British Library Licensor Scran

How bloom thy gardens crown'd with soft delight
And spread successive beauties to the sight:
What airy prospects! What romantic views!
Surprise the fancy, and inspire the Muse!
Through the long vista, or the casual break,
Glitter the blue canal, or silver lake;
Sweetly bewilder'd the spectator roves
Midst hills, and moss-grown rocks, and hanging groves;
With care the eye examines every part,
Too form'd for Nature – yet too wild for Art:
(Chalmers 1810, 14, 533)

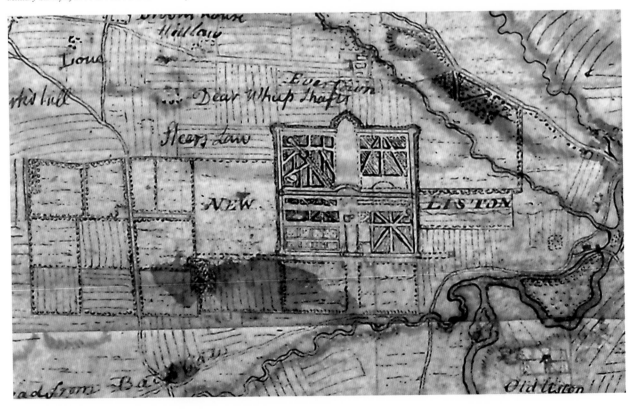

Fig 416 Aerial view of Newliston from the south. The pond and matching earthworks occupy the centre of the photograph. SC1018819

Fig 417 A sketch of the probably seventeenth century tower house at Newliston. SC1252475

Culhorn, where Field Marshall Stair lived when he visited Wigtownshire, was also looked after by McCalla, although he found the time that he had to take travelling there from Castle Kennedy prevented him from keeping the workmen up to the mark. As at Castle Kennedy there were many avenues and a great mount or belvedere, the summit of which was to be planted in a circle open towards the house and the rest grassed (Dalrymple 1908, 19, 21, 22).

Stair's other main property was **Newliston** (Fig 414), not far from Edinburgh. A plan for the gardens was prepared by William Adam about 1725 and a copy was made in 1759 for the new owner, Roger Hog, after the property had been sold by the Stair family following the death of the second earl (RCAHMS Collections WLD\43\21P) (Fig 413). The surviving original plan is now at Blenheim; Stair sent a copy to Sarah, Duchess of Marlborough, the widow of his former commander-in-chief, who was engaged in the construction of the palace there. A new house was designed by William Adam in 1723 (Adam 1980, Plate 35) (Fig 418), but, as at Castle Kennedy, it was never realised and the tower house continued to be inhabited until the later eighteenth century (Fig 417); William Adam, who was paid £150 sterling in 1723 (NRS GD 135/144), was probably responsible for the building of the stables. The present mansion, the plan for which, by Robert Adam, is dated 1789, now forms the focal point for the garden (Bolton 1922, 2, 279).

In contrast to Castle Kennedy with its varied natural setting, Newliston was situated on a site which sloped gently from west to east; the terrain would have permitted the adoption of a strictly symmetrical design, but, in spite of this, a degree of deliberate asymmetry,

*Fig 418 An engraving of the south front of the proposed Newliston House designed by William Adam (*Vitruvius Scoticus, *Plate 35) © University of Strathclyde. Licensor Scran*

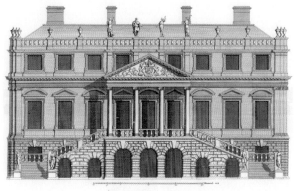

The South Front of Newliston toward the Court

Fig 419 A detail from a plan of the Carmichael estate showing the policies immediately around the mansion house. This was constructed in stages and the tower house, the L-shaped building next to the walled garden, remained in use. DP065808

although very orderly asymmetry, was chosen (Figs 415, 416). The garden was enclosed within a stone wall or sunk fence fortified with corner towers, with an angled bastion on the north side and semi-circular ones to east and west; a terraced walk was constructed along the wall allowing views both inside and outside the garden. A raised horseshoe-shaped lawn enclosed by a sunk fence broke the line of the walls on the south. The fashion for fortified gardens has been associated with the wars of the earlier eighteenth century and the admiration given to the fortifications of the French military engineer, Vauban, although there were seventeenth century predecessors (Williams 2000, 49–56, 69). A canal, accompanied by a terrace walk, was designed running at an oblique angle across the policies; it began on the west with an octagonal pond, fed from a diverted stream, and led to a cascade down which water fell into a semi-oval basin matched by a semi-oval lawn; another cascade led to the eastern section of the canal from where the water was led below ground to a small oval pool and out beyond the garden wall to a channelled stream. A second shorter and narrower canal with a series of water steps ran from the north-west with intricate walks laid out to both sides. Avenues and walks were laid out providing varied views including those towards the mansion of Craigiehall and Niddry Castle. The plantation to the east of the house was laid out like an asymmetric Union Jack with a statue of Hercules as its focus and a regular serpentine walk on two of its sides. The use of bastions and towers as major features in the garden and the presence of a statue of Hercules reflect the celebration of the field marshal's military career. The suggestion that the disposition of the plantings at Newliston was intended to represent the disposition of the armies at the Battle of Dettingen in 1742 (Mackenzie 1927, 242) is countered by the fact that the plan, which was actually carried out at Newliston, dates from about 1725.

Speculation on the influence that foreign travel for military and diplomatic purposes had on choices made in respect of garden design can be explored further at the less well known **Carmichael House** in Lanarkshire, which is remarkable for the preservation of its mid eighteenth century landscape (Figs 419, 421). This was designed by John Carmichael, third Earl of Hyndford, who belonged to a younger generation than Stair, being born in 1701. He was a captain in the third regiment of foot-guards from 1733 before succeeding his father in 1737 and sitting in parliament as a Scottish representative peer (Fig 420). After the outbreak of the War of the Austrian Succession, Hyndford was sent by George II as an envoy extraordinary and plenipotentiary to mediate between Frederick II of Prussia and Maria Theresa of Austria, a mission leading to the Treaty of Breslau. Between 1744 and 1749 he was in Russia and was engaged in forwarding the Treaty of Aix-la-Chapelle, which was concluded in 1748. Seeds brought from Russia are believed to have been used in the

Fig 420 *Portrait of John Carmichael, third Earl of Hyndford, by John Richardson the Elder. © National Galleries of Scotland. Licensor Scran*

plantations on his estate. He left Moscow late in 1749, and was attached to the embassy in Vienna between 1752 and 1764 (*DNB* 10, 176–7). The persistence of garden designs of extreme formality in Prussia, Russia and Austria may be relevant to his choices for Carmichael. This extensive foreign service would appear to leave little time for works on his estate in Lanarkshire, but he erected a new mansion in two parts in the 1730s and laid out an extensive formal landscape around it; there is no record of him employing a professional architect or surveyor. He was much concerned with agricultural developments on his estates and granted leases of fifty-seven years to his tenants to encourage improvements. As at Newliston and Castle Kennedy before the fire, accommodation was provided by a tower house which appears on the surviving copy, made in 1882, of the plan of the policies surveyed in 1750, and they appear in a similar form on the Military Survey. The tower lay close to the two pavilions which were built by the Earl of Hyndford during the 1730s and which were probably intended to be part of a larger building (RCAHMS Collections DP 065807). John Carmichael died in 1767 and left no direct heirs; his second wife lived to 1807. There seems to have been no impetus to change the design of the gardens and they remain an excellent example of a style of gardening that ceased to be fashionable in the later eighteenth century (Fig 419).

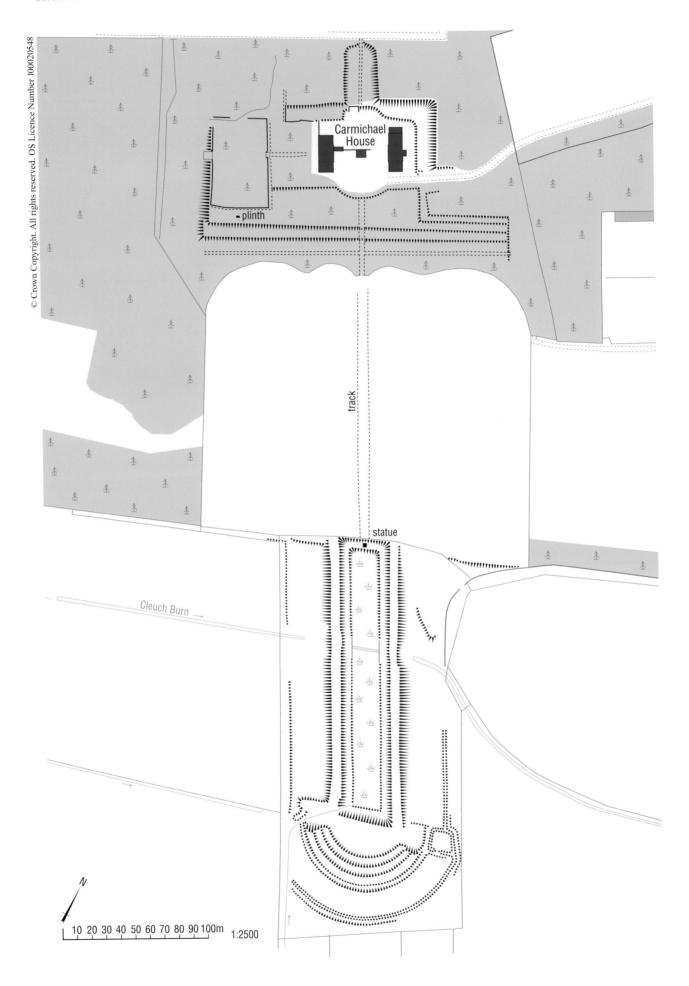

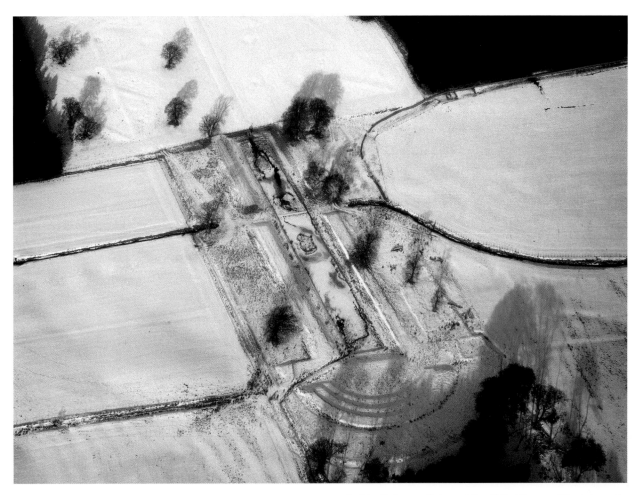

Fig 422 Aerial view of the policies at Carmichael from the north with light snow revealing the outlines of the former criss-cross walks within the wildernesses bordering the way down to the canal and amphitheatre. Some of the surviving design for small tree plantations arranged in a quincunx pattern can be seen on the left of the photograph. SC1037617

The gardens lie across the valley of the Cleuch Burn with Carmichael Hill to the north-west and Tinto to the south-east. The whole design, as at Newliston, is slightly asymmetric, and there has been a deliberate choice not to align the policies on the prominent peak of Tinto towards which a vista could have been designed with relatively little extra effort, given the amount of earth moving required for the creation of the present landscape. The plan of the earthworks around the site of the house as surveyed by the Royal Commission shows the slight misalignment between the house and the canal. The house stands facing south-east on level ground with terracing to the rear and to the front, all of which was densely planted with evergreens in the 1950s, and a walled garden to the north-west. Below the terracing was a long grassy walk with a central path leading down to one end of the canal. On each side were plantations with walks, laid out in wilderness fashion, which can still be detected in the grass under

Fig 421 Plan of the gardens at Carmichael House. GV004967

suitable light conditions (Fig 422). The rectilinear canal, always known as the curling pond, measures some 34m in length with broad terraced walks on each side. It is fed by the Cleuch Burn, but there seem to have been problems in arranging for it to be filled consistently. At its south-east end is a semi-circular amphitheatre of three steps beyond which was a level area formerly planted with trees backing on to a broad avenue ending on the skyline as viewed from the site of the house. Fields on both sides of this avenue are separated by narrow plantations, which would have served as shelter belts, and decorated with circular plantations, five to a field, arranged in quincunx fashion. Avenues and shelter belts divide up the remainder of the policies (Fig 423).

Alan Tait (1980) has enlarged on the transition to a greater informality in garden design in his book *The Landscape Garden in Scotland, 1735–1835*, marking the developments in taste between these dates, but he also documents its antecedents during the preceding twenty years. How early William Adam's move towards a less extended rectilinear approach to garden design began is uncertain. Tait places it in the 1730s, but notes that within the formal landscape Adam designed at **Taymouth Castle** in 1720 was a curving riverside walk, in addition to the massive avenues running north and south extending across the River Tay and the parallel lines of plantations arranged at 45 degree angles across

Fig 423 The Carmichael estate as depicted on Roy's Military Survey of 1747 to 1755 with its full array of decorative plantations. © British Library Licensor Scran

the landscape. There were parterres of a relatively plain design and an orchard in the immediate area of the house; the planting holes for the trees which edged the grass plots in front of the house can still be seen in what is now a golf course (Figs 424, 425). The line of the river favoured the form of a curving walk, and its creation may be seen as a response to the natural landscape in contrast to the major features of the design, which take no account of the varied terrain.

From 1720 Adam rapidly became the favoured architect for Scottish proprietors who wished to rebuild their country houses. Owners might ask and pay for proposals and a plan but often the house concerned was

not rebuilt or remodelled because the scheme proved too expensive for the proprietor. Many of these designs were later published in *Vitruvius Scoticus*, the plates for which were being put together from the mid 1720s (Adam 1980). Adam worked on plans for houses at Floors, Redbraes, Hamilton, Mavisbank, Newliston, Castle Kennedy, The Drum, Mellerstain, Lawers and Arniston among others. Garden designs at Hopetoun, Taymouth and Arniston followed the plans for the buildings (Tait 1980, 12). Adam was usually on good terms with his clients, some of whom were amateurs of architecture and might influence the design of the mansion and its surrounding landscape.

The foremost theorist among the owners was Sir John Clerk of Penicuik whose work on his own gardens at **Penicuik** and **Mavisbank** influenced the taste of the landowning and garden designing classes in Scotland.

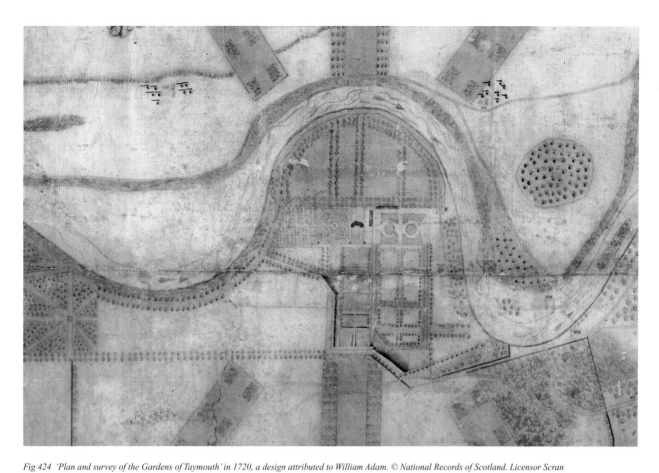

Fig 424 'Plan and survey of the Gardens of Taymouth' in 1720, a design attributed to William Adam. © National Records of Scotland. Licensor Scran

Fig 425 Aerial view of Taymouth Castle with the planting holes for the trees bordering the walks showing as a darker green in the short turf of the golf course. SC1238227

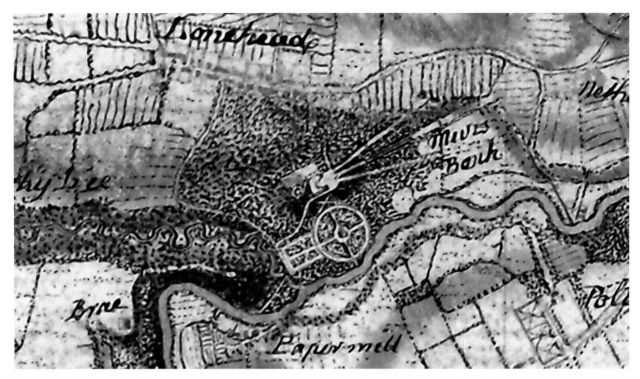

Fig 426 Sir John Clerk of Penicuik's estate at Mavisbank with its extensive planting along the River Esk as depicted on Roy's Military Survey of 1747 to 1755. © British Library Licensor Scran

Much has been written about the gardens with which he was involved (Piggott 1970, 110–17; Spink 1974, 31–40; Tait 1980, 21–4; Gifford 1989, 94; Cooper 2002, 47–62). He had made a two year long *grand tour* through Germany, Austria, France and Italy beginning in 1697 (Gifford 1989, 81–2). His poem in blank verse, *The Country Seat*, which Clerk indicates he had largely perfected in 1724 and which was completed in 1727, was transcribed by Samuel Boyse in Edinburgh in 1732 and circulated widely in manuscript. Boyse's verses on Yester and Castle Kennedy have already been noted, and he also wrote about Dalkeith and Mavisbank, as well as gardens in England, and appreciated and echoed Clerk's views on garden design (Chalmers 1810, 14). These drew on the writings of Addison and Pope, as well as ideas set out in Switzer's *Ichonographia Rustica* (1718) and attempted to apply them in a more practical manner (Tait 1980, 18–21). In 1727 William Adam was travelling in England with Sir John Clerk of Penicuik, visiting various houses around London and arranging the preliminaries for the publication of *Vitruvius Scoticus* (Gifford 1989, 108). Clerk's garden and landscape at Mavisbank and Penicuik are discussed extensively by Tait (1980, 21–4), but he comments that Adam's plan for Arniston was perhaps a better realisation of the more liberal aspects of *The Country Seat* than Clerk's own properties (Tait 1980, 26–33) (Figs 426, 427). There was a gradual increase in the perception of the value of the natural landscape, even in its wildness. Adam's work on the gardens at Hamilton

Palace and the building of Chatelherault in the 1730s provided a contrast between the view down Alexander Edward's long avenue towards the Palace and the rear and sideways views to the Avon Gorge, the ruined Cadzow Castle and the park with its wild white cattle. There were no avenues or allées in this direction and the planting along the Avon followed the winding of the river (Tait 1980, 40–41; Gifford 1989, 146–7).

Apart from Adam, William Boutcher, who was based at his nursery at Comely Bank, Edinburgh, was the most prominent Scottish designer. In his designs and those of Thomas Winter and William Taylor, Tait detects a lack of vigour and self-assurance, reckoning that the formal style had degenerated into unimaginative repetition, and points out the inappropriateness of Boutcher's scheme for the estate at The Grange (later Lamancha) in Peeblesshire and his lack of appreciation of its natural surroundings (Tait 1980, 9–11). His plan of changes to the policies at Airth Castle in 1721 (Fig 428), show an elaboration of what was already there, rather than the simplification Adam introduced at Hopetoun. However, the close involvement of some owners with the design and development of their estates led to gardens, as at Castle Kennedy, Newliston and Carmichael, which exhibit a robust and inventive treatment of the ground, taking into account their prominent natural features, and stamped with their own signature.

John Clerk was not the only Scottish landowner concerned about writing his thoughts on the design of gardens and policies in the 1720s. George Dundas, who inherited the **Dundas Castle** estate in 1707, wrote an account of his experiences in tree planting there which survives in manuscript. He also recorded his conclusions on the design of gardens, probably in about 1724.

Fig 427 Arniston with its mansion and policies designed by William Adam and showing a greater involvement with the landscape as it is depicted on Roy's Military Survey of 1747 to 1755. © British Library Licensor Scran

These owe a great deal to *The theory and practice of gardening* by Antoine-Joseph Dézallier d'Argenville, which was translated from the original French by John James in 1712. The list of the subscribers includes more than thirty of the foremost of the nobility and gentry in Scotland, but not Dundas himself or the earls of Stair and Hyndford. His own gardens have not survived (Fig 429) but, in contrast to Sir John Clerk (another non-subscriber), he favoured gardens on the lines of those of his near neighbour, the Earl of Stair at Newliston, to whom he sold some of his trees for the garden. He declared:

The true size of a handsome garden is 30 or 40 acres not more. The building should descend the parterres 3 steps at least Nixt to the house both upon the back front and side should parterres of different kinds present themselves. Next to the parterres (if the ground be plane and the view pleasant) should be quarters of grass and other flat work to make the best of the view taking [notice] not to shut up the view with groves unless they are placed in Quincunx or opened with large hedgerow. If there be no Vista, but Mountains Hills forests, woods or villages verry near you may then edge the parterre with palisades and Groves to hide these Objects.
To accompanie parterres you should make choice of such designs of wood work as Groves opened in Compartment Quincunxes, Verdant Halls wt Bowling greens, Arbour work and fountains in

the Middle and especially near the house groves of evergreens. The [he]ad of a parterre is usually adorned wt basons or waterworks wt a circular line of palisades cut into a goose foot which leads into the Great Walks and the space between the bason and the palisade is filled wt small pieces of Embroidery or Grasswork set out wt yews, cases and flower pots.
In gardens that have terrasses, sideways or in front of the building to continue the view you must not shut it up wt palisades but lay several compartments of a parterre together such as embroidery, green plots or cut grass which should be divied att convenient distances by cross walks the embroidery always being nixt the house ... Without the parterre ... should be many different designs as Tall Groves, Quincunxes, close walls, galleries and halls of verdure, green arbours, labyrinths, bowling greens and Amphitheatres adorned with fountains canals figures &c which renders a garden Magnificent. You should observe in distributing several parts to oppose always the one to the Other, as a wood to a parterre or a bowling green and not to put all the parterres on one side and all the wood on the other (NLS 80.6.3, 30–2)
Parterres may be reduced to these following: Parterres of Embroidery Parterres of Compartment, parterres after the English manner, parterres of cut [work] parterres of grass with a border of flowers bursting through it which has best a mean appearance and is the worst of all the others. And parterres of water which are also at present quite out of use.

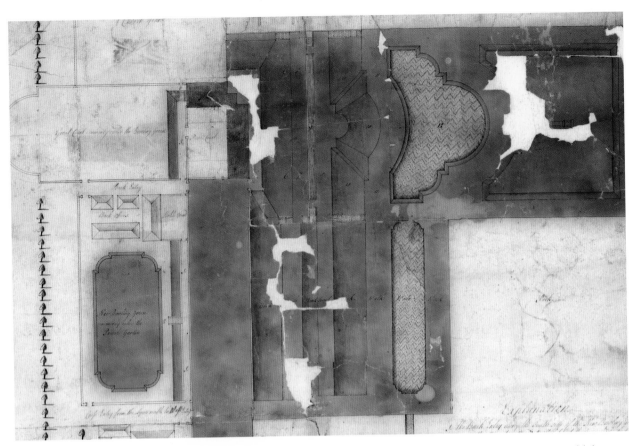

Fig 428 'A Plan of the West Avenue Garden Banks Terrasses pieces of Water and offices about the House of Airth The Seat of Mr James Graham of Airth', William Boutcher's plan of 1721 for the elaboration of the gardens at Airth Castle (STD50/14). DP090705

Parterres of Embroidery are so called because the box wherever they are planted imitates Embroidery on the Ground. These are the finest and most magnificent of all and are accompanied sometimes with knots or scrolls of cut grass work. Their bottom should be sanded or gravelled the better to distinguish the Embroidery which is usually filled with Smiths dust or black coal the narrow paths about the scrolls of grass should be filled with powered tile sherds or brick dust. Parterres of Compartment differ from the former in that the design of its sides and ends is the same but they are filled more up in the Middle with scroll and other grass works, knots and borders for flowers with a little well disposed Embroidery. They should be grounded and pathed as the former.
Parterres after the English manner are the plainest and meanest they compst only of large grass plots all of a piece or cut but a little and Encompassed with a border of flowers separated by a path of 2 or 3 foot wide laid smooth and sanded or gravelled ...
Parterres of cutwork tho not so fashionable at present are not unworthy our regard they differ from the others in that all the parts which compose it be cut with symmetry and they admit neither grass nor Embroidery, but only borders edged with box that serve to raise flowers in, and by means of a path of sufficient breadth that runs round each piece you may walk round the whole parterre which should be sanded or gravelled. Parterres of Embroidery being the finest should lie nix to the building those of Compartinent should accompanie yt and parterres after the English manner or those with the twisting borders of low flowers should serve to fill up the greater spaces, or in the Orangeries those of cut work are proper for small places where you would raise flowers and then it is called likewise parterres Fleurisse. The breadth of a parterre should be that of the whole house or somewhat more. Their length should not exceed a just proportion but that you may from the building discover all the Embroidery and Compartments. You may dispose parterres several ways either by cutting them into two long quarters with an Alley between them or making only one large square of Embroidered works with walks on the sides; or cutting it by diagonal walk in form of a St Andrews cross or sometimes into quarters arched att one end as the ground shall require.
There should be very few yews in a parterre and those not above 4 or 5 foot high for taking away the sight and beauty of the Embroidery.

Parterres are finest at first planting because
throw time the box spreads, the grass slope
loos it colour and the ground its level. (NLS
80.6.3, 34–7)

Dundas may have been more typical of the practice of
his contemporaries in his conservatism than Sir John
Clerk, and changes in garden design were slow to
make themselves felt, but by the middle of the century
there had been a pronounced shift in taste which,
however, took many years to make itself manifest in the
wider landscape.

Drumlanrig Castle in Dumfriesshire provides an
example of continuity into the period of the landscape
garden (Fig 431). The rebuilding of the castle and
gardens there began in the time of the first Duke of
Queensberry who was one of the main beneficiaries
of the fall of the Duke of Lauderdale before himself
losing the support of James II and VII. The form of
the gardens that accompanied the reconstruction of
the castle between 1675 and 1697 in the time of the
first duke is uncertain but, as Sir William Bruce was
consulted about the design of the building, they may
have incorporated some of the underlying principles
which were employed in his own gardens at Balcaskie
and Kinross. The area immediately around the house
was enclosed by stone walls with six stone built
pavilions with ogee roofs resembling those on the
castle. Like those on the castle, their 'bellcast roofs'
were to be covered in lead according to a contract of
1686 which included the leading of water through
the gardens and the installation of a 'clanging clock'
(Dunbar and Davies 1990, 314–16). The main entrance
was approached through a gate opening onto a drive
around an oval lawn leading to the double stairway
from which the front door was reached. The second
duke, who inherited in 1695, employed as his gardener
James Wood, son of Hew Wood of Hamilton, of whom
nothing is known after he travelled to London in 1696
'to improve himself for the Duke's better service'
(Jamieson 1992). The name of the next gardener
responsible for both Drumlanrig and the garden at
Queensberry House in Edinburgh was Cornelius van
Nerven, who was of Dutch origin. In 1698 the duke
sent instructions to Drumlanrig for the quarrying of
stone for stairs, a summer house, a fountain base and
pedestals for statues; a cascade was introduced.

In their long careers Charles Douglas, third Duke
of Queensberry from 1711 to 1778, and his gardener
David Low, who held the post between 1714 and
1747, saw a period of transition to the adoption of
the ideas of the landscape garden. Changes under the
superintendence of Low saw work on the west side of
the house, with a new bowling green and a great bank
cut out of whin rock to allow the eye to pass along an
avenue to the canal and the cascade where rock was
cut to improve its flow. Two drawings of a design for

*Fig 429 Dundas Castle and the estate of George Dundas, as depicted on
Roy's Military Survey of 1747 to 1755. Evidence of its owner's deliberations
on the design of gardens does not emerge from the map. © British Library
Licensor Scran*

*Fig 430 A sketch for the cascade at Drumlanrig in 1732 by Sir John Clerk of
Penicuik. DFD\58\14. SC1238230*

Fig 431 Aerial view of Drumlanrig from the north showing the partial recreation of the formal gardens of the earlier eighteenth and nineteenth centuries. SC1018915

the cascade were made by Sir John Clerk of Penicuik in 1728 and 1732 (RCAHMS Collections DFD\58\11 and DFD\58\14) (Fig 430). Two plans show the gardens in 1738 and 1739 in considerable detail with the network of avenues running out from the parterres around the castle (Jamieson 1996, 2; Gibson 2007, 28–9), one of which appears in Vitruvius Britannicus (1967, Vol 4, BR45, 46) (Figs 432, 433). The focus from the mansion is the cascade with the canal at its foot on which is depicted a miniature galleon.

There are extensive references to the gardens at Drumlanrig in the 1720s. As a preamble to his account of the house and gardens Macky provided a short aside

on the Gusto Grande, which he says is often mentioned by the Italian architects who attributed it to Louis XIV, giving as an example his choice for the site of 'the finest Palace in the World' of 'the barrennest Part of his Dominions, Versailles, and bringing Rivers over Mountains to supply it with Water, shew'd the Greatness of his Taste: ... The first Duke of Queensbury, who built this noble Palace in the Reign of Charles the Second, may seem to have had the oddest Taste in the World in the Situation of it; for it stands on a Rock, environ'd with high Mountains on every side' (Macky 1729, 13–14). He obviously considered the site sufficiently remarkable to require such a form of comparison. Similarly, when Daniel Defoe visited Drumlanrig at about the same time, he described it as 'a fine Picture in a dirty Grotto, or like an Equestrian Statue set up in a Barn; 'tis environ'd with Mountains, and that of the

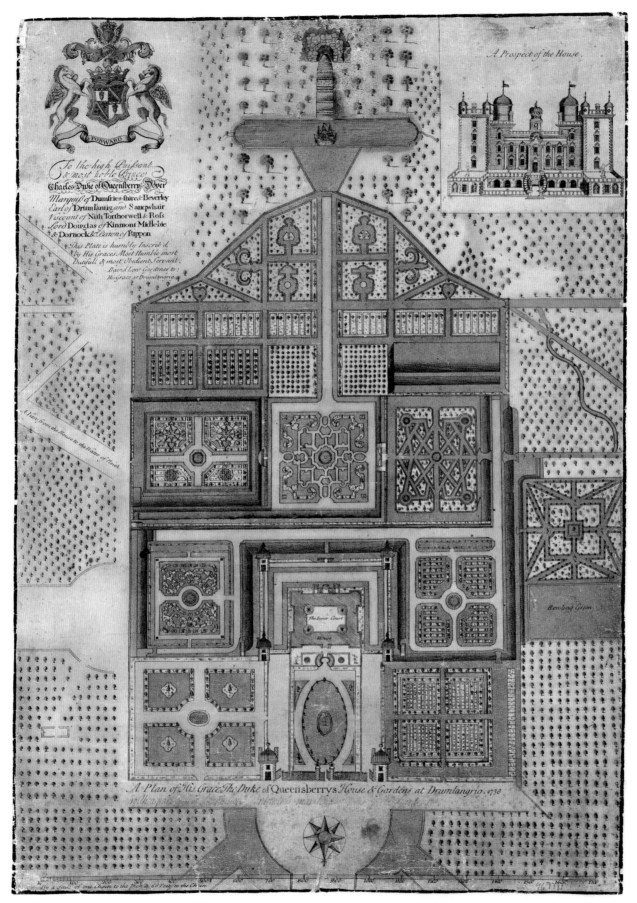

Fig 432 'Drumlanrig Castle and gardens' about 1739 showing the extensive parterres and water features including the canal and cascade by the gardener David Low.
DP1238226

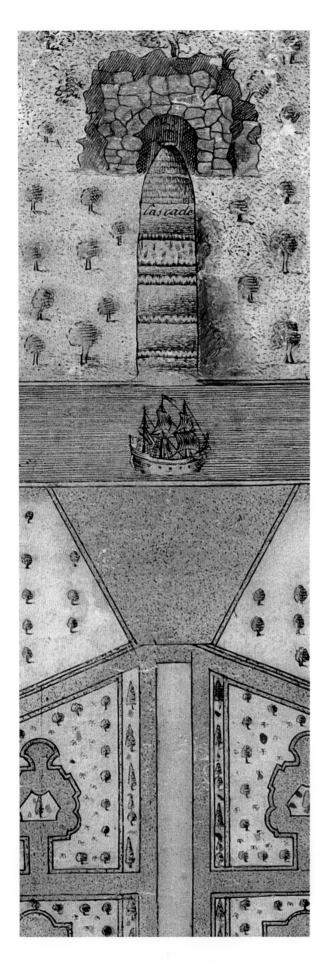

most hideous Aspect in all the South of Scotland' and likened its setting to that of Chatsworth (Defoe 1968, 727). He went on, 'But that which was more surprising than all the rest was to see a Palace so glorious, gardens so fine and every Thing so truly magnificent, and all in a wild mountainous Country' (Fig 434). His versifying companion wrote:

> Just thus, with horrid Desart Hills embrac'd,
> Was paradise on Euphra's border plac'd.
> The God of Harmony to grace the View,
> And make the Illustrations just and true,
> Strong contraries presented to the Eye,
> And circled Beauty in Deformity.
> The happy Discord entertains the Sight,
> And as these show more black, that shews more bright. (Defoe 1968, 727)

> The house stands on the Top of a rising Ground, which at its first Building, lay with a steep and uncouth Descent to the River, and made the Lookers on wonder what the Duke meant to build in such a disproportion'd Place: But he best understood his own Design; for the House once laid out, all that unequal Descent is so beautifully levelled and lay'd out in Slopes and Terrasses, that nothing can be better design'd, or indeed, better perform'd than the Gardens are, which take up the whole South and West Sides of the House; and when the whole Design will be done, the rest will be more easy, the Ground being a Plain the other Way, and the Park and Avenues compleatly planted with Trees.
> At the Extent of the Gardens there are Pavillions and Banquetting-Houses, exactly answering to one another, and the Greens trimmed, Spaliers and Hedges are in Perfection. (Defoe 1968, 728)

This perception of the house and garden as absolutely inappropriately sited may be contrasted with the descriptions of two visitors some twenty and fifty years later which provide examples of a major change in taste. In 1750 Bishop Pococke wrote:

> This fine improvement is a very beautiful situation; – there is a gentle ascent to the house of about half-a-mile, which is on a flat on the side of the hill, with a descent from it of 100 feet perpendicular to the rivlet, the hills rising up every way, except to the north, are covered with wood and cut into ridings. The house is something in the castle way, with a mixture of Roman architecture in a bad taste:– they were at first hanging gardens, but the present Duke has

Fig 433 Detail from the plan of 'Drumlanrig Castle and gardens' showing the cascade and a miniature galleon on the canal. DP1238226

Fig 434 Drumlanrig Castle set 'in a wild mountainous country'. SC764708

turned them all into slopes except the upper one which is thirty feet high, and could not so easily be formed into a slope. His Grace has likewise planted this part with forest trees, and made a large piece of water at the bottom with keeping up the rivlet; there 20 acres in the garden, and 700 under plantations: the prospect to the north is of the valley and hills and high mountains (Pococke 1887, 9–10).

Pococke disliked the architecture of the house and commented with mild approval, on the changes in the gardens which reduced their formality while the surrounding natural landscape was the subject of admiration.

Twenty-six years later in 1776 Gilpin in his *Observations, relative chiefly to picturesque beauty* (1789) found the house to be magnificent, 'tho there is little beauty in the architecture', approved of the scenery and was inspired by the garden to express the deepest condemnation. He writes:

The garden front of Queensberry-house opens on a very delightful piece of scenery. The ground falls from it, near a quarter of a mile, in a steep, sloping lawn; which at the bottom is received by a river; and beyond that rises a lofty wooded bank. All these objects are in the grandest style, except the river; which, tho not large, is by no means inconsiderable.
It is amazing what contrivance has been used to deform all this beauty. The descent from the house

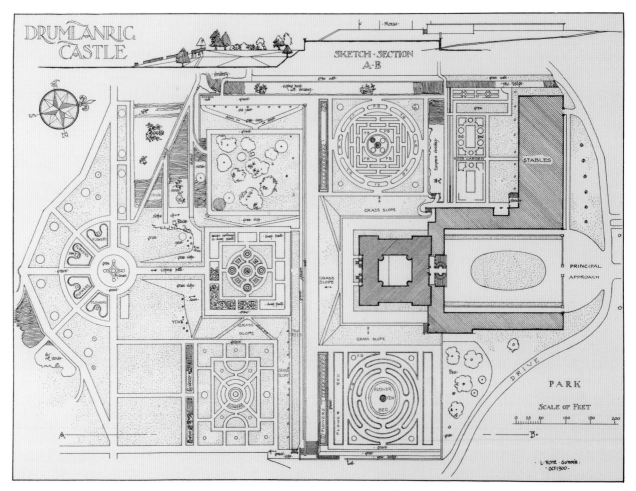

Fig 435 Bird's eye view of Drumlanrig from Inigo Triggs' 1902 volume, Formal Gardens in England and Scotland Plate 83.

has a substratum of solid rock, which has been cut into three or four terraces; at an immense expence ... How much less expensive is it, in general, to *improve* the face of nature rather than to *deform* it! In improving we *gently follow*: in deforming, we *violently oppose* ...

The rough hand employed in these scenes having dispatched the slope, proceeded next to the river. All it's winding simplicity, it's rocky channel, it's woody furniture, and fringed banks, were destroyed at once; and formed, by making a head, into an oblong canal. The grand wooded bank beyond the river still remained an object for improvement. At great expence a little stream was conducted from the neighbouring hills to it's summit. There a most immense cascade, constructed of hewn stone, and consisting of innumerable steps, received it; and conducted it in state to the canal. – So vile a waste of expence, as this whole scene exhibits, we rarely meet with. Deformity is spread so wide through every part of it, that it now exceeds the art of man to restore it again to nature. The indignation of the poet seems to have been levelled at this very place;

– deformities of hardest cure.
The terrace mound uplifted; the long line
Deep delved of the flat canal; and all that toil,
Misled by tasteless fashion, could atchieve
To mar fair Nature's lineaments divine.
(Gilpin 1789, 2, 83–5)

He does, however, commend 'the Duchess of Queensferry's taste ... a simple walk which winds beautifully, and at every turn commands some part of the rocky river below' (Gilpin 1789, 2, 87).

Following David Low's death in 1747 the maintenance of the garden decreased, with only eight or ten men employed at lower wages, while the new head gardener was paid a lower fee (Jamieson 1996, 2). The gardens at Drumlanrig, after a period of neglect and depredation in the time of the fourth Duke of Queensberry, were inherited in 1810 by the third Duke of Buccleuch and by his successors. Sir Walter Scott was consulted about the form of the gardens there and various plans were produced in the earlier nineteenth century, which looked back to the glories of the formal gardens of the late seventeenth and early eighteenth centuries, resulting in one of the greatest of examples of the revival of the formal garden in Scotland (Fig 435).

Afterword

Scotland as depicted on William Roy's Military Survey of Scotland of 1747 to 1755 was a country with formal gardens and policies set in a landscape of agricultural change with extensive areas enclosed and others subject to alternative forms of division and regulation. In contrast, some hundred years later, the First Edition of the Ordnance Survey 6-inch to the mile maps, dating from 1843 onwards, present a very different landscape. While some formal gardens survived, the vast majority had been redesigned and extended on an informal plan, an approach to the garden very different in many ways from the ideas of the seventeenth and earlier centuries, as well as that of the first half of the eighteenth century. The intervening years had seen a sequence of developments characterised in broad terms by the construction of curving drives, deliberately irregular planting of trees and shrubs and the cultivation of smooth turf running up to the house. Policies were often surrounded by a belt of trees, cutting off a view of the middle and foreground. Kitchen and walled gardens were frequently moved a short distance from the dwelling house, and hothouses and greenhouses of various forms for forcing such fruits as peaches, nectarines and grapes became more widespread. Although the production of food for the inhabitants of the mansion house was still a major concern and a matter of pride, improvements in transport and markets meant that the growing of fruit and vegetables was no longer crucial to the household. The gardens of the medieval and early modern periods were depicted as an enclosed Paradise surrounded by wild country; these later gardens from the later eighteenth century onwards enclose a modified natural landscape set in a countryside which has been enclosed and regulated, providing a sense of wilderness preserved in an orderly geometric utilitarian countryside. This movement between the formal and the natural, the Paradise and the Wilderness, is an underlying theme in the design of gardens of which the gardens of Scotland, lost and surviving, provide a remarkable example.

Distribution Maps

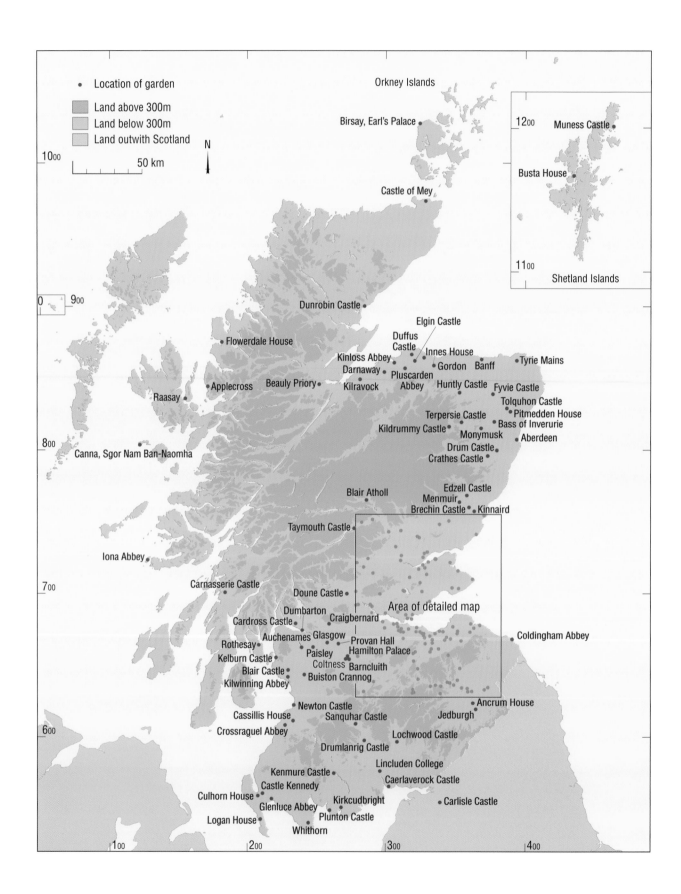

Location of garden

Land above 300m
Land below 300m
Land outwith Scotland

N

50 km

1000

900

800

700

600

0

Orkney Islands

Birsay, Earl's Palace

Castle of Mey

1200   Muness Castle

Busta House

1100

Shetland Islands

Dunrobin Castle

Elgin Castle

Duffus Castle   Innes House

Kinloss Abbey   Gordon   Banff   Tyrie Mains

Flowerdale House

Darnaway   Pluscarden Abbey

Applecross   Beauly Priory   Kilravock   Huntly Castle   Fyvie Castle

Raasay   Tolquhon Castle

Pitmedden House

Terpersie Castle   Bass of Inverurie

Kildrummy Castle   Monymusk   Aberdeen

Canna, Sgor Nam Ban-Naomha   Drum Castle

Crathes Castle

Edzell Castle

Blair Atholl   Menmuir

Brechin Castle   Kinnaird

Taymouth Castle

Iona Abbey

Area of detailed map

Carnasserie Castle

Doune Castle

Dumbarton   Craigbernard

Cardross Castle   Coldingham Abbey

Auchenames   Glasgow

Rothesay   Provan Hall

Paisley   Hamilton Palace

Kelburn Castle   Coltness   Barncluith

Blair Castle   Buiston Crannog

Kilwinning Abbey

Newton Castle   Ancrum House

Cassillis House   Sanquhar Castle   Jedburgh

Crossraguel Abbey   Lochwood Castle

Drumlanrig Castle

Lincluden College

Kenmure Castle   Caerlaverock Castle

Castle Kennedy

Culhorn House   Kirkcudbright

Glenluce Abbey   Carlisle Castle

Logan House   Plunton Castle

Whithorn

100   200   300   400

Grandtully Castle

Castle Menzies

Clunie Castle

Dunkeld Cathedral

Forfar Castle

Glamis Castle

Dunninald Castle

Coupar Angus Abbey

Kettins

Arbroath Abbey

House of Nairne

Castle Lyon

Scone Abbey

Moncur Castle

Carse Grange

Firth of Tay

Perth

Balmerino Abbey

Monzie Castle

Flisk

Earlshall

Lawers

Ballinbreich Castle

Dunbog

Drummond
Castle

Tullibardine

Lindores Abbey

Melville House

St Andrews
Cathedral

Balcomie Castle

Balvaird Castle

Falkland Palace

Balcarres House

Balcaskie House

Dunblane Cathedral

Kinross House

Lochleven Castle

Leslie House

Castle Campbell

West Wemyss

Cambuskenneth Abbey

Alloa Tower

Stirling Castle,
King's Knot

Clackmannan Tower

Dunfermline Abbey

Firth of Forth

Airth Castle

Culross Abbey

Fordell Castle

Aberdour

Donibristle House

Inchcolm Abbey

Kinneil House

Hopetoun House

Ballencrieff
House

Tyninghame House

Lochend House

The Binns

Royston House

Biel

Linlithgow Palace

Duntarvie

Dundas Castle

Northfield
House

Haddington

Niddry Castle

Craigiehall

Holyrood

Seton
Palace

Whittingehame Tower

Kirkliston

Prestonfield

Newliston

Ravelston

Edinburgh

Inch

Pinkie House

Winton
House

Lennoxlove
(Lethington)

Hatton House

Brunstane House

Craigmillar Castle

Dalkeith Castle

Fountainhall

Saltoun
Hall

Yester House

Mavisbank

Newbattle Abbey

Shank House

Crichton House

Penicuik House

Arniston
House

Soutra Aisle

Brunston Castle

Coltness House

Lamancha (The Grange)

Black Barony

Thirlestane Castle

Neidpath Castle

Whytbank
Tower

Langshaw

Carmichael House

Plora Burn

Torwoodlee Tower

Old Gala House

Kelso Abbey

Traquair House

Elibank
Castle

Old Melrose

Mertoun
House

Posso Tower

Melrose Abbey

Roxburgh
Castle

Douglas Castle

Newholm Hope

Langhaugh

Hangingshaw

Dryburgh Abbey

Gazetteer

The majority of gardens and designed landscapes discussed in the text are in private ownership. Inclusion of a site does not mean that there are established, formal access arrangements. Some gardens, notably those in the care of Historic Scotland and the National Trust for Scotland, are open to the public, either regularly or occasionally. The sites are listed with their historic county and their present district.

Garden	Historic County	Council	National Grid Reference
Aberdeen, Bishop's Palace	Aberdeenshire	City of Aberdeen	NJ 9398 0877
Aberdeen, King's College	Aberdeenshire	City of Aberdeen	NJ 9395 0814
Aberdour Castle	Fife	Fife	NT 1923 8546
Airth Castle	Stirlingshire	Falkirk	NS 9000 8683
Alloa	Clackmannanshire	Clackmannan	NS 8889 9251
Ancrum House	Roxburghshire	The Scottish Borders	NT 6297 2505
Applecross House	Ross and Cromarty	Highland	NG 7188 4569
Arbroath Abbey	Angus	Angus	NO 6431 4133
Arniston House	Midlothian	Midlothian	NT 3258 5946
Auchenames	Renfrewshire	Renfrewshire	NS 3953 6284
Balcaskie House	Fife	Fife	NO 5246 0357
Balcarres House	Fife	Fife	NO 4740 0440
Balcomie Castle	Fife	Fife	NO 6259 0982
Ballencrieff Castle	East Lothian	East Lothian	NT 4880 7827
Ballinbreich Castle	Fife	Fife	NO 2718 2049
Balmerino Abbey	Fife	Fife	NO 3582 2468
Balvaird Castle	Perthshire	Perth and Kinross	NO 1698 1153
Banff, Pennant's Mount	Banffshire	Aberdeenshire	NJ 6900 6381
Barncluith	Lanarkshire	Hamilton	NS 7298 5450
Bass of Inverurie	Aberdeenshire	Aberdeenshire	NJ 7809 2059
Biel	East Lothian	East Lothian	NT 6336 7589
Birsay, Earl's Palace	Orkney	Orkney Islands	HY 2480 2777
Black Barony	Peeblesshire	The Scottish Borders	NT 2363 4726
Blair Castle	North Ayrshire	Ayrshire	NS 3045 4803
Blair Atholl	Perthshire	Perth and Kinross	NN 8657 6618
Bog of Gight (Gordon Castle)	Morayshire	Moray	NJ 3498 5955
Brechin Castle	Angus	Angus	NO 5978 5989
Brunstane House	City of Edinburgh	Midlothian	NT 317 724
Brunston Castle	Midlothian	Midlothian	NT 201 582
Buiston Crannog	Ayrshire	North Ayrshire	NS 4155 4352
Busta House	Shetland	Shetland Islands	HU 3451 6680
Caerlaverock Castle	Dumfriesshire	Dumfries and Galloway	NX 0254 6563
Cambuskenneth Abbey	Stirlingshire	Stirling	NS 8085 9396
Canna, Sgor Nam Ban-Naomha	Inverness-shire	Highland	NG 2299 0439
Cardross	Dunbartonshire	West Dunbartonshire	NS 3850 7587
Carlisle Castle	Cumbria	Cumbria	NY 3969 5622
Carnasserie Castle	Argyllshire	Argyll and Bute	NM 8390 0084
Carmichael House	Lanarkshire	South Lanarkshire	NS 9364 3901
Carse Grange	Perthshire	Perth and Kinross	NO 2712 2540
Cassillis House	Ayrshire	South Ayrshire	NS 3404 1281
Castle Campbell	Clackmannanshire	Clackmannan	NS 9613 9926
Castle Kennedy	Wigtownshire	Dumfries and Galloway	NX 1125 6081
Castle Lyon	Perthshire	Perth and Kinross	NO 3019 2910
Castle Menzies	Perthshire	Perth and Kinross	NN 8376 4961
Castle of Mey	Caithness	Highland	ND 2903 7388

Garden	Historic County	Council	National Grid Reference
Clackmannan Tower	Clackmannanshire	Clackmannan	NS 9065 9195
Clunie Castle	Perthshire	Perth and Kinross	NO 1132 4401
Coldingham Abbey	Berwickshire	The Scottish Borders	NT 917 687
Coltness House	Lanarkshire	North Lanark	NS 7995 5626
Coupar Angus Abbey	Perthshire	Perth and Kinross	NO 2232 3980
Coupar Grange	Perthshire	Perth and Kinross	NO 2298 4266
Craigmillar Castle	Midlothian	City of Edinburgh	NT 2880 7087
Craigbernard	Stirlingshire	East Dunbartonshire	NS 594 790
Craigiehall House	West Lothian	City of Edinburgh	NT 1667 7542
Crathes Castle	Kincardineshire	Aberdeenshire	NO 7341 9680
Crichton House	Midlothian	Midlothian	NT 4003 6247
Crossraguel Abbey	Ayrshire	South Ayrshire	NS 2753 0833
Culhorn House	Wigtownshire	Dumfries and Galloway	NX 0787 5914
Culross	Fife	Fife	NS 9888 8624
Dalkeith Castle	Midlothian	Midlothian	NT 3332 6790
Darnaway Castle	Morayshire	Moray	NH 9946 5502
Douglas Castle	Lanarkshire	South Lanarkshire	NS 8424 3184
Doune Castle	Perthshire	Stirling	NN 7284 0107
Drum Castle	Aberdeenshire	Aberdeenshire	NJ 7987 0064
Drumlanrig Castle	Dumfriesshire	Dumfries and Galloway	NX 8519 9921
Drummond Castle	Perthshire	Perth and Kinross	NN 8447 1807
Dryburgh Abbey	Berwickshire	The Scottish Borders	NT 5915 3170
Duffus Castle	Morayshire	Moray	NJ 1892 6725
Dumbarton Castle	Dunbartonshire	West Dunbartonshire	NS 3998 7448
Dunblane Cathedral	Perthshire	Stirling	NN 7815 0138
Dunbog	Fife	Fife	NO 2851 1803
Dundas Castle	West Lothian	City of Edinburgh	NT 1183 7671
Dunfermline Abbey	Fife	Dunfermline	NT 0896 8731
Dunkeld Cathedral	Perth	Perth and Kinross	NO 0239 4259
Dunninald Castle	Angus	Angus	NO 7035 5427
Dunrobin Castle	Sutherland	Highland	NC 8504 0082
Duntarvie Castle	West Lothian	West Lothian	NT 0905 7647
Earlshall	Fife	Fife	NO 4647 2108
Edinburgh Castle	Midlothian	City of Edinburgh	NT 2511 7349
Edinburgh, Heriot's Hospital	Midlothian	City of Edinburgh	NT 2553 7315
Edinburgh, Kirk o' Field	Midlothian	City of Edinburgh	NT 2596 7331
Edinburgh, Trinity Hospital	Midlothian	City of Edinburgh	NT 2599 7394
Edzell Castle	Angus	Angus	NO 5848 6908
Elgin Castle	Morayshire	Moray	NJ 2118 6281
Elibank Castle	Selkirkshire	The Scottish Borders	NT 3969 3630
Falkland Palace	Fife	Fife	NO 2534 0745
Flisk	Fife	Fife	NO 3138 2248
Flowerdale or Gairloch House	Ross and Cromarty	Highland	NG 8141 7536
Fordell Castle	Fife	Fife	NT 1469 8538
Forfar Castle	Angus	Angus	NO 4561 5081
Fountainhall	East Lothian	East Lothian	NT 4265 6771
Fyvie Castle	Aberdeenshire	Aberdeenshire	NJ 7639 3930
Glamis Castle	Angus	Angus	NO 3858 4805
Glasgow Castle	Lanarkshire	City of Glasgow	NS 6015 6559
Glasgow University, Old College	Lanarkshire	City of Glasgow	NS 5983 6512
Glenluce Abbey	Wigtownshire	Dumfries and Galloway	NX 1850 5866
Gordon Castle	Morayshire	Moray	NJ 3498 5955
Grandtully Castle	Perthshire	Perth and Kinross	NN 8911 5134
Haddington	East Lothian	East Lothian	NT 5133 7383
Hamilton Palace	Lanarkshire	South Lanarkshire	NS 7264 5592
Hangingshaw	Selkirkshire	The Scottish Borders	NT 3982 3016
Hatton House	Midlothian	City of Edinburgh	NT 1285 6881
Holyroodhouse, Palace of	Midlothian	City of Edinburgh	NT 2684 7400
Hopetoun House	West Lothian	West Lothian	NT 0885 7901
House of Nairne	Perthshire	Perth and Kinross	NO 0738 3284
Huntly Castle	Aberdeenshire	Aberdeenshire	NJ 5319 4074
Inch House	Midlothian	City of Edinburgh	NT 2767 7082
Inchcolm Abbey	Fife	Fife	NT 1897 8265
Innes House	Morayshire	Moray	NJ 2793 6500
Iona Abbey	Argyll	Argyll and Bute	NM 2868 2451
Jedburgh	Roxburghshire	The Scottish Borders	NT 6505 2078
Kelburn Castle	Ayrshire	North Ayrshire	NS 2171 5670
Kelso Abbey	Roxburghshire	The Scottish Borders	NT 7284 3381
Kenmure Castle	Kirkcudbrightshire	Dumfries and Galloway	NX 6353 7639
Kettins	Angus	Perth and Kinross	NO 2370 3900
Kildrummy Castle	Aberdeenshire	Aberdeenshire	NJ 4548 1693
Kilravock Castle	Nairnshire	Highland	NH 8140 4936
Kilwinning Abbey	Ayrshire	North Ayrshire	NS 3032 4327
Kinloss Abbey	Morayshire	Moray	NJ 0657 6150
Kinnaird Castle	Angus	Angus	NO 6341 5711
Kinneil House	West Lothian	Falkirk	NS 9819 8055
Kinross House	Kinross-shire	Perth and Kinross	NO1236 0204
Kirkcudbright	Kirkcudbrightshire	Dumfries and Galloway	NX 6823 5106
Kirkliston	West Lothian	City of Edinburgh	NT 1295 7329

341

Garden	Historic County	Council	National Grid Reference
Lamancha (The Grange)	Peeblesshire	The Scottish Borders	NT 1994 5225
Langhaugh	Peeblesshire	The Scottish Borders	NT 2030 3100
Langshaw Tower	Roxburghshire	The Scottish Borders	NT 5169 3976
Lawers	Perthshire	Perth and Kinross	NN 7992 2302
Lennoxlove (Lethington)	East Lothian	East Lothian	NT 5150 7204
Leslie House	Fife	Fife	NO 2596 0183
Lincluden College	Dumfriesshire	Dumfries and Galloway	NX 9664 7791
Lindores Abbey	Fife	Fife	NO 2439 1847
Linlithgow Palace	West Lothian	West Lothian	NT 0019 7732
Lochend House	East Lothian	East Lothian	NT 6776 7796
Lochleven Castle	Kinross-shire	Perth and Kinross	NO 1374 0177
Lochwood Castle	Dumfriesshire	Dumfries and Galloway	NY 1374 0177
Logan House	Wigtownshire	Dumfries and Galloway	NX 0964 4282
Mavisbank	Midlothian	Midlothian	NT 2880 6514
Melrose Abbey	Roxburghshire	The Scottish Borders	NT 5484 3417
Melville House	Fife	Fife	NO 2989 1380
Menmuir	Angus	Angus	NO 5342 6436
Mertoun House	Berwickshire	The Scottish Borders	NT 6198 3195
Moncur Castle	Perthshire	Perth and Kinross	NO 2835 2951
Monymusk	Aberdeenshire	Aberdeenshire	NJ 6848 1542
Monzie Castle	Perthshire	Perth and Kinross	NN 8737 2450
Muness Castle	Shetland	Shetland Islands	HP 6295 0116
Neidpath Castle	Peeblesshire	The Scottish Borders	NT 2361 4048
Newbattle Abbey	Midlothian	Midlothian	NT 3334 6602
Newholm Hope	Peeblesshire	The Scottish Borders	NT 1941 3071
Newliston	West Lothian	City of Edinburgh	NT 1108 7353
Newton Castle	Ayrshire	South Ayrshire	NS 3390 2230
Niddry Castle	West Lothian	West Lothian	NT 0952 7437
Northfield House	East Lothian	East Lothian	NT 3891 7392
Old Gala House	Selkirkshire	The Scottish Borders	NT 4916 3589
Old Melrose	Roxburghshire	The Scottish Borders	NT 588 340
Paisley Abbey	Renfrewshire	Renfrewshire	NS 4855 6395
Penicuik House	Midlothian	Midlothian	NT 2172 5920
Perth Charterhouse	Perthshire	Perth and Kinross	NO 1154 2339
Perth, Dominican Friary	Perthshire	Perth and Kinross	NO 1178 2386
Perth, 'Gilten Arbour'	Perthshire	Perth and Kinross	NO 1170 2395
Pinkie House	Midlothian	East Lothian	NT 3494 7267
Plora Burn	Peeblesshire	The Scottish Borders	NT 3609 3629
Plunton Tower	Kirkcudbrightshire	Dumfries and Galloway	NX 6049 5073
Pluscarden Abbey	Morayshire	Moray	NJ 1420 5761
Pitmedden House	Aberdeenshire	Aberdeenshire	NJ 8845 2803
Posso Tower	Peeblesshire	The Scottish Borders	NT 2001 3324
Prestonfield	Midlothian	City of Edinburgh	NT 2780 7210
Provan Hall	Lanarkshire	City of Glasgow	NS 6675 6632
Raasay	Inverness-shire	Highland	c NG 55 36
Ravelston House	Midlothian	City of Edinburgh	NT 2178 7402
Rothesay Castle	Buteshire	Argyll and Bute	NT 2780 7210
Roxburgh Castle	Roxburghshire	The Scottish Borders	NT 7130 3372
Royston House	Midlothian	City of Edinburgh	NT 2258 7727
St Andrews Castle	Fife	Fife	NO 5110 1698
St Andrews Cathedral	Fife	Fife	NO 5147 1664
Saltoun Hall	East Lothian	East Lothian	NT 4606 6844
Sanquhar Castle	Dumfriesshire	Dumfries and Galloway	NS 7850 0923
Scone Abbey	Perthshire	Perth and Kinross	NO 1144 2664
Seton Palace	East Lothian	East Lothian	NT 4173 7508
Shank House	Midlothian	Midlothian	NT 3343 6114
Soutra Aisle	Midlothian	The Scottish Borders	NT 4525 5840
Stirling Castle	Stirlingshire	Stirling	NS 7895 9410
Stirling Castle, King's Knot	Stirlingshire	Stirling	NS 7889 9364
Taymouth Castle	Perthshire	Perth and Kinross	NN 7844 4652
Terpersie Castle	Aberdeenshire	Aberdeenshire	NJ 5464 2023
The Binns	West Lothian	West Lothian	NT 0508 7856
Thirlestane Castle	Berwickshire	The Scottish Borders	NT 2812 1535
Tolquhon Castle	Aberdeenshire	Aberdeenshire	NJ 8726 2862
Torwoodlee Tower	Selkirkshire	The Scottish Borders	NT 4669 3774
Traquair House	Peeblesshire	The Scottish Borders	NT 3307 3548
Tullibardine	Perthshire	Perth and Kinross	NN 9098 1391
Tyninghame House	East Lothian	East Lothian	NT 6193 7984
Tyrie Mains	Aberdeenshire	Aberdeenshire	NJ 9393 6293
West Wemyss	Fife	Fife	NT 3189 9462
Whittingehame Tower	East Lothian	East Lothian	NT 6022 7324
Whithorn	Wigtownshire	Dumfries and Galloway	NX 4447 4031
Whytbank Tower	Selkirkshire	The Scottish Borders	NT 4418 3766
Winton House	East Lothian	East Lothian	NT 4381 6949
Yester House	East Lothian	East Lothian	NT 5434 6716

Bibliography

Printed, Manuscript and Online Primary Sources with Abbreviated Titles

Adair Adair Manuscript maps in the National Library of Scotland

CH NRS Church Records

CSP Calendar of the State Papers relating to Scotland and Mary Queen of Scots, 1547–1603, edited by J Bain *et al*, 1898–, Edinburgh

DNB Dictionary of National Biography, Oxford University Press 2004

DOSL Online Dictionary of the Scottish Language

ER *The Exchequer Rolls of Scotland*, edited by J Stuart *et al*, 1878–1908, Edinburgh

HMSO Her Majesty's Stationery Office

Historic Scotland Online Inventory of Gardens and Designed Landscapes in Scotland

MW *Accounts of the Masters of Works for Building and repairing Royal Palaces and Castles* Vol 1 1529–1615, edited by H M Paton *et al*, 1957, HMSO

NLS National Library of Scotland

NRAS National Register of Archives for Scotland

NRS National Records of Scotland

NSA *New Statistical Account of Scotland* 1845, Edinburgh

Pont Pont Manuscript maps in the National Library of Scotland

RCAHMS Collections held by the Royal Commission on the Ancient and Historical Monuments of Scotland

RMS *Registrum Magni Sigilli Regum Scotorum*, edited by J M Thomson *et al*, 1882–1914, Edinburgh

RPS *The Records of the Parliaments of Scotland to 1707*, University of St Andrews 2007, online resource

RSS *Registrum Secreti Sigilli Regum Scotorum*, edited by M Livingstone *et al*, 1908, Edinburgh

Regesta Regesta Regum Scottorum 1959–87, Edinburgh: Edinburgh University Press

Stat Acct *The Statistical Account of Scotland*, edited by J Sinclair, 1791–7, Edinburgh

TA Treasurers Accounts *Accounts of the Lord High Treasurer of Scotland*, 13 vols, edited by T Dickson and J Balfour Paul, 1877–1916, Edinburgh

Select Bibliography

Aa, P van der 1729
La Galerie Agréable du Monde, Leide

Adam, W 1980
Vitruvius Scoticus, Edinburgh: Paul Harris

Adamson, J 1618
Mouson eisodia: The Muses Welcome to the high and mightie Iames by the grace of God King of Great Britaine, France and Ireland, Defender of the Faith &c. At his M. Happie returne to his old and native kingdom of Scotland, after XIIII yeeres absence, Edinburgh

Addyman, T & McGowan, P 2006
Pitmedden Garden and Estate, *Discovery Excavation Scot* (new series) 9, 19

Adomnan of Iona 1995
Life of St Columba, translated by R Sharpe, London: Penguin

Airey, O (ed) 1884–5
The Lauderdale Papers, London: Camden Society

Alberti, L B 1988
(De Re Aedificatoria) On the art of building in ten books, translated by J Rykwert with N Leach and R Tavernor, Cambridge, Massachusetts and London: MIT Press

Alexander, J E 1864
An account of the excavations at Cambuskenneth Abbey in May 1864, *Proc Soc Antiq Scot* 6, 14–25

Allan, D A 1997
'Commendation of the Private Countrey Life': Philosophy and the garden in seventeenth-century Scotland, *J Garden Hist* 25:1, 59–80

Allan, D A 1999
'In the Bosome of a Shaddowie Grove': Sir George Mackenzie and the consolations of retirement, *Hist European Ideas* 25:5, 251–73

Anderson, A 1922
Early Sources of Scottish History, AD 500 to 1286, Edinburgh: Oliver & Boyd

Anderson, P D 1982
Robert Stewart: Earl of Orkney, Lord of Shetland 1533–1593, Edinburgh: John Donald

Androuet du Cerceau, J 1559a
Livre d'architecture ... contenant les plans et desseings de cinquante bastiments tous differens, Paris

Androuet du Cerceau, J 1559b
Livre D'Architecture ... contenant plusieurs & diverses ordonances de Cheminees, Lucarnes, Portes, Fonteines, Puis & Pavillons, Paris: André Wechel

Androuet du Cerceau, J 1988
Les plus excellents bastiments de France, Paris: Sand & Conti

Angus, W (ed) 1914
Protocol Book of Gilbert Grote, Scottish Record Society, 34, no 161

Anon 1683
A brief account of the province of East: New: Jarsey in America: Published by the Scots proprietors having interest there. For the information of such as may have a desire to transport themselves, or their families thither. Wherein the nature and advantage of, and interest in a forraign plantation to this country is demonstrated, Edinburgh: John Reid

Anon 1929
The Douglas Garden Window from which the body of William Earl of Douglas was thrust out after his assassination by James II, *Scottish Country Life*, July, 223

Anthony, J 1991
The Renaissance Garden in Britain, Princes Risborough: Shire

Apted, M R 1984
Arnold Quellin's statues at Glamis, *Antiq J* 64, 53–61

Apted, M R 1985
Aberdour Castle, Edinburgh: HMSO

Apted, M R 1986
The buildings and other works of Patrick 1st of Strathmore, 1671–95, *Antiq J* 66, 91–115

Apted, M R & Snowden, R L 1984
The de Wet paintings in the chapel at Glamis Castle, in Breeze 1984, 232–48

Arnot, H 1779
The History of Edinburgh, Edinburgh: William Creech

Aspinall, A & Pocock, J A 1995
Geophysical prospection in garden archaeology: an appraisal and critique based on case studies, *Archaeol Prospection* 2, 61–84

Atlee, H 2006
Italian Gardens, London: Frances Lincoln

Bain, J 1881
Calendar of documents relating to Scotland preserved in Her Majesty's Public Record Office, London, Edinburgh: HM General Register House

Baird, R 2003
Mistress of the House: great ladies and grand houses 1670–1830, London: Weidenfeld & Nicholson

Baird, W A 1930
Lennoxlove, *Trans East Lothian Antiquarian Fld Natur Soc* 2, 9–28

Balfour, J 1824
The historical works of Sir James Balfour, Edinburgh: W Aitchison

Balfour-Melville, E M W 1936
James I, King of Scots, 1406–1437, London: Methuen

Ballerini, I L 2006
The Medici Villas, Florence: Giunti

Bannatyne, R 1836
Memorials of transactions in Scotland, A. D. MDLXIX – A. D. MDLXXIII, edited by Robert Pitcairn, Edinburgh: Bannatyne Club

Barbour, J 1996
The Bruce, Edinburgh: Mercat Press

Bardgett, F D 1989
Scotland Reformed: the Reformation in Angus and Mearns, Edinburgh: John Donald

Barrow, G W S 1976
Robert Bruce and the Community of the Realm of Scotland, Edinburgh: Edinburgh University Press

Barrow, G W S 1980
The Anglo-Norman Era in Scottish History, Oxford: Clarendon Press

Bartos, J 2010
The Spirituall Orchard: God, garden and landscape in seventeenth-century England before the Restoration, *J Garden Hist* 38:2, 177–193

Bartow, E P 1879
Bartow genealogy. Containing every one of the name of Bartow descended from Doctor Thomas Bartow (and other descendants of ... Thomas Bartow) who was living at Crediton, in England, A.D. 1672 ... Baltimore

Bath, M 2003
Renaissance decorative painting in Scotland, Edinburgh: National Museums of Scotland Publishing

Bath, M 2007
Ben Jonson, William Fowler and the Pinkie Ceiling, *Archit Heritage* 18, 73–86

Bawcutt, P & Hadley Williams, J (eds) 2010
A Companion to Medieval Scottish Poetry, Woodbridge: D S Brewer

Benedict 1995
The Rule of St Benedict, London: Sheed and Ward

Billings, R W 1845–52
The baronial and ecclesiastical antiquities of Scotland, Edinburgh: William Blackwood & Sons

Blaeu, J 1654
Theatrum Orbis Terrarum, sive Atlas Novus, Vol 5, Amsterdam

Blunt, A 1982
Guide to Baroque Rome, London: Granada

Bolton, A T 1922
The architecture of Robert and James Adam (1758–1754), London: Country Life and George Newnes

Bonehill, J & Daniels, P (eds) 2009
Paul Sandby: picturing Britain, London: Royal Academy of Arts

Boney, A D 1988
The Lost Gardens of Glasgow University, Bromley: Christopher Helm

Boorde, A 1550
The boke for to learne a man to be wyse in buyldyng of his howse for the helth of body [and] to holde quyetnes for the helth of his soule, and body The boke for a good husbande to lerne. [Imprynted by me Robert Wyer, dwellynge at the [sy]gne of S. Iohn Euangelyst, by s. Martyns parysshe in the felde besyde the Duke of Suffolkes place, at Charynge Crosse], London

Boorde, A 1574
A compendyous regyment or a dyetary of healthe made in Mountpyllyer, by Andrewe Boorde of physycke doctour, newly corrected and imprynted with dyuers addycyons dedycated to the armypotent Prynce and valyent Lorde Thomas Duke of Northfolke. [Imprynted at London: In Fletestrete at the sygne of the George nexte to saynte Dunstones churche by Wyllyam Powell, In the yere of our Lorde god. M. CCCCC. LXVII], London

Boorde, A [1562]
The first boke of the introduction of knowledge, London: William Copland

Boudon, F 1999
Jardins d'eau et jardins de pente dans la France de la Renaissance, in Guillaume 1999a, 137–84

Bourgeois, J & Meganck, M (eds) 2005
Aerial Photography and Archaeology 2003. A Century of Information Archaeological Reports Ghent University 5, Gent

Boyse, S 1735
Retirement: a poem, occasioned by seeing the palace and park of Yester, Edinburgh

Brann, M 2004
Excavations at Old Caerlaverock Castle 1998–9, Dumfries: Dumfries and Galloway Natural History and Antiquarian Society

Breeze, D (ed) 1984
Studies in Scottish Antiquity, Edinburgh: John Donald

Breeze, D 1987
A Queen's Progress, Edinburgh: HMSO

Broun, D, Finlay, R J and Lynch, M (eds) 1998
Image and identity: the making and re-making of Scotland through the ages, Edinburgh: John Donald

Brown, A E (ed) 1991
Garden Archaeology, CBA Res Rep78, London: CBA

Brown, A L & Moss, M 1996
The University of Glasgow: 1451–1996, Edinburgh: Edinburgh University Press

Brown, J 1999
The pursuit of paradise: A social history of gardens and gardening, London: HarperCollins

Brown, K M 1991
From Scottish Lords to British Officers: state building, elite integration and the army in the seventeenth century, in Macdougall 1991a, 133–69

Brown, K M 2004
Noble Society in Scotland, Edinburgh: Edinburgh University Press

Brown, K M 2011
Noble Power in Scotland from the Reformation to the Revolution, Edinburgh: Edinburgh University Press

Brown, M M 2005a
The gardens of Glamis: an aerial view, *Proc Soc Antiq Scot* 135, 19–39

Brown, M M 2005b
Aerial survey and designed landscapes in Scotland: detection and documentation, in Bourgeois & Meganck 2005, 243–54

Brown, M M 2009
The water garden at Brunston Castle, Midlothian, *Archit Heritage Soc Scot: Mag 25*, Spring 2009, 20–1

Brown, P H 1904
Scotland in the time of Queen Mary, London: Methuen

Brown, P H (ed) 1978
Early Travellers in Scotland, Edinburgh: James Thin

Calder, J T 1887
Sketch of the civil and traditional history of Caithness, Wick: William Rae

Calkins, R G 1986
Piero de'Crescenzi and the Medieval Garden, in Macdougall 1986, 157–73

Cameron, A 2011
Fyvie Castle, *Discovery Excavation Scot* (new series) 12, 19

Cameron, J 1998
James V: the personal rule, 1528–43, East Linton: Tuckwell

Campbell, K 2007
Policies and Pleasances: a guide to the gardens of Scotland, London: Barn Elms

Campbell, N D 1913
An Inventory of Archibald, 7th Earl of Argyll's Castle of Campbell (formerly called Castle Gloume), in the Shire of Clackmanan, taken on 21 February, 1595. Transcribed from the original, preserved in the Argyll Charter Chest, *Scot Hist Rev* 10, 299–305

Carpenter, S 2003
Performing Diplomacies: The 1560s Court Entertainments of Mary Queen of Scots, *Scot Hist Rev* 82:2, 194–225

Caus, S de 1612
La Perspective, avec la raison des ombres et miroirs, London: I Norton

Chalmers, A (ed) 1810
The works of the English poets, London

Chalmers, G 1887–1902
Caledonia, Paisley: Alexander Gardener

Chamberlayne, J 1710
Magnae Britanniae notitia: or, the present state of Great-Britain, London

Chatenet, M (ed) 2006a
Maisons des champs dans l'Europe de la Renaissance, Paris: Picard

Chatenet, M 2006b
Les maisons des champs de papier ... de Jacques Androuet du Cerceau, in Chatenet 2006a, 69–86

Cherry, A 1987
Princes, Poets & Patrons: the Stuarts and Scotland, Edinburgh: HMSO

Clancy, T O & Markus, G (eds) 1995
Iona: The Earliest Poetry of a Celtic Monastery, Edinburgh: Edinburgh University Press

Coffin, D R 1982
The 'Lex Hortorum' and Access to Gardens of Latium During the Renaissance, *J Garden Hist*, 2, 201–232

Cole, M A, David, A E U, Linford, N T, Linford, P K & Payne, A W 1997
Non-destructive techniques in English gardens: geophysical prospecting, *J Garden Hist* 25:1, 26–39

Colonna, F 1499
Hypnoteromachia Poliphili, Venice: Aldus Manutius

Colonna, F 1546
Le Songe de Poliphile, Paris

Colville, J 1825
The historie and life of King James the Sext: being an account of the affairs of Scotland from ... 1566 to ... 1596; with a short continuation to 1617, Edinburgh: Bannatyne Club

Colvin, H M 1986
Royal Gardens Medieval England, in Macdougall 1986, 9–22

Colvin, H M 1995
A Biographical Dictionary of British Architects 1600–1840, New Haven and London: Yale University Press

Colvin, H M 1999
Essays in English Architectural History, New Haven and London: Yale University Press

Colvin, H M & Harris, J (eds) 1970
The Country Seat: studies in the history of the British Country House, London: Allen Lane

Comrie, J D 1932
History of Scottish Medicine, London: Wellcome Historical Medical Museum

Cooper, D E 2006
A Philosophy of Gardens, Oxford: Clarendon Press

Cooper, J 2008
Scottish Renaissance Armies, Oxford: Osprey

Cooper, N 2006
Houses of the London countryside: the first English villas, in Chatenet 2006a, 257–68

Cooper, S 1999
Ornamental structures in the medieval gardens of Scotland, *Proc Soc Antiq Scot* 129, 817–39

Cooper S 2000
A history of ornamental buildings and structures in Scotland's gardens and designed landscapes, Ph D Thesis, Edinburgh College of Art/Heriot Watt University Department of Architecture

Cooper, S 2002
Sir John Clerk's garden buildings at Penicuik, *Archit Heritage* 13, 47–62

Coppack, G 1991
Mount Grace Priory North Yorkshire, London: English Heritage

Coryate, T 1611
Coryats Crudities : hastily gobled vp in five Moneths trauells in France, Sauoy, Italy, Rhetia co[m]monly called the Grisons country, Heluetia alia_s Switzerland, some parts of high Germany, and the Netherlands; newly digested in the hungry aire of Odcombe in the county of Somerset, & now dispersed to the nourishment of the trauelling members of this kingdome, London

Cosgrove, D 2008
Geography and Vision: seeing, imagining and representing the world, London & New York: I B Tauris

Cosh, M 1994
The Adam family and Arniston, *Archit Hist* 27, 214–25

Cowan, I B 1983
Darker vision of the Scottish Renaissance, in Cowan & Shaw 1983, 125–40

Cowan, I B 1972
The enigma of Mary Stuart, London: Sphere

Cowan, I B 1995
The Monastic History of the Diocese of St Andrews, in Higgitt 1995, 7–15

Cowan, I B & Easson, D E 1976
Medieval Religious Houses in Scotland: with an appendix on the houses in the Isle of Man, London: Longman

Cowan, I B & Shaw, D (eds) 1983
The Renaissance and Reformation in Scotland, Edinburgh: Scottish Academic Press

Cox, E H M 1935
A History of Gardening in Scotland, Edinburgh: Chatto & Windus

Craig-Brown, T 1886
The history of Selkirkshire or chronicles of Ettrick Forest, David Douglas

Cramond, W 1891–4
The Annals of Banff, Aberdeen: New Spalding Club

Crawford, B E (ed) 1999
Church, chronicle and learning in Medieval and Renaissance Scotland, Edinburgh: Mercat Press

Crescentius, Petrus (Pietro de'Crescenzi) 1474
Liber ruralium commodorum in alma Vniuersitate Louaniensi: per Joannem de Vvestfalia, Louvain

Cruden, S 1999
Castle Campbell, revised edition edited by C Tabraham, Edinburgh: Historic Scotland

Cruft, C H, 1984
James, 2nd Duke of Atholl and John Cheere, in Breeze 1984, 285–301

Cruft, C H 1991
The state of garden archaeology in Scotland, in Brown 1991, 175–89

Cruft, K, Strachan, S, Dunbar, J G, Gifford, J, Fawcett, R & Gow, I 2006
Borders, The Buildings of Scotland series, New Haven and London: Yale University Press

Cunningham, I C (ed) 2006
The Nation Survey'd: Essays on late sixteenth-century Scotland as depicted by Timothy Pont, Edinburgh: John Donald

Curle, J 1935
Melrose: the precinct wall of the monastery and the town, *Hist Berwick Natur Club* 29:1, 29–50

Curle, J 1935
Some notes upon the abbey of Melrose, *Hist Berwick Natur Club* 29:1, 51–70

Currie, C K 1990
Fishponds as garden features, *J Garden Hist* 18:1, 22–96

Daley, B E 1986
The 'Closed Garden' and the 'Sealed Fountain': Song of Songs 4:12 in the Late Medieval Iconography of Mary, in Macdougall 1986, 255–78

Dalrymple, H H (ed) 1908
A description of Castle Kennedy, a seat belonging to the Right Honble. the Earl of Stair. 1798. (Letters of Thomas McCalla, gardener at Castle Kennedy, to 2nd Earl of Stair, between 1731 and 1740), Edinburgh: Privately printed

Dawson, J E A 2007
Scotland Re-formed, 1488–1587, Edinburgh: Edinburgh University Press

Defoe, D 1727
A tour through the whole island of Great Britain, London: G Strahan

Defoe, D 1968
A tour through the whole island of Great Britain, London: Frank Cass & Co

De Jonge, K 1999
L'environnement des chateaux dans les Pays-Bas méridionaux au XVI siècle et au début du XVII siècle, in Guillaume 1999a, 185–206

De Moulins, D & Weir, D A 1997
The potential and use of environmental techniques in gardens, *J Garden Hist* 25:1, 40–6

Dennison, P 2006
Timothy Pont's portrayal of Towns, in Cunningham 2006, 125–38

Dennistoun, J (ed) 1841
Coltness Collection M.DC.VIII. – M.DCCC.XL. Memorials of the Stewarts of Allanton, Coltness, and Goodtrees by Sir Archibald Stewart Denham, 1608–1698, Edinburgh: Maitland Club

Dewar, A D 1980
Castle Menzies, Weem, Perthshire, Derby: Pilgrim

Dézallier d'Argenville, A-J 1712
The theory and practice of gardening, translated by John James of Greenwich, London

Dickson, C & J H 2000
Plants and People in Early Scotland, Stroud: Tempus

Dilworth, M 1994
Franco-Scottish Efforts at Monastic Reform, *Records Scot Church Hist Soc* 25, 204–21

Dilworth, M 1995
Scottish monasteries in the late middle ages, Edinburgh: Edinburgh University Press

Dingwall, C 1992
The Hercules Garden at Blair Castle, Perthshire, *J Garden Hist* 20:2, 153–72

Dingwall, C 1994
Gardens in the wild, *J Garden Hist* 22:2, 133–55

Dingwall, C 2000
Glamis Castle: a history of the designed landscape, Strathmore Estates

Dingwall, H M 2003
A History of Scottish Medicine, Edinburgh: Edinburgh University Press

Ditchburn, D 2001
Scotland and Europe: the medieval kingdom and its contacts with Christendom, 1214–1560, East Linton: Tuckwell Press

Dixon, P, O'Sullivan, J & Rogers, I 2000
Archaeological Excavations at Jedburgh Friary 1983–1992, Edinburgh: Scottish Trust for Archaeological Research

Dobie, J S (ed) 1876
Cunninghame, topographized by Timothy Pont MA 1604–1608, Glasgow: John Tweed

Donaldson, G (ed) 1952
Protocol Book of James Young 1485–1515, Edinburgh: Scottish Record Society

Donaldson, J 1908
A description of Castle Kennedy, a seat belonging to the Right Honble. the Earl of Stair, Edinburgh

Dougall, M & Dickson, J 1997
Old managed oaks in the Glasgow Area, in Smout 1997, 76–85

Douglas, G 1827
The Palice of Honour, Edinburgh: Bannatyne Club

Douglas, G 1874
Poetical Works, Edinburgh: William Patterson

Dowden, J (ed) 1903
Chartulary of the Abbey of Lindores 1195–1497, Edinburgh: Scottish History Society

Drummond, W 1617

Forth feasting A panegyricke to the Kings most excellent Maiestie, Edinburgh: Andro Hart

Drummond, W 1976

Poems and Prose, edited by R H MacDonald, Edinburgh and London: Scottish Academic Press

Dunbar, J G 1964

The Palace of Holyroodhouse during the first half of the sixteenth century, *Archaeol J* 120, 242–54

Dunbar, J G 1970

Kinross House, Kinross-shire, in Colvin & Harris 1970, 65–9

Dunbar, J G 1973

The building of Yester House, 1670–1878, *Trans East Lothian Antiq Fld Natur Hist Soc* 13, 20–42

Dunbar, J G 1975

The building activities of the Duke and Duchess of Lauderdale, 1670–82, *Archaeol J* 132, 202–30

Dunbar, J G 1984

Some aspects of the planning of Scottish royal palaces in the sixteenth century in 'Design and practice in British architecture; studies in architectural history presented to Howard Colvin', *Archit Hist* 27, 15–24

Dunbar, J G 1991

Sixteenth-century French parallels for the Palace of Falkland, *Review of Scottish Culture* 7, 3–8

Dunbar, J G 1995

Two late seventeenth century designs for Kinnaird Castle Scotland, in Gow & Rowan 1995, 43–51

Dunbar, J G 1999

Scottish Royal Palaces, East Linton: Tuckwell

Dunbar, J G 2000

Notes on a copper-plate engraving of Glamis Castle, in Slade 2000, 110–11

Dunbar, J G & Davies, K 1990

Some late seventeenth century building contracts, *Miscellany Scot Hist Soc* 11, 269–323

Dunbar, W 1998

The Poems of William Dunbar, edited by P Bawcutt, Glasgow: Association for Scottish Literary Studies

Dunlop, A I 1942

Scots abroad in the fifteenth century, London: Historical Association

Durkan, J 1986

Glasgow Cathedral: the precinct of Glasgow Cathedral, Glasgow: Glasgow Cathedral

Durkan, J & Ross, A 1961

Early Scottish Libraries, Glasgow: J S Burns

Durkan, J & Kirk, J 1977

The University of Glasgow, 1451–1577, Glasgow: University of Glasgow Press

Edington, C 1995

Court and Culture in Renaissance Scotland, East Linton: Tuckwell

Evelyn, J 1658

The French Gardiner instructing how to cultivate all sorts of fruit trees and herbs for the garden, London: John Crooke

Evelyn, J 1666

Kalendarium Hortense or the gard'ners almanac, London: Jo Martin and Ja Allestry

Evelyn, J 1679

Sylva, or A discourse of forest-trees, and the propagation of timber in His Majesties dominions, London: John Martyn

Everson, P, Taylor, C C and Dunn, C J 1991

Change and Continuity: Rural settlement in North-West Lincolnshire, London: HMSO

Everson, P 1996

Bodiam Castle, East Sussex: castle and designed landscape, *Chateau Gaillard*, 17, 79–84

Everson, P 1998

'Delightfully surrounded with woods and ponds': field evidence for medieval gardens in England, in Pattison 1998b, 32–8

Ewart, G & Gallagher, D B 2008

The history and archaeology of Stirling Palace (Stirling Castle Palace Archaeological Research 2004–2008), Edinburgh: Historic Scotland

Ewart, G & Sharman, P 1995

Stirling Castle Phase I, *Discovery Excavation Scot (new series)*, 15

Ewart, G & Gallagher, D B forthcoming

Monastery and Palace: archaeological excavations at Holyroodhouse, 1996–2009, Edinburgh: Historic Scotland

Fawcett, R 1995

Stirling Castle, London: Batsford/Historic Scotland

Fawcett, R (ed) 1998

Medieval Art and Architecture in the Diocese of Glasgow, British Archaeological Association Conference Transactions 23, Leeds: W S Maney

Fawcett, R 2003

The buildings of Scone Abbey during and after the Reformation, in Welander *et al* 2003, 169–80

Fawcett, R & Oram, R 2004

Melrose Abbey, Stroud: Tempus

Fenwick, H 1970

Architect Royal, Kineton: Roundwood Press

Ferguson, J 1910

Linlithgow Palace, its history and traditions with peeps from its windows at the burgh and surrounding district, Edinburgh: Oliver & Boyd

Fergusson, J 1963

The White Hind, London: Faber

Findlay J R 1875

Hatton House, Edinburgh

Findlay J R 1875a

Notes on Hatton House, Mid-Lothian, *Proc Soc Antiq Scot* 11, 124–39

Fittis, R S 1885

Ecclesiastical annals of Perth, to the period of the Reformation, Edinburgh

Fleet, C 2006

Pont's Writing: Form and Content, in Cunningham 2006, 35–47

Fleming, D H 1910

The Reformation in Scotland, London: Hodder and Stoughton

Fleming, J V 1986

The Garden of the Roman de la Rose: Vision of Landscape or Landscape of Vision, in Macdougall 1986, 201–34

Fontaine, M M 2006

Plaisirs, hospitalité et profits, in Chatenet 2006a, 9–48

Fradenburg, L O 1991

City, Marriage, Tournament: Arts of Rule in Late Medieval Scotland, Wisconsin: University of Wisconsin Press

Franck, R 1694

Northern memoirs, calculated for the meridian of Scotland wherein most or all of the cities, citadels, seaports, castles, forts, fortresses, rivers and rivulets are compendiously described: together with choice collections of various discoveries, remarkable observations, theological notions … : to which is added the contemplative & practical angler … / writ in the year 1658, but not till now made publick, London

Fraser, A 1969

Mary Queen of Scots, London: Weidenfeld and Nicholson

Fraser, W (ed) 1872

Registrum Monasterii S. Marie de Cambuskenneth, A.D. 1147–1535, Grampian Club no. 4, Edinburgh

Frew, J & Jones, D (eds) 1989

Aspects of Scottish Classicism: the house in its formal setting, 1690–1750; proceedings of a symposium held at Chatelherault, Hamilton, May 18th 1988, St Andrews: St Andrews University

Froissart, J 1805
Sir John Froissart's Chronicles, London: Hafod Press

Fullarton, J (ed) 1858
Topographical account of the district of Cunningham, Ayrshire. Compiled about the year 1600, by Mr Timothy Pont, Glasgow: Glasgow Maitland Club

Furnivall, F J (ed) 1870
The fyrst boke of the introduction of knowledge made by Andrew Borde … A compendyous regiment, or A dietary of helth made in Mountpyllier, compiled by Andrewe Boorde … Early English Text Society extra series 10, London

Fyfe, W W 1852
Summer life on land and water at South Queensferry, Edinburgh

Gairdner, J & Brodie, R H 1903
Letters and Papers Foreign and Domestic Henry VIII, Vol 19 Pt 1, London: HMSO

Gallagher, D B 1998
Holyrood Abbey: the disappearance of a monastery, Proc Soc Antiq Scot 128, 1079–99

Gardham, J & Weston, D 2004
The world of Chaucer: medieval books and manuscripts and early printed books from Glasgow University Library, held at the Hunterian Museum 15 May to 28 August 2004, Glasgow: University of Glasgow Library

Gerard, J 1597
The herball or Generall historie of plantes. Gathered by Iohn Gerarde of London Master in Chirurgerie, London: Edm. Bollifant for [Bonham Norton and] Iohn Norton

Gibson, R 2007
The Scottish Countryside, Edinburgh: John Donald Birlinn

Gifford, J 1988
Fife, The Buildings of Scotland series, New Haven and London: Yale University Press

Gifford, J 1989
William Adam 1689–1748, Edinburgh: Mainstream Publishing

Gifford, J 2007
Perth and Kinross, The Buildings of Scotland series, New Haven and London: Yale University Press

Gifford, J & Walker, F A 2002
Stirling and Central Scotland, The Buildings of Scotland series, New Haven and London: Yale University Press

Gilbert, J M 1979
Hunting and Hunting Reserves in Medieval Scotland, Edinburgh: John Donald

Gilpin, W 1789
Observations relative chiefly to picturesque beauty made in the year 1776 on several parts of Great Britain, particularly the High-lands of Scotland, printed for R Blamire, London

Glenn, V 1998
Court Patronage in Scotland 1240–1340, in Fawcett 1998, 111–21

Glendinning, M, McInnes, R & MacKechnie, A 1996
A History of Scottish architecture from the Renaissance to the present day, Edinburgh: Edinburgh University Press

Goodare, J 1999
State and Society in Early Modern Scotland, Oxford: Oxford University Press

Goodare, J & Lynch, M (eds) 2000a
The Reign of James VI, East Linton: Tuckwell Press

Goodare, J & Lynch, M 2000b
The Scottish State and its Borderlands, 1567–1625, in Goodare & Lynch 2000a, 186–207

Gordon, J 1661
Abredoniae novae et veteris description A description of new and old Aberdeens, with the places nearest adjacent auctore Jacobo Gordono.

Gow, I & Rowan, A (eds) 1995
The Scottish Country House 1600–1914, Edinburgh: Edinburgh University Press

Greig, M K 1990
'Pennant's Mount' (Banff Parish), mound, Discovery Excavation Scot 1989, 19–20

Grose, F 1789–91
Antiquities of Scotland, London: S Hooper

Guillaume, J (ed) 1999a
Architecture, Jardin, Paysage: L'environnement du chateau et de la villa aux XV et XVI siècles, Paris: Picard

Guillaume, J 1999b
Le jardin mis en ordre: jardin et chateau en France du XV au XVII siècle, in Guillaume 1999a, 103–36

Gunter, E 1624
The description and vse of his Maiesties dials in VVhite-Hall Garden, London: Bonham Norton and John Bill

Hadfield, M 1979
A History of British Gardening, London: John Murray

Hagopian van Buren, A 1986
Reality and Romance in the Park at Hesdin, in Macdougall 1986, 115–34

Haldane, E S 1934
Scots Gardens in Olden Times, London: Alexander Maclehose

Halkerston, P 1831
A treatise on the history, law, and privileges of the palace and sanctuary of Holyroodhouse, Edinburgh: Maclachlan and Stewart

Halkett, A 1875
The autobiography of Anne Lady Halkett Edited by John Gough Nichols, London: Camden Society

Hamilton, T 1954
Forest Trees: some directions about raising forest trees, London: Nelson

Hamilton, W 1831
Descriptions of the Sherriffdoms of Lanark and Renfrew, compiled about M.DCC.X, Glasgow: Maitland Club

Hannay, R K (ed) 1915
Rentale Dunkeldense, translated and edited by R K Hannay, Edinburgh: Scottish History Society

Hariot, T 1590
A briefe and true report of the new found land of Virginia of the commodities and of the nature and manners of the naturall inhabitants. Matis Speciali, Francoforti ad Moenum: Typis Ioannis Wecheli, sumtibus vero Theodori de Bry anno M D XC. Venales reperiuntur in officina Sigismundi Feirabendii

Harrison, J G 2011
Rebirth of a Palace: The Royal Court at Stirling Palace, Edinburgh: Historic Scotland

Harrison, R P 2008
Gardens: an Essay on the Human Condition, Chicago and London: University of Chicago Press

Harvey, J 1954
English Medieval Architects: a biographical dictionary down to 1550, London: Batsford

Harvey, J 1989
Garden Plants of around 1525: the Fromond List, J Garden Hist, 17:2 122–34

Harvey, J 1990
Mediaeval Gardens, London: Batsford

Harvey, J 1992
The Garden plants of Moorish Spain, J Garden Hist, 20:1, 71–82

Hay, D 1983
Scotland and the Italian Renaissance, in Cowan & Shaw 1983, 114–24

Hay, D 1984
Scottish Renaissance Architecture, in Breeze 1984, 196–231

Hayes, C 2007
Historic Orchards of the Carse of Gowrie: report to the Perth & Kinross Countryside Trust, Cupar

Hazlitt, C R (ed) 1895
Early Popular Poetry of Scotland and the Northern Borders, London: Batsford

Henderson, P 1999
The Visual setting of the English Country House; 1500–1625, in Guillaume 1999a, 207–18

Henderson, P 2005
The Tudor House and Garden, New Haven and London: Yale University Press

Henryson 1968
The Poems and Fables of Robert Henryson, edited by H H Wood, London: Oliver & Boyd

Hewitt, G R 1982
Scotland under Morton 1572–80, Edinburgh: John Donald

Hibbert, S 1931
A description of the Shetland Islands, Lerwick: T & J Manson

Higgitt, J (ed) 1995
Medieval Art and Architecture in the Diocese of St Andrews, British Archaeological Association Conference Transactions 23, Leeds: W S Maney

Higgitt, J 1998
Manuscripts and Libraries in the Diocese of Glasgow before the Reformation, in Fawcett 1998, 102–10

Hill, P 1997
Whithorn and St Ninian: the excavation of a monastic town 1984–91, Stroud: Sutton

Hist MSS Comm 1904
Sixteenth Report of the Royal Commission on Historical Manuscripts, London: HMSO

Hogg, B J 1975
Garden Works at Hopetoun House, Typescript RCAHMS D7.33 Hop

Holden, T G 1996
The plants and people from Buiston Crannog, Ayrshire, Scotland, *Antiquity* 70, 954–9

Holloway, J 1989
Patrons and Painters: art in Scotland 1650–1760, Edinburgh: Scottish National Portrait Gallery

Holloway, J 1995
Views in Scottish Houses, in Gow & Rowan 1995, 109–17

Howard, D 1995
Sir William Bruce's Design for Hopetoun House and its Forerunners, in Gow and Rowan 1995, 53–67

Howard, D 1999
Chasse, sports et plaisirs autour des chateaux d'Ecosse, in Guillaume 1999a, 295–305

Howard, M 2007
The Building of Elizabethan and Jacobean England, New Haven and London: Yale University Press

Howard, M 2006
The hunting lodge in England, 1500–1650, in Chatenet 2006a, 283–90

Hume, D 1644
The history of the house and race of Douglas and Hume, Edinburgh: Evan Tyler

Hume, J R 1985
Lincluden Collegiate Church, Edinburgh: HMSO

Hunt, J D 1986
Garden and Grove: The Italian Renaissance Garden in the English Imagination: 1600–1750, London: J M Dent & Sons

Hutcheon, J 1838
Views of Edzell Castle, Forfarshire, Edinburgh: Leith & Smith

Hynd, N 1984
Towards a study of gardening in Scotland from the 16th to the 18th century, in Breeze 1984, 269–84

Hynd, N & Ewart, G 1983
Aberdour Castle Gardens, *J Garden Hist* 11:2, 93–111

Innes, C (ed) 1840
Liber cartarum sancte crucis munimenta ecclesie Sancte Crucis de Edwinesburg, Edinburgh: Bannatyne Club

Innes, C (ed) 1842
Aberdoniae vtrivsque descriptio. A description of both touns of Aberdeen / by James Gordon, Parson of Rothiemay. With a selection of the charters of the burgh, Edinburgh: Spalding Club

Innes, C (ed) 1843
Registrum episcopatus Glasguensis. Munimenta ecclesie metropolitane Glasguensis a sede restaurata seculo ineunte XII ad reformatam religionem, Edinburgh: Bannatyne Club

Innes, C (ed) 1845
Registrum Episcopatus Aberdonensis. Ecclesie Cathedralis Aberdonensis Regesta Que Extant in Unum, Aberdeen: Spalding Club

Innes, C (ed) 1855
The Black Book of Taymouth, Edinburgh: T Constable

Innes, C (ed) 1867
Ledger of Andrew Halyburton, conservator of the privileges of the Scotch nation in the Netherlands, 1492–1503, Edinburgh: HM General Register House

Jack, R D S 1985
Alexander Montgomerie, Edinburgh: Scottish Academic Press

Jackson, K H 1971
A Celtic Miscellany, London: Penguin Books

Jackson-Stops, G, Schochet, G J, Orlin, L C & Macdougall, E B (eds) 1989
The fashioning and functioning of the British Country House, Hanover National Gallery of Art, Washington, Studies in the History of Art 2

Jacques, D 1997
The progress of garden archaeology, *J Garden Hist* 25:1, 3–10

Jacques, D 2000
The formal garden, in Ridgeway & Williams 2000, 31–48

James VI 1599
Basilikon Doron, Edinburgh: Robert Waldegrave

Jamieson, F 1992
Drumlanrig Castle Gardens: Notes written for Garden History Society's excursion to Drumlanrig and Leadhills 7 June 1992 Typescript RCAHMS Collections 20096

Jamieson, F 1994
The royal gardens of the Palace of Holyroodhouse, 1500–1603, *J Garden Hist* 22:1, 18–36

Jamieson, F 1996
Drumlanrig Castle gardens, Typescript produced for the Drumlanrig Castle study day, organised by the AHSS, 18 May 1996, to celebrate the publication of the Buildings of Scotland Dumfries and Galloway volume. RCAHMS Collections

Jennings, A 2005
Tudor and Stuart Gardens, London: English Heritage

Jervise, A 1857
Notice of the ruins of baths discovered at Edzell, Forfarshire in May 1855 &c, *Proc Soc Antiq Scot* 2, 226–9

Jestaz, B 1999
La villa de Giovanni Ruccellai a Quaracchi et ses nouveautes, in Guillaume 1999a, 21–8

Johnson, M & Campbell, K 2010
Elements of an eighteenth-century landscape revealed: excavations within the former gardens of Caroline Park House, Granton, Edinburgh, *J Garden Hist* 38:1, 81–98

Kay, W 1989
Development of the formal landscape at House of Dun, 1723–1750, in Frew & Jones 1989, 41–8

Keay, A 2008
The Magnificent Monarch: Charles II and the Ceremonies of Power London: Continuum UK

Keil, G 1986

Hortus Sanitatis, Garten der Gesundheit, gaerde der Sunthede, in Macdougall 1986, 37–41

Kerr, H F 1932

An interpretation of a drawing entitled 'Our Lady Kirk of Field, Edinburgh', in H.M. State Paper Office, *Proc Soc Antiq Scot* 66, 140–5

Kerr, J 2008

Balmerino Abbey: Cistercians on the east coast of Fife, *Citeaux: Commentarii Cistercienses* 59, 37–60

Kirke, T 1689

A modern account of Scotland; : being, an exact description of the country, and a true character of the people and their manners Written from thence by an English gentleman, London

Kirke, T & Thoresby, R 1892

Tours in Scotland 1677 & 1681 by Thomas Kirke and Ralph Thoresby, edited by P Hume Brown

Kolbert, C F & Mackay, N A M 1977

History of Scots and English land law, Berkhamsted: Geographical Publications

Laing, D 1857

Notice of the death of Robert Blackader, Archbishop of Glasgow, during a pilgrimage to the Holy Land, in the year 1508, *Proc Soc Antiq Scot* 2, 222–6

Laing, D (ed) 1875

Correspondence of Sir Robert Kerr, First Earl of Ancram, and his son, William, Third Earl of Lothian, Edinburgh: Bannatyne Club

Landsberg, S 1995

The Medieval Garden, London: British Museum Press

Langford, T 1681

Plain and full instructions to raise all sorts of fruit-trees..., London: Richard Chiswel

Lauder, J 1900

The Journals of Sir John Lauder, Lord Fountainhall, Edinburgh: Edinburgh University Press

Lazzaro, C 1990

The Italian Renaissance Garden, New Haven: Yale University Press

Lazzaro, C 1999

The sixteenth century central Italian villa and the cultural landscape, in Guillaume 1999a, 29–44

Lee, M 1980

Government by pen: Scotland under James VI and I, London: Urbana

Lee, M 1983

King James' Popish Chancellor, in Cowan & Shaw 1983, 170–82

Lee, M 2010

'Dearest brother': Lauderdale, Tweeddale and Scottish politics, 1660–1674, Edinburgh: John Donald

Lees, J C 1878

The Abbey of Paisley from its foundation to its dissolution with notices of the subsequent history of the church and an appendix of illustrative documents, Paisley: Alexander Gardner

Lewis, J 1992

Excavations at Balvaird Castle, Perthshire, *Proc Soc Antiq Scot* 122, 365–82

Liddiard R (ed) 2007

The Medieval Park: new perspectives, Macclesfield: Windgather Press

Liddiard, R & Williamson, T 2008

There by Design? Some Reflections on Medieval elite Landscapes, *Archaeol J* 165, 520–35

Lindsay, A W 1849

Lives of the Lindsays, London: John Murray

Lindsay, D 1879

The Poetical Works of Sir David Lyndsay, Edinburgh: W Patterson

Lindsay, R, of Pitscottie 1899–1911

The historie and cronicles of Scotland from the slauchter of King James the First to ane thousande fyve hundreith thrie scoir fyftein zeir, edited by A E J G Makay, Edinburgh: Scottish Text Society

Lithgow, W 1633

Scotlands vvelcome to her native sonne, and soveraigne lord, King Charles wherein is also contained, the maner of his coronation, and convocation of Parliament; the whole grievances, and abuses of the common-wealth of this kingdome, with diverse other relations, never heretofore published, Edinburgh: John Wreitton

Lithgow, W 1640

The totall discourse, of the rare adventures, and painefull peregrinations of long nineteene yeares travailes from Scotland, to the most famous kingdomes in Europe, Asia, and Affrica ... And of his last and late returne from the Northern Isles, and other places adjacent, London: I Okes

Loomis, R S 1956

Scotland and the Arthurian Legend, *Proc Soc Antiq Scot* 89, 1–21

Lorimer, R S 1899

Scottish Gardens, *Archit Rev* 6, 194–205

Lorimer, R S 1910

Scotch Gardens and garden architecture, *Trans Edinburgh Archit Assoc* 5, 58–66

Loudon, J C 1842

Recollections of a Gardening Tour, *Gardeners Magazine* 8, 596–606

Lowe, C E 1991

New light on the Anglian 'minster' at Hoddom: recent excavations at Hallyards Quarry, Hoddom, Annandale and Eskdale District, Dumfries and Galloway Region, *Trans Dumfries Galloway Natur Hist Antiq Soc* 66, 11–35

Lowrey, J 1987

'A Man of Excellent Parts' Alexander Edward: Minister, Architect, Jacobite. 1651–1708, St Andrews: St Andrews University

Lowrey, J 1989a

Development of the formal landscape at Hamilton Palace, 1700–1732, in Frew & Jones 1989, 25–32

Lowrey, J 1989b

Sir William Bruce and his circle at Craigiehall 1694–1708, in Frew & Jones 1989, 1–8

Lowrey, J 2007

Practical Palladianism: The Scottish Country and the concept of the villa in the late seventeenth century, *Archit Heritage* 18, 151–65

Lowther, C 1894

Our Journall into Scotland AD 1629, Edinburgh: David Douglas

Lynch, M 1990

Queen Mary's Triumph: the baptismal Celebrations at Stirling in December 1566, *Scot Hist Rev* 69:1, 1–21

Lynch, M 1991

Scotland A New History, London: Century

Lynch M 1998

A nation born again? Scottish identity in the sixteenth and seventeenth centuries, in Broun *et al* 1998, 82–104

Lynch M 2006

The Age of Timothy Pont, in Cunningham 2006, 27–34

Macaulay, J 1987

The Classical Country House in Scotland, 1660–1800, London: Faber and Faber

Macaulay, J 1989

The seventeenth century genesis of Hamilton Palace, in Frew & Jones 1989, 17–24

Macaulay, J 2009

Sir William Bruce's Hopetoun House, *Archit Heritage* 20, 1–14

McDiarmid, M P 1973

The Kingis Quair of James Stewart, London: Heinemann

MacDonald, A A 1972
The Poetry of Sir Richard Maitland of Lethington, *Trans East Lothian Antiq Fld Natur Hist Soc* 13, 7–19

Macdougall, E B (ed) 1986
Medieval Gardens, Washington: Dumbarton Oaks

Macdougall, N 1982
James III: a political study, Edinburgh: John Donald

Macdougall, N (ed) 1991a
Scotland and War, AD 79–1918, Edinburgh: John Donald

Macdougall, N 1991b
'The greatest scheip that ewer saillit in Ingland or France': James IV's 'Great Michael', in Macdoughall 1991a, 36–60

Macdougall, N 2006
James IV, Edinburgh: John Donald

M'Dowall, W 1886
Chronicles of Lincluden as an abbey and as a college, Edinburgh: Adam and Charles Black

Macfarlane, W 1906–08
Geographical Collections relating to Scotland. Made by Walter Macfarlane, edited from Macfarlane's transcript in the advocates' library, by Sir Arthur Mitchell & J T Clark. Scottish History Society vols 51–3, Edinburgh

MacGibbon, D & Ross, T 1887–1892
The Castellated and Domestic Architecture of Scotland from the twelfth to the eighteenth century, Edinburgh: D Douglas

MacIntosh, G H 2007
The Scottish Parliament under Charles II 1660–1685, Edinburgh: Edinburgh University Press

MacIvor, I & Petersen, B 1984
Lauderdale at Holyroodhouse 1669–70, in Breeze 1984, 249–68

Mackay, S 2001
Early Scottish Gardens, Edinburgh: Polygon

Mackechnie, A 1995
Design Approaches in Early Post-Reformation Scots Houses, in Gow & Rowan 1995, 15–33

Mackechnie, A 2000
James VI's architects and their architecture, in Goodare & Lynch 2000, 154–169

Mackechnie, A 2005
Court and Courtier Architecture, 1424–1660, in Stell & Oram 2005, 293–326

Mackenzie, H 1927
The anecdotes and egotisms of Henry Mackenzie, 1745–1831, London

MacKenzie, R 1990
A Scottish Renaissance Household: Sir William Hamilton and Newton Castle in 1559, Ayrshire Archaeological and Natural History Society

MacKenzie, W M (ed) 1939
Kingis Quair, London

M'Kerlie, P H 1870–1879
History of the Lands and their Owners in Galloway, Edinburgh: William Patterson

Mackie, J D 1924
The Secret Diplomacy of King James VI. in Italy prior to his Accession to the English Throne, *Scot Hist Rev* 21, 267–82

MacIvor, I & Gallagher, D B 1999
Excavation at Caerlaverock Castle, 1955–66, *Archaeol J* 156, 143–245

Macky, J 1729
A journey through Scotland. In familiar letters from a gentleman here, to his friend abroad. Being the third volume, which compleats Great Britain. By the author of the journey thro' England (2nd edn), London: printed for J Pemberton and J Hooke

McKean, C 1995
A Plethora of Palaces: Some 'Castle-wise' Country Houses in Early Renaissance Scotland, in Gow & Rowan 1995, 1–13

McKean, C 2001
The Scottish Chateau, Stroud: Sutton

McKean, C 2003
The Scottish renaissance country seat in its setting, *J Garden Hist* 31:2, 141–62

McKean, C 2006a
Timothy Pont's Building Drawings, in Cunningham 2006, 111–24

McKean, C 2006b
Quelques maisons de champagne ecossaises de courtisans de Jacques VI, in Chatenet 2006a, 171–80

McLean, T 1989
Medieval English Gardens, London: Barrie & Jenkins

McNeill, W A & McNeill, P G B 1996
The Scottish Progress of James VI 1617, *Scot Hist Rev* 75, 38–51

Macpherson, A 1862
Handbook of Hamilton, Bothwell, and Uddingston, Hamilton

McRoberts, D (ed) 1976a
The medieval church of St Andrews, Glasgow: Burns

McRoberts, D 1976b
The sixteenth century panoramic view of St Andrews, in McRoberts 1976a, 151–2

Mahon, R H 1930
The tragedy of Kirk o' Fields, Cambridge: Cambridge University Press

Maitland, R 1829
The History of the House of Seytoun to the year MDLIX by Sir Richard Maitland of Lethington, Glasgow: Maitland Club

Malcolm, C A 1925
The gardens of the castle, *Book of the Old Edinburgh Club* 14, 101–20

Malden, J 1993
The Abbey and Monastery of Paisley, Renfrew: Renfrew District Council

Manson, T M Y 1983
Shetland in the Sixteenth Century, in Cowan & Shaw 1983, 200–13

Markham, G 1623
Cheape and good husbandry for the well-ordering of all beasts, and fowles, and for the generall cure of their diseases printed by T[homas S[nodham] for Roger Iackson

Marshall, D 1881
Notice of three contracts betwixt Sir William Bruce of Balcaskie ... , *Proc Soc Antiq Scot* 35, 324–37

Marshall, R K 1973
The days of Duchess Anne: life in the household of the Duchess of Hamilton, 1656–1716, London: Collins

Marshall, R K 1995
Scarce a finer seat in Scotland, in Gow & Rowan 1995, 35–51

Marshall, R K 1998
The Winter Queen: The Life of Elizabeth of Bohemia, Edinburgh: National Galleries of Scotland

Marshall, R K 2001
Mary of Guise, Edinburgh: National Museums of Scotland

Martin, M 1999
A description of the Western Islands of Scotland, ca 1695; and A late voyage to St. Kilda. A description of the Occidental, i.e. Western Islands of Scotland by Donald Monro, Edinburgh: Birlinn

Maxwell, Sir Herbert 1908
Scottish Gardens being a representative selection of different types, old and new, London: Edward Arnold

Maxwell-Irving, A M T 1997
Kenmure Castle, *Trans Dumfries Galloway Natur Hist Antiq Soc* 72, 41–54

Maxwell-Irving, A M T 2000
The Border Towers of Scotland: Their History and Architecture The West March, Blairlogie: A M T Maxwell-Irving

Melville, J 1929
Memoirs of Sir James Melville, London: George Routledge

Meyvaert, P 1986
The Medieval Monastic Garden, in Macdougall 1986, 25–53

Mignot, C 2006
La villegiatura cardinalice en France, in Chatenet 2006a, 123–43

Millar, A H (ed) 1890
The Book of Record: A Diary written by Patrick Lyon, First Earl of Strathmore and other documents relating to Glamis Castle 1684–89, Scottish History Society Monograph 9, Edinburgh

Millar, A H 1890a
The historical castles and mansions of Scotland: Perthshire and Forfarshire, Paisley: Andrew Gardner

Miller, N 1986
Paradise Regained: Medieval Garden Fountains, in Macdougall 1986, 135–54

Miller, N F & Gleason, K L (eds) 1994
The Archaeology of Garden and Field, Philadephia: University of Pennsylvania Press

Moffat, B 1989
Third Report on Researches into the Medieval Hospital at Soutra, *Soutra Hospital Archaeoethnopharmacogical Research Project* 3, Edinburgh

Moir, J (ed) 1894
Hectoris Boetii Murthlacensium et Aberdonensium Episcoporum Vitae, Aberdeen: New Spalding Club

Mollet, A 1670
The garden of pleasure, containing several draughts of gardens, both in embroyder'd-ground-works, knot-works of grass, as likewise in wildernesses, and others, London: John Martyn ... and Henry Herringman

Montgomerie, A 1887
The Poems of Alexander Montgomerie edited by J Cranstoun, Edinburgh and London: William Blackwood and Sons

Monteith, R 1845
Description of the Islands of Orkney and Zetland, Edinburgh: Thomas G Stevenson

Moorhouse, S 1991
Ceramics in the medieval garden, in Brown 1991, 100–17

Morford, M 1987
The Stoic Garden, *J Garden Hist* 7:2, 151–75

Morrison, I 1995
Climatic change in Scotland, *Scot Archives* 1, 3–16

Moryson, F 1617
An Itinerary written by Fynes Moryson, gent. First in the Latin tongue and then translated by him into English: containing his ten yeeres travell through the twelve Dominions of Germany, Boermerland, Switzerland, Netherland, Denmarke, Poland, Jtaly, Turky, France, England, Scotland, and Ireland, London

Murray, A C 1932
The memorials of Sir Gideon Murray of Elibank, Edinburgh: John Orr

Murray, A L 1983
Financing the royal household, in Cowan & Shaw 1983, 41–59

Murray, H K & Murray, J C 2008
Drum Castle, *Discovery Excavation Scot* (new series) 9, 18–19

Murray, J 2008
Sir Herbert Maxwell: Chairman of the Royal Commission on the Ancient and Historical Monuments of Scotland 1908–1934, *Trans Dumfriesshire Galloway Natur Hist Antiq Soc* 82, 115–35

Mylne, R S 1893
The Master Masons to the Crown of Scotland and their works, Edinburgh: Scott & Ferguson and Burness & Co

NADFAS Garden History Group c2000
Cowane's Hospital Garden in Stirling, Stirling

Neill, P 1813
On Scottish gardens and orchards: Drawn up, by the desire of the Board of Agriculture, Edinburgh

Neville, C J (ed) 1990
A plea role of Edward I's army in Scotland, 1296, *Miscellany Scot Hist Soc* 11, 5th series, 3, 7–134

Newte, T A 1791
Prospects and observations on a tour in England and Scotland: natural, oeconomical and literary, London: Printed for G G J and J Robinson,

Nicholson, R 1974
Scotland: the Later Middle Ages, Edinburgh: Oliver & Boyd

Nimmo, W 1880
The History of Stirlingshire, London

Nuttgens, P 1972
The Landscape of Ideas, London: Faber & Faber

Omond, G W T 1887
The Arniston Memoirs, Edinburgh: David Douglas

Opsomer-Halleux, C 1986
The Medieval Garden and Its Role in Medicine, in Macdougall 1986, 93–113

Ordnance Survey 1963
Field Archaeology, London: HMSO

Ottenheym, K 2007
Dutch influences in William Bruce's Architecture, *Archit Heritage* 18, 135–49

Paca, B 2010
Landscape architecture from the heart: Chatelherault and Teackle Mansion garden, *J Garden Hist* 38:1, 99–111

Page, R & Page, C 1996
Blackfriars of Stirling, *Proc Soc Antiq Scot* 126, 881–98

Parrott, V 2010
Celestial expression or worldly magic? The invisibly integrated design of Uraniborg: a look at some philosophical aspects of the ground plan of Tycho Brahe's house and gardens, *J Garden Hist* 38:1, 66–80

Parry, M L & Slater, T R (eds) 1980
The making of the Scottish countryside, London/Montreal: Croom Helm McGill Queen's University

Paterson, R C 2003
King Lauderdale: the corruption of power, Edinburgh: John Donald

Pattacini, L 1998
André Mollet, Royal Gardener in St James Park, London, *J Garden Hist* 26:1, 3–18

Pattison, P 1998a
Giant Steps: fieldwork in London's royal parks, in Pattison 1998b, 39–46

Pattison, P (ed) 1998b
There by Design: field archaeology in parks and gardens. Papers presented to a conference organised by RCHME and the Garden History Society, BAR British Series 267, Oxford: British Archaeological Reports

Pattison, P, Field, D & Ainsworth, S (eds) 1999
Patterns of the Past Essays in Landscape Archaeology for Christopher Taylor, Oxford: Oxbow

Paul, J B 1904–14
The Scots Peerage, Edinburgh: David Douglas

Pearsall, D 1986
Gardens as Symbol and Setting in Late Medieval Poetry, in Macdougall 1986, 237–51

Penman, M 2004
David II, East Linton: Tuckwell

Pennant, T 1776
A Tour in Scotland MDCCLXXII Part 2, London: Benjamin White

Pennant, T 2000
A Tour in Scotland 1769, Edinburgh: Birlinn

Pennecuik, A 1815
Works, Leith: A Allardyce

Piggott, S 1970
Sir John Clerk and 'The Country Seat', in Colvin & Harris 1970, 110–17

Pliny 2006
Complete Letters, edited by P G Walsh, Oxford: Oxford University Press

Pococke, R 1887
Tours in Scotland 1747, 1750, 1760, Edinburgh: Scottish History Society

Potter, R 1975
The English Morality Play: origins, history, and influence of a dramatic tradition, London and Boston: Routledge

Pringle, D 1990
Craigmillar Castle, Edinburgh: HMSO

Pringle, R 1995
Rothesay Castle, Edinburgh: Historic Scotland

Proctor, C 2007
Physician to The Bruce: Maino de Maineri, *Scot Hist Rev*, 86:1, 16–26

Proudfoot, E & Aliaga-Kelly, C 1997
Excavations at Niddry Castle, West Lothian, 1986–90, *Proc Soc Antiq Scot* 127, 783–842

Quest-Ritson, C 2003
The English Garden: A Social History, London: Penguin

Rackwitz, M 2007
Travels to Terra Incognita. The Scottish Highlands and Hebrides in early modern travellers' accounts c. 1600 to1800, Munster/New York/Munchen/Berlin: Waxmann

Rawcliffe, C 2008
Gardens and Health in England, *J Garden Hist* 36:1, 3–21

RCAHMS 1912
Fourth Report and Inventory of Monuments and Constructions in Galloway, Volume I, County of Wigtown, London: HMSO

RCAHMS 1914
Fifth Report and Inventory of Monuments and Constructions in Galloway, Volume II, County of the Stewartry of Kirkcudbright, London: HMSO

RCAHMS 1920
Seventh Report and Inventory of Monuments and Constructions in the County of Dumfries, Edinburgh: HMSO

RCAHMS 1924
Eighth Report and Inventory of Monuments and Constructions in the County of East Lothian, Edinburgh: HMSO

RCAHMS 1928
Ninth Report and Inventory of Monuments and Constructions in the Outer Hebrides, Skye and the Small Isles, Edinburgh: HMSO

RCAHMS 1929
Tenth Report and Inventory of Monuments and Constructions in the Counties of Midlothian and West Lothian, Edinburgh: HMSO

RCAHMS 1933
Eleventh Report and Inventory of Monuments and Constructions in the Counties of Fife, Kinross and Clackmannan, Edinburgh: HMSO

RCAHMS 1946
Twelfth Report with an Inventory of the Ancient Monuments of Orkney and Shetland, Edinburgh: HMSO

RCAHMS 1951
An Inventory of the Ancient and Historical Monuments of the City of Edinburgh, Edinburgh: HMSO

RCAHMS 1956
An Inventory of the Ancient and Historical Monuments of Roxburghshire, Edinburgh: HMSO

RCAHMS 1957
An Inventory of the Ancient and Historical Monuments of Selkirkshire, Edinburgh: HMSO

RCAHMS 1963
Stirlingshire: An Inventory of the Ancient Monuments, Edinburgh: HMSO

RCAHMS 1967
Peeblesshire: An Inventory of the Ancient Monuments, Edinburgh: HMSO

RCAHMS 1982
Argyll: An Inventory of the Ancient Monuments, Volume 4, Iona, Edinburgh: HMSO

RCAHMS 1990
North-east Perth: an archaeological landscape, Edinburgh: HMSO

RCAHMS 1992
Argyll: An Inventory of the Ancient Monuments, Volume 7, Mid Argyll and Cowal: Medieval and Later Monuments, Edinburgh: HMSO

RCAHMS 1994
South-east Perth: an archaeological landscape, Edinburgh: HMSO

RCAHMS 2007
In the Shadow of Bennachie: A Field Archaeology of Donside, Aberdeenshire, Edinburgh: RCAHMS and Society of Antiquaries of Scotland

Reid, J 1988
The Scots Gard'ner published for the Climate of Scotland, Printed by David Lindsay in Edinburgh in 1683, Edinburgh: Mainstream Publishing

Reid, R C 1931
Lincluden, Edinburgh: Neill

Richardson, S 2010
A room with a view? Looking outwards from late medieval Harewood, *Arch J* 167, 14–54

Richardson, J S & Root, M E 1948
The Castle of Stirling, Edinburgh: HMSO

Ridgeway, C & Williams, R (eds) 2000
Sir John Vanbrugh and Landscape Architecture in Baroque England 1690 to 1730, Stroud: Tempus

Robertson, A N 1953
Icehouses of the eighteenth and nineteenth centuries in Edinburgh and the Lothians, *Book of the Old Edinburgh Club* 28, 131–3

Robertson, F W 2000
Early Scottish gardeners and their plants, East Linton: Tuckwell Press

Robertson, F W 2007
A history of apples in Scottish orchards, *J Garden Hist* 35:1, 37–50

Robertson, J (ed) 1843
Collections for a history of the shires of Aberdeen and Banff, Aberdeen: Spalding Club

Robertson, U A 1995
The Gardens at Hopetoun: a story of development and change, Hopetoun House Preservation Trust

Rogers, C (ed) 1879–80
Rental Book of the Abbey of Cupar-Angus, London: Grampian Club

Rohr, R J 1986
A sun, moon and tidal dial, *Antiq Horology* 16, 227–32

Ross, D J 1993
'Musick fyne': Robert Carver and the art of music in sixteenth century Scotland, Edinburgh: Mercat Press

Ross, T 1890
Ancient sundials of Scotland, *Proc Soc Antiq Scot* 24, 161–273

Rowan, A 1984
The building of Hopetoun, *Archit Hist* 27, 183–202

Roy, W 1747–55
Military Survey of Scotland

Sadler, R 1809
The state papers and letters of Sir Ralph Sadler, edited by A Clifford, Edinburgh: Constable

Sanderson, M H B 1982
Scottish Rural Society in the 16th Century, Edinburgh: John Donald

Sanderson, M H B 1983
The Edinburgh Merchants in Society, 1570–1603; the Evidence of their Testaments, in Cowan & Shaw 1983, 181–99

Sanderson, M H B 1987
Mary's People, Edinburgh: James Thin

Sanderson, M H B 2002
A kindly place? Living in sixteenth-century Scotland, East Linton: Tuckwell Press

Scot, J 1872
The staggering state of Scottish statesmen from 1560 to 1650. With a memoir of the author and historical illustrations by Charles Rogers, Edinburgh

Scott, A 1902
The Poems of Alexander Scott, edited by A K Donald, London: Early English Text Society

Scott, P H 1995
Defoe in Edinburgh and other papers, East Linton: Tuckwell Press

Scott, W & Laing, D (eds) 1827
The Bannatyne Miscellany, Vol 1, Edinburgh: Bannatyne Club:

Scott, W 1998
The journal of Sir Walter Scott from the original manuscripts at Abbotsford, Edinburgh: Canongate

Sharman, J 1889
The library of Mary Queen of Scots, London

Shaw, D 1983
Adam Bothwell, Conserver of the Renaissance, in Cowan & Shaw 1983, 141–169

Shepherd, I A G 2006
Aberdeenshire: Donside and Strathbogie, Edinburgh: Royal Incorporation of Architects of Scotland

Shirra, W 1889
Stirling in early times, *Trans Stirling Natur Hist Archaeol Soc*, 1–34

Sibbald, R 1710
The history, ancient and modern, of the sheriffdoms of Fife and Kinross, Edinburgh: James Watson

Sibbald, R 1710
The history ancient and modern, of the sherrifdoms of Linlithgow and Stirling, Edinburgh: Andrew Symson

Sibbald, R 1803
The history, ancient and modern, of the sheriffdoms of Fife and Kinross, with the description of both, and of the firths of Forth and Tay, and the islands in them ... with an account of the natural products of the land and waters, Cupar: R Tullis

Sibbald, R 1833
The autobiography of Sir Robert Sibbald, knt., M.D., Edinburgh

Sibbald, R 1892
Sibbald's History and Description of Stirlingshire, Ancient and Modern 1707, Reprinted by J S Shearer, Stirling

Sieveking, A F 1908
Sir William Temple upon the gardens of Epicurus, with other XVIIth century garden essays, London: Chatto & Windus

Simpson, G G 1999
The Heart of King Robert I: Pious Crusade or Marketing Gambit?, in Crawford 1999, 173–86

Simpson, W D 1922
The architectural history of Huntly Castle, *Proc Soc Antiq Scot* 56, 134–63

Simpson, W D 1925
The Augustinian Priory and parish church at Monymusk, Aberdeenshire, *Proc Soc Antiq Scot* 59, 34–71

Simpson, W D 1931
Edzell Castle, *Proc Soc Antiq Scot* 65, 115–76

Simpson, W D 1933
Further Notes on Huntly Castle, *Proc Soc Antiq Scot* 67, 137–60

Simpson, W D 1938
Tolquhon Castle and its builder, *Proc Soc Antiq Scot* 72, 248–72

Simpson, W D 1939
Fyvie Castle, *Proc Soc Antiq Scot* 73, 32–47

Simpson, W D 1945
Hatton House, Midlothian, *Proc Soc Antiq Scot* 78, 15–26

Simpson, W D 1948
Tolquhon Castle Aberdeenshire, Edinburgh: HMSO

Simpson, W D 1952
Edzell Castle Angus, Edinburgh: HMSO

Simpson, W D 1954
Craigmillar Castle, Edinburgh: HMSO

Simpson, W D 1959
The Northernmost Castle of Britain: Muness Castle, Unst, Shetland, *Scot Hist Rev* 38, 1–9

Simpson, W D 1960
Huntly Castle Aberdeenshire, Edinburgh: HMSO

Skelton, R A 1967
The Military Survey of Scotland 1747–1755, *Scot Geogr Mag* 83,1, April 1967, 1–12

Slade, H G 1995
John Elphinstone and the Castle of Glamis, in Gow & Rowan 1995, 119–27

Slade, H G 2000
Glamis Castle, Soc Antiq London Monogr, London

Slater, T R 1980
The mansion and policy, in Parry & Slater 1980, 223–47

Slezer, J 1693
Theatrum Scotiae.: Containing the prospects of their Majesties castles and palaces: together with those of the most considerable towns and colleges; the ruins of many ancient abbeys, churches, monasteries and convents, within the said kingdom. All curiously engraven on copper plates. With a short description of each place. Printed by John Leake for the author, London

Slezer, J 1718
Theatrum Scotiae: containing the prospects of his majesty's castles and palaces, together with those of the most considerable towns and colleges ... within the said kingdom ... with a description of each place, Printed for D. Browne ... J. Senex ... W. Taylor ... W. Mears, J. Browne, and F. Clay ... and A. Johnston ..., London

Slezer, J 1719
Theatrum Scotiae: containing the prospects of his majesty's castles and palaces, together with those of the most considerable towns and colleges ... within the said kingdom ... with a description of each place, Printed and sold by J. Smith, London

Slezer, J & Jamieson, J S 1874
Theatrum Scotiae, with life of the author and large additional illustrations Edinburgh and London: W Paterson; H Sotheran and Co

Smith, J S (ed) 1990
North-East Castles: castles in the landscape of North-East Scotland, Edinburgh: Mercat

Smout, T C (ed) 1997
Scottish Woodland History, Edinburgh: Scottish Cultural Press

Smout, T C 2006
Woodland in the Maps of Pont, in Cunningham 2006, 77–92

Somerville, A R 1986
The sundials of John Bonar, Schoolmaster of Ayr, *Antiq Horology* 16, 233–41

Somerville, A R 1987
The ancient sundials of Scotland, *Proc Soc Antiq Scot* 117, 233–64

Somerville, A R 1990
The ancient sundials of Scotland, London: Rogers Turner

Spalding, J 1829
History of the troubles and memorable transactions in Scotland in the reign of Charles I, Aberdeen: George King

Spink, W 1974
Sir John Clerk of Penicuik: landowner as designer, in Willis 1974, 31–40

Stannard, J 1986
Alimentary and Medicinal Uses of plants, in Macdougall 1986, 69–91

Steane, J 1993
The archaeology of the medieval English monarchy, London: Batsford

Steele, V & Cooper, S 1998
Yester House: notes for AHSS visit, 15 August 1998, Typescript RCAHMS 42808

Stell, G P & Oram, R D (eds) 2005
Lordship and Architecture in Medieval and Renaissance Scotland, Edinburgh: John Donald

Stevenson, D 1984
Masonry, symbolism and ethics in the life of Sir Robert Moray, FRS, *Proc Soc Antiq Scot*, 114, 405–31

Stevenson, J (ed) 1870
Documents illustrative of the history of Scotland from the death of King Alexander the Third to the accession of Robert Bruce MCCLXXXVI – MCCCVI, Edinburgh: HM Register House

Stevenson, J & Davidson, P 2009
Ficino in Aberdeen; the continuing problem of the Scottish Renaissance, *Journal of the Northern Renaissance* 1:1, 64–87

Stevenson, K 2006
Chivalry and Knighthood in Scotland, 1424–1513, Woodbridge: Boydell Press

Stevenson, S & Thomson, D 1982
John Michael Wright: the King's Painter, Edinburgh: National Gallery of Scotland

Stewart, A 2003
The Cradle King: The Life of James VI and I, London: Chatto & Windus

Stewart, D 2004
Edzell Castle Garden, *Discovery Excavation Scot* (new series) 5, 19

Stewart, M C H 1989
Lord Mar's garden at Alloa, in Frew & Jones 1989, 33–40

Stewart M C H 1998
The Earl of Mar and the Scottish Baroque, *Archit Heritage* 9, 16–30

Stewart, M C H 2002
The metaphysics of place in the Scottish Historical Landscape: patriotic and Virgilian themes 1700 to the early nineteenth century, *Stud Hist Gardens Designed Landscape* 20:3, 240–64

Stewart, M C H 2007
Regenerating a Highland Heritage – Lord Mar's approach to the historic house and landscape, 1700–1732, *Archit Heritage* 18, 115–33

Stirling, W M 1815
Notes historical and descriptive on the Priory of Inchmahome, Edinburgh: William Blackwood

Stokstad, M 1986
The Garden as Art, in Macdougall 1986, 177–85

Stone, J C 1989
The Pont Manuscript Maps of Scotland, Tring: Map Collector Publications

Stone, J C 2006
An Assessment of Pont's Settlement Signs, in Cunningham 2006, 49–54

Stone, J C 2006
Timothy Pont: Three Centuries of Research, Speculation and Plagiarism, in Cunningham 2006, 1–27

Strong, R 1973
Splendour at court: Renaissance spectacle and illusion, London: Weidenfeld & Nicolson

Strong, R 1984
Art and Power: Renaissance festivals, 1450–1650, Woodbridge: Boydell Press

Strong, R 1986
Henry Prince of Wales and England's Lost Renaissance, London: Thames & Hudson

Strong, R 1998
The Renaissance Garden in England, London: Thames & Hudson

Stuart, G M T 1955
The origins of gardening in Scotland, *The Stewarts* 10:1, 74–87

Stuart, J (ed) 1872
Records of the monastery of Kinloss with illustrative documents, Edinburgh: Edmonston & Douglas

Summerson, H 1993
Medieval Carlisle: the city and the Borders from the late eleventh century to the mid-sixteenth century, Cumberland and Westmorland Antiquarian and Archaeological Society Extra Series 25, Kendal

Sutherland, J 1683
Hortus Medicus: or Catalogue of the plants in the Physical Garden at Edinburgh, Edinburgh: Printed by the heirs of Andrew Anderson

Swan, J & Leighton, J M 1828
Select views of Glasgow and its environs, Glasgow, Edinburgh and London: Joseph Swan; Blackwood; Basil Stuart

Switzer, S 1718
Ichnographia rustica: or, the nobleman, gentleman, and gardener's recreation. Containing directions for the general distribution of a country seat, London

Symes, M 1996
Garden Sculpture, Princes Risborough: Shire

Symes, M 2000
A Glossary of Garden History, Princes Risborough: Shire

Symes, M 2005
The English Rococo Garden, Princes Risborough: Shire

Symson, A 1823
A large description of Galloway, Edinburgh

Tait, A A 1980
The Landscape Garden in Scotland 1735–1835, Edinburgh: Edinburgh University Press

Tait, A A 1989
The view from the road: Joseph Spence's Picturesque Tour, in Jackson-Stops *et al* 1989, 353–71

Taylor, C 1974
Fieldwork in Medieval Archaeology, London: Batsford

Taylor, C 1983
The Archaeology of Gardens, Aylesbury: Shire

Taylor, C 1997
The place of analytical fieldwork in garden archaeology, *J Garden Hist* 25:1, 18–25

Taylor, C 1998
From recording to recognition, in Pattison 1998b, 1–6

Taylor, C, Everson, P & Wilson-North, R 1990
Bodiam castle, Sussex, *Med Archaeol* 34, 36–57

Thomas, A 2005
Princelie Majestie: the court of James V of Scotland, 1528–1542, Edinburgh: Birlinn

Thomson, D 1974
The Life and Art of George Jamesone, Oxford: Clarendon Press

Thomson, M W 1964
Reclamation of waste ground for the Pleasance at Kenilworth Castle, *Med Archaeol* 8, 222–3

Triggs, I 1902
Formal Gardens in England and Scotland, London: Batsford

Tudor, J R 1883
The Orkneys and Shetland, London: Stanford

Urquhart, S 2005
The Scottish Garden, Edinburgh: Birlinn

Vitruvius Britannicus 1967
Vitruvius Britannicus or the British Architect edited by J Woolfe & J Bandon, New York: Benjamin Blom

Vitruvius Pollio 1988
Ten books on architecture, New York: Cambridge University Press

Von Bülow 1895
Journey through England and Scotland made by Lupold von Wedel in the years 1584 and 1585, *Trans Royal Hist Soc* 9, 223–70

Waldie, G 1894
A history of the town and palace of Linlithgow, with notices historical and antiquarian of places of interest in the neighbourhood, Linlithgow: Waldie

Walker, J 2002
Dunkeld House: a documentary study, unpublished typescript in RCAHMS

Walker, N H 1990
Kinross House and its Associations, Privately Published

Webster, D 2004
Little acorns and tall oaks: Project Pont and after, *Scot Archives* 10, 93–108

Wedderburn, R 1979
The complaynt of Scotland, Edinburgh: Scottish Text Society

Welander, R, Breeze, D and Clancy, T O (eds) 2003
The Stone of Destiny: artefact and icon, Society of Antiquaries of Scotland Monograph 22, Edinburgh

Weldon, A 1644
A perfect description of the people and country of Scotland, London

Whiteley, M 1999
Relationship between garden, park and princely residence in medieval France, in Guillaume 1999a, 91–102

Whittle, E 1989
The Renaissance gardens of Raglan Castle, *J Garden Hist* 17:1, 83–94

Whittle, E 1992
The Historic Gardens of Wales, London: HMSO

Whittle, E & Taylor, C 1992
The early seventeenth century gardens of Tackley, Oxfordshire, *J Garden Hist* 20:1, 37–63

Whyte, D 1986
John Reid: pioneer landscape gardener, *Scot Genealogist* 33:2, 174–81

Whyte, I D 1979
Agriculture and Society in Seventeenth Century Scotland, Edinburgh: John Donald

Whyte, I D 1980
The emergence of the new estate structure, in Parry & Slater 1980, 117–35

Whyte, I D 2002
Landscape and History since 1500, London: Reaktion

Whyte, T 1792
Account of the Parish of Liberton, *Archaeol Scotica* 1, 192–388

Williams R 2000
Fortified Gardens, in Ridgeway & Williams 2000, 49–72

Williamson T 2000
Estate management and landscape design, in Ridgeway & Williams 2000, 12–30

Willis, P (ed) 1974
Furor Hortensis: essays on the history of the English landscape garden in memory of H F Clark, Edinburgh: Elysium Press

Wilson, D R 1991
Old gardens from the air, in Brown 1991, 20–35

Wilson, D R 2000
Air Photo Interpretation for Archaeologists, Stroud: Tempus

Wilson, J J 1891
The Annals of Penicuik, Edinburgh: Constable

Wilson, J 1982
The site of the Elvetham entertainment, *Antiquity* 56, 46–7

Wilson, J M (ed) 1854
Imperial Gazeteer of Scotland, Edinburgh: A Fullarton & Co

Wilson, W D (ed) 1839
Ferrerii Historia Abbatum de Kynlos: una cum Vita Thomae Chrystalli Abbatis with a preface by James Patrick Muirhead, Edinburgh: Bannatyne Club

Withers, C 2006
Pont in Context, in Cunningham 2006, 139–54

Wittkower, R 1958
Art and architecture in Italy, 1600 to 1750, London: Harmondsworth

Wood, H H (ed) 1968
The Poems and Fables of Robert Henryson, London: Oliver & Boyd

Wormald, J 1981
Court, kirk and community: Scotland 1470–1625, Edinburgh: Edinburgh University Press

Wormald, J 1988
Mary Queen of Scots: a study in failure, London: George Philip

Woodbridge, K 1986
Princely Gardens, London: Thames & Hudson

Young, A 1987
Tudor and Jacobean Tournaments, London: George Philip

Zeepvat R 1991
Roman gardens in Britain, in Brown 1991, 53–9

Index

Abercorn Castle 194
Abercrombie, James 81, 84
Abercrombie, John 27
Abercromby, Henry, prior of Scone 35
Aberdeen 7, 44, 46, *46*, 49, 50–1, *51*, *207*, 208, 209
Aberdeen University 46, *207*, 209
Aberdour Castle 15, 113–15, *114*, *115*, 116, 117, 121, 172, 195, *195*, *196*, 239, 243
Adair, John, maps 6, 269–70
    see also Balcaskie; Ballinbreich; Belton; Biel; Broxmouth; Castle Huntly; Craigiehall; Dalkeith House; Drummond Castle; Dunbog; Falkland Palace; Flisk; Kinneil; Lawers; Lennoxlove; Leslie House; Lochend; Niddry; Presmennan; Seton Castle; Shank House; Tullibardine Castle; Tyninghame; Winton Castle; Yester
Adam, Robert 321
Adam, William 313, 325, 326, 328
    Airth Castle 277
    Arniston House 326, 328, *329*
    Castle Kennedy 315, 317, *318*, 321, 326
    Hamilton Palace 15, 307, 326, 328
    Hopetoun House 298, 300, 301, 303–4, 307, 313, *314*, 326, 328
    Lawers 255, 326
    Newliston *319*, 321, *321*, 326
    Taymouth Castle 325–6, *327*
Addison, Joseph 328
Adomnan, Abbot of Iona 18
aerial surveys 3
    Brunstane 229
    Castle Kennedy 316
    Castle Menzies 111
    Dunkeld House 289
    enclosure discovery 61
    Glamis Castle 260, 261, 263, 264
    Glenluce Abbey 35, 37
    Hopetoun House 298
    House of Nairne 304
    Kinnaird Castle 292, 293
    Lawers 255
    Linlithgow Palace 73
    Monzie Castle 5
    Shank 108
    Stirling Castle 179
Airth Castle 5, 276–8, *279*, 280, 328, 330
Akinhead, Robert 94
Albany, Duke of 55, 76
Albemarle, Earl of 296
Albert, Prince 181
Albert VII, Archduke of Austria 181

Alberti, Leon Battista 117, 118, 119
Albertus Magnus 43, 60
Album Amicorum 149
Alesius (Alexander Alane) 81
Alexander II, King of Scots 55
Alexander III, King of Scots 62
Alexander, Sir James 27
Alexander, Robert 33
Allan, David 15, *278*
alleys 101, 114, 178, 215, 220, 240, 330
    see also avenues; walks
Alloa House 15, 65, 172, 222, 244, 267, 296, 307–11, *308–11*
Alston, Charles 243
Alva 301
ambassadors 49, 62, 65, 83, 102, 103
amphitheatres 286, 325, 329
Ancram, Earl of 39, 168–71, 172
Ancrum House 39, 169–71, *170*, 172
Anderson, David 101
Anderson, Henry 253
Anderson, John 187, *187*, 197
André de Toulongeon 55, 56
Androuet du Cerceau, Jacques 130, 181
Angus, Earl of 76, 88
Anna, Marchioness of Hamilton 172, 248
Annabella, Queen (consort of Robert II) 58
Annandale, 1st Earl of 180
Annandale, 3rd Earl, later 1st Marquess of 297
Anne, Queen 240
Anne, Queen (Anne of Denmark) 97, 117, 133, 140, 152, 168, 173, 177, 181
Applecross House *315*
arbours 100
    Aberdour Castle 114
    Ancrum House 170
    Dalkeith House 294
    Dundas on 329
    Gylten Herbar / Gilten Arbour 43
    Hatton House 233
    herbarium 43
    Hotel de St Pol 55
    Kinnaird Castle 290, *294*
    Old Gala House 167
    Stirling Castle 183
    Strife of Love in a Dream woodcuts 119
    Yester House 236
Arbroath Abbey 24, 39, *39*, 105
archaeological excavations 18
    Aberdeen 44

Aberdour Castle 113, 114
Buiston Crannog 18
Caerlaverock Castle 86
Cambuskenneth 27
Castle of Mey 175, 177
Edzell 149, 150, 151
Elgin 44
Howe 18
Iona 18
Jedburgh 39, 44
Lincluden College 181
Paisley Abbey 42
Pennant's Mount 194
Perth 44
Rothesay Castle 290, 294
Soutra 46
Stirling Castle 79
town gardens 95
Whithorn 18
Archer, Alexander 130, *158*, 159
archery butts 63, 68, 81, 94, 102, 125, 141, 171, 186, 285–6
architecture 119, 120, 257, 266
    see also Adam, Robert, Adam, William; Bruce, Sir William;
      Lorimer, Sir Robert; Smith, James
Ardchattan monastery 24
Argyll 216, 313
Argyll, Earls of 91, 121–2, 132, 216
Argyll, Marquess of 210
Argyll's Lodging 122
Arnhall 144
Arniston House 108, 326, 328, *329*
Arran, Earl of 47, 83–4, 90, 93–4, *94*, 106, 115, 116, 253
Arthur, King 179
Arthur, Prince of Wales 73, 179
Ashton Hall, Lancashire 304
astronomy/astrology 133, 146–7, 188, 189
Atholl, Marquesses of 244, 304
Auchenames 91
Auchterlonie/Ochterlonie, Mr, of Guinde 39, 218
    see also Ouchterlonie, Rev
Auchtermuchty 70
avenues 269–70
    Airth Castle 278
    Alloa House 308, 311
    Ancrum House 169
    Balcaskie House 218
    Brechin Castle 293, *296*, *297*
    Brunstane House *229*
    Carmichael House 325
    Castle Kennedy 316, 319
    Culhorn House 321
    Dalkeith House/Palace 294, 295
    Drumlanrig Castle 331, 332
    Drummond Castle 255, 270
    Glamis Castle 260, *262*, 263, 267, *268*, 269
    Hamilton Palace 250, 252, 304, 305, 307, 328
    Hangingshaw 275
    Hatton House 233
    Hopetoun House 298, 303–4
    House of Nairne 270, *270*, 304, *305*
    Kenmure Castle 174
    Kinnaird Castle 289, *290*, *291*, 292–3
    Kinneil House 253, 269
    Kinross 284, 287
    Lawers 255
    Lennoxlove (Lethington) 230–1
    Leslie House *219*, 220
    Melville House 294, *299*
    Mollet's advice 215
    Moncur Castle *269*, 270

Newliston 323
Niddry Castle 196, *199*
Rome 218
Shank 108, 257
Taymouth Castle 270, 325
Thirlestane Castle 226
Tolquhon Castle 136
Tyninghame House 281
Yester House 235, 237, 269
    see also drives
aviaries 55, 56, 215
axiality 9, 97, 101, 175, 223, 264, 284
Ayala, Pedro de 62
Aytoun, William 203

Bain, James 274
Balcarres House 144, 145, 149
Balcaskie House 216–18, *216–18*, 219, 240, 256, 283, 284, 303, 331
Balcomie Castle 113, 138, *140*
Balfour, Andrew 241, 242
Balfour, Michael 149
Balfour, Robert 296
Ballencrieff House 60, 164
Ballinbreich Castle 112–13, *112*, *113*, 117, 219
Ballintroddo 108
Balliol, David 55
Balliol, John 55
Balloch Castle 111
Balmerino Abbey 32, 105
balustrades 55, *182*, 183, 226, 263, 264
Balvaird Castle 113, 138, *139*
Banff, Pennant's Mount 194
Banff Castle 60, 88
Bangor, Northern Ireland 188–9
Bannatyne, Janet *158*, 159
banqueting houses
    Barncluith 272
    Drumlanrig Castle 334
    Dundas Castle 190
    Duntarvie Castle 132
    Edzell Castle 128, *146*, 149
    Hamilton Palace 249
    Holyroodhouse 103, 104
    Kenilworth Castle 55
    Melville House 293
    Moray House 202, *202*
    Muness Castle 128
Barbour, John 100, 179
Barncluith 271–3, *272*, *273*
Barras, Edinburgh 58
Barras Green, Fyvie Castle 151, *152*
Barton, John 186, *187*
Bass of Inverurie 88
Bassandyne, Thomas 95
bath houses 103–4, *105*, 149, 233
Bauchope/Bauchop, Tobias 266, 287
Baxter, James 94
Beaton, James, Archbishop of Glasgow 50
Beaton, Patrick 60
Beatson, Robert 71
Beattie, Margaret 211
Beaufort, Joan, Queen (consort of James I) 55, 56, 62
Beauly Priory 24
bee boles 136, 168, *169*
beehives 71, 76, 136, 160, 162
Belton *8*
Benham, Bishop of Aberdeen 51
Bening, Simon 77, 79
Bentinck, William, Earl of Portland 236, 296
Biel House 8, 270–1, *270*, 271

Binning Woods *282*
Binns, The 269
Birkenside 108
Birsay *see* Earl's Palace
Bishops' Palace, Orkney 125, 127
bishops' residences 6, 47, 48–51, 209
Blackadder, Robert, Archbishop of Glasgow 57
Blackbarony/Darnhall 161, 193
Blackfriars, Perth 43
Blaeu, Johannes 90, 108, 173, 175, 177, 205, 207
Blair Atholl 105, 111–12, *111*
Blair Castle 173
Blair Drummond 301
Blakhall, Andro 116
Blois, France 80, 241
Blore, Edward *187*
Boboli Gardens, Venice 173
Bodiam Castle, Sussex 85
Boece, Hector 51
Boethius 150
Bog of Gight *see* Gordon Castle
Bonar, John 188, *188*
Bonnefons, Nicholas de 247
Boorde, Andrew 11, *12*, 47, 57, 97–8
Bothwell 67
Bothwell, Earl of 106, 121, 125, 132, 174
Bothwell, Adam, bishop of Orkney 125, 127
Boutcher, William 5, 276–8, *280*, 315, 328, *330*
Bowes, Sir Robert 152
Bowie, John 180
bowling greens
    Airth Castle 277
    Alloa House 311
    Castle Huntly/Castle Lyon 258
    Castle Kennedy 317, 318
    Clackmannan Tower 276
    Cowane's Hospital 244, *245*
    Drumlanrig Castle 331
    Dundas on 329
    Earl's Palace 125
    Fyvie Castle 151, *152*
    Glamis Castle 261, 263, 264
    Hamilton Palace 249
    Hatton House 232, 233
    Holyroodhouse 210, 240–1
    Kinnaird Castle 290
    Kinross House 286
    Lawers 255
    Lennoxlove (Lethington) 231
    Leslie House 220
    Lincluden College 181
    Sanquhar Castle 292
    Stirling Castle 183
    Taymouth Castle 297
    Yester House 237, 239
box, use of 78, 117, 118, 198, 199, 244, 247, 250, 264, 330
Boyd, Thomas 274
Boyse, Samuel 320, 328
Brahe, Tycho 133
Braun, Georg 30
Braun and Hogenberg, plan of Edinburgh 107
Breadalbane, Earl of 296, 297
Brechin Castle 15, 293, *296*, *297*
Brechin Cathedral, canon of 56
Brechin hospital 47
Brereton, Sir William 207
Bridgeman, Charles 239
Brochel Castle 50
Bronckhorst, Arnold 116–17, 119
Broughton House *11*, 189

Broun, Bishop of Dunkeld *50*
Broun, Andrew (Holyrood lion-keeper) 75
Broun, James (sundial-maker) 189
Broun, John (Dunkeld gardener) 49
Brown, Andrew (Leslie House gardener) 220
Brown, James, Prayer Book *51*
Brown/Broun, John (Holyroodhouse gardener) 211, 241
Brown, Peter Hume 11, 14
Brown, William 103
Broxmouth House *8*, 194
Bruce, Alexander, Earl of Kincardine 221–2, 225
Bruce, Grisel 241
Bruce, John 287–8
Bruce, Laurence, of Cultmalindie 127, 129
Bruce, Robert *see* Robert I (the Bruce), King of Scots
Bruce, Sir William 11, 15, *216*, 217, 224, 266, 281, 283, 313
    Balcaskie House 216, 218, 219, 256, 283, 303, 331
    Brunstane 224, 229
    Craigiehall House 297, 301
    Drumlanrig Castle 331
    Dunkeld House 289, 304
    Edward and 244, 283–4, 289, 293–4, 297, 298, 304
    Holyroodhouse restoration 239, 240
    Hopetoun House 298, 302, 303, 314
    House of Nairne 304
    Kinnaird Castle 289
    Kinross 283–9, 301, 303, 331
    Lennoxlove (Lethington) 224, 229
    Leslie House 219–20
    Melville House 298
    Moncreiffe House 289
    Panmure House 219, 283
    Stirling Castle 244
    Thirlestane 224
    Yester House 235, 237
Brunston/Brunstane Castle 10, 156–9, *156–8*, 165, 224, 229, *229*
Bry, Theodor de 101
Buccleuch, 3rd Duke of 336
Buchan, John 14
Buchanan, David 202
Buchanan, George 105, 117
Buckam/Buckham, Richie 178
Buiston Crannog 18
Burghley, Lord 106, *106*, 115, *116*, 121, 152
    Theobalds 121, 173
Burgundy, Duchess of 63
Burgundy, Duke of 56
Burkmair, Hans 81
Burnett, Sir Thomas 177
Busta House *128*, 129, *129*, 193
Bute, 3rd Marquess of 290

Cadzow Castle 63, 328
Caerlaverock Castle 85–6, *86*, *87*, 189
Caithness, Earls of 175
Caldwell, Andrew 186, 210
Caldwell, Hendry, John and Thomas 210
Cambuskenneth Abbey 26, 27, *27*, 29, *29*, 43
Campbell, Lady Anne 172
Campbell, Archibald, 2nd Earl of Argyll 91
Campbell, Archibald, 5th Earl of Argyll 132, 216
Campbell, Archibald, 7th Earl of Argyll 121
Campbell, Archibald, 9th Earl of Argyll 121
Campbell, Archibald, Marquess of Argyll 210
Campbell, Colin, 1st Earl of Argyll 91, 121–2
Campbell, Colin, 6th Earl of Argyll 121
Campbell, Sir Colin, of Glenorchy 57, 172, 223, 248, 251
Campbell, Sir Duncan, of Ardbrek/Auchenbreck *215*, 216
Campbell family, Loudon 189
Campbell, George 67, 68, 69, 76

Campbell, Sir James 255
canals
    Airth Castle 278, *280*
    Biel House 270
    Carmichael House 325
    Castle Kennedy 316, 318
    Dalkeith Palace 295
    Dampierre, France 120
    Drumlanrig Castle 331, 332, *333, 334*, 336
    Dundas on 329
    French gardens 121
    Hamilton Palace 305, 307, *307*
    Lennoxlove (Lethington) 231
    Mollet's advice 215
    Newliston 323
    Stirling Castle 182
    Theobalds garden 121
    Villa Doria Pamphili, Rome 237
    Yester House *1*, 236, 237, 238
Canna, Sgor nam Ban-Naomha *2*, 19–20, *20*
Cardono, Girolamo 49
Cardross Castle 59, 60–1
Carlisle Castle, Cumbria 59
Carmichael House *322*, 323, *324*, 325, *325–6*, 328
Carmichael, John, 3rd Earl of Hyndford 323, *323*
Carmichael, William 67
Carnasserie Castle *215*, 216
Caron, Antoine 103
Carpenter, Andrew 300
Carr/Kerr, Robert, 1st Earl of Somerset 160
Carscreuch 319
Carse of Gowrie 67, 94
Carse Grange *40*, 41
Carswell, John, Bishop of the Isles 216
Carwall, Andrew 185
cascades 236–7, *238*, 323, 331, *331*, 332, *333, 334*, 336
Cassanate, William 49
Cassie, Margaret 248
Cassillis, Countess of 90
Cassillis, Earls of 90, 315
Cassillis Castle 88, 90, *90*
Castle Campbell 91, *92, 96*, 97, 105, 121–2
Castle Huntly/Castle Lyon 258, 259, 260, *260–1*, 266, 301
Castle Kennedy 9, *313*, 314–20, *316–18*, 321, 326, 328
Castle Menzies 4, 6, 9, 68, 97, 109–11, *109–10*, 112, 246
Castle of Mey 175
Castle Semple 91
Catherine of Aragon 73
Cauldwell, Friar John 65
Caus, Salomon de 140, 173, 181
Cecil, William, Lord Burghley *see* Burghley, Lord
Chalin de Vinario, Raymond *48*, 49
Chapman, Peter 40
Charles I, King of Great Britain and Ireland
    Alexander Seton and 152, 222–3
    Holyroodhouse 187, 198
    imprisonment 218
    Keirincx paintings 184, *184*, 195
    Linlithgow Palace 183
    in Spain 168
    statue at Glamis 263, 267
    Stirling Castle 179
    Treaty of Carisbrooke 223
    visit to Scotland 177, 186, 195
Charles II, King of Great Britain and Ireland 243, 273
    Falkland Palace 184
    Gordon Castle 210
    Hampton Court 223
    Holyroodhouse 213, 240
    King's House, Perth 210, *211*

Linlithgow Palace 183
    Restoration 11, 186, 213, 224
    St James Park, London 244
    statue at Glamis 263, 267
    Stirling Castle 213, 244
Charles V, Emperor 62, 90
Charles V, King of France 55, 60
Charles VI, King of France 55
Charles VII, King of France 57
Charles VIII, King of France 119
Charpentiere, Andries 300
Charterhouse, Perth 42, 46, 57
Chatelherault 307, 328
Chaucer, Geoffrey 60, 61, 88
Cicero 150
Clackmannan 59, 60
Clackmannan Tower 275–6, *277, 278*
classical influences 9, 17, 44, 117–18, 143, 150, 213, 215, 313
Clement, James 77
Clement, Sir Walter 77
Clephane, Arthur 301
Clerk, John (Terpersie tenant) 51
Clerk, Sir John, of Penicuik 326, 328, 329, *331*, 331, 332
Cliddesdale, Alexander, prior of Cambuskenneth 27
Clien mansion 34
Cliveden, Buckinghamshire 304
Clunie, bishop's residence 49
Clunie Castle 49, *50*, 63
Cobbett, William 273
Cockburn, Agnes 156
Cocks, John 253
Coldingham Abbey 20, *20*
Coldingham Priory 32
Coldstream nunnery 55
Colinton 301
Collace, Margaret 158
Coltness House 211
Columella 144
Colville, John 116
Colvin, Howard 53
Comrie Castle 110
Cook, Moses 247
Cooper, Scott 63
Coryate, Thomas 12
Coupar Angus Abbey 31, 32–4, *32, 33*, 51, 68, 100
    see also Carse Grange; Coupar Grange
Coupar Grange 41–2, *41*
courtly love 61, 86
Cowane's Hospital 244, *245*
Cox, Euan 13, 14–15, 17, 25
Craigbarnet/Craigbernard 74
Craigiehall House 297, *301*, 323
Craigmillar Castle 88, 132–4, *133*, 135
Cranston, Sir William 57
Crathes Castle 177
Crawford, Earls of 252, 253, 257
Crawford, Andrew 127
Crawford, David 250, 251
Crawford, James 91
Crawfordmuir 145
Crescentius (Pietro de' Crescenti) 60, 127
Crichton Castle 105
Crichton, Edward 156
Crichton family 156, 157
Crichton House 143
Crokatt, Charles 301
Cromwell, Oliver 149, 203, 210, 211, 223
Cromwell, Thomas 47
Cromwell's Mount 194
Crossraguel Abbey 29, 37, *38*, 97

Cruft, Kitty (Catherine) 15
Culhorn House 315, 317, 319, 321
Culross Abbey 68, 93, 221, *221*
Culross House *220*, 221–2, *221*, 301
Cumberland, Duke of 111
Cunningham, Walter 76
Cupar *205*, 207

Dalgetty 91
Dalkeith Castle 88, 133, 294
Dalkeith House 114, 116, 294, *300*, 328
Dalkeith Palace 294–5
Dalrymple, Sir David 267
Dalrymple, John, 2nd Earl of Stair 313–14, 315, 317, 319, 320, 321, 329
Dampierre, France 120
Darnaway (Tarnwa) Castle 105, *111*, 112
Darnhall/Blackbarony 161, 193
Darnley, Lord 65, 103, 105, *105*, 106–7, *106*, 115, 116, *116*, 121, 132–3
Daueson, Thom 37
David I, King of Scots 27, 59
David II, King of Scots 55, 59, 61
Dean, Alexander 160
Dee, John 150
Defoe, Daniel 11, 182, 239, 244, 267, 295, 332, 334
design and layout 11, 97, 100–1, 108–9, 117–18, 129, 143
    avenues 269–70
    axiality 9, 97, 101, 110, 284
    bowling greens 183
    classical models 9, 117–18, 143, 213, 215, 313
    Dundas on 329–31
    French gardens 101, 120–1, 329
    health and 46, 97–8
    historic monument views 11, 216–18, 284, 303–4, 305, 308, 311, 325
    informality 101, 293, 325–6
    Italian influence 100–1, 118–21
    Kerr's letter on 39, 168, 169–71
    medieval gardens 53, 61, 77, 85, 119
    Mollet's advice 214–15
    monastic gardens 23, 27, 32–3, 35, 43
    mounts 193–4
    Neill on 15
    octagonals 181
    owners' names incorporated 134, 135
    statuary 266–7
    sundials 187–93
    terraces and terraced gardens 101, 117, 121, 270–7
    town gardens 199–209, *200–2*, 203–4, *204*, 206, *243*
    university gardens 46
    water features 101, 120, 121, 132, 134–5, 157–8, 182, 236–7
    Wode Partbooks' illustrations 107–8
    woodland 171–2, 278–81, 286, 292–3
    see also Bruce, Sir William; Edward, Alexander; knots and knot gardens; landscapes; *Scots Gard'ner, The*
Devosse, Cornelius 116
Dézallier d'Argenville, Antoine-Joseph 299, 329
Dickson, Camilla and James 18
Douglas, Archibald, Earl of Angus 76, 88
Douglas Castle 88
Douglas, Charles, 3rd Duke of Queensberry 331
Douglas family, Dalkeith 88
Douglas, Gavin 53, 73, 100
Douglas, James, 4th Earl of Morton 103, 113–14, 115–17, 118, 119, *119*, 121, 125, 150
Douglas, James, 9th Earl of Douglas 57
Douglas, James, 11th Earl of Morton 243
Douglas, Sir James 57, 116
Douglas, Janet, Lady Glamis 88
Douglas, Robert, provost of Lincluden 180
Douglas, William, 3rd Duke of Hamilton 248, 252–3

Douglas, William, 6th Earl of Morton 94
Douglas, William, 7th Earl of Morton 115, 195, 196
Douglas, William, 8th Earl of Douglas 56–7, 63
Douglas, William, of Drumlanrig 180
Douglas, William, of Lochleven 116
Doule, Dande 67
Doune Castle 59, *59*, 60, 70, 122, 301
drives *1*, 130, 313, 331, 337
    see also avenues
Drum, Midlothian *8*
Drum Castle, Aberdeenshire 101, 175, *175*, 177, 210
Drumlanrig Castle 180, 248, 292, 294, 331–6, *332–6*
Drummond, Lord 74
Drummond Castle 74, *190*, 191, *191*, 193, 246, 253–5, *254–5*, 270, 301
Drummond, George 242
Drummond, Margaret 71, 74
Drummond, William, of Hawthornden 150, 168–9, 177–8, 257
Dryburgh Abbey 24, *24*
Dumbarton Castle 60, 73, *73*, 74, 105, 177
Dunbar friary 75
Dunbar, Gavin, Bishop of Aberdeen 50
Dunbar, William 62, 86
Dunblane 25
Dunbog 113
Duncan, Mrs 301
Dundas Castle *189*, 190–1, *190*, 328, 331
Dundas, George 108, 328–31
Dundas, Sir Walter *189*, 190, 191
Dundrennan Abbey *9*
Dunfermline, 1st Earl of 150, 152, 153, 154, 155, 161, 223, 234
Dunfermline, 2nd Earl of 210
Dunfermline, 4th Earl of 234
Dunfermline Abbey 24, 140, *141*, 152, 177
Dunfermline Palace 59, 94, 97
Dunkeld, bishopric of 40, 49
Dunkeld House 289, 304
Dunninald Castle 194
Dunnottar Castle 105
Dunrobin Castle 174–5
Dunsapie Loch 103, *104*
Duntarvie Castle 129–32, *130–2*
Durham, James, of Duntarvie 130
Durie, Andrew, abbot of Melrose 31–2
Dysart, Countess of 220, 224, *224*, 225, 234

Earl's Palace *124*, 125, *125*, *126*
Edinburgh *57*, 58, 107, 160
    'English spy's map' 81, 84, *85*, 140–1, 184
    Gordon of Rothiemay's maps 81, 84, 107, *107*, 109, 140, 184, *185–6*, 197–8, 199, *200–1*, 202–4, *202–4*, 206–7, 244
    town gardens 84, 199–204, *200–1*, 202–4, 206–7
    see also Edinburgh Castle; Edinburgh University; Grange, the; Heriot's Hospital; Holyrood; Holyroodhouse; Kirk o' Field; Moray House; Physic Garden; Prestonfield House; Priestfield; Queensberry House; Trinity Hospital
Edinburgh, Bishop and Dean of 240
Edinburgh Castle 57–9, *57*, 83, *85*, 177, 197
Edinburgh University 106, 240
    see also Kirk o' Field
Edward I, King of England 11, 40, 55, 85
Edward II, King of England 179
Edward VI, King of England 83, 84, 90, 121
Edward, Alexander 15, 283, 297, 313
    Brechin Castle 15, 293
    Craigiehall House 297, 301
    English gardens 304
    Falkland Palace 244
    Hamilton Palace 15, *272*, 283, 304–7, *306–7*, 328
    Hopetoun House 15, 298, 299, 302, 303, 314
    House of Nairne 304

Kinnaird Castle 289, *291*, 293, *294*
Kinross 15, 283–4, *285–6*
Melville House 293–4, 298
tour 295–6, 300, 308
Edward, Robert 283
Edzell Castle 10, 14, 133, 143–50, *144–5*, *147–8*, 171, 172, 188, 191
banqueting hall 128, *146*, 149
English garrison 210
Lindsay fess chequy 146, *151*
Mary, Queen of Scots 105, 143
philosophy and 15
sculpture 144, 145–9, 150, 267
summer house 136, 149
walls 101, 145, 149
Edzell, Lord *see* Lindsay, Sir David
Eleanor (of Castile) Queen 55
Eleanor (of Provence) Queen 55
Elgin 44
Elgin Castle 59
Elibank Castle *4*, 10, 160–2, *160–1*
Elizabeth I, Queen of England 115, 121, 134–5
Elphinstone, John 259, 263
Elphinstone, Nicol 108
enclosed gardens 53, 61, 63, 97, 100, 109, 119, 239
Balcaskie House 218
Ballinbreich Castle *112*
Biel House 270, *270*
Cambuskenneth Abbey 27
Clackmannan Tower 276
Darnaway (Tarnwa) Castle *111*
Dunbar's *Tretis of the Twa Mariit Wemen and the Wedo* 86
Duntarvie Castle 130
Edinburgh *85*
Glamis Castle *261*
Hamilton Palace 249
Iona Abbey 18
Kirk o' Field 106, 107
Muness Castle 128
Niddry Castle 92
Plunton Tower *138*, *139*
Presmennan *271*
St Andrews Cathedral *30*
Shank Place 108
Virgin Mary identified with 26, 63
Yester House 235
see also walled gardens
English gardens and influence 13, 15, 116, 304
Anne of Denmark's 97, 140, 181
Edward's tour 296
Lauderdale's 228–9, 231
monarchs' 55, 198–9
octagonals 181
Pegasus statue 300
public access 244
seed imports 40–1
see also Ham House; Hampton Court; Richmond Palace; St James Palace; Somerset House; Theobalds; Whitehall Palace; Wimbledon
'English spy's map' 81, 84, *85*, 140–1, 184
entertainment and leisure 63, 84, 102–4, 171
see also archery butts; fishing; football; golf; hawking; hunting; masques; tennis courts; tournaments
Epictetus 150
Erasmus 49
Erskine, Anne, Countess of Rothes 117
Erskine, James, Lord Grange 308, 310, 311
Erskine, John *see* Mar, 2nd Earl of; Mar, 6th Earl of
Estienne, Charles, and Liebault, Jean, *La Maison Rustique* 144
Etienne, Charles 283
Eugenius IV, Pope 56

Evelyn, John 213, 247, 283, 296, 308
Eyck, Jan van *54*, 56

Falconer, John 235
Falkland Palace 59, 62, 70–1, *70–1*, *182*, 183–4, *183–4*, 244, 246
courtyard *82*
cross house 79, *83*
gardeners 70, 79
gates 71, 80, 183
James V 76, 79–80
James VI 113, 141, 161, 177
Mary of Guise 76, 80
Mary, Queen of Scots 105
Morrison's visit 12, 113
parks 63, 184, 244
roundels from interior facade *83*
Slezer's illustrations 80, *82*, *182*, 183, 244, 246
tennis court 63, *70*, 79, 80, 183
trees 71, 79, 183, *183*, 213, 244
Falkland Tower 70
Fast Castle, laird of 55
Fechtenburg, Bernard 149
Fenton, Thomas 103
Ferdinand, Grand Duke of Tuscany 135
Ferdinand, King of Aragon 57, 62, 65
Fergusson/Ferguson, Henry 235, 250
Ferrerio/Ferrerius, Giovanni 37
Fetternear, bishop's residence 50
feuing 99–100, 108, 172
church property 27, 29, 32, 99–100, 108
James IV 75–6, 162
town gardens 95
fish ponds 61, 132, 134–5, 157–8
Alloa House 308
Ancrum House 171
Brunston Castle 157, 165
Carse Grange *40*, 41
Coltness 211
Coupar Grange 41–2, *41*
Craigmillar Castle 88, 132, 133, *133*, 134, *134*, 135
Duntarvie Castle *130*
Glamis Castle 88, 260, 263
Hallyards *61*
Hamilton Palace 250, 251
Hesdin, France 55, 56
Holyroodhouse 81, 83, 94
Posso Tower *163*, *164*, 165, 166
Sanquhar Castle 292
Stirling Castle 182
fishing 115, 157
Fitzbaldwin, William 59
Fleming, George 231
Fletcher, Andrew, of Saltoun 258
Fletcher, Henry 258
Fleury monastery, France 23
Flisk 113
Flowerdale/Gairloch House *315*
Fontainebleau, France 80, *103*, 120, 121, 173, 198
football 171, 261
Forbes, Dame Isobel 145
Forbes, William 135–6
Fordell Castle 101
Forfar Castle 59, 60
Foster, Duncan 296–7
Foulis, George *158*, 159
Fountainhall 143
fountains 10, 100, 143
Alloa House 308
Dalkeith Palace 295
Drumlanrig Castle 331

Dundas Castle *189*, 190–1, *190*
Dundas on 329
Dunrobin Castle 175
Edinburgh Castle 59
Falkland Palace 80
Glamis Castle 263
Hamilton Palace 250, 305
Hatton House 232, 233
Heriot's Hospital 206
Holyroodhouse 240
Hopetoun House 300, 301
Hotel de St Pol 55
Italian influence 158
Kelburn Castle 173
Kinnaird Castle 290
Kinross House 286, 287
Leslie House 220
Linlithgow Palace 79, 80
Mollet's advice 215
Pitmedden House 223
Ravelston House 159, *159*
Rome 218
Saltoun Hall 258
Somerset House, London 140
Stirling Castle 177
Theobalds garden 121
Virgin Mary identified with 26
Whitehall Palace, London *10*
Yester House 236, *236*, 237, 239
see also water features
Francesco Colonna 77, 119
François I, King of France 80, 119, 120, 121
François II, King of France 81, 84, 91, 93, 101, 102, 132
French gardens and influence 11, 120–1, 213–15, 223–4
Alloa House 308, 311
Charles II familiar with 240
design and layout 101, 120–1, 329
Duntarvie Castle 130
Edward's plan for Hamilton 305
Edward's tour 296–7
Falkland Palace 79–80
fortified gardens 323
The French Gardiner 247
Holyroodhouse 81, 198
Hopetoun House 299
Kinross House 286, 287–8
monarchs' gardens 55
monasteries 24
public access 243–4
Sibbald on 241
Stirling Castle 79
water features 121, 132, 173, 237
see also Blois; Fontainebleau; Hesdin; Hotel de St Pol; Marly;
   Meudon; Versailles
Froissart, Jean 179
fruit 34, 62, 69–70, 337
Alloa House 310
Ancrum House 170
Castle Kennedy 318
Coltness 211
Dalkeith House 294
Dunrobin Castle 175
Earl of Crawford's list 252, 253
Falkland Palace 70
Glasgow University 209
Hamilton Palace 250, 251
Kinross House 286
Linlithgow Palace 71, 73
monastic gardens 25, 27, 30
Newton Castle 91

Saltoun Hall 258
Scone Abbey 34
Stirling Castle 69
town and village gardens 95
fruit trees
Aberdeen bishop's garden 50
Aberdour Castle 243
Alloa House 310
Balcaskie House 218, 240
Banff 194
books concerned with 247
Carse of Gowrie 67, 94
Castle Kennedy 318, 319
Castle Menzies 111
Coupar Angus Abbey 32, 33, 68
Cowane's Hospital 244
Culross House 221
Cupar 207
Edinburgh town gardens 199
Gala House 167, 172
Glasgow University 46
Hamilton Palace 250, 252
Hatton House *232*, 233
Heriot's Hospital *204*, 244
Hopetoun House 301
Jedburgh 34, 39, 170
Kinloss Abbey 37
Kinnaird Castle 290
Kinneil House 94
Kirk o' Field 107
Leslie House 220
Lindores Abbey 68, 71
Linlithgow Palace 71, 73
monastic gardens 25, 39
Newbattle Abbey 170
Newliston 318
Niddry Castle 310
nurseries 218
Paisley Abbey 42
St James Palace, London 198–9
in *The Scots Gard'ner* 248, 250
Seton Palace 195
Stirling Castle 67, 68, 69
terraced gardens 118
Thirlestane Castle 229
trade 67
see also orchards
Fuchs, Leonhart 46
Fyvie Castle 150–2, *152*, 209–10

Gairloch House *315*
Gala House 167, 172
Galbraith, William, abbot of Kinloss 37
Gallotre, Bertrand 81
Galloway 69, 173
Garden of Eden *see* Paradise
garden gates
Aberdeen bishop's residence 50
Aberdour Castle 115, 195
Ancrum House 170
Brunston Castle 157, *158*
Busta House *128*
Carnasserie Castle *215*, 216
Craigmillar Castle 132
Falkland Palace 63, 71, 80, 183
Glamis Castle 263
Hatton House 233
Heriot's Hospital 244
Holyroodhouse 81, 185–6, 210, 294
Kerr's advice 170

Kinross House 285
Lennoxlove (Lethington) 230
Moray House *202*
Newton Castle 91
Pitmedden House 223, *223*
Stirling Castle 141, 178, 179, 183
Thirlestane Castle 226, *227*
Yester House *14*, 236, 239
Gardener, John 71
gardeners 266
    Alloa House 65, 244, 308, 310
    Auchenames Tower 91
    Cardross Castle 60
    Castle Kennedy 315, 317, 319
    Castle Menzies 246
    Coupar Angus Abbey 32–3
    Cowane's Hospital 244
    Craigbarnet 74
    Culhorn House 321
    Dalkeith Castle 88
    Douglas Castle 88
    Doune Castle 60, 70
    Drumlanrig Castle 248, 331, 336
    Drummond Castle 74, 191, 253
    Dumbarton 74
    Dunkeld bishopric 49
    Dunrobin Castle 175
    Edinburgh Castle 59
    English Queens' 53, 55
    Falkland Palace 70, 79
    Fordell Castle 101
    Forfar Castle 60
    Glamis Castle 88
    Glasgow 209
    Grange, Edinburgh 246, 253
    Haddington 60
    Hamilton Palace 218, 240, 241, 246, 248
    Hatton House 233
    Heriot's Hospital 203, 244
    Holyroodhouse 69, 75, 81, 83, 94, 103, 186, 199, 210–11, 241, 248
    Hopetoun House 298
    Houston House 158
    Iona 18
    Kildrummy Castle 60
    Kilravock Castle 37, 86
    Kincaid, James 107
    Kinneil House 94, 241, 248, 253
    Kinross House 288, 289
    Kirk o' Field 94, 106
    Lawers 257
    Lennoxlove (Lethington) 231
    Leslie House 220
    Linlithgow Palace 71, 73, 79, 94, 253
    Menmuir 60
    monastic gardens 26, 27, 37
    Niddry Castle 196, 246
    Priestfield, Edinburgh 246
    Quakers 248
    Reid family 246
        see also Reid, John
    royal gardens 59–60
    Scone Abbey 67
    Shank Place 108, 257
    Stirling Castle 63, 65, 67, 68–9, 75, 76, 77, 78, 178, 179, 183
    Taymouth 297
    Traquair 59
    visits to French gardens 296–7
    see also Balfour, Robert; Campbell, George; Hampton, John;
        Mollet, André; Sharp, Sir John
Gardiner, John 59, 70

Gardiner, Robert 40, 49
Gartmorn Dam 308
Geddy, John 29–30, *30*, *77*, 100, *206*, 207
Gerard, John 101
Gibbons, Grinling 267
Gifford family, Busta House 129
Gifford Village *1*, 237
Gilbert de Rerick, Archdeacon of Glasgow 56
Gilmour family, Craigmillar Castle 134, 135
Gilpin, W 335–6
Gilten Arbour 43
Glamis, Lady 88
Glamis Castle 88, 105, 171, 209–10, 258, 260–9, *261–8*, 292
Glasgow 26, 49, 50, *50*, 209
Glasgow University 46, 47, *47*, 209
Glendoick House 14, 34
Glenesk 145
Glenluce Abbey 35, 37, *37*, 105
Gogar 301
golf 102
Gordon Castle 123, *123*, 125, 196–7, *199*, 210
Gordon of Cluny 209
Gordon, George, 4th Earl of Huntly 122–3
Gordon, George, 6th Earl and 1st Marquess of Huntly 123, 135, 196–7
Gordon, James, of Rothiemay, maps/plans 6
    Aberdeen *7*, 46, 50, *51*, *207*, *208*, 209
    Cupar *205*, 207
    Edinburgh 81, 84, *107*, 107, 109, 140, 184, *185–6*, 197–8, 199,
        200–1, 202–4, *202–4*, 206–7, 244
    St Andrews *205*, *206*, 207
Gordon, Jean, Countess of Sutherland 174, *175*
Gordon, Sir John, of Lochinvar 174
Gordon, Robert, of Gordonstoun 175
Gordon, Robert, of Straloch 113, 125, 173, 177, 197
Gordon, Sir Robert, of Glen 174
Gordon, Sir Robert, of Lochinvar 180
Govane, John 209
government 121
Gowrie, Earls of 43, 210
Gozbert, abbot of St Gall 20
Graham, James, Judge-Admiral 276
Graham, James, Marquis of Montrose 149
Graham, James, of Monzie 166
Grandtully Castle 111
Grange, the, Edinburgh 246, 253
Grange, the (later Lamancha), Peeblesshire 328
Grant, Robert 231
Grassmarket, Edinburgh 58
Gray, John 37
Great Michael 87, 88
Gregory XIII, Pope 150
Greig, Robert 220
Greyfriars Kirkyard, Foulis and Bannatyne tomb *158*
Grose, Francis 29
grottoes 100, 121, 173, 215, 237, 272, 305, 311
Guise, Charles de, Cardinal of Lorraine 120–1
Gylten Herbar/Gilten Arbour 43

Haddington *58*, 59, 60, 156
Haddington, Earls of 197, 279, 281
Hadfield, Miles 25
Hadrian's Villa, Tivoli 290
Haito, abbot of Reichenau 20
Haldane, Elizabeth 13–14, 25
Halkett, Anne 172
Halkett, Dr James 287, 288–9
Halkett, Mary 289
Hallyards 61–2, *61*, 68
Halyburton, Andrew 47, 77
Ham House, London 181, 224, 225, 228, 231

Hamilton, 1st Duke of 210, 251
Hamilton, 3rd Duke of 248, 252–3
Hamilton, 4th Duke of 296, 297, 304
Hamilton, Marchioness of 172, 248
Hamilton, Dukes of, keepers of Holyroodhouse 241
Hamilton, Anne, 3rd Duchess of Hamilton 241, 243, 248, 252–3
Hamilton, Friar Archibald 65
Hamilton, Lord Basil 273
Hamilton, Daniel 253
Hamilton, Elizabeth 210
Hamilton House (Kirk o' Field) 94, 106
Hamilton, James, 2nd Earl of Arran 47
Hamilton, James, 3rd Earl of Arran 83–4, 90, 93–4, *94*, 106, 115, 116, 253
Hamilton, James, of Finnart 79
Hamilton, James, Lord Claneboye 188
Hamilton, Sir James 57
Hamilton, John, 1st Lord Belhaven and Stenton 271
Hamilton, John, Archbishop of St Andrews 49
Hamilton, John, of Barncluith 271, 273
Hamilton, John, of Biel House 271
Hamilton, John, of Bothwell 94
Hamilton Palace 15, 94, 248–53, *249–52*, 294, 304–7, *306–7*, 328
    Adam's work 15, 307, 326, 328
    Barncluith and 272
    Edward's work 15, *272*, 283, 304–7, *306–7*, 328
    gardeners 218, 240, 241, 246, 248
    knot gardens 155, 234, 251–2
    Pinkie House compared to 234
    statues 249, 266, 305
Hamilton, Quentin 273
Hamilton, Robert, Lord Presmennan 271
Hamilton, Thomas *see* Haddington, Earls of
Hamilton, William, 3rd Duke of Hamilton 248, 252–3
Hamilton, William (son of Lord Basil) 273
Hamilton, Sir William 90–1
Hampton Court, London 7, 92, *93*, 141, 223, 296, 311
Hampton, John 246
Hangingshaw 274–5, *276*
Harborne, John 158
Hariot, Thomas 101
Harlaw, Thomas 244, 308, 310
Harvey, John 25
Hatton House 223, 231–3, *232*, *233*
hawking 63, 102, 117
Hay, John, 1st Marquess of Tweeddale 11, 233, 234, 274, 281
Hay, John, 2nd Marquess of Tweeddale 233, *233*, 234, 235, 237
Hay, John, 4th Marquess of Tweeddale 239
Hay, Margaret, Countess of Dunfermline 153
Hay, William, 5th Lord Yester 234
health
    garden design and 97–8
    see also medicinal plants; physic gardens
Hebrides 76, 313
    see also Canna; Raasay
Henri II, King of France 55, 101, 121
Henri III, King of France 144, 150
Henri IV, King of France 173, 198
Henri, Duc de Rohan 139, 172
Henrietta, Marchioness of Huntly 196
Henrietta Maria, Queen (consort of Charles I) 187, 198, 199
Henry IV, King of England 55
Henry V, King of England 55, 56
Henry VI, King of England 71
Henry VII, King of England 73, 92
Henry VIII, King of England 7, 29, 47, 83, 90, 92, 93
    see also Hampton Court
Henry, Prince (son of James VI) 9, 168, 173, 177, 179
Henry de Lichton, Bishop of Aberdeen 51
Henryson, John 60

Henryson, Robert 46, 95, *95*, 100
Hepburn, James, abbot of Scone 34
herb gardens 101
    Coupar Angus Abbey 32, 33, 34
    Earl's Palace *124*, 125, *126*
    Edinburgh town gardens 199
    Heriot's Hospital 204
    hospitals 44, 46
    Iona Abbey 18
    monastic gardens 43–4
    Scone Abbey 34
    Seton Castle 91
    university gardens 46–7
    Wedderburn's list of plants 46
    Whithorn 18
    see also kitchen gardens
Heriot, George 199, 203, 267
Heriot's Hospital 195, 199, 203–4, *204*, 206–7, 242, *243*, 243, 244
hermeticism 150
Hertford, Earl of 93
Hesdin, France *54*, 55–6
Hibbert, Samuel 129
Hill, Octavia 13
Hilliard, Nicholas 116
historic monument views 11, 216–18, 284, 303–4, 305, 308, 311, 325
Hoddom 20, *21*
Hog, Roger 321
Holyrood 7, 57–8, 241
Holyrood Abbey 24, 26, 32, 43, 46, 75, 83, 100
Holyroodhouse, Palace of 15, 62, 74, *74*, 80–1, 83, 108, 140–1, 210, 240–3, *241*, 274
    archery butts 81, 94, 102, 186
    banqueting houses 103, 104
    beer store 184
    Charles I 187, 198
    Charles II 213, 240
    Cromwellian army occupation 213
    drainage 75, 94
    Duke's Walk 240
    Dunsapie Loch 103, *104*
    dykes 75, 94
    'English spy's map' 81, 84, *85*, 140–1, 184
    fish ponds 81, 83, 94
    garden access *186*, *187*
    garden design and layout 84, 184–5, *185*, 198, 240
    garden doors 81, 186
    gardeners 68, 69, 75, 81, 83, 94, 103, 186, 199, 210–11, 241, 248
    gates 81, 185–6, 210, 294
    Gordon of Rothiemay's map 81, 84, 109, 140, 184, *185–6*, 197–8, *202*
    Henrietta Maria, Queen 187, 198
    James IV 74–5
    James V 75, 76, 80–1, 84, *186*, *187*
    James VI 103, 141, 160, 177
    knot garden 81, 184, 185, 198
    lion house 75
    Mary of Guise 81, 83, 84, 94
    Mary, Queen of Scots 102, 103, 104, 141
    masques 104, 240
    menagerie 103
    north-west tower *84*
    nurseries 248
    orchards 103, 184, 210
    parks 63, 74, *74*, 103, 184
    parterres 109, 184, 185, 198, *202*, 240
    Privy Garden 186, 240
    Queen Mary's Bath House 103–4, *105*
    Queen's Park 103, *104*, 240
    restoration 232, 239–40
    St Anne's Yards 240, 241

seeds 94, 103
'Siege of Troy' yard 141
South Garden 75, 94, 102, 185, 186, 210, 241
sundial 186–7, *187*, 191, 198, 240
tennis courts 240
tournaments 74–5, 83, 141
trees 84, 94, 184, 240, 301
vegetable gardens 185, 242
walled gardens 80, 81, 83, 84, 184
de Wet's paintings 233
see also North Garden, Holyroodhouse
Holywood Abbey 156
Hondius, Henricus 108
Hope, Helen, Countess of Rothes 279, 281
Hopetoun, Earl of 298, 301, 313
Hopetoun House 15, 193–4, 298–304, *302–3*, 307, 313, 314, *314*,
    326, 328
Hotel de St Pol, Paris 55
House of Nairne 270, *270*, 304, *304*, 305
houses
    gardens and 11, 15, 97–8, 119, 121, 213, 247
    see also axiality
    in 'garden' definition 1
    in James IV's feu charters 76
Houston House 158
Howe, Orkney 18
Howyson, Robert 49
Hume, Sir Alexander 57
Hume, George 231
Hume Brown, Peter 11, 14
Hunter, George 231
Hunterian Psalter *25*, *95*
hunting 63, 76, 102, 105, 115, 117
Huntly Castle 122–3, *123*, 135, 210
Huntly, Earl of 123
Huntly, Marquess of *7*, 123, 135, 196–7, 209
Hutchinson, Robert (Hamilton Palace gardener) 248
Hutchisone, Robert (Glasgow gardener) 209
Hynd, Neil 15
Hyndford, 3rd Earl of 323, *323*

Inch House 134, 135, 143
Inchcolm Abbey 35, *36*
Inglis, Robert 274
Innes, John 151
Inveresk Lodge 193
Inverurie *see* Bass of Inverurie
Iona Abbey *16*, 18, *19*, 24
Irvine, Ayrshire 67
Isabella of Castile 57, 62, 65
islands in gardens 132, 135, 157, *157*, 158, *163*, 165, 239, 292
Italian influence 130, 135, 160, 217–18
    garden design and layout 100–1, 118–21
    grottoes 173
    knot gardens 77–8
    terraced gardens 117
    water features 132, 158, 236–7
    see also Medici villa; Villa dell' Ambrogiana; Villa Doria
        Pamphili; Villa Farnese; Villa Lante

Jackson, James 41
Jackson, Robert 158
Jacobite rebellions 10, 12, 111, 149, 311, 313
Jacques de Lalain 57
James I, King of Scots 42, 43, 55–6, 57, 59, 61, 70, 73, 79
James II, King of Scots 55, 56, 63, 70, 100
James III, King of Scots 27, 47, 55, 57, 62, 63
James IV, King of Scots 49, 55, 57, 62–76, *62*, *67*, 79, 90, 91, 179
    Drummond Castle 191
    Elibank Castle 162

Falkland Palace 70–1
Glenluce Abbey 35
Great Michael 87, 88
Holyroodhouse 74–5
Huntly Castle 122–3
Linlithgow Palace 71, 73
Stirling Castle 62–3, 65, 87, 106, 179
tournaments 58, 62, 74, 75
see also King's Old Building/King's House
James V, King of Scots 55, 76–81, *76*, 83, 88, 90, 92, 93, 94
    Coldingham Priory 32
    Craigmillar Castle 88, 132
    Crown and Church land yields 98–9
    Falkland Palace 76, 79–80
    Glamis Castle 260
    Holyrood Abbey 32, 83
    Holyroodhouse 75, 76, 80–1, 84, *186*, *187*
    Lindsay, Sir David 76, 102
    Linlithgow Palace 76, 79, 80
    monasteries and 29, 30–1, 32
    St Andrews Priory 32, 76
    Stirling Castle *52*, 62, *64*, 76, 77–9, *80*, 81, 106
James VI and I, King of Scotland and England 7, 9, 113, 117, *117*,
    133, 138, 139–41, 156, 177–8, 179
    Castle Campbell 122
    Craigmillar Castle 133, 135
    Crossraguel Abbey 37
    Darnley's murder scene 116, *116*
    Drumlanrig Castle 180
    Edzell Castle 143, 144
    Falkland Palace 113, 141, 161, 177
    Ferdinando de Medici and 135
    Glamis Castle statue of 263, 267
    grottoes 173
    Holyroodhouse 103, 141, 160, 177
    Lincluden College 180
    Linlithgow Palace 141, 177
    Scottish visit 1617 160–1, 172, 177, 178, 179, 180, 181, 195, 197
    Stirling Castle 7, 9, 105, 141, 161, 178
    succession to English throne 97, 143, 177, 195, 240
    Tolquhon Castle 135
James VII and II, King of Scotland and England 223, 234, 240, 263,
    267, 296, 331
James, Duke of Rothesay 69
James, Prince (son of James V) 76
James, John 329
Jameson, George 197, 209, *209*, 210, 279
Jameson, Mark 46
Jamieson, Fiona 15
Jedburgh Abbey 24, 34, *34*, 39, 156, 169, 170
Jedburgh Castle 59
Jedburgh Friary 44
John, Lord Fleming 103
John of Arderne 44, *45*
John Hectoris Macgilleon, Bishop of the Isles 56
Jones, Inigo 117
Jonson, Ben 140
Jonston, James 186

Katherine, Queen (consort of Henry V) 55
Keirincx, Alexander 184, *184*, 195, *197*
Kelburn Castle 173
Kelso Abbey 24, 32
Kenilworth Castle 55, 61–2, 85
Kenmure Castle *172–4*, 173–4, 180, 188, *188*, 193
Kennedy, Bishop 56, 88
Kennedy family, Cassillis Castle 88
Kennedy, Gilbert, 2nd Earl of Cassillis 90
Kennedy, Janet 44
Kennedy, John, 7th Earl of Cassillis 315

Kent, Duke of 297
Keppel, Arnold Joost van, Earl of Albemarle 296
Kerr, Anna, Countess of Lothian 169
Kerr, Mark, Abbot of Newbattle 121, 122
Kerr/Carr, Robert, 1st Earl of Somerset 160
Kerr, Robert 170
Kerr, Sir Robert, Earl of Ancram 39, 168–71, 172
Kerr, William, 3rd Earl of Lothian 169, 193
Kildrummy Castle 59, 60, 88, *89*
Kilgour, Thomas 79
Kilmaluig Castle 50
Kilravock Castle 37, 86
Kilwinning Abbey 24, 42, 100, 252
Kincaid, George 26
Kincaid, James 107
Kincardine, Earl of 221–2, 225
Kincardine castle 63
Kingis Quair, The 53, 56, 61, 73, 78
King's College, Aberdeen University 46, *207*, 209
King's House, Perth 210, *211*
King's Knot, Stirling Castle 7, *66*, 67, 77, 78, 140, *142*, *176*, 177–9, *177–8*, 181–3, 193
King's Old Building/King's House, Stirling Castle *52*, *64*, 65, *66*, 78, *80*, 91, 122
King's Park, Falkland Palace 244
King's Park/Old Park, Stirling Castle 62, 76
Kingston, Viscount 196
Kinloss Abbey 32, 37, *38*, 39, 125
Kinman, Robert 60
Kinnaird Castle 213, 289–95, *290–4*, 299
Kinneil House 94, 241, 248, 253, *253*, 269
Kinross House 15, 283–9, *284–7*, 301, 303
Kirk o' Field, Edinburgh 65, 94, 105, 106–7, *106–7*, 108, 109, *116*, 133
Kirke, Thomas 12, 220, 234, 244, 252, 290
Kirkforthar House 193
Kirkliston 46–7, 68
kitchen gardens 337
 Aberdour Castle 195
 Airth Castle 277
 Alloa House 296, 308, 311
 Balvaird Castle 138, *139*
 Busta House 129
 Castle Huntly/Castle Lyon 258
 Coltness 211
 Culross House 221
 Dalkeith House/Palace 294, 295
 Drummond Castle 253
 Edinburgh Castle 59
 Edzell Castle 149
 Glamis Castle 267, *268*
 Glasgow University 46
 Hamilton Palace 250, 305
 Hangingshaw 275
 Heriot's Hospital 204
 Hopetoun House 301, 303
 Kinneil House 253
 Kinross House 284–5
 Lawers 256
 monastic gardens *22*, *23*
 Seton Castle 91
 in *The Scots Gard'ner* 204
 Thirlestane Castle 229
 Yester House *1*, 236
 see also herb gardens; vegetable gardens
Knight, John 115
knots and knot gardens 77–8, *79*, 119
 Aberdour Castle 114
 Ancrum House 170
 Auchenames Tower 91
 Blair Atholl 111–12, *111*

Castle Campbell 122
 Dundas on 330
 Elibank Castle 162
 Hamilton Palace 155, 234, 251–2
 Heriot's Hospital 206
 Holyroodhouse 81, 184, 185, 198
 Lincluden College 179–80
 Mollet's advice 215
 Pinkie House *153*, 155, 234, 251–2
 Stirling Castle 77, 78
   see also King's Knot
 Wimbledon 199
 Winton Castle 92

Lalain, Jacques de 57
Lamancha (The Grange) 328
landholding 9, 29, 32, 51, 97, 98–100
 see also feuing
Lando, Pietro, Doge of Venice 152
landscapes 15, 97, 101, 118, 119, 307–8, 311, 326, 328, 331–6
 Alloa 308, 311
 Drumlanrig House 335
 Glamis Castle 262, 264
 Hamilton Palace 305, 307
 Kinross House 284
 medieval gardens 61, 85
 Yester House 239
Langhaugh 165
Langshaw Tower 162, *162*, 164
Lasren (Iona gardener) 18
Lauder, Elizabeth 232
Lauder, Sir John (later Lord Fountainhall) 155, 220, 232–3, 234, 250
Lauder, Margaret 223
Lauder, Sir Thomas Dick 315–16
Lauderdale, Earls and Duke of *see* Maitland
Lawers House 246, 255–7, *256*, 326
Le Moyne de Morgues, Jacques 101
Le Nôtre, André 223, 226
Learmont, William 38
Learmonth, Sir James 138
Learmonth, John 138
Leckie 60
Lee, David 333
Lee, Nathaniel 240
Lee, Sir Richard *85*
Leiper, Thomas 136, 149
Lely, Peter 234
Lennox, 4th Earl of 116
Lennox family 137
Lennoxlove (Lethington) 172, 213, 223, 224, 229–31, *230–1*, 235
Leslie House 113, *212*, 219–21, *219*, 224, 266, 281, 290
Leslie, John 49
Leslie, Lady Margaret 279, 281
Leuchars 269
Lincluden College 179–81, *180*, *192*, 193
Lindores Abbey 39, 40, *40*, 68, *68*, 71, 100, 252
 see also Wode, Thomas
Lindores, abbot of 71
Lindores, Philantus 231
Lindsay, Lord 172
Lindsay, Master of 102
Lindsay, Sir David (of the Mount), poet 100
 Ane Satyre of the Thrie Estaitis 46, 102, *102*, 172
 Complaint/Testament of the Papingo 172, 179
 Lindsay, Sir David (Lord Edzell)
  Edzell Castle 133, 143–5, *145*, 146, 149, 150, 161, 172
 James V and 76, 102
Lindsay family, Edzell 10, 143, 149
Lindsay, Lady Henrietta *215*, 216
Lindsay, John, 17th Earl of Crawford 257

Lindsay, John, Lord Menmuir 144, 145, 149, 150, 172
Lindsay, Robert, of Pitscottie 87
Lindsay, William, 18th Earl of Crawford 252, 253
Linlithgow Palace *10*, 59, 62, 63, 70–3, *72*, 94, 160, *182*
    Ane Satyre of the Thrie Estaitis at 102
    Charles I/Charles II 183
    Cromwell's forces 210, 213
    gardeners 71, 73, 79, 94, 253
    James IV 71, 73
    James V 76, 79, 80
    James VI 141, 177
    James VII and II 240
    Mary, Queen of Scots 105
    Slezer's illustrations *182*, 183, 210
lion houses 75, 79, *80*, 186
Lipsius, Justus 150
Liston 68
literature 61
    Strife of Love in a Dream 77, 119
    see also masques; poetry
Lithgow, William 12, 172, 175
Lochend House *8*, 269
Lochleven Castle 114, 116, 117, *118*, 133, 284, *284*
Lochwood Castle/Tower 3, 194, *194*, 195, *195*
Logan House 194
London and Wise 234
Longueville, Duke of 79
Loretto School 156
Lorimer, Sir Robert 231
Lorraine, Duke of 79
Loudon, John Claudius 316
Louis XI, King of France 91
Louis XII, King of France 88, 92, 119, 120
Louis XIV, King of France 223, 244, 267, 296, 332
love 61, 86
Low, David 331, 336
Lowis of Plora 164
Lowther, Christopher 167
Lubias, William 37
Lundy, Sir John 65
Luss 69

McCalla, Thomas 313, 315, 317, 319–20, 321
Macdougall, William 103
Macgill, Alexander 237, 307
Macgilleon, John Hectoris, Bishop of the Isles 56
Mackenzie, Sir George, of Rosehaugh 108, 257
Maclary, Malcolm 63
Mclellan, John 173
MacLellan, Sir Robert, of Bombie 189
MacLellans Castle *11*, 189
Machaut, Guillaume de 56
Macklehose, Giles 63
Macky, John 11
    on Alloa House 311
    on Barncluith 272, 273
    on Culross 222
    on Drumlanrig Castle 332
    on Glamis Castle 263
    on Hamilton Palace 307
    on Heriot's Hospital 244
    on Hopetoun House 300, 301, 303
    on statuary 267
    on Tyninghame House 281
    on Yester House 237, 239
Madeleine, Queen, (consort of James V) 79, 80, 81
Maineri, Maino de 60–1
Maitland, Charles, Lord Hatton 223, 226, 228, 231–2, 233, 239
Maitland family, Brunstane 157
Maitland, John, 1st Earl of Lauderdale 172, 223, 229

Maitland, John, 5th Earl of Lauderdale 232
Maitland, John, Duke of Lauderdale 221–2, 223, 224, *224*, 234, 240, 241, 257, 331
    Sir William Bruce and 224, 229, 240, 283
    Brunstane 224, 229
    Holyroodhouse restoration 239, 240
    Lennoxlove (Lethington) 224, 229–30
    Thirlestane Castle 224–5, *224*, 226, 228, 229
Maitland, Mary 233, 234
Maitland, Richard, 4th Earl of Lauderdale 232
Maitland, Sir Richard, of Lethington 91, 92, 121, 195
Malcolm III (Canmore), King of Scots 55
Malcolm IV, King of Scots 46
Malcolm, Charles 57, 58
Malin, Walter, abbot of Glenluce 31
Malynson, John 60
Manchan of Liath 18
maps *see* Adair; Blaeu; Gordon, James, of Rothiemay; Pont; Roy
Mar, Earl of 60, 281
    see also Stewart, James, Earl of Moray (and of Mar)
Mar, 2nd Earl of 171–2, 179
Mar, 6th Earl of 237, 307–8, 310, 311, 313, 314
    Alexander Edward and 295, 296, 297, 304, 307–8
    see also Alloa House
Mar, Earls of, governors of Stirling Castle 244
Mar and Garioch, Earl of (John Stewart) 132
March, Earl of 274
Marcus Aurelius 150
Margaret, Countess of Moray 202
Margaret, Princess (daughter of James I) 56, 91
Margaret, Queen (Margaret of Denmark) 27, 55
Margaret, Queen (Margaret Tudor) 67, *67*, 71, 73, 75, 76, 77, 79, 88
Marjoribanks, John 118
Markham, Gervase 157–8
Marly, France 296, 300
marriage 55, 56, 86, 102
Marshall, Alexander 71
Martin, Moyse/Mogin 80
Mary Erskine's School 159
Mary of Gueldres 55, 56, 63, 70, 71, 85
Mary of Guise 46, 76, 77, 86, 94, 101, 102, 123, 138
    Falkland Palace 76, 80
    Holyroodhouse 81, 83, 84, 94
    Stirling Castle 79
Mary, Queen (Mary of Modena) 240
Mary, Queen of Scots 7, 83–5, *84*, 94, 101–5, 116, 121, 123, 139, 150
    Castle Campbell 105, 122
    Craigmillar Castle 132–3
    Earl of Morton and 115, 116
    Edzell Castle 105, 143
    Glenluce Abbey 37, 105
    Holyroodhouse 102, 103, 104, 141
    Lochleven Castle 133, 284
    marriage to Darnley 103, 115
    marriage to Earl of Bothwell 106, 125, 174–5
    marriage to François II 81, 84, 91, 93, 101, 102, 132
masques 102, 103, 104, 105, 122, 140, 141, 179, 240
Massoun, Walter 59
mathematics 150, 188, 193, 247
Mathieson, Mr 181
Mavisbank 326, 328, *328*
Maxwell family, Caerlaverock Castle 86
Maxwell, Dame Grissel 189
Maxwell, Sir Herbert 13
Maxwell, Margaret 253
Maxwell, Robert, 1st Earl of Nithsdale 180
mazes 141, *204*, 206, 236, *237*
Meager, Leonard 283
Mediceners House, Aberdeen University 46, *46*
Medici, Catherine de 55, 103, 120

Medici, Cosimo de, Grand Duke of Tuscany 173
Medici, Ferdinando de, Grand Duke of Tuscany 135
Medici, Francesco I, Grand Duke of Tuscany 120
Medici, Lorenzo de' (the Magnificent) 118, 119
Medici villa 119, 173, 181
medicinal plants 18, 35, 43–4, 46, 49, 95, 127, 203, 240, 242–3
    see also physic gardens
Megginch 269–70
melancholy 193
Melrose Abbey 20, *21*, 24, 30, 31–2, *31*, 56, 99, 162
Melrose, abbot of 31–2, 57
Melville, 1st Earl of 293, 294
Melville House 293–4, *298*, *299*
Melville, Sir James 116
Melville, Thomas 79
menageries 55, 56, 103
    see also lion houses
Menmuir 60
Menzies, James 110, *110*, 111
Mertoun House 270
Metsys, Quintin 49
Meudon, France 120, 121
Midhope nursery 301
Midlothian, Pont's map 108
Miller, George 241, 248, 253
Miller, Hugh 251
Miller, Isaac 248, 249, *249*, 250, *250*, 251, *251*
Miller, James 241, 253
Miller, Margaret 255
Miller, William 241, 248, 253, 301
Mitchell, Andrew 211
Modane, John 63
Mollet, André 198–9, 202, 204, 206, 213–15, 226, 244, 290, 299
Mollet, Jacques 198
monastic gardens 2, 6–7, 9, 16–51, *20*, *22*, 23, *23*, 99, 100
Moncur Castle *269*, 270
Moncur, Hob 67–8
Monimail Tower 293
Monk, General 283
Monk's Tower, Perth 43
Monro, Donald, Dean of the Isles 49–50, 139
Montgomerie, Alexander 140, 193
Montrose 60
Montrose, Marquis of 149
Monymusk Priory 34, *35*
Monzie Castle 5, 101, 166–7, *166*, 193
Moray, Pont's map *6*
Moray House 202, *202*
Morer, Thomas 11
Morison, Robert 241, 243
Morrison/Moryson, Fynes 12, 15, 113, 171
Morrison, John 71, 83, 94, 103
Morton, 4th Earl of 103, 113–14, 115–17, 118, 119, *119*, 121, 125, 150
Morton, 6th Earl of 94
Morton, 7th Earl of 115, 195, 196
Morton, 11th Earl of 243
mottes *see* mounts
Mount Grace monastery, Yorkshire 42
mounts 193–4
    Ancrum House 171
    Banff Castle 60
    Blackbarony/Darnhall 161, 193
    Busta House 129, 193
    Castle Kennedy 317
    Culhorn House 321
    Huntly Castle 123, *123*
    Kinnaird Castle 289, 290
    Lincluden College 179, 180, 181, *192*, 193
    Lochwood Castle/Tower 3, 194
    Lord Burghley's London garden 121

Monzie Castle 166–7, 193
Muness Castle *126*, 193
Somerset House, London 181
Yester House 236, *237*, 239
    see also King's Knot
Mowbray, George 301
Muchalls Castle 149
Muness Castle 97, *126*, 127–9, *127*, 193
Munro, General 194
Munster, Sebastian 81
Murray, Sir Archibald 161
Murray, Elizabeth, Countess of Dysart and Duchess of Lauderdale
    220, 224, *224*, 225, 234
Murray family 137
Murray, Sir Gideon, Lord Elibank 160–1, 162, 164, 168, 177
Murray, Dne James 94
Murray, Sir James, of Kilbaberton 177, 178
Murray, John, of Hangingshaw 275
Murray, John, of Lochmaben, later Earl of Annandale 180
Murray, Patrick, Laird of Livingstone 242
Murray, William, 2nd Lord Nairne 304
Murray, Sir William 88
Myln, Walter 34–5
Mylne, Alexander 186, 191
Mylne, John 186–7, *187*, *190*, 191, 193, 219, 224, 253
Mylne, Robert 186, 239–40, 267, 294

Naesmyth, James 165, 168
Naesmyth, John 165
Naesmyth, Michael 165
Nairne, 2nd Lord 304
Nairne, Lady 304
Nairne, James 304
Napier, John, of Merchiston 155, 188, 193
Nasmyth, Patrick 276
Neidpath Castle 193, 234, 274, *274*, *275*
Neill, Patrick 15, 34, 39, 42
Nerven, Cornelius van 331
Newbattle Abbey 32, 39, 169, 170, *192*, 193, *193*
Newholm Hope 165
Newliston 301, 314, 318, *319–21*, 321, 323, 325, 326, 328, 329
Newte, Thomas 39
Newton Castle 90–1, *91*
Nicander Nucius 62
Nicholas V, Pope 56
Niddry Castle 91, 92, 150, 196, *199*, 246, 301, 310, 323
Nithsdale, 1st Earl of 180
Noltland Castle 127
Norie, James 271
North Berwick Abbey 156
North Berwick nunnery 46
North Garden, Holyroodhouse 184, 186, 198, *202*, 240, 241–2, *241*
    physic garden 243
    purchase of 81, 84, 94
    Queen Mary's Bath House 103–4, *105*
    sundial 186–7, *187*, 191, 198, 240
Northern Isles 139
    see also Orkney; Shetland
Northfield House 143
Nost, John van 267, 300

Ochterlonie/Auchterlonie, Mr, of Guinde 39, 218
Ogilvie, Lord 144
Ogilvy, Sir George 194
Ogilvy, Sir John, of Lintrathen 57
Old Gala House 167, 172
Old Rayne 50
orchards 6, 61, 101, 109
    Aberdeen town gardens 209
    Aberdour Castle 114, *114*, *115*

Alloa House 308
Ancrum House 39, 170
Arbroath Abbey 39, *39*
Balcomie Castle 138
Ballencrieff House 60, 164
Balvaird Castle 138, *139*
Biel House 270
Blair Castle 173
Burghley's London garden 121
Cambuskenneth Abbey 27
Cardross Castle 60
Carse Grange *40*, 41
Cassillis Castle 90
Castle Huntly/Castle Lyon 258
Castle Kennedy 315
Castle Menzies 109–10, *111*
Charterhouse, Perth 42
Clackmannan Tower 60, 275, 276
Clien mansion 34
Clunie Castle 49
Coldstream nunnery 55
Coltness 211
Coupar Angus Abbey 33, 34
Craigmillar Castle 88, 132, 133, *133*, 134, 135
Culross House 221
Cunningham 173
Dalkeith House/Palace 294–5
Doune Castle *59*
Drummond Castle 74, 253
Dunfermline Abbey 140
Dunrobin Castle 175
Duntarvie Castle 132
Earl of Crawford's list 252
Edinburgh Castle 58, 59
Edzell Castle 149
Elibank Castle 162
Falkland Palace 183, *183*, 184
Glasgow University 46, *47*, 209
'great gardens' 63
Haddington 60
Hamilton Palace 249–50, *251*, 305
Hampton Court 7, 92
Hangingshaw 275
Hesdin, France 55, 56
Holyroodhouse 103, 184, 210
Hopetoun House 298
Hotel de St Pol 55
in James IV's feu charters 76
Jedburgh Abbey 34
Kelburn Castle 173
Kildrummy Castle 60, 88
Kilravock Castle 37
Kilwinning monastery 42, 252
Kinloss Abbey *38*, 39
Kinnaird Castle 289, 290, *293*
Kinneil House 253
Kinross House 286, 287
Kirkliston 46
Lennoxlove (Lethington) 231
Lindores Abbey 39, *68*, 252
Linlithgow Palace 71, 73
monastic gardens 23, *23*, 34, 39
Neill's report 34
Newton Castle 91
Niddry Castle 92, 196, *199*
Old Gala House 167
Paisley Abbey 42, *42*, 252
Posso Tower 165
Raasay 50
Roxburgh Castle *59*

St Andrews 207, *207*
Seton Castle 12, 91, 93
Shank Place 108
Stirling Castle 7, 68, 179, 182, 183
Taymouth Castle 326
Torwoodlee Tower 137
Tyninghame House 281
Whytbank Tower 168
Winton Castle 196
Yester House *1*
see also fruit trees
Orkney 18, 76, *124*, 125, *125–6*, 127, 313
Orkney, Earls of 125, 127, 304
Ormiston, Laird of 250
Ouchter, John 83
Ouchterlonie, Rev 149
    see also Auchterlonie/Ochterlonie, Mr

Paganson, Malcolm 59
Pages, Bastien 105
painted posts 7, 10, *10*, 92, 93, *93*
Paisley Abbey 26, 42, *42*, *43*, 252
Paisley, abbot of 56
Palazzo Piccolomini 119, 137
Panmure, Earl of 149, 218, 307
Panmure House 218–19, *218–19*, 274, 283, 296
Paradise 7, 25, 26, 27, 46, 56, 337
parks 61, 63, 105, 213
    Ancrum House 170, 171
    Arnhall 144
    Ballinbreich Castle 112
    Biel House 270
    Blackbarony/Darnhall 161
    Cardross Castle 60, 61
    Dalkeith House/Palace 294, 295
    Drummond Castle 255
    Dunbog 113
    Edzell Castle 149
    Falkland Palace 63, 184, 244
    Flisk 113
    Glamis Castle 260
    Gordon Castle 125
    Hamilton Palace 94, 248, *250*, 251, 252, *272*, 304, 307, 328
    Hangingshaw 275
    Hatton House 232
    Hesdin, France 55, 56
    Holyroodhouse 63, 74, *74*, 103, 184, 240
    Hopetoun House 303
    Huntly Castle 123
    in 'garden' definition 1
    Kinneil House 253
    Kinross House 286, 287
    Lennoxlove (Lethington) 230, *230*, 231
    Linlithgow Palace 63
    Old Gala House 167
    Panmure House 219
    Pinkie House 155
    Pont's maps 109
    Presmennan *271*
    Shank Place 108
    Stirling Castle 62, 63, *63*, *64*, 68, 76, 77, 78, 112, 179, 183, 244
    Tyninghame House 281, *281*
    Yester House 235, 237
parterres 173
    Aberdeen *207*, 209
    Aberdour Castle *115*
    Airth Castle *5*, *280*
    Alloa House 308, 311
    Ancrum House 169
    Blair Castle 173

Brunston/Brunstane Castle *156*, *157*
Busta House 129
Castle Huntly/Castle Lyon 259
Castle Kennedy 317
Castle Menzies 109
Coltness 211
Cowane's Hospital 244
Craigiehall House 297
Dalkeith House 294
Drum Castle 177
Drumlanrig Castle 332, *333*
Drummond Castle 253
Dundas Castle *190*
Dundas on 329–31
Edinburgh College 207
Edinburgh town gardens 199, 202
Edzell Castle 150
Falkland Palace *183*
Glamis Castle 263, 264
Ham House, London 181
Hamilton Palace 249, 304
Heriot's Hospital 203–4, *204*, 206, 207, *243*, 244
Holyroodhouse 109, 184, 185, 198, *202*, 240
Hopetoun House 298, 299, 300, 301, *302*, 303, 313, 314
Houston House 158
Kenmure Castle *173*, 174, *174*
Kinnaird Castle 289, 290, *292*
Kinneil House 253
Kinross House 286
Lawers 255
Leslie House 220
Lincluden College 180, 181
Mollet's advice 215
Moray House 202
Neidpath Castle 274
Posso Tower *164*, 165
Presmennan 271
St Andrews *206*, 207, *207*
St James Palace, London 198
in *The Scots Gard'ner* 244, 247
Stirling Castle 179
Taymouth Castle 326
Thirlestane Castle 226, *227*
Trinity Hospital 203
Versailles, France 299
Villa dell' Ambrogiana, Tuscany *120*, 135
Wimbledon, London 199
Yester House 236, *236*, 237, 239
Patterson, John 183
Peebles, David 30, 100
Peebles friary 75
Peers, Sir Charles 181
Pembroke, Countess of 150
Pencz, Georg 147
Penicuik House 326, 328
Pennant, Thomas 39, 180, 182
Pennant's Mount 194
Perth 42, 43, 44, 46, 57, 210, *211*
Perth, Earl of 297
Perth, Earl and Countess of *190*, 193
Philip the Good, Duke of Burgundy 56
philosophy 15, 133, 143, 150, 155, 191
Philpson (supplier of trees to Stirling) 67
Physic Garden, Edinburgh 35, 240, 241–3, *242*, 247
physic gardens 35, 46, 240, 241–3, *242*, 247, 258
    see also medicinal plants
Pinkerton, William 253
Pinkie House 3, 11, 125, 152–6, *153*–5, 191, 193, 234, 239, 251–2
Pitmedden House 222–3, *222*, *223*
Pius II, Pope 118–19

Place of Weem *see* Castle Menzies
plantations 278, 281
    Airth Castle 278, *280*
    Alloa House 311
    Biel House 270
    Carmichael House 325, *325*, 326
    Castle Kennedy *316*, 319
    Drum *8*
    Drumlanrig House 335
    Flowerdale/Gairloch House *315*
    Glamis Castle 267, 292
    Hangingshaw 275
    Hopetoun House 303, 313
    House of Nairne 304, *305*
    Kinnaird Castle 292–3
    Kinross House 286
    Neidpath Castle 274
    Newliston *320*, 323
    Presmennan 271
    Reid's patterns *281*, *305*
    Taymouth Castle 325–6
    Tyninghame House 278–9, 281, *283*
    Versailles, France 296
Pliny the Younger 44, 117–18, 135, 150
Plora Burn 164
Plummar, Nicolao 59
Plunton Castle 3, 13
Plunton Tower 137–8, *138*, *139*
Pluscarden Abbey 24, 39, 125
Pluscarden Priory 150
Pococke, Bishop 239, 334–5
poetry 53, 61, 76–8, 85, 86–7, 100, 175, 193
    Clerk's *The Country Seat* 328
    pastoralism 150
    Yester House 239
    see also Boyse; Chaucer; Douglas, Gavin; Drummond, William;
        Dunbar, William; Henryson, Robert; *Kingis Quair*; Lindsay,
        Sir David; Lithgow; Montgomerie; *Tayis Bank*
Pollen evidence 18, 44, 46, 114
Pollock, Laird of 172, 248
ponds
    Aberdour Castle 114
    Alloa House 308, 310, 311
    Biel House 270
    Carse Grange 41
    Castle Kennedy 317
    Coupar Angus Abbey 32, 33
    Hamilton Palace 250, *251*, 305, *307*
    Hatton House 232
    Holyroodhouse 81
    Hotel de St Pol 55
    Kilravock Castle 37
    Kinnaird Castle 289–90
    Lennoxlove (Lethington) 231
    Mollet's advice 215
    Newliston *321*, 323
    nobles' gardens 10
    Old Gala House 167
    Pinkie House 234
    Stirling Castle 178–9, 182
    Yester House 239
    see also fish ponds; pools
Pont, Timothy 30, 42, 90, 100, 172–3
    maps 9, 100, 101, 105, 107, 108–9, 129, 137, 138–9
    see also Ancrum House; Auchenames; Ballinbreich; Balloch;
        Blair Atholl; Cambuskenneth; Castle Menzies; Castle Semple;
        Darnaway; Edzell; Glamis Castle; Gordon Castle; Grandtully;
        Huntly Castle; Kinloss; Lindores; Midlothian; Monzie;
        Moray; Paisley Abbey; Scone; Spynie; Stirling Castle;
        Tullibardine Castle; West Highlands

pools
    Hangingshaw 275
    Hotel de St Pol 55
    Kinross House *287*
    Newliston 323
    Saltoun Hall 258
    see also ponds
Pope, Alexander 328
Portland, Earl of 236, 296
portraits 92, 116–17, 197, 234, 264, 266, 279, 283
Posso Tower *163*, 164, 165–6, *165*, 168, 170
Postel, Simon, abbot of Chaalis 31
Presmennan 271, *271*
Preston, David 133, 135
Preston, George 132
Preston, John, Lord Fentonbarns 156, 158, 161
Preston, Simon 132, 133, 134
Preston, Sir William 132
Prestonfield House 263
Prestongrange *122*
Priestfield 246
Primaticcio, Francesco 121
Pringle family 164, 167–8
Pringle, George 136, 164, 167
Pringle, James 164, 168
Pringle, Sir James 167, 172
Pringle, Robert 167

Quakers 241, 246, 248, 255, 257
Queensberry, Duchess of 336
Queensberry, Dukes of 248, 274, 292, 331, 332, 336
Queensberry House 331
Queenshaugh 70
Quellin, Arnold 263, 267
Quhitbrow, Alexander 178

Raa, William 101
Raasay 50
Raglan Castle, Gwent 158
Rait, John 160
Ramsay, William, Earl of Dalhousie 197
Rankeillour, Lord 281, 298, 301
Rankin, Provost of Stirling 181
Ravelston House 159–60, *159*
Rawlinson, Ralph 248, 249
Reformation, the 29, 97, 98, 100, 101
Reichenau drawings *2*, 20, *22*, 23, *23*, 26
Reid, Alexander 246
Reid, James 246
Reid, John 108, 196, 241, 246–8, 257, 258
    see also Scots Gard'ner, The
Reid, Robert, abbot of Kinloss, later bishop of Orkney 37, 125
Reid, William 246
religious aspects 7, 25–6, 61, 97
    see also Paradise; Quakers; Reformation, the; Virgin Mary
Richardson, John, the Elder 323
Richmond Palace, London 73, 173, 237, 239
Rizzio, David 115
Robert I (the Bruce), King of Scots 57, 60, 73, 116
Robert II, King of Scots 55
Robert III, King of Scots 43
Robertson, Forbes W 15
Roger de Mowbray 25
Rome 218, 237
Ronsard, Pierre de 121
Rook, James 71
Rose, Hugh 37
Rose, John 283
Ross, Duke of 51
Ross and Cromarty 313

Ross, Elizabeth 104
Rossellini, Bernardo 119
Rossie Priory *61*, 62
Rothes, Countess of (Anne Erskine) 117
Rothes, Countess of (Helen Hope) 279, 261
Rothes, Earl (later Duke) of 113, 213, 219, 220, 319
Rothesay Castle 290, 292, *294*, *295*
Rouch, David 26
Roxburgh Castle 59
Roy, William, Military Survey 6, 11, 270, 313, 337
    see also Alloa House; Ancrum House; Applecross; Arniston;
        Balcaskie; Ballinbreich; Brechin Castle; Carmichael House;
        Castle Huntly; Castle Kennedy; Castle Menzies; Craigiehall;
        Dalkeith Palace; Drum; Dundas Castle; Duntarvie; Flowerdale;
        Hangingshaw; Hopetoun; House of Nairne; Kenmure;
        Langshaw; Mavisbank; Melville House; Newliston; Pinkie;
        Shank House; Tyninghame
Royston House 143
Ruskin, John 13
Ruthven, Lord 141
Ruthven, William, 1st Earl of Gowrie 43
Rynd, James 175

Sadler, Sir Ralph 83–4
St Andrews 29–30, *30*, *44*, 49, *77*, 97, 100, 104, *205–7*, 207
St Andrews Castle *206*, 207
St Andrews Cathedral *28*, 29–30, *30*, 49
St Andrews Priory 29–30, 32, 76, 100
St Andrews University 30, 46, 100
St Columba 18
St Gall monastery *see* Reichenau drawings
St James Orchard, Cambuskenneth 27
St James Palace, London 187, 198–9
St Leonard's College, St Andrews 207, *207*
St Machar's Cathedral *51*
St Margaret's Well, Edinburgh Castle 58
Saltoun Hall 258, *259*
Sandby, Paul 313
Sandby, Thomas 264
Sandilands, James 108
Sanquhar Castle 292
Scalloway Castle 127
Schevez, William, Archbishop of St Andrews 47, *48*, 49, *49*, 60
Schoner, Sophia 168
science 11, 150
    see also architecture; astronomy/astrology; mathematics; surveying
Scone Abbey 29, 34, *35*, 67
Scone, abbot of 34, 56, 67
Scots Gard'ner, The 12–13, *13*, 168, 246, 247–8, 257
    avenues 269
    fruit trees 248, 250
    Hamilton Palace and 249–50
    house and garden relationship *247*, *258*
    kitchen gardens 204
    melons 250
    parterres 244, 247
    paths 247, 248, 255–6
    terraces 270
    tree plantation patterns *281*, *305*
Scott, Marion, Lady Fordell 101
Scott, Sir Walter 218, 273, 336
Scoughall, Tom 81
sculpture 10, 143
    Edzell Castle 133, 143, 144, 145–9, 150, 267
    Foulis and Bannatyne tomb, Greyfriars Kirkyard *158*
    Fyvie Castle 151–2
    Heriot's Hospital 207
    Mount Parnassus subject of 181
    Ravelston House fountain 159
    Somerset House, London 181

Winton 196
see also statues; sundials
seeds 223, 248, 251, 296
    Alloa House 172
    Cardross Castle 60
    Carmichael House 323
    Castle Kennedy 319
    Clackmannan 60
    Doune Castle 59
    Edzell Castle 144
    Falkland Palace 70
    Hamilton Palace 94, 248, 250
    Holyroodhouse 94, 103
    Hopetoun House 298, 301
    Kinneil House 253
    Kinross House 287, 288, 289
    Linlithgow Palace 71, 94
    Physic Garden 242–3
    Stirling Castle 65, 67, 68, 69, 77, 94, 106
    Taymouth Castle 297
    trade in 7, 40–1
    Whithorn 18
    Yester House 235
Seller, W 209
Semple family 42
Seneca 150
Servi, Constantino de' 173
Seton, Alexander, 1st Earl of Dunfermline 140, 150, 152, 153, 154,
    155, 161, 223, 234
Seton, Sir Alexander, Lord Pitmedden 222–3, *222*
Seton Castle 10, 12, 91, 92, 93, 105, 150, *197*
Seton, Charles, 2nd Earl of Dunfermline 210
Seton family 7, 91, 93, 150, 246
Seton, George, 10th Lord Seton and 3rd Earl of Winton 195
Seton, George (builder of Winton) 7, 92
Seton, James, 4th Earl of Dunfermline 234
Seton Palace 184, 195, *197*
Seton, William, 1st Lord Seton 91
Seymour, Edward, Earl of Hertford 135
Sgor nam Ban-Naomha *2*, 19–20, *20*
Shakespeare, William 121, 193
Shank House/Shank Place 108, *109*, 246, 257, *257*
Shanks, James 288, 289
Sharp, John (sundial maker) 187
Sharp, Sir John 68–9, 75
Sharp, John, of Houston 158
Shaw, George Bernard 13
Shaw, William 150
Sheill, Alexander 231
Shetland 97, *126–9*, 127–9, 193, 313
Shireburn, Sir Nicholas 300
Sibbald, Sir Robert
    on Balcaskie House 218
    Castle Kennedy information to 314
    Edward and 283
    on Falkland Palace 244
    gift to Sir Hans Sloane 296
    on Hamilton Palace 252
    on Hatton House 233
    on Hopetoun House 298, 304
    James VII and II and 240
    on Kinross 287
    on Linlithgow Palace 183
    on Melville House 293
    Physic Garden 35, 241–2
    on statuary 267
    on Stirling Castle 182
Sinclair, Katherine, Lady Seton 91
Sixtus V, Pope 217–18
Skougal, Robert 40

Slezer, John 225
    see also Cambuskenneth; Culross House; Dalkeith House;
        Dumbarton; Dunfermline Abbey; Falkland Palace; Glamis;
        Glasgow University; Gordon Castle; Hamilton Palace; Hatton;
        Heriot's Hospital; King's House; Kinnaird; Kirk o' Field;
        Lennoxlove; Linlithgow Palace; Newton; North Garden; Perth;
        Physic Garden; Thirlestane
Sloane, Sir Hans 296
Smith, James 235, 237, 266, 294
Smythson, Robert 181
Soest, Gerard 234
Somerset, Earl of, later Duke of 121, 160
Somerset House, London 140, 181
Somersham, Cambridgeshire 62
Somerville, Andrew 189
Sommelsdyke, Veronica van 221
Sorgvliet, Holland 236
Southesk, Earl of 289, 292
Soutra hospital 46
Spalding, John 196
Spence, Bishop of Aberdeen 50
Spernic, John 47
Spicer, John 40
Spink, Robert 59
Spynie Castle *6*, 105
Stair, 2nd Earl of 313–14, 315, 317, 319, 320, 321, 329
stanks *see* ponds
statues 266–7
    Alloa House 267, 308, 310, 311
    Castle Huntly/Castle Lyon 258
    Craigiehall House 297
    Drumlanrig Castle 331
    Glamis Castle *262*, 263, 264, 267
    Gordon Castle *199*
    Hamilton Palace 249, 266, 305
    Hatton House 233
    Heriot, George 267
    Hesdin, France 56
    Holyroodhouse 240
    Hopetoun House 300, 301
    Kinnaird Castle 290
    Leslie House 220, 266
    Melville House 294
    Mollet's advice 215
    Newliston 323
    Paisley Abbey 42
    Thirlestane Castle 226, *227*, 266
    Yester House 235, *235*, 236, *236*, 239, 266–7
Steven, Agnes 244
Stevenson, James 298
Stevenson, William 244
Stewart, Alexander, Archbishop of St Andrews 49
Stewart, Barbara 110, *110*, 111
Stewart, Bernard 74–5
Stewart family, Garth 110, 111
Stewart, Henry, *see* Darnley, Lord
Stewart, James, Earl of Moray (and of Mar) 32, 35, 102, 105, 115–16
Stewart, Sir James (keeper of Rothesay Castle) 292
Stewart, Margaret 15
Stewart, Patrick, Earl of Orkney 125, 127
Stewart, Robert, Earl of Orkney 125, 127
Stewart, Sir Walter 211
Stimson, Frances 13
Stirling *64*, 122, 244, *245*
Stirling Castle *52*, 62, 63–9, *64–5*, 70, 74, 77–9, 94, 141, 178–9, 244
    Chapel Royal 7, 9, 62, 63, 65
    Charles II 213, 244
    Cromwellian siege 213
    garden below the castle 7, 65, *66*, 69, 76, 79, 141, 181, *181*
        see also King's Knot

garden within the castle 63, *64*, 65, *66*, 69, 77, 179, 183, 244
Great Hall 62, *64*, *80*
Harvey's *Mediaeval Gardens* 25
herbs 34, 67, 178
James IV 62–3, 65, 87, 106, 179
James V *52*, 62, *64*, 76, 77–9, *80*, 81, 106
James VI and I 7, 9, 105, 141, 161, 177, 178
James VII and II 240
King's Knot 7, *66*, 67, 77, 78, 140, *142*, 176, 177–9, *177–8*, 181–3, 193
King's Old Building/King's House *52*, 64, 65, *66*, 78, *80*, 91, 122
King's Park/Old Park 62, 76
Ladies Hole 79
Lion's Den 79, *80*
Mary, Queen of Scots 105
New Park 62
Pont map *63*, 112, 179
Queen's Knot 182
tournaments 58, 63
trees 65, 67–8, 87, 179
views 98, *98–9*, 141
vines 7, 67
water features 178–9, 182
Stirling, John 74
Stobhall 193
Stoicism 150, 155
Stone, Jeffrey 111
Strachan, John 79
Strang, John 209
Strathbogie 123
    see also Huntly Castle
Strathmore, Earl of 233, 258–9, 260, 261, 263–6, 267, 269
Strife of Love in a Dream, The 77, 119
summer houses
    Aberdeen bishop's garden 50
    Aberdour Castle 195
    Barncluith 272
    Drumlanrig Castle 331
    Edzell Castle 136, 149
    Kinross House 286, 287
    Monzie Castle 167
    Neidpath Castle 274
    Perth 210
    Pinkie House 155, 234
    Yester House 239
    see also banqueting houses
sundials 10, 143, 186–93, *189*, *190*, *192*, *193*, 267
    Aberdour Castle 195, *196*
    Airth Castle 278
    Broughton House *11*
    Cowane's Hospital 244
    Craigmillar Castle 134, 135
    Dalkeith House 294, *300*
    Drummond Castle *190*, 191, *191*, 193, 253
    Edward's notes on 283
    Falkland Palace 183
    Glamis Castle 260, 263, *264*
    Hamilton Palace 248, 249, 250
    Heriot's Hospital 206, 207
    Holyroodhouse 186–7, *187*, 191, 198, 240
    Inch House 134
    Kenmure Castle 174, *174*, 188
    Lennoxlove (Lethington) 231
    MacLellans Castle *11*
    Marquess of Huntly's Aberdeen garden *7*, 209
    Neidpath Castle 274
    Posso Tower 165–6, *165*
Surgeon Apothecaries Company 242
surveying 150, 247, 258
Sutherland, James 242–3, 247, 250, 283

Swan, Joseph 50
Switzer, Stephen 328
Sympsone, Robert 211
Symson, Andrew 314

Tacitus 150
Tackley, Oxfordshire 158
Tait, Alan 15
Taket, Dean Mathew 65, 68
Tantallon Castle 114
Tavis Bank 74
Taylor, John (the Water-Poet) 140
Taylor, William 328
Taymouth Castle 270, 296, 297, 325–6, 327
tennis courts 63, *70*, 79, 80, 121, 183, 240
Terpersie Castle 51
terraces and terraced gardens 100, 101, 117–18, 120, 121, 143, 270–8
    Aberdour Castle 114–15, *114*, *115*, 117, 195
    Airth Castle *5*, *279*, *280*
    Alloa House 311
    Balcaskie House 216, 218
    Barncluith 271–3, *272*, *273*
    Biel House 270–1, *270*, 271
    Brechin Castle 293
    Busta House *128*, 129, *129*
    Carmichael House 325
    Castle Campbell 91, *96*, 122
    Castle Huntly/Castle Lyon 259, *260*
    Castle Kennedy 316–17
    Clackmannan Tower 275–6, *277*, 278
    Clunie Castle 49
    Coltness 211
    Cowane's Hospital 244
    Culross House 221, 222
    Dalkeith Palace 295
    Drum Castle 101, 175, *175*, 177
    Drumlanrig Castle 335
    Drummond Castle 193, 253
    Dundas on 329
    Elibank Castle *4*, *160*, 161, 162
    Falkland Palace 79, *182*, 183
    Hamilton Palace *251*, 305
    Hangingshaw 274–5, *276*
    Hatton House *232*, 233
    Kenmure Castle *171*, 173, 174
    Kinnaird Castle 289
    Kinross House 286, 287
    Langhaugh 165
    Langshaw Tower *162*, 164
    Lawers 256
    Leslie House 113, *212*, 219, 220
    Lincluden College 181, *192*
    Linlithgow Palace *182*, 183
    Lochwood Castle/Tower 194, *194*
    Meudon, France 121
    Mollet's advice 215
    Monzie Castle *5*, 101, 166, *166*
    Muness Castle *126*, 128
    Neidpath Castle 274, *274*, *275*
    Newliston 323
    nobles' gardens 10
    Panmure House *218*, 219, *219*
    Pitmedden House 222, *222*, 223
    Plora Burn 164
    Plunton Tower *138*
    Posso Tower *163*, *164*, 165, *165*, 166
    Somerset House, London 181
    Stirling Castle 79
    Thirlestane Castle 224, 226

Torwoodlee Tower 137
Tyninghame 281
Villa Medici 119
Whittingehame Tower 121, *121*
Whytbank Tower *167*, 168, *168*, *169*
Winton Castle 195–6, *198*
Yester House *1*, 235, 237, 239
Theobalds (Lord Burghley's garden) 121, 173
Thirlestane Castle 223, 224–9, *224–8*, 231, 266
Thomson, William 70
Tibbermore 49
Tolquhon Castle 135–6, *136*, 149
Torwoodlee Tower 136–7, *137*, 167
tournaments 58, 62, 63, 74–5, 83, 141
town gardens 95, 199, *200–1*, 202–4, 206–7, 209
Toynbee, Arnold 13
trade 7, 25, 40–1, 67–8, 242–3, 248, 250, 296
Traile, David 65
Traquair House 59, 63
travel, source of influences 116, 123, 223–4, 241, 287
    clerics 23, 24–5, 49, 56, 57
    Edward's tour 295–7
    pilgrims 56–7
    soldiers 55, 323
Trenan (monk) 18
Trinity Hospital 85, 203, *203*, 242, *242*
Tudor, Margaret, Queen (consort of James IV) 67, *67*, 71, 73, 75, 76, 77, 79, 88
Tullibardine Castle 87–8, *88–9*, *269*, 270
Tullibardine, Marquess of 237
Turner, Dr William 121
Tweeddale, Marquesses of 11, 233, *233*, 234, 235, 237, 239, 274, 281
Tyninghame House *8*, 220, 278–9, 281, *281–3*, 301
Tyrie 194
Tyrwhitt, Robert 135

university gardens 46–7
Uraniborg, Denmark 133
Utens, Joost/Giusto 135

Vanson, Adrian 117
Vavasour, Sir Thomas 181
vegetable gardens 27, 30, 39–41, 101
    Coupar Angus Abbey 32, 33
    Culross House 221
    Doune Castle *59*
    Duntarvie Castle 132
    Earl's Palace 125
    Edinburgh town gardens 199
    Elibank Castle 162
    Glasgow University 46
    Hamilton Palace 249, *251*
    Holyroodhouse 185, 242
    Kenmure Castle *173*, 174
    Linlithgow Palace 73
    monastic gardens *22*, *23*, 27, 30, 39–41
    see also kitchen gardens
Versailles *214*, 223, 224, 264, 287, 294, 296, 299, 308, 332
Victoria, Queen 181
Villa dell' Ambrogiana, Tuscany *120*, 135, *135*
Villa Doria Pamphili, Rome 237
Villa Farnese 237
Villa Lante 158, 237
Villa Medici 119, 173, 181
Villiers, George, Marquess of Buckingham 172
Virgin Mary 3, 26, 61, 63, *79*
Vitruvius 118
Vorsterman, Johannes 181
Vredeman de Vries, Hans 122

walks
    Aberdeen town gardens 209
    Airth Castle *280*
    Ancrum House 170–1
    Barncluith 272
    Biel House 270
    Carmichael House 325, *325*
    Castle Huntly/Castle Lyon 259
    Castle Kennedy 315, 317, 318, 319
    Castle Menzies 109
    Clackmannan Tower 276
    Coltness 211
    Cowane's Hospital *245*
    Craigiehall House 297
    Culross House 221
    Dalkeith Palace 295
    Drumlanrig Castle 336
    Duntarvie Castle 130
    Glamis Castle 263
    Hamilton Palace *251*, 305
    Hangingshaw 275
    Heriot's Hospital 204
    Holyroodhouse 240
    Hopetoun House 301, 303
    Kenmure Castle 174
    Kinnaird Castle 290, *294*
    Kinross House 286, 287
    Lennoxlove (Lethington) *230*, 231
    Leslie House 220
    Lincluden College 179
    Mollet's advice 214–15
    Neidpath Castle 274
    Newliston *320*, 323
    Posso Tower 165
    Presmennan 271
    St James Palace, London 198–9
    in *The Scots Gard'ner* 247, 248, 257
    Taymouth Castle 325, 326, *327*
    terraces 270
    Thirlestane Castle 226, 228–9
    Torwoodlee Tower 137
    Villa dell' Ambrogiana, Tuscany *120*
    Whytbank Tower 165, 168, *169*
    Wimbledon, London 199
    Yester House 235
Wallace, John, of Craigie 90
Wallace, Mungo 287
Wallace, William (mason) 195, 203
walled gardens 9, 11, 62, 97, 109, 143, 185, 337
    Aberdeen town gardens 209
    Aberdour Castle 115, 195, *195*
    Airth Castle 277, 278
    Ancrum House 169, 170
    Balcomie Castle 138, *140*
    Balvaird Castle 138, *139*
    Banff 194
    Blair Atholl castle 111–12
    Busta House 129, *129*
    Cambuskenneth Abbey 27, 29
    Carmichael House 325
    Castle Huntly/Castle Lyon 259
    Castle Kennedy 316, 318–19
    Castle Menzies 109, 111
    Coltness 211
    Craigmillar Castle 134
    Culross House 221
    Drum Castle 175
    Drummond Castle 253
    Dundas Castle 190
    Earl's Palace 125

Edzell Castle *144*, 145, *145*, 149
Elibank Castle 162
Falkland Palace 71, *182*, 183–4, 244
Fyvie Castle 151
Glamis Castle 261, 263, 264
Glasgow University 209
Gordon Castle *199*
Hamilton Palace 249, 250, *251*
Hangingshaw 275
Hatton House 233
herbarium 43
Heriot's Hospital 204, 206
Holyroodhouse 80, 81, 83, 84, 184
Huntly Castle 210
Kenmure Castle 173–4, *173*
Kinneil House 253
Kinross 286
Kirk o' Field 106
Langshaw Tower *162*, 164
Lawers 255, 256
Lennoxlove (Lethington) *230*, 231, *231*
Lochwood Castle/Tower 194, 195
Moray House 202
Newliston 323
Niddry Castle 196
Panmure House 218
Pinkie House 153, *153*, 155
Ravelston House 159
in *Roman de la Rose* 61
Rossie Priory *61*
St Andrews 207
Saltoun Hall 258
Seton Castle 91, 93
Seton Palace 195
Shank Place 108
Stirling Castle 79
Thirlestane Castle 226, 228–9
Tolquhon Castle *136*
Torwoodlee Tower 137
Trinity Hospital 203
Tyninghame House 281
Yester House *1*, *234*, 235
see also enclosed gardens
wars, effect on gardens 7, 25, 55, 93, 111, 209–10, 211, 213
see also Jacobite rebellions
water features 97, 101, 135, 143
Alloa House 308, 311
Biel House 270, *271*
Brunston Castle 157, 158
Craigmillar Castle 132
Dalkeith Palace 295
Drumlanrig Castle *333*
Dundas on 329
Duntarvie Castle 132
Edinburgh Castle 59
French gardens 121, 132, 173
Hopetoun House 298, 300
Italian influence 120, 132, 158
Lochwood Castle/Tower 194
Mollet's advice 215
Raglan Castle, Gwent 158
Stirling Castle 178–9, 182
Tackley, Oxfordshire 158
Tolquhon Castle 136
Yester House *1*, 236, *238*
see also canals; cascades; fish ponds; fountains; islands in
gardens; ponds; pools
Watts, William 179, 183, 186
Webb, Sidney and Beatrice 13
Wedderburn, Robert 46

Wedel, Lupold von 105, 141
Weem *see* Castle Menzies
Weir, John 244
Weldon, Anthony/Antony 12, 178
West Highlands 177, 313
see also Argyll; Hebrides; Ross and Cromarty
West Kers 301
West Wemyss 269
Wet, Jacob de 233–4, 235–6, 237, 239, 263, 264, 266, 267
Whitehall Palace, London 7, *10*, 92, 296
Whithorn 18, 49, 189
Whithorn Priory 35, 105
Whittingehame Tower 115, 121, *121*
Whytbank Tower 10, 164, 165, *167–9*, 168, 170
Wigtown, Earls of 189
wildernesses 337
Airth Castle 278, *280*
Alloa House 308, 310, 311
Carmichael House 325, *325*
Castle Kennedy 319
Dalkeith Palace 295
Hamilton Palace 305, *307*
Heriot's Hospital 244
Hopetoun House 194, 300
Kinnaird Castle 289
Kinross House 286, 289
Lennoxlove (Lethington) 231
Mollet's advice 215
Wilhelm IV, Duke of Bavaria 75
William of Culross, abbot of Kinloss 37
William I (the Lion), King of Scots 55, 59, 60, 62
William III, King of Great Britain and Ireland 223, 236, 242, 293, 296
Wilson, Mary 13, 14
Wilsoun, James 63
Wimbledon, London 199, 206
Winter, Thomas 263, 264, 265, 266, 267, 328
Winton, 3rd Earl of 223
Winton Castle 7, 91, 92, 93, 150, 195–6, *198*
Wise (London supplier of plants) 235
Wode Partbooks *3*, *26*, *69*, 71, *72*, 100, *100*, 107–8, *107–8*, *116*
Wode psalter 116
Wode, Thomas 71, *72*, 100, *100*
see also Wode Partbooks
Wolsey, Cardinal 90
Wood, Hew 218, 240, 248, 250, 253, 331
Wood, James 248, 331
Wordsworth, William and Dorothy 273
Wright, John Michael 283
Wyck, Jan 225–6, 230, 231, 244
Wyngaerde, Antonis van 10, 92, 93

Yester House *1*, 11, *14*, 233, 234–9, *234–8*, 266–7, 269, 294
York Buildings Company 10, 149
Yronsyde Wood, Lindores Abbey *68*

Zeno 150
Ziegler, Hans 149